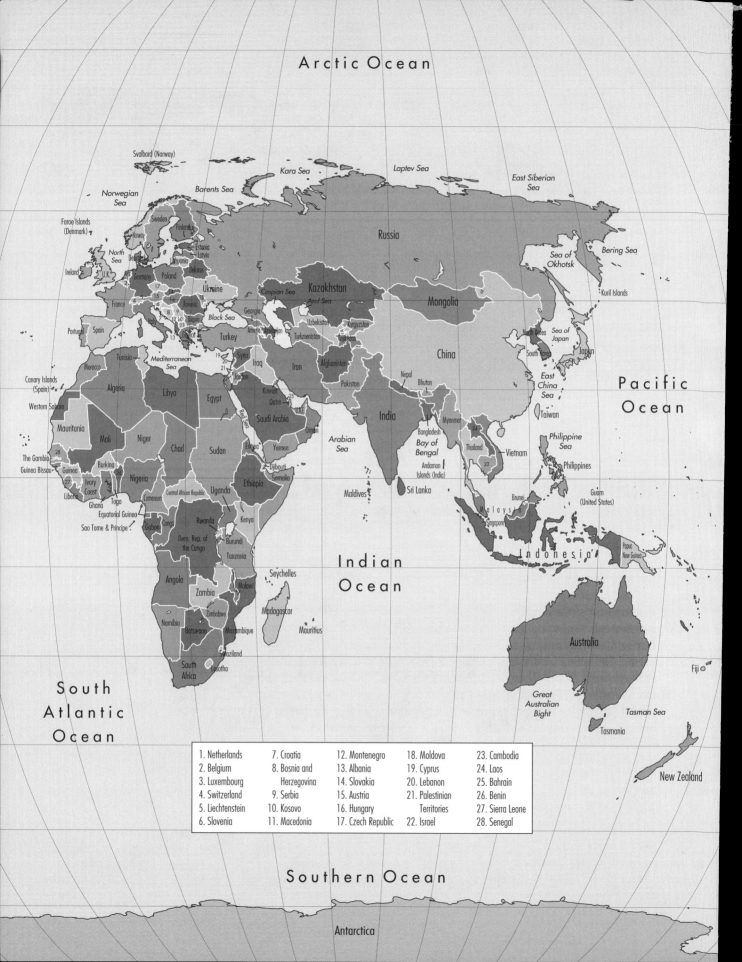

A

COMPARATIVE INTRODUCTION

TO

POLITICAL SCIENCE

CONTENTION AND COOPERATION

ALAN G. SMITH

CENTRAL CONNECTICUT STATE UNIVERSITY

ROWMAN & LITTLEFIELD

Lanham • Boulder • New York • London

Executive Editor: Traci Crowell
Associate Editor: Molly White
Senior Marketing Manager: Karin Cholak
Marketing Manager: Deborah Hudson
Interior Designer: Kathy Mrozek
Cover Designer: Meredith Nelson

Credits and acknowledgments borrowed from other sources and reproduced, with permission, in this textbook appear on appropriate page within the text or in the credit section on page C-1.

Published by Rowman & Littlefield
A wholly owned subsidiary of The Rowman & Littlefield Publishing Group, Inc.
4501 Forbes Boulevard, Suite 200, Lanham, Maryland 20706
www.rowman.com

Unit A, Whitacre Mews, 26-34 Stannary Street, London SE11 4AB, United Kingdom

Copyright © 2017 by Rowman & Littlefield

British Library Cataloguing in Publication Information Available

Library of Congress Cataloging-in-Publication Data

Names: Smith, Alan G.
Title: A comparative introduction to political science : contention and cooperation / Alan G. Smith.
Description: Lanham : Rowman & Littlefield, [2017] | Includes bibliographical references and index.
Identifiers: LCCN 2015046401 (print) | LCCN 2016003258 (ebook) | ISBN 9781442252585 (cloth : alk. paper) | ISBN 9781442252592 (pbk. : alk. paper) | ISBN 9781442252608 (electronic)
Subjects: LCSH: Comparative government. | Political science—Cross-cultural studies.
Classification: LCC JF51 .S5448 2017 (print) | LCC JF51 (ebook) | DDC 320—dc23
LC record available at http://lccn.loc.gov/2015046401

♾™ The paper used in this publication meets the minimum requirements of American National Standard for Information Sciences—Permanence of Paper for Printed Library Materials, ANSI/NISO Z39.48-1992.

Printed in the United States of America

CONTENTS

FIGURES

TABLES

TODAY NATIONS CONFRONT complex challenges, such as economic crisis and change, global warming, wars and their refugees, and the political role of religion. At this historical juncture, it is especially important for people to understand the fundamentals of politics. This book aims to enable students to traverse the terrain between their first impressions of politics and the realities of the subject. It focuses on clear, logical, and compelling explanation of what they need to know about today's politics, to be good citizens of their nations and the world. The book's strategy has several features that work in tandem: (a) an overall theme: politics as the interplay of contention and cooperation in and around government, (b) the book's conception of political science as the exploration of causal factors and consequences related to political phenomena, (c) exploration of the subject in a diversity of real-world contexts, including two country cases per chapter, (d) an effective, intuitive pedagogical approach to topic sequencing, and (e) an accessible, practical approach to concepts and their application to the real world.

A THEME: POLITICS AS THE INTERPLAY OF CONTENTION AND COOPERATION

I have found that students focus better on a subject when they have an overall theme to help integrate the whole. I think of politics as the interplay of contention and cooperation by individuals and groups, to affect authoritative decision making (in this case, decision making by government). Here the word "group" is meant expansively, including not only interest groups but also a wide range of other entities such as political parties, factions within them, sociopolitical movements, institutions, schools of thought about policy, and other types of groups. My meaning for the term "contention" is also expansive, based on how the word is used in ordinary language: any sort of striving in the face of difficulty, rivalry, competition, or opposition. (Thus I use the word much more broadly than what a few political scientists call "contentious politics"—protest, usually involving sociopolitical movements, outside established political channels.)

Thinking about the interplay of contention and cooperation stimulates interesting and important questions. The United States, for example, displays an increasingly polarized society, politically, economically, and socially, and we see vigorous contention within other nations, too, as well as among nations in international politics. What brings individuals to cooperate in maintaining such groups as political parties, interest groups, and social movements? What factors can contribute to division within such groups into different contending factions? In legislative assemblies, when do legislators tend to cast votes in cooperation with their party and its leadership, and when do they go their own way? When and why do different parties ally with one another, and when do such coalitions break down? When and why do different governmental institutions seem to be contending or cooperating with each other, and which has the most influence over the other as they do so? In international politics, when and why do nations contend with each other, and when are they more likely to cooperate (sometimes in contending alliances)?

Regarding the *intensity* of intergroup contention, more questions arise. When and why do groups contend sharply, sticking to their most important priorities? When and why do they engage in more gentle rivalry, at times engaging in cooperation and compromise? What are the consequences of differences in the intensity of contention or cooperation? And what about the consequences of patterns of contention and cooperation? I believe that the theme of political contention and cooperation can motivate student interest as well as help tie the course together.

POLITICAL SCIENCE, CAUSAL FACTORS, AND CONSEQUENCES

This book defines political science as the systematic examination of causal factors and consequences of political phenomena. For students to be good citizens of their nations and the world, they need to be able to think in terms of causal factors and consequences regarding important developments around them. At various points in this book, I highlight one or more of three types of causal factors that affect patterns of contention and cooperation in politics: (a) the main types of political framework that surround and structure politics, (b) influence, the most common form of power in politics, and (c) values, among the goals of policies and at times among the motivations of contending groups, alongside (or even occasionally instead of) material interests.

For example, multiparty parliamentary democracy displays very different patterns of contention and cooperation from those that we see under two-party presidential democracy or military authoritarian rule. In another example, the influence of a political party's top leadership over its legislators and mid-level leaders is a key factor in the degree of cooperation within the party, as it contends with other parties. And in the financial crisis of 2008–2009, shared concern about a value—public well-being in the particular form of minimal financial stability—contributed to cooperation among parties and interest groups that normally contend with each other, often sharply. An especially important cluster of values, human rights, is a recurring topic over the course of the book as either causal factor or consequence.

COUNTRY CASES

Moreover, good citizenship requires being able to view events and patterns in a comparative context. Some awareness of what goes on elsewhere enriches one's perspective on how things are done domestically, so that what is happening at home does not seem to be "the only game in town." In addition to many brief examples from various countries within the narrative, each chapter ends with two in-depth country cases, drawn from many different parts of the world, to illustrate political contention and cooperation with an eye to the chapter's topic. In understanding politics, it is important for students to situate concepts in the stories of particular nations. Over the course of this book, a wide range of nations are represented.

TOPIC SEQUENCING

A further challenge for a text introducing political science revolves around topic sequencing. The field of politics is a sprawling tapestry with many interrelationships among topics. How can the student understand one topic without the others? Yet a text must start somewhere, and proceed in some order. If the student's understanding of politics is not built systematically, from the ground up, the result may be a complex jumble of information that can even discourage students from good, thoughtful citizenship.

This book emerged from my thirty years of teaching the course to undergraduates, in which I used my syllabus to rearrange the sections and chapters of the available textbooks to achieve what I considered to be a more natural and logical sequence of coverage. For example, the distinction between parliamentary and presidential democracy is commonly first presented in the chapter on the legislative process, which tends to come toward the middle of texts or later. But a preliminary and simplified version of the distinction is also useful for understanding topics that should come earlier in the book, such as power and interest groups. I concluded that for the subject of politics to unfold in a natural, logical, synchronized way, concepts and topics need to be sequenced carefully to reduce confusion and build understanding systematically, step by step. Eventually it occurred to me that the market needed a book that did a better job of topic sequencing.

A second major aspect of topic sequencing is the overall order of the chapters in the book. For introductory students, chapters need to flow in a logical order to build a feel for politics and government. I believe that this book's table of contents presents such a sequence. However, a qualification is in order here. Often instructors using the same text vary in how they want to use it in the course, and may prefer a different sequence. And they may not want to assign every chapter, every section of a chapter, every box feature, or every country study, as required reading for students. For this reason, I have tried to craft each chapter and section to be sufficiently comprehensive and self-contained to be able to stand alone, so that each may do its job as part of a different sequence or strategy. Such modular construction can provide a book that is a flexible and powerful multi-use tool, capable of being employed effectively in various roles in a wide range of higher education settings, from community colleges to regional and primary state universities, liberal arts colleges, and other universities.

TERMS, CONCEPTS, AND THEIR REAL-WORLD APPLICATION

Another feature of this book's pedagogical approach addresses challenges that students sometimes face when they are confronted by new terms and try to apply them to often messy realities. Clarity and accuracy in applying terms to the real world is important in preparing students for good citizenship as well as for further study of politics. Contending politicians sometimes use vague, emotionally charged, and extreme language to characterize events or their opponents.

Media coverage does little to reduce the resulting confusion, and many voters are tempted to throw up their hands in frustration or disgust. Being a responsible citizen requires some awareness of the shades of gray between polar extremes, and having a feel for when exaggeration or outright falsehood may be afoot. This text attempts to make a start on this problem, in the nonpartisan context of introducing political science.

In addition to using clear terms and definitions, most chapters contain a "Concept in Context" section, explaining further the meaning of a key term or phrase in the realistic context of its actual use. And where appropriate, this text includes examples that illustrate and invite critical thinking about the application of terms. To be sure, this book relies on terminology widely used in political science, defined as simply and directly as possible. But occasionally a term that is widely used by political scientists to label a phenomenon may unintentionally create a misleading or confusing impression of what it refers to. At the few points where such confusion is possible, this book adds more intuitive terminology that is direct, revealing, and clear, in relation to both ordinary language and political reality.

The most important occasions for this seem to arise as political scientists use typologies to classify phenomena. Sometimes contrasting labels suggest extremes, whereas most of the empirical reality actually occupies the spectrum between the extreme poles. For example, in the chapter on political parties, I take note of the terms "catchall" and "programmatic," used by many political scientists to classify political parties. The first word implies vacuous pandering, while the other seems to go to the opposite extreme: a party that always displays and pursues a specific and detailed program of policy prescriptions. These terms are fine for the extremes, but in reality, most parties lie somewhere in between. In this case, it may be better to enrich our terminology for introductory students by adding a pair of words from ordinary language—"broad" and "focus"—to classify parties by their segment of the continuum.

In another example, political scientists who study voting tend to draw a contrast between (a) voting by policy preference, with the voter choosing a party because its policy on a key issue is closest to the voter's own policy preference (called "proximity" voting), and (b) voting without regard for policy, either on a gut feeling or on whether things seem to be going well or poorly for oneself or one's country. But many votes seem to be on a continuum between these poles. To help here, at points in the chapters on parties (10)

and elections (11), I employ the notion of general policy direction preference. This involves preferences that government policy move in one or more of four types of general direction: (a) toward a value (e.g., national security or social justice), (b) in the direction of a particular ideology, (c) toward support for an interest group, or (d) in the direction of a general policy prescription to address an important issue (e.g., toward restricting or expanding access to abortions). Often voter motivations and party appeals seem to center on preferences for such general policy directions, rather than on specific policy positions, retrospective assessment of events, or affective attraction, or involve mixtures of these factors.

SPECIAL FEATURES

To enrich student learning, this book also includes revolving selections of boxed sections under the following titles:

- ***Concept in Context*** (noted above) expands on some of the most important key terms and concepts by showing how they may be viewed in the context of their use in politics and political science.

- ***Contention and Cooperation in Focus*** zeroes in on a particular issue, event, or process in a country that illustrates the interplay of political contention and cooperation.

- ***The Philosophical Connection*** takes note of the views of one or two important political philosophers on topics discussed in the chapter.

- ***The Human Rights Connection*** examines how the human rights outlook bears on aspects of the chapter's topic.

- ***Applying the Models*** uses the models of the distribution of influence (majority preference, elite, pluralist, and personal leadership, introduced in chapter 2) to help explain some part of the chapter topic.

- ***Country Case Studies*** at the end of each chapter help illustrate each chapter's themes, give a feel for the politics of particular nations, and provide helpful background for examples that are found in subsequent chapters.

- ***Critical Thinking Questions*** at the end of each chapter expand on the chapter's concepts for students to consider the implications and relate to other situations.

- *Key Terms* are found in bold and defined in the text, listed at the end of each chapter for easy review, and defined again in the glossary at the end of the book.

The book also contains tables, figures, maps, and photos that are designed to underscore the major concepts and take-home points in each of the chapters, and enhance student comprehension of the topics.

SUPPLEMENTS

- **Test Bank.** For each chapter in the text, there is a test bank section that includes multiple choice, true/false questions, and essay questions. The Test Bank is available to adopters for download on the text's catalog page at https://rowman.com/ISBN/9781442252592.

- **Testing Software.** This customizable test bank is available as either a Word file or in Respondus. Respondus is a powerful tool for creating and managing exams that can be printed to paper or published directly to the most popular learning management systems. Exams can be created offline or moved from one learning management system to another. **Respondus LE** is available for free and can be used to automate the process of creating print tests. **Respondus 3.5**, available for purchase or via a school site license, prepares tests to be uploaded to any of the most popular course management systems such as Blackboard. Visit the Respondus Test Bank Network at http://www.respondus.com/products/testbank/search.php to download the test bank for either Respondus 3.5 or Respondus LE.

- **Companion Website**. Accompanying the text is an open-access Companion Website designed to engage students with the material and reinforce what they've learned in the classroom. For each chapter, flash cards and self-quizzes help students master the content and apply that knowledge to real-life situations. Students can access the Companion Website from their computer or mobile device; it can be found at http://textbooks.rowman.com/smith1e.

- **eBook.** The full-color eBook allows students to access this textbook anytime and anywhere they want. The eBook for *A Comparative Introduction to Political Science* includes everything that is in the print edition in vibrant color, and features direct links to the Companion Website where students can access flash cards and self-quizzes to help test their understanding of the major concepts and terminology in each chapter. The eBook can be purchased at https://rowman.com/ISBN/9781442252608 or at any other eBook retailer.

- **PowerPoint Slides.** A set of line art PowerPoint slides provides all the tables and figures from the text. The slides are available to adopters for download on the text's catalog page at https://rowman.com/ISBN/9781442252592.

ACKNOWLEDGMENTS

This book owes much to many. I have received thoughtful feedback at every stage of its development from countless reviewers (you know who you are), including William T. Daniel, Francis Marion University, and Laurie Sprankle, Community College of Allegheny County, South. Insightful readings of the whole manuscript were generously provided by an old friend, Norwegian professor Bernt Hagtvet, and by my son Daniel, a recent college graduate who majored in political science and offered the perspective of a student. I am also much in debt to the understanding and energetic support of Traci Crowell, executive editor for political science at Rowman & Littlefield. I much appreciate the perspective and skillful editing provided by developmental editor Sara Wise, as well as the help on a variety of tasks provided by associate editor Molly White. And this book could not find its audience without the efforts of marketing manager Deborah Hudson. I also thank the production supervisor for my book, Anita Singh from Deanta Global Services, and her staff, copyeditor Deepika Davey, and Jehanne Schweitzer, senior production editor at Rowman & Littlefield. Finally, I am deeply in debt for the moral support and patience of my wife, Rhona, and my sons, Andrew and Daniel.

THE BASICS
OF POLITICS

I   II   III   IV   V

PART   PART   PART   PART   PART

Politics, Government, and Policy

FOCUS QUESTIONS

- **WHAT** is politics?
- **WHAT** is a policy?
- **WHAT** is government?
- **WHAT** is representative democracy? What are its main forms?
- **WHAT** are the main forms of nondemocratic government?
- **WHAT** are some major policy areas that governments address?
- **WHAT** are the purposes of government and policy?

IMAGINE THAT YOU ARE A CITIZEN of Greece in 2012 in the middle of an extended European economic slump that followed a financial crisis. The economy is in depression, and businesses are failing. More than a quarter of working-age Greeks are unemployed. Meanwhile, the Greek government is spending much more than it takes in taxes, and faces huge debt payments that it cannot make. Government services and benefits such as pensions have been sharply reduced, economic distress is widespread, and mass protest demonstrations occur frequently. Depending on your point of view, you may have urgent questions, and such questions contend with one another for attention.

Some point out that Greece shares a common currency (the Euro) and certain institutions with the strongest economies in Europe; why don't other European countries and institutions come to Greece's aid? Others may ask a different question: since Greece's economy is obviously unable to generate enough tax revenue for the government to be able to repay its debts on time, why not just declare a government default (inability to pay creditors) and negotiate down the debt? A third group asks, why doesn't Greece just keep cutting wages and government spending until it can produce products cheaply enough to succeed in world trade? A fourth view asks, what led to this mess, and who is responsible? What role is being played by Germany, whose economy did quite nicely during this period?

Accurate answers to these questions would involve various factors, including economic, historical, and cultural ones. But no answer to any of them would be complete without a look at the patterns of contention and cooperation among various groups in Greece and Europe around government decision making. This is the realm of politics, the subject of this book.

BASIC CONCEPTS

Why study politics? Politics may seem to you to be little more than a spectator sport, with people cheering one side or another. You may ask, what does it have to do with me? Well, in reality, politics affects each of us on an immediate and personal level. It can influence the cost of college tuition, the size of financial aid packages, and the terms of student loans. On a broader scale, politics and government affect the availability of jobs, our personal freedoms, national security, the safety of our transportation systems, and the protection of consumers and businesspeople from fraud and harm. In countless ways that we are mostly unaware of, politics and government help determine the conditions under which we live.

Also, politics has been involved in a range of important historical events: the onsets of World Wars I and II, the 1930s' economic decline into the Great Depression, the Cold War between the West and the Communist countries between 1950 and 1990, the fall of Communism at the beginning of the 1990s, the abolition of racial segregation in the southern United States (during the 1960s) and South Africa (during the 1990s), the financial and economic crisis of 2008–2011, the European economic stagnation of 2013–2014, and the absence of serious action to address global warming since the phenomenon was discovered by scientists in the 1990s. In every one of these cases, politics played a key role.

This book aims to help you understand politics. It uses the approach of political science to examine factors affecting politics, and to explore the consequences of political phenomena. Along the way, the text frequently highlights patterns of contention (any sort of striving or competition) and cooperation among individuals and groups as they try to affect government.

This first chapter introduces the basics, beginning with definitions of the terms *politics, government,* and their main product, *policy* (e.g., laws and programs). Individuals and groups normally contend under an overarching organizational framework with which they cooperate: government. Thus at the outset, we need a preliminary picture of what governments look like. The chapter turns next to the most common forms of government that surround and shape politics. Finally we need to move on to the purpose of government: the point of all the contention and cooperation. Hence the chapter finishes with a brief look at various areas of policymaking and their goals.

Politics, Contention, and Cooperation

People often use the term *politics* without thinking much about what it means. Politics arises in a wide variety of settings, including workplaces (e.g., "office politics"), religious organizations, schools, economic enterprises, clubs, and even families, not just around government. In political science, attempts to define politics have tended to focus on its outcomes—decisions by people in positions of authority—and the resulting distributions of things that people value (see "Concept in Context"). But much of politics goes on informally in society: outside, around, and prior to authoritative decision making. And some government decisions regulate behavior rather than distributing things. Something else seems

CONCEPT IN CONTEXT | Politics

Giving a simple definition of politics is not easy. In the 1930s, political scientist Harold Lasswell described political science as the study of "who gets what, where, when, and why."* This idea suggests that politics might amount to whatever concerns the *distribution* of things. Three decades later, political scientist David Easton added that the distribution of things that people value must be done by those in formal positions of *authority*; he defined politics as "the authoritative allocation of values."† But while this seems to be a good account of what *government* does, it doesn't seem to capture very well all that we mean by the word "politics."

In some ways, these approaches to defining politics seem too narrow. First, as noted above, politics can also go on informally in social interactions around decision-making bodies, and prior to authoritative decisions. Moreover, some authoritative decisions involving distribution do not seem political, such as businesspeople making a deal and signing a contract, or a contestant winning a prize on a reality TV show. Furthermore, both Lasswell's and Easton's definitions view politics as concerned with distributing things. But some of politics are related to government's *regulation* of behavior, such as setting rules to assure the safe disposal of toxic waste by chemical companies. Here it seems like a stretch to view such decisions as "allocating" anything.

A somewhat broader approach to defining politics is simply to equate it with collective decision making. But this idea might include activities that people do not tend to call "political." Imagine a group of technical experts exchanging ideas to solve a problem, such as a manufacturing company's team of engineers collaborating to modify a production process. Or students may work together on a group project for a college class. Is this politics? In another way, however, "collective decision making" seems too narrow. For example, it leaves out the jockeying for influence prior to the actual decision making, which also seems to be part of politics. We need to add something else to our explanation of politics to better capture how we use the word in ordinary language today. This additional aspect seems to be the role of contention among individuals and groups.

---

* Harold D Lasswell, See *Politics: Who Gets What, When, How* (New York, London: Whittlesey House, McGraw-Hill Book Company, 1936).
† David Easton identified politics with the "authoritative distribution" of things that people value. See *The Political System, an Inquiry into the State of Political Science* (New York: Knopf, 1953).

necessary to adequately characterize politics. In what follows here, I focus on the interplay of contention and cooperation among individuals and groups, to affect authoritative decision making.

Occasionally we say that a person or group is being "political" when they seem to be maneuvering to gain influence, advantage, or popularity in a community or organization. This usage invokes the idea of striving or competition by an individual or a group, to achieve a goal. A good term for this dimension of politics is "contention," as the word is used in ordinary language. In talking about sports, for example, we say that teams in a league are "contending" for the championship. If you are simply stating your opinion in a discussion, you might preface your comment with "I contend that" such and such. Contention can be either against a challenge or against other contenders, or both.

To be sure, this contention aspect of politics can make political news seem confusing and off-putting. When you see and hear political debate on television or online, you may ask yourself, "How could I possibly figure out who is right? They're probably just trying to sell me something." However, alongside the idea of self-interested competition, at times we find a more high-minded aspect of politics.

The Greek philosopher Aristotle wrote that to be human is to be a "political animal," one who can contribute to defining and pursuing the good of the whole community. At least at times, contending political rivals may be viewed as also cooperating, to some extent, in pursuit of values shared by the entire community.

In important ways, politics continually involves elements of both contention and cooperation. For example, in politics individuals cooperate in groups in order to contend effectively with other individuals and groups. And typically contenders cooperate to some extent in observing the rules or customs under which they engage in their political contention.

Such realities are consistent with one of these phenomena appearing to mostly prevail over the other at times. Occasionally, periods with politics primarily displaying contention seem to alternate with much more cooperative phases. In the Egyptian "Arab spring" uprising of 2011, for example, at first prodemocracy opposition groups cooperated in demonstrations to remove the old regime's leader, President Hosni Mubarak. But subsequently, the protest movement divided into multiple contending groups in trying to prepare a new constitution, elect a government under it, and resolve the subsequent conflict between the military and the Muslim Brotherhood—the long-standing Islamist opposition party that had been formally illegal under Mubarak's rule. In particular, secular groups were unable to cooperate sufficiently with each other to be able to organize effectively in opposition to Islamist ones, led by the Muslim Brotherhood (who proved much better at cooperation). Still later, in 2013, the military seized power and imposed cooperation on everyone else to suppress the Muslim Brotherhood. Up to 1992 in the United States, the contending Republican and Democratic parties cooperated frequently in Congress, but did so less from 1992 through 2010, and much less after that. Contention and cooperation are inextricably entwined in politics.

With pairs of concepts like contention and cooperation, we may be tempted to see one as good and the other as bad. For example, decisions are made and things get done faster with cooperation, while contention often seems to stand in the way. However, the emergence of a good decision by an organization may require sharp contention. And people can cooperate for the wrong reasons, as in the case of a real estate developer who bribes a politician to approve a project.

In discussing contention and cooperation in and around government, I mean the word "group" in a broad and expansive way, to designate a wide variety of entities in various contexts. For example, one type of group incorporates the word in its title, and is commonly mentioned in political science. It is the "**interest group**": a category of people or organizations (e.g., occupational, such as farmers, steel manufacturers, or child welfare organizations) that shares policy-related concerns and tries to affect government decision making, or an organization that aims to represent such a category, without running candidates for office under its own label. But another important type of group is a **political party**. Minimally defined, a political party is an organization that runs candidates for office under its own banner. And there are many other types of groups that engage in political contention and cooperation: majorities, minorities, institutions, economic strata, regional populations, ethnic groups, social movements, religious faiths, schools of thought regarding policy issues, supporters of particular values, alliances of political parties (called "coalitions"), alliances of interest groups, and even whole nations and alliances of them (in "international politics"). Some of these groups are fairly clearly defined, and some much less so. And of course, there can be a lot of overlap of membership between different groups.

Egyptians hold flags and shout slogans as tens of thousands gathered for a demonstration at Cairo's Tahrir Square in April 2011, two months after President Hosni Mubarak was ousted, to demand that former regime officials including the veteran strongman be purged and tried.

Contention among groups can range from extremely sharp and intense to quite mild, with a lot of accompanying cooperation. Examples of intense contention include protest marches and sit-ins by social movements such as the 2011 "Arab Spring" democracy movements in North Africa and the Middle East, or the 2011–2012 "occupy" protests against inequality in the United States.[1] Political contention can even become so sharp as to break down into outright conflict, such as revolution, civil war (e.g., in Syria from 2012 on), or the takeover of the government by the armed forces (e.g., Egypt in mid-2013). But again, political contention can also be much less intense. It can be consistent with bargaining and compromise, in which contention and cooperation overlap directly. Indeed, political contention and cooperation display a continuum, from intense contention with minimal cooperation at one end, to nearly harmonious cooperation at the other, with a large middle range with much overlap and interplay of contention and cooperation.

Whether political contention is gentle and civil or sharp and intense, whether it is out in the open or is only implicit, and whether the best policy decision in a particular situation results from cooperation and compromise or from continued sharp contention, we may define **politics** as the interplay of contention and cooperation among individuals and groups to affect decision making in authoritative organizational frameworks.

As we will see in chapter 2, an important factor in politics is influence, the most common form of power in politics. In this book, following political scientist Jack Nagel, I define **power** as the causal impact of the preferences of one individual or group on the actions of others.[2] Influence is informal power, and often affects patterns of contention and cooperation. For example, the influence that a group's leaders have over its members can enhance the level of cooperation within the group. In the mid-2010s in the United States, within the Republican Party the extent of the influence possessed by the party's traditional leadership had a lot to say about its ability to hold the Republicans together in the face of contention by the party's arch-conservative "tea party" faction. This is important for contention more broadly. In any group, the level of cooperation within it can be a big factor in the group's effectiveness in contending with rival groups for influence in the political process overall. In this book, influence is frequently highlighted among the many types of causal factors that we will see affecting patterns of contention and cooperation.

Policy and Organizational Authority

To make and implement decisions, typically a group employs an organizational structure. For example, a corporation normally has a chief executive officer, a chief financial officer, other leading executives, and a supervisory board of directors. Such structures can be found in a wide range of groups such as business offices, religious congregations, clubs, or even families. A central feature of a group's organizational structure is that people or units in it possess degrees of authority. **Authority** is formal power, defined in this book as people complying, fairly systematically, with the preferences of an individual or group as a matter of formal (often legal) obligation. For example, authority is at work when a chief executive officer of a corporation directs the chief financial officer to implement a new accounting directive.

The most comprehensive decisions made by organizational structures concern the group's policies. A **policy** in the broadest sense is a group's practical approach to solving a problem or achieving a goal. For example, student absenteeism can be a problem for schools. To address this problem, the school administration has rules specifying the legitimate excuses for absence, how many unexcused absences result in a penalty, what the penalty will be, how individual cases will be handled, and so on. This package of rules and procedures is the school's policy on class attendance. Students, parents, and school officials tend to cooperate with its implementation, contributing to its goal of student attendance. Whatever the degree of contention that went into making the policy, a key consequence of the policy is the cooperation by group members that follows due to the organization's authority.

Government

An especially important type of group that needs policies is a territorial community. This may be a town, county, city, region, or country. For a territorial community, the leading organizational units with the authority to make policy and carry it out are referred to as its **government**.

At a very general level, we may say that the function of government is to evaluate the basic arrangements surrounding citizens' lives and, if necessary, adjust them. Making adjustments is done through creating and applying policies. For this purpose, government must have *comprehensive* authority over the whole community. That is, governmental structures must be capable of setting limits on what may be done by other groups and authorities within the community, when necessary. (As we shall see in chapter 2, governmental authority can be especially strong when the government possesses "political legitimacy": the widespread sense among the people that the system of government is rightful and just for them.)

Government policies are often formal and specific, such as a law or program, or a rule to be used in applying a law or program. However, government's approach to a problem may also be less formal, such as a policy of shifting resources in ways that strengthen or weaken a law or program. For example, in the United States in 2012 and 2013, the Republican Party was actively working to reduce or deny resources to units that were charged with implementing laws that it opposed: both a new financial regulation law and a new program to make health insurance more affordable and comprehensive for Americans. In addition, a government can adopt a policy of taking no action with regard to a problem or goal, in what can be called a policy of inaction. In many ways, the key goal of political contention and cooperation is to affect government policymaking. The last sections of this chapter will briefly introduce the major areas of policy that tend to be addressed by national governments.

In addition to making policy, government helps to structure political contention itself. For example, from 2011 on, political parties in Greece and Spain contended vigorously over how to respond to the demands by some other European nations that the countries sharply cut their government spending (in return for receiving outside financial aid to help them pay their debts). But despite the differences between the parties, the system of government required that ultimately, at least some of the contending parties had to cooperate enough to pass budget proposals that they could agree on. And then, at least those in government are required to cooperate—however grudgingly—with the resulting policy.

The entire array of governmental structures possessing comprehensive authority over the national territory is referred to collectively as **the state**. This is what we mean when we make a distinction between "state" and "society," or speak of "state ownership" of an enterprise, or of national defense as a "state function."[3]

FORMS OF GOVERNMENT

The overall system of government amounts to a pattern of cooperation surrounding politics. It allows political contention and policymaking to proceed within orderly bounds. As we shall see in this book, there are a range of forms of government. Each type of governmental system helps to structure political contention in its own particular ways. At the most abstract level, we may say that governmental structures fall into two broad categories: representative democracy and authoritarian government.

Representative Democracy

Under **representative democracy**, the people, in free and fair elections, choose the officials who set the main outlines of the government's key laws and programs. Representative democracy's most prominent political institutions include:

a) legislative assemblies, which must approve laws and programs, alongside

b) an executive leadership, which directs how laws and programs are to be applied and makes important policy proposals to the legislative assemblies.

In representative democracy, political contention tends to be open and lively within and around these institutions.

Legislative assemblies are large elected bodies whose members have equal voting power and represent the various portions of the nation's territory that voted them into office. The leadership of the executive branch of government is itself led by a chief—usually called either "president" or "prime minister"—who may or may not be directly elected. But the executive leadership also includes the heads of the various ministries or departments (e.g., labor, defense, or foreign relations) in the executive branch. They are called "ministers" or "secretaries," and are appointed by the chief executive. Less prominent, but at times important in democratic politics, are (a) the professional bureaucracy ("civil service") that implements policies and makes up the great bulk of the executive branch, and (b) an independent judicial branch, whose courts oversee the application of policies and resolve disputes about them.

Essential Features Two essential features of representative democracy are especially important as it structures the contention and cooperation of individuals and groups. First, representative democracy respects and protects key human rights that are necessary for free and fair elections. These include the rights to freedom of expression, association, the press, and religion, and to fair trial, that make possible free political contention. Without open debate and free formation of associations, countries cannot have free and fair elections. Related to these freedoms is another important feature. Key groups such as political parties and interest groups must possess **autonomy**: independence in decision making. In a representative democracy, associations will not be controlled or dominated by government; they must be able to contend and cooperate freely.

In addition, democracy provides **political accountability**: the capacity of the citizens to hold leading public officials responsible for their performance in office. If citizens dislike the performance of an official or a political party, they can vote for someone else next time. For example, from 2010 on some governments in southern Europe had to approve very unpopular government spending cuts (e.g., cuts in pension payments) in return for outside aid in paying their debts; in several cases, the leaderships who agreed to these concessions were removed in the next election. Over some period of time, we expect a representative democracy to display alternation in power, the replacement of one leadership with another. When we do not see such alternation, the public may doubt whether the substance underneath the formalities is democratic.

Two other key principles also help to structure democratic political contention. **Formal political equality** means that each person's vote counts equally, and virtually every citizen may aspire to office.[4] And **majority rule** means that at least in legislative assemblies, bills must receive a favorable majority vote to become law.[5] But majority rule does not mean that a majority of the people or of an assembly can do anything it wants. Under representative democracy, fundamental rules govern the basic structures, procedures, and authority of governmental institutions, including protecting human rights. Such rules are typically included in a special document called the nation's constitution, which is normally insulated from easy modification.

Accompanying the constitution in a representative democracy should be an independent judiciary. A leading part of that is a constitutional court (in the United States called the "Supreme Court") charged with ensuring the observance of human rights and of the constitution itself.

Basic Types of Democratic Governmental Structure The most important distinction between forms of representative democracy centers on two matters: how the top leader of the executive branch is chosen, and what is the length of her or his term of office. On one hand, the people may vote to choose the chief executive directly, in an election that is formally separate from the election of the legislators. This "president" then appoints the heads of the various ministries or departments into which the executive branch is subdivided (collectively these officers are referred to as the "cabinet"). This type of governmental structure formally "separates" the legislative and executive structures and personnel; no one is a member of both branches at once. Most importantly, the president serves a fixed term of office (e.g., four years) until the next presidential election. This form of democratic governmental structure is called **presidential**. It is the type of democratic government that we find in the United States and Latin American nations, for example.

On the other hand, a democratic system could have the chief executive be a leading member of the most important legislative assembly, selected to the top executive post by a majority vote of that assembly. This type of governmental structure is called **parliamentary**. The "prime minister" (PM) is usually the leader of the party with the most seats in the key legislative assembly. Once in office, the PM also appoints the cabinet, but in this case draws from the ranks of the supporting legislative majority. Here the PM and the other executive chiefs continue to be members of the legislative assembly (though they spend most of their time in their executive branch jobs).

A key feature of parliamentary government is that normally the prime minister and her or his fellow cabinet ministers serve in their top executive positions *only so long as they continue to have the support of the legislative majority for their key policy proposals*. Normally if a significant bill fails, the PM and cabinet are expected to resign, making way for a new parliamentary election or parliament's selection of a new PM. Parliamentary government is the most common type in Europe, for example. (Chapter 13 discusses another type of democratic government called "semi-presidential," which blends certain features of both presidential and parliamentary government.)

These differences between presidential and parliamentary forms of representative democracy can have important consequences for the patterns of contention and cooperation within and between political parties. For example, we shall see in chapters 10–12 that under parliamentary government, legislators who are members of the same party tend to vote the same way on bills. They follow the example of the party or parties holding the parliamentary majority, who must stick together in passing the cabinet's bills to keep their leaders in their cabinet positions atop the executive branch. In contrast, under presidential government, the president serves a fixed term of office regardless of whether her or his policy proposals pass in the legislature and become law. Thus there is less pressure on legislators of the president's party to always vote in favor of the president's bills, and for opposition parties to always vote against them.

Another organizational distinction among representative democracies concerns the number of significant political parties. Regardless of whether a representative democracy is parliamentary or presidential, the political framework may be either "two-party" or "multiparty." In a **two-party** system, political contention is dominated by two main parties contending with each other. Normally one or the other of the big parties wins the majority in any given legislative assembly. (A more accurate phrase—but too cumbersome for general use—would be a two "prevailing" party system.) In contrast, a **multiparty** system includes a larger number of significant parties, usually five or more. In this case, too many parties are present in legislative assemblies for any one of them to hold a majority on its own. To build the majority necessary to pass bills, two or more parties have to form an alliance, called the "majority coalition." Thus the number of significant parties is another factor that affects patterns of contention and cooperation.

Notably, democratic countries' organizational frameworks are often labeled with a phrase that designates *both* its governmental structure and its party system. For example, Latin American political systems are "multiparty presidential," the United States is "two-party presidential," the British political system is normally "two-party parliamentary," and the continental European systems are "multiparty parliamentary." I refer to this phrasing as designating the country's type of "political framework."

Authoritarian Government

The main category of nondemocratic system today is **authoritarian government**. It may be defined as government in which the basic outlines of key laws and programs are *not* set by officials chosen in free and fair elections. Rather, some ruling group chooses the key government officials (typically from among its own ranks), though that group does not try to assert total control over the lives of the citizens. While authoritarian government imposes a great deal of cooperation on political participants, and lacks the open and free political contention that characterizes representative democracies, we will see that political contention is found in this category of government, too.

Authoritarian governments are most often classified according to the type of group that dominates their politics. This ruling group may be a single political party, the armed forces ("military rule," as in Egypt in 2012–2013), a religious hierarchy and its armed supporters ("theocratic" government, as in Iran after 1978), an individual leader with his or her advisors in a long-established system (e.g., Saudi Arabia's monarchy), or a personal dictator with his or her associates (e.g., Mobutu Sese Seko in the Congo from 1965 to 1997). Other groups may be influential behind the scenes in specific areas of policy. But again, the choice of which individuals will lead the government comes from informal contention and cooperation within the dominant group.

To get a sense of authoritarian government, just put the word "not" in front of almost everything mentioned above about democracy. First, legislative assemblies and political parties other than the dominant one may exist, but they do so only formally, without substance and autonomous impact. Either the legislature is a tightly controlled "rubber stamp" supporting executive branch proposals, or it lacks authority over significant policy areas, or both. Where

Francisco Franco (1892–1975), Spanish General and authoritarian dictator of Spain from October 1936 until his death in 1975.

the dominant group is a political party, it may ban other parties altogether (e.g., a "single-party" regime such as in China). Or the regime may allow certain other parties in the legislature as a mere formality, while ensuring that the ruling party always holds the bulk of the seats and dominates the assembly (a "single-party dominant" or "electoral authoritarian" regime; see the Belarus country case study at the end of this chapter).

Under authoritarian rule, accountability, political equality, and majority rule are not practiced. Key civil and political human rights are not guaranteed. While they may be respected to varying degrees, this happens at the discretion of the

TABLE 1.1	Regime Types and Frequencies

Regime Types	Countries	% of Countries
Representative democracy	104	54%
Semi-democratic	17	8.9%
Electoral authoritarian	46	23.9%
Politically closed authoritarian	25	13.0%

Source: These data are from Larry Diamond, "Thinking about Hybrid Regimes," *Journal of Democracy* 13, no. 2 (2002). They still roughly reflect the proportions of different broad categories of governmental structure today.

government. Groups outside of the government and its direct supporters have limited ability to contend for their goals. At times, the government forces them to cooperate with its strategies. Political contention is greatly constrained under authoritarian government, in contrast to representative democracy.

Some national governments fall into a gray area between representative democracy and authoritarian government. These are sometimes called "semi-democratic" or "hybrid" regimes, and will be discussed later in this book. While today most countries are classified as representative democracies at least formally, there are substantial numbers in the other categories, too (see Table 1.1).

Totalitarian Rule

There is another category of nondemocratic governmental system, called "**totalitarian**." Today only a few clearly totalitarian systems exist, including North Korea and areas controlled by radical Islamists, such as major parts of Syria and Iraq and smaller portions of Afghanistan, Pakistan, Yemen, Somalia, Libya, Nigeria, and the Central African Republic. Totalitarian government tries to assert total control over the lives of its citizens. Like authoritarianism, it lacks free and fair elections, accountability, and civil rights guarantees, but it also

a) strongly imposes an official political or religious ideology on social life, the media, and education;

b) requires leading members of significant organizations to be members of the ruling political party or organization, greatly reducing their independence in decision making; and

c) regularly monitors society and infringes the human rights of anyone it has suspicions about.

Such societies are sometimes described as "closed," with few avenues of access to alternative information or ideas.

Examples of past totalitarian governments include Hitler's Nazi Germany of the mid-1930s to 1945, Stalin's Soviet Union at least from around 1930 until his death in 1953, Pol Pot's Cambodia in the mid-1970s, China during its most heavily Maoist periods (at least from 1957 to 1959 and from 1965 to 1971; see Country Case Studies in chapter 6), and Taliban-ruled Afghanistan prior to the American/NATO invasion in 2001. Today, the most prominent totalitarian areas are Kim Jong Un's North Korea and the areas of Syria and Iraq controlled by a radical Islamist political and military force called Islamic State.

Some authoritarian nations display elements of totalitarian rule, but not the full picture. For example, in the latter decades of the Soviet Union, the range and intensity of totalitarian controls were somewhat reduced in comparison to the Stalin years. Systematic state terror was largely gone (though selective detention of active dissidents might still occur), and private conversation had become largely free. But people in responsible management positions still had to be members of the Communist Party, and the party and state still controlled public expression and organization.

Before we go further into how individuals and groups contend and cooperate in and around these forms of government, however, we need a preliminary sense of what governments do—what the contention is all about. As we saw above, government's main product is policy. We now turn to a look at the sorts of policy that governments make and apply.

POLICY AREAS

Government policies are diverse, but three broad categories stand out: (a) sociocultural policies, which affect personal and group freedoms, (b) policies that affect the economy, and (c) policies that concern foreign relations and national defense. Each of these types of policies may be divided into various policy areas. For example, the economic category might include policies that address the environment, education, transportation, health, the financial system, or economic growth (see Table 1.2).

Sociocultural Policy

Sociocultural policy concerns the bounds of acceptable personal freedom, in self-expression, individual and group autonomy, and politics. In these policy

TABLE 1.2	Policy Areas

Policy Category	Example Areas
Sociocultural policies	Civil liberties (freedoms of speech, association, religion), privacy, police powers, rights of criminal defendants, church v. state
Policies that affect the economy	Taxation, regulation, and government spending in such areas as social welfare, central bank lending, transportation, the environment, health, and education
Foreign relations and defense policies	Size of the military, foreign military intervention, treaties, diplomacy, participation in international organizations, foreign aid

THE HUMAN RIGHTS CONNECTION | The United Nations Contribution

In this broad category of public policy, an important factor is the universal human rights agreements under the U.N. umbrella. Definitions of a wide range of key freedoms can be found in the U.N.-sponsored international human rights agreements. First came the U.N.'s proclamation of the importance of human rights, in the 1948 "Universal Declaration" of human rights. Then, after many years of negotiation and refinement came the U.N.'s "Covenants" of human rights—one civil-political and the other economic-social—which were meant to obligate signatory governments. These documents were finished in 1966, and went into effect for signatory governments a decade later, in 1976.

Most relevant to sociocultural policy is the civil-political Covenant. It focuses on protection of freedoms of thought, expression, association, privacy, movement, and religion, freedom from slavery and arbitrary detention, the right to fair trial and equal treatment under the law, and protection of life against violence.* Press freedom is especially important.

In addition, governments must guarantee key *political* rights, most importantly the right of citizens to participate in "genuine elections" of government officials by secret ballot. This includes the opportunity to run for office "without unreasonable restrictions" (Article 24). If implemented, these last political provisions, together with the freedom guarantees, result in what we call "free and fair elections."

Each nation has the obligation to enforce respect for human rights respect domestically. But no systematic international enforcement mechanism exists to assure that governments do so. And the rights are defined in general terms, giving nations leeway to adapt them to their circumstances and cultures. Human rights affect government policy mainly as compelling values that may affect debates and their outcomes (see chapter 3).

_____

* For more on these rights, see chapter 3.

areas, strong advocates of freedom contend with those who favor curbs for the sake of social order or other traditional values.

Not surprisingly, nations differ as to what kinds of personal freedom are protected, and in the nature and degree of protection. Political contention in these policy areas is, in effect, about how narrowly or broadly human rights should be interpreted and applied. For example, if a country is at war, a vigorous nationalist may ask, "Should speech that is critical of the government's war strategy be considered acceptable, or be condemned as unpatriotic?" In nations where the majority religion plays a prominent political role (e.g., in some Muslim nations), clerical conservatives may believe that too much emphasis on personal and political freedoms can lead to excess and disorderly behavior. In particular, they may press the government to act against speech that they consider hostile to their religion.

In the realm of freedom of action, policy issues in one country may get no attention in another. Abortion and birth control are debated in the United States and a few Catholic nations, but in most of Europe the option of abortion is assured and the issue is not on the political agenda. In the United States, homosexuality is increasingly accepted. However, Iran has seen the murders of some gay men, and a recent president has declared that homosexuality does not exist in Iranian society. Whether women should be allowed to drive cars is an issue in Saudi Arabia (they are not, at present), and whether women should be allowed to attend school or walk in public without being accompanied by a male relative may be an issue in Taliban-controlled parts of Afghanistan and Pakistan or Islamic State-controlled parts of Syria and Iraq (often they are not, at present). Yet these issues provoke no controversy elsewhere.

Other key sociocultural issue areas are immigration and minority rights. How much immigration should be allowed? Should the government or groups in society be allowed to harass ethnic, racial, and religious minorities? What government services and benefits should recent immigrants be allowed to receive? And what role should religion play in government? "Church-state" questions, such as whether to have children say prayers in public schools, have arisen in the United States, for example. Some Latin American nations have traditions of Catholic Church involvement in public education, and in some Muslim nations Islam plays a prominent role in both education and criminal justice. Here the cultural rights of religious minorities may be a subject of political contention.

In addition, concerns about physical security and social order prompt some citizens to contend for increased powers for the police and prosecutors in law enforcement. Crime is a concern in many nations of the world. Even where street crime is not a prominent problem, court cases involving a heinous crime or a prominent personality may get tremendous attention in the press. The perception of a threat of terrorism can prompt extensions of police power, such as the American "Patriot Act" that was passed in the wake of the 9/11 attacks of 2001, and the subsequent National Security Agency program of surveillance of phone and Internet data that came to light in 2013. These moves may in turn clash with the concern for privacy and the rights of defendants in court.

As we shall see in chapter 6, generally policies that favor individual freedoms and rights, resisting government intervention in personal behavior, are classified ideologically as "left of center." In contrast, policies that favor government intervention in sociocultural areas to bolster traditional values are called "right of center," or conservative.

Policies Affecting the Economy

Economic policy in the broadest sense encompasses a wide range of government activities that affect the economy, often through domestic spending, taxation, and regulation. Issue areas include education, transportation, the environment, the financial system, relief for people in economic distress, and overall economic growth.[6]

For example, much government spending goes toward providing resources and social services. **Social welfare** services aim to assure minimal well-being to the disadvantaged, including the elderly, the unemployed, the ill, or the poor generally. Key questions include how much should government provide for pensions for the elderly, unemployment benefits, job training, health insurance, or food or housing aid? How should these services be delivered?

Other government spending targets the society generally. Governments typically provide certain necessary services that might not otherwise be available at affordable prices, such as public schools, the mail system, major roads, police protection, parks, and military bases. Political contention arises over how much a government should be spending on these things. And should government own and produce other key goods, such as the main water supply, electric power, railroads, and even production of such things as iron, steel, automobiles, and energy resources such as oil and gas?

In these areas and others, a government may want only to **regulate** (impose rules on) the provision of key goods and services, rather than owning and running them. It does so in pursuit of such goals as public health, safety, fairness, environmental protection, and overall prosperity, for example. In 2008 and 2009 in the United States, many observers placed some blame for the financial crisis on the failure of American regulatory agencies in the late 1990s and the 2000s to adequately monitor and regulate such things as complicated investment products, banks' capital reserves, and deceptive practices in home mortgage lending. How much should government regulate the financial system to avoid a repetition of the recent crisis?

In addition, governments may want to provide **subsidies**: low-cost loans, grants, or special tax breaks mostly for private organizations and activities that are viewed as serving the public interest. For example, governments provide subsidies for such activities as education or job training, transportation improvements, production for national defense, and alternative energy research and development (e.g., solar power research). A government may want to spend more along these lines during an economic downturn to reduce unemployment and stimulate more spending on local businesses. To preserve a nation's domestic food supply capacity, a country's government may give aid to farmers who cannot grow food as cheaply as competitors elsewhere in the world. A key question is how much should governments be involved in these areas?

Moreover, government spending requires funds that governments collect, mainly through taxes. But a lot of contention arises over who and what should be taxed. Should taxes fall mainly on individual incomes, or corporations' incomes, commercial transactions, or wealth? Should tax rates be higher on higher incomes (a practice known as progressive taxation), because higher-income individuals can best afford to pay additional taxes without reducing their normal spending? Or should all be taxed at the same rate, in the name of equality? How much do various forms of taxation restrain the economy? Again, we will see much more on economic policy in chapter 7 on "political economy."

As we shall see in chapter 6, policy approaches that favor government intervention in policy areas affecting the economy are generally referred to as ideologically "left of center." Policies that oppose government intervention in the economy are classified as "right of center" or "conservative." But it is important to remember that many people look at policies without ideological lenses; instead they ask pragmatically, does the policy take care of the problem, or not?

Foreign and Defense Policy

A third broad policy category includes foreign relations and defense policy (the focus of chapters 16 and 17). Nearly all nations maintain armed forces to defend their boundaries and interests. However, their traditions and needs differ based on the different kinds of challenges they face. For instance, countries with long histories of peace with their neighbors, such as Sweden and Switzerland, do not feel that they need large military establishments. In contrast, other countries such as the United States, Britain, France, Russia, and Israel have a history of contending with military threats and projecting power. They feel the need for substantial armed forces. How large should the armed forces be in each of these countries? How well should they be equipped?

Issues also arise around when and how a nation should use its military forces. As we shall see in chapter 2, in 2003 the French government ultimately decided not to participate in the American-led invasion of Iraq. In the United States and Britain, supporters of the intervention in Iraq defended it as a fight against terrorism, while many critics considered it to be a battle for control over oil. Nations frequently face decisions about whether to join international interventions for peacekeeping or ending human rights abuse. The question has emerged with crises like the ethnic-religious conflict in the former Yugoslavia in the 1990s, the Rwandan ethnic genocide of 1994 (see chapter 18), and the violence in the Congo and in the Darfur region of Sudan in the 2000s. Some nations (e.g., Scandinavian nations, India, and Nigeria) have been quite ready to send troops on peacekeeping missions, while others have not done so.

In April of 2009, A U.N. Rifleman stands watch as Indian United Nations peacekeepers look for rebels who shot at a patrol near a U.N. mission base in Kiwanja, in North Kivu Province of the Democratic Republic of Congo.

Foreign policy issues that do not involve the military tend to get less public attention. Differences among nations may arise, for example, over aid to disadvantaged developing nations. Such policies receive wide support in Scandinavia, for example, but much less among American voters. Some nations support an active role in international agencies such as the U.N., while in others such involvement is controversial. In some nations, international financial agreements produce lively debate. Within the European Union, the question of whether to join the single-currency "Eurozone" has been controversial in some nations.

Ideologically (as we shall see in chapter 5), approaches that tend to favor a bigger defense establishment and strong exertion of military power related to national security tend to be classified as "right of center" or conservative. Left-of-center approaches typically favor less exertion of military power (except for certain humanitarian purposes), and greater use of diplomacy. But again, many people look at these issues in pragmatic terms rather than through ideological lenses.

What's It All For? Public Values and Interests

If the main function of government is to make and apply policies, then one place to look for purpose behind government is among the ultimate aims of the policies. Implicit in most policy proposals are one or more values that they aim to pursue. In this book I refer to **public values** as values pursued for the whole community.

The public values that policies appear to pursue tend to come under broad value categories such as order, justice, freedom, well-being, and equality. But these words, by themselves, are very abstract; each is subject to interpretation, and can take various particular, substantive forms (see Table 1.3). For example, "order" can mean social order, as in obedience to law or stability in social structure or custom. But the word can also refer simply to peaceful dispute resolution, or the stability of government institutions. Justice can refer to criminal justice as in effective law enforcement, to social justice as in fair return for effort, or to simple fairness ("equity").

Freedom can be entrepreneurial, in the form of absence of government regulation of business. Or the word can be used in a "civil" sense, as in the "civil liberties" of free expression and association. "Political freedom" tends to refer to freely competitive representative government. Equality can refer to treatment under the law, to the distribution of opportunity to get ahead, or to the distribution of income and wealth.

Well-being has an especially wide range of meanings. It can be defined minimally, in terms of physical security against assault, as in protection from street crime, terrorist attack, or military invasion ("national security"). But well-being can also be defined in economic ways, such as overall economic growth on one hand, or minimal economic security for anyone who becomes disadvantaged, on the other. Other forms of well-being are the physical health of the public and the development of people's capacities. Some people may even consider the dignity of the people or their spiritual or psychological health (as they define these conditions) to be forms of public well-being.

In this book, I use the word "values" to refer to public values such as these particular forms of the broad value categories. Values such as national security, social justice, and civil liberties are the ultimate substantive goals of public policy, in contrast to merely instrumental values such as "efficiency," "competence" (e.g., in economic management) or problem-solving skill in governing, without reference to what the skill possessor is actually trying to achieve.

As we shall see in chapter 3, at times public values can affect political contention and cooperation. To be sure, groups' material interests comprise the most common and prominent single motivational driver in politics. This is reflected heavily in political science generally and in this book. For example, when a nation's coal industry fights a costly regulatory proposal, it is clearly pursuing the group's financial interest. However, a strong attachment to one or more public values can also form a foundation of a group's support and activism as it contends in politics. A low-income environmental activist, for example, is driven mainly by concern for public well-being in the form of environmental health.[7] Such questions as whether advantaged European governments should provide aid to combat high unemployment in southern Europe, and whether social life in the Middle East and northern Africa should be controlled by rules derived from the Islamic

TABLE 1.3	Examples of Public Values
Value Category	**Examples of Particular Public Values**
Order	Social order, law enforcement, political stability, economic stability
Justice	Criminal justice, social justice, basic fairness
Freedom	Civil liberties (freedoms of expression, association, religion), entrepreneurial freedom, political freedom
Well-being	National security, individual security against assault, GDP growth, minimal income floor, health, environmental health, individual development
Equality	Equality of income, equality of opportunity, equal treatment by law

religion, invoke contention among values as well as material interests. Shared values can contribute not only to support for policies aimed at them, but also to the maintenance of ongoing alliances between political parties (called "coalitions").

SUMMARY: CONTENTION AND COOPERATION IN POLITICS AND GOVERNMENT

Certain basic concepts are important for us at the outset: politics, influence, government, and policy. Politics is focused on the interplay of contention and cooperation by individuals and groups in and around government. Ultimately, that contention and cooperation is about making policies to address problems or achieve goals.

Then the chapter turned to introducing the main types of governmental system, representative democratic and authoritarian, and the main forms of each. Among democracies, a key difference for the overall pattern of contention and cooperation was how the executive branch leadership is chosen, and for authoritarian government a key criterion of difference was what sort of group dominates the regime. Next the chapter described the main categories of government policy, around which political contention arises: sociocultural, economic, and foreign policy/defense.

We have seen that politics and government encourage individuals and groups to contend with each other, but also to cooperate at times. Government helps to structure political contention with enough cooperation to allow policymaking. In the next chapter, we turn to an important factor affecting political contention and cooperation: power, and its most common form in politics, influence.

COUNTRY CASE STUDIES

The United Kingdom is a representative democracy in which the party that wins an election is held accountable primarily by having to contend in the next election. Belarus is an authoritarian government in which the party in control of government does not have to face real political contention; it disadvantages other parties to the extent that it is impossible for them to win elections.

The United Kingdom: A Two-Party Parliamentary System

The United Kingdom has a representative democracy with a parliamentary type of government. In practice it has a one-house legislature, called the House of Commons, referred to as "parliament." (The House of Lords, a nondemocratic vestige of the centuries-earlier effort to represent the landed nobility, has no significant political role today.) By majority vote, parliament selects one of its members to head the executive branch, called the "prime minister" (PM). The PM then appoints the chiefs of the various departments of the executive branch, also from the ranks of the parliamentary majority. Altogether, the PM plus these department heads are called the "cabinet." The PM and cabinet continue to lead the executive branch only as long as they continue to receive majority support in parliament for their major policy initiatives. This is called retaining the "confidence" of parliament.

The parliamentary majority normally comprises the parliamentary membership of one or the other of Britain's two prevailing parties, Labor and Conservative. Thus, Britain's political framework is normally two-party parliamentary. Ideologically, Labor is moderately left of center, while the Conservatives are what their name declares, "conservative." To be sure, the "two-party" aspect of the political framework does not mean that there will be no small parties in parliament; only that normally, they will be too small to be needed to help form the parliamentary majority for choosing the prime minister and passing legislation. Almost always, either Labor or the Conservatives will hold a majority of the parliamentary seats on its own.

As we shall see in more detail in chapter 3, the main reason why one or the other of the two big parties typically wins the majority of seats lies in the voting rules. Each small district sends to parliament only the one candidate who wins the most votes; second place yields no benefits. This gives the advantage to large parties with broad voter support, and many voters avoid "wasting their votes" on parties with no chance of winning. So in party formation, small groups tend to combine or join larger ones to have a chance of winning seats. The most successful party in an election will win numerous seats by small margins, producing a bigger proportion of the parliamentary seats than its proportion of the vote. Consequently, for example, the parliamentary elections of 1997, 2001, and 2005 saw the Labor Party winning the majority of seats in the House of Commons.

This means that when British citizens vote in parliamentary elections, in effect they are choosing which party's leadership will direct *both* the legislative and the executive branches of government. The members of parliament from the majority party, to keep their leaders in the cabinet, will stick together in legislative voting for the bills proposed by their leader, the prime minister. Hence the majority party can pass its policy program. For example, from 1997 when Labor took power until 2010 (when it lost a parliamentary election), the Conservative Party, holding only a minority of the seats, was not able to stop Labor-supported legislation or force the cabinet to compromise. Thus, after the election British voters supporting the Labor Party could expect to get the government policies that Labor pledged to support in the election campaign.

This situation allows the government to take aggressive action in addressing a problem. The cabinet does not have to worry about its policy proposals being blocked or watered down much in parliament. For example, during the economic and financial crisis of 2008–2009, Prime Minister Gordon Brown's Labor government intervened strongly to avoid a general financial collapse. It injected money into big financial enterprises (such as Lloyds and the Royal Bank of Scotland) to avoid their bankruptcy, which would have set off a whole series of other bankruptcies and "runs" on the banks (mass withdrawals by depositors). In addition, the government mounted a program of spending to provide jobs and stimulate the flagging economy.

To be sure, the United Kingdom has a few parties other than Labor and Conservative, but normally they tend to remain small, with strength in just a few local areas. The most notable of these is the Liberal Democrats (LDP), who are generally classified as an ideologically "centrist" party. They are mildly left of center on sociocultural issues (generally opposing government intervention in matters of personal freedom). But on economic issues, they experience contention between (a) a moderate left-of-center faction favoring mild government intervention in the economy, and (b) a moderate right-of-center group that opposes most government intervention in the economy. Usually the Liberal Democrats get enough voter support to win seats only in a few small areas (e.g., in such "outsider" regions as parts of Wales, Cornwall, and northern Scotland). The Scottish National Party (SNP), what I call an ethnic-regional party, usually runs well only in parts of Scotland. Again, in these circumstances either Labor or the Conservatives will be likely to win a majority of the seats in the House of Commons.

However, what if exceptional circumstances allow neither of the two big parties to win a majority of the seats in the House of Commons? Prior to the parliamentary election of May 2010, the Labor government's policies regarding the financial crisis and recession had avoided a catastrophic meltdown and depression. But the economy was only just beginning to recover from the deep recession stemming from the crisis. With prosperity not yet restored and the budget deficit widening, the Labor government was becoming less popular and the opposing Conservatives stood to win more seats than Labor.

Nonetheless, due to very unusual circumstances, the Conservatives did not win a parliamentary majority. As it happens, both Labor and the Conservatives had been somewhat discredited by a scandal involving members of parliament who charged personal expenditures to their taxpayer-funded expense accounts. Moreover, the Conservatives' main economic policy direction proposal—cutting spending to reduce the budget deficit—did not seem to be bringing much public enthusiasm at a time when public spending seemed necessary to prop up employment and the consumer economy. Meanwhile, the third party, the Liberal Democrats (LDP), had not been sullied by the parliamentary expense scandal and had a popular leader espousing centrist policies. It thus was likely to do unusually well at the expense of the two traditionally prevailing parties.

In the election outcome, the Conservatives won only 36 percent of the vote, Labor got 29 percent, and the Liberal Democrats won an unusually large 23 percent. As the most successful party in the election, the Conservatives won significantly more than 36 percent of the seats. But in an extremely rare situation, their seat total in the House of Commons (306 out of 650) came in at only 47 percent of the body, not enough to hold the parliamentary majority in its own hands.

Thus forming a parliamentary majority would require an alliance of at least two parties, a "majority coalition." But which two parties, and with what common ground between them to enable them to cooperate in government? The third-running Liberal Democrats' campaign rhetoric had much in common with Labor's favored policy directions, but the two parties' seat totals together did not quite add up to a majority in Commons. They would have had to find yet another small party to join their coalition.

In the end, the Liberal Democrats chose to join in coalition with the Conservatives, whose party leader, David Cameron, became prime minister. They did so despite major differences in the policy directions that the two parties had supported in the campaign.

On economic issues, Nick Clegg, the Liberal Democratic leader, proceeded to favor the moderate conservative faction in his party and its leading economic specialist, Vince Cable. The Conservative-dominated cabinet led by Cameron tilted heavily to the right in its economic policies. It proposed rapid and deep cuts in government spending. But in the proposed shake-up of the health-care system, some contention arose from the LDP, requiring compromise by Cameron. And in the two years leading up to the next election in 2015, Cameron eased off on the budget-cutting, to assure further economic recovery.

The 2015 election seemed hard to predict beforehand. In the months leading up to it, the Scottish National Party (SNP) was surging in voter support in Scotland following a popular 2014 referendum there on Scottish independence (which got wide support but ultimately failed), a new U.K. Independence Party (UKIP) seemed to be rising around opposition to immigration and British membership in the European Union, and the race seemed tight between Labor and the Conservatives. The Liberal Democrats, having tilted rightward in coalition with the Conservatives—contrary to their 2010 campaign posture—were losing their traditional centrist and left-of-center supporters. Meanwhile, the economy was trending upward (thus helping the Conservatives), and Cameron had promised a referendum on EU membership, which weakened the UKIP vote. In the election outcome, the Conservatives won a surprisingly large victory outside Scotland (where the SNP won nearly all the seats, weakening Labor's total), and a solid majority in parliament. No longer having to deal with a coalition partner, Cameron and the conservatives were free to pursue their rightward, budget-cutting tradition. And Britain returned to its classic two-party pattern of having a single majority party running the executive branch of government.

Belarus: Democratic Formalities, Authoritarian Substance

Belarus is a former Soviet republic in Eastern Europe that in 1991 became an independent nation when the Soviet Union was dissolved.

The institutional structure of Belarus's government is quite similar to France's, but its government is authoritarian rather than democratic.

In the last years under Communism in the 1980s, small groups of democracy activists in the nation operated under the banner of the Belarusian Popular Front (BPF). However, they were not the main factor responsible for Belarus gaining independence and free elections. When the Soviet Union collapsed, national independence was actually thrown in the lap of Belarus, and no elections were held immediately. Thus a major factor in many post-Communist democratic transitions—a bottom-up democracy movement pressing the nation to leave the old Soviet orbit and democratize its politics—did not play a strong role in Belarus's independence. In fact, the holdover parliament from the last year of the Soviet era kept itself in power, illegally nullifying a lawful and successful petition drive by BPF to elect a new parliament. The holdover parliament then drafted a new constitution that roughly followed French semi-presidential lines, with an elected president appointing a prime minister who had to be approved by an elected two-house legislature.

The existing government eventually agreed to hold elections three years after independence. But suffering heavily from economic problems and yearning somewhat for the security of the past, Belarusians elected a mainly traditionalist parliament in 1994. The president elected at that time, Alexander Lukashenko, had campaigned as a corruption fighter but proved instead to be a traditionalist authoritarian leader. Lukashenko got the parliament to expand his presidential powers, including the power to dissolve parliament and be reelected indefinitely without term limits. In effect, he subordinated parliament to his authority.

In Belarus, human rights infringement plays a key role in politics. Western observers have consistently refused to judge Belarusian elections to be free and fair. In a number of ways, opposition parties are heavily constrained in their campaigning. The government limits candidates' expenditures and access to the paper that campaign brochures and newspapers are printed on. The government also controls the media in ways that prohibit real debate and publicity for candidates, for instance, by withdrawing accreditation from opposition journalists. The government and its allies have used violence, detention, criminal prosecution, and the threat of them against opposition party activists, nongovernmental organizations (NGOs), independent journalists, and ethnic minorities such as ethnic Poles. In the 2006 election, the government detained and beat up a presidential candidate and detained some outside election observers.

In both presidential elections of 2006 and 2010, Lukashenko was officially declared the winner with over 80 percent of the vote. But independent election observers considered the official vote counts unreliable, with numerous irregularities and indications of fraud. Amid the demonstrations that followed the two elections, the police detained and/or used violence against hundreds of demonstrators. Seven of the nine opposition presidential candidates were detained, and ten or more of the people detained after the 2010 election remain political prisoners, including one presidential candidate. In response, European Union officials have imposed an EU travel ban on Belarusian officials. However, poor relations with Europe do not create many foreign policy problems for the regime because it favors tight integration with Russia rather than connections with the rest of Europe and the West.

Under these circumstances, Belarusian opposition political parties have remained small and have not been able to build substantial support among the people. In the 1990s and 2000s, they could not win more than a handful of seats in the parliament, which is dominated by traditionalist managers supporting Lukashenko, many without party affiliation.

In the parliamentary election of September 2012, again there were few real controls on election fraud, and the announced 75 percent turnout seemed unrealistic to independent observers. As usual, opposition parties were denied access to TV coverage and other effective means of informing the public about their candidates and policy proposals. Looming in the background was the fact that prior to the 2010 presidential election, the leader of a group with a website publicizing opposition candidates (and press secretary of a presidential candidate), Oleg Bebenin, had been found hanged with no evidence of suicide.

Under these conditions, and with at least eleven dissidents from the 2010 protests still held as political prisoners, the main opposition parties—the BPF and the United Civil Party—withdrew from participation in the 2012 parliamentary election a week before election day, urging their supporters to boycott the vote. The other smaller opposition parties, the Belarusian Social Democratic Party and Just World, were unable to win a single parliamentary seat. Observers from the Organization for Security and Cooperation in Europe declared that the election was not run impartially and questioned the counting of the vote, while EU foreign policy officials noted an "overall climate of repression and intimidation" surrounding the elections. Thus with the legislative branch fully under the control of the president, Belarusian democratic formalities remain an empty shell. This example reveals the importance of considering the full political framework and its distribution of influence when classifying governments, rather than relying solely on formalities such as the presence or absence of multiparty elections.

Interestingly, in recent years, Lukashenko has seemed to be entertaining links with Europe. Belarus is a member of the European Union's Eastern Partnership Program, was critical of Russia's annexation of the Ukrainian province of Crimea in 2014, and failed to join Russia's trade sanctions against Europe (in retaliation for European sanctions against Russia due to its intervention in eastern Ukraine).

Considering the track record, though, these moves look more like public relations than substance, and it is unlikely that Belarus will cast its lot with the EU. Belarus continues to have most of its economy under state ownership, remains a member of the Eurasian Economic Union (the Russian-sponsored alternative to the EU), is heavily dependent on low-priced, subsidized oil and gas from Russia, and has an authoritarian political system that is anathema to EU standards and much more compatible with that of Russia. Notably, former Ukrainian boss Viktor Yanukovych also had public skirmishes with Putin and postured as considering EU links, in the months leading up to his ultimate decision to reject the EU and embrace Putin. (This stance by Yanukovych led to demonstrations, regime repression of them, and his ultimate removal by the Ukrainian parliament). Belarus, for its part, does not have Ukraine's history of anti-Russian nationalism, and Lukashenko is unlikely to envision much public protest if (or when) he ultimately casts Belarus's lot clearly with Russia.

◅ **PRACTICE AND REVIEW ONLINE**

CRITICAL THINKING QUESTIONS

1. How is politics more than just collective decision making?

2. How is the authority of government different from other authorities?

3. Which democratic form requires the most cooperation among contending groups? Why?

4. What public values are most directly served by representative democracy? Authoritarian government?

5. How do sociocultural policy and economic policy differ in the main values they pursue?

KEY TERMS

interest group, 5
political party, 5
politics, 6
power, 6
authority, 7
policy, 7
government, 7
the state, 8
representative democracy, 8
autonomy, 9
political accountability, 9
formal political equality, 9
majority rule, 9
presidential, 9
parliamentary, 10
two-party, 10
multiparty, 10
authoritarian government, 11
totalitarian government, 12
sociocultural policy, 13
economic policy, 15
social welfare, 15
regulate, 16
subsidy, 16
public values, 17

FURTHER READING

Birch, Anthony. *The Concepts and Theories of Modern Democracy*. New York: Routledge, 1993.

Brooker, Paul. *Non-Democratic Regimes: Theory, Government, and Politics*. New York: Palgrave Macmillan, 2009.

Cheibub, Jose Antonio, Robert A. Dahl, and Ian Shapiro, eds. *Democracy Sourcebook*. Boston: MIT Press, 2003.

Crick, Bernard. *Basic Forms of Government*. Magnolia, MA: Peter Smith, 1994.

Dahl, Robert A. *Democracy and Its Critics*. New Haven: Yale University Press, 1989.

Dahl, Robert A., and Bruce Steinbrickner. *Modern Political Analysis*, 6th ed. Upper Saddle River, NJ: Prentice-Hall, 2003.

Held, David. *Models of Democracy*, 3rd ed. Palo Alto, CA: Stanford University Press, 2006.

Heywood, Andrew. *Key Concepts in Politics*. Basingstoke: Palgrave, 2000.

Lijphart, Arend. *Patterns of Democracy: Government Forms and Performance in Thirty-Six Countries*. New Haven, CT; London: Yale University Press, 1999.

Sartori, Giovanni. *Democratic Theory*. New York: Cambridge University Press, 1965.

NOTES

[1] A few political scientists have focused on this sort of phenomenon occurring outside conventional political channels, calling it "contentious politics." See Doug McAdam, Sidney Tarrow, and Charles Tilly, *Dynamics of Contention* (New York: Cambridge University Press, 2001).

[2] This definition is derived from that of Jack Nagel; see *The Descriptive Analysis of Power* (New Haven: Yale University Press, 1975), 29. I view power as having three major forms: authority, coercion, and influence.

[3] To be sure, in international relations, the word "states" refers to countries as well as their governments, and in some countries the regions or provinces within the country are also referred to as "states." In these cases, the context makes clear the meaning.

[4] This is in contrast to what some refer to as substantive political equality, involving voter impact on policy. See the section on "meaningful voter choice" in chapter 11.

5 As ordinary voters choose their representatives, some voting systems require a majority vote to fill a position with an individual, while others require only a "plurality"—more votes than anyone else.

[6] Chapter 7 will treat this policy category more extensively. Here we shall only introduce the sorts of policy issues that economic policy addresses.

[7] See chapter 9, under the heading of "value-related interests."

Power and the Distribution of Influence

FOCUS QUESTIONS

- **WHAT** is power?
- **WHAT** main forms does power take? Which form is the most common in politics?
- **WHAT** is a model in political science?
- **WHAT** are the main models of how influence may be concentrated or dispersed in politics?

IN LATE OCTOBER 2014 in the central African country of Burkina Faso, large-scale demonstrations arose in the capital, Ouagadougou, against the government. The president, Blaise Compaoré, had ruled the country for nearly thirty years—originally through a military takeover and then by largely preordained presidential elections. He was coming to the end of his second term after an earlier constitutional amendment had set a two-term limit for the presidency. The protests followed Compaoré's attempt to get the term limit removed so he could stay in power. After out-of-control protesters burned down the parliament building where the constitutional change was about to be made, Compaoré ended up fleeing the country.

The president was no longer "in power," but who was? The protesters had numbered in the thousands, but they were not themselves organized in a way that could quickly substitute for the prior government. They could contend, but not cooperate sufficiently for the task. But the country's army could. As had occurred many times in Africa and elsewhere in the developing world since the 1960s, the military again stepped into the vacuum, led by a senior general, Honoré Nabéré Traoré. But within a day, it became unclear whether Traoré had sufficient influence within the upper ranks of the officer corps to stay on top. It turned out that a junior officer from the presidential guard, Lieutenant Colonel Yacouba Isaac Zida, had more support. He took over the leadership of the regime, and was able to suppress further street protests.

At the time, all this left many questions related to the possession of political power. Would the military continue to cooperate in support of Zida? Would the weak government be able to consolidate its authority over the population and the frustrated urban protesters? Would Zida carry through on his pledges to schedule new elections and hand the government over to civilians? Would the current military government or a future one continue to cooperate with American and French efforts to combat Islamist jihadists in north and central Africa? To answer such questions, one requirement is clear thinking about power. What forms does it take, and what are their sources? It is this topic that we now take up.

FORMS OF POWER

In chapter 1, we noted that politics is driven by the interests and values of the individuals and groups that are involved in political contention and cooperation, and is structured by surrounding political frameworks. But the type of political framework is not the only fundamental factor that structures politics. Another factor that helps both to drive and to structure political contention and cooperation is power.

Imagine that you are living in the late 1780s in the American state of Virginia. You are persuaded to support the country's new constitution by reading essays by founding fathers James Madison and Alexander Hamilton. Or imagine that you are starting a new job. Your supervisor instructs you on how to do one of your tasks, or mentions an aspect of your job that is especially important for your future prospects for promotion. You proceed to do what is suggested, as well as you can. In both of these examples, a type and degree of power is being exercised over you.

What is power? This word is very flexible in its usage. It can refer to holding the highest government offices, such as when we say that a particular leader or party is "in power" in her or his country. But power can also characterize an informal leader-follower relationship, such as when we say that a cult leader had "a strange power" over his followers, enabling him to get them to do almost anything.

In addition, power can vary widely in its intensity. The word may refer to coercion, affecting someone's actions by force or the threat of unacceptable penalties for noncompliance. Or it can refer merely to persuasion, such as suggesting that American founding father James Madison made "powerful" arguments in the Federalist Papers in 1788 on behalf of the new national constitution. We may say, for example, that someone has "a lot of power" in his or her organization, while another person has "very little power." In international relations, we speak of the difference between "hard power" (e.g., coercion such as military threats) and "soft power" (efforts to persuade another nation's citizens and policymakers of a shared interest or value).

Political scientist Jack Nagel provided a definition of power that usefully accommodates the wide variety of uses of the word in relation to politics: the causal impact of the preferences of one individual or group on the actions of others.[1] Whether someone's preferences exert a mild effect (Madison's persuasiveness) or a much more intense effect (your boss's instructions), power is affecting your behavior.

Another distinction that we can make among forms of power concerns what could be called its "mode" of exercise. **Directive power** aims to get people to take specific actions. If a foreign minister orders embassy officials to deny a visa to someone, (s)he is using directive power. In contrast, **limit-setting power** sets boundaries and leaves people free to act within those limits. For example, speed limits on highways rely on limit-setting power. People may drive at any speed below the maximum or above the minimum. (Of course, as with many other distinctions in politics, there can be a gray area between these categories: such narrow limits may be set that the resulting behavior seems somewhat directed.)

Whether power is directive or limit setting, it can take two main forms: authority and influence. As we shall see below, authority is formal power, involving compliance as a matter of formal or legal obligation. Influence is informal power, which is normally less intense and constraining than authority. Also worth mentioning is a special, extremely intense type of influence, coercion, which is compliance due to the threat or application of unacceptably harsh penalties.

Each type of power may play a part in political contention, and may produce cooperation. We now turn to examining each form of power and its most important sources.

AUTHORITY

As was noted in chapter 1, authority is power that is widely accepted as a matter of formal obligation. The authority holder typically has a legal right to have his or her preferences obeyed. For example, when the chief executive officer of a corporation issues a directive, (s)he expects it to be carried out by subordinates. And in a courtroom when a judge makes a decision about procedure, the contending parties and their lawyers must cooperate with the judge's decision. Authority is a widespread source of cooperation.

Like any form of power, authority can operate in both a directive and a limit-setting way. As noted above, highway speed laws exert limit-setting authority over drivers. They don't tell you exactly at what speed to drive. But if you drive over the speed limit and a police car comes up behind you with its lights flashing, the officer is exercising directive authority. You know what to do. You pull over and stop because you recognize the authority of the police to enforce the law.

In a society under the rule of law, citizens know that generally people will stay within the limits of the law, and that laws will be enforced by those in authority. By and large, this knowledge enables us to usefully predict what other people will do in many situations, and thus fosters cooperation in society.

Police officer writing a speeding ticket.

In the case of authority, power is linked to the official position of the power holder. Tied to any official position in an organization is a **scope of authority**—the particular field that the authority covers, and who is subject to it. A chief executive of a company usually has no authority outside that company. Similarly, a minister of environmental affairs lacks authority outside the matters and organizations that the environment ministry oversees. If lines of authority within an organization are confused or overlap, it can be a source of contention that disrupts patterns of cooperation.

State Authority

We also speak of the authority of the state overall. Probably the earliest recognizable governments in recorded history were the ancient principalities or monarchies, each with one leader at the top. Often small states could not effectively defend themselves against larger ones. When the territory governed was relatively large, for example, in the case of the Persian Empire in the Middle East and central Asia in the fifth and fourth centuries BCE, such units were called empires. Many were the product of little more than military conquest and the threat of overwhelming force against anyone who disobeyed. Under this crude authority, cooperation was systematic and obligatory, but tied primarily to the fear of punishment for disregard for government's decisions. As we shall see in chapter 4, subsequently most states settled into an intermediate size that we now call the "nation-state."

Some governments may have relatively weak authority. In a "weak state" situation, the government has limited capacity to enforce laws and implement programs. This may be due to inadequate resources, organization, training, or commitment, or perhaps a consequence of war or economic collapse. For example, the authority of the government of Somalia in East Africa has been extremely weak for two decades now, with most of the country under the control of either contending local clans, Islamic jihadist terrorists, or occupying Kenyan military forces. Similarly, since 2014, Libya has been largely under the control of contending regionally based clans and Islamist groups. In the Central African Republic recently, state authority was virtually absent.

Even in a developed nation with a strong central government, in certain areas of life some citizens may fail to respect the law. In these cases, cooperation with laws depends on the effectiveness of enforcement rather than authority per se. Enterprises or individuals may use loopholes or deceptions to evade the intent, if not the letter, of the law, if they think they can get away with it. For example, in the early 2000s, the big American corporations Enron and WorldCom falsified their accounting to conceal losses. In the preceding decade, policies of deregulation and budget cuts had weakened the authorities who enforced accounting regulations. The stockholders weren't concerned much because the roaring economy seemed to be lifting all boats. However, when the boom ended after 2001, Enron and WorldCom were caught, their stock dove in value, and the U.S. government passed new financial and accounting regulations and dedicated new resources to enforcing them.

We can also speak of the distribution of authority within the state. For example, among representative democracies, the difference between the presidential and parliamentary types of government structure may be described in terms of the distribution of key forms of authority. In a presidential system, the voters

CONCEPT IN CONTEXT | Formal-Legal Legitimacy and "Trust in Government"

Note that political legitimacy is different from merely formal-legal legitimacy. Legal legitimacy concerns whether the rules of the regime have been followed properly in a particular case. For example, in a military authoritarian regime, a "president" who was appointed officially, according to the procedures specified by the generals for their system, is legally legitimate in that system. This contrasts with the self-declared "presidency" of a colonel who has just led junior officers in a takeover of the government. But distinct from legal legitimacy, as a separate matter, the citizens of the country may or may not regard the whole *system* of military rule as politically legitimate.

Note also that the question of whether the political system has political legitimacy is also quite different from that of whether people affirm their "trust in government" in response to a poll question on this. In a representative democracy, many people may say in a poll response that they lack "trust" in their government. But this does not necessarily mean that they no longer accept their democratic system of government overall. It may be because they don't like the current leadership of the government and are eagerly awaiting the chance to remove the party or parties currently in power in the next election, without having any problem with the democratic system. I would urge polling organizations to rephrase their trust in government question to ensure that respondents understand what the poll is asking about.

hold the authority to choose both the chief executive and the members of the significant legislative assemblies, in formally separate elections. In a parliamentary system, the voters hold the authority to choose the legislators, who in turn have authority when it comes to choosing (or replacing) the chief executive.

Political Legitimacy

The authority of government can be enhanced by its enjoyment of **political legitimacy**. This is the public's sense that their system of government is rightful and just. If people regard the system of government as the right one for them, the laws made under it will command greater respect and voluntary compliance, and there will be fewer instances of disregard for state authority and the need for law enforcement.

To be sure, state authority can exist without enjoying political legitimacy. Even under an illegitimate military dictator, most people feel obligated to obey the laws that were in effect before the military coup. However, in the absence of political legitimacy, we are likely to see larger numbers of people who comply only due to fear of enforcement. The government may thus have to rely more on threats and punishments to enforce its authority. Again, where authority is legitimate, people tend to cooperate voluntarily without keeping a close eye on enforcement. As we shall see in chapter 4, the foundations of political legitimacy in the West have evolved over recent centuries, and attaining it remains a challenge facing many national governments today.

INFLUENCE

The most common form of power in political contention and cooperation is **influence**. Influence is informal power that is typically less intense than coercion, and may work through positive as well as negative inducements. Many

TABLE 2.1	Forms of Power and Their Properties		
Form of Power	**Intensity Level**	**Degree of Limitation**	**Example**
Authority	High	Highly limited by formal rules and area of behavior	A transportation ministry deputy obeying the minister's instructions
Coercion	High	Moderately limited; usually temporary, tied to a situation	Police threatening a dissident
Influence	Wide variation; often mild	Informal and less limited by area, situation, and timeframe	A high party official getting the cooperation of a fellow party legislator on a bill

political contenders who have some authority, or even the capacity to coerce, prefer to pursue their objectives through influence (see Table 2.1). As we shall see, individual and group influence can have various sources, and vary in its strength.

Influence can be a resource and a tool in political contention, and sometimes may be among its goals. Success in political contention may depend partly on how much influence the individual or group has over others. But influence may also be a source of cooperation. Within a group, its leaders' influence over members can be a major factor behind the internal cooperation that is necessary for the group to contend successfully in politics. In a political party, for example, the degree of cooperation that exists between contending groups may be a product mainly of patterns of influence across them. In the United States in 2014, the top leadership of the Republican Party exerted its influence to the utmost to get the party's arch-conservative Tea Party faction to cooperate in supporting the party's nominees who had the best chance of winning in the general election in November. In key Senate races, they got the desired cooperation, and the Republicans were successful, winning back the Senate majority that they had lost in 2008.

Influence is so directly involved in politics that one might be tempted to include influence in a definition of politics. However, participation in politics may not involve influence. Contention can exist without it. If someone at a meeting of a political organization voices a proposal that gets no traction, we cannot say that that person has exerted influence. But we certainly should not deny that that person is participating in politics in expressing the idea.

Nonetheless, at least the *potential* for influence seems to be entwined in most of politics. In this book, I discuss influence as an especially important factor affecting politics. Influence regularly affects the interplay of contention and cooperation, but it also is regularly *affected by* patterns of contention and cooperation.

Sources of Influence

The most common source of influence is control over rewards and penalties. These often include the granting or withholding of such things as money, employment, or political support. For example, a political party official may be able to influence party activists partly because (s)he can affect their chances for promotion or demotion within the party's organizational structure. To be sure, control of resources does not in itself guarantee influence. A person must know how to use them effectively to exercise influence.

A second source of influence is the capacity to persuade, often based on perceived analytical resources. These include qualities such as real or perceived intelligence, expertise, persuasive skill, or charisma. For example, a party's expert on energy issues may have influence over other party members in that policy area. And an "elder statesman" who is known to have sound judgment can exercise influence behind the scenes.

A third source of influence is control over information. This can be especially important if an individual or small group is the only source of information on a topic. For example, many U.S. and British critics of the 2003 invasion of Iraq argued that their two governments had selectively released intelligence information favoring invasion prior to the war, while suppressing other information under their control that did not support invasion. Later on, we found out that before the invasion there was intelligence that cast doubt on the view that Iraq's leader, Saddam Hussein, had a program to develop weapons of mass destruction and ties to the terrorist group al-Qaeda. Post-invasion inspections found no facilities to produce weapons of mass destruction (other than a few old weapons left over from the 1980s that had escaped destruction), confirming the doubters' view.

U.S. Secretary of State Colin Powell, in advocating the invasion of Iraq before the U.N. Security Council in February 2003, held up a vial that could contain enough anthrax to kill large numbers as he alleged that Saddam Hussein's Iraqi government had ongoing programs of "weapons of mass destruction."

Contending individuals and groups often use information that is available to others but not widely so, presenting some of it selectively to affect others' behavior. Candidates campaigning for office usually try to exercise this form of influence by presenting only the information that shows them and their favored policies in the best light.

An important factor in politics that involves both analytical resources and control over information is the news media. Media sources have an aura of expertise in presenting and commenting on events. At least partly to attract a larger audience, broadcast media outlets often adopt a single, simplified interpretation of political events (see "The Personal Leadership Model" below). Facts that support the dominant storyline tend to be reported, while those that do not may be left out. If this occurs at times even in democracies with an independent press, imagine the effect in authoritarian states with government-controlled media. In states such as Russia, media coverage tends to favor the government's interests.

Those who control information can exercise limit-setting influence by keeping issues off the public and governmental agendas. In the early 1980s, at the beginning of the AIDS crisis, members of the French health ministry learned that the national blood supply was contaminated with HIV, the virus that causes AIDS, but did not immediately release this information and stop the use of the blood. Some AIDS cases resulted from blood transfusions, and the French health minister had to resign when the concealment was discovered. In the early 2000s, a major American drug company kept from the public and regulators information that a drug for arthritis pain relief, Vioxx, could cause heart problems. In 2004, a Japanese maker of air bags discovered in testing that their bags could

TABLE 2.2 | **Modes of Power**

Mode of Power	Authority	Coercion	Influence
Directive	A police officer issuing a ticket	Arresting a criminal	Asking a favor
Limit Setting	Highway speeding laws	Secret police threatening dissidents	Controlling information on alternatives

malfunction in inflating in a way that caused shrapnel injuries, but kept it secret for years.

Issues that find their way into public discussion via the media may still fail to generate government action, partly due to influence. Groups opposing a policy can barrage the public and politicians with misleading information that raises questions even about what most scientists agree on, such as the dangers of cigarette smoke (from the 1960s on) or the extent, causes, and consequences of global warming. Influence, as well as the other forms of power, can operate in both a directive and a limit-setting mode (Table 2.2).

Exchange and Patron-Client Relationships

Influence does not always flow in only one direction. Influence can be reciprocal between two political participants or groups. One influences the other in one situation, while the reverse may be true in another setting. Imagine that you are a member of a legislative assembly and you come from a mainly rural district. You become friendly with another legislator who is a fellow member of your party but represents an urban area. Because you know more about farm policy, you can occasionally influence your urban friend on farm issues. Similarly, occasionally the city-dweller may affect your decisions on urban policy. At various times, the result is cooperation; each supports the other's proposals in legislative politics.

Political scientists call this an **exchange relationship**, since both you and your friend have the expertise and ability to help one another. Exchange relationships tend to be governed only by the customary rule that normally, favors should be returned. Such relationships in legislative assemblies often contribute to the cooperation needed to get legislation passed.

Sometimes two people in an exchange relationship have very unequal amounts of influence. For example, a party leader or legislative committee chairman typically has much more influence than a new rank-and-file party member or legislator. A continuing exchange relationship between the two may be described as a **patron-client relationship**. The patron has much more to offer the ordinary member than vice versa: advancement within the party, good committee placements, or favorable treatment of the client's proposals. The only resource that the client can offer the patron is political support for her or him in policymaking or party leadership contention. This is an exchange relationship, but the patron's scope of influence is greater than the client's. Patron-client relationships play an important role in cooperation in politics, as well as in contention.

At the extreme of influence inequality, patron-client influence can seem almost like coercion. For example, in rural areas of a less developed country such as Bangladesh, well-off landowners often hire labor and rent out land to poor tenant-farming families. Such landowners (the patrons) often represent the only source of employment opportunities and tenancies in the area. The poorer clients may depend on these opportunities to be able to feed their families. In these circumstances, patrons may have preferences regarding the social and political behavior of their clients.[2] It may be understood in the village that clients are expected to cooperate in supporting the patron-preferred candidate(s) or group in local political contention. Insofar as a would-be client needs the job, land rental, or other benefit that is at the discretion of the patron, the patron can have a strong degree of informal influence over the client (see Figure 2.1).

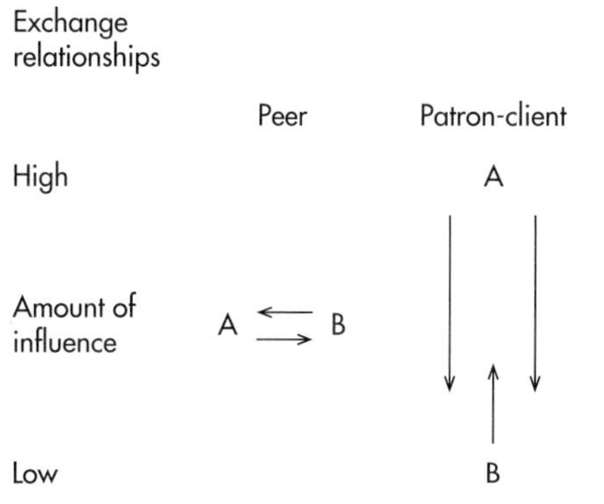

Of course, economic dependencies need not always produce greatly unequal patron-client relationships and heavy patron influence. Particularly in informal settings, even economic clients may contend sharply with groups to which their patrons belong.[3]

FIGURE 2.1

Influence in Exchange Relationships, Peer and Patron-Client

Exchange relationships

	Peer	Patron-client
High		A
Amount of influence	A ⇄ B	
Low		B

Influence by Anticipated Reaction

Recall that influence, as a form of power, involves the causal impact of preferences. If you are a political client, you may *anticipate* what your patron's reaction *would be* to a choice you might make, and act accordingly. You might perceive that the patron is likely to frown on your doing one thing but be happy with your doing another, and feel pressure to choose the latter. This phenomenon is influence by **anticipated reaction**. In this way, a patron may end up influencing behavior even when he or she does not intend to do so. The client might even be wrong about the patron's actual preferences in the particular situation, but the compliant behavior still demonstrates the patron's influence.[4] Again, as we saw in the definition of power, it is the perceived preferences that have the impact.

In representative democracies, voters can sometimes be said to influence their elected officials through anticipated reaction. The key factor is an elected official's (or party's) perception of the voters' preferences on an issue. A negative voter reaction could reduce support for the officeholder in the next election. Such perceptions may influence the official's decision on an issue. For example, a European conservative party might want to reduce the government's involvement in the economy. But it may not want to anger voters by proposing major cuts in health insurance benefits or pensions. Similarly, a U.S. senator may be deterred from backing cuts in the military budget at a time of perceived threats to national security.

Finally, however, a note of caution is in order about "causal" factors that explain behavior. As we shall see in chapter 3, it is typical in political science that several factors affect an outcome, rather than just one causal factor. When we talk about influence, we need not mean that someone else's preference is the *only* factor that determines an action. Other factors, too, may weigh in. For example, if you are a legislator, a top leader of your party may ask for your vote for a bill that you don't favor. The leader's offer of rewards for support (or penalties for

CONTENTION AND COOPERATION IN FOCUS | Influence by the International Monetary Fund

Influence can operate internationally. Over the last half of the twentieth century, many developing nations ran up large debts to international lending institutions such as private banks, United Nations-related bodies like the World Bank, and donor governments. The recipient nations appreciated the cooperation of donor/creditors in making funds available for the development of local resources and infrastructure. However, it became clear by the 1980s that some debtor nations had little prospect of ever being able to repay the debts in full, usually because they had few comparative advantages in international trade. The debtor nation and the creditor contended with each other over what to do, with the creditors holding the greater influence because they controlled future access to credit.

This is where the International Monetary Fund (IMF) comes in. The IMF is like an international bank that can offer its own loans to help governments get past financial crises. But the IMF has another function: in effect, the creditor banks and governments use it as a negotiating representative. Through the IMF, creditors may agree to stretch out, reduce, or postpone payments on the debt, or extend new loans to help the debtor governments through financial crises.

This possibility gives the IMF influence over the debtor governments. In return for the help, the IMF typically requires that debtor governments fulfill certain conditions aimed at fixing the problems that led to the debt. For example, the debtor government may have to agree to cut its budget deficit by downsizing government spending (laying off government workers and cutting programs and benefits) and reducing regulation of the economy. Such measures may narrow the range of policy options that governments can seriously consider. For example, IMF-imposed restrictions may rule out broad efforts to alleviate poverty if those efforts would increase the government's budget deficit. The IMF, on behalf of the creditors, exercises powerful limit-setting influence over the debtor nation governments, and it normally gets much of the cooperation that it desires.

However, IMF influence is not unlimited. The debtor nation may have some room to contend over the terms. This is because the creditor banks want to avoid an official default on the loans—publicly conceding that they will not be repaid. A default would mean not only that the debtor loses access to future credit, but also that the creditor bank has to declare that the money lent is lost, which can threaten its balance sheet and stock price. To avoid outright default, the IMF must at least listen to the debtor government's concerns. In this situation, other factors may intervene. People within the debtor nations may oppose the budget cuts, and the popular opposition may be so great that the government's political costs of complying with IMF requirements are simply too high to pay. This is particularly true if the government can find other options to help it fulfill its immediate financial needs, like emergency aid from a friendly foreign government or the proceeds from a natural resource.

Ultimately, while the IMF and the debtor nation may contend over the terms, they both have incentives to cooperate enough for negotiations to proceed. Upon satisfactory agreement, the IMF can ease the payment terms and/or make new loans, and the creditors will follow.

Notably, many of these same factors—familiar fare among developing nations from the 1980s on—have come home to Europe since the 2008–2009 financial crisis. By 2011, several southern European countries with large debts to banks and other governments, including ones with large economies such as Spain and Italy as well as smaller ones such as Greece and Portugal, faced the same dilemmas and pressures to reduce their domestic spending.

nonsupport) may be more or less successful depending on your personal values, needs, beliefs, and reelection prospects (see chapter 3). Similar dilemmas can arise in the case of international influence as well, where governments are faced with decisions about whether to comply with demands from influential international institutions (see "Contention and Cooperation in Focus").

COERCION

Coercion is a particular form of influence with special characteristics. It involves compelling an individual to obey by threatening or using force or other extremely harsh penalties. Coercion tends to be temporary and specific to a situation.

Coercion is normally extralegal, or outside the law. However, in the exercise of law enforcement, coercion may be legitimate. For example, if a suspect resists arrest, police may legitimately threaten or use appropriate force sufficient to assure the cooperation of the alleged lawbreaker. Again, however, in a well-established state with political legitimacy, law enforcement coercion should be infrequent. If people consider the state to be politically legitimate, they will generally obey the law voluntarily. Implicitly, the state remains in the position of *threatening* to coerce those who break the law.

In politics, the coercion that gets the most attention involves extralegal power, and is typically quite intense. Under an authoritarian regime, a member of the secret police might, outside the law, casually warn a citizen not to become involved with a dissident group. The message to the citizen may be that ignoring the warning could lead, for example, to violence or death for the victim or a family member. This represents informal limit-setting coercion.

When government officials engage in a pattern of violent coercion, the results may qualify as human rights abuse. In the mid-1990s in Bosnia (in the former Yugoslavia), Bosnian Serb security forces engaged in the "ethnic cleansing" of Muslims. They used murder, rape, and house burning to coerce ethnically non-Serb—usually Muslim—populations into leaving their villages. If this activity is conducted systematically by government agents, it becomes **state terror** (see The Human Rights Connection). State terror is the systematic threat and use of violence by government officials, or by others with the backing of government officials, to compel obedience.

For the perpetrators, such coercion helps them contend against their opponents, and secure cooperation with the dominant group. The aim may be directive (e.g., to evacuate the villages) or limit setting (e.g., to deter any organized resistance).

Similar results follow when governments allow paramilitary groups, armed units outside the official ones of the state, to use coercive measures. In Myanmar between 2012 and 2014, members of the Rohingya Muslim minority in the coastal Rakhine region were murdered or driven from their homes by Buddhist fanatics as the military rulers looked the other way. In the mid-2000s in the Darfur region of Sudan, an Arab militia called the janjaweed, armed and informally encouraged by the Sudanese government, used murder and rape to empty black Muslim villages. (They did so in part to punish the area's population for a rebellion by a small minority of its members.) At times from the 1960s through the 1980s, Latin American military regimes such as those in El Salvador, Guatemala, Chile, and Argentina used informal paramilitary groups (sometimes led by off-duty police officers or soldiers) to coerce. Such "death squads," operating under tacit regime approval, made many of their government's alleged opponents "disappear" by kidnapping and murdering them. Human rights groups are still trying to bring the perpetrators of these abuses to account.

As the world well knows, individuals and groups without a connection to a state may also use terror (see chapter 18). Starting in 2013, the Muslim sect

THE HUMAN RIGHTS CONNECTION | Coercion and Genocide

The recent history of human rights abuse shows us that coercion can be particularly brutal and vicious. Terror may be directed against members of a group to silence them or prevent them from organizing or joining a political party. Such limit-setting terror infringes on people's rights to freedom of expression and association, as well as their right to life. In the United States in the first half of the twentieth century, members of the Ku Klux Klan practiced lynching (mob killing) of African Americans, primarily in the southern states. They did so to intimidate the African American community and prevent its members from organizing, expressing themselves, and voting. Whites in state courts and juries did not punish lynching. However, in the 1960s the national government passed new civil rights laws protecting freedom of expression and association. It successfully used those laws to prosecute lynching in federal courts. The rationale was that racially motivated murder deprived victims of their civil rights. These prosecutions effectively ended lynching as a form of terror.

Terror by security or paramilitary forces can sometimes qualify as full-fledged genocide. The 1948 United Nations Convention on Genocide defines genocide principally as killing or harming members of a group "with intent to destroy, in whole or in part, a national, ethnical, racial or religious group as such" (Article II). Genocide may be preceded or accompanied by attempts to coerce, but the goal is the victims' death, not obedience. During World War II, the Nazis attempted to kill or remove all of the Jews within the territories held by Germany. The resulting six million Jewish deaths probably constituted the largest genocide in history. Other examples are the ethnic Hutu genocide against Tutsis in Ruanda in the mid-1990s, or that in the Darfur region of Sudan in the 2000s. A genocide may occur in the context of a war to take over and control territory. In northwestern Iraq, Islamic State terrorists sought to exterminate the Yazidi people in 2014, believing their religion to be satanic and believing the Koran to authorize the penalty of death—the same punishment they apply for apostasy (falling away from the true Islam) and for adultery, for example—for this.

calling itself the Islamic State (IS) has employed brutal terror on a large scale as its main engine of rule. In areas under the group's control in Eastern Syria and northern and western Iraq, anyone unwilling to obey the rules of their strict form of Sharia (Islamic) law faced brutal punishment. For someone exhibiting dissident behavior or believing in a religion other than the radical Sunni Islamism of IS itself, this could include being killed on the spot. Often families in conquered territory had little choice but to give up their children to be soldiers in IS's army, if demanded. In their domains, IS was often financed through kidnapping for ransom, control of the drug trade, and theft of oil.

Terror by independent groups may be more selective and targeted, related to who they want to coerce and what they want to accomplish. In Iraq and Afghanistan, for example, Islamist radicals and members of previous regimes have used roadside bombs and assassinations to threaten foreign and local government forces. They also seek to deter locals from working with those forces.

FOUR MODELS OF THE DISTRIBUTION OF INFLUENCE

The most common form of power in politics, by far, is influence. Many contending groups and individuals use influence to try to affect government policy.

Who has the most influence? How is it distributed within a political system? Is it concentrated in the hands of a few individuals or groups, or is it more widely dispersed?

Whether explicitly or implicitly, some observers view politics in terms of a theoretical "model." A **model** is a simplified impression or picture that aims to represent what is really happening on a larger and more complicated stage: in this case, how influence tends to be distributed in policymaking in some country, institution, or other body. This section considers a series of four such models of influence distribution:

The **majority preference model**, in which government policymaking carries out the preferences of the majority of the citizens.

The **elite model**, in which policymaking implements the preferences of some small, dominant group in society.

The **personal leadership model** (prominent in the media), in which policy-making stems from the intentions of individual leaders.

The **pluralist model**, in which influence over policymaking is dispersed among a wide range of interest groups that contend and bargain with one another.

These four impressions should be treated as hypotheses to be tested against empirical reality. They concern how influence *is* distributed, *not* how it *should be* distributed.

These models of the distribution of influence should not be confused with the forms of government introduced in chapter 1 (e.g., military authoritarian rule vs. parliamentary democracy). The models are rival pictures of how influence may be distributed in *any* political system. To be sure, we may think of a particular model as a good explanation for the politics of a nation under a particular type of governmental structure. For example, many observers associate the idea of majority-preference politics with Britain's normally two-party parliamentary political system (see chapter 1, country case study on the United Kingdom). China's single-party authoritarian regime certainly looks elite based. But such a view is a theory to be tested, not a logical connection to be assumed.

Finally, note that the models of the distribution of influence may be applied to *parts* of a political system as well as entire systems. For example, a model may be applied to only voting behavior, or representation, or a political party. And the models are not mutually exclusive. Sometimes a combination of two or even three models may provide the best explanation of a particular phenomenon in the political process. Which of the models may be at work in a situation is not only a matter or theoretical curiosity. Whether the preferences of an elite or a particular leader determine the outcome, rather than the preference of the majority or of multiple groups, may play a big role in whether a nation goes to war, or responds to an economic slump with a jobs program (e.g., spending on roads and bridges) to spur economic recovery.

The Majority Preference Model

One of the first arguments in favor of democracy involved the simple idea that in dealing with sharp conflict in society, counting votes is better than counting the dead bodies that result from military conflict. Of the models, the majority preference model most resembles our traditional sense of representative democracy. It suggests that the political process carries out the desires of the majority of the citizens (within constitutional limits). In this perspective, government's overall job is to translate the preferences of the majority into policy. The majority preference model assumes that the most important contenders in politics are the majority and one or more minorities. It views government officials as charged with cooperating in the identification and implementation of the majority preference in any given policy area.

The oldest version of the majority preference model is **direct** ("participatory") **democracy**. The ancient Greek city-state of Athens in the fifth century BCE, for example, had the people deliver their preference directly in the public square, instead of electing representatives to decide on laws. Where the public business had to be carried out by individual officials, the people chose most of them by lot, "drawing names out of a hat," rather than by voting.

This image of democracy has had its admirers. However, the classical Greek philosophers Plato and Aristotle of the fourth century BCE saw problems with direct democracy. They argued that amid political contention, ordinary citizens were vulnerable to the shortsighted and selfish passions of the moment. Those passions could be incited by the oversimplifying rhetoric of manipulative leaders (called "demagogues"), and produce what is called "mob rule." In addition, direct democracy seems only practical for small states, where the citizenry can come together physically in the public square. From the fourth century BCE in Greece to the sixteenth century in Italy, small city-states usually proved militarily vulnerable to defeat by larger units. In larger states, policymaking assemblies had to be made up of representatives of the citizens, not the citizens themselves. As James Madison, the leading architect of the American Constitution, argued in *Federalist* #10, in principle enlightened representatives have the time to examine the issues in detail. They can refine the citizens' views to make them workable.

Many who favor the majority preference model primarily follow the "delegate" or "mandate" theory of representation, with representatives following the wishes of the voters who elected them. In election campaigns, when people view contending candidates and parties as taking their policy ideas to the voters in search of majority support, they are applying the majority preference model to party contention in elections. Some early commentators on politics took a dim view of this. Eighteenth-century conservative Edmund Burke instead favored the "trustee theory" of representation, which has representatives using their own independent judgment. And in the 1830s in the United States, visiting Frenchman Alexis de Tocqueville noted unpleasant conformist pressure on Americans from what he called "majority opinion" (see "The Philosophical Connection").

However, today's public opinion polling generally shows that on most issues, there is no majority possessing knowledgeable, clear, and strong views. At most, we can say that at times on one or two very prominent issues, majorities seem to have preferences that government policy move in a certain *direction*. Such policy directions may be defined in different ways, such as toward a certain value (e.g., national or economic security; see chapter 1), along the lines of an ideology, toward better protection of some group interest, or even in the direction of a particular policy. Again, though, when a majority seems to favor some sort of policy direction, it is unlikely to be sure of how far it wants the government to go

THE PHILOSOPHICAL CONNECTION | Tocqueville and the Tyranny of Majority Opinion

Frenchman Alexis de Tocqueville was a political philosopher who thought deeply about how we can be influenced by our perceptions of the views of the majority around us. Writing about American democracy in the 1830s,* he argued that in relatively egalitarian democratic societies (which the United States was at the time, by the world's standards), people tended to see each other as equals. This approach freed them from the influence of individual leaders or educated aristocratic groups. But when people in democratic societies heard about the opinion of the majority about something, representing the view of large numbers, they tend to fall under its spell. Majority opinion could be so powerful, Tocqueville suggested, that those who rejected it might find themselves intimidated or shunned. Thus, democracy opens the possibility of an omnipotent majority controlling policymaking.

However, Tocqueville further observed ways in which the Americans had partially avoided the "tyranny of majority opinion." One of these points focused on the shortcomings of "general ideas," the packaging in which majority opinion tends to come. For him, general ideas tend to picture human behavior in uniform and oversimplified ways. In his view, educated people rightly greet such characterizations with skepticism. To be sure, Tocqueville noted, a generalization can be sound if it is backed by systematic examination of the facts. But in his view, egalitarian democracies tend to invite simplistic generalizations about behavior. People tend to assume that everyone behaves more or less alike (and like themselves). And in any case, people are usually too busy to do systematic study and dig into the details. They are inclined to take any shortcut that claims to yield comprehensive understanding without much intellectual work.

However, Tocqueville observed that while general policy decisions may be made at the state level where majority opinion tended to prevail, nonetheless the Americans tended to decentralize the administration of those policies to the local level. In *local* matters, he thought, people looked into the details of government policy. People discovered that government policy can affect their particular interests in specific ways (like whether a road will be built past one's house). On such matters, Tocqueville observed, people do possess real knowledge stemming from daily practical experience, like that of a merchant who is skeptical on issues concerning trade despite buying trendy general ideas regarding everything else. Thus, he maintained, participating in local democracy can draw people past the oversimplifying generalizations of regional or national majority opinion.

Related to all this was Tocqueville's observation that Americans readily form associations to get things done. Notably, voluntary associations often focus on particular issues that may not catch the attention of majority opinion. Tocqueville discussed voluntary associations in a pluralist vein as a useful check on central government power in America, given the absence of the checking capacity of the landed nobility in Europe.

_____

* Alexis de Tocqueville, *Democracy in America*, ed. J. P. Mayer, trans. George Lawrence (New York: Harper Perennial, 2000).

in the desired policy direction. People tend to leave those details to the elected policymakers.

The Elite Model

Our second model views political contention as principally between an advantaged minority and the rest of society. The elite model of influence distribution suggests that regardless of the type of governmental structure, a small top group (the elite) dominates the political process. It assumes that on major issues, the shared interests of members of the elite tend to outweigh their differences, producing mainly cooperation rather than contention at the elite level.

Outsider groups must cooperate with the dominant group to have any indirect influence.

The elite model clearly applies to authoritarian regimes. In imperial China (c. 211 BCE–1912 CE), the government was in the hands of an elite group of officials extensively trained in the teachings of the ancient Chinese philosopher Confucius. In the former Soviet Union, it was easy to identify the dominant role of the Communist Party officials and their governmental hierarchies. In past right-wing authoritarian regimes (such as Hitler's Germany), the elite included high-ranking party and government officials along with segments of the military, big business, and family allies.

Ruling authoritarians, such as the Nazis and Communists, tried to color their elite-dominated systems with majority preference hues—at least in rhetoric and propaganda. They often claimed that the elite understood the "true" or "real" interests of the majority better than the majority itself did. Thus, there was no need to ask the majority what they wanted through democratic procedures.

While the elite model may seem most appropriate for authoritarian states, some theorists have also applied it to representative democracies. One form of this model presents the elite's power as directive, actually controlling government policy. For example, some early twentieth-century Marxists saw business and the wealthy as actually controlling democratic policymaking behind the scenes. But this view was hard to reconcile with the apparent contention among political parties and interest groups in democratic politics.

Other critics held that the elite mainly used limit-setting power rather than directive power. Instead of controlling the government directly, business and the wealthy limited the policy agenda to prevent the government from acting against their interests. Some other critics thought that the elite-dominated socio-economic system itself served to narrow the citizens' conceptions of their own interests, keeping them within the boundaries of what was harmless to the elite's interests.[5]

In contrast, some free-market-oriented conservatives have claimed that a left-of-center elite often dominates. They consider this elite in negative terms, as favoring strong government intervention in the economy, and consisting of government bureaucrats, left-of-center intellectuals, and the media. This view alleges that such groups cooperate to keep policymaking within left-of-center boundaries.

Ordinary citizens often express the idea that some sort of *political* elite controls the government. Popular phrases such as "it's not what you know; it's who you know" draw from this model. According to this perception, a class of political insiders makes the key decisions, distant from average people. A milder and more democratic picture of influence by a political elite is possible, too. Joseph Schumpeter (1947) saw voters electing an elite when they choose a leadership, a party, or a coalition of parties to govern them.[6] For Schumpeter, the distinctive nature of representative democracy is that through elections, voters are able to hold the current political elite *accountable* for the results of its policymaking.

The use of "elite" in this model contrasts with a general, everyday usage that refers to any highly advantaged social group. Such a category may be defined by income, wealth, education, social status, or position in an organization. But members of such a category do not necessarily have or pursue common interests relevant to politics. This merely classificatory use of the term "elite" does not actually reflect or prove an elite model explanation of political decision making.

Some political scientists stress the divisions within the most advantaged portions of the population. They use the word "elite" in the plural. According to this **plural elites** view, a small number of elites may heavily influence their areas of life or politics. An influential party organization may be viewed as one type of elite, alongside business, financial, bureaucratic, military, religious, and other "elites." Political scientists with a plural elites perspective may consider officials of prominent interest group organizations (e.g., business "trade associations" or labor union federations) as elites, rather than as leading representatives of categories of ordinary people or organizations.

In the 1980s, a "new institutionalism"[7] in political science suggested that in part, government officials in any given institution amount to an elite. According to this view, much of government behavior reflects officials' commitments to their governing institutions, to the missions and procedures of those institutions, and to individual officials' roles and duties within them. This perspective considers institutional elite influence to be compatible with democratic influence, stemming from the popular election of key officeholders.

Some observers (including Plato, Aristotle, and Edmund Burke) have seen an occasional positive role for an elite in representative government. This view holds that if things go poorly under democracy, it is because of a prevailing majority preference that is shortsighted, selfish, and/or impassioned. On the other hand, if things go well, it must be because of guidance by a wise, community-minded informal elite. Again, the elite model does not require that the elite always rule solely in its own interest. It only holds that the key decision makers must share some interests and constitute an elite that dominates politics.

The Personal Leadership Model

Individual leaders as well as groups can wield heavy influence in political contention. The personal leadership model of the distribution of influence emphasizes the role of leaders and their personalities and contentions, especially in what is often considered the "horse race" of electoral contention. This model pays less attention to other factors such as issue positions, surrounding conditions, group pressures, or institutional history. What counts here are the preferences of leaders, which others tend to follow. For example, the personal leadership perspective might view Jacob Zuma, the president of South Africa, as the embodiment of the economic and social aspirations of the black majority. In the personal leadership model, individual leaders are the main contenders in politics and the focal points for group cooperation.

In democracies, broadcast news media reports tend to emphasize personal leadership. Personality and personal rivalry carry great weight. In media coverage of elections, polls measuring candidate support and the popularity contest often take center stage. In some authoritarian nations, state-run news coverage sometimes reduces the political process to the decisions of the leader, with whom the whole government is identified.

Even an entire legislative assembly might be discussed as if it were a personality, with a single "reaction" to something that the chief executive said or proposed. The Brazilian Chamber of Deputies (the lower house of the legislative branch) might be said to have "rejected" the president's bill, even though 45 percent of the deputies voted in favor of it. Division over a proposal within an institution or between institutions may be presented as a dramatic personal confrontation between

Winston Churchill giving a radio speech to bolster British resolve at the beginning of World War II.

the leaders of the two opposing sides. For example, American television news in the mid-1990s often portrayed legislative business in terms of the contention between the president, Democrat Bill Clinton, and the arch-conservative House Republican leader Newt Gingrich. In 2015 and 2016, a similar dynamic was highlighted between Democratic president Barack Obama and Republican senator Mitch McConnell, the leader of the Senate Republican majority. In actuality, this was a great over-simplification of political contention; a variety of views existed within each party on the issues.

In a similar vein, in election campaigns, candidates and commentators often talk about which candidate has the aura of "leadership." For many ordinary voters, this idea of "leadership" may come down to little more than how engaging and forceful the leader seems to be on camera.

The fact that broadcast radio and TV news so often seem to feature the personal leadership model is probably related to their need to appeal to a mass audience. The personal leadership focus makes events easier for listeners or viewers to grasp, and personal drama serves as appealing entertainment.

All of these observations apply less to other media sources, such as newspapers, the Internet, and much of cable TV. These formats generally have more space available to delve into issues, interests, and a greater diversity of viewpoints. Particularly online, a huge variety of sites attract small niche audiences who share the sites' viewpoint rather than trying to compete for the mass audience by aligning with its tastes. For example, the American left-of-center website MoveOn.org appeals to liberals, while the Drudge Report website appeals to conservatives.

Of course, personal leadership does matter in many political situations. Some political scientists study the role of leaders, using memoirs, interviews, diaries, and such. Someone may exert leadership in private, even if he or she lacks in charisma in public speeches. This was the case with American president Lyndon Johnson in the 1960s, for example. Johnson's skill lay in privately persuading reluctant legislators in his party to support his proposals. Some of these, including government medical aid for the elderly and the poor, were striking new policy departures at the time.

Other examples involve stirring public rhetoric. U.S. president Franklin Roosevelt's radio "fireside chats" boosted American morale during the depression of the 1930s, and the radio speeches of British prime minister Winston Churchill during World War II helped maintain the resolve of the British people amid devastating German air raids on British cities.

The Pluralist Model

The pluralist model suggests that modern representative democracies seldom display a clear "majority opinion" on issues. Nor is there a dominant elite, given the importance of democratic elections. Instead, pluralists see a variety of opinions held by members of groups and organizations representing them, on issues that affect those groups.

As noted in chapter 1, an interest group is any group with shared concerns related to government policy, or any organization representing such a group, that tries to influence policymaking without running candidates for office under its own banner. Examples of interest groups include farmers, textile workers, supporters of animal rights, the railroad industry, women, members of a minority ethnic group or religion, and any of the organizations that represent such group interests. The pluralist model views the political process primarily as one of interest groups contending, bargaining, and often compromising with each other. Unlike the plural elites perspective, pluralists tend to see interest group organizations and their officials mainly as representing groups in society, rather than as elites in themselves.

Some political scientists accept that the pluralist account accurately describes much of the overt political process of democratic politics, but criticize the system itself. Some view pluralist bargaining as frequently leading to watered-down half-solutions to problems. Other critics suggest that pluralist politics gives away too much to representatives of the best-organized contending groups in exchange for their support.[8] As we shall see in chapter 3, some critics point to inequality of influence between groups with different amounts of resources, such as money, personal connections, and political skills. Ultimately, a leading founder of the pluralist model, Robert Dahl, provided his own form of such criticism.[9]

Using and Combining the Models

Which model, or combination of models, best explains the distribution of influence in some arena of politics? To some extent, this question will be left to you to answer as you read on in this book. In each of the following chapters, an "Applying the Models" box will ask which model best explains influence distribution in some part of the political process. For instance, which model best helps us understand the distribution of influence within a legislative assembly? Within a political party? In policymaking in a particular issue area? Within the elite of an authoritarian military regime?

In explaining the political process, the models often contend with each other. But in some cases, the best explanation flows from two or more of the models cooperating with each other to explain the particular phenomenon better than any single model. When we look at a leader trying to persuade the majority on a contentious issue, we may want to combine the personal leadership model with the majority preference one. For example, in 2008, then British prime minister Gordon Brown led the rescue of big British banks and appealed to the public to support the action. Brown exercised political leadership, but he was also trying to influence the majority preference to gain its support in the next election. And when someone comments on the powerful influence of a business trade association, the observation adds to the pluralist model a degree of policymaking influence by an elite of business and wealth.

SUMMARY: CONTENTION AND COOPERATION IN POWER AND ITS DISTRIBUTION

Power is both a resource for political contention and a source of cooperation. Individuals and groups use power in contending to affect policymaking, and often power relations play a key role in cooperation in making and applying policy.

As we have seen, power can be directive, controlling another person or group's actions, or limit setting, setting boundaries within which a person or group must function. It can take the intense forms of authority and coercion, but its most common form in politics is influence, which is milder and more informal. Influence can have different sources, such as an official position, perceived expertise, or control over rewards and penalties. And influence can take different forms. Exchange relationships can be mutual and roughly equal, or they can be unequal, as in patron-client relationships. In either case, they play important parts in producing the cooperation needed to get decisions made.

Four models help explain how influence can be distributed in political systems or in parts of them: majority preference, elite, personal leadership, and pluralist. The models differ as to the most important contending groups and the pattern of their contention and cooperation. The majority preference model displays the majority contending against one or more minorities, with enough strength to impose cooperation on the political process around the majority's preferences. The elite model has a top group with most influence concentrated in its hands (at least as long as its members cooperate internally), capable of imposing cooperation on minorities. The personal leadership model views political contention as between prominent leaders (each with their cooperative followers), whether or not one leader-follower group is able to win out. The pluralist model considers the key contenders to be interest groups, whose contention and bargaining produce policy outcomes (see Table 2.3).

TABLE 2.3	Models of the Distribution of Influence			
Model of Distribution of Influence	**Key Actor(s)**	**Common Sources of Influence**	**Common Mechanisms of Influence**	**Example**
Majority Preference	The electorate	Votes in reelection, public opinion poll results	Policymakers anticipating voters' reactions	In 2008, officials striving for recovery from recession
Elite	Dominant group	Ability to coerce, money, control over official positions	Patron-client distribution of rewards and penalties, anticipated reaction	The Communist Party in China
Personal Leadership	Individuals	Official position, expertise, indispensability, charisma	Inspire followers, patron-client distribution of rewards and penalties	Consumer advocate Ralph Nader pressing for consumer protection laws
Pluralist	Interest groups	Group's votes, money, information	Exchange, bargaining, threats of withdrawal of cooperation	Banking representatives pushing for lighter regulation

COUNTRY CASE STUDIES

Our two country cases provide a contrast between a representative democracy in a developed nation and an authoritarian regime in a fast-developing one. Canada combines the majority preference and pluralist models, while China presents an elite model pattern with dashes of personal leadership.

Canada: A Complex Democracy

The Canadian political process provides an example of how the distribution of influence in a representative democracy can evolve over time. In such a democracy, the voters are able to hold the government accountable through elections, and thus can at least have important limit-setting influence over government. A former British colonial possession, Canada has the same parliamentary form of government as does the United Kingdom. The voters elect the House of Commons, and that legislative assembly selects the chief executive by majority vote.

Canada also shares Britain's electoral system, single-member district plurality (SMDP). As we shall see in chapters 3 and 11, this voting system tends to limit the number of significant parties in the national political process. With only the biggest vote-getter winning a district's single seat, only very large parties—typically two—can win a lot of seats across the nation. In a British-style two-party system, the majority preference model looks fairly good as an explanation; typically the most successful party in an election wins at least a near majority of the votes and a clear majority of the seats in parliament. The winning party is then able to pass its program in parliamentary fashion.

Interestingly, though, in Canada it is not the case that only two parties prevail. Canada's party system is now minimally a multiparty one (though we might view it as falling into the "few party" gray area between two-party and multiparty). To be sure, from the mid-1920s through the 1980s, two large parties were the main contenders in Canadian politics: the moderately left-of-center Liberal Party and the moderately conservative Progressive Conservative Party. Often one or the other of these two parties won a majority of the seats in the House of Commons and ran the government more or less in the fashion of the governing party in

the United Kingdom. However, sometimes the leading party did not have a majority. In that case, it occupied the cabinet (in what is called "minority government"), but without assured majority support for its proposals to parliament. It had to seek support from a small third party to pass bills.

However, by the 1990s we saw the emergence of a multiparty pattern of politics on a regular basis, despite Canada's SMDP voting system. Why? First, if a nation's regions differ very much culturally and economically, regionally based parties can emerge. A regional party can win many seats in its home region(s), even as it finds little support elsewhere. A classic example arose in the 1990s in Quebec, a French-speaking province that historically comprised French Canada and contains almost a quarter of Canada's population. The Bloc Quebecois (BQ) runs well in Quebec and has established a strong minority presence in Canada's politics. Originally, it was based on a demand for separation of the province from the rest of Canada, but today it focuses mainly on preserving Quebec's autonomy and protecting its regional interests.

In addition, a smaller party on the left has gained a foothold. After World War II, a socialist party with strong union ties called the Cooperative Commonwealth Federation began to win a significant minority presence in British Columbia, Saskatchewan, Manitoba, and a bit later, the Northwest Territories. In the late 1950s, the party dropped socialism from its program and became today's New Democratic Party (NDP), toward the left end of the Canadian ideological spectrum. Until recently, the party could win only 5–10 percent of the seats in Commons, but seemed to be gradually expanding its appeal in Ontario and a few other provinces. The 2011 elections, however, saw a real breakthrough for the New Democrats, giving them a third of the seats in Commons and the position of second largest party there. (The previously leading left-of-center party, the Liberals, was suffering from a scandal related to campaign spending that cost it much public support, and sharp contention for its party leadership that brought division within the Liberal ranks.) The NDP did especially well in Quebec, where it swamped the Liberals and even the Quebecois, as the latter's separatist appeal seemed to be fading.

To be sure, in 2013 and 2014, the NDP's public support fell back to a bit over 20 percent. This was related to the recent resurgence of the Liberals, now united under their new young leader, Justin Trudeau (son of popular Liberal PM in the 1960s and 1970s, Pierre Trudeau). But the NDP will remain significant in Canadian politics.

In Canada's western regions of British Columbia and Alberta, the mid-twentieth century saw the emergence of a small populist and arch-conservative party, Social Credit. It disappeared in the 1980s, but in effect reemerged as the Reform Party in the 1990s. The latter expanded its appeal into Ontario and elsewhere and by the early 2000s had become the Canadian Alliance. Members of Alliance paired their strongly held free-market views with resentment over what they perceived as the prevailing dominance of Canada's eastern provinces over the nation's politics. They held an elite-model picture of Canada's past, viewing the leaders of the two moderate parties of the east, the Liberals and the Progressive Conservatives, as an elite cooperating to control national politics. Remarkably, by the end of the 1990s, the Alliance party, to the right of the Progressive Conservatives, was unseating and replacing the latter in the rest of Canada, too. In 2003, as support for the Progressive Conservatives was dwindling, their national activists had little choice but to merge with the Alliance to form what is now the Conservative Party, the top right-of-center party in Canada. On the ideological right, party contention has been replaced by cooperation under the leadership of Prime Minister John Harper, who led minority governments in the 2000s and majority-holding governments in the 2010s. Harper has hewed to a strongly conservative line, cutting government spending, regulation, and taxes, even to the point of increasing budget deficits (as the late 2014 drop in oil prices has cut into government revenues).

The recent emergence of strongly conservative views on the Canadian right, and the establishment of the left-wing New Democrats alongside the center-left Liberals, defies a long-standing prediction about voting behavior: the Downsian view. In 1957, political scientist Anthony Downs generalized about the behavior of the leading political parties in single-member district, two-party systems. Among Downs's predictions was that the two big parties would tend to converge in their ideas toward the middle of the ideological spectrum (sometimes referred to as the "median voter"). That was where the more independent swing votes often provided the margin of victory. But Canada seems to provide a counterexample, with ideological polarization winning out and at least two of the three leading parties displaying a distinct left-right ideological division as they contend for the majority preference. With the wide array of interests represented in various ways by these three large parties, the pluralist model seems more applicable than either the majority preference or the elite models.

Insofar as John Harper and Justin Trudeau now appear as especially prominent leaders, though, the personal leadership model should not be counted out. In the weeks preceding the parliamentary election of late 2015, an anti-Harper campaign in the media urged voters to choose whichever parliamentary candidate seemed to have the best chance of defeating the Conservative in the district. Trudeau and the Liberals swept to a large victory, gaining the parliamentary majority and installing Trudeau as the new prime minister. An immediate consequence was that Canadian policy switched to favoring aggressive action on global warming, in advance of the December world summit meeting on the problem in Paris.

China: Elite Influence

In China, the elite model of influence distribution best explains governmental decision making. Since the Communist Revolution in 1949, the top leadership of the Chinese Communist Party (CCP) has directed policy in China. Everyone in the legislative and executive branches of government must belong to the Communist Party, and the top Party leadership decides who will serve in key governmental posts. Thus the outlines of policy come from officials who are not freely and fairly elected. The overall elite is a combination of the top full-time party officials (who may have honorific government titles too) and top government officials who also serve on high-level party bodies.

Within the party-government elite, however, the distribution of influence becomes more complex. The highest level of the Communist Party's administration is the five-to-nine-member "standing committee" of the larger (25–30-member) board of directors of the national party (known as the Politburo). This elite within the elite guides the regime. However, the personal leadership model plays a role within the elite. Most of the time, there are two leaders who receive constant attention in the Chinese press and are considered partners at the top: the general secretary of the CCP and the prime minister.

The most important figure is the top party leader, Xi Jinping, who holds three key positions today: general secretary of the Communist Party, state president, and chairman of the Central Military Commission of the party and government. Mr. Xi seems to supervise the second most prominent individual, the prime minister, Li Keqiang, who is the formal manager of government policymaking. The PM leads the State Council—a large cabinet formally chosen by the legislative branch, the 3,000-member National People's Congress (NPC). But the latter body has little real power, meeting only once a year for a couple of weeks to approve key policies announced by the top party figures in the government.

The NPC is elected every five years (most recently in March of 2013) by regional people's congresses, which are in turn elected by local people's congresses. Multi-candidate elections by the people occur only in the villages at the lowest local level. But elections are confined to candidates screened or chosen by the Communist Party. In reality, the top party leadership designates the prime minister. This appointment gets rubber-stamp approval from a national party Congress that meets once every five years in the fall before each newly elected National People's Congress convenes the following spring. The last such party congress was held in October of 2012, approving the top leadership choices for the government that were formally adopted by the National People's Congress in March 2013.

This brings us to two more elements in the personal leadership aspect of Chinese politics: the successors in the wings. Succession to the positions of party leader and PM is telegraphed well before power is actually handed over by the earlier appointments of the chief deputies of the party leader and PM. In March 2008, when Hu Jintao was in the middle of his decade as party leader and overall chief of the regime, Xi Jinping was named to the positions of state vice president and vice chairman of the Central Military Commission. Similarly on the government executive side, the somewhat popular PM Wen Jiabao took on a first deputy prime minister, Li Keqiang. In 2012 and 2013, the formal succession of Xi Jinping and Li Keqiang to the positions of party leader and PM, respectively, took place. So judging from formal positions alone in 2010, these four people made up a majority of the standing committee of the CCP Politburo, and comprised an elite within an elite. Should we think of them as personal leaders, or as the tip of an elite iceberg? The truth is that since political scientists cannot get access to the inner workings of this regime, we cannot know who ultimately holds influence, individual leaders or a wider elite.

In the recent past, the pattern of top personal leadership has varied. At times the most influential leader overall has not even held one of the highest governmental positions. For example, Mao Zedong was "chairman" of the Communist Party for a quarter century until his death in 1976; however, he was state president only from 1954 to 1959, and he was never prime minister or party general secretary. Yet it was Mao who spearheaded the "great leap forward" in the late 1950s, in which China attempted to decentralize the production of steel to small "backyard furnaces" and to get farmers to join in large communal farms. Following the massive failure of the Great Leap and the roll-back of its policies, Mao was excluded from significant influence in the early 1960s, in favor of his chief rival at the time, Liu Shaochi. But Mao began a comeback with a new ideological training campaign in the army, and by the mid-1960s was able to mount the "Cultural Revolution." This movement removed—and sent to the countryside to be poor farmers—large numbers of managers in the Communist Party, the government, educational institutions, and economic enterprises.

After Mao's death, his successor as paramount leader was Deng Xiaoping. Formally, however, he led China only from the position of chairman of the Central Military Commission of the party and government, and held no formal position at all in the early and middle 1990s. It was Deng who spearheaded China's earth-shaking policy shift toward capitalism in the 1980s and 1990s. His successor, Jiang Zemin, continued to be influential (along with associates from Shanghai) into the 2000s, the years of Hu Jintao's reign.

The closest thing to unpredictability comes when a prominent leader suddenly falls from grace. In 1987, the removal of party general secretary Hu Yaobang signaled a significant (though ultimately temporary) slowdown in the momentum toward capitalism in China. In 2012, a rising leader, Bo Xilai, seemed to have been proposing a policy shift back toward socialist goals. But he (and his wife) suddenly came under attack in the press for alleged corruption and abuse of power, and he lost all of his positions.

China's authoritarian single-party political system, then, displays the elite model overall, but with the personal leadership model also playing a part. In the 2000s, the Hu-Wen leadership's commitment to a "harmonious society" suggested pursuing greater equality between the developed and growing eastern urban areas and the poorer and more rural ones in the center and west of the country. The announced "scientific approach to development" involves shifting industry gradually into more high-tech production. However, the people have no chance to judge whether such announced policies are actually pursued or whether they achieve their goals. At all levels, patron-client patterns of influence prevail, and rising officials often bring their clients with them up the ladder.

The government struggled with an economic slowdown that resulted from the financial and economic crisis of 2008–2009 in the United States and Europe, as foreign demand for Chinese exports temporarily fell. The Chinese government responded by announcing a large program of spending for jobs in infrastructure, health, education, and other areas, along with some tax cuts, in part to try to keep Chinese consumers buying goods and services (called "consumer demand"). Part of the problem is that because of poor government funding for pensions for the elderly, unemployment insurance, health, and education, China's citizens tend to save their money to insure against such needs, rather than spending it.

Local protests do occur over unemployment, government seizures of land for new projects that displace ordinary people from their homes and farms, and other hardships. But such protests are not coordinated nationally in a way that might politically challenge the regime, partly due to a vigilant secret police. The one-party elite suppresses independent labor organization, and in practice has achieved little in addressing environmental pollution. Thus Chinese costs of production remain comparatively low, despite occasional labor shortages in the most dynamic eastern coastal regions that can cause upward wage pressure there; enterprises can always shift to the hinterland, where wages are lower.

Meanwhile, the party-government elite is flush with funds from China's growing success in international trade. It can do whatever it wants to help Chinese business capture more international markets for manufactured goods and more access to the world's raw materials. In 2008, government spending on infrastructure for business brought China's economy out of the recession early. It regained double-digit growth rates by 2010, in part because the government could spend whatever it took to keep the Chinese currency (the yuan, sometimes called renminbi) from increasing in value relative to the dollar. This policy of "pegging" its currency to the dollar keeps Chinese goods cheap in world trade, undercutting the prices of competitors in the Pacific basin and around the world. Over a few recent years, the government allowed its currency to rise slowly relative to the dollar. But when Chinese economic growth seemed to be slowing in 2015, the government abruptly devalued the Yuan to keep the prices of its exports low in world markets. And China's corporations and government continue to buy up mineral and energy resources in Africa and elsewhere to feed Chinese industry.

Elite dominance in China seems to face few threats. The new post-2012 leadership under party general secretary (and chair of the Central Military Commission) Xi Jinping and his deputy, prime minister Le Keqiang, continues to suppress any would-be opposition, and is orchestrating a campaign to boost Chinese nationalism. Despite a property investment bubble (with whole complexes of unoccupied new housing units), the regime continues to manage the economy to keep growth in the high single digits.

⟁ **PRACTICE AND REVIEW ONLINE**

CRITICAL THINKING QUESTIONS

1. Why is "causal impact by preferences" a better definition of power than getting someone to do what one wants?

2. How are authority and coercion more intense forms of power than influence? Explain whether that makes them better or worse as sources of cooperation in politics.

3. Why does neither the majority preference model nor the pluralist one seem sufficient alone to explain representative democracy?

4. Under what conditions might the elite model best explain the distribution of influence in a representative democracy? Would that situation be desirable? Why or why not?

5. Under what condition might the personal leadership model be necessary to explain the distribution of influence in a representative democracy? Does that situation seem like a good one to you? Why or why not?

KEY TERMS

directive power, 27
limit-setting power, 27
scope of authority, 28
political legitimacy, 29
influence, 29
exchange relationship, 32
patron-client relationship, 32
anticipated reaction, 33
coercion, 35
state terror, 35
model, 37
majority preference model, 37
elite model, 37
personal leadership model, 37
the pluralist model, 37
direct democracy, 38
plural elites, 41

FURTHER READING

Bentley, Arthur. *The Process of Government*. Chicago: University of Chicago Press, 1908.

Clegg, Stewart R., and Mark Haugaard, eds. *SAGE Handbook of Power*. Los Angeles; London: SAGE, 2009.

Dahl, Robert. *Democracy and Its Critics*. New Haven: Yale University Press, 1989.

Dahl, Robert. *On Democracy*. New Haven: Yale University Press, 1998.

Haugaard, Mark, ed. *Power: A Reader*. Manchester and New York: Manchester University Press, 2002.

Haugaard, Mark, and Howard H. Lentner. *Hegemony and Power: Consensus and Coercion in Contemporary Politics*. Lanham, MD: Lexington Books, 2006.

Hay, Colin. *Political Analysis: A Critical Introduction*. Basingstoke and New York: Palgrave, 2002.

Lindblom, Charles E. *Politics and Markets*. New York: Basic Books, 1977.

Lukes, Stephen. *Power: A Radical View*. London: Macmillan, 1993.

Nagel, Jack. *The Descriptive Analysis of Power*. New Haven: Yale University Press, 1975.

Schumpeter, Joseph A. *Capitalism, Socialism, and Democracy*. New York: Harper & Row, 1950.

NOTES

[1] Jack Nagel, *The Descriptive Analysis of Power* (New Haven: Yale University Press, 1975), 29. This definition was subsequently adopted by a leading political scientist and theorist of democracy, Robert Dahl, in his *Modern Political Analysis* (New Haven: Yale University Press, 1976), 29–30.

[2] For excellent examples of this, see Eirik G. Jansen, *Rural Bangladesh—Competition for Scarce Resources* (Oslo: Norwegian University Press, 1986).

[3] See James C. Scott, *Weapons of the Weak: Everyday Forms of Peasant Resistance* (New Haven: Yale University Press, 1985).

[4] See Dahl, *Modern Political Analysis* (New Haven: Yale University Press, 1976), 30–31.

[5] For example, see Herbert Marcuse, *One Dimensional Man* (Boston: Beacon, 1964).

[6] Joseph Schumpeter, *Capitalism, Socialism, and Democracy* (New York, London: Harper & Brothers, 1947).

[7] See James G. March and Johan P. Olsen, "The New Institutionalism: Organizational Factors in Political Life," *American Political Science Review* 78 (September 1984): 734–49.

[8] See Theodore Lowi, *The End of Liberalism* (New York: Norton, 1969).

[9] See Robert A. Dahl, *Dilemmas of Pluralist Democracy: Autonomy vs. Control* (New Haven, CT: Yale University Press, 1982).

Political Science

FOCUS QUESTIONS

- **WHAT** is political science?

- **WHERE** did political science come from?

- **HOW** does political science look at cause and effect in politics?

- **WHAT** sorts of collective decision making involve politics?

IMAGINE THAT AT YOU ARE A STUDENT at a public college or university in your country and one day you pick up the college newspaper to discover that government funding for your institution has been cut. The result will be a big increase in your tuition costs in the coming fall. In addition, you read that a legislative representative from the district encompassing the college voted for the cuts to public colleges and universities. Whether or not you are outraged, you may be curious about the overall decision and the vote by your representative. To fully understand how these things happened, both here and elsewhere in your country, you would have to engage in what is called "political science." This chapter's goal is to explain to you what political science is.

CAUSAL FACTORS AND CONSEQUENCES IN POLITICS

In studying politics, political science goes beyond description to the examination of causal factors and consequences. Why did a government adopt this policy, and not that one? How did the president of Colombia gain office, and what have been the consequences of his victory? Why did a nation's government allocate a certain percent of its budget to higher education, and not more or less? Is there a way of organizing democracy that would allow people to deliberate more thoughtfully and knowledgeably about issues? If so, what is it? Overall, **political science** may be defined as the systematic investigation and explanation of what happens, why things happen, and the consequences of what happens, in politics and government.

Any attempt to answer such questions requires critical thinking. In political science, critical thinking involves a reasoned, deliberate, objective, and systematic examination of political events and processes. As we shall see below, political scientists don't want to attribute an event to a single cause when there may have been several contributing factors.

THE DEVELOPMENT OF CONTEMPORARY POLITICAL SCIENCE

Politics has been studied at least since the time of the ancient Greeks in the fourth century BCE. In the first half of the twentieth century, students of government tended to consider either the institutional structures and procedures, such as how a legislature passes bills, or the effects of social structure (especially social classes) on government. At mid-century, however, the study of politics took a new turn.

Behavioral Pluralism

The "behavioral revolution" in political science may be traced to the 1950s in the United States. In analyzing politics, many were put off by propaganda such as that of the Nazis and the Soviet Communists in the 1920s and 1930s, with its distorted and biased perceptions of politics in the service of ideological agendas. Political scientists sought a more rigorously objective and scientific approach. Regarding their focus, many wanted to understand why certain prominent European experiments in democracy broke down during the 1920s and 1930s, whereas other democracies managed to survive the sharp party and class contentions of the era. Political scientists turned away from the prior preoccupation with governmental institutions and procedures and toward the study of observable behavior.

Among other things, this shift revealed a prominent role for interest groups in and around government policymaking. Recall from chapter 1 that an interest group may be defined as a group of people or organizations with shared concerns relevant to politics, or an association representing such a group, that tries to influence policymaking without running candidates for public office under its own banner. Again, interest group associations represent a variety of groups, such those defined economically (e.g., senior citizens, doctors, or chemical manufacturers), or by ethnic or racial affiliation, or religion, region, gender, or shared political opinion. At least in some democracies, political contention was found to be much more complex than a single conflict between haves and have-nots and their party representatives. Political contention was instead fragmented into competition and rivalry among countless interest groups, who sometimes negotiated their way toward compromise and cooperation. **Behavioral pluralism** was born as a general theoretical approach to the study of representative democracy.[1]

Some political scientists adopted new descriptive terminologies to highlight what they saw as beneficial consequences of pluralist politics. For example, as we shall see in our discussion of theory later in this chapter, Gabriel Almond suggested that pluralist politics performs a series of useful functions for society.

David Easton suggested that pluralist democracy produces effective societal adjustment to changes in the economic and social environment on the model of information-processing systems using feedback loops.[2] Ultimately, behavioral political science reached beyond concern with interest groups and voters to examine the whole range of political phenomena.

Challenges to Behavioral Pluralism

However, behavioral pluralism faced challenges in explaining policy decision making. Pluralist perspectives seemed to imply that at least in political systems that were open to interest group influence, the bulk of such groups could be heard. Some critics argued, however, that the playing field among interest groups was not level. Some groups had advantages with regard to resources, skills, and connections for gaining influence in policymaking.

In addition, much of politics goes on in private. Political participants do not always tell political scientists what happens behind the scenes. For example, potential new issues that could be threatening to established interests might be quashed by them informally and not be considered by government officials.[3] And citizens' ideas of their own interests and values may be constrained or influenced by conventional habits and surrounding pressures reinforcing the status quo.[4]

Moreover, some critics accused strict behavioralists of not paying enough attention to important factors. These included institutional settings, the economic and cultural backgrounds of politics, political change, and the perspectives of social movements (e.g., on ethnic-racial, gender, environmental, and lifestyle issues). In subsequent decades, many political scientists took up these topics. Two early pluralists, Robert Dahl and Charles Lindblom, later analyzed what they had come to see as substantial inequality of influence in pluralist democracy.[5]

THE APPROACH OF EMPIRICAL POLITICAL SCIENCE

In its scientific aspects, political science primarily takes an **empirical** approach. In empirical inquiry, scientists consider the observed facts of the subject and look for patterns that shed light on why the phenomena occur. Empirical political scientists generally make observations and draw inferences in a neutral, analytical, and objective manner rather than approving or disapproving of what they discover. They reject analysis that distorts the facts with biased or selective presentation of information.

You may wonder: How can the study of politics be a science? A student might say, "What do you mean science? I took this course to hear interesting debates about politics." The sections below are intended to demonstrate how, in the hands of empirical political science, the study of real-world politics can indeed be both scientific and interesting.

Terms and Concepts

Political scientists try to use terms that refer to actual political behavior in specific ways. In defining a term, for example, an empirical political scientist wants to specify just what observable facts it designates. To do so is to **operationalize** the term: to put it into practical operation in referring to clearly identifiable behavior. For example, if the term in question is "protest," the political scientist will want to know exactly what behaviors the term refers to (its "indicators"). Does protest include a formal presentation of a grievance, a demonstration with people carrying signs, a personal confrontation with someone, or all of these?

Using terms to designate behavior accurately can be challenging. For example, using a pair of words to classify a phenomenon into two contrasting types can be misleading. Often the two words suggest an extreme, either/or division, when most examples of the phenomenon lie somewhere between the extremes. A good example of this problem concerns some of the terms used to describe political parties. In political science, the term "catchall party" originally referred to an extreme case. A catchall party tried to appeal to nearly *all* voters with vague slogans that would sound attractive to anyone.[6] Such a party might pledge to stand for "the people," or be able to "fix" the nation's problems, or restore the nation's past glory. But the catchall party would not indicate how it actually wanted to do such things. The opposite extreme is the "programmatic" party, with a clear ideology and specific policy preferences organized into a program.

Unfortunately, some political scientists have applied the term "catchall" to political parties with broad concerns that are not at the catchall extreme of breadth. As we shall see in chapter 10, such parties do possess an ideological identity and do support certain policy directions that do not appeal to everyone. (Regarding some of those policy directions, though, they may lack many *specific* policy proposals on which all party members agree). On the other side, few parties are fully "programmatic" in the sense of having a specified policy program covering all issues. Such terms are fine for referring to the extremes, but for the bulk of parties between the extremes, it may be better to use ordinary words like "broad" and "focus" to classify them. In practice, the point is to refer to segments of a continuum, rather than the extreme poles of that spectrum.

To express matters of degree, numbers can be an attractive option. However, often important causal factors and consequences in politics cannot be meaningfully measured quantitatively. Attempts to come up with quantifiable indicators or rating systems that turn political phenomena into numbers often leave us with just numbers rather than real measures of what we claim to be explaining. And differences in data that are large enough to be called "significant" by statisticians may not be enough to reflect genuine *political* significance in the real world. Most importantly, qualitative conditions such as the breadth of political parties, political culture, and characteristics of government institutions also play powerful roles as causal factors or consequences, or both.

Causal Factors

In natural science, the ideal research design is the scientific experiment. In experiments in the physical sciences, some factors cause other things to happen. This sort of factor is called the **independent variable**, such as the addition of one chemical to another in a test tube. The next step is to observe what happens. The result, or outcome, is called the **dependent variable**. The solution in the test tube turned red because of a chemical reaction that produced a new red compound. This could be described as a "controlled experiment." Everything is kept "constant" except the independent variable (the addition of a certain amount of the chemical) and the dependent variable (the outcome). Nothing foreign contaminated the solution in the test tube; nothing shook it or altered its temperature, and so on.

CONTENTION AND COOPERATION IN FOCUS | How the Electoral System Affects the Number of Parties

In chapter 1, I noted that a key part of the organizational framework around politics that affects patterns of contention and cooperation is the number of significant political parties in the political system. The two main possibilities are two-party versus multiparty (four, five, or more parties). But a question immediately arises: what causal factor(s) are primarily responsible for whether a democracy's party system is two-party or multiparty? The most commonly cited factor here is the voting system—called the **electoral system**. One type of electoral system has large districts sending multiple representatives, with parties winning seats in them according to their percentages of the vote—what is called "proportional representation" voting (PR). Under PR voting, even small political groups will be able to form parties and contend on their own to win seats. Following what is sometimes called "Duverger's law,"[*] the result will be both small and large parties, and thus a multiparty system. Here interparty cooperation is required after the election; multiple parties must ally with one another in contending coalitions to have a chance of building majorities to pass bills.[†]

The main electoral alternative to this approach is to have small districts, each filling just one seat with the candidate winning the most votes (sometimes referred to as "first past the post"). In this "single-member district plurality" voting system (SMDP), only large parties will be able to gain significant numbers of seats. Small parties tend to have little chance of coming in first in many districts, so many of their supporters—not wanting to waste their votes—will instead vote for one of the large parties if they have a preference between them. To be sure, some small parties will persist and gain some votes (but not seats in significant numbers), such as the British Liberal Democratic Party and the Scottish National Party prior to 2010. But most small groups see that they are unable to contend successfully on their own as distinct political parties, and tend to coalesce into large parties.

Moreover, with SMDP voting the largest parties will tend to win numerous seats by moderate vote margins. That means that the most successful party's proportion of the legislative seats will be significantly greater than its proportion of the votes overall (just as small parties' proportion of the seats will be much smaller than their proportion of the votes). With far fewer significant parties overall, two are likely to be sufficiently dominant that one or the other will hold a legislative assembly majority in its

own hands. We call this a "two-party system" (though a more accurate phrase might be a two "prevailing" party system). Normally, at any given time each legislative assembly will possess one "majority party."

Considering these effects, however, we need to be careful about how we judge the type of electoral system as a causal factor for producing party system outcomes. Take SMDP voting; is it a **sufficient condition**—always producing the outcome—for a two-party system? It does look like a **necessary condition**; we hardly ever see a two-party system without SMDP voting. However, as we shall see in later chapters, SMDP is not *sufficient* to produce a two-party system; on occasion, we see multiparty outcomes with SMDP voting. How so? There may be *regionally based* parties that are each very big vote-getters in its home region, especially if it seeks to represent a distinctive ethnic group that dominates the region and its sense of social identity. Such parties may be big enough in their home areas of concentrated support to be the top vote-getters in numerous SMDP races there, but weak or missing in the rest of the country and hence small nationally. If enough such regional-strength parties are present to prevent the largest parties from winning legislative majorities (as in India, for example), then the party system can be multiparty despite an SMDP electoral system.

For its part, fully PR voting comes close to being a sufficient condition to produce a multiparty outcome; more numerous parties—typically at least four or five—virtually always result. But PR voting is *not* a *necessary* factor for multiparty politics because, as we just saw, with regional parties SMDP can also produce multiparty politics. So neither type of electoral system can be regarded to be both necessary and sufficient to produce the outcome associated with it. (As we shall see later in this book, a lot of other factors can affect just how many parties can win noticeable numbers of votes—termed "effective" parties by some political scientists.) So we cannot say that the type of electoral system is *the* cause of either two-party or multiparty outcomes.

---

[*] See Maurice Duverger, *Political Parties: Their Organization and Activity in the Modern State*, trans. Barbara and Robert North (London: Methuen; New York: Wiley, 1954).

[†] Dutch political scientist Arend Lijphart stressed this difference in his *Democracies: Patterns of Majoritarian and Consensus Government in Twenty-one Countries* (New Haven: Yale University Press, 1984).

Ideally, scientists begin a controlled experiment by formulating a **hypothesis**: a prediction about how the independent variable, by itself, is likely to affect the dependent variable. Then they proceed to design the experiment to test the hypothesis, isolating the role of just the causal factor under study. This type of inquiry gives us the idea of one thing "causing" another.

Political scientists, however, cannot run controlled experiments in the style of the natural sciences. They can only look for causal factors in ongoing political processes, where normally, multiple variables affect outcomes. Political scientists do this in a systematic way, choosing examples of the phenomenon they are studying in a way that holds the basic situation constant as much as possible. But they know that usually, multiple causal factors will be at work. Very rarely do political scientists discover a causal factor that is *both* (a) necessary and (b) sufficient (always producing the outcome) to yield a type of result—what we think of as *the* cause of the outcome (see "Contention and Cooperation in Focus").

MULTIPLE CAUSAL FACTORS AND CHALLENGES IN CAUSAL ANALYSIS

Often, however, the number of causal factors affecting an important political phenomenon is more than just two. Imagine that you are trying to understand how members of legislative assemblies vote on bills in presidential democracies. As we saw in chapter 1, in countries with the presidential type of democratic governmental structure, legislators of the same party don't all have to vote together in support of their leader's proposed bills to keep him or her in control of the executive branch; the president serves a fixed term of office regardless of whether her or his policy proposals pass the legislative assemblies. Thus at times, individual legislators may cast votes contrary to the preference of their party leaders.

Your hypothesis may be that at least in election years, legislators will tend to cast votes on bills in ways that please the voters in their districts (to help with reelection). However, your research results may turn up mixed on this question. Survey data and follow-up interviews are likely to reveal that individual legislators' voting on bills can be affected by several factors in addition to their interest in pleasing the voters to get reelected. A few possible causal factors are:

- Party leadership influence,
- Legislators' personal values,
- Legislators' empirical beliefs regarding the issues of the day (for example, on economic issues, the degree of accuracy of representatives' understanding of the principles of economics),
- Legislators' past patterns of support for interest groups,
- Big campaign contributions that the legislator may have received recently or may hope to get,
- The level of voters' awareness of the legislative voting record of the officeholder,
- Whether there is a viable opponent in the district for the next election.

Complicated, huh? You may discover that even with an upcoming election looming, legislators do not always vote with the majority preference in their district. For example, if there is no strong rival on the horizon, and if the legislator's party leaders are pressing hard for a party-supported vote that may be controversial in the district, and such a vote fits the legislator's personal values, he or she may cooperate with the party leadership and cast a vote contrary to the views of most voters in the district represented. This happened with several Democrats in the American Congress who voted for new health insurance legislation in 2010. Even some who had a serious Republican contender in their reelection race stuck with their party leaders on the legislative vote, and lost their seats.

Factor Interactions and Intervening Variables

Correlations between independent variables and the outcome do not automatically mean causation. The researcher should explore *mechanisms* of causation—*how* the independent variables affect the dependent one. This task may require further investigation and an extra dose of critical thinking to dig into the meaning of the data. What sorts of complications might turn up?

First, one causal factor may affect another, as well as affecting the dependent variable. Let's return to the example of legislators voting with or against public opinion. We noted that if there is no strong opponent and reelection seems assured, party leader influence may prevail and lead the legislator to cast a vote that is contrary to majority opinion in the legislator's district. However, what if new polling indicates that a weak opponent has suddenly started to look strong, perhaps due to a heavy influx of outside campaign contributions for negative advertising against the officeholder? This change in district competitiveness can affect another causal factor that we just noted: the amount of party leadership pressure. Party leaders may drop their pressure on our unfortunate legislator to vote for a party-backed bill that is controversial in her or his district. The party leaders want to see their fellow party member reelected in what has now become a tight contest. Sometimes one causal factor is affected by another causal factor within the field of behavior being studied.[7]

Moreover, an independent variable may affect the outcome only *through* its impact on another causal factor, which more directly affects the dependent variable. That other factor may be labeled an **intervening variable**, coming in between the independent and dependent variables. For example, an economic downturn in the community—an independent variable—may damage an officeholder's chances of reelection—the dependent variable. But this may occur only through another contributing factor: the public's sense that the officeholder or his/her party was somehow responsible for the downturn (just how so, need not be understood by the voters). This question of whether or not voters blame a bad outcome on the party in power points to an intervening variable: public opinion about politicians' responsibility for external events.

In the United States, the public's answer to this question about governing party responsibility for bad results seemed to be yes when the Republican Party suffered big election losses in 2008 in the midst of a financial crisis. But in other situations, the answer seemed to be no, with the voters not considering the leading officeholders to be responsible:

- When America's Republicans won the most seats in the 2002 legislative elections despite the devastating terrorist attacks on American soil in September 11, 2001, and

- When German voters kept the Christian Democratic Party in power in the mid-2009 parliamentary election despite the financial crisis and economic downturn of 2008–2009.

Sometimes another independent variable affects the intervening variable. For example, what the news media or "the experts" say about the causes of a bad outcome, and how much of the public listens to which media sources, may affect public opinion about officeholder responsibility for negative events. The key point is that intervening variables can help connect the dots between independent and dependent variables in explaining important political phenomena.

In sum, understanding politics is a bit like the basics of chemistry. You start with the basic elements, but with the understanding that most often we find their atoms combined into multielement compounds which, in turn, interact with one another. Each chapter in this book, in one way or another, starts out by identifying the most important types of group and/or causal factor at work in the chapter topic. Then it proceeds to explore how those elemental factors contend, cooperate, or combine, to produce outcomes, which may then play the role of causal factors producing more outcomes.

Comparative Methods

Further complexity can arise when political scientists *compare* research results from different settings, places, or times. To be sure, almost all research in political science involves comparison to some extent. Analyzing the results of a single opinion poll is actually comparing the answers given by different respondents to the survey questions. But often comparison plays a more prominent and conscious role, such as when the researcher looks into what can be discovered about a phenomenon in different regions, periods, political organizations, or countries. As we shall see below, a major subfield within political science is "comparative politics."

If an explanation of some political phenomenon holds up across several nations, or several periods or locales in one nation, then it seems to carry more weight generally. But comparison also introduces more variables and complexity, and may require further critical thinking. Increasing the number of cases in the comparison may make it more difficult to find common patterns of cause and effect, leave less opportunity to explore each case deeply enough, and increase the chances that the diverse cases may not really be comparable (see "Concept and Context"). One answer is to settle on two or three carefully selected cases for comparison. This approach allows for some multicase explanatory power but also permits in-depth examination of cases.

Values as Causal Factors

This book discusses myriad causal factors and consequences related to politics. But periodically our exploration highlights certain causal factors that are important to contention and cooperation in politics, but do not always get the attention that they deserve. A factor that was introduced in chapter 1 was political frameworks (combining the type of governmental structure with the type of party system), which especially affect contention and cooperation within and between political parties.[8] A second key factor is influence, introduced in chapter 1 and explored further in chapter 2.

CONCEPT IN CONTEXT | Intensive and Extensive Comparison

Two lines of approach to comparing political phenomena were laid out first by the nineteenth-century British political philosopher John Stuart Mill,* and explored more recently by political scientist Adam Przeworski.† One approach carefully selects just a few locations where a phenomenon occurs, in which most of the surrounding conditions are the same, and explores them intensively. This approach is modeled on the scientific method noted above, in which researchers try to isolate just the variation in the causal factors and outcomes under study. They attempt to keep everything else fairly constant between cases. The small number of carefully selected cases lessens the chance that other causal factors may be involved. For example, someone interested in explaining military interventions (takeovers, or "coups") in politics might compare only the right-wing military coups in Brazil, Chile, and Argentina between 1964 and 1975. Przeworski called this the "most similar systems design." With only a few related cases, a deeper focus on variables is possible (though more causal factors may turn up than originally expected). But results may be harder to generalize to the world at large.

The other comparative approach is more extensive; it considers the phenomenon in a wide range of different cases without trying to keep the cases similar. In contrast to the above study considering just two or three military interventions, a researcher might look at all of them anywhere in the world in the twentieth century. Among the many differences in the cases, the researcher may spot one or two variables that seem to be similarly linked to an outcome in virtually all cases. In another example, Robert Dahl compared all established democracies (the outcome) in a great variety of national contexts. Among the factors that he noticed across them all were freedom of expression and independent decision making (**autonomy**) among groups.‡ Political scientists may feel confident that the few similarities they see across so many different cases may indicate important factors for the phenomenon they are trying to explain. Przeworski called this the "most different systems design."

So with a wide range of diverse cases, results may be more generally applicable. However, researchers run the risk of overlooking factors such as cultural, institutional, or historical differences that can cause the "data" to mean different things in different cases. In practice, often comparative research tries to mix and balance the two approaches and their advantages and disadvantages.

---

* See *A System of Logic* (New York: Harper & Brothers, 1884).

† See Adam Przeworski and Henry Teune, *The Logic of Comparative Social Inquiry* (New York: Wiley-Interscience, 1970).

‡ See Robert A. Dahl, *Polyarchy: Participation and Opposition* (New Haven, CT: Yale University Press, 1971).

In addition, at the end of chapter 1, I introduced public values as the aims that are implicit in policies, and hence among the ultimate aims of government. Again, I was referring to particular forms of broad value categories such as order, justice, freedom, well-being, and equality. For example, justice-oriented policies may pursue criminal justice or social justice. Or well-being may be interpreted in different ways to yield particular forms, such as overall economic growth, or minimal economic security for all, or wider access to health care. The idea of freedom may take entrepreneurial, political, and civil liberties forms. These goals of public policy may be referred to as public values—values pursued for the whole community.

As I noted in chapter 1, most often my mention of values in this book will refer to such substantive goals of policies. Only occasionally will I refer to merely instrumental values such as "competence" or "efficiency," independently of what someone is efficiently or competently trying to accomplish.

The idea of substantive public values suggests an empirical question: to what extent can public values be another type of causal factor affecting patterns of contention and cooperation? As was noted in chapter 1, values do sometimes seem to play a part in motivating the supporters of policy ideas. To be sure, the role played by public values in politics may be difficult to pin down using behavioral methods. A particular policy's implicit value objective might not supply the main motivation for the support that the policy receives from all of the policy's backers. Indeed, the type of political motivation in politics that is most often cited or assumed by political scientists is self-interest in some form. Group and individual self-interest will play an important part in explaining politics in this book, as in any political science textbook.

However, the fact that public values may be harder to trace and define clearly in political motivation does not mean that they are never relevant to the causal explanation of policymaking. At times, such values clearly help motivate groups in their political efforts, whether alongside or even instead of group self-interest. Differences over which public values should have priority in a given situation, over their meaning, and over how best to pursue them, can heighten the intensity of political contention. And shared concern for public values can contribute to political cooperation in making and applying policies. For example, in the U.S. Congressional debate in 2013 over whether to keep the government operating and raise the U.S. debt limit, surely shared concern about national and international financial stability (alongside Republican worries about their party's waning public support over the issue at the time) played a part in driving many Republican legislators to suddenly switch from contention to cooperation with the Democrats, and allow the necessary legislation to pass.

As we shall see in coming chapters, public values can also affect an array of other political phenomena. For example, values may contribute to:

1. The ongoing goals of certain types of interest group,[9]

2. The aims of social movements,

3. The motivations of some voters as they cast their ballots,

4. The capacity of a party or coalition to stay together and cooperate despite internal contention, and

5. Transitions from one type of political framework to another

It is not only overlapping material interests that can bring contending groups toward cooperation or compromise in a particular case; such outcomes can also get a boost from shared values.

One important example of the impact of values on politics is in the domain of human rights. The first official U.N. human rights document, the Universal Declaration of 1948, articulated human rights as goals especially under the headings of freedom and well-being. The subsequent U.N.-sponsored international Covenants of Human Rights (in effect for signatory nations in 1976) went further to obligate signatory nations to have laws protecting rights such as those to freedom of expression, freedom of association, and the right to a fair trial.

However, the U.N. Covenants provide no mechanism of international authority to enforce the creation or implementation of such laws. And specific duties imposed by the Covenants are limited to requiring that signatory governments report to the Human Rights Commission regarding human rights conditions

THE HUMAN RIGHTS CONNECTION | National Obligations under the Civil-Political Covenant

The specific obligations imposed by the U.N.'s International Covenant on Civil and Political Rights (ICCPR) under international law pertain mostly to monitoring human rights conditions. The Covenant imposes requirements for regular reporting of human rights conditions by U.N. member nations, and assessment of the reporting by an international Human Rights Committee (HRC). The committee meets three times a year and is comprised of eighteen members selected by the signatory states. The HRC and its staff may ask probing questions and get a subsequent response from a representative of the country's government. The reports and results are public and are submitted to the U.N.'s Economic and Social Council, and then on to the U.N. General Assembly. In addition, nations have the option of signing the First Optional Protocol under the Covenant, which allows individuals and groups who have exhausted all national avenues to appeal to the HRC about their human rights plight.

These reporting and assessment requirements do not directly address human rights problems, of course, but they do make way for publicizing them and mobilizing the "shame" factor, for what that is worth. In practice, the most serious punishment for severe violations is international sanctions of one sort or another, such as the trade embargo imposed on the new Serbia-Montenegro republic in the mid-1990s due to its support for human rights abuse in neighboring Bosnia-Herzegovina.

Notably, a very important nation in the history of human rights respect, the United States, formally ratified the ICCPR in 1992. However, it did so with a sweeping reservation, stating that it did not regard the ICCPR as "self-executing." That is, the United States does not consider any of the Covenant's reporting and other requirements as obligatory on itself unless the nation explicitly adopts enabling legislation to that effect. (Observers noted that without the reservation, it would have been unlikely that the U.S. Senate—which in practice requires a 60 percent vote for passage of such legislation—would have approved the ratification.) In fact, the United States, extremely conscious of its national sovereignty and confident in its own national protections of civil-political rights, has not adopted such legislation.

What laws or constitutional provisions in your country are related to protecting human rights? Are they applied effectively?

in their countries (see "The Human Rights Connection"). Thus the practical importance of the Covenants is to provide a set of internationally and officially accepted values, serving to bolster the claims of victim groups in politics and hopefully steer governments' policies in their direction.

THEORY IN POLITICAL SCIENCE

Theory about anything involves large-scale explanation of its subject matter. In political science, theory suggests broad patterns of cause and effect that are presented as permeating politics generally. Theories may be considered as generally supported by the facts, or may remain at the level of hypothesis or conjecture, either not yet established as valid or just hard to establish, or both.

In political science, there are two types of such broad explanation of patterns of cause and effect: empirical and normative. **Empirical theory** concerns causal factors and consequences among observable phenomena in politics studied scientifically. Normative theory examines and tries to justify values as important consequences, and explores what are the best causal means to pursue them, as paths that ought to be followed.

Empirical Theory

What do we mean by the word "theory" in empirical political science? In one sense, any conceptual hypothesis is theoretical until it is supported by empirical investigation. But what is most often meant by "theory" is better indicated by the phrase "grand theory," regarding the widespread impact of a whole class of causal factors. For example, the above-discussed pluralist approach to politics emerged first as a general argument that the interaction and bargaining among interest groups plays a powerful role in policymaking. In contrast, Karl Marx (see chapter 4) argued that the preferences of the ruling economic class play a powerful role in determining policy.

Some early theoretical initiatives by political scientists concerned the consequences—typically beneficial, they thought—of pluralist politics. These theorists served to highlight aspects of pluralist democracy that foster political stability. For example, Gabriel Almond presented a list of what he considered to be key functions of the government, such as "aggregating" interests (getting related interest groups to compromise and cooperate in support of broad policy programs such as the election platforms of large political parties), "political recruitment," and "rule making."[10] Almond suggested that if these functions are spread out among various political institutions, the chances are better for political stability because the process avoids overloading any one institution with too many demands.

David Easton[11] pictured democratic government as an information-processing system. The system is driven in large part by its desire to adapt to changes in the economic, social, or political environment around it. Interest group "demands" (e.g., expressions of policy preference) and "supports" (e.g., effort and money contributed to political causes and government) served as "inputs," which political processes "convert" into policy "outputs." When the impact of a policy—say, a tax cut with some degree of impact on a stalled economy—is noticed by society, the information is fed back into the political system in its next round of demands. In Easton's view, this "feedback loop" provides for organizational adaptation to change (see Figure 3.1). Another political scientist, Samuel Huntington, emphasized that the "institutionalization" of parties and government units—stabilization of their structures and procedures over time—was key for overall political stability.[12]

Descriptive perspectives such as these provided some overall context for students of politics. They helped to map the political process and relate its parts to each other as aspects of a functional whole. The underlying thrust was positive and reassuring that the democratic political process was at least capable of providing political stability by responding to policy challenges and resolving intergroup contention peacefully. As was noted above, however, this positive view has been challenged. And in American politics, the original home of multiple institutions checking and balancing each other, some critical observers point to the frequency of deadlock that overdoes stability at the expense of addressing serious problems.

Among empirical political scientists today, some additional theoretical approaches play the role of

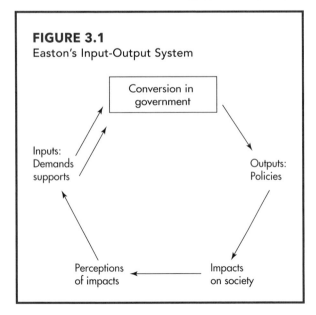

FIGURE 3.1
Easton's Input-Output System

"schools of thought," concerning what clusters of variables are especially power-ful causal factors in politics. For example,

- Institutionalist analysis stresses the impact of political institutions (e.g., legislative or executive), and the rules, norms, and incentives they create, on political outcomes.

- Political culture emphasizes the effects of deeply held cultural values, beliefs, and customs that stem from the surrounding culture of society.

- Modernization analysis attempts to explain the development of democracy in terms of the impact of "modern" factors such as economic growth, urbanization, industrialization, education, modern forms of communication, and the size of the middle class.

- Rational choice analysis stresses self-interested calculation as a motivator of political action, with individuals and groups applying cost-benefit analysis to their alternatives, and choosing the one that maximizes their own benefit.

Political scientists who subscribe to one of these schools of thought may treat their favored type of causal factor as a widespread independent variable, or only as an intervening one, and may see its role only in certain major areas of politics. For example, a rational choice-oriented political scientist might concede that public values may play roles at times in raising issues and proposing policies, but might nonetheless contend that when policy decisions are finally made, the self-interested calculations of groups and individual participants will prevail.

Political scientists who rigidly adopt only one of these orientations and deny the validity of the others may encounter major opposition within the discipline. For example, the rational choice orientation has contributed much to political science by highlighting the role that the rational self-interest of groups and individuals can play in the political process. But some proponents of rational choice theory seem to overlook the possible roles of other factors. Such additional factors may include history, culture, attachment to particular groups or individuals, social solidarities, personal and group beliefs and values, and the customs and missions of government institutions. Sometimes rational choice analyses amount to little more than laying out an assumed sequence of logic for a group in a situation, without thorough empirical demonstration that political participants actually act on that logic in numerous particular cases. The result has been a contentious debate between rational choice-oriented political scientists and other political scientists with different views.[13]

Because political science tends to produce less conclusive "truths" than natural science, political scientists tend to be skeptical of theories that claim to explain the political world too completely. As philosopher of science Karl Popper suggested,[14] explanatory theories must be "falsifiable." That is, their explanations must always allow for the possibility of **counterexamples**—data contrary to the hypothesis. Theories that claim to be able to "explain away" all seeming counterexamples (Marxism, for example, has been accused of this) are suspect. Counterexamples often prove useful by pointing the way to further research that explores more variables and their impacts.

Normative Theory

Many political scientists consider the scope of political science to include only the empirical and scientific approach that the current chapter has embodied up to this point. But some political scientists add an element of judgment. They ask: What *should* politics and society be like? What goals are most important, and how are they best pursued?

Such approaches are commonly referred to as **normative**. The linguistic root of the term is "norm," in the sense of a standard to be pursued. Normative inquiry examines political phenomena in terms of their consequences for important values. Normative discussion includes not only devising ideal ways to pursue values, but also *evaluating* empirical realities as to how well they realize some value. It adds the "ought" to the "is." For example, normative thinking asks, how is democracy good, what achievable form of it is best, and how might this or that form of democracy fall short?

A branch of normative inquiry is called **normative theory** or political philosophy. Normative theory engages in one or more of the following: examining normative concepts, exploring human nature, history, and current society in light of them, and suggesting what arrangements may be required to pursue public values effectively.

Notably, normative theory includes empirical observations about causal factors and consequences, as well as normative exploration. Generalizations about "what is" often play a supporting role in justifying "what ought to be." Indeed, most of the important normative theorists did what they considered to be serious empirical analysis long before the mid-twentieth-century development of the methods of modern political science. But they asked about causal factors and consequences in a way that is more expansive and value related than what we see in behavioral research (see "The Philosophical Connection"). For example, political philosophers may debate about human nature and the broad course of history. And the empirical analysis in their works varies in its objectivity, accuracy, and comprehensiveness. Nonetheless, the bulk of the empirical thought on politics that can be found in the Western tradition prior to the twentieth century appears in the writings of the political philosophers.

Today, some political philosophers show disdain for much of behavioral political science. They see narrow "number-crunching" as abstaining from consideration of the big questions that really matter. For their part, on the other hand, many empirical political scientists are uncomfortable in the realm of political philosophy. Concepts such as freedom, public happiness, political ethics, equality, and justice can be interpreted in different ways, and can be difficult to operationalize (put into practical operation) behaviorally. It can be hard for people to agree on the terms, criteria, and standards of reasoning for discussing these concepts. And when such concepts are employed in the form of ideological rhetoric, they can be used in self-serving ways that distort or conceal empirical reality, rather than confronting it honestly.

Nonetheless, most political scientists recognize that normative inquiry can be done well. It can respect the need for empirical accuracy and maintain high standards in normative and empirical reasoning. While normative theorists are only a small minority within political science, they share in the overall enterprise of trying to understand causal contributions and outcomes related to politics and government. Normative theory is the focus of chapter 5 and the "Philosophical Connection" boxes throughout this book.

The other main branch of normative political thought and discussion is **ideology**. Rather than open-ended and comprehensive exploration, ideology focuses on systematic prescription. An ideology collects and connects, into a

THE PHILOSOPHICAL CONNECTION | Thomas Aquinas

Observing the behavior of politicians and some of the decisions they make, many people wish for a world in which politics was dominated by ethical considerations. What might the whole political process look like if the bulk of political participants were trying to be ethical, first and foremost? One such picture is found in the normative and empirical thinking of the Christian theologian and political philosopher Thomas Aquinas (1225–1274).*

Aquinas laid the foundation for centuries of subsequent Catholic thought on politics and society, and influenced later political thought generally. Aquinas stressed order and justice as the key values for government to pursue. He believed that to pursue these values, governments had to operate primarily through *law*.

In key empirical aspects of his thought, Aquinas borrowed from ancient Roman thinkers such as the Roman Stoics and Cicero. They had observed that certain practices were commonly found in societies that seemed to be harmonious and flourishing. Positive examples of these included support for the public good and appreciation of moral virtue, alongside, more negatively, prohibitions against harming others and unfairness in commerce. The Stoics referred to these basic rules collectively as "natural law." Building on both these earlier thinkers and the Christian context, Aquinas saw natural law as rational and given by God. Thus its principles became ethical standards for human behavior.

For Aquinas, ordinary human reason was capable of seeing the general principles of natural law. But to apply them to real-world cases, people needed additional help from "human law" applied by governments. This realm of human law, however, could be a challenge. Human law had to adapt natural law to local circumstances, allowing for some diversity among nations in their laws and customs. And these practical rules for applying natural law could sometimes have exceptions, and could even be improved by human reason.

To be sure, for Aquinas, people and governments got some help from "old Divine law," God's biblical revelation of rules such as the prohibitions of murder and theft in the Ten Commandments. But even these rules remained general. As for the "new Divine law"— the teachings of Jesus of Nazareth in the New Testament, such as "love thy neighbor" and forgive your enemies—such maxims were too idealistic and perfectionist to be enforced by the state. For Aquinas, this "new Divine law" was left to the individual conscience, the pulpit, and God's judgment in the afterlife.

For the often difficult task of practically specifying and applying human law, Aquinas followed classical Greek and Roman thought in requiring the reason and virtue of leading statesmen, pursuing the common good. Overall, Aquinas looked favorably upon monarchy because of the unity it provided at the top of government, but he also suggested consultation with a group of wise statesman in the framing of laws. Ultimately, for Aquinas, the best form of government was "law sanctioned by lords and commons." (If the people were free of corruption, he thought—a big "if"—they could be allowed to elect their governmental leaders.)

---

* See Thomas Aquinas, *Treatise on Law* (*Summa Theologica*, I-II, questions 90 through 97), trans. Richard J. Regan (Indianapolis: Hackett Pub. Co., c 2000), and *On Kingship*, trans. Gerald B. Phelan (Toronto: Pontifical Institute of Mediaeval Studies, 1949).

single approach to policy and politics, the following: (a) one or more preferred values, (b) related empirical beliefs about society and politics, (c) evaluations of society and politics, and (d) prescriptions for government's structures and policies that follow logically from those values, beliefs, and evaluations. An ideology such as Marxism-Leninism or classical liberalism typically adopts views—some of which may be drawn from the work of the political philosophers—on these matters, and proceeds directly to prescriptive solutions for the current era. Ideologies, the topic of chapter 6, often play an important role in the identities of political parties.

THE SCOPE OF POLITICAL SCIENCE AND THE SEQUENCE OF POLICYMAKING

The scope of politics is broad, and thus the same can be said about political science. Spatially, politics and political science reach out into society, beyond the confines of formal political institutions. But the scope is broad in a temporal sense, too. Political scientists study the whole process of policymaking, all the way from the selection of the policymakers through the steps of policymaking to the impacts of policies on society after the policy decision is made.

Selecting the Policymakers

First, who are the people in office who make the decisions, and how did they get there? Politics plays a prominent role in the selection of those who will serve as the leading government officials, such as members of legislative assemblies (in democracies) and the top officials of the executive branch of government. As we shall see in detail in chapters 9, 10, and 11, people engage in political contention to decide who will be the parties' nominees for public office. Then parties and supportive interest groups contend, cooperate, and try to exert influence to get their nominees elected to government posts. In doing so, they appeal for support from groups among the voting population. In authoritarian governments, various individuals and subgroups within (or associated with) the dominant group contend, use influence, and cooperate to place their members or supporters in important government jobs.

Raising and Defining Issues

Next, how did a given policy issue first arise? In a single organization like a club or an economic enterprise, new challenges or opportunities may just pop up, such as when a trucking company confronts a big rise in diesel fuel prices. In national policymaking, too, sometimes an issue forces itself onto the agenda, like the Great Depression of the 1930s or the economic and financial crisis and downturn of 2008–2009 in Europe and North America (see Figure 3.2).

Normally, however, the arrival of an issue on the agenda of national politics tends to require political effort. At any given time numerous problems exist, and getting people to pay serious attention and to one of them involves contention, cooperation, and influence. A blogger, a newspaper editor, a book (see photos), a piece of scientific research, a report produced by an interest group, the coordination of the efforts of multiple related interest groups, a social movement engaged in protest, or a political party's leaders holding a press conference can each contribute to getting an issue onto the political agenda.

Different groups have different capacities to elevate problems or goals that are important to them into national issues that government must address.[15] For example, environmental groups face challenges in getting the issue of global warming (due to carbon dioxide and methane emissions) onto the government's agenda. Correlatively, a group may aim at keeping *off* the agenda issues that could lead to government action that is contrary to the group's goals.[16] The traditional fossil-fuel industries (e.g., oil, gas, and coal) generally work to keep the issue of global warming off the agenda. Opportunities for this may be provided not only by the structure and procedures of government, but also by any possibility of

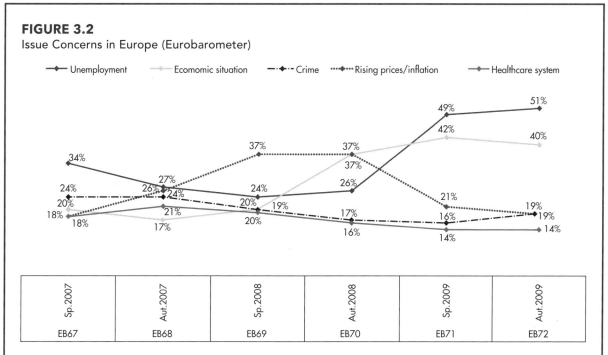

FIGURE 3.2
Issue Concerns in Europe (Eurobarometer)

Source: Adapted from TNS Opinion & Social, "Public Opinion in the European Union," *Standard Eurobarometer* 72/Autumn 2009 (Brussels: Directorate-General for Communication, European Commission, 2009).

affecting the prevailing values in a society's culture and public opinion through advertising. Often multiple groups must work together to raise an issue, contending with other groups that would like to keep it off the agendas of public opinion and government.

Once an issue is getting attention, its problem or goal must be defined. Various contending groups will dive in to try to "frame" (characterize) the issue. Take the issue of weak performance by public schoolchildren in poor areas. Groups that generally oppose government spending may frame this issue as a problem of poor teacher performance. They may blame administrators for allowing teachers (or whole schools) whose students score poorly on standardized tests to remain in place, and press to allow parents to choose their kids' schools. Contending with this view are groups that favor government spending to address such challenges. They may frame the problem in terms of lack of resources for public schools in poor neighborhoods, pointing out that well-off areas receive more money and thus can hire more teachers and pay them better. Other groups may point to poverty as a stress on families that tends to reduce parents' engagement in student learning.

In authoritarian frameworks, issue raising is largely limited to the executive structures of government, along with whatever interest groups or political party the government favors or depends on. Under certain conditions, a mass movement engaging in repeated large-scale protests may be able to force an issue onto the public agenda. For example, youth unemployment, government corruption, and police suppression of dissent sparked the uprisings that toppled regimes in Tunisia and Egypt in 2011.

Individuals can be important in raising issues. Simone de Beauvoir (1908–1986), author of the Second Sex (1952), at left, raised feminist issues in France; Rachel Carson (1907–1964), author of Silent Spring (1962), center, raised the issue of environmental pollution in the United States; and Ralph Nader (1934–), author of Unsafe at Any Speed (1965) raised consumer safety issues in the United States.

Proposing and Evaluating Policy Ideas

Once an issue is on the agenda, the next step is proposing policy options to address it. Political contention again emerges, as various individuals and groups come forward with policy ideas that get varying levels of attention. Such groups may include interest groups, schools of thought among experts, candidates or parties in election campaigns, parties or their factions in legislative assemblies, and other parts of the government. A policy proposal may emerge in any of a variety of forms, such as a newspaper opinion piece, an interest group's report, or a speech by a party leader at a hearing of a legislative committee. Generally, policy proposing includes framing the policy idea in terms of the value(s) that it is crafted to pursue.

Alongside policy proposing comes political contention in evaluating the proposals. People comment on the costs and benefits of various alternative policy options, in light of the values that they consider to be the key goals in the policy area. Groups' differing goals make for different criteria for evaluating proposals. For example, we shall see in chapter 7 that in getting an economy out of a slump, people who mainly want to avoid inflation or reduce government debt evaluate a policy differently from those who want to reduce unemployment. In addition, contending groups may present different empirical views of whether a policy option can actually achieve its desired goals, or instead may produce bad consequences.

Making Policy Decisions

Clearly, a key part of politics is the final decision making on issues. In the "rational actor" model of policymaking that is used by many students of decision making in single organizations, this next step would be straightforward. As if the organization were an individual mind making a decision, decision makers compare the ratios of benefits to costs for each alternative, in relation to agreed-upon values. Then they rationally choose the option that yields the most favorable preponderance of benefit over cost in pursuit of the key value(s). In national politics, though, things are not so simple. Contending groups tend not to be on the same page about what the key proposals are, how they should be evaluated, and what the key objective is.

At this early point in our exploration, to address how decisions are actually made in and around government would be jumping ahead into topics that are considered later in this book. It is appropriate here, however, to note a couple of aspects of policy decision making that people often fail to consider: (a) the step of narrowing the policy option list, and (b) the possibility of taking no action at all on the problem.

Narrowing the Range of Options to a Short List Often another phase in political decision making is excluding some options in order to produce a short list of what seem like the most feasible and acceptable alternatives. Political scientist Charles Lindblom addressed this stage twice in his career, in different ways. In his early work, Lindblom stressed that government decision making tends to rule out ideas for big changes. Rather, decision makers tend to favor small policy steps addressing one part of a problem at a time. He suggested that this "disjointed" and "incremental" approach was partly because of the limitations of the human mind, but also because big changes pose the greatest risk of bad unintended consequences.[17] In some of his later work, however, Lindblom adopted a somewhat different approach. He suggested that business groups can often block consideration of policy proposals that they consider adverse to their interests, by threatening not to pursue objectives such as investment and hiring that reduces unemployment.[18] These objectives are especially important to government in democracies because, among other things, if the unemployment rate is too high, elected officials may not be reelected.

Voters, too, can sometimes narrow the list of policy options. For example, senior citizens vote regularly, and cutting old-age pensions to reduce a budget deficit is not generally a good way to gain reelection. In addition, general moods among policymakers may narrow the option list, as in the case of the antiregulation mood of the 1980s and 1990s around the world. Values such as human rights can also serve to narrow the range of policy alternatives under consideration; for example, people tend to be unwilling to give up their privacy rights for the sake of an all-out war on illegal drugs. As you can see, a variety of factors can rule things out, shortening the list of policy proposals that are seriously considered.

Policies of Inaction The extreme of narrowing the range of policy options is narrowing it to zero. The policy decision may be to not take any action on the issue. Action may be prevented by such factors as the influence of opposing groups, the failure of key participants to agree on a policy, or technological obstacles to effective action.

In the United States in 1993–1994, health insurance reform made it onto the American governmental agenda, but no further. A proposal for universal health insurance encountered heavy opposition from influential medical business groups representing drug companies, health insurance companies, hospitals, and most doctors, who were all accustomed to few regulations and high incomes. The widespread satisfaction of most people with their employer-provided insurance at the time, and a big television campaign by the medical business to raise fears of change, led to no significant action on the

TABLE 3.1	Some Factors In Policies of Inaction
Process-related factors	Issue fails to get on the public agenda. A group opposing action exerts influence. Policymakers cannot agree on an option.
Issue-related factors	Absence of cost-effective and feasible options. A clash between available options and deeply held values.

issue. Notably, however, when the issue of universal health insurance reemerged in 2009–2010, the economic context was very different. A deep recession had cost many people their jobs—and thereby their health insurance. This time a formal program on the issue was adopted, though only after much contention, debate, and difficulty in getting enough cooperation to achieve majority support in legislative assemblies.

A policy of inaction may also stem from barriers to the effectiveness of *any* policies to address a problem. For example, the problem of illegal drugs such as heroin, cocaine, and methamphetamines presents huge challenges standing in the way of good intentions to address it: a lack of economic alternatives for peasants growing the raw materials (e.g., in Afghanistan or Peru), poor governments low on resources and authority to limit the trade, long and porous national borders in producing and consuming countries, transportation systems that are too economically and technologically complex and diverse to allow easy tracing and interdiction of smuggling, and wealthy drug-trafficking enterprises that are only too willing to use bribery and violence to protect their trade.

In addition, as was noted above, policymakers may encounter a clash between more powerful enforcement methods on one hand, and on the other, deeply held values concerning respect for personal freedom, privacy, and fair trial rights. A society may be unwilling to sacrifice these rights to a war on illegal drugs, especially if it would be unlikely to win that war in any case. This value clash arose again in 2013, with the revelation of the American government's access to the world's Internet communications (e.g., email and social media such as Facebook) and American phone records, for the purpose of preventing terrorist attacks. Table 3.1 summarizes some key characteristics of policies of inaction.

Monitoring Policy Implementation and Its Consequences

During the policy implementation stage in the process, the chosen policy is put into effect. Group contention affects this stage, too. Within and among the political executive, bureaucracy, courts, and affected interest groups, further decisions may influence how a policy is carried out. Then the policy will be monitored periodically by technical experts, political participants, and other interested observers. To be sure, usually few have the time to pay much attention to follow-up studies of a policy's success or failure. But if something goes wrong in a big way with a policy, the situation will garner headlines, invite examination and evaluation, and perhaps give rise to new issue raising and policy proposing. Other social (and natural) sciences can tell us scientifically whether a policy is working or not, but the key is whether the public or influential groups *perceive* it to be working—where political contention and cooperation may come into play.[19] In any case, the perceived impacts of yesterday's policies take us back to the agenda setting and policy proposing that begins the next round of the policy sequence.

FIELDS AND SUBFIELDS WITHIN POLITICAL SCIENCE

Another way in which the terrain of political science may be divided concerns the fields and subfields within the discipline. Among empirical political scientists, we see differences in the types of causal factors and consequences that attract their attention. Some of these areas of study can be found in the table of contents of this book, for example: interest groups, political parties, governmental institutions, policies, attitudes among the public, and governments' behavior toward other nations. Overall, though, the broadest subfield divisions within political science concern either the domain of nations studied or the methods used:

- **The politics of one's own country.** American politics is studied by many political scientists in the United States, French politics in France, etc. Within that domain, the methods of empirical political science are applied to a range of smaller subfields, such as interest groups, political parties, and other topics mentioned above.

- **Comparative politics.** A second major empirical heading within the discipline includes these same topics and subtopics, but in the context of foreign nations and comparisons between the nations of the world. This field is called comparative politics. It includes studying phenomena in a particular foreign country, a few in a region, or comparisons among larger numbers of nations (see "Concept in Context").

- **International relations.** A third empirical field involves the interactions among nations and their governments. This area includes such subfields as the foreign policies of individual nations, patterns of diplomacy among nations (regionally or globally), international organizations such as the United Nations or the European Union, national security/war, international terrorism, and international political economy (see chapters 17 and 18).

- **Normative theory/Political philosophy.** A fourth broad heading for study in political science departments is normative theory, introduced above. Some of its subfields divide the history of political thought into historical periods, such as the ancient-medieval period, the "modern" era (roughly from the sixteenth through the nineteenth centuries), and the twentieth century/contemporary period (see chapter 5). Another subfield studies ideologies (see chapter 6). Other areas stem from subjects of frequent debate including examinations of values such as freedom, justice, and equality and their practical implications; conceptual analysis of the language of politics; political ethics; and "postmodern" issues assessing the moral and political implications of such topics as race, gender, sexual orientation, human rights, and local democracy.

SUMMARY: CONTENTION AND COOPERATION IN POLITICAL SCIENCE

Political science tries to understand the key causal factors and consequences that are involved in political contention and cooperation. The modern form of the discipline began with a concern to be scientific in explaining politics, focusing on observable behavior and defining concepts in terms of their explicit indicators. Multiple factors may contend with each other to affect politics and policymaking, and interact with each other in doing so. "Theory" in political science is concerned with the impact of some particular cluster of causal factors, affecting much of politics across the board. At times, different theoretical approaches may contend with each other to explain a phenomenon. Normative theory focuses on what patterns of contention and cooperation are best for pursuing key values.

The temporal scope of political science ranges through the whole sequence of policymaking, from who the policymakers are and why, to how issues get onto the agenda of policymaking, how policy options are proposed and evaluated, how decisions are made, and what happens in carrying out policy decisions and monitoring the results. Political contention is found in each phase.

COUNTRY CASE STUDIES

Our two country cases each illustrate the multiple causal factors that can contribute to political outcomes. The coverage of France focuses on just one important foreign policy decision, to stay out of the invasion of Iraq in 2003. The coverage of Zambia focuses on the overall pattern of party contention and cooperation over the last century.

France: Multiple Causal Factors in the French Refusal to Join the Invasion of Iraq

A concrete example of the wide range of factors that can influence a political outcome is the case of the decision by the government of France to avoid participating in the invasion of Iraq in 2003. In early 2003, France refused to join the American-led invasion of Iraq without the approval of the U.N. Security Council, and indicated that it would veto any new Security Council resolution backing the invasion. This meant that the intervention would not have U.N. backing.

Many factors contributed to France's vigorous policy stance in this case. The French position on the issue followed the anti-invasion stance taken by the French president at the time, Jacques Chirac. Chirac led the main conservative party in France—the Union for a Popular Movement—a new combination (just formed in 2002) of diverse groups that included much of the old center-right Union for French Democracy as well as Chirac's own (Gaullist conservative) Rally for the Republic. Conservative parties in the United States and Britain at the time favored the invasion, but the UMP seemed divided. Thus, the personal beliefs and values of Chirac and his close advisors likely contributed to the French decision.

How was President Chirac personally able to influence the decision so heavily? The French governmental framework was a relevant factor. Chirac was not the prime minister (the operational chief of the executive branch), foreign minister, or defense minister. But the

French political system gives the president potent powers in the foreign policy area. Major foreign and defense policy decisions require the president's signature, and Chirac had always been a staunch defender of French foreign policy independence (of U.S. leadership) and a supporter of the U.N. as a vehicle for resolving major international disputes. Accordingly, Chirac's prior election to the presidency also contributed to the policy decision.

In addition, Chirac had much clout as the leader of his political party, which held the majority in the main legislative house, the National Assembly. That meant that President Chirac could freely pick people for the positions of prime minister, foreign minister, and defense minister who would be willing to follow his lead in such matters. Thus, his party's big victory in the last parliamentary election, unusually giving the UPM a parliamentary majority in its own hands, contributed to the French refusal to join in the invasion of Iraq. But there is much more to the story.

France's past policies and their consequences were another factor. The views of older senior officials in the French defense ministry, foreign ministry, and intelligence community surely played a role. It was well known that past French experience with invasion and military occupation to control the direction of a developing nation that is culturally different had been particularly disastrous in the last half century. The French suffered a humiliating defeat at Dien Bien Phu in Vietnam in 1954 in trying to hold on to their empire. A decade later, France was forced out of Algeria, a Muslim country in North Africa, where there were many French settlers. In the latter experience, the French military and settlers had bitter encounters with "urban guerilla warfare"—involving small-unit ambush, sabotage, and bombing in city streets.

Recent French interventions had been few, small-scale, brief, and in former French colonies with cultural ties to France. France had even opposed U.N. intervention in the 1994 genocide in the East African nation of Rwanda. Surely, French officials, knowledgeable about the nation's past experience in Vietnam and Algeria, held a dim view of the American prospects for holding and controlling Iraq, a country with which the United States had no past connections.

In addition, various interest groups undoubtedly played a role in the French reluctance to join the invasion of Iraq. In the business sector, there were some French firms involved in Iraq. Their business interests would surely be threatened in the case of invasion,

and some of them no doubt worked vigorously to discourage it. Moreover, France has the largest Muslim Arab minority population in Europe (mostly of North African ancestry). This group generally opposed Western intervention in Iraq, and wields votes in French elections. The presence in France of numerous young militant Islamists, perhaps ready for terrorism should France join the invasion, was also something French foreign policy decision makers had to ponder.

The surrounding economic circumstances should be considered as well. The French economy was struggling to recover from an economic slowdown and competition in the new Eurozone. It could ill afford to risk the disruption of the Middle East oil supplies, which some feared at the time, or the heavy cost of supplying French troops and paying for reconstruction. Officials in France's finance ministry were likely critical of the idea of French involvement in the invasion.

Political attitudes played a role, too. Many French are skeptical toward the United States and its motives, and French public opinion overall ran against the invasion and French participation in it. For comparison, some Americans in U.S. intelligence-related units of government were aware that the claims supporting invasion—that Saddam Hussein had active programs for developing "weapons of mass destruction," or was somehow involved in the 9/11 terror attacks—were based on weak evidence, but they were pressured not to talk publicly about it. In France, there was no informal embargo on such information. If France were to join in the invasion and it did not go well, President Chirac and his party might have paid a heavy price in the next elections.

To be sure, factors and pressures weighing in against French participation were not the only ones. In favor of intervention, there was horror at Saddam Hussein's brutality toward some of his people and toward Iran. This included earlier use of chemical weapons, not only against the Iranians during the war but also against northern Kurdish villages at the end of the 1980s. This likely invited some from the human rights community to be sympathetic to the impulse to invade. Also, concern over Iraq's alleged pursuit of weapons of mass destruction led others to support intervention.

However, human rights supporters were divided, too, by other concerns. Both of the U.N.'s human rights Covenants include in their opening preambles the right to national self-determination. And as a practical matter, invading Iraq might itself bring on the use of chemical weapons, and might produce other negative consequences for human rights in Iraq and elsewhere. Removal of the government might mean the removal of the rule of law, and unleash contentions between Sunni and Shia Muslims, for example, which might get out of control, produce human rights infringements, and spread more widely in the region. As you can see, many factors, some no doubt selfish, and some not so, were at work in the conscious and considered French decision not to join in the invasion of Iraq.

When the invasion was successful in taking Baghdad, Chiraq saluted the outcome, while pressing for involving the United Nations in any transitional administration of Iraq. The Americans, however, were opposed to any such U.N. role, as well as to any involvement of French companies in the subsequent reconstruction. Looking back from the vantage point of the present (see Country Case Studies, chapter 4), many would wish that the French pre-invasion position had prevailed.

Zambia: Causal Factors in a Developing Nation

The African country of Zambia has taken a journey from British colonial rule to representative democracy that provides us with examples of common causal factors that affect contention and cooperation in developing countries. It has gone from a period of minimally democratic single-party dominance after independence from 1964 to 1972, to two decades of single-party authoritarian rule, and then back to minimally democratic single-party dominance from 1991 up to the present.

Zambia held its first postindependence elections in 1964. The preceding colonial experience had a big impact on Zambia's initial party system. The United National Independence Party (UNIP) had led the anticolonial struggle, and thus was the only widely organized and well-known party at the time. A second contributing factor was the electoral system: single-member district plurality (SMDP), which Zambia inherited from the British. As we saw earlier in this chapter, this "first past the post" procedure rewards only the largest party in each small district with its sole seat. Large parties with their strength spread across many districts tend to gain large numbers of seats, and a proportion of the legislative assembly that is larger than their proportion of the vote. Inevitably UNIP would win big victories, at least initially.

A third key factor was the type of representative democracy. Zambia adopted a semi-presidential system, with a directly elected president (serving for a fixed term of office) who selects the PM from among the members of parliament. Semi-presidential democracy is parliamentary in a key way: once appointed, the PM and cabinet must have the support of the parliamentary majority to stay in office. But the directly elected president has some key powers in addition to nominating and removing the PM and approving the PM's choice of the other cabinet ministers, such as the power to dissolve the assembly and call new parliamentary elections. Especially in the common case where the president is the party leader of the biggest party in the parliamentary majority, the president is much more the recognized leader of the government than is the PM. Thus this type of representative democracy adds a strong dash of the personal leadership model to the mix of factors that affect it. UNIP embraced a left social democratic ideology (see chapter 6) espoused by its leader Kenneth Kaunda, with the state playing a leading role in furthering economic development and modernization.

In practice, however, UNIP was a large and diverse umbrella party. As was noted above, it was widely organized and won numerous seats with moderate margins of victory in the SMDP elections. But if a country has different regions each dominated by a distinct ethnic identity—another causal factor that can have an impact in a developing country—ethnic-regional parties might form that are large in their home areas (though small nationally) and thus can win seats in those areas. Zambia has such ethnic-tribal minorities. The most significant are the Bemba people in the north and parts of the central "Copperbelt" (where the copper mines are concentrated), the Lozi in the West, the Nyanja in the east, and the Tonga to the south. To avoid having to contend with such parties, Kaunda followed a conscious strategy of representing these various tribal groups in UNIP's own National Executive Committee (NEC) and the cabinet. But periodically, ethnic-regional leaders in or outside UNIP would feel disaffected and form a party to challenge UNIP.

At a high point in the party's strength, Kaunda shut down the opposition parties and declared a single-party state in 1972. But the regime did not turn to repressing the other groups' leaders and activists. Instead Kaunda continued to co-opt leading figures of the regions and other parties into UNIP and the government. (UNIP was organized outside parliament, too, with a Central Committee and committees for each ministry's policy area to help keep tabs on ministers' performance.) With significant state ownership and intervention in the economy, there were a lot of jobs to distribute to keep people happy. Legislative seats were filled by competition among UNIP-screened candidates, who were free to voice local concerns.

Eventually the UNIP single-party regime's support began to erode significantly. Here we find the impact of another key factor: economic conditions, whether they arise domestically or in response to economic events or forces originating outside the country (or both). Hard economic times started in the 1970s, and by the end of the 1980s Zambia faced many tough problems, including inflation, reductions in subsidies imposed by the International Monetary Fund (IMF) (especially cuts in the maize subsidy that kept urban food prices down), uneven world copper prices, increasing unemployment, and illegal strikes. With rising dissatisfaction, in 1990 the UNIP government had to legalize other parties; after a roughly twenty-year run, the single-party regime was over.

A number of former UNIP government officials flocked to a new party, the Movement for a Multiparty Democracy (MMD) headed by a top trade union official, Frederick Chiluba. In 1991 the MMD, campaigning mostly against the preceding UNIP management of the economy, soundly defeated UNIP for control of the 150-member one-house parliament, and Chiluba won election as president. He then largely broke with his trade union base and moved toward free-market liberalization and privatization of state-owned enterprises. This approach was required by the IMF—the lead bargaining agent for the creditors in dealing with debtor nations who fell behind in their payments—in order to renegotiate terms of debt and to allow new aid.

At first, the MMD ruled in a single-party-dominant style with presidential formalities, somewhat like Mexico prior to the 1980s. Over time, Mr. Chiluba faced broader challenges in maintaining public approval. One was that he is a Bemba and had appointed several Bemba to high positions in the MMD and his government, giving the appearance of favoritism. In addition, his IMF-favored policies of economic austerity, free-market liberalization, and privatization—including the all-important copper industry—allowed fewer opportunities to offer clientelistic benefits for public support (see chapter 2), and were often unpopular among the voters. Third, he alienated many with his repeated attempts to get the constitution changed to allow him to extend his presidency beyond the two-term limit.

Chiluba's chosen successor to run for president was a former minister and anticorruption campaigner, Patrick Mwanawasa. Here we encounter another factor that affects polities that are in a transition to democracy: vote manipulation in elections. In a disputed election with accusations of ballot box stuffing and double voting, Mwanawasa won by a slim margin. For the SMDP-chosen assembly, MMD's broad organization and name recognition allowed it to gain a narrow majority, but Mwanawasa's position was fragile.

His policies were initially centrist to center-left, favoring more state economic intervention while trying to reduce corruption. By the mid-2000s, however, under pressure from aid donors and a modernized economics/planning ministry, the government's policies were tilting toward more free-market reforms. But any negative political fallout was limited by other favorable economic factors that were operating at the time: rising copper prices, reduced inflation, strong maize harvests that kept food prices down, continuing donor aid that supported government finances and agricultural subsidies, and pursuit of some high-level corruption cases (including investigations of Chiluba himself).

Politically, Mwanawasa continued the old pattern of co-opting some leaders of smaller parties into cabinet positions to maintain a supportive Assembly majority. But he also employed another less pleasant tactic: Mwanawasa would publicly criticize and remove anyone in current or past cabinet office who began to look like a serious rival. The tenures of ministers were sometimes short. Mwanawasa's successor (upon his death in 2008) as president and MMD leader was Rupiah Banda, who more or less continued the former's policy approaches. The international financial contagion of 2008–2009 temporarily reversed some of the above-noted favorable factors, but the beginnings of worldwide recovery in late 2009 and 2010 were again favorable for the administration.

The most significant opposition party in the late 2000s was the Patriotic Front (PF), associated with the personal appeal of its leader, the late Michael Sata. Sata was a former MMD leader who quit the party to start his own after losing out to Mwanawasa for the party's presidential nomination in 2001. Sata's strength was in the north, the Copperbelt, and now around the capital, Lusaka. He campaigned with a leftist tilt as a vigorous prolabor and antipoverty critic of the MMD's privatization efforts. Sata's promises of new jobs appealed to urban youth and shantytown dwellers. Despite the fact that the PF remains somewhat personalistic (partially built around its leader's personality) and is not well organized in rural areas of the country, Sata only lost the 2008 presidential election narrowly (claiming fraud), and the PF won 44 of the 150 elected seats in the assembly.

By 2010, Banda and the MMD were facing new challenges: fresh evidence of corruption, widespread doubts about how much average Zambians were benefiting from the good macroeconomic numbers, and informal contention within the MMD between President Banda and some former Mwanawasa supporters. And contention had arisen over Chinese economic influence and bad labor practices (especially in the copper industry). Notably, Banda at times displayed the old pattern of accusing critics within the MMD of improper past behavior and removing them from ministerial positions. Sata was able to capitalize on negative public reaction to these factors to win the 2011 presidential election by 42 percent to Banda's 35 percent, which represented the first alternation in power since the end of single-party authoritarian rule in 1991.

In office, Sata followed a moderate left-of-center approach, with his characteristic dashes of nationalism and populism. Labor practices in Chinese-owned copper mines have improved, and taxes have been cut for lower-income earners. However, he did not deliver on a prominent campaign promise of a new constitution. And division arose within Sata's main ethnic base, the Bemba of the north, after he intervened to impose his own pick as the Bemba traditional paramount leader. Sata fired his (Bemba) defense minister for opposing the move, leading to the latter's exit from the PF along with his followers. In office, Sata followed his predecessors' intolerance of vigorous criticism, whether from within his cabinet, leaders of opposing parties (detained on occasion), or dissenting press and NGOs. And in 2013 and 2014, public dissatisfaction with the

government increased as copper prices weakened, slowing down economic growth. Nonetheless, Sata's program for infrastructure improvement (especially road building and repair) was making a difference through most of the country, including many rural areas that were not part of Sata's traditional support base.

When Sata's health failed and he died in late 2014, he was succeeded as president by his white vice president, Guy Scott, and a factional fight broke out over who would be the PF nominee for the January 2015 presidential election. Scott favored Sata's nephew and cabinet minister, Miles Sampa, while many of the party regulars preferred the PF secretary-general, Eduard Lungu. After dueling nominating conferences, in the end Lungu won the nomination, and narrowly won the presidential election of January 2015.

The third significant party in Zambia is the United Party for National Development (UPND). It is southern based and mainly Tonga led. Ideologically, the UPND began as moderate left of center, but has evolved to become center-right. Its leader in the early 2000s, Anderson Mazoka, almost defeated (some would say did defeat, but for election fraud) Mwanawasa for the presidency in 2001, but he subsequently died. Since then the UPND's presidential candidate has been Hakainde Hichilema, who got 15–25 percent of the votes in presidential elections until 2015, when he was barely edged out, 48 to 46 percent. The party normally wins between 25 and 35 of the 150 parliamentary seats (now holding 34).

The MMD, for its part, suffered a major blow in late 2014 due to its own factional fight over the presidential nomination. The party president, former televangelist Nevers Mumba, insisted on himself as the MMD nominee, in the face of opposition from the majority of the party's National Executive Committee who favored former president Banda. In the end, Mumba was handed the MMD nomination by a Supreme Court decision, and he expelled the opposing party national secretary and his deputy from their offices. Following Mumba's power play and the factional hostility that it engendered, Mumba failed disastrously in the election, getting less than 1 percent of the vote (Banda no doubt would have done much better). In contrast, after PF's contention over its nomination, sufficient unity was achieved to win. All of this highlights a significant cluster of causal factors (and sometimes outcomes) in democratic politics: factional contention and the distribution of influence within political parties.

◥ **PRACTICE AND REVIEW ONLINE**

CRITICAL THINKING QUESTIONS

1. What did interest groups have to do with the origins of modern political science?

2. When and how might a correlation between two factors actually fail to reveal causation?

3. Why might empirical analysis be more attractive to someone in studying politics than normative theory? And vice versa?

4. When and how might the issues on the agenda of national politics fail to include important problems?

5. Why isn't policymaking simply a matter of weighing the costs and benefits of the alternative policies?

KEY TERMS

political science, 52
behavioral pluralism, 52
empirical, 53
operationalize, 53
independent variable, 54
dependent variable, 54
electoral system, 55
sufficient condition, 55
necessary condition, 55
hypothesis, 56
intervening variable, 57
empirical theory, 61
normative, 64
normative theory, 64

FURTHER READING

Dahl, Robert A. *Modern Political Analysis*, 5th ed. Englewood Cliffs, NJ: Prentice-Hall, 1991.

Evans, Peter B., Dietrich Rueschmayer, and Theda Skocpol, eds. *Bringing the State Back In.* Cambridge: Cambridge University Press, 1985.

Goodin, Robert E., and Klingemann, Hans-Dieter, eds. *A New Handbook of Political Science.* New York: Oxford University Press, 1997.

Harrison, Lisa. *Political Research: An Introduction.* New York: Routledge, 2001.

Manheim, Jarol B., Richard Rich, and Lars Willnat. *Empirical Political Analysis: Research Methods in Political Science*, 5th ed. New York: Addison Wesley Longman, 2002.

Monroe, Alan D. *Essentials of Political Research.* Boulder, CO: Westview Press, 2000.

Peters, B. Guy. *Comparative Politics, Theory and Method.* New York, NY: New York University Press, 1998.

White, Louise G. *Political Analysis: Technique and Practice*, 3rd ed. Belmont, CA: Wadsworth, 1994.

NOTES

[1] At first, political scientists tended to describe the role of interest groups; See David Truman, *The Governmental Process: Political Interests and Public Opinion* (New York: Knopf, 1953), and Yale colleagues Robert Dahl and Charles Lindblom, *Politics, Economics, and Welfare: Planning and Politico-economic Systems Resolved into Basic Social Processes* (New York: Harper, 1953). Soon Dahl spearheaded the development of behavioral research methods with his *Who Governs? Democracy and Power in an American City* (New Haven, CT: Yale University Press, 1961).

[2] The simple idea is that an organization takes action on a problem, gathers information on the results, and that information is "fed back" into the next sequence of decision making on the problem.

[3] See Peter Bachrach and Morton S. Baretz, "The Two Faces of Power," *American Political Science Review* 56 (1962): 947–53.

[4] See Herbert Marcuse, *One Dimensional Man: Studies in the Ideology of Advanced Industrial Society* (Boston: Beacon, 1964); and Steven Lukes, *Power: A Radical View* (London, New York: Macmillan, 1974).

[5] See Robert A. Dahl, *Dilemmas of Pluralist Democracy: Autonomy vs. Control* (New Haven: Yale University Press, 1982), and Charles E. Lindblom, *Politics and Markets: the World's Political Economic Systems* (New York: Basic Books, 1977).

[6] See Otto Kirchheimer, "The Transformation of the Western European Party System," in *Political Parties and Political Development*, ed. Joseph LaPalombara and Myron Weiner (Princeton: Princeton University Press, 1966), 177–200.

[7] Political scientists have a piece of jargon for a contributing factor that is a purely independent one, coming solely from the outside and not affected at all by other variables within the field of observation: an "exogenous variable." This word has Latin roots, made up of "genous" (meaning "generated" or "emerging") alongside "exo" (meaning "outside"). In contrast, interactions between contributing factors within the field of observation—perhaps even impacts of the dependent variable on one of the causal factors—are called "endogenous effects." The word "endogenous" is made up of the same root "genous" (again, "emerging"), now paired with "endo," meaning "within" or "from within."

[8] See chapter 1, "Contention and Cooperation in Focus."

[9] See chapter 9.

[10] See Gabriel A. Almond and G. Bingham Powell, Jr., *Comparative Politics: A Developmental Approach* (Boston: Little Brown, 1966).

[11] See note 1.

[12] Samuel Huntington, *Political Order in Changing Societies* (New Haven: Yale University Press, 1968).

[13] See Donald P. Green and Ian Shapiro, *Pathologies of Rational Choice Theory* (New Haven, CT: Yale University Press, 1994), and Jeffrey Friedman, ed., *The Rational Choice Controversy* (New Haven, CT: Yale University Press, 1996).

[14] If you are interested in the philosophy of all this, see Popper's *Logic of Scientific Discovery* (London: Hutchinson, 1959) or *Objective Knowledge; an Evolutionary Approach* (Oxford: Clarendon Press, 1972).

[15] This aspect of influence was stressed by E. E. Schattschneider in his *The Semi-sovereign People: A Realist's View of Democracy* (New York: Holt, Rinehart and Winston, 1960).

[16] See chapter 2's section on "the elite model."

[17] See "The Science of Muddling Through," *Public Administration* 19 (1959): 78–88, and, *the Intelligence of Democracy; Decision Making Through Mutual Adjustment* (New York: Free Press, 1965).

[18] See *Politics and Markets* (New Haven: Yale University Press, 1978).

[19] For more on this, see chapter 2.

Building the Contemporary Nation-State

Challenges and Responses

FOCUS QUESTIONS

- **WHAT** major challenges do political communities have to overcome to establish the stable nation-state as we know it today?

- **WHO** contends in each challenge?

- **HOW** do the contention and cooperation among groups affect political frameworks, and how are patterns of contention and cooperation affected by such frameworks?

- **WHAT** role does influence play in the unfolding and resolution of the challenges?

IN EARLY 2011, demonstrations arose in Syria as part of the "Arab Spring" democracy movement. Feeling threatened by the growing protests, Syria's authoritarian regime increasingly employed violence, which led to open civil war by 2012. By 2015, over 200,000 had been killed and millions displaced.

Some in Western nations saw the conflict mainly as another phase in the wave of democratization that many developing nations have experienced over the last thirty years. However, there is much more to the story. Syria had not actually been a recognizable nation-state for long. A strong military power in ancient times, Syria had been overwhelmed by the Mongols in the late middle ages, and later was incorporated into the Turkish-based Ottoman Empire. Only with the post–World War I dissolution of the Ottoman Empire and the Western powers' allocation of present-day Syria to French colonial control did the country's current boundaries emerge. The French brutally suppressed a rebellion in 1925 and kept control until after World War II, when rising Arab nationalism helped bring independence. Thus by the mid-twentieth century, Syria had gained a measure of national identity. But the prior decades of instability had provided the people little sense of the legitimacy of its government or of full extension of government authority over the whole territory.

The Arab nationalist Ba'ath Party arose and gained control in the 1950s. By the mid-1960s, its leadership had been taken over by a group of military officers led by members of the minority Alawite sect (concentrated in a mountainous coastal area), a secretive offshoot of

Shia Islam. Within that group, in 1970 another military coup installed an Alawite, Hafez al-Assad, atop the Ba'ath Party and the country. Assad put fellow Alawites in the key positions in the government, and forcefully centralized authority over the territory. He ruled until his death in 2000, when he was succeeded by his son, Bashar. Behind the current uprising, in addition to democratic aspirations, was long-standing resentment among the majority Sunni Muslims over Alawite dominance, along with stirrings of Islamic fundamentalism among the Sunnis. Certainly one dimension of today's civil war is the political cleavage between Sunnis on the one hand and the Alawites and other religious minorities on the other. But 2013 saw a further sectarian cleavage emerge within the rebel camp between moderate Sunnis and the radical, Salafist Sunni jihadis of the Islamic State and the Nusra Front.

This raises a question: Is every country's story unique, or are there distinct types of challenges that nations tend to confront on their way to political stability and peaceful citizen participation, that can help us organize our thinking about political development? If so, what are those challenges, and how can they be overcome in ways that build foundations to support the modern nation-state?

CHALLENGES AND FOUNDATIONS

In nations that have long-established and stable political frameworks, people tend to take certain things for granted. Most people think of the government's authority as extending across the country, and of themselves as citizens of their nation. In most countries, people think of their governments as legitimate and have at least some opportunity to participate safely in politics. In one form or another, most of these underlying building blocks have developed in most of today's stable nation-states. However, these foundations have not always been present, and have not been installed to the same extent and in the same ways everywhere. Today's nations have gone through sequences of political development to reach the point where they are today. And in many countries, the process of installing these building blocks continues.

Borrowing from a body of political science literature on "crises and sequences" in political development,[1] this chapter will explore four such foundations:

- Penetration by state authority—the extension of state authority throughout the country.
- National identity—widespread self-classification by people as citizens of their nation.
- Legitimacy—a widespread sense that the system of government is rightful and just.
- Participation—the opportunity for citizens to safely participate in government.

Building and strengthening these foundations of modern politics has required—and in many cases continues to require—overcoming challenges. The above-noted political scientists who have studied political development refer to this process in terms of sequences of "crises" in political development. But rather than stressing the "crises," I put more emphasis on the positive, on how the list can also refer to state-supporting foundations that may be built in overcoming the challenges.[2] Second, I use the term "challenge" rather than "crisis." The word "crisis" tends to convey the idea of a short-term emergency, a connotation that indeed is often appropriate. But in many cases these encounters in political development build gradually, and are resolved only partially and over extended periods of time.

In addition, political scientists who discussed political development in terms of "crises and sequences" included a fifth challenge, that of "distribution." Certainly, economic crises and tensions over distribution have affected political development at times. But as the events of 2008–2009 have shown, contention over distribution is more an ongoing feature of both established and developing nation-states, than a challenge distinctive to the latter. (We shall treat "political economy" in chapter 7.)

The list of challenges presented in this chapter—state authority, national identity, legitimacy, and participation—is not meant to suggest any typical sequence in which the challenges tend to arise in countries. Different nations have experienced different sequences of development on the way to their current political frameworks. For example, some nations achieved a minimal sense of national identity before substantially extending state authority, while for others the sequence was reversed. Some nations experienced a long period of seeming legitimacy of authoritarian rule before facing and accommodating demands for greater participation, while other nations' first experience with political legitimacy came only after a challenge of participation was overcome, with the establishment of some form of representative democracy. Some nations have to revisit challenges that they were content to think they had overcome earlier.

Great Britain is often considered a classic favorable case. It had the luxury of overcoming the challenges one at a time over an extended period. But more recently in many countries in the developing world, multiple challenges have arisen at once. And in some cases the process remains very much unfinished. Egypt established national identity and penetration by state authority early on, but continues to grapple with legitimacy and participation. For a given nation, some of these supporting foundations exist substantially and may only need maintenance in the present, while in other nations some foundations still need to be installed pretty much from scratch.

The following sections amount to an extended exercise in political science as presented in chapter 3. The chapter considers causal factors and consequences regarding the chapter topic and its patterns of contention and cooperation. In this case, we explore what factors affect positive or negative outcomes regarding each challenge in building the modern nation-state.

THE CHALLENGE OF PENETRATION BY STATE AUTHORITY

Penetration by state authority is an important political resource that helps ensure the stability and effectiveness of government. As we saw in chapter 1, "the state" refers to all units of a country's government considered as a single entity with comprehensive and sovereign authority over a territorial community. For a representative democracy, for example, the state encompasses the whole array of institutions of government—legislative, executive, and judicial—and levels of government: national, regional, and local, taken together as a single whole.

In a simple principality, the state may amount to little more than the king, his or her agents, and the police.

Early Penetration: The First Establishment of the State

Early governments tended to be monarchic, ranging from small principalities to great empires. In the early establishment of the state, new technologies could be important. The invention of writing (first among the ancient Sumerians in the Middle East) led to systematic record keeping, which enabled governments to collect taxes efficiently. Without writing, maintaining the huge Persian Empire of the sixth century BCE, for example, would have been impossible. Early transportation improvements were important, too. The Romans created a vast network of roads to maintain their empire, enabling the quick movement of troops, food and other resources, and information. The empire of Genghis Khan in the fourteenth century relied heavily on horses for fast transportation as well as effective war making.

In Europe, from the fourteenth through the seventeenth centuries, we saw the rise of some durable monarchies over fairly large territories, such as those of France, Spain, and England. Their extent was greater than that of the city-state or small principality, but less than what we think of as an empire. Before then, rule in the Middle Ages had been mostly by the old feudal landowners, often with some influence by the Catholic Church. Later, feudal obligation was gradually replaced by growing national bureaucracies under the king, accompanied by a more regular application of law. At least dating from the 1300s, when the French king Phillip the Fair began challenging the international influence of the Papacy, independent "national" states began to emerge as the primary actors.

This early development of a recognizable state proceeded unevenly. As late as the 1600s, savage wars over religion and territory in central Europe rendered security of life and property shaky at best. But gradually the old idea of government by "divine right" was replaced. What took its place was pragmatic cooperation with government based on a crude exchange imposed by the king (or king and parliament, in England). In effect, kings and queens declared to the people: "You pay taxes and obey the law, and I'll assure military defense and social order, and will protect your safety and property."[3] In comparison with such horrors as the sixteenth-century French Wars of Religion and the seventeenth-century Thirty Years' War in central Europe, this looked to most people like a pretty good deal.

Regarding this first enlargement of principalities toward a "national" scope of territory, a different approach to European state formation has focused on the economic requirements of military defense. Modern weapons (especially guns and artillery), navies, and fortifications were very expensive. Kings had to gather substantial resources to pay the bill by extracting taxes over a large area. This was not only a matter of organizing centralized bureaucracies to tap commerce in the reviving towns and cities. In addition, kings needed to assure a fairly lawful and stable commercial environment—preserving the peace and protecting property—to support the prosperity required to supply the needed taxes.[4]

Broader Penetration: The Full Extension of State Authority

However, there is an aspect of the challenge of penetration that is not a matter of ancient history, but rather is very much with us today. This is the spread of the authority of government's laws and programs out from its core of greatest strength to cover the whole national territory and society. While the state may be strong at the center—around the capital city or among the middle class—its authority may still remain weak in peripheral (outlying) areas or among certain socioeconomic groups or strata.[5]

One indicator of the extension of state authority is the effectiveness of tax collection throughout the territory and in all sectors of the economy. But beyond this, how effective is other law enforcement? How well do government programs reach all regions and groups, including rural as well as urban areas? Here we are looking for a "just right" solution: we don't want our government to have too much power over our lives, but we need it to have the authority to do its job throughout the country.

In the extension of state authority, if we include program implementation as well as lawfulness we get what political scientists call **state capacity**. This can be a matter of degree. **Weak states**—those with poor extension of state authority— are sometimes on the verge of being **failed states**, with anarchy prevailing over much of the territory, as in Somalia in East Africa in the 2000s and much of eastern and southern Libya in the 2010s.

What factors can contribute to overcoming the challenge of penetration by state authority? One powerful factor was noted in chapters 1 and 2 and will be examined below: the pervasive sense of governmental legitimacy. If groups throughout the country consider the nation's political framework to be rightful and just, with its decisions arrived at fairly, people are more likely to cooperate with governmental authority. This sort of compliance contrasts with the less even lawfulness that follows when people obey the law based only on calculations of the likelihood of getting caught and suffering serious punishment for law break- ing. However, assuming realistically that the sense of governmental legitimacy does not lead everyone to lawful behavior in all circumstances, other factors may be needed to extend law enforcement capacity.

The Roles of Technology and War

As we saw above, new transportation and communication technologies played important roles in the establishment of states in ancient times. In the nineteenth and early twentieth centuries, too, new technologies helped central states to extend their authority toward the fron- tiers. Railroads and the telegraph played powerful roles in many nations, provid- ing for the rapid movement of troops, goods, and communication over long distances. The resulting enlargement of areas of stability, trade, and interdepen- dence brought wider demands for law enforcement to protect property. Today, many countries in the developing world still have poor transportation (e.g., bad roads) and communication networks that make it difficult to extend govern- ment authority.

A train on the Trans-Siberian Railway traveling toward Mongolia.

War can also contribute to greater extension of authority. In wartime, people must accept government mobilization of resources and coordination of military defense, and the central government's authority must extend to the border with the enemy. For example, Germany was a fragmented collection of small states until the Franco-Prussian War. The most important of these states, Prussia, led by Otto von Bismarck, asserted military leadership that led to German unification in 1870.

The Role of Cultural and Economic Circumstances

In some areas of the developing world, cultural barriers stand in the way of the extension of government authority. In rural Africa, for example, sometimes traditional clan elders and chiefs have more influence with local people than do the agents of the national government. In a nation's peripheral areas, like the northwestern tribal areas of Pakistan or the eastern part of the Congo, many locals view the central government as an alien elite trying to force its will on the population. This situation has added to the difficulties that central governments have encountered in trying to put down rebellions, such as those of the radical Islamist Taliban in Pakistan. As we shall see in the next section on national identity, a region's distinctive language, ethnicity, and culture can make for such strong resistance by some to central authority that outright hostilities can result (e.g., today's eastern Ukraine, where some ethnic Russians resist the central government in Kiev and its use of the Ukrainian language).

In contending with groups on the periphery that resist its authority, the central government has the advantage of control over the national budget. Leaders trying to extend national authority can offer new economic benefits (or stabilize the delivery of old benefits) that can bring greater prosperity to outlying regions. Such benefits might include projects, investments, jobs, and subsidies. They would be offered on the condition that people in the recipient regions cooperate with the government on other matters. However, to extend its authority in this way, the central government needs the resources to offer such help to regions.

For example, Russia is a major exporter of oil, and world oil prices in the early to mid-1990s were low. This reduced the resources available to the new democratic government that had replaced the Soviet regime in 1991. The slump in oil prices contributed to the sharp economic downturn that accompanied the country's fragile transition to capitalism in the 1990s. In that decade, the central government led by President Boris Yeltsin often found itself short of the resources that it needed to aid and control Russia's regions. In the early 2000s, however, a rise in world oil prices brought substantial new funds to government coffers. This greatly aided the new Russian president, Vladimir Putin, in his efforts to get the regions under central control. In the developing world, many poor governments do not have the resources to support the extension of state authority.

Especially when the scarcity of resources weakens state capacity, laws and programs may be unevenly applied. This situation is evident in some poor developing nations. If agents of the central government are few and poorly paid, and law enforcement is not automatic, then the presence or absence of law enforcement can more easily be bought and sold through bribery and corruption. Influence replaces authority, and government-funded benefits may go mainly to personal supporters of administrators and leaders rather than to everyone who may be legally eligible. The resulting climate of corruption can weaken governmental legitimacy, which can further reduce the extent of state authority.

THE CHALLENGE OF NATIONAL IDENTITY

What turns a geographical territory with a state structure into a nation? In the phrase "nation-state," "nation" refers to the large scope of the territory and people over which the state has authority. It suggests a land area encompassing multiple cities and their environs. (This contrasts, for example, with the ancient Greek "city-state.") As we saw in chapter 1, a nation comprises a group of people sharing a sense of a common history, cultural heritage, and usually an official language, as well as territory. The countries discussed in this book, from very large ones such as the United States, Russia, India, and China, to tiny Benin in West Africa or Belize in Central America, are all nation-states.

National identity is achieved when the inhabitants of a territory classify themselves, at least minimally, as citizens of the whole political community rather than primarily as members of an ethnic group or a region within it. The sense of national identity does not require the intense patriotism that we associate with nationalism (see chapter 6). It is more a minimal habit of self-classification than a sense of mission. But it does typically mean that people are at times aware of the well-being of the whole nation as a public value, in addition to the well-being of oneself, one's family, clan, ethnicity/tribe, region, religious community, or other unit.

Of course, a pervasive sense of national identity among a country's citizens in no way eliminates political contention between groups. In some cases, it may contribute to it; regions that were previously unaware of each other may now perceive themselves to be competing for scarce resources. But typically a sense of common national identity does make group contention in the area more peaceful, and facilitates the cooperation that is necessary to preserve a stable nation-state.

Contributors to National Identity

Some contributions to national identity are familiar to us today. Throughout the world, schools teach history and literature in ways that influence children to think of themselves as citizens of a nation with a shared and respected past.[6] In addition, governments help build national awareness by creating and emphasizing national symbols, such as national sports teams, a national flag, a national anthem, and grand government buildings in the capital city. A sense of national identification is also fostered by shared national rituals such as Independence Day celebrations, a pledge of allegiance to the nation for schoolchildren, or national elections. These things encourage people to feel a sense of community and solidarity with their country.

Events, too, can play an important role. For example, a war with a neighboring nation or a war for national independence against colonial occupation can call on contending groups to cooperate and depend on each other in the collective effort. This unity can heighten the citizens' sense of solidarity with their country.

Another factor is the perception of events from a national point of view. With the advent of new media technologies such as radio and television in the twentieth century, broadcast news media could highlight events as if they were affecting the nation as a whole, and address the people as a single audience. Mass popular culture can help, too, such as movies and literature with themes that reflect the national experience.

THE PHILOSOPHICAL CONNECTION | Friedrich Nietzsche (1844–1900)

Friedrich Nietzsche was a sharp social critic of the modern state.* He lamented what he saw as its use of moral and legal rules to suppress life's passions. For Nietzsche, the key unit of political society was not the state but rather the "people." Over each people, he wrote, is a "tablet of values," a "tablet of good and evil." In his view, each people's tablet of values includes what that particular people considers to be most glorious, sacred, or worthy, in contrast to the values of other peoples. Nietzsche thought that pursuit of these distinctive values, and conventions and norms related to them, should guide society rather than the state.

According to Nietzsche, a people's prevailing cultural ideals come from its leading past and present writers, poets, philosophers, religious reformers, or historians. These sources of national culture present the people with ideals toward which to strive. Nietzsche's concept of well-being lay in struggle and striving for high standards, not in enjoying the achievement of a goal. He decried the materialism of his day, whether in the form of capitalism or socialism, as representing a decadent decline into animal-like physical enjoyments and contentment. His view was that if you focus on striving to pursue the difficult aims put forth by your culture, you will spend less time in psychologically unhealthy envy of those who have been more successful than you.

Nietzsche's view of the impact of the state focused on political psychology. For him, laws and moral rules aimed at regulating human behavior only serve to stifle passions and aspirations that are natural in human life. If someone wrongs you, Nietzsche thought, the healthy answer is to ventilate your anger on the spot. In his view, not to do so risks an unhealthy buildup of "resentment," which could fester over time into a desire for revenge. By delaying the satisfaction of the wronged party, Nietzsche argued, the state's law enforcement and the modern justice system amount to one big engine of obsession with revenge, causing resentment to fester and build while the impersonal wheels of justice slowly grind on.

At the top of the healthy society for Nietzsche were "the good," those who were most successful in striving toward the cultural ideals of the people. In his view, members of this healthy nobility were often impulsive and passionate, and rarely calculating and prudent. Most importantly, they should be psychologically open, confident, and positive about themselves. In their evaluations, this informal nobility mainly made distinctions between good and "bad," not between good and evil. They merely disdained "the bad" as falling short of the ideal, rather than hating it as something evil. They were capable of respect for their rivals or enemies.

Nietzsche as a political philosopher was characteristically given to excesses, both in the way he presented the alternatives and in his expressed preferences. Obviously, today's society cannot do without government. Finding value in Nietzsche's thought requires lifting elements from it for application to contexts (e.g., psychology) other than that of his world view overall.

---

* See Friedrich Nietzsche, *The Portable Nietzsche*, trans. and ed., Walter Kaufmann (New York: Viking Press, 1980).

While the sense of one's particular nationality with its distinctive political culture can be important to how people understand politics (as the late twentieth-century communitarians suggest), it is not something that can entirely replace the state, as the late nineteenth-century political philosopher Friedrich Nietzsche argued (see "The Philosophical Connection").

A Special Challenge to National Identity: Coinciding Political Cleavages Involving Regional Division

In some cases, the inhabitants of a nation-state largely share a single ethnic identity. Over time, the Franks came to think of themselves mainly as French (despite some regional differences), the Swedes as Swedish, and so on. However, most nation-states are more complex socially and ethnically. Multiple ethnic groups may exist and contend in politics without getting in the way of the country's overall sense of national identity. Under certain circumstances, though, ethnic attachment and interethnic contention may indeed produce a challenge to national identity.

Before African countries gained their national independence (mostly in the 1960s), the European colonial administrators often drew territorial boundaries without regard for shared ethnicity. "Divide and conquer" strategies sometimes led them to split an ethnic group into minority status in different territories. The colonial authorities might not want to concentrate an ethnic group or tribe in one territory where its dominance might contribute to a sense of its own national identity, encouraging resistance to colonial control. In the Middle East, for example, this divide-and-conquer approach was used against the Kurdish people, tough fighters whose settlement area ended up distributed among Turkey, Iran, Iraq, Syria, and the former Soviet Union.

Ethnic division within a nation is an example of what political scientists call a **political cleavage**: any enduring division within a population that can contribute to political disputes. Political cleavages may also arise over other differences, such as race, religion, language, economic stratum or role (e.g., upper socioeconomic class versus lower socioeconomic class), and region. Ordinarily, such cleavages do not interfere with a broad sense of national identity. However, a challenge of national identity may arise when two conditions exist:

- Multiple lines of political cleavage divide one group off against another, and
- One of those lines of cleavage is region.

If two or more lines of political cleavage are superimposed on one another, dividing one group from another over multiple sources of difference at once, we call the situation one of **coinciding cleavages**. For example, two ethnic groups may also differ as to religion, and perhaps over language and social stratum, as well. In this situation, the sense of attachment to one's own group and political contention between the groups may intensify.[7] The reason for this is that on a wide range of political issues—say, ethnic, religious, and economic—members of the groups tend to always have the same opponents and the same allies. The longer the list of cleavages that coincide, the greater the intensity of intergroup contention. (The opposite of this is **cross-cutting cleavages**, wherein each group is internally sectioned by other lines of cleavage that cut across the group, making members of the same group opponents on some issues and rendering members of different groups allies on some issues, thus softening the intensity of group attachment and intergroup contention.)

Even this intensification of political contention, however, is not likely by itself to seriously challenge national identity. But if one of the groups has a territorial home base where it is the dominant group (especially if the group has its own language), chances are it may at some point aspire to break away and have its own nation-state (see "Contention and Cooperation in Focus: Nigeria"). In 2011, largely Christian and racially black South Sudan split off (after years of conflict) from Sudan's Muslim and Arab-ancestry north to become an independent country. Such deep divisions mark present-day Iraq, for the southern Shia Muslims, the northwestern Sunni Arabs, and the moderate Sunni Kurds of the northeast (see Country Case Studies below).

A Response to the Challenge: Federalism

Nations can take several approaches to building and maintaining national identity. Where superimposed cleavages exist and involve regional differences, one approach that a government can take is **federalism**. This involves establishing a regional level of government and delegating some responsibilities (such as education, roads, criminal justice, etc.) to it. Under such an arrangement, issues that provoke sharp contention between ethnicities at the national level may be delegated to the different regions' governments. There, each region has more homogeneous attitudes and can agree on the issue. In this approach, which political scientist Robert Dahl called "consensual decision,"[8] national politics can focus on issues that do not invite sharp contention between regions, and overall national identity comes more easily (see "Contention and Cooperation in Focus").

Certainly, federalism cannot resolve every sensitive issue that involves regional contention. An issue may touch so deeply on important human rights values for the whole nation that it cannot be delegated to its regions. In the United States in the mid-nineteenth century, slavery proved to be so contrary to freedom as a public value that it could not be left to each region (or state in the United States) to handle as it wished. Ultimately, a bloody civil war had to be fought to eliminate American slavery. However, within a decade, the United States returned to federalism with regard to the sensitive issue of how the freed slaves were to be treated; for ninety years after the end of Reconstruction in 1876, white majorities in the southern states were allowed to confine African Americans' activities with racial segregation, discrimination, and exclusion from voting.

Especially large and diverse nations such as the United States, Brazil, Nigeria, and India tend to have federal forms of government. Where the national government is democratically elected, typically the regional governments are, too.

CONTENTION AND COOPERATION IN FOCUS | Nigeria

Nigeria has many ethnic groups and languages, but three have been especially important historically, each with a regional area of concentration: the Christian Ibo in the southeast, the mostly Christian Yoruba of the southwest, and the Muslim Hausa-Fulani of the north. In the late 1960s, Christian Ibo farmers of the southeast resisted what they saw as dominance by the Muslim north by mounting a war of secession (the Biafra Civil War; see Country Case Studies, chapter 16). After a long siege, the Ibos had to surrender.

In areas where the ethnic-religious groups coexist, another cleavage may intensify contention. In parts of the "middle belt" area of Nigeria, for example, Muslim cattle-herders may find themselves in land disputes with a Christian farming tribe. Disturbances in the street are not uncommon when sources of dispute have arisen.

As these divisions reinforce one another, attachment to one's own group intensifies. Hostility may grow toward the opposing group to the point that contention overwhelms cooperation. If the two groups speak different languages, even communication to settle their differences can be difficult. Each group then forms a very strong subculture within the nation. To help tamp down sources of contentious dispute, the Nigerian government has taken a federal form. Contending groups cooperate in allowing key issues to be handled by the elected governments at the regional level, where consensus and cooperation is easier to reach. For example, Nigeria's federal structure has allowed regions to decide the contentious issue of the role of Islamic Sharia law in the criminal justice system for Muslims. The northern Islamic regions can choose to adopt it, while the southern and more Christian regions do not.

The opposite approach is a **unitary state**, which does not grant a regional level of government independent responsibility for any policy areas (see Figure 4.1). Nations with unitary government tend to be smaller and to lack deep divisions from superimposed cleavages.

Leadership Attitudes Toward National Identity

In the case of multiethnic and multicultural nations, another key factor for national identity is the attitudes of leaders of political parties and ethnic groups. If contending groups' leaders identify with the nation and influence their followers to do so as well, national identity is enhanced. In the early and middle twentieth century in the United States, for example, leaders of immigrant ethnic minorities tended to embrace identification as Americans and urge it on their followers. In contrast, if leaders of a religious or ethnic group emphasize its own cultural values in ways that explicitly go against national identification, group contention may intensify.

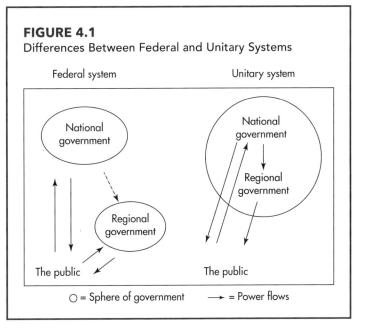

FIGURE 4.1
Differences Between Federal and Unitary Systems

Notably, leaders of a *majority* ethnic or religious group can also disrupt shared national identity. If such a majority feels threatened by minorities, it may try to tie the nation's identity too much to its own ethnicity or religion. For example, in recent decades in India the rise of Hindu nationalist leaders threatened to revive ethnic and religious tensions that had been successfully tamped down during the earlier postindependence decades. This development has to some extent resurrected the challenge of identity for India (see Country Case Studies, chapter 11).

Immigrants being processed at Ellis Island in New York harbor.

THE CHALLENGE OF LEGITIMACY

Another step in political development beyond establishing a national identity is achieving a widespread consensus on the "rules of the game" of government. For government to effectively regulate political contention, contenders must recognize its authority and cooperate with its basic rules. As we saw in chapter 2, a system of government has political legitimacy when citizens accept its institutions and practices as rightful and just for them. How and why do nations' political arrangements gain legitimacy in the eyes of the public?

On the one hand, citizens may cooperate with the government partly out of shared interests and pragmatism, a practical sense that the nation's system "works well for us." However, a stronger form of political legitimacy is present when the public believes that its governmental system is rightful and just for the country. Such a sense of legitimacy strongly bolsters the authority of government and its laws. Citizens obey willingly because they believe that the rules are arrived at fairly—rather than complying only in proportion to their fear of punishment for rule breaking.

To be sure, the concept of legitimacy can be hard to "operationalize" (see chapter 3) and measure. For example, in the old Soviet Union after the death of Soviet leader Joseph Stalin in 1953, the threat of widespread state terror ended. Economic conditions gradually improved for the bulk of the population. At the same time, the regime continued to use its control over the media, education, and culture to transmit positive messages about its role and performance. The people seemed to quietly accept the regime, but it was difficult to tell how much legitimacy the system actually enjoyed. However, at least by the time Communism fell in 1991 with hardly a whimper of public protest, the regime had clearly run short of legitimacy.

Similarly, in pre-2011 Egypt, it was hard to tell how much political legitimacy President Hosni Mubarak's authoritarian regime commanded. But after huge protests in early 2011 forced Mubarak to step down, it seemed that the public's sense of the regime's legitimacy had been weak. Under Mubarak's rule, the strength of opposition had been concealed because elite groups suppressed key opposition ones (especially the Muslim Brotherhood). When the opportunity arose, a broad movement quickly emerged in favor of democracy. A variety of otherwise contending secularist and Islamist groups cooperated in the Tahrir Square protests, and then afterward to work out the outlines of a transfer of power from a military council to a representative democracy. However, the Egyptians had not yet settled on the contours of the actual transition and the new democracy, and soon cooperation was replaced by multisided political contention (see Country Case Studies, chapter 12).

What factors contribute to establishing and preserving political legitimacy, or to challenging the legitimacy of an existing government? Some factors are largely out of government's control, while others can be affected by government.

The Role of Culture Regarding Political Legitimacy

One set of factors affecting political legitimacy relates to a nation's cultural values surrounding politics.[9] If the type of government is a good fit with those values, it is more likely to enjoy political legitimacy. For example, up through the nineteenth century, Russia's monarchy seemed to enjoy substantial legitimacy. It found powerful support in Russia's brand of Christianity, which valued order and hierarchy. The Russian Orthodox Church was itself ruled in a hierarchical fashion under its "patriarch." And it taught its congregations that the monarch (the "Czar") ruled by divine right, so the citizens had a religious duty to obey their government.

This contrasts with the individualistic culture of the early colonial Americans. The new settlers were mainly small farmers who had fled (or were descended from those who fled) class-bound Europe with its official religions. They cherished their independence. In addition, most were Protestant Christians whose religious tradition encouraged them to read the Bible on their own rather than relying on a priestly hierarchy to interpret it for them. And most of the colonies practiced some degree of local self-government, not having to pay much attention to the distant British crown. In the 1770s, the colonies rejected new taxes imposed by a British king and a parliament that did not represent the American colonists. Within a decade, revolution had brought independence to the colonies. Individualistic contention against what they saw as excessive British authority later enhanced the legitimacy of the new government: a presidential democracy with divided and weak national institutions and strong protections for personal freedom against national government. The resulting political framework tended to decentralize group contention in American life until the Civil War of the 1860s.

As in the case of the challenge of national identity, governments and societies can do things to try to sustain legitimacy. Again, the schools can play a role; the system of government can be presented to children as good and fair. Parents may reinforce these ideas at home, as may religious figures from the pulpit.

However, leaders may also influence people to oppose political legitimacy. If members of a racial, ethnic, or religious group feel victimized by a dominant group, they may consider the system to be unfair. Their local leaders may contend against their plight in community or religious gatherings in ways that undermine the government's legitimacy among such groups. Such opposition arose, for example, against ethnic Pashtun domination under the Taliban government in Afghanistan in the early 2000s, ethnic Serb domination of the former Yugoslav government, Sunni Arab minority domination of the former Iraqi government of Saddam Hussein and the current government of Bahrain, and minority Alawite (a religious sect related to Shia Islam) rule over the Sunni majority in Syria. In each of these cases, the dominant group's suppression of contention by other groups no doubt detracted from the sense of the legitimacy of those regimes among opposing groups.

The Rule of Law and a Constitution

Another legitimacy-enhancing factor is the **rule of law**, which involves three shared values: justice as fairness, order as consistency in government authority, and equality as equal treatment under the law. A government that accepts the rule of law operates consistently by rules that apply equally to everyone. Such a government does not treat different individuals or groups in different ways, or rely on the discretion of officials who might favor certain individuals or groups. The Roman republic and empire certainly helped its legitimacy with its new emphasis on law. France did the same in the early nineteenth century after the introduction of the Napoleonic Code—emperor Napoleon Bonaparte's updating of Rome's old Justinian code of law. Going from lawless, arbitrary rule to lawfulness tends to boost legitimacy. The same can be said for progress in reducing bribery and corruption, factors that corrode legitimacy, especially in many developing nations.

However, promising the rule of law while failing to deliver it can undercut legitimacy. When the American forces invaded Iraq in 2003, the American government hoped that its transitional Coalition Provisional Authority (CPA) would be a bridge to a new democratic government that the Iraqis would consider legitimate. The CPA stressed that it had replaced Saddam Hussein's often arbitrary authoritarian rule, which had favored the Sunni Arab minority and had engaged selectively in state terror. However, the American policy of removing the entire old government down to its lower levels actually created lawlessness on a large scale. Early on, this hindered trust in the occupiers' efforts toward a new regime that Iraqis might consider legitimate.

Governments can enhance their legitimacy by adopting explicit, formal rules to govern the decision-making process: a **constitution**. A constitution lays out the basic structures, procedures, powers, and limitations of government. The American Constitutional Convention in 1787 created such a document. The constitution's subsequent ratification by the American states enhanced the legitimacy of the national government. To effectively structure how government works over time, constitutions normally make themselves difficult to amend.

Recently, many newly democratic nation-states in the post-Communist and developing worlds have drafted constitutions to enhance the legitimacy of the new order. As we shall see in chapter 15, constitutions may be drawn up by large conferences representing most of the significant groups in the community (the "social pact" approach), or instead by commissions appointed (and often influenced) by the previously dominant group. However, if the new government does not actually follow its rules in practice, the document will not enhance the government's legitimacy. To prevent this, many of these countries have also established independent constitutional courts to judge whether the government is following its constitution (see chapter 14).

Longevity and Policy Effectiveness

Some factors can encourage support for governments under certain circumstances for periods of time, but may not instill a lasting sense of political legitimacy. When institutions and procedures remain over time without instability, people know what to expect and become accustomed to cooperation with the government. German political sociologist Max Weber referred to this phenomenon as "traditional" legitimacy.[10]

However, the twentieth and twenty-first centuries have seen numerous instances of long-standing regimes losing legitimacy and falling. Longevity of a governmental structure seems to help legitimacy only if the governmental institutions also have a record of effective policy-making in relation to key public values. For example, the old Soviet government in Russia existed for a long time and provided its people with well-being in the form of economic security. However, toward the end of the Soviet era in the late 1980s, scarcity of key consumer goods led to people having to stand in line for hours hoping for a chance to buy basic items such as soap. Meanwhile, influential members of the ruling party and government had easy access to goods. Citizens began to doubt the effectiveness of Soviet economic policies, which no doubt helped to undermine the government's legitimacy.

Leadership Charisma and Ideology

Sometimes public attachment to the personality of an inspiring national leader can help spearhead and stabilize new institutions, at least temporarily. Max Weber called this "charismatic" legitimacy,[11] evident in such regimes as those of Adolph Hitler in Germany in the mid to late 1930s, and Mao Zedong in China in the 1950s and late 1960s. Often the charismatic leader tries to inspire the population with a new ideology. In Egypt in the 1950s, Gamal Abdul Nasser used Arab nationalism to rally support, and in Tanzania in the 1970s, Julius Nyerere used "Ujamaa" socialism (harking back to traditional African village customs of cooperation). However, while charismatic leadership and new ideology can help undermine the legitimacy of the previous system, by themselves they generally cannot secure enduring public attachment to the new institutions. Often when the charismatic leader passes from the scene, the ideology declines, group contention breaks out within and against the regime, and it undergoes significant change.

Representative Democracy

Finally, the form of government itself, and its degree of respect for individual and group freedoms, may also impact its legitimacy. Since the mid-1970s, there has been a noticeable worldwide rise in the adoption of multiparty elections. Representative democracy seemed to be an answer to authoritarian situations in which an ethnic or religious minority dominated the government and excluded the majority from influence. As recently as 2011, in North Africa and the Middle East we have seen an array of opposition groups cooperating in social movements for democracy. They contended against situations of ethnic or religious minority dominance such as those mentioned above in Iraq and Syria, as well as the Libyan government's control by the nation's Western tribes and the supremacy of Bahrain's Sunni minority over its majority Shia.

Under representative democracy, contending groups seem more willing to live with problems and inefficiencies without trying to bring down the whole political system. People know that in the next election, they will at least be able to get new leadership. Moreover, election-day procedures give citizens a sense of connection to their nation and its government.

Related to this is democracy's assurance of respect for particular individual and group freedoms, such as those of expression, association, the press, and fair trial. Particularly when peaceful protest is met by government violence and detention (e.g., in Iran in 2009 and Egypt and Syria in 2011), the people often demand respect for individual freedoms. Especially if reinforced by international support related to human rights awareness, these values can come to be

---

THE HUMAN RIGHTS CONNECTION | The Influence of U.N. Human Rights Covenant Obligations

Representative democracy got a boost as a contributor to legitimacy from an international factor: the incorporation of free and fair elections into the United Nations' civil-political human rights Covenant (see chapter 3). But in practice, the international Covenants of human rights cannot directly control what sort of government a nation will consider legitimate. And as noted in chapter 3, nor does the International Covenant of Civil and Political Rights (ICCPR) direct nations in the particulars of how they should set up democratic government. This gives nations some flexibility as they seek to comply, but it also may allow the adoption of mere election formalities without true democracy.

Moreover, the ICCPR does not authorize direct international intervention against a signatory nation that violates human rights. (Near the beginning of the ICCPR is an article asserting the right of national self-determination.) The reporting requirements that the ICCPR imposes can help *publicize* patterns of violation of civil and political rights. Such publicity can both mobilize international opinion and also inform the citizens of the offending nation. But arguably, the cumulative effect of the ICCPR is to promote the basic principles of representative democracy as criteria or standards for what peoples may consider legitimate government.

viewed as requirements for governmental legitimacy (see The "Human Rights Connection").

In some nations, individual freedom values had enhanced political legitimacy long before the twentieth century. For example, over the centuries the British developed strong customs of respect for individual liberty. And in the late 1780s, the Americans amended their new constitution by adding the protection of key individual freedoms (e.g., freedoms of expression, association, and religion) against national government interference, thereby bolstering the legitimacy of the new national government.[12] In this case, shared support for freedom values enabled enough intergroup cooperation among otherwise contending groups to allow the amendment of the constitution in line with those shared values.

Internationally, a twentieth-century boost in this direction came from the U.N.'s human rights agreements: the Universal Declaration of human rights (1948), and Covenants of human rights (1966, in effect for signatory nations in 1976; see chapter 1). They have contributed to bottom-up pressure by national social movements for human rights and democracy (e.g., the East European democracy movements at the end of the 1980s), as well as international influence of governments on each other to view human rights respect as legitimacy enhancing.

THE CHALLENGE OF PARTICIPATION

The **challenge of participation** involves contention with the government to allow more citizens to take part in politics. Often a challenge of participation leads to the adoption of representative democracy, especially if the challenge takes the form of cooperation among the contending groups in a broad, umbrella-style democracy movement. But challenges of participation and resulting gains may be more limited than this.

The earliest examples of challenges of participation did not demand full democratization. In medieval times in parts of Europe, when the king asked his subjects for more taxes (usually to fund a war), they often wanted to be consulted about why he needed the money. Some monarchs had to call an assembly of representatives of the nobles, gentry, towns, and the church to make the case. When people in Africa and Asia rose up against European colonial rule in the 1950s and 1960s, most expected national independence to bring greater access to political participation than they had under colonial rule.

As we shall see below and in chapter 15, however, many postindependence efforts to expand participation fell short. In some cases, the government was only trying to mobilize the public behind the government's goals, or particular groups aimed only to increase their own access around narrow interests. These efforts tended not to yield broad and lasting expansions of the opportunity for participation.

Challenges of participation may stem in part from struggles to secure or expand **civil liberties** such as freedoms of expression, association, religion, and the press. To be sure, groups in civil society may possess a degree of such liberties under some types of authoritarian rule, as in Egypt and Tunisia prior to 2011. However, people can only secure their civil liberties via assured *political* rights: representative democracy with free and fair elections.

Factors behind Challenges of Participation

Political scientists have suggested numerous reasons for the rise of demands on nondemocratic governments to grant wider opportunities for participation in politics and government (chapter 15). Some explanations include long-term, general developments across many countries, such as the "modernization" factors noted in chapter 1. These trends include economic growth, industrialization, urbanization, education, modern communications, and the rise of a broad middle class. Such developments tend to produce increased numbers of minimally educated people in cities and towns. A range of economic and social groups arise with organizations to represent their interests: community groups, labor unions, professional organizations (e.g., of teachers, lawyers, and doctors), and social movements that may develop around major issues. Such groups' activists may spearhead efforts to reduce constraints on freedoms, provide local institutions for broader participation, and remove limitations on voting rights and electoral fairness. This presents a largely pluralist model picture of pressures for more political participation.

Portrayal of protesters dumping tea into Boston harbor during the Boston Tea Party of 1773.

Medium-term developments may contribute to challenges of participation. In the early twentieth century in Europe and Latin America, extreme inequality and economic hardship led workers and other lower-class urban groups to protest their conditions and their exclusion from politics. At mid-century, poor conditions under colonial rule contributed to the national independence movements of the 1950s and 1960s. From the late 1970s through the early 1990s in the developing world, citizens challenged authoritarian regimes against the backdrop of mounting economic problems: stagnation, inflation, deteriorating government finances, heavy national indebtedness, and expanding inequality. In the late 1980s in Russia and Eastern Europe, adverse conditions facing consumers contributed to the uprisings that brought down Communism. And in Egypt in 2011, several conditions were important, including (a) numerous educated youth with no job prospects; (b) ongoing public resentment over the regime's corruption, election-rigging, and suppression of opposition groups; (c) the government's use of extralegal detentions and torture; and (d) a recent sharp rise in food prices.

In addition, short-term events can provide the immediate spark to a challenge of participation. The American Revolution occurred in part because of resentment over new British colonial taxes. Protests provoked British retaliation, including closing the port of Boston, leading to new protests until the cycle spiraled out of control. In the Egyptian case, the mid-2010 police killing of a young man in Alexandria (with the news spread via the Internet) and the example of an uprising in neighboring Tunisia both played important roles.

Early Democratic Responses

A challenge of participation may lead to representative democracy, or may fail altogether, bringing some new authoritarian regime. Where democracy results, its form often relates to the circumstances of the events that led to it. Examples of this are provided by the attention-getting first examples of representative democratic development, Great Britain and the United States.

The British and American Forerunners A series of challenges of participation set the institutional contours of England's government in the mid to late seventeenth century. By 1640, a largely Protestant parliament was struggling to take over leadership of the government from a Catholic king who needed parliament to approve new taxes for his wars against European powers. The parliamentary forces overthrew the monarchy in a civil war and ruled for a decade under their chief general, Oliver Cromwell. However, Cromwell became a virtual dictator. The republican regime collapsed soon after his death, and the monarchy was restored with a more agreeable king in 1660.

A generation later, however, another Catholic king wanted to impose his religion over largely Protestant Britain. The result in 1689 was a "bloodless revolution" that installed a different hereditary line and a much weaker king, with parliament's influence greatly bolstered. The measure of victory was the depositing of the executive leadership in the hands of the leaders of the parliamentary majority. The monarch's role subsequently withered, and power became concentrated in the hands of a prime minister and cabinet supported by the parliamentary majority. When new challenges arose over extending voting rights to all adult males in the nineteenth century and to women in the early twentieth century, the basic system of government was not in question.

In contrast, the Americans of the late eighteenth century faced a very different situation. The former colonies had been practicing a degree of self-government for some time, but without representation in Parliament. They came to resent taxation efforts by a distant king and parliament. After the Revolution, each state found itself largely independent, with the Continental Congress representing each state equally under the loose Articles of Confederation. When the states conceded by the late 1780s that they needed a stronger national government for defense and a national free trade area, many still distrusted distant state authority. They kept the executive chief weak and separate from the legislative power. But they also wanted to limit the legislative authority, granting the president a limited veto power over legislation. Also, the small states demanded that in addition to a legislative assembly that gave weight to population (the House of Representatives), a second powerful legislative house be set up that would give each small state the same voting power possessed by the largest state, as had been the case under the Articles. Both houses had to approve a bill for it to become law. The result was a divided and, at the time, fairly weak "presidential" system of government (see "Concept in Context" below).

Continental Europe and Voting Systems In contrast, the continental European monarchies encountered their main challenges of participation much later, in the late nineteenth and early twentieth centuries. As in the earlier British experience, these continental challenges contended against monarchic tradition for greater opportunities for participation. The other European nations followed the British example in adopting the parliamentary form of government. But they did not follow the British and American examples regarding their SMD (single-member district) voting systems. Why not?

As was noted briefly in chapter 3, Great Britain and the United States share the single member district plurality (SMDP) electoral system in which small districts each select the one candidate who got the most votes. With only the top vote-getter winning the one seat in each district, only the largest parties will see their candidates win in significant numbers of districts. Consequently, small groups tend to combine into a few large parties—at the extreme, only two big contenders—to get representation for their views and leaders. The result is usually a party system with two parties that are so big that one or the other will win the majority in any given legislative house. This outcome has important consequences for party contention and cooperation in the legislative process. Normally (that is, in the absence of special rules requiring supermajorities to enact legislation) one of the two dominant parties will be able to pass bills without having to cooperate with other parties.

But when the continental European countries were challenging their monarchies to allow expanded participation in the late nineteenth century, conditions had changed a lot since Great Britain and the United States had adopted SMDP centuries earlier. Industrialization and urbanization had produced several important political cleavages. Those divisions sprang from social class (working class vs. "white collar"), religion (Catholic vs. Protestant versus secular), region (center vs. periphery), urban versus rural residence, and sometimes ethnicity. With all these cleavages, numerous groups wanted to represent their contending interests in politics. Meanwhile, the Europeans could see that in the United States and Britain, SMDP elections tended to produce only two large parties in national politics. To preserve the viability of several contending groups, European nations generally chose some form of **proportional representation** (PR) voting.[13] Under PR, large election districts each send a number of representatives to the key legislative assembly, and these seats are allocated to the parties in proportion to their shares of the vote in the district. As we saw in chapter 3,[14] this allows small parties as well as big ones to win seats. Again, the outcome is numerous contending parties in legislative assemblies, not just two big ones. This has major consequences; typically there are too many parties for any one of them to hold legislative majorities in its own hands, so alliances (called "coalitions") must form to gain the majorities that are necessary to support a prime minister and pass favored legislation.

Authoritarian Responses

In some nations, the challenge of participation is met by repression and fails to significantly expand participation. At the conclusion of the challenge, one group is dominant—whether a particular political party, the armed forces, a single leader with his or her associates, or a religious hierarchy. Outsiders are suppressed or marginalized, and the nation is forced back into public quietude and deference. This occurred in China after the Tiananmen Square massacre in 1989. In that incident, student protesters demanding democracy were driven from China's most prominent public square in Beijing, and democracy activists were arrested throughout the country.

Alternatively, a challenge of participation may result in what seems like the beginnings of democracy, followed by a new authoritarian regime. In early 1917 in Russia, amid the nation's setbacks in World War I and an accompanying severe economic downturn, protests in the biggest cities forced the monarch (the "czar") to resign. A provisional government was established to rule until an assembly could be elected to write a democratic constitution. But by the end of 1917 this fragile government was suffering difficulties similar to those that had confronted the czar earlier. It was overthrown by a revolutionary socialist party called the Bolsheviks, which imposed a nondemocratic single-party regime later to be called Communist.

Another example is Iran in 1978. An unpopular monarch was overthrown by an Islamic movement led by Shia cleric Ayatollah Ruhollah Khomeini. The Iranian revolution at first appeared to be a broad-based, democracy-spirited rejection of authoritarian government, but Khomeini and his followers soon undermined the fledgling postrevolution democratic processes and instituted an authoritarian regime under their own leadership. Today the clerics have been joined at the top by the revolution's military arm, the Islamic Revolutionary Guard Corps.

In some cases in the early-mid-twentieth century, a new democracy emerged and lasted for a decade or two before succumbing to authoritarian or totalitarian takeover. Established elites were fearful of Russian-style socialist revolution amid the economic disruptions from World War I and the Great Depression of the 1930s. For example, the 1915–1940 period in Italy, Germany, Spain, and Portugal saw democracies yield to either totalitarian or authoritarian single-party rule. (Those regimes ended in Germany and Italy with defeat in World War II). In the newly independent developing nations from the 1950s through the early 1970s, shaky democracies with fragile economies often gave way to authoritarian regimes that were military, single-party, or personal-autocratic.

By the 1980s and 1990s, however, these authoritarian regimes faced major policy difficulties, a new democratic mood, and new challenges of participation. Many became representative democracies (see Country Case Study on Brazil below). But others took up little more than the formalities of multiparty elections. In these countries, a single dominant party prevented opposing parties from contending freely, and continued to control the government (see the Country Case Study on Belarus, chapter 1).

THE TIMING OF THE CHALLENGES

What if a country must cope with two or three nation-building challenges at once? Countries that only have to deal with only one challenge at a time seem more likely to respond to them successfully, and gain durable foundations in the outcome. For example, England already enjoyed a strong sense of national identity when, in the seventeenth century, it faced conflict over legitimacy between those favoring parliamentary power and the supporters of the king. The settlement of 1689 and its aftermath secured basic legitimacy for king and parliament, with the latter increasingly holding the primary influence. Later, Great Britain handled its challenge of penetration by state authority with the final defeat of the Scottish highland clans at the Battle of Culloden in 1742. It was not until the nineteenth century that demands for participation in Britain led to the extension of voting rights to all males. By this time, the pattern of party contention within a well-established political framework could easily handle mass participation.

However, not all nations have the luxury of addressing one challenge of development at a time, as Great Britain did. For example, poor penetration by government benefits to a remote region can produce a challenge of participation, demanding more autonomy and control over such programs (e.g., eastern Mali or the delta region of Nigeria). Or legitimacy may be shaken by a challenge of participation, as in the Arab Spring demands by youth and other groups for replacement of authoritarian rule with genuine representative democracy.

The simultaneous challenges problem was especially evident among many African and Asian nations after gaining independence from colonial rule. During the colonial era, none of the foundations that we have examined—pervasive national identity, political legitimacy, avenues for participation, and full penetration by state authority—had seen much progress. When the colonial powers withdrew, questions often lingered about national identity, the new governments had little time to build an enduring sense of legitimacy, experience with participation was largely absent, and penetration by state authority was often weak. Demands related to the various challenges came all at once, again intensified by the unmet challenge of continuing poverty. The result in many developing nations was instability and authoritarian rule. Only in the 1980s and 1990s, as authoritarian regimes lost their meager legitimacy, could developing nations focus on challenges of legitimacy and participation by embarking on transitions to representative democracy.

SUMMARY: CONTENTION AND COOPERATION IN POLITICAL DEVELOPMENT

As we have seen, responses to challenges in political development serve to install state political resources that support its stability and effectiveness. These include the penetration by state authority throughout the country, a sense of identification with the nation, a sense that the system of government is rightful and just, and access to political participation. Each challenge may involve sharp contention, and each resolution of a challenge involves a new form of cooperation.

Political contention within a nation is softened by a sense of a common national culture and shared perceptions of events, and arrangements that localize forms of contention that are especially divisive. Political legitimacy is the sense that political arrangements are basically rightful and just. It enhances voluntary cooperation with government's procedures and laws due to the sense that decisions are arrived at fairly. Political legitimacy results from building institutions that fit the society's culture, operate by rules that apply equally to all, produce results that benefit nearly all contending groups at one time or another, and in recent decades, provide for free political contention and cooperation.

Penetration by state authority spreads cooperation with the law by the imposition (sometimes contentious) of national government authority and influence over outlying areas or disaffected groups. Participation expands due to political contention from hitherto excluded groups, and results in structuring political contention and facilitating cooperation. Responses to the challenge of participation have produced different forms of democratic government: parliamentary and presidential, which each may have two prevailing parties or a larger number of significant ones. Recent international human rights treaties have helped establish representative democracy as a norm for both participation and legitimacy.

COUNTRY CASE STUDIES

On this topic we consider two developing nations, Iraq and Brazil. Iraq's path of political development was deeply affected by the policies of former colonial occupiers in the nineteenth and early twentieth centuries, and by coinciding cleavages involving region. Brazil was independent by the early nineteenth century and has not suffered from coinciding cleavages involving ethnic regions and religion. Accordingly, its experience of the challenges of political development has differed significantly from that of Iraq.

Iraq: A Nation in Flux

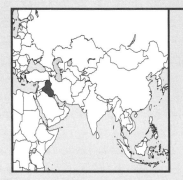

It is difficult to imagine a country in which problems of political development are more overwhelming than Iraq. In terms of national identity, the country suffers from major coinciding cleavages. Iraq is divided ethnically between Kurds and Arabs, and religiously between the two major sects of Islam. The Sunnis are the majority of Muslims worldwide but only a minority of Muslims in Iraq, while the Shia are the majority in Iraq (and dominant in neighboring Iran). Each of these three resulting groups has a regional base: the Sunni Kurds in the northeast, the Sunni Arabs in the central-northwest, and the Shia Arabs in the south.

Under the Ottoman Empire from the sixteenth century through the early twentieth, the minority Sunni Arabs had been installed as the dominant group in the government of Iraq. With the crumbling of Ottoman rule during World War I, Britain created the protectorate of Iraq out of three former Ottoman provinces. The British divided Iraq into the three major regions mentioned above. Political cleavages along lines of religion, ethnicity, language, and region coincided, a recipe for continuing tensions.

In 1921, Shia Muslims in the south rose up against the British, and the rebellion was put down with brutal force. A powerful central government seemed necessary to hold the country together and ensure national authority. The British relied on the Sunni Arab minority, which had dominated local affairs under the Ottoman Turks, to facilitate the extension of national authority throughout the protectorate. When British rule formally ended in 1932, they installed a Sunni Arab

foreigner as king and retained heavy influence over policy. In 1958, Sunni Arab nationalist army officers overthrew the monarchy and eliminated British influence, but authoritarian rule continued. A decade later, a Sunni Arab political party, the relatively secular Ba'ath Party, united and stabilized the central government while opposing Shia Islamic fundamentalism.

The new Ba'ath Party regime was backed by a powerful and brutal security chief, Saddam Hussein. He claimed that he could forcefully project central authority over the country, particularly over the restive Shia majority in the south and the Kurds with their strong ethnic nationalism in the northeast. With the extension of state authority at the top of his agenda, Saddam assumed formal political leadership in 1979. He proceeded to further centralize power within the Ba'ath Party and the army in the hands of himself, his family, and close associates from his home district of Tikrit. Saddam used violence freely against political opponents to extend the government's authority. He also used the media to glorify himself as the leader and built numerous presidential palaces.

By the early 1980s, fear of the new radical Shia government in neighboring Iran (and perhaps the desire to seize strategic lands there) contributed to a war that lasted through the decade. The war continued to bolster authoritarian rule and may even have stimulated Iraqi national identity somewhat. Outside the center-west Sunni areas, however, there was little to support a sense of legitimacy other than the government's provision of monthly food rations and its ability to fight off attacks from Iran. The regime instead had to rely heavily on the threat of coercion. Upon the conclusion of the bloody war with Iran in stalemate at the end of the 1980s, Saddam made an example of a number of Kurdish villages. He accused them of disloyalty and attacked them with chemical weapons, leading to thousands of deaths.

Saddam then invaded the small border state of Kuwait, but he was ultimately repulsed by the United States and its allies in the first Gulf War of 1990–1991. The subsequent ongoing confrontation with the United States, together with Saddam's guarantee of food rations, no doubt provided some nationalistic support for his rule. Nonetheless, penetration by his authority in Iraqi territory in the 1990s was severely limited. American air power shielded the southern Shia areas and the Kurds in the northeast from the worst of central government intervention. Under this stress, Saddam apparently destroyed his old chemical weapons and was unable or unwilling to develop usable new ones.

Following the American invasion and occupation of Iraq in 2003 (ostensibly to preempt Saddam's use of weapons of mass destruction), the challenge of national identity remained. The invading Americans abolished the remnants of state authority by removing the entire Baathist governmental structure without providing anything to replace it on the ground. The resulting lawlessness undermined any legitimacy the new order might have otherwise gained. Militias of each ethno-religious sect became the unofficial local governments in their base areas, often infiltrating and controlling new government police units. Increasingly in 2006 and 2007, acts of terror broke out between Sunnis and Shias. In many mixed communities, the majority sectarian group drove the minority one from their homes.

And yet, despite the failure to surmount the challenges of national identity, legitimacy, and penetration by state authority, the challenge of participation would not wait. Both the Shia and the American forces pushed for the establishment of representative government. But the Kurds in the north and the Sunnis of the central-northwest feared that the majority Shia might oppress them in any new government.

By early 2009, the deaths from sectarian attacks were much reduced. In many areas, sectarian cleansing had run its course, leaving neighborhoods composed of either all one group or all the other. A moderate "Awakening" movement of tribal leaders in the Sunni Arab areas arose with American encouragement and support, expelling many al-Qaeda supporters there. The Shia-dominated government led by Nuri al-Maliki in Baghdad had gained strength in many areas, and defeated the militias in the southern city of Basra. Both the Awakening and Maliki benefited from increased American troop presence and willingness to intervene.

By 2014 the Americans had ended their ground troop presence in Iraq. But the challenge of national identity remains largely unmet. The Maliki government was mostly successful in elections in the Shia areas, but the reinforcing ethnic and religious cleavages between the three communities will probably require a federal system of government if Iraq is to stay together. By 2014, the oil was flowing more reliably, helping the government provide rewards for cooperation. But many Sunnis feared that the Shia-dominated government would not allocate a proper share of the oil revenues to the minority Sunni areas, and Sunnis remained largely shut out of politics.

Then came the 2014 invasion of much of Western Iraq by the former al-Qaeda in Iraq (now renamed the Islamic State—IS). In a rapid blitz, IS drove eastward out of its Syrian base areas, bolstered by (a) a growing influx of militant Islamist foreign fighters, (b) a wide array of military equipment and vehicles captured in Syria from the army and the rebels, and (c) the disintegration and flight of Sunni officers and men from army units that were often based more on patronage and corruption than fighting capability. In Iraq, IS took advantage of both Sunni resentment at their treatment by the Shia government in Baghdad, and IS's own reputation for killing anyone suspected of opposition or dissent, to coerce Sunni populations into cooperation. This involved not only local Sunni populations' silent acquiescence with strict Sharia law and its violent punishments without fair trial procedures, but also families having to provide any available young men to serve as IS soldiers.

The United States, Great Britain, and other countries responded with precision air strikes in support of Kurdish and Iraqi government forces, and the gradual reintroduction of small numbers of American military trainers into Iraq. However, driving back IS's advances in Sunni areas was not easy. American air strikes could not be indiscriminate, so their numbers were limited. And taking back territory required substantial involvement by Shia militias (aided by Western air strikes) on the ground, who sometimes loot and kill when they win, and difficult engineering work to disable IS land mines and booby traps. Restraining revenge-motivated Shia militia abuses against Sunnis proved to be a long-running task, though the militias seemed to display better behavior in reclaiming the city of Tikrit in early 2015.

Iraq continues to confront its simultaneous challenges of extension of state authority, legitimacy

(Sunni and Kurdish resistance to a purely Shia-run government in Baghdad), and participation (the absence of fair representation of Sunnis and Kurds in the official government of eastern Iraq). In the long run, either a division of the country or a federation of some sort seems likely.

Brazil: Intertwined Challenges

Brazil's political development showed long encounters with most of the challenges of nation building. They often overlapped and interacted with each other. However, one state political resource was installed early—national identity. Brazil originally was the Portuguese Empire in South America, largely united by language, culture, and religion, and set apart from the Spanish-speaking areas around it. From the beginning, Brazil functioned as a federal system, with substantially autonomous regions (called states). There were no regions with sufficiently different ethnic, racial, linguistic, or religious identities to propel a separate sense of nationality. Large numbers of slaves of African descent worked the sugar plantations of the northeast and the coffee plantations of the southeast (until the abolition of slavery in 1888), but they were not concentrated in any one region. In the late nineteenth and early twentieth centuries, large numbers of immigrants from such countries as Italy, Germany, Portugal, Spain, and Japan soon embraced Brazilian nationality.

Penetration by state authority, however, was more of a challenge. Brazil was formally ruled by a monarchy based in Rio de Janeiro from the point of national independence in 1822 until 1890. But King Dom Pedro and his son did not substantially alter the relative independence of Brazil's states, which were dominated by their agricultural elites. The landowners of each area controlled their areas, led by local bosses referred to as the "colonels," in a system called "coronelismo." The bosses were in turn led by each state's governor. Few modern transportation and communication links existed between states. When the "military republic" era (of unstable military rule) began in 1891, the traditional oligarchies based on the landed estates continued their autonomous domination of regional politics.

Real penetration by state authority began only in 1930 with the military-backed ascendancy of the charismatic Getulio Vargas. Vargas was a nationalist and a populist (presented as a "man of the people") who represented not only military modernizers but also newer urban groups. He was able to replace the state governors with his own appointees, and he founded the Social Democratic Party largely to represent the new state governors. In addition, Vargas also founded the union-based Brazilian Labor Party, and used patron-client relationships through both parties to help extend state influence. The central government's authority extended further in 1937, when plans for democracy were dropped in favor of Vargas's authoritarian "new state" (Estado Nuovo). Democracy was restored after World War II, and in the 1950s new infrastructure programs expanded modern transportation and communications networks, which more effectively connected the states and further extended the authority of the national center.

The challenge of legitimacy, however, has had a more difficult history in Brazil. In the nineteenth century, the monarch oversaw contention between elite-based political parties, with the eligible electorate restricted (e.g., by a literacy requirement) to under 3 percent of the population. The king played a moderating role in national politics, stepping in to replace one governing party with another when trouble arose.

But this national political system was largely irrelevant to ordinary people. What counted most was that the government be considered somewhat legitimate in the eyes of powerful groups in society, especially the sugar and coffee landowning elite. In 1889, after Emperor Dom Pedro II led a successful campaign to end slavery, he was overthrown and a "military republic" ensued. The new national government, operating without much legitimacy, suffered frequent instability as powerful groups and regions contended with one another. The role of "moderator" was taken up by the armed forces, though less efficiently since the military officers were sometimes involved in the quarrels of others and were often divided among themselves. Legitimacy remained weak.

A new attempt at legitimacy came with Great Depression of the 1930s, when the challenge of participation entered the picture amid economic distress. In 1930, the military, exercising its inherited "moderator" role, installed Getulio Vargas (mentioned above) as president after a disputed presidential election result. Vargas embodied the desire for participation by urban and middle-class interests that had hitherto been largely excluded from politics. He sought legitimacy based on his charisma and policy effectiveness in the face of the Great Depression. Vargas's government spurred some redistribution of political influence from the rural to the urban sectors, aiming to build modern industry with state support and tariff protection from imports. The main impact was in job creation, accompanied by new welfare benefits in the growing urban areas.

Along the way, Vargas began to respond to the challenge of participation. He established unions and allowed them a role in the administration of new social benefits, as well as establishing the Brazilian Labor Party and the Social Democratic party. But the new political organizations were established in a largely top-down fashion, rather than emerging from spontaneous bottom-up organization. Vargas was charismatic and widely popular, but in 1937 he and his military backers cut short the legitimacy and participation gains by ending democratization in favor of the authoritarian "new state." Under it, the new organizations were subjected to top-down political control.

At the end of World War II, amid a rising challenge of participation and concerns among elites about Vargas's power, the military removed him and instituted a competitive democratic system. Over the subsequent years, despite a few brief military forays into politics, the basic legitimacy of representative democracy was established in Brazil. The challenges of legitimacy and participation had begun to be addressed, alongside a spurt in economic development that increased modern employment and lasted into the early 1960s.

The 1946 constitution, however, implicitly preserved the moderating role of the military by subjecting it only to civilian rule that the military judged to be consistent with "the laws." By 1964, the government was led by an aggressively change-oriented successor to Vargas, Labor party leader Jango Goulart. Opposition had arisen over big rises in inflation, government budget deficits, and numerous strikes. Ideological tensions and polarization built up related to economic inequalities on one hand and cold war fears of Communism on the other. Large landowners, big business, foreign interests, and the military itself feared expansion of government ownership and intervention in the economy. The military intervened, suppressed the unions, and this time stayed in power for over twenty years.

The military government tried to maintain some legitimacy by keeping many of the formal trappings of representative democracy. The generals even passed through a controlled Congress the notorious "fifth institutional act" that authorized the state of siege and suspension of civil rights and liberties. They decided not to dismantle union federations and other organizations that had been set up under civilian rule, preferring instead to install compliant new leaders to head them. And military officers tended to take over only the top rungs of management of the executive branch of government, preferring to employ civilian bureaucrats to carry out governmental functions generally.[15] The generals enjoyed early policy successes in spurring further modernization of industry and economic growth.

Overall, however, legitimacy was out of reach. The generals lacked popular and charismatic leaders, and relied on heavy political repression and widespread detentions (with torture) in the late 1960s. As soon as oil price spikes brought economic stagnation in the early to mid-1970s, a new challenge of participation built up steam. The generals decided to permit a very limited form of two-party competition, between their own party vehicle (called "ARENA") and an opposing broad democratic movement party (BDM). By the mid-1970s this umbrella alliance of diverse prodemocracy groups was clearly winning elections against the military-supporting party. The generals kept majority control of Congress only by manipulating its representative formula and other rules. Meanwhile, the list of policy failures under the military government lengthened to include even higher inflation, ballooning national debt, stagnating economic growth, and corruption scandals.

By the late 1970s, the military had had enough of the hassles and challenges of government. A faction among the generals that favored transition to civilian rule won out. In 1978, they chose President Joao Baptista Figuereido, under whom "l'abertura" ("the opening") became a reality. Detainees were released, exiles returned in safety, and union organization became free. A democratization process finally transferred power formally to civilians in 1985. In 1987 and 1988, a new constitution was drawn up by an assembly that was freely and fairly elected. The legitimacy of representative democracy has finally been accepted by the generals as well as the people, with the help of presidents in the 1980s and 1990s who generally pursued conservative policies that the generals were comfortable with. Some of the unrealistic economic guarantees of benefits and protections in the 1988 constitution were modified, and regional government spending was brought under control by 1999.

The last element of the challenge of participation was met in 2002. Amid broad dissatisfaction over widening inequality and low growth, a left-of-center candidate won the presidency: Luis Inacio da Silva (known as Lula) of the Workers Party. The new government was generally committed to financial discipline, but focused new spending on targeted aid to the disadvantaged. Most notable was the "Bolsa familia" program of food aid to poor families who kept their children in school and got them vaccinated.

Current president Dilma Roussef, Lula's successor at the head of the Workers' Party, has largely continued in the policy directions of the previous decade. The economy recovered fairly well from the worldwide challenges of 2008–2009, and new offshore oil prospects promise help in the future (though not at present, with the recent plunge in the price of oil). It is fair to say that Brazil has substantially met its challenges of penetration by state authority, national identity, participation, and the legitimacy of democratic institutions.

However, this is not to say that major problems do not continue to face government. The policy challenges of crime, deteriorating infrastructure, and uneven provision of government services persist. In 2014, substantial public spending on World Cup football (soccer) facilities brought protests at what seemed like lavish waste on frivolities in the face of major public needs for improvement in education, health care, infrastructure, and public safety. Meanwhile, growth began to slow in 2014, and in 2015 Brazil seemed headed into recession. But politically, Roussef seems unable to increase government spending to address such challenges, with the budget deficit and inflation running high. Indeed, she responded by appointing a new finance minister, Joachim Levy, who began

cutting government spending to reduce the budget deficit. And the central bank began increasing interest rates to contain inflation. Recession through 2015 seemed inevitable.

As if these problems weren't enough, perhaps the most attention-getting political challenge facing the Roussef administration by 2015 was a scandal related to a long-running investigation of allegations of past bribery and corruption. It was alleged that going back to the mid-2000s, (a) large bribes were paid by construction and engineering companies to secure contracts for work in projects of Petrobras, the state-owned Brazilian oil company, and (b) much of this money was funneled through PT figures in the government to pay some legislators, especially of the centrist Democratic Movement Party and the conservative Progressive Party, to remain in the majority coalition and support the president's proposals in the Chamber and the Senate.

Roussef, who chaired the Petrobras board during much of the period covered by the allegations, says she was unaware of the corruption (as does Lula, president at the time). But the cloud of scandal was enveloping the administration, prompting protests and weakening the financial support for some current Petrobras-related projects. Roussef's support in polls plummeted in 2015, and the influence of her main coalition partner, the centrist Democratic Movement Party, rose (despite the involvement of some of its leading figures in the scandal). It gained the speakership of the Chamber of Deputies for one of its leaders, received new cabinet seats at the PT's expense, and exerted new influence in Congress over finance minister Levy's budget proposals.

The Petrobras scandal may be linked to a key problem of multiparty presidential democracy: the difficulty of maintaining majority legislative support for presidential proposals under this political framework. With the president's party typically in the minority in legislative assemblies, and given the relative autonomy of parties, party factions, and individual legislators in the assemblies, the cabinet coalition and its control of the budget can go only so far in gaining enough legislative cooperation to enable the passage of bills to address problems. But this is a practical challenge associated with Brazil's type of democratic framework, not a threat to its legitimacy for Brazilians.

⚐ PRACTICE AND REVIEW ONLINE

CRITICAL THINKING QUESTIONS

1. Can coinciding political cleavages that include regional differences be overcome? How?

2. Rank the factors affecting political legitimacy as to how potent they are in producing it. Why are some stronger than others?

3. How might legitimacy affect the penetration by state authority? How might a legitimate government fail to control the national territory?

4. How might the challenge of participation affect legitimacy?

KEY TERMS

penetration by state authority, 81
state capacity, 83
weak states, 83
failed states, 83
national identity, 85
political cleavage, 87
coinciding cleavages, 87
cross-cutting cleavages, 87
federalism, 88
unitary state, 89
rule of law, 91
constitution, 92
challenge of participation, 94
civil liberties, 94
proportional representation, 97

FURTHER READING

Binder, Leonard, et al. *Crises and Sequences in Political Development*. Princeton, NJ: Princeton University Press, 1971.

Dahl, Robert A. *Polyarchy: Participation and Opposition*. New Haven, CT: Yale University Press, 1971.

Diamond, Larry, and Marc Plattner, eds. *The Global Resurgence of Democracy*, 2nd ed. Baltimore: Johns Hopkins University Press, 1996.

Grew, Raymond, ed. *Crises of Political Development in Europe and the United States*. Princeton, NJ: Princeton University Press, 1978.

Huntington, Samuel P. *Clash of Civilizations and the Remaking of World Order*. New York: Simon & Schuster, 1996.

Huntington, Samuel P. *The Third Wave: Democratization in the Late Twentieth Century*. Norman, OK and London: University of Oklahoma Press, 1991.

Sorensen, Georg. *Democracy and Democratization: Processes and Prospects in a Changing World*, 2nd ed. Boulder, CO: Westview Press, 1998.

Taras, Raymond, and Rajat Ganguly. *Understanding Ethnic Conflict*, 2nd ed. New York: Longman, 2002.

United Nations. *International Bill of Human Rights: Final Authorized Text of the United Nations*. New York: American Association for the International Commission of Jurists, 1977.

Weiner, Myron, and Samuel P. Huntington. *Understanding Political Development*. Boston: Little Brown, 1987.

NOTES

[1] See Leonard Binder et al., *Crises and Sequences of Political Development* (Princeton, NJ: Princeton University Press, 1971), and *Crises of Political Development in Europe and the United States*, ed. Raymond Grew (Princeton, NJ: Princeton University Press, 1978).

[2] I do not extend the analysis, as the "crises and sequences" authors did, into measuring progress toward certain modernization endpoints: "capacity, equality, and differentiation."

[3] As we shall see in chapter 5, some normative theorists idealistically referred to this as the "social contract" basis for the state.

[4] See Charles Tilly, *Coercion, Capital, and European States, AD 990–1992* (Cambridge, MA and Oxford, UK: Blackwell, 1992).

[5] This was the phase of extension of state authority that the "crises" authors were referring to when they wrote of crises of "penetration," and they tended to present it late in the sequence of crises, not first.

[6] This is an example of what political scientists call "political socialization," the conveying of long-held values and norms to other people; see chapter 8.

[7] Political scientists call such cleavages "coinciding," "reinforcing," or "superimposed"; see chapter 8.

[8] See Robert A. Dahl, *After the Revolution? Authority in a Good Society* (New Haven: Yale University Press, 1990).

[9] Political scientists call this "political culture"; see chapter 8.

[10] Weber, Max, *The Theory of Economic and Social Organization* (Berkeley, CA: University of California Press, 1957; first published 1922).

[11] Ibid.

[12] These were the first ten amendments to the U.S. Constitution, referred to as the "Bill of Rights." Only in the early-mid-twentieth century, however, were similar protections assured against the *regional*, or "state," level of government in the United States. This was done through U.S. Supreme Court decisions that "incorporated" the rights in the national Bill of Rights under the post–Civil War Fourteenth Amendment to the constitution, which guaranteed individual "life" and "liberty" to the former slaves in the American South. To be sure, however, the full implementation of those protections for African Americans did not occur until the success of the civil rights movement in the 1960s.

[13] See Seymour M. Lipset and Stein Rokkan, eds., *Party Systems and Voter Alignments: Cross-national Perspectives* (New York: Free Press, 1967).

[14] In chapter 3, see "Contention and Cooperation."

[15] The system came to be referred to as "bureaucratic authoritarian"; as applied to Argentina, see Guillermo O'Donnell (translated by James McGuire in collaboration with Rae Flory), *Bureaucratic Authoritarianism: Argentina, 1966–1973, in Comparative Perspective* (Berkeley, CA: University of California Press, 1988).

NORMATIVE
POLITICAL
THOUGHT

I   II   III   IV   V

PART   PART   PART   PART   PART

Political Philosophies and Theories

- **WHICH** of the contending schools of political thought favor elected government? How do they differ from one another?

- **TO** what extent do aristocratic traditionalist and humanitarian law thinkers agree on which groups contend with each other in politics?

- **HOW** and why might power checkers and free marketers cooperate with each other? Do they share pursuit of certain values? How might they contend against each other?

- **ACCORDING** to Marx, what are the main contending forces in politics, and which have the most influence? Under what circumstances would the majority of human beings cooperate in establishing socialism?

- **HOW** might the humanitarian law and free self-development currents cooperate?

IMAGINE THAT YOU ARE A PARENT of teenagers living in Lagos, Nigeria. Your family income is stable, and every day you see your son and daughter off to school. But the problem of street crime is an ever-present reality and you sometimes worry that your children will not make it home safely. Usually all goes well, but occasionally you lament to yourself, "All I want from government is for me and my family to be able to walk in our neighborhood safely! Crack down on these thugs!" This view reflects what may be the most ancient concern in political thought, a desire for physical security. You want a government that is so powerful and fearsome that people would not dare break the law. There is a political philosopher for you: Thomas Hobbes (1588–1679; see below). In Hobbes's writings, you can find a whole world view built around, and justifying, what you want. But keep in mind that there are a number of other political philosophers whose writings disagree with Hobbes. And they can be persuasive, too.

CURRENTS IN POLITICAL PHILOSOPHY AND THEORY

Political philosophies include explorations of human nature, of the values that government ought to pursue, of how society and politics work, and of how government should be crafted to achieve its goals. Normative theory (see chapter 3) is not the same thing as ideology, which focuses especially on strategies and prescriptions for today's problems. But the political philosophers provided many of the elements that underlie present-day ideologies.

Political scientists consider normative theory to be a significant part of their discipline. One major reason for this is related to empirical political science itself. Normative theory includes empirical as well as normative observations. Indeed, for the first 2½ millennia of recorded commentary on politics prior to the twentieth century, attempts to understand key causal factors and consequences related to politics appeared mainly in the works of the political philosophers.

Normative Theory and Political Contention

Often innovative normative thought was prompted by empirical situations of political contention. In the early sixth century BCE in China, imperial order was threatened by contention among feudal warlords. In the early fourth century BCE in Greece, the Athenians faced challenges and conflict related to the loss of their empire. In the first century BCE in Rome, supporters of republican institutions had to contend with new leaders who seemed to foreshadow—and want—monarchy. In the seventeenth century in England and the eighteenth century in France, sharp contention over religion challenged traditional monarchies. In the last half of the nineteenth century and again in the 1930s, contention arose over industrialization's inequalities and financial crises. Each of these situations gave rise to new initiatives in normative theory by observers of society and politics. Thinkers sought new recipes for solving pressing problems, moderating contention, and facilitating cooperation. They ended up contributing to the founding, modification, and justification of today's governmental arrangements, as well as to today's ideologies.

Regarding normative theory, we will apply the theme of contention and cooperation at two different levels. First the theme appears within the thinkers' arguments. For each political philosopher's empirical views of social and political life, we will identify the key groups that contend and sometimes cooperate in political society. But contention and cooperation also arise between the outlooks of the political thinkers themselves. Despite the rich diversity of individual viewpoints, these thinkers can be grouped into different general approaches that contend with each other to some extent.

Contending Currents in Normative Political Thought

Commentators have classified normative political theorists in various ways, such as by ideological affinities, shared concepts, or historical periods (see "Concept in Context"). Here I group key political philosophers according to their general approaches to how political communities should deal with the interplay of contention and cooperation in politics. Each approach amounts to a "current" or "strand" of thought, which may be seen as contending with the other currents.

Members of each **strand (current)** share a general project, within which individual initiatives nonetheless display distinctive features. As we shall see below, thinkers within the same strand tend to broadly agree about on the main problems related to contention and cooperation that should be addressed, the primary values that government should pursue, and at least some aspects of their practical solutions. Among the more ancient currents, one focused on concentrating power for security, while another stressed a virtuous elite, and a third

CONCEPT IN CONTEXT | Classification of Political Thinkers

Some commentators have grouped political thinkers under ideological headings, as precursors to the ideologies that began to spring up in the eighteenth and nineteenth centuries, such as conservatism, classical liberalism, and Marxism-Leninism. But that view tends to impose later models of thinking on earlier thinkers who don't necessarily fit them well.

Other analysts of political thought group political philosophers around shared ideas. For example, we might group together Hobbes, Locke, and Rousseau, as "social contract" thinkers. This classification points to the shared idea of people in an area consciously agreeing to join in a formal community and be governed by a structure of authority—thereby leaving behind their natural freedom (of the "state of nature"). But as we shall see below, these three thinkers viewed and employed the social contract idea in very different ways.

Other commentators classify political thinkers by historical era, such as the "ancient" (up to the fall of the Roman Empire), "medieval" (from then to the Renaissance of the fifteenth and sixteenth centuries), "modern" (from the Renaissance through the nineteenth century) and "contemporary" (the twentieth century to the present) eras. But again, there could be wide divergence in lines of thought within the same historical era.

Notably, the most important political thinkers considered themselves to be addressing eternal issues, such that their initiatives could contribute insights for meeting today's challenges. The treatment below groups thinkers into categories of approach to contention and cooperation that are relevant to today's political and policy challenges.

emphasized benefiting all citizens through law. In more recent centuries, one approach centered on checking power, and another on fostering the commercial market, while a third trumpeted the demise of that market, and yet another concerned itself with developing the potential of each citizen.

In some ways, thinkers sharing a strand are part of a cooperative enterprise, each building on its previous initiatives and engaging in a dialogue with them. Although the currents contend with each other, at times we shall also see elements of cooperation between them.

POWER CONCENTRATION

From the beginnings of government, many people looked to it to provide order, one of the key value categories noted in chapters 1 and 3. They wanted to be protected from chaos and conflict, seeking to avoid the perils and uncertainties of **anarchy**—the absence of government. In the search for order, one key focus was stability in the governmental system. To this end, some observers preferred **monarchy**, rule by one person. They considered unity at the top of government to be necessary for it to take the lead in resolving disputes, repressing wrongdoing, and bolstering social order.

In ancient times, religion tended to supply a primary support for kingship. In medieval Europe, this approach had culminated in the doctrine of the "divine right of kings," meaning that the monarch derived the right to rule directly from God. From the fourteenth century on, however, Christianity in Europe was weakening in its capacity to prop up kings, and the papacy itself was becoming politicized. Monarchs were building their nation-states to some extent independently of church support, as had the French king Phillip the Fair by 1300. In the sixteenth and seventeenth centuries, wars over religion in Europe had become very disruptive and destructive. Writing in mid-1600s England, English philosopher Thomas Hobbes argued that religious differences could only serve as a source of factional contention and ultimately war. Obedience to government as a matter of religious duty had to be abandoned in favor of the only foundation he considered to be a sufficiently powerful substitute—fear. For Hobbes, only fear of concentrated governmental power could save people from the alternative: constant fear of the anarchic violence that accompanied lack of concentrated governmental power.

In his most famous work, *Leviathan* (1651), Hobbes argued that people were naturally selfish pursuers of power. Only the unchallenged authority of centralized government, based on fear of certain punishment, could deter disorder and violence. Without such an all-powerful government, people would be in what Hobbes called a "state of nature." Competition, suspicion, and contention over insults would prevail, and the resulting struggle for power would render life "poor, nasty, brutish, and short." Economic progress, he argued, was impossible without security.

Hobbes argued that shared fear of violence could bring sufficient cooperation to set up the right sort of government, in what he called a "social contract." The agreement was to officially recognize an unchecked, all-powerful king or assembly. (Of these two options, he made it clear that he preferred monarchy.) The fear of certain punishment by this "sovereign" would repress wrongdoing. As long as the people submitted to such a supreme power, Hobbes didn't even mind if it was the result of military conquest (what he called "commonwealth by acquisition"). In this sense, the "contract" as a voluntary agreement was only a metaphor; what Hobbes really meant was a tacit consent to the rule of the sovereign, revealed by an evident pattern of cooperation with it.

For Hobbes, "justice" must mean whatever the king or the reigning assembly says it means. Otherwise, the pursuit of justice might itself produce conflict. Since people sometimes contended sharply over religion, the government must establish a single official religion in the nation. With all power concentrated in this way, people would settle into a peaceable pursuit of conveniences, trade, the arts, or other personal concerns.

ARISTOCRATIC TRADITIONALISM

However, the rule of one person could also be arbitrary, impulsive, lawless, and self-interested, often referred to as "tyranny." Under these conditions, kingship could ultimately prove to be quite disorderly, and invite overthrow and further disorder. In the outlook of **aristocratic traditionalism**, the pursuit of order had to allow the expansion of political leadership to a group of wise leaders who could check each other's passions. But for the aristocratic traditionalists, this required an idealistic political psychology of elite leadership, which in turn pointed to the need for the elite to receive moral education to justice.

Justice is a broad value category with various particular forms, but they all seem to have in common the notion of somehow assuring fair rewards and penalties for people's actions. The ancient Chinese thinker Confucius and the classical Greek philosophers Plato and Aristotle thought of justice as a positive personal quality that led to fair treatment of people. In this approach, justice is viewed not in terms of rules, rights, or governmental structures, but rather as a personal virtue that society should try to nurture, especially among advantaged leaders.

These thinkers wrote in a largely pre-commercial era (up through the late Middle Ages), in which agriculture was the dominant feature of the economy. They were sympathetic to **aristocracy**, which they defined as public-spirited rule by the few best citizens, aimed at the common good. They tended to view the landowning nobility as having the most potential for supplying virtuous leaders to achieve order and justice in government. According to this view, the landowners had a long-term stake in the community, and they possessed the necessary resources to educate their children to pursue the common good, and to engage in public service for its own sake rather than for personal gain.

As we shall see below, the aristocratic traditionalists opposed direct ("participatory") democracy. But they also opposed **oligarchy**, defined as self-interested rule by a propertied and wealth-oriented elite. In their recommendations for cooperation in the state, the Western thinkers in this group preferred that the people elect a virtuous leadership, rather than having it imposed on them.

Confucius (551–479 BCE)

The first renowned aristocratic traditionalist was the Chinese philosopher Confucius. He wrote to persuade the contentious feudal warlords of his day to adopt a path to social order and harmony. According to Confucius, the source of order was an elite of virtuous leaders who possessed wisdom and benevolence. A successful Confucian leadership did not operate primarily by applying rules. Instead, the leaders' compassion and concern for accurate understanding should set the tone for orderly behavior by others.

The leaders would pay careful attention to the *li*, or "rites" (sometimes called "rituals"). The goal was, first, to set examples of virtuous behavior, including respect for one's elders and loyalty to the group and the community. The *li* were to be followed with an appreciation for their underlying purpose of social cooperation and harmony. Second, in judging disputes a leader must be wise and must accurately target the facts of the situation. Confucius's doctrine of "rectification of names" referred to the accurate application of terms to reality, as opposed to today's "spinning" of a story to fit someone's own interests. In this view, Confucius made a powerful point that remains relevant today: distortion or misrepresentation of the facts contributes to extreme contention and can make cooperation nearly impossible.

Confucianism was important in East Asia right up to the early twentieth century. In political practice, it developed into rule by an elite group that included Confucian scholars alongside regional and local rulers governing between the emperor and the people. In real-world practice, however, Confucianism could not guarantee that these rulers would follow Confucian teachings and avoid distorting the facts and pursuing only their self-interests. And, leaving little room for individualism, Confucianism did not acknowledge that the people themselves might want to affect their government. To deal with these difficulties, next we will consider ancient Greek forms of aristocratic traditionalism.

Plato (427–347 BCE)

The fifth and fourth centuries BCE was an era in Greece in which most people lacked education. The most common contenders for political control were "the many"—the middle- and lower-class majority—and "the few"—the wealthy property holders. Politically, the former tended to support direct democracy, participatory rule by the citizens in the fashion of Athens in its mid-fifth-century "golden age." The well-off tended to advocate oligarchy, the self-interested rule by the propertied few. The aristocratic traditionalists in ancient Greece opposed both models and sought ways to replace the political contention between them with more cooperation in politics.

In the view of the Classical Greek philosopher Plato, direct democracy led to the self-interested, impulsive, and unthinking rule by the poor. (This group might include farmers, laborers, artisans, or traders in the towns). He considered them uneducated and vulnerable to manipulation by demagogues, clever orators who distort reality and manipulate their audiences to gain power. Alongside the democratic poor and the oligarchic rich, Plato also considered another not-so-desirable contending group: people with spirited, military inclinations. Plato sought a resolution of the contentions among these groups by means of leadership by a morally educated elite.

Plato's most well-known work was a long dialogue, *the Republic*, which was presented as an exploration of the meaning of justice. It had three main features: a scheme of education, the presentation of an imaginary three-class state, and a political psychology. His program for education ranged from children's literature presenting gods and eminent people as good and steady role models, to higher education stressing mathematics and clear reasoning about enduring concepts, and ultimately the goal of seeing "the good" in things. In Plato's view, properly educated people could make decisions about the common good by way of rational and cooperative discussion, rather than by factional contention.

The second major aspect of Plato's *Republic* was the imaginary city that it laid out. This city was divided into three social classes, with each class remaining separate and specializing solely in its own activities. The governing class would be the philosophic and virtuous rulers. They would exercise control over a spirited and courageous warrior class that was denied property in the later chapters of the *Republic*. These "auxiliaries" were most concerned about status and honor, and were always ready to deal vigorously with anything the rulers might consider to be really bad. These top two classes, in turn, would control the third and largest portion of the citizens, the "desiring" class. The latter would engage in farming or trades, possess property, and focus on their practical arts and making money. People would be assigned to their respective classes at the end of the early phase of the education, based on the results of prior testing of their ability, character, and dedication to the city.

Strikingly, however, *the Republic* described this three-class state as imaginary and impossible. Accompanying it in the dialogue was an analogous three-part picture of the individual mind or soul. In this political psychology, Plato favored having the rational part of one's mind guide and limit the soul's spirited part. Spirited inclinations included anger and indignation, concern for status and honor, and at best courage (defined as vigorous defense of the rational part's views of what is terrible). In turn, rational thought and spirited opinion would limit one's moneymaking impulses and activities. The *Republic's* final definition of justice was having each of the three parts of the soul stick to its proper role in this hierarchy of subordination and not meddle in the other parts' roles.

At times in the *Republic*, Plato seemed to be thinking of the three-class state not as a recommendation for cities at all, but rather as an elaborate metaphor symbolizing the individual mind, with its three parts and their virtues: wisdom in the rational part, courage in the spirited part, and moderation and justice spread throughout. Will the real Platonic justice please stand up—the three-part state or the ideal three-part soul? Sometimes political philosophy leaves us with questions as well as answers.

Plato's practical recommendations for real-world states seem to be found in two other dialogues, the *Laws* and *the Statesman*. In the *Laws*, inequality would be limited (partly by equal land ownership among the households), and virtuous government officials would be elected. In the *Statesman*, Plato saw a natural contention in assemblies between those who were primarily peace loving and those who were primarily spirited and warlike. Both types of people had to be mingled in government institutions to balance each other. And when necessary, they would hopefully listen to leading individuals for whom, within their own souls, both sides were subordinate to the reasoning part.

Overall for Plato, good governance in the real world should be based on law, the consent of the governed, and the pursuit of the common good by elected officials. But for aristocratic traditionalism's perspective on the whole range of real-world governments, we must turn to Aristotle, Plato's most well-known student.

Aristotle (384–322 BCE)

Much more than Plato, Aristotle ventured into comparative analysis of real-world regimes. He compared forms of government not only in their institutional variations but also in their socioeconomic settings. And he reasoned empirically about causal factors and consequences related to governmental change. In these ways, Aristotle resembled a modern political scientist. But he also reasoned about the good state and made recommendations which, in his view, could help real-world communities pursue the common good.

Like Plato, Aristotle sought a lawful society, the election of virtuous public officials, and the rule of rationality over the passions. But in his view the common good included more than a good and just way of life. It also had to include values that matter to less-than-ideal people: freedom and wealth—the values, respectively, of the democrats and the oligarchs. Aristotle's practical recommendations combined elements of the rule of the many with features of rule by the few, in what he called "mixed government."

On behalf of the many, Aristotle made an argument that profoundly affected later political thought. He suggested that the mass of the citizens could usefully contribute their diverse perspectives and capacities of judgment to politics. But in what political role? Especially if most voters were moderate "middle-class" property owners—folks who Aristotle considered most likely to be impartial and law abiding—the citizenry as a whole would be qualified to elect their government officials and judge them at the end of their term of office.[1]

However, as to making laws and other important political decisions, for Aristotle the elected officials should govern. This was partly a bow to wealth, because normally in his era only well-off people had the leisure time and the economic security to engage in full-time public service without being tempted to steal from the public coffers. As the citizens voted, though, Aristotle wanted them to favor candidates who were qualified by moral wisdom and justice—not just by their property—to direct policymaking.

Thus Plato and Aristotle contributed an idea that was to take hold later in Western political thought: having the citizens *elect* the government officials who made laws and other key decisions. However, Plato and Aristotle differed in important ways from today's view:

- As aristocratic traditionalist thinkers, they did not consider the elected leaders to be *representatives* of the voters. They conceived of government by elected officials as a form of rule by the few—whether it be aristocratic if the few were wise and just, or oligarchic if the few were rich and self-interested.

- They agreed that government must intervene in education and culture—at least for the young—to foster the healthy soul, patriotism, and support for traditional institutions and the prevailing religion. Neither Aristotle nor Plato defended individual rights or private freedom of thought and action. For the aristocratic traditionalists, the citizen should think of himself or herself first as part of the republic, and not make claims against it.

- They stressed moderation in property ownership. The two thinkers looked down on moneymaking as necessary but not deserving of much respect or attention in political philosophy.

Edmund Burke (1729–1797)

In the late Middle Ages, the growth of commerce in Europe and Asia began to rival the importance of agriculture, and the idea of an elite education grounded in moral justice began to fade. The most influential European redrawing of aristocratic traditionalism to fit these new times, while retaining the idea of electing the aristocratic elite, emerged in the work of a late eighteenth-century British thinker and statesman Edmund Burke. He wrote in a time when modern commerce had given rise to extensive inequality. For him, selfish and ill-conceived passions could be contained only if they remained under the sway of traditional values and institutions, such as the church, the nobility, and the monarchy. In Burke's view, old institutions and laws surely contained wisdom if they had lasted so long, and people should view projects for change with skepticism. Burke valued liberty, but he viewed it in terms of the ancient customs surrounding the traditional rights of Englishmen, rather than rational, general rules about freedom.

Regarding property ownership, Burke abandoned the ancient Greek emphasis on moderation. He wrote in an era of rising commercial power, heightened inequality, and, especially in France, widespread public resentment over that inequality. Frightened by the French Revolution (which removed the nobility from its position of economic and political power), Burke believed that owners of substantial property should be heavily represented in government. Only they were strong enough to defend property against the threat of ambitious leaders and their envious followers.

In line with Plato's and Aristotle's recommendations for the real world, though, Burke accepted elections as the way to choose lawmakers. But he stressed that elected officials should not try to represent the policy preferences of the voters in their district. Rather, members of parliament should use their independent judgment about the common good of the whole nation, and be judged by the voters at the end of their term. Overall, he advised that decision making be left to the discretion of a "natural aristocracy" of leaders of wisdom and virtue, supported by experience and property. Burke did not oppose all change, but he would only accept very limited changes that built on traditional institutions.

In sympathy with Burke, today's aristocratic traditionalists tend to be skeptical of adopting new laws to solve problems. Instead, they prefer the judgments of wise leaders who apply traditional values and established approaches to new circumstances (see "The Philosophical Connection" on Michael Oakeshott in chapter 6), relying on custom wherever possible.

However, does the aristocratic traditionalist conception of the common good really include the good of everyone? Aristocratic traditionalism never abandoned the idea that the interests of some may have to be sacrificed for the sake of the supreme good—the good and just life of the elite—to pursue the public interest. To see an approach that more consciously addressed the good of everyone, we turn to our next strand in political thought.

HUMANITARIAN LAW

Although the **humanitarian law** current also focused on government for the common good, its definition of the good differed from that of aristocratic traditionalism. Rather than focusing on the virtue of a leadership class, the humanitarian law current stressed benefiting the whole citizenry through law,[2] and providing in some way for citizen consent to laws. To make this work, the humanitarian law thinkers also had to undertake a political psychology, this time involving the whole citizenry and not just the elite. To tame group contention, the humanitarian law thinkers asked three questions: (1) how can the natural social feelings of citizens be enlisted to support the entire community, (2) how can government be channeled by law to benefit all, and (3) how might citizen consent to laws be allowed?

Natural Law

By the end of the Roman Republic in the first century BCE, the humanitarian law approach was emerging. It first appeared among the Roman Stoic philosophers, who in turn influenced Marcus Tullius Cicero (143–106 BCE), a Roman statesman and philosopher. Cicero saw government as based on the Stoics' idea of **natural law**. Natural law was a body of principles of conduct that the Stoics had observed to be common to the practices of harmonious and flourishing societies (e.g., "no harming"). Such principles seemed to be the embodiment of reason, to such an extent that they had to have been given by God. For Cicero, natural law was also an expression of humans' inherent love of others and concern for the community's well-being.

These social inclinations could discourage offensive behavior and help reconcile otherwise contending groups such as the top statesmen, the nobility, and the common people. The aristocratic Senate, largely representing the landowning nobility, would contribute its wisdom in framing laws that treat the citizens equally and encourage virtue. (Outside politics, the nobles should treat peasants generously, stimulating peasant gratitude.) The people's representatives, the tribunes, had their veto power to defend the common people's concern for liberty. And benevolent personal leadership, whether in the form of a father-figure king or public-spirited "consuls" (the two major executive chiefs in the Roman

Republic), would oversee the application of the law and set a positive example. Everyone will gratefully honor the virtuous statesmen.

Thomas Aquinas (1225–1274), the leading Catholic theologian of the late Middle Ages, integrated many of these themes into Christian thought. As we saw in chapter 3 ("The Philosophical Connection"), Aquinas followed Cicero in arguing that government should be based on natural law principles, which embodied reason and concern for the common good.

To be sure, government could get help from Christian "divine law," in two ways. First, such Ten Commandments rules as the prohibition of murder, theft, and "bearing false witness" (from the Hebrew bible) could bolster the application of natural law in the laws of the state. Second, the Christian New Testament maxims such as "love they neighbor," while too perfectionist to be enforced by the state on individuals, should serve as ethical ideals to be pursued as a matter of conscience, with expectation of reward in the afterlife. Subsequent Catholicism urged both governments and individuals to care for the poor.

For Aquinas, the duty of government stemmed from a basic fact: while ordinary people could recognize the general principles of natural law, they often had trouble applying them to specific situations. People need "human law" made by governments to supply particular rules for applying natural law to diverse circumstances and nations. Part of the challenge was that these rules may have occasional exceptions, and might need improvement over time. Following Cicero, Aquinas concluded that wise statesmen were needed to rise to this challenge by specifying and applying the rules of human law. As to the structure of government, Aquinas followed Cicero in favoring a mixed government with a monarch and "law sanctioned by lords and commons." If the people were not corrupt, they could elect some officials. Aquinas's ideas became the foundation of subsequent Catholic thought regarding government.

However, did these mixed institutions give sufficient influence to the citizenry as a whole? A "no" answer was given by a later contributor to the humanitarian law current, Jean-Jacques Rousseau, who also had a major impact on subsequent thought.

Jean-Jacques Rousseau (1712–1778)

Writing in the third quarter of the eighteenth century, Rousseau was among those who saw government as based on a social contract, people coming together to cooperate in achieving their ends. But in his approach to the sort of government that should be formed, he continued the humanitarian law approach, moving it in a more democratic direction. Rousseau also placed humanitarian inclinations and law at the center of his strategy for the best state. But he dropped the previous reliance on the concept of natural law; for Rousseau, laws were the positive creations of well-established governments. His contribution to the humanitarian law current had two major components: (1) his idea of the "state of nature" outside society and government, and its disappearance, and (2) his picture of good government.

If law is not natural, the idea of the "natural" must refocus on human motivation. In lieu of Cicero's general "love of mankind," Rousseau found in human nature a natural concern for others in need, which he called "natural pity." His *Discourse on the Origins of Inequality* (1755) began with an imaginary portrait of an original state of humankind, coming before the development of reason, society, agriculture, commerce, and government. Rather than Hobbes's conflictual and violent picture of society outside government, life for Rousseau's "natural man" was free, innocent, and peaceful. Individuals roamed independently, pursuing only their natural needs. Whenever their own self-preservation was not at stake, they felt natural pity toward others in need.

In the last half of the *Discourse on Inequality*, Rousseau indicated what would happen if society were to develop *without* good government. Humankind's venture into society would produce a long list of social ills, including commercial interdependence, inequality, obsession with status, social opinion, and wealth, and loss of authenticity and self-reliance. Ultimately the outcome would be outright oppression. In this pessimistic scenario, natural pity would be drowned by vain and unhappy self-interest.

To avoid these negative possibilities, societies need law and good government. Laws should be few and simple, and in part aimed at reining in the selfish struggle for individual reputation, wealth, and power. Rousseau's ideal society was small and mainly agricultural. Government would restrain inequality through taxes on luxuries, protect the poor by making farmland or work available, encourage the independent farmers, and provide a public education and an artistic culture that emphasized simple morality and patriotism. The laws would reinstate the natural human capacity for compassion by focusing it socially toward one's fellow citizens. Ideally, for Rousseau, poverty would be prevented and the weak would be protected from injustice.

Rousseau favored popular election of government officials, whom he wanted to be wise and morally upright. But he did not accept the idea of having the officials make laws on their own. For him, the people themselves must make the final decision. However, no bill could come before the people for a vote unless it was first proposed by the elected officials.

Due to Rousseau's requirement of popular approval for bills to become law, he focused a lot on the citizens' attitudes as lawmakers. When the citizens decided on a proposal by their elected officials, Rousseau wanted them to consider the common good rather than their interests as members of contending social or economic groups. Each citizen should consciously rise above his or her surrounding social and economic relationships, to think and vote independently, as if (s)he were "John Q. Public." The citizen would thus express what Rousseau called the "general will." In his view of lawmaking, only such an attitude could bring cooperation among contending groups.

This conceptual and ethical exertion by the citizens was not easy. Despite Rousseau's high regard for individual freedom, he argued that getting the citizens to focus on their common interest required that leaders steer education and culture toward concern with the community. Again, this approach seems to be related to his requirement that all citizens vote directly on laws.

Subsequent Humanitarian Law Thought

If one departs from Rousseau by accepting the idea of lawmaking by elected officials, as Cicero and Aquinas had done, the average citizen does not need to be guided toward generality of viewpoint and the common interest. Subsequent humanitarian law thinkers turned away from the tactic of having leaders steer culture toward close identification with the republic and the common interest. Instead, these thinkers embraced individual freedom of thought, expression, and association.

In the late eighteenth and early nineteenth centuries, the German thinkers Immanuel Kant (1724–1804; see "The Philosophical Connection" in chapter 17) and Georg Friedrich Hegel (1770–1831; see "The Philosophical Connection" in chapter 16) also saw law as the recipe for reconciling and harmonizing the contending forces in society. In the twentieth century, numerous countries' governments used laws and programs to reconcile socioeconomic tensions, and protected the weaker members of the community (see "Country Cases" at the end of this chapter) with such measures as universal health insurance, old age pensions, and public education. The human rights approach added a strong emphasis on freedoms of individual expression, association, religion, and the press, as well as humanitarian concern with well-being challenges such as hunger, ill health, and unemployment.

POWER CHECKING

Our next current of philosophical thinking about politics is primarily focused on limiting government power. The **power-checking** thinkers did not rely on humanitarian virtue or compassion to direct politics, and did not undertake an idealistic political psychology. Like Thomas Hobbes (see above), they assumed that humans are basically self-interested. But for that very reason, unlike Hobbes they did not trust any governing group with unlimited power. For the power checkers, arrangements must channel self-interest to protect people from overly concentrated power.

Social Class Checking through Institutions: Machiavelli and Montesquieu

In the last period of the Roman republic, the Greek historian Polybius (200–118 BCE) suggested that the king, nobility, and common people each needed a veto power to check each other's ambitions. Much later during the Renaissance, the Italian Niccoló Machiavelli (1469–1527) focused especially on checking the wealthy nobles and their natural tendency (in his view) to oppress the people and foster disorder. He wanted strong leaders to enforce the rule of law against the nobles and protect the people. But he also favored an independent assembly in which the people's representatives could check the nobility directly, so that the king could mostly retire to more benign activities. Thus Machiavelli preferred that monarchies evolve into mixed republics similar to the ancient Roman one prior to the Caesars. The people's representatives (e.g., the tribunes at Rome or the English House of Commons), those of the nobles (the Roman Senate, or later, the British House of Lords), and the executive branch chiefs (the king and his or her advisors) would each have a role in checking each other. The state would thus remain free and prosperous. For Machiavelli, only occasionally would the executive have to move harshly against a few lawbreakers to set an example (see "The Philosophical Connection," chapter 13), thus revitalizing respect for the laws.

In the early to mid-eighteenth century, Frenchman Baron de Montesquieu (1689–1755) praised Britain's use of multiple institutions to protect liberty. The House of Lords represented the nobility, the House of Commons represented the people, and the king represented the executive. Each had a veto to check the others.

John Locke (1632–1704)

With the Englishman John Locke, power-checking thought turned away from contending social classes in favor of institutional checks on governmental power, independent of their links to social classes. Like Hobbes before him and Rousseau after, Locke saw government as founded on a social contract rather than divine right. And as Rousseau would later do, Locke presented a more peaceful "state of nature" outside government than Hobbes had. But Locke's state of nature was not just imaginary, as would be the case with Rousseau's. Instead, Locke looked back historically to earlier, simpler social and economic conditions. In Locke's state of nature, humans were rational, lived in society, and sought to observe a minimal version of the old "law of nature": respect the life, liberty, and property of others. In the state of nature, individuals were free to enforce that law on their own, by punishing offenders to deter future wrongdoing and by making the guilty compensate victims.

Why leave the state of nature to join in a social contract? In the state of nature, in Locke's view, spontaneous informal enforcement of natural law was not sufficiently consistent and effective to protect life, liberty, and property. So communities set up government as an independent judge and enforcer to more efficiently apply the law of nature. Once people in an area had joined in a social contract, by majority vote they set up a specific form of government.

For Locke, in the earliest, simplest times, government, too, could be simple, perhaps in the hands of a monarch as war leader. The right to property extended only to as much land and crops as a family could use without allowing them to spoil. Few disputes existed because properties were small, and thus little law enforcement was needed. Plenty of unused land was available for the needy, and there was little contention for scarce resources. Change came, however, with the invention of money. A means of exchange like gold and silver never spoiled, and could be accumulated boundlessly. People could then farm far more land than they needed for their own consumption because they could trade the surplus grain for money before it spoiled. Farming became more productive. But as properties grew, unused land became scarce and contention increased.

Now government could no longer be simple. A monarch might also be gripped by selfish ambition, and for Locke a check was needed on government's ability to tax. Since government existed to protect both property and liberty, it should impose taxes only with the free consent of the taxpayers. If the citizens could elect representatives in an independent legislative assembly, those representatives could convey the people's consent to taxes.

Behind an independent legislative branch was one more potential check on government, in Locke's view. Like everyone else, the king and the legislature were under the laws. But what if either the king or the legislature (or both) ignored the law of nature and began oppressing people? This scenario would recreate a state of nature between the government and the victims, and the latter could resist if the law provided no recourse. But Locke observed that in practice, people would run the risks of rebellion only if the government had revealed a clear design against the lives, liberties, and properties *of the majority*. In this case, the people might legitimately rise up and replace or restructure the government, again by majority decision.

This approach worked if the problem was a bad king who needed to be checked by a popular majority. But what if the majority itself was inclined to tyrannize a minority? This question gave rise to the next stage in power-checking thought, which focused on checking a majority faction.

Checking Majority Faction: James Madison (1751–1836)

In the late eighteenth century, Madison was the leading architect of the American constitution. In the new nation, the voting property holders were no longer identifiable with an elite of wealth, as in England at the time. Rather, they were the average farmers of a more genuinely representative democracy. Accordingly, for Madison the perceived threat from government that needed checking was not a king or a nobility, but instead a majority ruling to the detriment of a minority. Madison's attention thus shifted to the contending groups in society, and how a majority faction might arise. He thus employed the majority preference model as an empirical one, an undesirable pattern to be avoided. But the bulk of the contending groups he saw were not the social classes of the earlier power checkers. For Madison, they were more like today's "interest groups" (see chapter 9), from bankers and debtors to farmers and merchants.

To counter the danger of majority tyranny, Madison's main argument centered on the need for nations to be large and for their government to be internally divided into separate units. If the country were large, interest groups would be too numerous for any one of them to claim a majority in legislative assemblies. (In contrast, a small political community like ancient Athens had fewer factions, increasing the risk that one of them would gain majority control.) In addition, to a large territory, nations needed separate governmental units to be able to check each other. The legislative branch could be comprised of two assemblies, which could "check and balance" each other, and the separate executive branch (see chapter 8, "The Philosophical Connection").

Checking Majority Opinion: Alexis de Tocqueville (1805–1859) and the Pluralists

In the early nineteenth century, Frenchman Tocqueville visited the United States and wrote about its politics. Like Madison, he saw a role for the majority preference model as an undesirable empirical scenario, but he saw the majority threat in terms different from those of Madison. He noted that the real political action in the United States was at the regional or state level (where the political community was smaller, increasing the threat of majority tyranny). Even with institutional separation of powers, Tocqueville saw a remaining risk of tyranny by majority opinion, which might pervade and dominate multiple institutions at once. How so?

In an era of equality without a highly educated landed aristocracy, Tocqueville argued, most citizens had nowhere to turn to but their own judgment, in which they had little confidence. He suggested that in this situation people tend to be unduly swayed by reports about the views of the huge "majority." In practice, majority opinion could intimidate and silence thoughtful minority views.

For Tocqueville, America's answer to the dangers of majority opinion under democracy lay in *local* democratic participation. Where citizens participate in the politics of their towns and districts, they know and are interested in particular local concerns. Going into the details of policy issues enables people to see through the overly simple general ideas brought forth by majority opinion (see "The Philosophical Connection" in chapter 2). Tocqueville also related to Madison's focus on interest groups as contenders in democratic politics, but in a different way. In America, he saw numerous associations—moral and intellectual as well as economic—fruitfully taking over the independent government-checking role that the landed nobility played in the old European monarchies.

To be sure, the idea that interest groups influence government and check power really came into its own only in the mid-twentieth century, with the establishment of modern political science by the pluralists (see chapter 3). Recall from chapter 2 that according to the pluralist model of the distribution of influence in democratic societies, influence is dispersed among numerous interest groups. Political scientist Robert Dahl (1915–2014) suggested that it was interest group pluralism in elections, not institutional checks or natural rights doctrines, that exercised the main limit-setting influence over democratic government.[3]

However, might interest groups themselves become centers of power that need to be checked? Pluralists have argued that certain aspects of interest groups tend naturally to moderate their claims (see chapter 9).[4] However, others became troubled by tendencies toward inequality of influence among interest groups (including Dahl himself, later on[5]), especially the superior influence often wielded by groups that were advantaged economically. It is in markets that such inequality originates, and we now turn to free-market thought.

FREE MARKET

By the mid-eighteenth century, entrepreneurs in Europe were increasingly intent on breaking free of the many restrictions on trade that remained from the Middle Ages and the early modern period. The **free-market** current of thought, associated with the French phrase *laissez-faire* (literally "leave alone to do"), proposes letting people in the market economy do or make things as they see fit. The values pursued by free-market thought are commercial and financial freedom and well-being. Freedom here means autonomy in controlling one's own earnings, property, enterprises, and pursuit of wealth. Well-being is identified with overall prosperity in the market. The free-market current tends to be critical of government interventions in the economy, such as taxation, regulation, and government spending.

Adam Smith (1723–1790)

Adam Smith, writing in the eighteenth century, was the founder of free-market thought as we know it today. Smith interpreted the goal of well-being in terms of "the wealth of nations" (the title of his major work), the sum of the monetary value of the properties of individuals. His key contending groups were the government, with its traditional "mercantilist" policies of taxes on imports and commerce to build gold in the treasury, versus entrepreneurs and their companies.

For Smith, the best way to maximize the wealth of nations was for people and enterprises to be left entirely free to work, invest, trade, and compete with one another. He stressed that free competition encourages people to specialize in functions they do best and reap the rewards of their work. Because success will come to those who use the nation's resources most efficiently, the free-market naturally steers resources to their optimal uses. On this view, the result is the greatest possible wealth of nations and the best possible goods and services for consumers at the lowest possible prices.

Smith's views did not leave much for governments to do. He did want government to provide for the national defense, build schoolhouses, and support improvements such as roads and bridges needed for the economy—at least where market incentives were insufficient for private enterprise to build them on its own. Government also needed to operate an impartial system of law enforcement and justice, especially to protect property. For Smith, people do have a capacity for sympathy, but the most that sympathy can do—in the context of an "impartial spectator" viewpoint—is restrain outright wickedness.

Economic "Social Darwinism"

The extreme of free-market thought may be found in the theories of the economic Social Darwinists of the late nineteenth century. The Englishman Herbert Spencer (1820–1903) and the American William Graham Sumner (1840–1910) applied to economics the notion of competition for survival that was put forward by biologist Charles Darwin in explaining the biological evolution of species. Spencer and Sumner, observing the rise of industry in the last half of the nineteenth century, thought that unregulated economic competition would ultimately be good for society by favoring the economically strongest companies and individuals.

For Spencer,[6] economic conduct must be allowed to produce its natural consequences, without government interference. Harmful practices and bad products must be allowed to proceed and be resolved through market choice alone. Only according to this "law of conduct and consequence" could humanity learn what it needed for survival. No government regulations in the economy were permissible for Spencer, not even sanitation laws or building codes. Spencer suggested approvingly that increasingly people were interacting on the individualistic principles of free "contract," as opposed to the old rules dictated by social status or military threats. His vision of the future was an "industrial society" in which corporations would order social life without much need for government.

In a similar vein, the American professor William Graham Sumner[7] argued that privately owned **capital** (productive resources) is the source of all employment, advance of civilization, and even human survival. He conceded that possessing wealth brings special access to leisure, luxury, and health care that people without wealth cannot have. But in Sumner's view, those rewards for gaining capital were necessary to keep others working hard to obtain it.

Sumner saw a few key contending groups: (1) the successful capitalists who stuck to competing in the marketplace, (2) the "social doctors" and philanthropists trying to get government to tax and redistribute resources, (3) the lazy poor who were the intended beneficiaries of those redistributions, (4) the wealthy "plutocrats" who tried to influence government to send material gains their way, and (5) the hardworking but not especially successful "forgotten man." Opposing groups 2 through 4, Sumner rejected nearly all government taxing and spending. For him, such government action amounted to little more than:

- rewarding the lazy poor and encouraging an increase in their population,
- allowing the social doctors and philanthropists to tell other people what to do, and
- giving undeserved subsidies ("jobbery") to the plutocrats, while
- exploiting the hardworking and taxpaying entrepreneur and "forgotten man."

Sumner argued that entrepreneurs should get their wealth honestly in the private marketplace instead of from government contracts, subsidies, or trade protections like tariffs. Sumner's version of social Darwinism is perhaps closest to the ideas of the present-day Tea Party movement within the American Republican party.

In the mid-twentieth century, free-market thought saw a return to Smith's emphasis on the assumed efficiency of the market in allocating resources. Economic thinkers such as the Austrian Friedrich von Hayek (1899–1992; see "The Philosophical Connection" in chapter 10) and the American Milton Friedman (1912–2006) stressed the innovation and progress produced by those who succeed in economic competition. They also noted the difficulty in exerting rational control over markets. Free-market advocates continued to stress individual self-reliance, deplore dependency on government benefits, and generally oppose taxation, regulation, and spending by government.

Supporters of the humanitarian law approach responded that if markets are entirely left alone, they produce inefficiency, waste, and harm. The strong could devour the weak, and economic collapse and depression might result. Humanitarian law advocates suggested that the advantages of the market could coexist with government programs and regulations to protect the health, safety, and security of consumers and the stability of the economy. The debate persists to this day in numerous free-market societies. But the deepest challenge to the free-market economy came in the mid-nineteenth century, in the thought of Karl Marx.

MARXISM

As economies industrialized and grew in the last half of the nineteenth century, they went through cycles of boom and bust. What might be the worst outcome of such developments, who is harmed the most, and what is the solution? Another economics-oriented philosophy emerged in the work of a German, Karl Marx (1818–1883),[8] in the mid-nineteenth century. The direct and indirect impact of Marx's ideas on the twentieth century was heavy.

The perspective and concerns of Marx were very different from those of the free-market theorists. Marx called the new system **capitalism**: a market system dominated by privately owned productive property (capital). For Marx, the main contending groups under industrial capitalism were the "bourgeois" capitalists—the owners of productive property—and the propertyless "proletariat" of workers. Secondary roles were played by the state and culture (which generally supported the ruling class) and a few small groups left over from the old feudal system based on agriculture.

Marx focused on the values of material security and equality. Ultimately, he favored **socialism**—public or state ownership of the economy's productive property. Much of the political philosophy of the twentieth century was a response to Marx.

Hegel and Marx's Critique

At the beginning of Marx's career as an intellectual, he was a student of the German philosopher Georg Frederick Hegel (1770–1831). Hegel was among those "idealist" philosophers who believe that we see and understand the world only through the lenses of our concepts.[9] But Hegel took the additional step of introducing development and history into the world in a major way, especially in the social world. He saw historical development as the evolution of the collective human experience, which he referred to as the "world spirit."

Hegel thought that things develop and change (and hence our understanding of them develops and changes) in a process that he called "dialectic." For Hegel, that process has three main stages: (a) first an organic whole, of which we have a simple, unified experience and impression—the "thesis" stage, (b) which then develops opposing parts within it ("contradictions"), competing with one another—the "antithesis" stage, (c) followed by a concluding stage of reintegration into a new, more complex, but more harmonized whole—the "synthesis" stage.

As applied to the sociopolitical world, for example, the thesis stage seems to be epitomized by traditional tribal society or middle ages feudalism. Here, life is simple, immediate, and fairly harmonious, as clan members and peasants take on functional roles according to qualities ascribed to them by the elders of the family, clan, tribe, or local lord. The antithesis stage seems to come with the rise of commerce with its rivalry and contention among households (as unfolds, e.g., in the second half of Rousseau's "Discourse on the Origins of Inequality"; see above). At this stage, individuals pursue achievement for themselves, not just trying to fit into some role in the group.

Hegel's synthesis stage involved the destination of the historical development of the world spirit: freedom, achieved through reason embodied in universal law. The synthesis stage was achieved with the rise of the modern state, the epitome of reason and freedom. Hegel saw the modern state as the collective assertion of human freedom, in rationally ordering and harmonizing the commercial contention rather than being pushed around by it (paralleling Rousseau's "social contract" with its "general will").

Here is where Marx's objections began. First, he thought Hegel had paid insufficient attention to the material world and economic developments. For Marx, the antithesis stage was not just the advent of commercial contention and rivalry. In the nineteenth century, commercial capitalism was to develop into industrial capitalism, and bring the rise of class conflict between a propertyless working class and the property-owning "bourgeoisie." But most importantly, Marx did not see the rise of the modern state as a harmonizing synthesis; actual states, he thought, simply aided and abetted the dominance of the capitalists that characterized the second, antithesis stage. For Marx, real synthesis could be gained only with revolution and takeover of productive property by the proletariat. This last major development in history would reunite humans with the physical world around them, abolishing what Marx called "alienation."

Capitalism and Alienation

The early writings of Marx were most concerned with the condition of the industrial laborer, which he characterized as "alienation." This condition did not exist among peasants in the preindustrial feudal era. Despite the overall reign of the landed oligarchy under feudalism, for Marx the peasants did have a sense of being at home on their plot of land, cultivating it and directly consuming its product (at least the half of the crop that didn't go to the landowner as rent). But by the early 1840s in England, peasants were being driven off the land by the enclosure movement, which removed the peasants from the land so that the owners could run sheep to provide wool to the new textile industry. To survive, many peasants had to move to the city, to work in the dangerous Manchester textile factories, for example.

In Marx's view, this new factory environment was entirely the realm of **capital** (privately owned productive resources) and the capitalist (the owner). Thus to the worker, the factory was alien territory, and work was regimented by the capitalist's machine-centered system. None of the product belonged to the worker, notwithstanding the fact (as Marx saw it) that the value of products comes from the labor that goes into them. Thus, for Marx, factory workers were engaged in "alienating"—making alien, as in selling off—their most human creative activity, labor. The meager wages received by workers amounted to only a portion of the prices that products fetched in the marketplace. The remainder of the retail price of goods—the "surplus value"—went to the capitalist owner.

Marx thought that over time capitalism also robbed the workers of all traditional sources of social stability, such as family life, status, culture, and religion. His answer was socialism, which would reunite the worker with his or her physical surroundings, restore the value of the product collectively to the workers, and guarantee material security. But how would socialism come about?

The Socialist Revolution

In his later work, Marx turned to empirical thought about economics. In history, he saw mostly systems of production and power in which one class ruled over others. Under feudalism, nobles dominated the peasants and townspeople. Later, under capitalism, owners dominated workers. Economically, each era had its own system, which Marx called its "relations of production." These relations coordinated what he called "forces of production," such as social classes, tools, and resources. In Marx's view, however, these systems were not set in stone. Forces of production tended to grow and develop over time. During the late Middle Ages, commerce and its new forces became too big for the old feudal relations of production. When the strain became too great, the old relations of production were broken by revolutions such as those in England in 1689 (peacefully) and France in 1789 (violently). Marx believed that in a very different way, capitalism would undergo the same fate.

Marx's later work focused on what he considered to be happening under capitalism. Once the early capitalists were victorious over the old feudal nobility, they settled into their own relations of production. The capitalists controlled ideas and culture in their own interest, much as the nobility had done previously. In time, in Marx's view, industrial capitalism would spread throughout the earth, undoing all of the old statuses, institutions, and values. It would reduce social, political, and economic contention into that between just two categories, the bourgeoisie (the capitalists), and the proletariat (the workers).

However, for Marx this new era was not static. He characterized the economic career of capitalism as a series of boom-and-bust business cycles. Capitalism's basic tendency was to increase production. With each expansion, however, production capacity tended to exceed what the consumer market could absorb. When such a "crisis of overproduction" occurred, prices would plummet, boom would turn to bust, and many businesses would go bankrupt. As the downturn gained momentum, so many businesses would fail and so many workers would become unemployed that few people would be left with enough money to buy the products. As a result, recession would worsen into depression.

Each recession or depression, Marx argued, would further swell the ranks of the proletariat and reduce the numbers of surviving capitalists. And each bust would be bigger and worse than the preceding one, until only a handful of capitalists would remain. There would be so few people left with enough income to be consumers that the collapsed engine of capitalism could not start again. For their very survival, the workers would forcibly take over ownership of the factories and begin operating them for themselves.

Note that at this point, the workers' dire situation of ever-intensifying poverty contrasted sharply with the situation on the eve of the earlier overthrow of feudalism by the bourgeois revolution. In the run-up to that revolution, the town entrepreneurs had been growing in wealth and political strength. Regarding the socialist revolution, Marx's view seemed to be that at the end of capitalism's career, the shared desperation of the workers (now the great bulk of the world's population), and the international homogenization of their social conditions under capitalism, would serve to unite and activate the proletariat enough for them to be able to seize power by force in their particular nations.

According to Marx, right after this revolution, the working class would have to exercise a "dictatorship" over its enemies, an idea that he left largely unexplained but that no doubt involved violent suppression. There would be a transitional era of socialism, with payment to each according to his work. But over time material abundance would lead to an ultimate **utopia**—an ideal, perfect society—with goods free on the shelves "to each according to his needs." The state, which in the past had always played the role of agent of the ruling class, would dwindle because Communism would have ended social classes and their contention with each other.

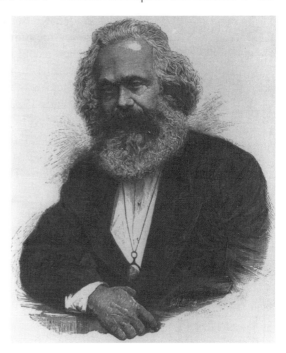

The German philosopher Karl Marx (1818–1883). His favored values were well-being and equality in their economic forms, and he favored socialism—collective social or governmental ownership of productive property—as the key means to pursue those values.

Subsequent Critiques of Marxism

Numerous free-market commentators doubted Marx's theories of economics and revolution, especially as governments learned to regulate and limit the swings in the business cycle. They argued that Marx misunderstood the modern economy and that socialism would not work. Power-checking thinkers worried that under socialism there would be nothing to check the threat of the concentration of power in the management of industry. And, indeed, at least some subsequent events confirmed their concerns.

Moreover, most socialists in Europe—even many who were sympathetic to Marx's economic analysis—argued against Marx's view that social change must proceed through violent revolution. They preferred to pursue socialism democratically, through peaceful parliamentary politics. Many people who stressed the humanitarian law approach argued that government programs and regulation could progressively address problems of poverty and economic instability, without the need for socialism.

Other supporters of socialism, such as Vladimir I. Lenin, the Bolshevik leader of the early 1920s, and Mao Zedong, the leader of China's Communist Party and government from 1949 to 1959 and from 1965 to 1971, had their own analyses. They approved Marx's critique of capitalism but were unwilling to wait for the full economic career of capitalism to unfold—and collapse—in their countries. As we shall see in chapter 6, they sought their own quicker roads to socialist revolution.

FREE SELF-DEVELOPMENT

Some thinkers have asked, if humans are endowed in principle with free choice, shouldn't the government pursue the full flourishing of individuality and individual capacity in society? **Free self-development** thought pursues freedom of thought, expression, culture, and contribution to society, alongside ready opportunity for the full development of one's distinctive capabilities. The free self-development thinkers saw pursuit of the latter goal through education, job training, job opportunity, and opportunity for growth in understanding and participation in social and political life. For the free self-development thinkers, realization of potential is a lifelong endeavor that enhances the individual's contribution to economic, social, and political life. Three key representatives of this strand of thought are John Stuart Mill, T. H. Green, and John Dewey.

John Stuart Mill (1806–1873)

We find the first broad initiative in free self-development thought in the work of a mid-nineteenth-century British thinker, John Stuart Mill. He was the son of James Mill, a prominent devotee of utilitarian philosophy. Utilitarianism had involved calculating any course of action's resulting balance of pleasure over pain, and adopting policies that produced what Jeremy Bentham, the founder of modern utilitarian thought, called "the greatest happiness of the greatest number." After a youth spent in studying the works of Bentham and his father, the mature son broke with classical utilitarianism by broadening the definition of utility. Mill wanted to include the free self-development of the individual, progressively over time. Certainly, society had a right to protect itself from harm, whether through law or (in less serious cases) social disapproval. But in the absence of harm to others, individuals should be able to develop freely. Society should not control adults "for their own good."

In his essay *On Liberty*, Mill considered freedom of expression and debate to be a key driver of human progress. For him, the main contending groups on any issue were the existing majority school of thought and the challenging minority view. Mill argued that only if a majority opinion is freely challenged, and the challenging view and its reasons are vigorously represented, can we:

- figure out which view is more right and useful,
- fully understand the meaning and justifications of the prevailing and challenging views, and

- sift out what is good and bad in both views, if "some of each" turns out to be the best answer.

Mill used the same argument to support liberty of pursuits and life plans, too. He defended "experiments in living," and protested "the despotism of custom." Exercises of individuality in thought, expression, lifestyle, and self-development had value both for the individual and for the improvement of society. In his essay *Utilitarianism*, Mill argued that cultivating one's higher mental faculties, especially out of concern about the world, brought deep and lasting satisfaction.

For Mill, human nature had both a selfish and a social side, with the latter bringing much satisfaction to life. In his *On Representative Government*, he praised what he called the "active" character: self-reliant, creative, and inclined to work to improve oneself and one's circumstances, but not inclined to look enviously on the attainments of others. Challenging the customs of his day, Mill and his wife wrote a major early feminist text, *The Subjection of Women*.[10] This was consistent with his view that protecting free self-development serves the deepest foundation of human utility, "the permanent interests of man as a progressive being."

Mill rejected authoritarian government. He did so in part because he thought it encouraged passivity among the people, and among politicians it prompted envious "place hunting" rather than purposeful public service. Representative democracy, however, invites the active character. It encourages people to protect their own interests and take on elevating roles in public activities. In representative assemblies, in Mill's view, every significant variety of opinion should be able to find its voice. He favored a form of proportional representation (see chapter 3) in which minority views would get representation in legislative assemblies in proportion to their voting support. Finally, Mill stressed education in an era in which few people were obtaining it. He wanted voters at least to be able to read and write, and he proposed giving extra votes to the better-educated.

Toward the end of his career, Mill became critical of capitalism and its social and economic inequality. He puzzled over how well it permitted the free self-development of all. But he also expressed fear regarding centralized socialism, as to whether it might give rise to a new despotism even under democratic control.

Thomas Hill Green (1836–1882)

The British thinker Thomas Hill Green extended free self-development thought into economic issues.[11] Like Mill, Green stressed free self-development and saw a social side of human nature as well as a self-interested side. Green respected Mill's concern for **negative freedom,** the protection of individual thought and action from inappropriate barriers presented by society or government.

However, Green also thought that certain conditions in industrial society inappropriately limited free action and self-development. These included abject poverty, unhealthy conditions in housing or the workplace, child labor, overly long work hours, and lack of education. Green saw such conditions as reducing the contributions that their sufferers could make to society.

For Green, democratic government should foster **positive freedom** by taking action to remedy such problems. Government should provide positive benefits such as minimal health care, public education, workday limits, and laws against child labor and unhealthy work conditions. With these supports, people

Child labor, then and now: (left) boys unloading new tomato cans from freight cars in 1908 in a cannery in Indianapolis Indiana, USA; (right) an eleven-year-old operating machinery recently in a mosquito net factory in Tamil Nadu in southern India.

would be better able to provide goods and services in the economy and care for their families and others around them. By providing such programs to make people freer to contribute to society, people would be exercising their freedom together to expand the scope of individual freedom.

Green supported private property as a useful social creation that enhanced individual development for contribution to society. But where property operated contrary to this purpose, Green favored its regulation.

John Dewey (1859–1952)

The American John Dewey, writing mainly in the 1920s and 1930s, argued that purely private control of economic and cultural resources runs contrary to the free self-development of the individual. For Dewey, the prevailing industrial market economy left the poor regimented and without access to resources needed for cultural self-development. These resources ranged widely, from art, science, and the use of scientific reasoning to understand and solve problems, to literature, theater, social life, and knowledge of society.

Dewey was discouraged that democratic public discussion in his day seemed to be dominated by self-serving and manipulative rhetoric. This often covered up private interests at work behind the scenes. He thought democratic politics needed not only more honesty, but also a greater role for science and its methods of thinking. He advocated organized experimentation in addressing public policy problems to discover which answers work for broad interests rather than narrow ones.

One possible direction for that experimentation had to do with distribution in the economy. Dewey suggested not only that the poor are directly regimented by the industrial order, but also that they are pressured by economic insecurity into an all-consuming materialism. For Dewey, material gain ought to be not an end, but rather the means to cultural self-development. As a prerequisite for cultural self-development, society overall needed to alleviate economic insecurity.

With regard to daily life, Dewey argued that the prevailing top-down style of decision making in economic, religious, and other organizations taught ordinary people that their views and aspirations did not matter. He thought that this pattern undermined individuals' self-concepts, training them *not* to consider their own wants and needs. For Dewey, a key job of democracy is to consider the values, needs, and aspirations of ordinary citizens in making public decisions. On a micro level, he argued that managers should consult their subordinates about workplace needs. At times, Dewey seemed sympathetic to socialism, but he stopped short of recommending it. In general, he advocated greater democratic control over finance and policy rather than government ownership of the economy.

The theme of cultural freedom is at work in many of today's concerns, often expressed in social movements for protection of the civil rights of minorities, gay rights, minority cultures, political participation, environmental protection, and women's rights. Some observers classify these new issues as rising to rival—or even supersede—the older post–World War II economic issues of wages, job security, and entrepreneurial freedom (see chapter 8). As we just saw, Dewey thought that economic security was a prerequisite for successful expansion of cultural horizons.

Criticism of free self-development philosophy came especially from three of the other currents we have examined. Aristocratic traditionalists doubted its rationalistic projects for human improvement and feared the effects of such individualism on time-honored values, customs, and arrangements. Free-market advocates feared the costs of having government regulate the private market, levy taxes, and spend money for individual self-development or any other purpose. They also questioned how well recipients would use the benefits that they received. Marxists did not think that workers could achieve self-development while still under the economic and cultural reign of capitalism. Such strategies, in their view, would only serve to support capitalism.

COOPERATION AMONG THE CONTENDING CURRENTS

In this chapter, we have viewed the six strands of thought as contending with each other. But can some of them work together? In the real world, different currents of thought may influence each other, sometimes resulting in a product of cooperation that differs from any of the contributing currents. For example, an individual can basically favor a free-market approach but make room for humanitarian law in environmental regulation for clean air, or in emergency humanitarian relief. Or someone with a free-market approach may view the power-checking current as the best way to limit government economic intervention.

Liberal democracy itself may be seen as a combination of some of these strands of thought. Liberal democracy brings together a number of aspects:

- features of free-market thought,
- a moderate emphasis on law and popular consent from humanitarian law,
- civil liberties from the "negative" part of free self-development thought, and
- an emphasis on the autonomy of groups and their associations found in power-checking thought.

Liberal democracy favors commercial prosperity and its market freedom to some degree, but it also defends the rule of law, individual freedoms, and popular representation.

Another example of cooperation among different currents of thought exists in the development of human rights thought. Today's human rights thinking has no single philosophical founder. It has emerged instead from developing social

THE HUMAN RIGHTS CONNECTION | Contributions of History and Practice

In the humanitarian law current—in the natural law thinking of Cicero, the later Roman Stoics, and to some extent Thomas Aquinas—we find a strong emphasis on human duty: to avoid harm, to exercise benevolence toward others where possible, and to use government and law to protect people from harm. A limited expression of these themes appeared much later in the power-checking thought of John Locke. As we saw earlier in this chapter, Locke viewed natural law as an obligation to refrain from injuring others' life, liberty, and property. He argued that the social contract set up the state to apply natural law, using its authority and law enforcement powers to provide those protections more efficiently, as long as the state itself does not violate natural law in the process.

From these beginnings, social consensus and political practice took over in the early development of human rights. In 1776, the Americans took a step beyond Locke in their Declaration of Independence. They turned from a human obligation to protect key values such as life, liberty, and property, to rights that are "inalienable," to "life, liberty, and the pursuit of happiness." The French, on the eve of their revolution, went further along these lines to make a more detailed list of the "rights of man."

Human rights reached the world stage in the World War II era and afterward. In 1941, the American president Franklin Roosevelt argued for protecting, among humanity generally, "four freedoms"—freedom of expression, freedom of religion, freedom from want, and freedom from fear. In reaction to the horrors of the Holocaust and the war, as we saw in chapter 3, the United Nations approved the Universal Declaration of Human Rights (1948). Later, by 1966, the U.N. had articulated the more detailed Covenants of civil-political and economic-social rights, which went into effect in 1976 upon approval by the required proportion of national governments. In seeking the historical origins of today's human rights, then, we are dealing first with the historical experiences of the Americans and the French, and much later with the developing international consensus around United Nations-related efforts. But we may still note elements of earlier strands in political philosophy that contributed to the human rights outlook.

consensus and political practice (see "The Human Rights Connection"). Nonetheless, we can identify contributions to the human rights outlook from three of the currents: humanitarian law, power checking, and free self-development.

Alternatively, the free-market approach may cooperate with a degree of aristocratic traditionalism, as it does in much of conservative ideology today (see chapter 6). A government may privilege a dominant religion without interfering much in the market economy. Or, in the name of traditional values, a government may actively suppress ideologies that object strenuously to the free-market economy (e.g., socialistic ones), as did mid-century Spain under the rule of Francisco Franco, and many of the authoritarian developing nations between the 1960s and the 1980s.

Some combinations are unlikely. For example, historically the aristocratic traditionalist current has been unwelcoming to the emphasis on rights that tends to accompany the free self-development current, especially in its human rights form.

SUMMARY: CONTENTION AND COOPERATION IN NORMATIVE POLITICAL THEORY

Past political philosophies and theories may be grouped into currents of practical thought about the best approach for political society to take in dealing with problems and pursuing values. The aristocratic thinkers emphasized cooperation within an elite engaged in pursuing justice and wisdom and preserving traditional values. For Plato, Aristotle, and Burke, the election of the moral elite fosters cooperation between the elite and the mass. The humanitarian law thinkers viewed law as reconciling and harmonizing otherwise contending segments of society, with the understanding of law led in part by elected officials. The power-checking thinkers stressed either the contention among social classes and the state administration (Polybius, Machiavelli, Montesquieu) or contention among interest groups (Madison, Tocqueville, and the later pluralists). Cooperation would ultimately result from bargaining and compromise.

Free-market thought argued for defusing contention in politics by barring the government from intervening in the economy. Marx saw the market as fostering class contention, with cooperation occurring only by the exertion of power by a dominant class; ultimately, for him the socialist revolution would eliminate classes and hence contention. Free self-development thought accepted a degree of cultural and political contention and debate as fruitful for individual self-development. But overall cooperation could be fostered by focusing policy on realizing the potential of all individuals. For the most prevalent attempts to interweave elements of these currents in today's politics, we will next explore the main ideologies and their favored policies.

COUNTRY CASE STUDIES

The cases of the United States and Sweden provide a sharp contrast that underlies much of economic policy contention today. Between 1875 and 1932, the United States leaned heavily toward the free-market model, but after 1932 it accepted some elements of the humanitarian law and self-development currents amid sharp political contention. Today, the free-market current is making a prominent and contentious comeback, as America's conservative party seeks to overturn the main thrust of policies that the United States has followed since the 1930s. Since 1932, Sweden has represented the humanitarian law current with elements of free self-development and, recently, some free-market modifications.

The United States: Free Market and Power Checking, then Humanitarian Law, and Back to Free Market and Power Checking

Before the 1930s, domestic American political economy basically followed the free-market current of political thought. As industrialization proceeded, there was very little government intervention in the economy. Large industrial enterprises exemplified the fundamental principle of division and specialization of labor, with many different functions working in harmony under the same roof.

The only government regulation involved occasional protection of competition against monopoly power and its abuses. Taxes were low and government spending was directed to the sort of economy-serving improvements (roads, bridges, canals, ports) that Adam Smith approved of. Welfare concerns were a matter of local benevolence, not the business of national government. The only major departure from Smith's general approach concerned international trade, in which tariff protections—which Smith disapproved of—often continued against imported goods.

Several circumstances encouraged laissez-faire practices, in addition to the strong role for power checking that was built into the American constitution. For example, the post–Civil War Fourteenth Amendment to the Constitution guaranteed the liberty and citizenship of the freed slaves. In subsequent decades, however, the American Supreme Court expanded on the view that corporations legally were also "persons." Thus, they should enjoy the same protections of their freedom of action. This basic idea contributed to the Court's striking down, as unconstitutional, a range of attempts to regulate corporations. In addition, the legal principle of limited liability for corporations discouraged attempts to get the courts to impose significant financial penalties to punish economic wrongdoing.

In addition, the United States has a federal system, and before the 1930s the Supreme Court considered many key policy areas to come only under state jurisdiction. Competing to attract business and investment, the states sharply limited taxes, regulation, and government spending for fear of losing business and investment to more lenient states. Only if a regulation was applied nationally could this competitive pressure against government intervention recede. But that was just what the Supreme Court ruled out by keeping most policy areas within the states' jurisdiction.

In key areas of the new industrial economy such as banking, steel, oil, and railroads, huge corporations arose. A corporation might become a monopoly and impose high prices through financial manipulation, buyouts of competitors, or threats against them. Regulatory efforts like the Interstate Commerce Act in 1887 and the Sherman Antitrust Act in 1890 were only applied selectively to the worst monopoly abusers. The Supreme Court limited such laws' impact on corporations, but before 1914 did allow the use of the antitrust legislation to break up labor unions and farmers' cooperatives. When a central bank was created in 1913 to help avoid financial panics like the ones in 1873, 1893, and 1907, it was owned and controlled by the banks.

As noted above, the Court interpreted the fifth amendment's guarantee of personal liberty—that "no person" can be "deprived" of his or her "liberty" by the national government without "due process of law"—to apply to corporations, too (as "legal persons"), further curbing the national government's chances of regulating corporations. In 1905 came the Supreme Court's Lochner decision, striking down a New York state law limiting bakers' working hours (to 10) and the work week (to 60 hours). In Lochner, the Court used the fourteenth amendment's guarantee of liberty— again, meant when adopted in 1868 to protect African Americans from re-enslavement by state law— to, in effect, ban regulation of corporations by state law, too. (The court also portrayed workday limitations as government "redistribution," which it prohibited as a reason for regulation.) In 1918, the Supreme Court struck down the first national child labor regulation, claiming that it interfered with the powers of the states. When the Great Depression arrived in 1929, President Hoover approved national government money for work on roads, river/harbor improvements, and public buildings, but he refused to approve any direct aid to the many citizens in need.

With the Great Depression of the 1930s, however, humanitarian law sentiment grew as large numbers of people needed help and protection. In the middle of the decade, the attitude of the Supreme Court's majority shifted (with one justice changing sides, producing 5–4 decisions in the opposite policy direction). It began to accept new government regulation in a wide variety of areas: banking, the stock market, home and farm mortgages, wages and hours (temporarily), union rights and labor relations, old age pensions (what Americans call "social security"), and even tax increases for higher incomes. The unemployed were offered jobs in public works such as rural water and electrification projects as well as building roads, schools, hospitals, and parks. The economy improved through the mid-1930s.

However, events in 1937 revealed that the free-market current was still very much alive. Apparently under pressure by people alarmed by the government deficits, the Roosevelt administration cut back heavily on government spending and raised some taxes. Consequently, the economy lurched back into depression. Despite the partial reversal of these cutbacks in 1938, it took World War II and its heavy spending to bring full employment and an end to the depression. After the war, the GI Bill enabled large numbers of returning veterans to get a college education. In the 1960s, the government made available food aid and medical care for the very poor and medical insurance for the elderly.

To be sure, late in the twentieth century, the free-market strand made a comeback. Government aid retreated, limiting help and restricting eligibility for it. Budget cutbacks in the enforcement of regulations also weakened the humanitarian law element and strengthened the free-market model. In the new century, however, the 2008 financial crisis brought humanitarian law inclinations back to center stage. Democratic president Barack Obama adopted programs to create and preserve jobs, regulate the excesses in the financial sector that had played a role in the crisis, and extend health insurance to the uninsured. But the congressional elections of 2010 put the free-market-oriented Republican Party in control of one of the two legislative houses, enabling them to block any further efforts in those directions. The later 2014 elections brought the Republicans control of the second house, the Senate. Power checking in support of the free-market current had returned in force.

In the political and sociocultural realms, however, the liberal democratic model has mostly prevailed. Opportunity for open political debate existed through the twentieth century, coming under strain only during the "red scare" of the early 1920s and the 1950s' McCarthy period (that of the persecutions of alleged Communists and those accused of associating with them). From the "counterculture" era of the late 1960s on, tolerance of different styles of behavior and dress has increased, in many ways culminating in the acceptance by the majority (and by the Supreme Court) of gay rights by 2015. Representative government persisted throughout, with a strong role for power checking in the style of Locke and the pluralists.

Sweden: Humanitarian Law, then Modified by Free Market

Sweden has exemplified mainly the humanitarian law outlook, but with a role for the free self-development approach as well. Up through most of the twentieth century, Sweden was rather homogeneous ethnically. (Immigrant minorities such as Vietnamese have recently become more significant.) Its early religious heritage is Lutheran, which encourages a sense of community responsibility. Sweden did not take the road of governmental ownership of economic assets, though its strong safety net programs and taxation to support them mean that the government steers a large piece of the country's income stream. Moreover, in line with humanitarian law thought, Sweden's political culture emphasizes law. Swedes tend to be respectful of laws, rules, and procedures. They have many social protections from harm and—unlike Americans—do not sue each other very often. In institutions and economic enterprises, leaders and managers must often consult with followers and subordinates in making decisions, and group consensus is highly valued. Thus, there is a tendency toward cooperation and compromise, if possible, before contention gets intense. In Swedish politics, the consequence tends to be a pattern of civility, cooperation, compromise, and consensus.

Sweden's first ventures into social welfare were humanitarian. In 1913, a national pension system was created for retired people, and in 1918 the state required all communities to take care of their homeless people. But, as in most countries, it was the Great Depression of the 1930s that provided the impetus for the establishment of a comprehensive welfare system. The government set up a system of substantial senior citizen insurance in 1937, along with direct aid to needy families, jobs programs, and the beginnings of unemployment insurance. In addition, in 1938 the government began sponsoring direct national wage negotiations between business and labor.

The decade after World War II saw a new wave of humanitarian government intervention. Retirement benefits and comprehensive health coverage increased. A Law on Social Help (1956) brought together a wide range of other benefits, and more were added in the 1970s. Job-related benefits included disability insurance and substantial unemployment compensation. Personal benefits included support to single parents and families with children, free maternity care, rent subsidies, subsidies for day care and nursery school, handicapped and survivor benefits, and housing subsidies for the needy. Higher education in Sweden is free.

Poverty was largely eliminated, and slums are nowhere to be seen. Environmental regulation can be heavy, given the strong Swedish concern to preserve the natural environment.

In the economy, both labor unions and employers play a strong role. For most of the twentieth century, centralized national negotiations involving unions, employers, and the government worked out national wage settlements and labor regulation, without government legislation. In recent decades, individual industries have handled such negotiations for their sectors. But the government has remained heavily involved in an active labor market policy, as it retrains workers in declining economic areas for employment in rising ones. In the distribution of income and wealth, Swedes traditionally opposed unlimited inequality. Most have supported a high level of governmental redistribution in the economy, even reducing gaps somewhat within industries and enterprises (called "solidaristic" wage policy). Meanwhile, Sweden had one of the most prosperous economies in the world, with unemployment consistently at 2 percent or lower and poverty hard to find.

All of these benefits, however, came at a high cost in taxes on individuals and businesses. With economic growth slowing in the 1980s, the free-market strand of thought began to have an impact on Swedish policy. One noticeable area was in financial deregulation; rules on bank lending were loosened. This contributed, by the end of the decade, to a financial "bubble"—a huge inflation in the price of some asset due to investors putting borrowed money into it in hopes of profiting from the rising price upon subsequent sale. The Swedish bubble was in real estate (as in the United States in the mid to late 2000s). All bubbles eventually burst, which happened in 1991–1992 in Sweden. Investors all tried to sell property at once, prices plummeted, and many loans could not be repaid (called a loan "default"). With bankruptcies and loan defaults ballooning in 1992, and people beginning to withdraw their deposits from banks, the financial health of some banks became questionable. Meanwhile, a worldwide economic slowdown was occurring, negatively impacting Swedish exports.

As the economy spiraled downward and unemployment shot up, government welfare spending necessarily shot up, and with it the budget deficit and the national debt. International traders began selling the kroner (the nation's currency), putting downward pressure on its value. By late 1992, interest rates were skyrocketing

and banks were beginning to fail. The general financial and economic crisis that resulted from all this shook Sweden to the bone.

How would the Swedish government respond to this crisis? The first emergency responses starting in 1992 were in line with the humanitarian law strand discussed above. The left-of-center Social Democrats cooperated with the ruling conservative Moderate Party (and other center-right parties) in backing decisive government interventions to protect the population from catastrophe. The government announced that it would guarantee all bank deposits and loans, and took over two large failing banks to stabilize them. Regarding the other banks at risk of failure, the government offered easy bailout loans as long as they opened their books to government inspectors. This was so that an independent government unit could see which assets were solid and which not, and take over the bad loans so that the remaining good assets (and the banks holding them) could stand. And strikingly, the government reversed course on Sweden's currency, devaluing it by 30 percent. This brought down the prices of the nation's exports to help exporters in international trade.

These moves, along with other social welfare measures to alleviate the crisis, caused the budget deficit to balloon to 15 percent of GDP. By 1994, the conservative Moderate-led government began to heavily reflect the free-market strand of politico-economic thought. (At times, the subsequent Social Democrat-led government cooperated with this striking shift.) The tax level of the top bracket has been reduced, unemployment benefits are now confined to about a year (accompanied by vigorous job training and job seeking incentives), pensions were cut back and eligibility rules for them tightened. Eventually pensions were privatized (with workers required to pay into them in the style of the American "401k"). "Temporary" hiring outside the standard labor market regulations—giving business greater flexibility in hiring and laying off—was extended to two years. These austerity measures provoked much resistance from the public, and unemployment rates came down only slowly through the 1990s (from 8 percent to 5 percent, still high by Swedish historical standards). However, with the help of a surge in Swedish exports (especially high-tech computer-related products) in middle and later years of the decade—related to the devaluation and the recovery of European demand—the Swedish economy gradually emerged from its slump.

The overall result is a blend of humanitarian law and free-market themes. Sweden still spends heavily to provide the public with a variety of services, employing a large portion of the working population, and the Swedish safety net remains substantial. Government spending continues to make up over 50 percent of the nation's gross domestic product, and taxes can still amount to more than 50 percent of incomes. Fast forwarding to recent years, Sweden was able to weather the 2008 crisis with continued growth, strong government finances, and little social and economic stress.

Woven into the Swedish approach is the free self-development theme, both economically and socioculturally. The government subsidizes culture and the arts and invests heavily in education. The above-described national emphasis on jobs and job training is directed to the economic side of self-development involving regulation of business as well as government spending.

Sweden's political system uses proportional representation, roughly similar to what Mill advocated. It allows a number of political parties and views to find expression in parliament. This means that forming and maintaining a parliamentary majority requires cooperation between two or more parties in a majority coalition. When no majority coalition of parties can be found that agrees on policies to deal with the issues of the day, a majority agrees to allow a "minority government" (see chapter 12): a single party or small coalition staffs the cabinet, without assured majority support for its bills in parliament. However, even minority governments are sometimes able to muster majority support for their bills to address pressing problems. This cooperative outcome follows from support by a parliamentary party outside the cabinet, either on a regular basis in one or more policy areas, or ad hoc, bill by bill.

◁ **PRACTICE AND REVIEW ONLINE**

CRITICAL THINKING QUESTIONS

1. Is it possible for government officials to share personal qualities in a way that eliminates intergroup contention, as the aristocratic traditionalists maintain?

2. Is it possible for a whole society to cooperate in supporting everyone in it, as the humanitarian law current seems to advocate? If so, how? If not, why not?

3. Do power-checking approaches automatically support the free-market? Might free-market supporters mobilize the cooperation of an overpowering majority that needs checking? If so, how?

4. Are there any similarities between the political frameworks advocated by the humanitarian law thinkers and the power checkers? If so, how do the different public values favored by the two currents explain the difference between their approaches?

5. Are there any similarities between the free-market and Marxist views regarding who the main contending groups are under capitalism, and which has the most influence?

KEY TERMS

strand (current), 109
anarchy, 110
monarchy, 110
power concentration, 110
aristocratic traditionalism, 111
aristocracy, 112
oligarchy, 112
humanitarian law, 116
natural law, 116
power checking, 119
free-market, 122
capital, 123
Marxism, 124
capitalism, 124
socialism, 124
utopia, 127
free self-development, 128
negative freedom, 129
positive freedom, 129
Liberal democracy, 131

FURTHER READING

Curtis, Michael, ed. *The Great Political Theories*, vols 1 and 2. New York: Avon, 1981.

Ebenstein, William, and Alan O. Ebenstein, eds. *Great Political Thinkers: Plato to the Present*. Fort Worth, TX: Holt, Rinehart and Winston, 1991.

Garner, Richard T., and Andrew G. Oldenquist, eds. *Society and the Individual: Readings in Political and Social Philosophy*. Belmont, CA: Wadsworth, 1990.

Losco, Joseph, and Leonard Williams, eds. *Political Theory: Classical and Contemporary Readings*, vols 1 and 2. Los Angeles, CA: Roxbury, 2003.

McDonald, Lee Cameron. *Western Political Theory*, parts 1–3. New York: Harcourt Brace Jovanovich, 1968.

Sabine, George. *History of Political Theory*. Hinsdale, IL: Dryden Press, 1973.

Sibley, Mulford Q. *Political Ideas and Ideologies: A History of Political Thought*. New York: Harper & Row, 1970.

NOTES

1 See "The Philosophical Connection," ch. 8.

2 My usage here should not be confused with the phrase as it is used in international law today, to refer to rules governing aid to refugees.

3 See Dahl's *Preface to Democratic Theory* (Chicago: University of Chicago Press, 1956).

4 Twentieth-century pluralists have suggested that two factors tend to exert moderating effects: (a) limitations on their internal unity due to cross-cutting divisions over issues (see chapter 4), and (b) the possibility of gaining more benefits from rational compromise than from all-out contention to win on all points.

5 See Dahl's *Dilemmas of Pluralist Democracy: Autonomy vs. Control* (New Haven: Yale University Press, 1982) and *Preface to Economic Democracy* (Berkeley, CA: University of California Press, 1985).

6 See *Social Statics*, abridged and rev., including "the Man versus the State" (New York: D. Appleton, 1899).

7 See *What Social Classes Owe to Each Other* (Caldwell, ID: Caxton Printers, 1961).

8 *The Marx-Engels Reader*, ed. Robert C. Tucker (New York : Norton, 1978).

9 Late eighteenth-century German philosopher Immanuel Kant argued that people cannot know "the thing in itself"; we only perceive things as they are processed through conceptual categories such as being and nonbeing, large and small, etc.

10 John Stuart Mill (with Harriet Taylor Mill), *The Subjection of Women* (London: Longmans, Green, Reader, and Dyer, 1869).

11 See *Lectures on the Principles of Political Obligation* (London: Longmans, 1966).

Contemporary Ideologies

FOCUS QUESTIONS

- **WHAT** is an ideology? What is the difference between "left of center" and "right of center"?

- **HOW** is moderate left-of-center thought different from democratic socialism? What do they contend over?

- **WHERE** in their prescriptions can classical liberals and conservatives cooperate? Where do they diverge?

- **WHICH** ideologies oppose democratic political frameworks? Why?

- **WHAT** are the main differences between conservatism and Fascism/ethnic ultranationalism?

IMAGINE THAT YOU ARE A YOUNG STUDENT, and that you've never considered yourself "political." One day, your friend sends you a news story, and instead of tuning it out you read that global warming threatens to cause widespread drought in your country in the future. Concerned, you go with your friend to a meeting about climate change, and hear that there is disagreement about how fast the earth is warming, why, and what should be done about it. You realize that there is more to a political issue than the facts and what may seem like obvious solutions.

You also learn that most of the ideas for addressing global warming involve government intervention in the economy, either by regulation, taxation, or government spending. And government economic intervention itself, in the abstract, proves to be a matter of contention between political parties. The contention between supporters and opponents of economic intervention seems to affect how some people view global warming and whether they believe the government can or should address it. You have encountered ideology, and an example of its impact.

MEANINGS OF IDEOLOGY

Ideology is one of the most important forces in politics, especially in relation to today's political parties and the policy directions that they pursue.

It is inconceivable to try to introduce politics without a systematic look at ideology and ideologies. They have had a wide range of impacts on world events. Consider the following:

- In the 1930s, governmental responses to the Great Depression established a new relationship between the state and society in many nations, with governments actively intervening in the economy to address pressing problems.

- Between 1939 and 1941, Germany attacked its neighbors in Europe, beginning World War II and the Nazis' attempt to eradicate Jews there.

- In 1958–1959, the Chinese government tried to decentralize industry and turn agriculture into a collective activity; the result was large-scale economic disruption, deprivation, and even famine in some areas (see Country Case Studies below). By 1960, the Chinese government was actively reversing these policies.

- In the 1980s and 1990s, numerous governments across the globe introduced policies that resulted in reducing the government's role in economies.

- In the 2000s in many areas of the developing world, the pendulum swung back in the opposite direction, as governments expanded their roles, especially in addressing poverty.

- In 2014, a militant Islamist group called the Islamic State swept from Syria into Iraq, creating a large area spanning portions of both countries, where it imposed its puritanical form of Islam on the local populations.

What do all of these outcomes have in common? Ideology was a key contributing factor to each of them. Each development followed in part from contention between ideological viewpoints. And for good or ill, in each case the victorious ideological orientation played a role in subsequent cooperation around the new strategy.

An **ideology** is a prescriptive strategy for dealing with society and its problems, linked to particular values and empirical perspectives that support the strategy. The realm of politics and policy is complex, and people look for ways to bring order to their understanding of it. They may adopt a particular view of the world that relates to their values and goals. Ideologies vary greatly in the approaches they take, from moderate to extreme.

Political philosophy and theory—the subject of chapter 5—engages in open-ended exploration of values, society, human nature, history, politics, and policy. An ideology typically draws conclusions on such topics, often from some of the political philosophers you met in chapter 5, and melds them into a program of action. The result is a logical and practical pattern that can accommodate new issues or observations.

Many people who are active in politics find that their ideological orientation feeds their focus and passion. Clearly, then, ideology can play a role in political contention. Also, however, shared ideology can be a major support for political cooperation, especially in political parties (see chapter 10) and social movements. To understand politics, we need to be familiar with ideologies.

Ideology in Policy Classification

One common way to use ideological terms is to classify policy approaches on a "left-right" scale. But we need to be careful in using these words, to avoid confusion. The meanings of the words "left" and "right" have each varied in different historical periods, parts of the world, and political groups and parties. For example, the meanings of the word "conservative" and of the phrase "social democratic" have changed substantially over the last century. And usage can vary from one region of the world to another. The word "liberal" means one thing in the United States and Canada, but something quite different in the rest of the world (see "Concept in Context").

Another possible source of confusion is the old association of the word "left" with change and of "right" with preserving the status quo. This usage originated at the time of the French Revolution in 1789. When the new National Assembly met, those who wanted more rapid change in the socioeconomic arrangements of France sat on the left side of the hall. The more moderate leaders, who wanted a slower pace of change, sat on the right. But this usage causes the meaning of each word to vary sharply according to what the status quo is. Was it meaningful to say, in the 1980s in the Soviet Union, that someone who wanted to preserve traditional bureaucratic socialism was "on the right," while those who wanted to move toward a market economy were "on the left" because they wanted change? In political science regarding ideology, we need terms and meanings that refer to defined policy directions, applied consistently.

Another problem is the tendency of some people to use ideological words that imply value judgments. For example, to describe a person or policy as "leftist" or "rightist," or "left-wing" or "right-wing," implies an extreme. Use of such labels tends to carry a negative connotation. Words may also be used to cast a positive light. Today people on the right often say that they favor "reform," implying positively that they are fixing something that is broken. On the left, some people refer to themselves as "progressive," which suggests a forward march of improvement. Whether positive or negative, such words can become weapons in contending ideological rhetoric rather than useful labeling tools for understanding reality. For purposes of classifying policies, it is better to use neutral terms that suggest broad ideological *directions*, in which governments and their policies might go in addressing problems. And terminology should include preferences that are moderate as well as extreme.

This book will adopt a clear and consistent terminology to refer to policy approaches ideologically. Today, a key feature distinguishing one ideological direction from another is its support or opposition to government action in addressing various policy areas. Recall from chapter 1 that most policy issues can be broadly classified as (a) economic, in the sense of affecting the economy, (b) sociocultural, involving the scope of personal freedoms, or (c) defense/foreign policy.

In the broadly economic category of policymaking, we will call policies that generally favor government intervention (e.g., spending, regulation, or taxation) **left of center**, and those that generally oppose government activity **right of center** or "conservative." The reverse terminology applies to sociocultural issues. Conservatives tend to favor government intervention to bolster traditional values associated with religion, nationalism, and social order, for example, whereas left-of-center adherents generally oppose such intervention and stress personal freedoms. Those to the right of center also tend to favor a bigger defense establishment and exertion of power abroad in the "national interest" (more government intervention), whereas those to the left of center tend to support less military intervention and greater use of diplomacy (see Table 6.1).

TABLE 6.1	Ideological Orientations in Policy Sectors		
Ideological Direction	**Government intervention should primarily be**		
	Economic	**Sociocultural**	**Defense**
Left of center	Greater	Less	Less
Right of center	Less	Greater	Greater

These classifications, however, refer mainly to general directions that policy can take. They don't specify *how far* people want to go in the designated policy direction. Even people who favor nearly all of the general policy directions linked to their ideological self-classification do not necessarily want to go equally far in all policy areas. And it is possible to lean in one ideological direction in some policy areas but take a different approach to others.

For example, a conservative may favor a very strong military and generally oppose economic regulation. But in certain areas of regulation such as the environment, he or she may be willing to accept a role for government. Such a person's views may be affected by their understanding of the empirical facts, such as those regarding the effect of human-produced greenhouse gases on climate change. Or someone may hold right-of-center, free-market views economically but be mostly left of center socioculturally (see "classical liberalism" below). Moreover, some people decide on individual issues without much awareness of ideological leanings. In other words, these ideological directions concern how ideological terms are used to classify policies, not how all people actually think about policy.

Notably, however, there is another type of ideological terminology that involves more than a simple left-right spectrum to classify policy directions. In contrast to the policy-classification sense of ideology, this other way of talking about ideology evokes particular constellations of values, beliefs, and preferences regarding not only policy directions but also forms of government and perceptions of human nature. I call this second usage the "grand system" approach to ideology.

Ideology as "Grand System"

The word "ideology" can also suggest something well beyond classification of policies. Ideology can describe a "grand system," including preferences on a range of other matters such as the type of government and of government-society relationship, and related empirical views on human nature, society, and history. For example, conservatism today tends to include not only the above-noted policy directions, but also several other preferences. It implies (1) a preference for a predominantly privately owned economy based primarily on free-market principles, combined with (2) a concept of human nature as largely self-interested and thus in need of limitation by traditional institutions, customs, religion, and nationalism.

Which ideologies in this grand system sense are most significant today? Certain lines of ideological thought have been central to political parties and movements from the middle third of the twentieth century to the present. These include Marxism-Leninism, democratic socialism, moderate left-of-center ideology, green ideology, feminism, classical liberalism, conservatism, Fascism, ethnic ultranationalism, and militant Islamism. For each of these ideological families, tone and content may vary among countries, but a common ideological direction remains.

We will explore these ideologies starting with those that are commonly considered to be on the far left, and move through the center to the far right. Notably, however, not all aspects of an ideology need fall on the same side of today's left-right spectrum for policy classification. For example, the above-mentioned "classical liberalism" is right of center on economic issues and moderate left of center on sociocultural and defense issues. For each ideology, its preferred type of economy and related policies will be considered first, followed by the ideology's perspectives on politics, sociocultural and defense policy, and human nature.

MARXISM-LENINISM

Over most of the last half of the twentieth century, political parties with the name Communist ran the governments of Eastern Europe and much of Asia. They still control China, North Korea, Vietnam, Laos, and Cuba. The official ideology of Communist parties around the world during most of the twentieth century was **Marxism-Leninism**. It began with key Marxist ideas, borrowing especially from Marxian class conflict theory (see chapter 5). But Marxism-Leninism proceeded to heavily emphasize seizing state power and using it to control the economy and sociocultural life. In practice, this ideology was crafted by the Russian revolutionary Vladimir I. Lenin (1870–1924)[1] and his successor as Soviet leader, Joseph Stalin (1879–1953).

As we saw in chapter 5, Karl Marx assumed that after a long period of capitalism and industrialization, a socialist revolution could take place. Lenin, however, was not a patient man. He argued that developing areas could rebel and break out of the orbit of capitalism without the lengthy time frame. Lenin thought that a socialist revolution in Russia might disrupt capitalism worldwide and speed up the timing of global crisis and revolution. By 1917, World War I had already disrupted capitalism somewhat, and the 1917 Russian Revolution did break Russia off from Western capitalism. But it failed to spark revolution in Western and Central Europe. The new Russian government had to try to survive on its own without help from a dreamed-of socialist Europe.

Economic Centralization

After nearly a decade of mainly market coordination of the economy in the 1920s (with farming private), in 1930 Stalin reversed that policy, initiating full state ownership and centralized control of all aspects of the economy. The aim of this "command economy" was rapid industrialization, along with state-controlled "collective farms" in agriculture to cheaply feed that industrialization. To advance industrial development, heavy industry such as iron, steel, energy, and transportation received more resources than consumer industry. The state's "Five-Year

Vladimir I. Lenin (left) and Joseph Stalin (right) were the early architects of Marxism-Leninism.

Plan" set Russian wages, prices, and resource allocation overall. In the view of Marxism-Leninism, central government control embodied rationality and efficiency.

The main values pursued by Marxism-Leninism are economic security and equality. Full equality was the professed goal for the future. In the meantime, however, a long period of "building socialism" would involve some inequality. Party leaders, government bureaucrats, and managers would get better income and perks than ordinary workers and farmers.

Social, Political, and Military Intervention

Given its heavy state intervention in economic structure and policies, Marxism-Leninism is commonly placed on the extreme left of the ideological spectrum. But with regard to its political framework, sociocultural policy, and defense policy, this ideology was not at all left of center in today's sense. The early Soviet Union saw itself as surrounded by capitalist enemies, and Lenin and Stalin thought that a strong dose of internal unity was required. In Lenin's concept of human nature, "the masses" mainly wanted economic security and would obey an elite who would give it to them.

According to Lenin, control of the state could never be secured without a tightly organized, hierarchical, and disciplined revolutionary party. As early as 1902, he had stressed that party propaganda had to always follow a single party line. After the revolution in 1917, other parties were banned and open opponents were dealt with harshly. To be sure, from 1917 to 1921 and at times in the 1920s, debates and contending opinions were evident among the Bolsheviks themselves. But regarding the country at large, soon after the revolution Lenin was extolling "unity of will," "iron discipline" in the economy, and rough justice by the "armed workers" against would-be opponents. With the civil war over in 1921, Lenin's "party unity resolution" banned factions even within the Bolshevik party. The party's new executive chief, Joseph Stalin, began suppressing political contention within the party.

Especially after Lenin's death in 1924, Stalin used the ban on factions, and his control over positions and their incomes, to vanquish all potential contenders for power in his party. He imposed ideological control over the nation's education, media, and culture. In the "great purge" of the mid to late 1930s, Stalin's secret police arrested all of his former rivals in the Communist Party, their followers, and then many others. Victims were either executed (in the case of former top leaders) or sent off to the Siberian *gulag* of prison labor camps, usually to their deaths. In 1938–1939 alone, more than a million people lost their lives. Totalitarianism (see chapter 1) was now fully in place in the Soviet Union.

After Stalin's death in 1953, the threat of state terror receded. But still, only members of the Communist Party could fill government managerial positions. Only the Communist Party candidate was on the ballot for elections, and the party continued its control of culture, the media, and education. The party heavily supported nationalism and a massive military establishment. The regime justified its actions by citing continuing security threats from the capitalist nations of the West, especially the United States.

Marxist-Leninist ideology remained dominant in the Soviet Union and Eastern Europe until change began in the 1980s. With the fall of Communist governments in Russia and Eastern Europe in 1989–1991, most of their former members gave up Marxism-Leninism, accepted capitalism and democracy, and formed new parties toward the left end of today's conventional ideological spectrum. The remaining Communist Party-run governments, such as those in Vietnam, Cuba, and especially China, have increased the role of private markets in their economies to varying degrees and thus have departed from classic Marxism-Leninism.

DEMOCRATIC SOCIALISM

In the early twentieth century, most European socialists contended sharply against Lenin's views. In contrast to Marxism-Leninism's stress on violent revolution led by a small, tightly controlled party, **democratic socialism** favored peaceful change through the democratic process. Supporters organized open parties of workers and argued that as workers became the majority of voters, socialism would come about through the ballot box. By the late nineteenth century, many socialists were pointing out that key predictions by Marx had not held up.[2] And some favored socialism for only philosophical or ethical reasons, without relying on Marxist economic theory.[3]

Economic Orientation

In theory, socialism is defined as state ownership of the means of production. In practice, democratic socialists vary in their preferences for state ownership, from near total (apart from personal property) to only ownership of key industries such as in iron and steel, energy, auto manufacturing, transportation, insurance, and banking. Thus, some socialists favor the kind of "mixed economy" found in the Scandinavian countries in the early to mid-twentieth century, for example, in which small- and medium-sized businesses were privately owned.

Socialists usually prefer substantial coordination of most of the economy by government. This includes steering investment through a mostly state-owned banking system. However, the 1960s' example of Yugoslavia demonstrated "market socialism," with competition between publicly owned enterprises. (Elected workers' councils served as the boards of directors for enterprises, empowered to hire and fire management teams.) But whatever their methods of economic coordination, socialists aim to use resources rationally for the benefit of the whole society, and to avoid what they see as capitalism's waste, duplication, and corporate bureaucracy.

Regarding values, socialists pursue a robust minimum of economic well-being for all, reducing inequality. They believe that employment should be assured to all, and state-owned or heavily subsidized housing should be available to those in need. Government should provide education, transportation, and health care at little or no cost to the users. Democratic socialists suggest that since most people use only the services they need, socialism will not produce significant waste. They argue that the frequent use of free or low-cost services such as public transportation will enhance people's quality of life.

Society, Politics, and the Military

Democratic socialists favor a democratic political structure, and support freedom in the sociocultural policy category. In the early twentieth century, in Europe and the developing world they fought to win workers the vote, civil liberties, and the right to organize unions. As to defense spending, in peacetime, socialists tend to want to limit the armed forces to national self-defense. But in wartime (or on the eve of it), while some democratic socialists remained pacifist (especially regarding World War I), most displayed patriotic solidarity, supporting the troops and military expenditures.

Regarding human nature, democratic socialists believe that most people are naturally generous, feeling a sense of solidarity with the community. People will be willing to pay high taxes for the greater good if government is efficient in providing the benefits they want. Democratic socialists believe that people will find meaning in working at jobs in the public sector of the economy. In their view, reducing economic competition and inequality will improve morality generally. They tend to see possessive individualism as a reflection of the impact of advertising and capitalism's materialistic and competitive economic habits, not of human nature.

In the early twentieth century, democratic socialists made up the left wings of social democratic parties, but today they tend to form their own parties that they tend to call "socialist."

MODERATE LEFT-OF-CENTER IDEOLOGY

Today the ideological identity of the largest parties on the left side of the spectrum tends to be moderate left of center—for example, that of the Democratic

CONCEPT IN CONTEXT | The Evolution of "Social Democratic" and "Liberal" Ideology

By the early twentieth century in some European countries, social democratic parties had made gains that were not related to state ownership of the economy, such as limiting the work day, banning child labor, and raising wages. Especially during the Great Depression of the 1930s, these parties extended their concerns beyond labor to include government-provided pensions, public health insurance, and education. By mid-century, such parties had become selective as to where they favored state ownership in the economy, and were dropping socialism from their party programs.

In the United States, the Democratic Party had come to embrace the policies of President Franklin Roosevelt's "New Deal," including government old age pensions, jobs programs, and protection of union rights. But in the United States, the word "liberal" came to be attached to this approach, in sharp contrast to the way the rest of the world uses the word. Outside the United States and Canada, the word "liberal" indicates an ideology to be examined later in this chapter: "classical liberalism," with its support for the free market in economic issue areas (now "conservative" in the United States) alongside personal freedom in sociocultural policy areas. How did the unique North American use of the word "liberal" arise?

We can trace this usage to the evolution of the Liberal Party in Great Britain. Over most of the nineteenth century, the Liberal Party was a standard classical liberal one, supporting free markets and opposing government regulation, spending, and taxation. However, partly under the influence of the writings of the nineteenth-century political philosopher John Stuart Mill (see chapter 5), in the early twentieth century the party accepted some moderate left-of-center innovations in economic

policy. For example, in 1909 party leader David Lloyd George (1863–1945) proposed state help for the ill and handicapped. By the late 1920s, George was supporting the views of British economist John Maynard Keynes. Also a member of the Liberal Party, Keynes favored government spending and deficits when a country is threatened by an economic downturn, to maintain employment and avoid recession (see chapter 7). In sympathy with George and Keynes was the American philosopher and educational reformer John Dewey (1859–1952). Like Thomas Hill Green (see chapter 5), he viewed poverty as a constraint to freedom. Dewey called for a new meaning of liberalism to supplement civil liberties and free elections (see Chapter 5). He proposed that governments provide minimal economic security, partly to allow the poor to turn away from materialistic pressures and toward their own cultural self-development. Dewey referred to this approach as a new meaning of "liberalism."

Meanwhile, few Americans in the 1920s were socialists. Especially following the Russian Revolution of 1917 and the subsequent persecution of American leftists during the "red scare" of 1918–1920, left-of-center Americans did not want to identify as "social democratic." They followed Dewey's usage by calling themselves "liberal." The renewal of persecution of American leftists during the intensely anti-Communist McCarthy period of 1947–1957 reinforced this usage among moderately left-of-center people.

Again, by the 1950s, social democratic parties in Europe had generally abandoned socialism. Today, they share the same moderate left-of-center ideology with Americans in the Democratic Party. But the unique North American usage of the word "liberal" was firmly set in ordinary language there.

Party in the United States, the Labor Party in the United Kingdom, the Socialist Party in France, and the Social Democratic Party in Germany. From the 1930s on in Europe, members of "social democratic" parties were increasingly accepting capitalism, dropping socialism from their party objectives, and moving beyond their earlier labor focus to broader concerns. In the United States, the New Deal period of the 1930s and its many social programs exemplified this latter approach. What shall we call it? The American usage, "liberalism," is contrary to how the rest of the world uses the term (see "Concept in Context"). The phrase "social democratic" risks confusion, due to a possible association with early twentieth-century forms of democratic socialism. Thus, here we will use the phrase **moderate left-of-center** ("MLC") **ideology**.

Economic Pragmatism

Moderate left-of-center ideology adopts a pragmatic and selective approach to state ownership. On this view, the state should own no more of the economy than is necessary to provide essential public services that private enterprise cannot provide at an affordable cost. For example, if private ownership of essential economic functions such as electrical and water supply might lead to monopoly's abuses, moderate left-of-center ideology favors either state ownership of the sector (in independently operated enterprises called "public utilities") or strong regulation by the government.

Moderate left-of-center ideology is influenced by the humanitarian law current of philosophical thought (see chapter 5). As to values, MLCers worry less about reducing economic inequality than do socialists. Rather, they interpret public well-being mostly in two ways. For the middle class and lower strata, MLCers support solid infrastructure, government services, affordable health care, and environmental protection. And to address poverty and middle-class economic insecurity, MLCers support government action to support a minimal economic floor. For example, they may favor food aid and housing subsidies to people below a certain low-income level. MLCers may also support targeted aid for particular disadvantaged groups such as ethnic or racial minorities, unemployed people, poor farmers, the handicapped, and the elderly. Supporters deny that such aid encourages a habit of dependency among the beneficiaries. In their eyes,

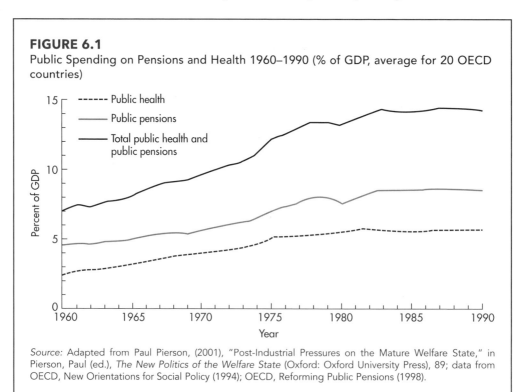

FIGURE 6.1

Public Spending on Pensions and Health 1960–1990 (% of GDP, average for 20 OECD countries)

Source: Adapted from Paul Pierson, (2001), "Post-Industrial Pressures on the Mature Welfare State," in Pierson, Paul (ed.), *The New Politics of the Welfare State* (Oxford: Oxford University Press), 89; data from OECD, New Orientations for Social Policy (1994); OECD, Reforming Public Pensions (1998).

unemployment compensation does not encourage idleness because the payments are minimal and those without jobs naturally prefer the dignity of employment.

In the 1960s and 1970s, moderate left-of-center parties in many established democracies significantly increased government spending on health and pensions (see Figure 6.1). Such spending leveled off in the 1980s and 1990s, when conservative parties were more commonly in power. Most of Europe still maintains fairly robust "safety net" protections. However, the ongoing financial crisis since 2008 has forced budget-cutting in southern Europe and Ireland that has significantly eroded the safety net there.

Moderate left-of-center ideology also favors a prosperous economy in which as many people as possible avoid the need for targeted aid. Its advocates may favor tariffs (taxes on imports) to combat what they see as unfair foreign trade practices that take domestic market share and cost domestic jobs. They may back subsidies (cheap loans or grants) to private enterprises for preserving jobs or expanding export potential. As we shall see in chapter 7, in an economic downturn or slump, moderate left-of-center supporters advocate (1) temporary deficit spending by the government to boost employment, and (2) low interest rates for business borrowing. Amid an economic slump MLCers tend to oppose major cuts in government spending ("austerity"; see chapter 7). And they support regulation of business to fight dangers such as fraud, excesses that pose risks to the financial system, and environmental harm. Drawing on the free self-development current (see chapter 5), moderate left-of-center ideology favors government spending on education, job training, and the arts.

Social, Political, and Military Policy

Politically, moderate left-of-center ideology encourages democratic practices, for example, by making it easier to vote. In sociocultural areas of policy, MLCers tend to support freedom of expression, reproductive choice, gay rights, and fair trial rights. As to defense policy, MLCers tend not to favor expanding military expenditures and commitments without an evident threat to the nation. However, they do support the use of troops where needed for peacekeeping or halting serious human rights abuses abroad, such as in Bosnia and Kosovo in the former Yugoslavia in the 1990s, and in the Darfur region of Sudan in Africa in the 2000s. Regarding active terrorists such as the militant Islamist group Islamic State in Syria, MLCers tend to back air power and are cautious when it comes to sending ground forces.

Those supporting moderate left-of-center ideology view people as gaining satisfaction and self-respect in their self-development. On the social side of self-development, they also consider humans to be open to generosity and community-mindedness in time of need. This includes aiding the least advantaged and responding to risks to key well-being values—for example, protecting a country from recession or environmental disaster.

Related Approaches

Some ideologies are in sympathy with MLC ideology, but have their own distinct concerns: left social democratic ideology, green ideology, and feminism. These ideologies are newer and less fully developed than the older ideological traditions that we explore in this chapter.

Left Social Democratic Ideology and Liberation Theology People who subscribe to MLC ideology range from those distinctly to the left to those near the center, or "center-left." Some people at the left end of the MLC category favor strong versions of MLC priorities and do not like the word "moderate." They tend to spearhead protest against wide gaps of inequality (e.g., in the American "occupy" movement of the early 2010s). Since no widely accepted label exists for this strongly left-leaning segment, here we will use a phrase adopted by some Europeans: "left social democrats." Today, left social democrats belong to such parties as Germany's Left Party, the American Green Party, Greece's Syriza, and Spain's Podemos. Left social democrats are especially critical of corporate power. Thus they may challenge certain MLC initiatives such as aiding a distressed banking sector or fostering new job opportunities in ways that erode traditional labor protections.

In mainly Catholic Latin America, religion has contributed to the left social democratic orientation in the form of "liberation theology." Citing Jesus of Nazareth's concern for the poor, liberation theology favors strong government action in pursuit of social justice, reduction of inequality, and minimal economic well-being, especially for peasants, indigenous hill peoples, and urban shantytown dwellers. Adherents to liberation theology urge the poor to become politically active. They favor social action such as building schools, health clinics, and small-scale credit-sharing cooperatives. At times, they have supported occupying unused agricultural land and dividing it among landless peasants.

Green (environmentalist) Ideology Green ideology seeks to rally people concerned about the environment. It is a fairly recent phenomenon, beginning in the 1960s.[4] In Europe, the Green orientation began developing as a party ideological identity in the 1970s. By the early 1980s, green parties had emerged in many of the nations of Western Europe, especially Germany and the Netherlands. The key value for the Greens is a form of well-being for the entire Earth: long-run physical health for all species of life.

Economically, Greens prefer state ownership only as necessary to curb environmental decline and preserve open space and nonrenewable resources. For example, Greens support public ownership of national and regional parks and forests to save wilderness from development. Some Greens also favor state ownership of key energy resources such as oil and gas. In economic policy, Greens advocate whatever degree of government intervention is required for environmental protection. Examples include aggressive regulation to reduce air and water pollution, ozone layer destruction, destruction or degradation of natural habitat, and greenhouse gas emissions. Greens tend to oppose nuclear power, at least until ways exist to safely dispose of nuclear waste and avoid earthquake risks.

Recently, Greens have been especially concerned about global warming and its consequences. Greens point not only to rising sea levels and turbulent weather, but also to water shortages due to droughts and to melting of mountain glaciers that feed the world's great rivers. Regarding climate change, Greens today face a difficulty concerning nuclear power. They traditionally oppose nuclear energy use because of the dangers of accidents and the unsolved problem of nuclear waste disposal. But nuclear energy is free of greenhouse gas production, and many energy analysts consider it to be a necessary component of any comprehensive strategy to reduce carbon dioxide emissions from burning fossil fuels.

Greens are not enthusiastic about conventional economic expansion. They see economic growth as often accelerating the general pressure on the environment and scarce natural resources. This orientation at times finds Greens in contention with some socialists and MLCers, who advocate industrial growth, jobs, and material gains. However, they believe that fundamental change in energy use will increase employment in new energy sectors such as solar, wind, and geothermal energy.

Green ideology puts less emphasis on sociocultural policies and the political system than do MLCers and socialists. But in practice Greens are strongly democratic and freedom oriented. They depend heavily on civil and political rights to broadcast their message, and on freedom-of-information rules to get access to closely held information about environmental effects. They are also notably to the left regarding defense. Generally critical of military expansion and war, Greens have been in the forefront of peace movements. They oppose the development of new weapons systems, especially nuclear ones that would devastate the planet if ever used.

As to human nature, Greens think that people appreciate the world of nature and have a psychological need for open space and wilderness. Greens see humans as potentially rational and farsighted, capable of making sacrifices to ward off future threats.

Like moderate left-of-center ideology, environmentalism has tremendous variation. Green parties often experience internal contention between their left and moderate wings. Especially in moderate green efforts, people who are otherwise democratic socialist, moderate left of center, classical liberal, or even conservative may cooperate with Green parties on particular issues.

Feminism Feminism supports women's self-development and gender equality. It seeks to raise women's self-esteem, mobilize women politically, help them realize their potential, and weaken inequalities and role differences between men and women.

In the nineteenth and early twentieth centuries, feminist thought focused on gaining the right to vote and rights to property and custody of children in divorce. In the mid-twentieth century, feminism moved on to combating women's subordination and the traditional family role of stay-at-home wife and mother. Feminism argues that economic dependency and cultural bias undermines women's efforts to work and succeed in the society outside the family. In these circumstances, women may feel a vague sense of emptiness and deprivation.[5] Feminists note the limited number of women in high positions in corporate boardrooms and government. They ask the government to provide women with equal opportunity to participate in the economy, culture, and politics.

Women marching on the U.S. Capitol in Washington, DC, in 1916 to gain the right to vote.

Some feminists stress cultural contention against the idea that males are natural leaders who should always be in control. Some have urged women to separate themselves from men to empower themselves. Others find in women special positive capacities for empathy, cooperation, relationship preservation, and mutual support, while men tend to overemphasize rationalism, rules, individualism, and competition.[6] However, many feminists do not see human nature as divided into these two camps. Instead, they blame the social, political, and legal environment for many of women's problems. For some feminists, fully equal treatment by gender will ultimately improve men's sense of dignity as well.

While a small portion of feminist intellectuals advocate socialism, feminism has no specific stance toward state ownership of the economy. In terms of economic policies, though, feminist priorities require MLC-style government intervention focused on the status of women. Examples include government support for education, maternity leave, childcare services, equal pay, protection from gender bias in hiring and promotion, and protection from sexual harassment in the workplace. Some feminists also support affirmative action to give a capable woman with fewer traditional credentials than male competitors a chance at getting a job. Many feminists also desire vigorous legal action to fight rape, prostitution, and the objectification of women by the media.

Pursuing these concerns politically requires democracy. In sociocultural policies, feminism favors individual freedom and self-development. To make progress, women must be free to assess their situation and to work with others for consciousness raising and political mobilization. While women's groups tend to be peace oriented and to favor a small military role, they are fully patriotic in wartime. Some favor the full integration of women into military roles, as is occurring even in some American units.

Thus the range of values that feminism emphasizes for women is wide: social justice, freedom, well-being in the form of enhanced economic security and dignity, and gender equality in the family and the economy. Humanitarian law and free self-development are the most important currents of political thought influencing feminism.

CLASSICAL LIBERALISM

As has already been noted, it is possible ideologically to be to the right of center regarding one policy sector while on the left of center on another. **Classical liberalism** focuses on individual freedom in both economic and sociocultural policy. It is on the right-of-center, free-market side of economic issues, but is moderately left of center and personal freedom oriented on sociocultural issues. Around the world today, many national party systems include a party with such an orientation.

Classical liberalism (CL) is one of the oldest ideologies. In the eighteenth and nineteenth centuries, classical liberals pursued freedom in all of its traditional forms. They led the fight for representative democracy and equal political opportunity. CLs opposed those eras' traditionalists among the landed nobility, the monarchy and its supporters, and the church. The traditionalists supported high taxes, trade restrictions to protect national wealth, special privileges for themselves, and sociocultural and political controls on society. In opposition to these policies, classical liberals fought for free markets in the economy as well as freedom of thought, expression, the press, and religion, and fair trial rights. Championing both property rights and civil-political freedoms, they played a role in the early development of civil-political human rights movements as well as democracy.

Today, such an orientation is referred to as "liberal" in most of the developed countries of world (with the exception of the United States and Canada; see "Concept in Context"), and "neoliberal" in the post-Communist and developing countries. To avoid confusion, here we will use the term classical liberal.

Free-Market Economics

Classical liberalism to some extent stems from the free-market outlook of Adam Smith, who favored *laissez-faire* economic policies (see chapter 5) and defined well-being in terms of the overall "wealth of nations." Classical liberals generally oppose state ownership of economic enterprises, as well as regulation, taxation, and redistribution. On matters relating to the economy, they reject almost everything favored by moderate left-of-center ideology.

In the CL view, the free market distributes resources most effectively. For CLs, government intervention diverts resources away from their natural channels in the private economy, where they are most efficiently utilized. As we shall see in chapter 7, they *oppose* (a) taxing the wealthy, viewing their savings as the key to investment and growth, (b) labor regulations that they see as impeding free hiring and firing of workers; and (c) government spending in excess of tax receipts ("deficit spending"), which they see as inherently encouraging inflation (excessive price increases).

CLs assume that economic actors behave rationally and price assets wisely; hence governments do not need to regulate finance and the economy. Some CLs do not believe that government intervention can effectively prevent recessions or even depressions, and view economic contractions (reductions in economic activity) as usefully eliminating inefficient uses of resources.

Moreover, for CLs government regulation and taxation run contrary to individual freedom, and should be minimized to protect property and support free entrepreneurship. These beliefs apply internationally as well as domestically. Classical liberals support free trade and globalization, and oppose nationalist government activities like tariffs (taxes on imports) and subsidies for exporting corporations.

Social, Political, and Military Orientation

In the sociocultural category of policy, classical liberalism joins MLC ideology in favoring civil liberties and personal freedom. CLs resist government attempts to bolster traditional values, and they oppose mixing religion with government. Classical liberals normally oppose aggressive military expansion. They regard war as mostly bad for business, and see heavy defense spending as siphoning off resources from their most efficient uses in the private economy.

In terms of human nature, classical liberalism emphasizes our inclinations toward individual freedom in all of its aspects: economic, artistic, cultural, political, scientific, and commercial. For classical liberals, human nature tends to be rational, so people can be trusted with wide ranges of freedom. Classical liberals believe that behavior and culture generally do not need the governmental steering or limit setting that aristocratic traditionalists call for. To limit such efforts by the government, classical liberalism often draws on the power-checking current in political thought as well as the free-market one (see chapter 5).

THE PHILOSOPHICAL CONNECTION | Michael Oakeshott and the Communitarians

The British thinker Michael Oakeshott was a leading twentieth-century conservative.* He saw modern politics primarily in terms of a contention between two approaches to politics and policy: (a) one that he liked, linked to what he called "political education," and (b) what he considered a harmful one characterized by "rationalism." In Oakeshott's view, rationalist policymakers see themselves as responding to pressing "felt needs" among the population. He saw their answer to a problem as always a general rule to be applied uniformly to all instances of that problem. According to Oakeshott, rationalists do not consider society's past experience when making decisions, but refer only to the logic of some rule, perhaps accompanied by their own personal experience.

What rationalist policymaking lacked, in his view, was something he called "political education." According to Oakeshott, those with political education have the advantage of understanding how society already works and what past experience can teach. They know that in new policymaking, unintended consequences were typical, loss was certain, and gain uncertain. If something has to be done, then, the conservative's first inclination will always be to take the smallest incremental step away from the status quo, and recognize its costs (as well as its benefits) before going further.

However, Oakeshott did not consider himself to be an opponent of reform. Faced with a problem, in his view, those with political education will search for society's own spontaneous momentum in relation to the issue. When women lacked the right to vote in the early twentieth century, he thought that policy reform should consider what is "intimated" by the direction already taken by society on that issue. Oakeshott suggested that people should notice that women's rights had already been expanding. For example, women had gained the right to own property and to claim it in divorce court proceedings. For Oakeshott, then, giving women the right to vote was an idea that was "intimated" (suggested implicitly) to policymakers by the direction that society was already taking. Giving women the right to vote was therefore the way to go.

In some ways following Oakeshott's stress on the inner momentum of society, the late twentieth-century **communitarians** saw a nation's ideas of justice as fundamentally embedded in, and derived from, the national community and its particular values, needs, and understandings.† Communitarian thought tends to assert that both the common good and the rights and well-being of individuals depend heavily on the community, rather than on the rationality of isolated individuals (as in classical liberalism, for example) or on state intervention.

Like MLCers, classical liberals vary in how far they lean in their characteristic ideological directions. In the United States, at the extreme they are represented by the "libertarian" wing of the Tea Party branch of the Republican Party. But classical liberalism can also be somewhat moderate. If a classical liberal party is very moderate in its free-market orientation—accepting some limited welfare programs and a degree of environmental regulation—and also moderate in its left-of-center stand for personal freedom in sociocultural areas, some commentators may call it "centrist." However, true centrism takes the middle position on most issues, in contrast to CL's positions to the right on economic issues and to the left in sociocultural ones.

CONSERVATISM

The root of the word "conservatism" is the verb "conserve." But again, this idea does not offer much help in understanding today's use of the word. What "conserving" means can vary widely depending on the status quo that is to be

To be sure, however, there are both conservative and left-of-center versions of communitarian thought. On the conservative side, communitarians tend to perceive in the community a prevailing way of life and conception of the common good, on which all good things depend. So the state should reinforce that prevailing perspective, and not succumb to abstract, universal principles of rights that are not favored by the existing community's mores (e.g., such as those articulated by John Rawls in his Theory of Justice; see "The Philosophical Connection," chapter 7). For some communitarians, this means that the state should refrain from action on many problems, leaving them to the community to handle. In this perspective, often the individual's sense of rights needs to be ready to yield to duties and the needs of society.

Among those who are sympathetic to communitarian ideas, however, are some observers who point out that a national community often contains within it multiple subcommunities that also provide these benefits, and question whether there is a single prevailing vision of the national common good. And notably, there are also left-of-center strands of communitarian thought. One approach is sympathetic to the classical liberal concern for the rights of individuals and minorities, but sees them as protectable only through a shared community appreciation of the reality of differences among people, of the contributions of different groups that may be present in the nation, and of the value of autonomous choice of lifestyle and pursuits.[‡] For some who hold this view, we cannot count on the free-marketplace of pursuits and ideas to naturally maintain the community's respect for individuality and diversity. For them, such respect must itself be part of the community's shared way of life and state concern, even to the point of occasional state intervention to bolster minority views and practices in the face of majority pressures. Regarding economic matters, such shared mutual respect may be necessary to maintain enough identification with the community to support sacrifice to meet the needs of the poor, for example.

---

[*] See Michael Oakeshott, *Rationalism in Politics and Other Essays* (New York: Basic Books, 1962).

[†] See Michael Sandel, *Liberalism and the Limits of Justice* (Cambridge, UK and New York: Cambridge University Press, 1982); Alasdair MacIntyre, *After Virtue: A Study in Moral Theory* (London: Duckworth, 1981); Michael Walzer, *Spheres of Justice: a Defense of Pluralism and Equality* (New York: Basic Books, 1983).

[‡] See Charles Taylor, *Philosophy and the Human Sciences* (Cambridge, UK: Cambridge University Press, 1985).

conserved. And this has changed considerably throughout Western history. Up through the nineteenth century, conservatism defended the king, nobility, and church against the classical liberal-led rise of democracy and commercial and sociocultural freedom. Then in the first half of the twentieth century, Western conservatism accepted representative democracy and the rise of nationalism around the two world wars. In the three decades following World War II, the nationalist theme in conservative ideology led many conservatives to accept a role for the state in planning economic recovery and building national economic strength. Then, by the 1980s, increasing numbers of conservatives were joining classical liberals in support of free-market policies.

The word **conservative**, when used to refer to someone's ideological stance, usually means moderately right of center. As with other ideologies, conservative political parties vary not only in their names, but also in how far right of center they are in their policies. For example, Germany's Christian Democratic Party is moderate in most of its views, while the British Conservative Party is moderate socioculturally but very free market oriented economically. Most of the Republican Party in the United States, in contrast, has moved strongly to the right in recent years on major issues in both the economic and the sociocultural policy categories.

Limited Economic Intervention

Today's conservatives join classical liberals in favoring limiting government intervention in the economy. Thus most of the economic details of conservatism have already been presented in the preceding section on classical liberalism. Except for a few comparative observations, those details do not need to be repeated here.

Like classical liberals, conservatives typically want to reduce government spending, whether for unemployment support, food aid, health care, or subsidies for environmental protection. They argue that such benefits from the government encourage dependency and lack of effort. Conservatives want to privatize as many state-owned functions, enterprises, and resources as possible. Along with their classical liberal economic allies, conservatives also want to reduce (1) the taxation that feeds such spending; and (2) government regulation, in such policy areas as labor market protections for workers, financial rules governing banking and investment, and special help for minorities and women. Today's conservatives tend to agree with classical liberals that such measures distort the optimal allocation of resources in the free-market economy. They might add, however, stress on what they see as the broader need to trust spontaneous developments among associations in society to address problems, rather than rational designs that they consider to be imposed on society (see "The Philosophical Connection").

However, in a few areas conservatives favor more economic intervention by the government than do classical liberals. For example, conservatives' attachment to nationalism may lead them to favor some tariff barriers and restrictions on immigration. Their belief in the broad value of order may include an emphasis on economic stability. Thus, in a time of financial and economic crisis, conservatives may accept emergency government interventions in the economy more readily than do classical liberals. For example, in late 2008 and early 2009, German chancellor Angela Merkel and her conservative Christian Democratic Union agreed with moderate left-of-center advocates in support of government intervention to save German banks from collapse, preserve jobs, and avert depression. At the same time in the United States, Republican president George W. Bush and a number of congressional Republicans backed the "Troubled Asset Relief Program (TARP)" program to rescue the banking system. Some conservatives also favor incremental change to reduce government economic intervention, rather than the rapid change that many classical liberals support.

In addition, conservatives tend to stress balancing the government's budget. To reduce budget deficits, some may be more willing than classical liberals to raise taxes—especially on the middle and lower levels of earners. Finally, some conservatives accept government regulation of the economy based on religious values, as in some nations with Muslim majorities. Thus, while conservatism generally favors free-market policies, it does so less consistently than does vigorous classical liberalism.

Social, Political, and Military Order

Conservatism views people as fundamentally self-interested; altruistic impulses are seen as generally limited to the family and patriotism. Traditional religious and patriotic values, institutions, and customs are needed to curb self-interest, keeping it within stable bounds. Conservatives favor bolstering the traditional family, including censoring images related to sex outside marriage. They tend to favor restricting practices related to extramarital sex, such as abortion and contraception. Favoring social order, conservatives advocate vigorous law enforcement and stiff penalties for criminals.

A key source of traditional values in many societies is religion (see below). As countries vary in their leading religions, the traditional values stressed by conservatism may vary. For example, Catholic Christianity influences France's conservative party, the Union for a Popular Majority, and Hindu values impact India's main conservative party, Bharatiya Janata. Islamic values certainly influence Turkey's governing Peace and Justice Party. In the United States, fundamentalist forms of Christianity prompt many American conservatives to support such policies as prayer in schools, restrictions on abortion, and exposing students in schools to creationist views of life's origins. Believers may cite sacred texts and commentaries on them to point out what the government should do in certain policy areas. For example, in some especially conservative Muslim countries such as Saudi Arabia and Pakistan, Islamic Sharia law is a heavy influence on the operation of their criminal justice systems.

A Variation in Emphasis: Nationalism and Neoconservatism

A key traditional value supported by conservatism is nationalism. Conservatives generally favor expanded spending on the military, and may support military intervention in foreign countries to protect their own national interests. Beginning in the 1970s, a portion of American conservatives began referring to themselves as **neoconservative**. Some early neoconservatives were new arrivals to conservatism, remaining moderate on economic issues but reacting strongly against the hippie counterculture of the 1960s and against what they saw as naïve efforts at peacemaking with the Soviet Union. By the 1980s, neoconservative thinking was focusing on the themes of nationalism, vigorous anti-Communism, and foreign military intervention in the service of their aims. For example, neoconservatives praised giving covert aid to the 1980s insurgency against the Soviet-allied government of Afghanistan.

After the collapse of eastern European and Soviet Communism in 1989–1991, neoconservative thinking shifted to projecting American military power in the Middle East against traditional authoritarian regimes there (most notably, that of Saddam Hussein in Iraq). The stated purposes were both to further American national security interests and to spread American values and democracy. After the 9/11 attacks against the United States by the radical Islamist group al-Qaeda, neoconservatives gained control over American foreign policy (coordinated by then deputy defense secretary Paul Wolfowitz), and achieved the desired invasion of Iraq in 2003. But the unintended consequences of neoconservative interventions—from (a) the late 1990s' Taliban takeover of Afghanistan to (b) the Iran-allied government of Iraq of the late 2000s, and (c) the Islamist election victories in Tunisia and Egypt in 2012—have led to some questioning and division among neoconservatives. Neoconservatives may be consolidating around targeting militant Islamism (see below) as the main cultural and military enemy.

But the new agenda for this aggressively internationalist branch of American conservatism is not yet clearly set.

ETHNIC ULTRANATIONALISM

Ethnic ultranationalism is an ideological stance that centers policy on the dignity, flourishing, and power of an ethnic group, usually comprising the majority in its society and identifying strongly with the nation-state. Its most prominent and fully articulated form in the twentieth century was pre-War Fascism in Germany, Italy, and Japan. More moderate forms are pursued by some late twentieth-century political parties such as France's National Front and Russia's Liberal Democratic Party.

Fascism

The ideology most commonly cited as "far right" is **Fascism**. Fascism mixes ethnic identification, extreme nationalism, and control of the state. It appeared most prominently from the 1920s through the 1940s in the views of Germany's Nazis, the Italian Fascists, and the Japanese militarists. According to Fascism, ethnic-national groups are naturally aggressive and find themselves in a struggle for survival and status against surrounding enemies. They are not surprised when one group dominates another, viewing people and ethnic-racial groups as naturally unequal and thus deserving of unequal outcomes. Fascists view leaders of their ethnic-nationalist cause as superior to their followers and much superior to those outside it.

Economic Coordination Despite some occasional socialist-sounding rhetoric, the Fascists of the 1930s and 1940s were virulently antisocialist along with their nationalism. In their view, egalitarianism could only serve to divide and weaken the nation. Fascists also saw commercialistic individualism as contending with the ethnic-national cause. They believed that the nation's struggle against surrounding enemies required substantial state control over capitalism. The economy had to emphasize military strength and preparedness, which required government regulation, substantial resources directed to the military, and subsidies to defense-related economic enterprises. German chancellor Adolph Hitler put Nazis in high places in important corporations, and Italian Fascist leader Benito Mussolini set up the "corporative state" to control the economy (see the Country Case Study on Italy). The Japanese militarists channeled their economy toward support for the military and imperial expansion around the Pacific Rim.

For Fascism, any unemployment problems that a nation might have would be solved by the expansion of an economy gearing up for war. However, the disabled and the elderly unable to work were abandoned to whatever fate befell them. In addition to the Fascist mix, Hitler's Nazism went to extremes of virulent anti-Semitism and prejudice against the disabled, homosexuals, and gypsies. Among the victims of their extermination efforts were the six million Jewish dead. In addition, for example, there were over twenty million civilian casualties of World War II in the Soviet Union alone, mostly from starvation and malnutrition-related disease.

Social, Political, and Military Control Fascist governments were politically authoritarian and antidemocratic. They used propaganda to persuade each citizen to identify solely with the nation and "the leader." Political contention of groups and parties in elections was illegitimate because it threatened the cohesion of the nation. Thus Fascists worked to undermine the democracies in which they first arose. These efforts typically included sponsoring a militia force for intimidation and street violence against opposing groups. Once the Fascist Party gained power and dismantled democratic frameworks, they outlawed overt opposition and punished protesters with violence and/or imprisonment. Along personal leadership lines, Fascists wanted to concentrate all power in the hands of the glorified single leader who personified the nation: the *Führer* (Hitler), *il duce* (Mussolini), or the emperor (Hirohito).

Accordingly, Fascist sociocultural policies allowed little room for individual freedom. Pervasive government propaganda, political use of police and judicial power against dissidents, discrimination in access to services, and government-encouraged private harassment combined to enforce nationalism and prejudice against foreigners or other alien groups. Among the Nazis, even church and family ran into trouble if they hindered national solidarity. (In contrast, Mussolini's Italy elevated religion and family). The seeming willingness of numerous Germans to join in rallies at which such views were extolled alarmed some critical observers.

The Nazis, the Italian Fascists, and the Japanese militarists saw human nature as irrational and rooted in ethnic and national identity. For them, humans can find a satisfying identity only in a sense of solidarity with an ancestral group, on which culture should be based. In addition, the Fascists saw humans as deeply in need of social order. People had to view society and the economy as cooperating in harmonious pursuit of a single national purpose. Groups whom they considered disruptive to the unity of society and the state had to be suppressed. The most prominent values of Fascism, then, were (1) well-being in the sense of ethnic and national dignity and status, (2) well-being in the sense of unquestioned military security (through military dominance) and (3) social order.

Ethnic Ultranationalism Today

The defeat of Nazi Germany, Fascist Italy, and Imperial Japan in World War II ended the large-scale, worldwide impact of Fascist ideology at the governmental level. It remained explicit only in a few cases, such as Spain under Generalissimo Franco (from 1936 until his death in 1975). Today Fascism may be found only in small, fringe skinhead or militia groups.

However, ethnic ultranationalism can still spur political action. Today it stresses ethnicity (sometimes coinciding with religion) more than national territory, and tends not to display a fleshed-out worldview across the various areas of ideology. In a few cases recently, intense ethnic solidarity whipped up by leaders has led to violence. For example, the 1990s saw conflicts in the former Yugoslavia, especially those involving the Serbs in the regions of Bosnia and Kosovo. And violence arose with even deadlier results between the ethnic Hutus and Tutsis in the nations of Rwanda and Burundi in east-central Africa (see Country Studies, chapter 18). In those two cases, the Serbs (mainly) and the Hutus, respectively, pursued ethnic cleansing to rid controlled territory of other groups viewed as rivals.

Ethnic ultranationalism takes a much more moderate form among some parties in such nations as France, Germany, Austria, and Russia. Small "national front" parties stress what they see as a need for identity and solidarity with the national ethnic majority, and pursue policies to benefit that group. Most importantly, they focus on reducing immigration. In Europe, they oppose EU policies of free migration within Europe, and are alarmed by the influx of Muslims from North Africa and the Middle East (e.g., in boats from Libya to southern Italy), fleeing the post–Arab Spring chaos there. In some cases, the result has been open campaigning to get their countries to leave the EU (e.g., the U.K. Independence Party in Great Britain).

Economically, national front parties tend to favor free-market capitalism with low taxes. However, they also support selective government intervention in the economy for nationalistic reasons, such as protectionist tariffs against foreign goods and rules banning state-provided benefits for immigrants. Their adherents strongly support national defense as well as strong police power against crime.

In other aspects of their views, however, ethnic ultranationalists seem caught in a contradiction. National front parties have accepted democratic politics and freedoms in order to make their case. They are small, typically facing a surrounding population that is mainly hostile to their extreme views. They need government to respect their rights to free expression and association to protect them from surrounding pressure against the hate messages that they sometimes deliver. But some observers wonder whether, if they were ever to gain sole power, national front parties might pursue a strongly interventionist approach in sociocultural policy areas, enforcing ethnic majority practices in ways that are contrary to the sociocultural freedom of minorities and immigrants.

MILITANT ISLAMISM

Islamism in general can be described as a social movement that seeks to revitalize the religion and heighten Muslims' attention to Islam in their lives. It varies in form and degree, looking quite different in Pakistan than in Indonesia, for example. **Militant Islamism** is a form of Islamism that stresses especially strict adherence to the religion found in the Koran (Allah's revelation through Mohammed) and the early hadith (reports and commentaries on Mohammed's words and actions). Militant Islamists advocate that the Koran and the early hadith should be the foundation of the state and law, in the form of Sharia law (legal practices derived from the Koran and the Hadith) as the code of the official justice system. Thus militant Islamism characteristically advocates **theocracy** (government run by a religion's clerics), and tends to see a sharp contention between Islam and Western lifestyles and values. Full-fledged militant Islamism is an ideology that encompasses only a small minority of the world's Muslims, but due to its heavy impact on world events today, we need to understand it.

Militant Islamism became prominent in three waves. The first, and by today's standards the mildest and most tolerant of religious diversity, is its Shia variant, expressed by the Iranian regime descended from the Iranian Revolution of 1978. The second, which first got attention in the 1990s, is represented by the Sunni radical group al-Qaeda, focused on striking at any sources of Western influence in what are regarded as Muslim lands. The third, and most important today, is the militant Islamism of the Islamic State (IS; alternatively, ISIL or ISIS[7]), which controls a large contiguous area of eastern Syria and western Iraq.

In most of the Middle East, Shia Muslims are a minority that have been periodically threatened and harassed by militants of the majority Sunni branch of Islam. Thus armed Shia militants tend to operate mostly in military defense of Shia populations against attack by Sunni militants. But the first Islamic theocracy, displaying how such a regime might work, arose in Shia and Persian Iran. More recently, we have seen how today's militant Sunni theocracy works in such places as Taliban-controlled parts of Afghanistan, al-Shabaab-controlled areas of Somalia, parts of southern Yemen, northeastern Mali and northeastern Nigeria, and most prominently today, IS-controlled portions of Syria and Iraq.

Economic Variation

The longest-established forms of Islamic theocracy are in Iran and Sudan, where militant Islamists' sociocultural views have some impact on the economy. In the area of regulation, for example, alcohol and tobacco are banned. In addition, the regime officially supports the Koran's ban on charging interest on loans. In practice, however, militant Islamist regimes have found this very difficult, and may resort merely to giving interest a different name. At times, the government economic policies of Iran and Sudan have favored Islamic banks and other Islamic enterprises. In Iran, the state owns some of the economy, especially in sectors such as big industry, banking, insurance, energy, telecommunications, natural resources, and transportation. In practice, however, the governments of Iran and Sudan have at times departed from Islamic rules, opening their economies to some extent to enhance foreign investment and economic development.

At the other extreme, IS tends to reject a wide range of practices and products that the group associates with Western values that it considers alien to its understanding of Islam. Private property is accepted in theory, but the regime seizes the property of dissidents who have refused to convert and have escaped or been killed. Harsh bans on alcohol, drugs, and music, for example, are enforced by violence. But to get money for its war, IS does whatever it takes. For example, IS in Syria engages in rough-hewn oil refining and sales to neighbors, drug smuggling, kidnapping of Westerners for ransom (conducting publicized beheadings of victims if ransom money is not forthcoming), and heavy taxation of entrepreneurs.

Sociocultural and Military Issues

For militant Islamists, justice is a key value, especially regarding swift and vigorous punishment of wrongdoing. Few rules protect the accused. Extreme versions of Sharia law can include such ancient and severe punishments as cutting off the hand of a thief, public flogging for premarital sex, or stoning an adulterer to death. Some such punishments, such as killing "apostates" (those judged to have abandoned the Muslim faith), can be found only in Sunni hadith, and are not found in the Koran.

A second key value for militant Islamists is order. They see most of today's Muslims as having been drawn away from their religious roots by Western ideas, lifestyles, and culture, which in their view bring social disarray. In the eyes of militant Islamists, human nature yearns above all for a stable personal and spiritual environment. For them, a Muslim's social identity should be rooted in her or his membership in the religious community (the *Umma*), and people must receive their values from that community.

Thus the religious authorities may prohibit a range of social behaviors. For example, gambling, smoking, drinking alcohol, dancing, and public mixing of the sexes may be banned, as may Western dress and hairstyles. Prohibitions are enforced either by the police or by informal religious militias supported by the government. The practical consequences of these regulations vary, however, from the relative tolerance found in Shia Iran (where nonetheless, there have been killings of homosexuals) to the tight clerical control in IS-controlled areas of Syria and Iraq and Taliban-run areas of Afghanistan, for example. Personal freedom is not a priority.

Militant Islam advocates an ancient, traditionalist view of the status of women. At the extreme—for example, in IS-controlled parts of Iraq and Syria or Taliban-controlled parts of Afghanistan—the Koran's admonition that women dress with "modesty" means covering their bodies fully with a loose-fitting *burka*. Regarding movement, militant Islamists believe that women belong primarily in the home. If a woman must work outside the home, she must do so separately from men. A woman may go out in public only if accompanied by a male relative. A woman walking alone may be accused of moral offenses, beaten, and/or incarcerated, as may a woman who tries to escape an abusive home environment or an arranged marriage. Boys may be required to attend Islamic religious schools (madrassas) that may include training in militant Islamism.

As to the political arrangements necessary to implement such goals, militant Islamism favors Sharia-inspired authoritarian government by clerics. But a range of forms exists. At the milder end, exemplified by Iran, the religious elite and its militia may permit the formalities of elected assemblies. However, clerics screen candidates for proper Islamic values and have a veto over legislation (see "The Human Rights Connection," chapter 12). At times, Iranian dissidents and prodemocracy advocates protesting electoral fraud may be met with violence, detention, and even long-term imprisonment. But these harsh actions seem to be primarily a matter of garden-variety authoritarian repression to keep the regime in power, rather than a use of terror to indoctrinate victims to adopt a set of religious beliefs.

At the totalitarian extreme of militant Islamism was, for example, the tight control and summary justice in Afghanistan by the Taliban clerics until their overthrow in 2002, and by IS in the areas of Syria and Iraq that it controls today. Militant Islamists view human rights such as freedom of expression and association as Western cultural prejudices. In this context, however, we need to remember that the vast majority of Muslims around the world are not militant. They are content to live under representative democracies in which they *may* aim, at most, to see Islamic values reflected more in government policy and the justice system.

Strategies for Change

A significant aspect of militant Islamism is its strategy for change. Here we encounter division among Islamists. The most minimalist among Islamists are those who seek primarily to protect their religious community from attack, rather than to impose their beliefs on others. Around the Middle East, Shia groups pursue a political role in governments, but seemingly less to impose their religious views and practices on non-Shias, than to assure the safety of the Shia community (and in effect, of other minorities) from invasion and subjection to control by other religious groups, usually militant Sunni ones.

Regarding terrorism, the most important militant Islamic groups are Sunni ones, and among them, the most attention-getting are those who practice "holy war"—violent jihad—against their perceived opponents. But such jihadists are a portion of a very important larger category, Sunni **Salafism**. The core of Salafism is support for state imposition of strict Sharia law—based on a literal reading of the Koran and the Sunni hadith—on the citizenries of nations. To understand these phenomena, we must first distinguish the key contending approaches within the ranks of Salafists, and how Salafist jihadists differ from non-jihadist Salafists.

Jihad and the Origins of IS and al-Qaeda The historical origin of Salafism as we know it today was a puritanical jihadist movement called Wahhabism that first emerged in Saudi Arabia in the last half of the eighteenth century. Then Abd al-Wahhab (a follower of the teachings of a fourteenth-century thinker, Ibn Taymiyyah) advocated a return to the literal meaning of the Koran and the early Sunni hadith. He rejected all kinds of subsequent developments in Islamic cultural practice, such as celebrating Muhammad's birthday or visiting shrines or graves of important Islamic figures or ancestors. Wahhab considered such practices to be idolatry (thus akin to the barbarous practices that preceded Muhammed), and tantamount to apostasy (leaving the faith), punishable by death according to the Sunni hadith. In Wahhabism, centuries of past interpretation and evolution in applying Islam to changing circumstances were rejected in favor of directly applying the literal wording of the Koran and the early Sunni hadith (the "Sunnah") to social, economic, and political life.

In the eighteenth century, an alliance was cemented between Wahhab's followers and one of the groups of nomadic raiders in the area, the Saud clan. That alliance yielded a zealous jihadist army that succeeded in conquering most of the Arabian peninsula. The Wahhabists created a caliphate (a domain ruled by a single top religious and political leader, the "caliph") there, much like that of IS in 2014 and 2015 in eastern Syria and western Iraq. Their policy toward both Muslims and non-Muslims seemed to be a choice: allegiance to the caliph and his creed, or death. Their deeds included an expedition into Iraq and a massacre of thousands of Shia in the Iraqi city of Karbala in 1801. The period of early Wahhabist rule in the Arabian Peninsula ended only with the bloody defeat of the Wahhabists by the forces of the Ottoman Empire in the 1810s.

A century later, after the post–World War I collapse of the Ottoman Empire, Saudi jihadist Wahhabism was revived in the form of the Isfahan ("brethren") movement of the 1920s. Again, the Isfahan jihadis behaved in ways that were strikingly similar to those of IS today, and again they could only be stopped militarily, this time by the Saudi king's forces in the early 1930s. The Wahhabists were then subordinated to the Saudi monarchy, and their project of international jihad was officially banned. The result was a less aggressive Wahhabism, stripped of the strategy of violent jihad, which became the main religion of Saudi Arabia. The Saudi clerics favored (a) strict governmental application of Sharia law (including beheadings for certain crimes, for example) and (b) literal application of the Koran and the Sunni hadith, with few adjustments to adapt to modern circumstances. (This is called the Shaf'i school of Sunni Islamic interpretation, as opposed to the looser Hanofi school favored by the Ottoman Empire and most of Turkish Islam today.)

While the Saudi monarchy did not advocate jihad against governments, it did provide financial support (out of its oil money, plenteous from the 1970s on) for spreading Wahhabism's doctrines, of scriptural literalism and strict state-imposed Sharia law, to other Muslim countries. By the 1980s, schools called madrassas were springing up across much of the Muslim world. Wahhabism's main ideas on the ideal Islamic society (minus some particular views peculiar to Wahhab's writings) became the broad approach called Salafism today.

Varieties of Salafism Within Salafism, however, are three broad categories of approach to change. In Saudi Arabia, most devotees focus on what is officially recommended: piously following Sharia in their own communities while avoiding politics. A second approach, more common outside Saudi Arabia, also avoids violent jihad but accepts involvement in politics to pursue the ultimate goal of government by Sharia law. Within this category are two subclassifications: (a) aggressive political action, as favored, for example, by many Salafists in Egypt's long-established Muslim Brotherhood, and (b) more pragmatic, tactical politics, such as the approach of Egypt's al-Nour party. The al-Nour Salafists supported the Brotherhood's moves in the direction of Sharia when the Brotherhood was leading the Egyptian government, but when the military took over in 2013, removing the Brotherhood from power, al-Nour cooperated with the new military regime.

The third major approach within Salafism is the jihadi one. To be sure, in Islam generally today, "**jihad**" need not be limited to the violent holy war that militant Islamists emphasize. In a widely cited verse in the Koran, it is given a broader meaning, involving any sort of struggle against injustice, evil, or any perceived enemy of Allah or the prophet Mohammed. This can include spiritual struggle against sin within oneself or contention in discussions with others. However, the most attention-getting form of jihad today, apparently referred to by the bulk of the Koran's references to jihad, is violent holy war.

Militant Sunni Islamists tend to read the Koran's passages on jihad literally, as a call for Muslims to join in war against all who "fight" Islam and even, in some verses, seemingly all infidels (nonbelievers in Islam). For example, IS in Syria and Iraq, the Taliban in Afghanistan, Al Shabaab in Somalia, and Boko Haram in Nigeria have burned non-Islamic schools and assassinated people who cooperate with the non-Islamist government or with Westerners. Again, the ultimate goal is to have religious officials control the government and install strict Sharia as the law of the land, whether efforts to accomplish these goals are nation by nation (e.g., for the Taliban in Afghanistan or the Syrian groups Jabhat al Nusra and Ahrar al-Sham) or on a world scale (for IS and, seemingly, al-Qaeda's central organization).

There are two major branches of Sunni Salafist jihadism today: al-Qaeda (AQ), which emerged first in the late 1990s, and IS. In part, the early Qaeda leader Osama bin Laden and his associates were inspired by the mid-twentieth-century Egyptian writer Sayyid Qutb.[8] For Qutb, the current era of Western influence is analogous to what he considered to be the ignorant barbarism that preceded the rise of Mohammed in the Arabian peninsula in the seventh century. In his view, nations with Muslim majorities should rid themselves of Western influence, especially Western military bases or outposts.

Al-Qaeda affiliates exist in many countries. While they attack the local regime and want to overthrow it, they tend to also focus attention on striking against westerners, whether private, governmental, or military. Notoriously, al-Qaeda and its affiliates conducted such operations as the September 11, 2001 terrorist attacks in New York and Washington, DC, that killed over 2,700 Americans, major bombings in England, Spain, Indonesia, Kenya, and Tanzania, and countless smaller suicide bombings in Iraq, Afghanistan, and Pakistan where Muslims are also frequently among the victims.

In their efforts to seize control of particular national governments, AQ-affiliated groups often cooperate with other salafist and jihadist Sunni groups that are not affiliates but share the goal of imposing strict sharia as the law of the land, such as Ahrar al-Sham in Syria (which reportedly has at times received support from, variously, Saudi Arabia, Qatar, and Turkey). Since all such groups believe that the Koran and the Sunni hadith are the only rightful sources of governmental legislation, they reject secular representative democracy.

In the late 2000s, however, al-Qaeda's unit in Iraq began to take its own path. It had spent more time fighting Western forces than had any other part of al-Qaeda, and it evolved into what is now called the Islamic State (IS). As noted above, by 2014 IS had attacked and taken over substantial areas in both Syria and Iraq. Soon some smaller al-Qaeda units around the Middle East and North Africa were signing up as IS affiliates. In contrast to al-Qaeda, IS seemed to focus on conquering territory and imposing strict Sharia law through violent terror, as much as on fighting the national regime in power in the area. Nearly any Muslim engaging in an activity that IS-sympathizing militants associate with Western culture or non-IS Islam may be labeled as an infidel (unbeliever), an idolater, or an apostate (someone who has abandoned Islam). If such a person is not willing to immediately convert to IS's brand of Islam and cannot escape, he or she may suffer the violent consequences. Notably, however, where IS has the resources it also tries to establish basic services in its areas such as electric power, water supply, bakery operation, and of course, crime control.

IS has developed an effective international social media effort to recruit foreign fighters from among disaffected and marginalized Muslim youths in countries such as Britain, France, Tunisia, and Saudi Arabia itself. With IS's growing numbers and their willingness to die in suicide missions to break through enemy defenses, the group has at times seized Syrian territory even from the local al-Qaeda unit, the Nusra Front. (Nusra, unlike IS, was at times willing to cooperate with other rebel groups fighting the Syrian regime, and seemed more wary of trying to impose strict Sharia on people in areas that it held.)

Again, it is important to understand that militant Islamism is only one branch of Islamic thought, adopted by only a small minority of Muslims worldwide. Most Muslims, including Shias generally and most Sunnis, accept Islam as somewhat pluralistic, and as coexisting peacefully with other religions. They seek creative ways of reconciling traditional Islam with the values and practices of the modern world. And even among those who support Sharia, many pursue it not as rule by a theocratic regime, but rather as a cluster of values that they wish to integrate more into their country's justice system via the electoral success of conservative political parties that support those values.

CROSS-CURRENTS AMONG IDEOLOGIES: NATIONALISM AND RELIGION

Some themes and values may affect multiple ideologies and encourage cooperation among their adherents. Two major cross-currents, nationalism and religion, have influenced how some ideologies express themselves. But neither of these has formed a coherent ideology of its own.

Pure nationalism is simply a strong feeling of attachment or solidarity with one's country. Thus, people view their freedom, security, prosperity, and dignity as linked to the nation as a unit. Many developing nations have built a sense of national identity based in part on the nationalism that arose in the struggle for independence from a colonial occupier. In wartime, a spirit of nationalism tends to arise and support the war effort.[9]

The most common role of nationalism, however, is to affect specific national expressions of other ideologies. As we have discussed, nationalism is a key feature of Fascism. And, in today's ethnic ultranationalism, members of a majority ethnic group may enlist nationalism in forming an ethnic-based political party. Moderate left-of-center ideology can at times advocate trade protection (tariffs and quotas on imports) to help the nation's producers. Nationalism can also be part of the traditional values that conservatives want the government to reinforce.

Particular national expressions of an ideology may also be affected by religion. Its role is obvious in liberation theology and in militant Islamism. But religion may also favor more moderate ideologies. Religions such as Christianity and Islam can provide some of the traditional values stressed by conservatism in some nations. Jesus's concern for the poor and his admonition to "love thy neighbor as thyself" may lead some Christians toward moderate left-of-center ideology. In parts of Asia, Buddhism plays a similar role, as can the social justice strand in Islamic thinking (e.g., Zakat, assistance to the poor).

SUMMARY: CONTENTION AND COOPERATION AMONG IDEOLOGIES

Ideological terms can easily be confusing; thus, it is important to find clear and consistent ways of using them. On one hand, we see broad contention between left-of-center or right-of-center ideological directions, and we can apply these phrases in classifying policies ideologically. The left-of-center direction tends to endorse strong government action in policies affecting the economy, but not in defense. It supports personal freedoms in sociocultural areas. The right-of-center direction leans the opposite way. Within each direction, more extreme policy ideas may contend with more moderate ones. But the broad category enables adherents of both to cooperate at times in support of a specific policy proposal.

On the other hand, we also talk about multiple ideologies in the sense of "grand systems." These more complex conceptions incorporate such features as a political framework, a specific kind of government-society relationship, preferred policy directions, and views of society and human nature. In the latter category, we glimpsed eight ideologies, presented roughly in order from left to right, from Marxism-Leninism and democratic socialism on the left to Fascism and militant Islamism on the right. In each case, sharing the ideology's worldview helps activists to cooperate, most commonly in a political party aligned with that ideology. Thus supporters can contend more effectively with ideological opponents.

At times, contending ideologies can find enough common ground to cooperate with one another. The most common basis for cooperation among ideologies seems to be shared values. For example, classical liberalism and conservatism today share support for market freedom and overall commercial prosperity (an interpretation of well-being). Consequently, their adherents may cooperate in support of free-market measures despite their differences over government intervention in sociocultural issues.

Similarly, left social democrats can cooperate with MLCers in support of government spending to expand job opportunities for the middle and lower economic strata, despite their differences over how far the government should go in job creation. This stems from their shared support for a floor of minimal well-being for the least advantaged in society. In addition, economic nationalism can sometimes bring together MLCers and moderate conservatives in support of tariffs on imports. Finally, advocates of some of the ideologies can cooperate around political frameworks. They can share support for representative democracy's formal mix of majority preference and pluralist distribution of influence (see "Applying the Models").

Finally, we should recognize that ideologies are just one cluster of factors affecting our attitudes toward policies and politics. At times, we may believe that a particular ideological orientation has the right answer. At other times, we may simply look for what seems to be the best policy on an issue, or the policy that best serves our self-interest, or the one that supports a value that is important to us. On a personal level, many people borrow elements from one ideology on one issue and from another ideology for another issue.

APPLYING THE MODELS | Patterns of Influence Within Ideologies

At least for some of the ideologies we have discussed, we can see patterns of influence distribution in their preferred systems. The elite model (dominance by a top group) exists in Marxism-Leninism, Fascism, and militant Islamism. Marxist-Leninists and Fascists favored a one-party state, with a party-state elite in power. Fascism also emphasized having a single leader at the top. Thus, it fused the personal leadership model with the elite one. After Stalin's death in 1953, most Marxist-Leninists (with the exception of North Korea, China, and later Cuba) rejected the glorification of a single leader. For militant Islamists, the elite of religious clerics should at least exercise limit-setting power, overseeing decision making to ensure that it stays within the boundaries of Islamic principles. In each case, the elite claim to know the real interests of the people better than the people themselves do.

In democratic contexts, the majority preference model also finds its way into some ideologies. Early twentieth-century socialists sought a peaceful, democratic transition to socialism based on the growing majority of workers among the voting population. Moderate left-of-center supporters suggest that people generally share an interest in their own self-development, thus providing an element of majority preference. For Greens, we all depend on the environment. Their goal is that electoral majorities recognize the threat to the environment. Ethnic ultranationalists favor the dominance of the majority ethnicity in their nations, the members of which should recognize and act on their common interests.

The majority preference conception also exists in combination with elite-model preferences in conservative ideology. Conservatives view the prevailing traditional institutions, religion, and culture, which should be bolstered by the government, as belonging to the majority. However, on the economic side, today's conservatives view the interests of all as dependent on the success of business, an economic elite that needs some limit-setting influence over politics to avoid too much government intervention.

The pluralist model can also be found in some of these ideological orientations. Because socialists, Greens, and ethnic ultranationalists tend to be minorities, they rely on pluralist aspects of the political process to be able to influence it. Although moderate left-of-center ideology seeks the support of majorities, it relies on pluralism as well. MLCers today pursue the interests not just of labor, but of a range of disadvantaged minorities who must stand up for themselves to get recognition. Classical liberalism's support of the self-expression of individuals and minorities implicitly suggests the pluralist model, though moderated by regard for free-market business interests.

COUNTRY CASE STUDIES

Each of the ideologies we have examined can include numerous variations. Here we consider two specific national variations, each exemplifying a more extreme ideology: Mussolini's version of Fascism and Mao Zedong's version of Marxism-Leninism. In each case, the ideology's founder, in contending with opposing views, sought to gain the cooperation of the mass of citizens. Mussolini emphasized action over intellectual understanding and organized private industry into a quasi-state structure for carrying out government policies; Mao included a phase in policymaking that invited "the poor majority" to participate in policy application.

Italy: Mussolini's Fascism

For Benito Mussolini, the Fascist leader of Italy from 1922 to 1943, the nation was the natural focus of human solidarity. While it was Italian ethnicity that modern Italy shared with ancient Rome and its glory, Mussolini emphasized the Italian nation-state. He did not embrace the racial preoccupation of Hitler and the Nazis. As closer links to (and dependency on) Nazi Germany developed, in 1938 Mussolini adopted laws taking rights and property away from the Jews. But the Italian government never persecuted Jews enthusiastically. Most of Italy's Jews were saved from the Holocaust, some even by high-level Fascists.

Mussolini claimed that the nation-state had a single collective will, expressed by the leader—*Il Duce*—and anything that divided this will was unacceptable. Legislative assemblies, parties, social classes, and individual rights were unnecessary and even harmful. Their contentions could only disrupt national cohesion, confuse the public, and detract from focus on the will of the leader, which represented the collective will of the people. The leader's job was to use rhetoric, propaganda, and myth to arouse the people's emotions so that they would identify with the leader, the state, and their yearning for national greatness. In particular, Italian Fascists sought to foster in the people a desire to emulate the past greatness of the Roman Empire.

Socioculturally, Mussolini reorganized the educational system, in part to socialize young people to his ideology. But he gave the Vatican autonomy and privileges and made Catholicism the state religion of Italy, in return for church support of the regime and allegiance to it.

For Mussolini, to arouse the desired emotions among the people, a leader must stimulate action. He used group violence to intimidate and crush opposition, first by paramilitary "Blackshirts" during his rise to power in the early 1920s, and later by the secret police. Such action was aimed at deepening the people's solidarity against their enemies. Mussolini's Fascism was openly anti-intellectual. He believed that truth is in feeling and acting on that feeling, and analysis and debate by intellectuals can only get in the way. Mussolini revised the criminal code of Italy to include vigorous enforcement of his policies.

Mussolini's Fascist state directed the economy to build the independent power and greatness of the nation. Having rejected his early socialist leanings, Mussolini for the most part preserved private property and big industry. However, the government intervened in the economy with whatever planning, control, and nationalization it needed to build national power. Such intervention included buying up large bankrupt companies during the Great Depression.

Ironically, the high level of state intervention in the economy mirrored that of socialism. Such intervention seemed necessary in light of Mussolini's stated goal of national economic self-sufficiency. Italy was struggling with shortages of raw materials. The regime had conquered Ethiopia in 1936 in an effort to build a colonial empire, resulting in economic sanctions against Italy by the League of Nations (the precursor to the United Nations). These sanctions, alongside the breakdown in international trade that accompanied the Great Depression, reinforced Mussolini's go-it-alone economic policy.

Mussolini called his economic system "corporativism." For each sector of the economy, such as transportation, communication, or steel manufacturing, the government created a "corporation" made up of multiple private companies. Corporations were to control and discipline their sectors to serve national needs. Each corporation's companies were encouraged to cooperate with one another in planning production levels and setting wages and prices. In Mussolini's view, this pattern would unite the efforts of labor with those of owners and managers. The result would be greater unity and productivity for the state. The corporations would replace parliament, with their representatives comprising a governmental "chamber" to advise the leader. In practice, the corporative structure served as a channel for communicating the regime's economic plans to economic enterprises.

What was the point of all this national greatness? Mussolini was likely influenced by ethnic and national social Darwinism—the view that ethnic groups and nations were in a "survival-of-the-fittest" struggle. Ethnic survival depended upon national self-sufficiency and greatness. Mussolini valued national collective self-sufficiency and dignity, not the well-being of the individual. Similarly, freedom meant only an imagined collective freedom of the people, not individual freedom. Order was an ultimate goal, but the means to it were at times impulsive, disorderly, and violent. Mussolini's Fascism lacked justice, equality, and human rights.

China: Mao's Marxism-Leninism

Mao Zedong was the most important Chinese revolutionary leader, and formally chairman of the Chinese Communist Party from the revolution in 1945 to his death in 1976. He was, in theory, a Marxist-Leninist. As such, Mao believed that in the developing world, a revolutionary elite party should seize power in each country and not wait for the full cycle of capitalism to be played out. Politically, he opposed free and open debate. Instead, he favored a centralized setting of the policy directions to be pursued by the Communist Party and the state. Mao favored the values of economic well-being and equality, but his ideology contained no regard for civil-political human rights. Order was not a preeminent value for Mao. In his strategy for change, order was a luxury that the "continuing revolution" could ill afford.

Economically, Mao favored social ownership and control of industry and property. Collectivism extended down even to peasant property, which eventually should be organized into rural communes. But within these general concepts, Mao allowed variation in strategy to fit the particular circumstances. In Mao's concept of party-government control, general policy direction would come from the center in periodic campaigns pursuing new policies. But in implementing these policies, there would be a cycle in which the mass of people could themselves apply "Mao Zedong thought" In what he called the "mass line."

Mao Zedong suspected that in China, the central government and party leaders could not effectively control policy implementation to the same degree as it had in Russia. But the top could use its control of mass communications, as well as the party and government hierarchies, to start campaigns for change. Maoist rule was characterized by a cycle with a general sequence:

1. The top level of the elite plans the campaign.
2. Party and government officials meet to study the campaign.
3. The campaign is announced, centering on slogans.
4. Party and government functionaries are decentralized to lower levels to try to get momentum going for the campaign.
5. A period of peak activity in the villages, economic enterprises, or neighborhoods ensues, with frequent meetings and attempts to rally people to implement the policy.
6. The campaign ends.
7. A period of quiet and consolidation allows party and government activists and officials to gather

information on the results in their particular area.

8. The leading party and government activists and officials go back up a level or two to their regular positions, for meetings to bring together information (what Maoists called "concentration of ideas") about what had been accomplished in their various areas.

9. The preparation for the next campaign begins.

This cycle played out for land reform in 1951–1953, peasant mutual aid teams in 1953–1954, small agricultural cooperatives in 1955, larger cooperatives in 1956–1957, and the ill-fated agricultural collectivization of 1958–1959 (the "Great Leap Forward"), as we will see below. It also occurred with the removal of moderate and conservative urban officials in 1966–1967 and their exile to the countryside (the "Cultural Revolution").

For leaders, ideology mattered more than specialized knowledge and expertise. Mao referred to this issue as the "red" versus "expert" problem. Yes, people had to have some training for their day jobs. But for the Maoists, not much specialization (or education for it) was necessary. People had to be ready at a moment's notice to shift into political gear. People in different jobs met frequently to coordinate their efforts around the aims of the latest campaign, even if abandoning their specialized functions for a while.

Mao held that people were naturally inclined toward cooperation and egalitarianism. They could be easily inspired by ideological meetings and slogans to undertake new activity. The popular will could achieve great social transformations. The "mass line" approach argued that much of the change could be accomplished not under the detailed direction of administrative hierarchies, but by people at the ground level, guided by local activists and general slogans. Consequently, campaigns often produced wide variation in their success from one area to another. And the methods of change adopted at the ground level also varied greatly.

The Maoists seemed to accept this variation. In cases where policy goals were not met on the ground, however, party and government officials often were pressured to report better results than had actually occurred. For example, many of the "cooperatives" of the mid-1950s may have been largely paper entities, with little more cooperation than building new dikes and irrigation networks in the winter off-season to expand agriculture. And much of the cooperation of the period occurred within village neighborhoods that already shared ancestral kinship linkages. But many Maoists, observing the seemingly smooth development of cooperatives, became convinced that the peasants were ready to embrace large-scale collective agriculture. They were wrong.

At times, part of the desired change was the removal or punishment of real or imagined political opponents. Especially during the land reform of the early 1950s and the Cultural Revolution of the mid to late 1960s, "struggle meetings" heaped criticism and ridicule on victims, who might then be dealt with brutally if they resisted. Again, Maoism did not promote principled respect for civil-political rights in theory or in practice.

The most disastrous outcomes of the "mass line" approach came with the Great Leap Forward (1958–1959) and the Cultural Revolution (1965–1971). The Great Leap's attempt at large-scale agricultural communes forced peasants to join large labor armies, which as a unit would perform one agricultural function at a time. These attempts and the resistance to them disrupted agriculture. The results were calamitous in a country with a huge population (600–700 million at the time), living on the production of a very limited amount of arable land with little margin for error. In some places, state authorities used falsely inflated food production figures to collect much of the harvest for the cities, leaving insufficient food for the peasants. Local famines may have killed as many as 20–30 million people, although actual numbers are unknown. By 1960, communal agriculture was cancelled, and China basically returned to family farming with some coordination by local authorities. The results of the Great Leap were so disastrous that by 1961 Mao had been forced out of power. The government came under the control of Mao's more conventional rival, Liu Shaochi.

By the middle 1960s, however, Mao had become worried by what he considered to be a trend toward Soviet-style bureaucratic conservatism and inequality in China. He started a campaign in the army first, which then emerged in 1965 as the Great Proletarian Cultural Revolution. Student and worker "red guard" units directed their animosity at officials and educated people whose attitudes, the Maoists claimed, were leading China down "the capitalist road." The movement engaged the egalitarian idealism of many students and greatly narrowed income differences. Officials who kept their positions were directed to spend some days every month working alongside their rank-and-file workers, to stay in touch with the masses and to insulate themselves from bureaucratic attitudes. Many others were brought before struggle meetings for humiliation, vilification, and often severe punishment.

Some top-level targets were imprisoned, with or without forced labor, and even killed. Most urban victims, however, were banished to the countryside to be "re-educated" by living as ordinary peasants, a life for which they were very poorly prepared. Some committed suicide. Ultimately, in schools, offices and factories, the Cultural Revolution replaced expertise with politics and ideology. It removed much of China's educated managerial talent.

Like earlier campaigns, the Cultural Revolution could not be centrally controlled. It became chaotic in some areas, as competing red guard units fought each other. Universities and economic organizations collapsed to the point that the army had to be called in to run things. The result was economic stagnation and decline at a time when some of China's newly industrialized neighbors were in take-off mode. By the early 1970s, Prime Minister Chou Enlai and other leaders were turning away from the Cultural Revolution, and many of its victims were allowed to return from the countryside. One of them was a former party leader in the late 1950s and early 1960s, Deng Xiaoping, who became army chief of staff and then, briefly, prime minister. When Mao died in 1976, Maoist resistance was broken. Deng became the nation's new paramount leader, and China began its move toward the economic capitalism that now reigns in most of the nation today.

⚐ PRACTICE AND REVIEW ONLINE

CRITICAL THINKING QUESTIONS

1. Why should we avoid identifying socialism with Communism?

2. What contending tendencies exist within moderate left-of-center ideology? When do shared values bridge the gap, and when do they not?

3. Why do people sometimes classify classical liberalism as "centrist" ideologically? When is that characterization somewhat appropriate? When is it wrong?

4. Why is it inaccurate to describe militant Islamism as Fascist? Over what values do the two ideologies contend? Under what circumstances might they cooperate?

5. When is religion a conservative force ideologically? When is it not? How do the values espoused by different religions explain the difference?

KEY TERMS

ideology, 140
left of center, 141
right of center, 141

Marxism-Leninism, 143
democratic socialism, 145
moderate left-of-center ideology, 148
green ideology, 150
classical liberalism, 152
communitarian, 154
conservative, 155
neoconservative, 157
ethnic ultranationalism, 158
Fascism, 158
militant Islamism, 160
theocracy, 160
Salafism, 163
jihad, 164

FURTHER READING

Ball, Terrence, and Richard Dagger. *Political Ideologies and the Democratic Ideal*, 4th ed. New York: Longman, 2002.

Baradat, Leon P. *Political Ideologies: Their Origins and Impact*, 7th ed. Upper Saddle River, NJ: Prentice Hall, 2000.

Ingersoll, David E., and Richard K. Matthews. *The Philosophical Roots of Modern Ideology*, 2nd ed. Inglewood Cliffs, NJ: Prentice Hall, 1991.

Kramnick, Isaac, and Frederick M. Wadkins. The *Age of Ideology: Political Thought, 1750 to the Present*. Englewood Cliffs, NJ: Prentice Hall, 1979.

Love, Nancy S., ed. *Dogmas and Dreams: A Reader in Modern Political Ideologies*, 3rd ed. Washington, DC: CQ Press, 2006.

Macridis, Roy C., and Mark Hulliung. *Contemporary Political Ideologies*, 6th ed. New York: Pearson Longman, 1996.

McCullough, H. B., ed. *Political Ideologies and Political Philosophies*, 2nd ed. Toronto: Thompson, 1995.

Sargent, Lyman Tower. *Contemporary Political Ideologies: A Comparative Analysis*, 12th ed. Belmont, CA: Wadsworth Thomson, 2003.

NOTES

[1] *Collected Works of V.I. Lenin* (New York: International Publishers, 1927).

[2] For example, Edward Bernstein, *Evolutionary Socialism: a Criticism and Affirmation* (New York: Schocken Books, 1961).

[3] For example, early twentieth-century British "Fabian socialism," which contributed to the founding of the British Labor Party. Key early twentieth-century writers in the Fabian socialist tradition in Britain are R. H. Tawney, Sidney and Beatrice Webb, and Harold Laski.

[4] In the United States, environmental awareness spread with Rachel Carson's *Silent Spring* (Greenwich, CT: Fawcett Publications, 1962), focused especially on pollution of rivers and streams.

[5] For example, the work of the American Betty Friedan, *The Feminine Mystique* (New York: Norton, 1974) and the Frenchwoman Simone de Beauvoir, *The Second Sex* (New York: Alfred A. Knopf, 1993).

[6] For the anti-patriarchal side of feminism, see Kate Millett, *Sexual Politics* (Garden City, NY: Doubleday, 1970). For the relationship-preserving side, called "difference feminism," see Carol Gilligan, *In a Different Voice: Psychological Theory and Women's Development* (Cambridge, MA: Harvard University Press, 1993).

[7] ISIL stands for Islamic State of Iraq and the Levant; the Levant is the traditional name for the whole area encompassing present-day Syria, Jordan, Lebanon, and Israel. This name was used by some members of the group itself in its early days. The alternative acronym, ISIS, stands for Islamic State of Iraq and Syria or Islamic State of Iraq and al-Sham (equivalent to "the Levant").

[8] *In the Shade of the Quran*, trans. M. A. Salahi and A. A. Shamis (Riyadh, Saudi Arabia: World Assembly of Muslim Youth, 1979), and *Social Justice in Islam*, trans. John B. Hardie (New York: Octagon Books, 1970).

[9] Arguments for devotion to the nation may be vigorously presented and elaborated, as they were, for example, by the Italian patriot Giuseppe Mazzini in mid-nineteenth-century Italy; see *The Duties of Man* (London: Chapman and Hall, 1862).

SOCIETY AND POLITICS

I — PART

II — PART

III — PART

IV — PART

V — PART

Political Economy

FOCUS QUESTIONS

- **WHAT** are the main functions that government performs in relation to the economy?

- **WHAT** services do governments typically provide?

- **WHAT** are the main approaches to economic policy?

- **HOW** did the economic and financial crisis that started in 2008 come about?

- **WHAT** do political economists who support the Keynesian and monetarist approaches propose to do about the recent financial crisis?

BY THE MID-2000s IN THE UNITED STATES and Europe, a "perfect storm" was brewing in the financial world. First, a trend of growing inequality since the 1970s had accelerated in the 2000s, producing floods of investment capital at the top that roamed the world in pursuit of higher returns. One result of this was a real estate **bubble** of highly inflated property values in the United States and parts of Europe (especially Spain and Ireland). A second, related factor was a big expansion of borrowing and investing by households and financial enterprises after 2000, much of it to try to profit from the real estate boom in one way or another. And thirdly, governments had failed to effectively regulate the financial system in three major areas: (a) mortgage lending, where borrower requirements had deteriorated, (b) the packaging and sale of complicated and poorly understood investment products based on mortgages, many of which were going into default, and (c) credit insurance on these bonds and other investments, which gave buyers confidence that their lending or investments could never end up costing them, a confidence that turned out to be unfounded (see "Contention and Cooperation in Focus").

When the real estate bubble burst in 2008—as all bubbles eventually do—the general absence of regulation meant that banks, other lenders and investors, and credit insurance issuers did not have adequate reserves set aside for a rainy day of widespread default on credit. The collapse in the market value of widely held bonds and other investments that were directly or indirectly based on mortgage loans led to the failure of a major American investment bank,

Lehman Brothers. Almost immediately after this, a huge multinational insurance company that had issued a lot of credit insurance, American Insurance Group (AIG), had to be bailed out by the U.S. government. Banks and other financial corporations, fearing big losses, lost confidence in one another and in many of their own assets, and lending froze up. Stock markets plummeted and much wealth evaporated. A sharp economic downturn followed, with big jumps in unemployment.

When many unemployed homeowners were unable to make their mortgage payments, banks took ownership of their homes (called foreclosure). They then tried to sell the homes into a very weak housing market, depressing real estate prices further in a vicious circle of continuing decline in property values. In addition, the downturn was further intensified as fearful businesses and consumers with incomes chose to forego spending in favor of paying down the debt that they had accumulated during the 2000s, causing further layoffs. We were off and running into the "great recession" and slump that began in 2008–2009 and continued in Europe into 2015.

It has been evident for a long time now that economic problems are affected by politics. At each step in the unfolding of the great recession, political contention and cooperation played a role in the development of these conditions. Clearly, an important topic in the domain of politics is political economy.

POLITICO-ECONOMIC SYSTEMS

A lot of politics and policymaking concern the economy. There are two main contending policy approaches to solving problems with economic implications. On one side are the free marketers who generally oppose government economic intervention in markets. On the other side are moderate left-of-center views that tend to support government intervention to solve economically related problems. More specifically, what do the two approaches favor, when do they contend sharply, and when can they cooperate? It is this dimension of political contention and cooperation that this chapter takes up.

For much of the last century, governmental approaches to the economy were more diverse than they are now. In today's political economy, markets play the leading role in economic coordination. The state's role is to modify the market where necessary. But the period from World War I through most of the twentieth century included prominent examples of state-led politico-economic models, too. Before launching into today's main contending approaches to issues affecting the economy, we will briefly discuss some of these patterns from the past that led up to the current context.

State-Led Economic Models

The international terrain heavily influenced political economy in the early twentieth century. The great colonial empires of the British, French, Dutch, and Portuguese were each somewhat insulated from each other. Each empire's colonies fed the raw materials produced by their farms and mines to London, Paris, etc., where they were turned into finished products. It was in the northern hubs that the empires' financial and technological resources were concentrated.

The colonial powers were not inclined to spread resources and expertise in the developing world further than was necessary to maintain and draw on their colonial possessions (see "Concept in Context").

CONCEPT IN CONTEXT | Colonial Rule

Colonial rule dominated the developing areas of Africa and Asia through the first half of the twentieth century. Rule was hierarchical in bureaucratic fashion, with some variations. In France's possessions, the French ran things right down to the local level, while the British favored "indirect rule," employing native chiefly figures at the local level of their rule.

The Main Colonial Powers and their Imperial Areas (with today's names):

Britain	East and southern Africa, south and Southeast Asia, parts of the Middle East
France	West Africa, part of Southeast Asia, parts of the Middle East
The Netherlands	Indonesia in Southeast Asia
Portugal	Angola and Mozambique in southern Africa
Belgium	Congo in central Africa
Germany	Cameroun in West Africa, Namibia in southern Africa, and Tanzania in East Africa

The British, French, Belgian, Dutch, and Portuguese colonial administrators wanted especially to preserve or expand the supply of raw materials, such as sugar, tea, coffee, or the products of mines (e.g., copper, iron, or diamonds) to the metropolitan countries. Investments in infrastructure such as roads, rails, and electricity were focused only on the commodity-producing locales, the main ports, and the neighborhoods where the colonial administrators lived. Economic benefits to the native population in these areas were uneven due to the rise and fall of world commodity prices.

Colonized areas thus missed out on the steady ground-level modernization (e.g., urbanization, industrialization, education, modern communications, and a growing middle class) that Europe and

North America had experienced in the nineteenth and early twentieth centuries. In most areas, the traditional cultural focus on status in the clan or tribe, and economically on food grains for nutrition, tended to restrain the growth of individualism and risk-taking for profit in cash crops. Especially in commercialized colonial areas, downturns due to agricultural disruption (e.g., drought), drops in world prices for agricultural exports, or other economic distress could lead to widespread malnutrition and land sales by small landholders to wealthier landowners. Many lost their land altogether and lived as either landless laborers or as sharecropping tenants, turning over 40–60 percent of the crop to the landowner. Over time, growing numbers fled rural poverty in favor of urban shantytowns (in Brazil called "favelas"), where people had somewhat better access to commercial opportunities but lacked sanitation, clean water, and electricity.

Especially in the decade after World War II, nationalist resistance began to arise in the colonized developing world. The spread of new forms of communication (especially the transistor radio) fostered greater awareness in the colonies of what life was like in London, Paris, Lisbon, or Amsterdam. The gap between there and here was stark. Anticolonial resistance leaders fed rising expectations that if colonial rule could be thrown off, development would take off and the new nation would charge into the modern world.

By the 1950s, for their part many Europeans felt increasingly uncomfortable with their empires. They had just fought World War II to defeat imperialism, and the United Nations had been born partly around the goal of national self-determination. Resistance by independence movements increased the costs of colonial rule, and in the end there was little durable enthusiasm for maintaining it. Most often peacefully, but sometimes pressed by mass protests and insurgent military efforts, the colonial administrators finally withdrew in the 1950s and 1960s.

In the decades after World War II came decolonization, which was followed by a new agenda: gradual movement toward freer trade and globalization. To be sure, the financial and technological advantages of Europe and North America remained, along with the developing nations' main role as suppliers of cheap raw materials to the industrialized northern economies. But now it was without the partitioning of the world that had characterized the earlier colonial period.

Both before and after decolonization, though, the developing world saw the rise of economic nationalist leaders of various sorts. They wanted to see their countries modernize and share in advanced development, especially in industrialization. Standing in the way, to some extent, was the status quo of mainly European and North American dominance in exports of finished goods. In this situation, numerous nationalist leaders in less-developed countries favored economic development paths that were more independent of the world market economy. That seemed to require models of modernization and development in which the state played a strong role. Usually in these cases, state-driven politico-economic coordination took one of four prominent forms: the Soviet-style command economy, the Fascist model, the state-led development approach, and the export-based approach.

Command-Economy Bureaucratic Socialism As we saw in chapter 6, the old Soviet system with its Marxist-Leninist ideology had virtually the whole productive economy owned by the state. Every economic sector had its ministry in the executive branch of government in Moscow. The system ran according to a detailed plan produced by the planning ministry of the government, in consultation with top managers in the various economic sectors. Middle-level and top managers were expected to be members of the Communist Party, but actual decision making in enterprises was largely top-down through the managerial hierarchies of the executive ministries. It was primarily in the nation's capital, Moscow, that top Communist Party officials indicated what directions they wanted ministerial policies to take.[1]

This model encountered major difficulties. To be sure, the state could command a rapid industrialization, as occurred in the early 1930s in the Soviet Union. But the system amounted to a huge network of interdependent monopolies. When a production problem occurred, there were no competitors to turn to. Any slowdowns tended to become bottlenecks that held up both those using the product and the suppliers feeding its production. Second, heavy centralization of decision making meant that often problems and disputes could not be resolved where they arose. Rather, they tended to be kicked upstairs through the party and government hierarchies, producing at least delay and often inaction. Third, the system could not easily innovate. Technological change meant interrupting the plan, causing the manager to fail to meet the quota. And by the last half of the 1980s, world prices were plunging for Russia's main sustaining export, oil. By the end of the decade, shortages and long lines for food and basic consumer goods increasingly irritated the public. By the early 1990s, the traditional Soviet model had largely disappeared with the fall of Communism in Eastern Europe and the Soviet Union.

Fascist State Coordination A second state-led approach could be found in the years leading up to World War II under Fascist governments such as those of Germany, Italy, and Japan. They envied the imperial status of the established colonial powers, and took control of their economies to prepare for war. As we saw in chapter 6, the bulk of the economy was privately owned, but in each case the ruling party made sure that it had friends within the leaderships of important corporations to influence them. Whether sectors of industry participated in formal coordinating bodies in the executive branch (as in Mussolini's "corporative" state; see Country Case Studies, chapter 6), or mainly in more informal councils, they had little choice but to cooperate with government strategies. Large-scale corruption could be rampant, but so long as managers and owners cooperated with the governmental leadership, they were shielded from problems. Intense nationalism prevailed. The defeat of Fascism in World War II more or less doomed this model in its fully developed form. However, milder versions of it seem to be emerging in Russia and China.

Import Substitution Industrialization (ISI) and North-South Relations In the world's south, from the 1930s on in Latin America and from the 1960s on in Africa and Asia after independence from colonial rule, milder forms of state-led development were prominent. Why so? The story begins in the colonial era. Again, the colonial powers saw developing countries merely as suppliers of raw materials for export. Crops, metals, and other minerals fetched fluctuating (and often low) prices in world commodity markets. Manufactured goods were imported from the northern developed countries for upper-strata consumers. When colonialism came to an end, in the early nineteenth century in Latin America and the mid-twentieth century in Africa and Asia, these basic economic relations remained in place between the world's developed north and the poor and undeveloped south. Political sociologist Immanuel Wallerstein thus stressed the inequality between the northern "core" of what he called the "world system," and the southern, dependent "periphery" of poor countries.[2]

The answer in many developing nations was the **import substitution industrialization** (ISI) model. The idea here was for industrialization, fostered and protected by the state, to substitute domestic products for foreign imports in local markets. In many countries from the 1930s on in Latin America and the 1960s on elsewhere, government subsidies and new state-owned enterprises aimed to expand labor-intensive domestic industrialization. Meanwhile, **tariffs**—taxes on imports—would keep import prices high, so domestic producers of the same goods could undercut the imports' prices. Often regulations also served to limit imports. Meanwhile, the state invested heavily in infrastructure—roads, rails, energy, and communications facilities. The hoped-for result would be modernization, self-sufficient prosperity, and near-full employment. ISI represented a rejection of the colonial and neocolonial relationships between developing countries and the world market.

Over time, however, this model ran into major difficulties. Factories could be built, but they often lacked the spare parts and expertise to make them work efficiently. And corruption was often endemic. But the most prominent problem was the cost. Keeping people employed in development projects was popular but expensive, and developing nations often were not very effective at collecting taxes to pay for them. To help cover deficits and pay for projects, governments either had their central banks print money—often producing rapidly rising **inflation** (prices rising faster than production)—or went heavily into debt to international lenders, or both.

The debt problems of developing nations paved the way for new modes of economic influence by the world's north. When developing countries' international debt payments could not be made, national governments had to negotiate with their northern financial creditors, through their bargaining agent, the IMF. As a condition for further northern aid and restructuring of debt to reduce payments, the IMF imposed reductions in state-led development: dropping regulations and tariffs on imports, privatizing state-owned enterprises, and cutting budget deficits, especially via big reductions in government spending. These cuts in government subsidies, state ownership, and tariff protection in developing countries tended to disadvantage domestic producers in competing with the imports domestically and for export markets internationally. The resulting globalization tended to restore the advantages of the technologically advanced northern producers in world trade, and shift the developing economies back toward their old (under colonialism) roles of supplying the north with needed raw materials. (For more on this aspect of political economy, see chapter 17's section on the relative economic power of individual nations over the course of the last century of globalization.)

Export-Led Development Another model had the state focus its coordination and subsidies on the development of strategic export sectors. In the postwar period in East Asia, we saw a few examples of what could be called the export-led development model. Examples of what Wallerstein called the "semi-periphery" were Japan, the postwar "Asian Tigers" of South Korea, Taiwan, Hong Kong and Singapore, and eventually China. Japan had already substantially industrialized prior to World War II, and its postwar recovery focused on producing a wide range of modern manufactured goods. South Korea did, too, eventually focusing especially on consumer electronics and computer-related products (e.g., Samsung's memory chips, flat-screen TVs, and smartphones). Taiwan's special corner was computer-related technology (e.g., motherboards for personal computers). The city-states of Hong Kong and Singapore aimed to provide financial services for the region. By the 2000s, the Chinese were producing almost anything that could be exported.

In these cases, the role of the state in development was typically less extensive than in the above models, but still strategic. It prioritized the private export sector to help manufacturers and service providers build footholds in world markets. In addition to providing subsidies (especially low-interest loans) to strategic export industries to get them off the ground, the government focused on building modern infrastructure for transportation, energy, and communication, and on education to provide a high-tech-capable workforce. Government industrial policymaking consulted and cooperated with exporting industries, coordinating the export effort.

In these particular countries, the state did not have to shoulder much of the burden of a social safety net. Their societies were broadly influenced by Confucian cultural traditions (see chapter 5), which emphasized extended family support, employer paternalism, and household saving rather than spending. Thus governments could keep welfare costs and taxes fairly low.

Capital supply was also aided by identity-related investment by ethnic Japanese, Korean, and Chinese entrepreneurs who had emigrated to other countries in the Pacific basin and operated successful businesses there. They had money and wanted nothing more than to be able to invest in their ancestral homes, where they could visit relatives and business associates and speak the language. For prosperity, these economies' growth relied not on domestic consumption—again, their people tended to be savers rather than spenders—but rather on foreign demand for their goods. Politics was characterized by strong single-party dominance.

The Present: Market-Led Political Economy and Globalization

In most countries today, wealth and income are distributed primarily by the private market economy. A major historical factor behind this prevalent situation has been globalization. In the 1980s and 1990s, nations made new agreements for freer trade: first the General Agreement on Tariffs and Trade (GATT) in the late 1980s, and then the establishment of the World Trade Organization (WTO) in the 1990s, to apply the new rules. These measures called for reducing or eliminating tariffs (taxes on imports), regulations, and government subsidies that had previously protected national producers.

These changes increasingly opened most nations' markets to much freer competition from the world's most advantaged producers. In the third quarter of the twentieth century, globalization's early winners were the traditional northern developed nations with advanced technology (see chapter 17). But increasingly, export gains also came to rising developing nations with cheaper labor but strengthening technology and adequate infrastructure (e.g., South Korea, Taiwan, and China). Over time, some local companies and jobs in both the world's North and South were displaced by the successful imports. In this context, many businesses in the developed northern nations argued that for them to be competitive in this new world of relatively free trade, their own domestic taxes and regulations should be reduced.

THE HUMAN RIGHTS CONNECTION | The U.N.'s Economic/Social Covenant

When the United Nations codified human rights principles in 1966, it produced an economic and social Covenant alongside the civil-political one. The International Covenant on Economic, Social, and Cultural Rights (ICESCR) set forth rights to access to things that are important to everyone. In its portions related to economic security, for example, the economic-social Covenant provides for a right to an "adequate standard of living" with regard to food, clothing, and housing. It also supports rights to health care, education, and employment under fair conditions.

Unlike the U.N.'s civil-political Covenant, however, the ICESCR does not impose direct obligations on signatory nations to provide laws implementing these rights. Instead, it declares only a general obligation to "take steps" to "progressively" realize its goals, "to the maximum of available resources."

In addition, the Covenant recognizes the need for "international assistance and cooperation" in attaining "the continuous improvement of living conditions" over time.

This limited form of obligation to fulfill economic-social human rights reflects the size of the problem and the barriers to addressing it. The world contains numerous nations with large populations of very poor people. Providing for economic security across the globe could require the transfer of substantial resources that are not easily available to most governments. This is especially true given today's global economic competition, resource scarcities, and government debt problems. In effect, what the ICESCR does is provide agreed-upon operational definitions of a range of well-being values, and urge signatory nations to move policy in their direction.

Still, though, some resources are distributed by government policies. How much influence should the state have, and what forms should it take? For example, should government policy focus on overall economic production and growth? Or, should its primary effort be to aid groups that are significantly disadvantaged by market outcomes, as was emphasized in the U.N.'s economic/social Covenant of human rights (see "The Human Rights Connection")? Or both? How should environmental, consumer safety, and financial system problems be dealt with? Now we turn to today's main contending lines of thinking on such questions.

ECONOMIC POLICY TODAY

Today political economy includes a wide range of government activities that affect the economy, typically involving domestic spending, taxation, and regulation. These activities address many policy areas, such as education, transportation, the environment, the financial system, relief for people in economic distress (social welfare), and economic growth in general. Here we define economic policy broadly, to include all of these policy areas and approaches.

Policies affecting the economy, like those in other policy categories, are aimed at least partly at public values. We tend to think first of well-being values, such as overall prosperity, minimal economic security, public health and safety, environmental protection, and the development of individuals' capacities. But economic policy can also engage other values, too, such as equality (whether of opportunity, results, or treatment by law), entrepreneurial freedom of individuals and enterprises in economic activity, justice as social justice in economic distribution or criminal justice for white-collar lawbreakers, and order in the form of overall economic and financial stability.

As was noted above, approaches to the various areas of economic policy involve two primary schools of thought contending with each other. On one side are the entrepreneurial freedom supporters, who favor reducing state involvement in the economy. Their general resistance to taxation, government spending, and regulation is considered ideologically right of center (see chapter 6). The following discussion of policy areas refers to them as "free marketers." For the other main contending school of thought, we borrow a label from chapter 6: "moderate left of center" (MLC). This approach supports what it considers moderate government interventions to solve problems affecting the economy.

Again, the contention between free marketers and moderate left-of-center supporters involves a spectrum rather than a bright line between two categories. There are degrees of intensity in each segment of the continuum, and there is a centrist area in the middle. Under certain circumstances, compromise and cooperation are quite possible between the contending orientations. At other times, contention reigns and cooperation seems almost impossible.

We first examine particular government activities and the contending approaches toward them. Then we take up the main contending strategies at the more general level of overall approaches toward government spending, taxation, and the supply of money for bank lending.

Social Welfare Spending

A major goal of government spending on social welfare is assuring minimal well-being to such groups as the elderly, the unemployed, the ill, and the poor. But how much should a government do in such policy areas as pensions for the elderly, unemployment benefits, job training, health insurance, and food and housing aid to those who need it? And how will the state provide these benefits? These activities involve an element of **redistribution**, transferring resources from the economically better-off to the less advantaged of a society. As you can see in Figure 7.1, in the last century such spending has grown more rapidly in times of economic downturn and stress, and leveled off somewhat in times of normal economic growth.

As we saw in chapter 6, the moderate left-of-center school of thought supports such spending, especially regarding two main values: (a) well-being as minimal economic security for disadvantaged groups and (b) social justice as opportunity for living-wage jobs for the unemployed. Moderate left-of-center advocates view both minimal economic security and social justice as valuable for all citizens, noting that people at every income level can experience economic reversals. They believe that people want to know that if a disaster happens, society will preserve their chance to attain a better future (see "The Philosophical Connection").

Moreover, moderate left-of-center supporters suggest that helping those who are comparatively disadvantaged serves the material prosperity of society as a whole. People with low incomes must put the bulk of their income into consumer spending on the basics. Thus aiding them supports local businesses and overall economic activity. Regarding health insurance, moderate left-of-center advocates make two arguments. First, they suggest that government support for universal health insurance can contribute to reducing medical costs via preventive and early stage medical interventions that help to avoid expensive curative care later. Second, moderate left-of-center supporters argue that universal coverage frees up household and enterprise money for consumer and business spending that would otherwise have to be set aside to cover present and future health costs.

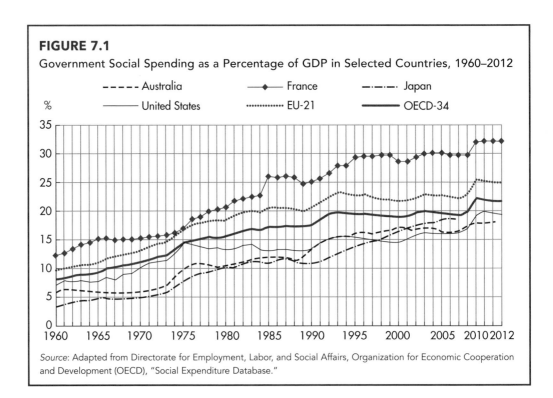

FIGURE 7.1

Government Social Spending as a Percentage of GDP in Selected Countries, 1960–2012

Source: Adapted from Directorate for Employment, Labor, and Social Affairs, Organization for Economic Cooperation and Development (OECD), "Social Expenditure Database."

THE PHILOSOPHICAL CONNECTION | John Rawls

For many, economic security is uncertain. The American political philosopher John Rawls (1921–2002) defined justice as fairness, and considered the question of what it meant for society to treat people fairly, especially the least advantaged.

To understand justice as fairness, Rawls argued, we must think of ourselves as determining what the basic structure of society ought to be like, from a special standpoint: what he called the "original position." The goal of this imaginary situation is to assure impartiality in our choice of social arrangements. Rawls assured impartiality by requiring that the decision be made behind a "veil of ignorance" about ourselves and our situation. In the original position, the chooser is not allowed to know anything about his or her own abilities, socioeconomic position, or even preferred life pursuits. This means that once the arrangements are set, choosers might find themselves at the bottom of society, the top, or anywhere in between. Thus, the original choice of the structure of society and its policies will be fair, without personal favoritism.

Because the chooser could end up at the bottom, Rawls argued, he or she would *not* approve a utilitarian solution (see chapter 5) in which some people must suffer in order to achieve the greatest overall sum of pleasures over pains. Instead, rational individuals would favor arrangements that benefited everyone. Thus a logical baseline option is the idea of equal distribution of things of value to everyone so that no one has to sacrifice. One might reject that and choose inequality, but to do so one must have a reason why things would work out better even for those at the bottom, whom Rawls referred to as "the least advantaged."

First, however, what things are important to everyone, and can be distributed by society? For Rawls, the "social primary goods" fall into three categories: (a) rights and freedoms, (b) positions of authority in organizations, and (c) income and wealth. Freedoms such as civil liberties must be allocated first because we need freedom in order to pursue any other goals that we might have. In allocating individual freedoms, Rawls stuck with equality, seeing no advantage to the idea of unequal distribution. Freedoms of expression, association, etc. are assured only when everyone has them equally, so the goal would be the greatest workable extent of such freedoms that can be assured to everyone equally.

Regarding the distribution of positions of authority, Rawls assumed that a rational chooser would have society permit inequality because everyone would be worse off without directors and managerial hierarchies in organizations. But that leads to another question: how to fairly distribute *opportunity* for people to *gain* positions of authority. Again, equality is the answer—equality of opportunity. For Rawls, this goal required more than merely protecting people from discrimination (e.g., based on race, religion, or age). Remaining socioeconomic disadvantages might still leave talented and motivated people unable to compete effectively. Education and extra recruitment efforts must be provided to achieve "fair equality of opportunity": actually equal chances for those with the same talent and motivation.

For Rawls, this still leaves a third key area for distribution: income and wealth. Even if individual freedoms and fair equality of opportunity are in place, people with less natural ability are at a disadvantage regardless of their willingness to strive. Here, however, Rawls argued that the approach of equality of income and wealth was unsatisfactory. Pursuing equal economic distribution dampens entrepreneurial incentives, so that incomes drop for everyone, including the least advantaged. Inequality can foster innovation and dynamism in ways that help even the least advantaged. But if equal results would actually reduce income levels of the least advantaged, then the opposite extreme—more inequality than is necessary to raise the least advantaged position—is also unjust and would require a degree of redistribution. The answer in each case is only enough inequality to maximize the minimum.

Certainly we might question how realistic it is to expect people to consciously transport their minds into Rawls's "original position." However, their surrounding circumstances in society might be one factor. Given a stable society, the psychological leap might be especially challenging. But the financial and economic crisis of 2008 reminded people around the world that the risk of reversals of fortune can be very real. In the United States, for example, many experienced a simultaneous loss of job, health insurance, and home, while others saw their retirement funds disappear. Thinking about Rawls's original position does not seem so far-fetched. The debate about whether and how to "maximize the minimum," in Rawls's phrase, continues.

The free-market school of thought opposes state intervention in the market economy, and thus seeks to reduce social welfare spending. Free marketers suggest that welfare spending requires either (a) taxation, which they see as drawing off money that would be better allocated to consumption, savings, and investment by citizens and businesses, or (b) government borrowing, which free marketers see as drawing money out of the credit supply that might otherwise be available for business investment. Regarding the recipients, free marketers suggest that household economic distress is often due to poor motivation to work and save. Social welfare support, they argue, encourages dependency. They suggest that if unemployment support is too strong, people who cannot find work in their current fields may resist switching to lower-paying jobs in other fields.

In response especially to this last point, some northern European governments (e.g., Germany in 2005, Sweden in 2007, and Denmark in 2010), facing discouraging rates of long-term unemployment, significantly reduced their levels of unemployment compensation for those out of work for more than two years (though they continued other forms of aid for the unemployed). Notably, however, these countries also added positive incentives and job training to expand lower-wage employment. Some center-leaning left-of-center advocates cooperated with moderate free marketers in support of these measures.

State Provision of Goods and Services

Governments typically provide certain services to the people, and they may own resources and facilities for this purpose. For example, in the developed nations the state normally owns and runs the public schools, the main mail system, major roads, police protection, parks, and military bases. These **public goods** that serve the whole population tend to be impractical for the private market to provide profitably. Moderate left-of-center supporters and many free marketers tend to cooperate in maintaining these policies (see Table 7.1).

For some other goods that are essential for nearly everyone, provision may be either public or private. Examples of such public necessities include the railroads, communications networks (e.g., telephone systems), and electrical and water supply. Traditionally, these are viewed as natural monopolies; technically, the only

TABLE 7.1	Types of Government Involvement in Economic Enterprises	
Approach and Frequency	**Common Examples of Sectors**
State ownership (often as independent utilities)	Schools, mail, roads, police, parks, health insurance
Occasional state ownership	Electricity, water, autos, rails, phones, steel, oil, gas, some hospitals, and some broadcast media
Subsidy (selective)	Strategic manufacturing industry as well as research and development for industry
Regulation (selective)	Electricity, water, and many other policy sectors, public and private

viable way is to have just one producer for a local area, as in one landline telephone company or electric company. If the producer is privately owned, consumers could be vulnerable to the abuses of **monopoly**. Under monopoly conditions the sole producer of something everyone needs can dictate terms to consumers to maximize profits, perhaps leading to unaffordable prices for many and low quality.[3]

For supplying a public necessity that does not technically require monopoly, some moderate left-of-center advocates have suggested having the government own the main enterprise, or adding a state-owned (or partially state-owned) enterprise to compete alongside private ones to keep prices affordable and retain standards. For example, today the vast majority of developed countries have state-run universal health insurance systems.

In recent decades, however, free marketers in many countries have pressed successfully for partial or complete **privatization** of public enterprises: governments selling their state-owned enterprises to the private sector. They suggest that government regulation can maintain affordable prices and quality, as in the case of Dutch and Swiss health insurance, for example. Moreover, free marketers argue, sometimes technological change may to some extent undermine natural monopoly and allow for competition, as in the case of the mid-twentieth-century growth of crop transport by trucks (competing with railroads) and today's telephone services (cell phones competing with landline systems). If monopoly-related problems do arise, however, some free marketers will cooperate with moderate left-of-center advocates to allow regulation of the sector.

Other categories of enterprises have sometimes been partly or wholly state owned due to their large size and strategic importance for maintaining national prosperity. Examples include banking; the manufacturing of iron, steel, automobiles, and aircraft; basic fuels for energy production (e.g., oil and gas); and, in many developing nations in the twentieth century, the marketing of staple food grains. At least some state ownership in these sectors has been justified as helping the government keep prices affordable, reduce unemployment, stimulate broad economic prosperity, and steer investment in directions that better serve the needs of the entire economy.

In the energy sector, at times governments have taken ownership of an important and lucrative resource such as oil or gas. The stated purposes might be to keep the resource's price low for the nation's consumers, to keep it out of the hands of foreign-owned or **multinational corporations** (corporations with significant international operations), and/or to have ready access to the resource's revenues to support government programs while keeping taxes low. For example, Mexico nationalized its oil business in the 1930s, the Russian government regained ownership of oil and gas assets in the 2000s that had been partially privatized in the 1990s, and Argentina renationalized its oil company in 2012. At the extreme, some national government budgets are heavily dependent on state oil and gas exports (or royalties from private production).

In most of these sectors, free marketers oppose public ownership and provision of services. Again, they believe that private ownership produces the most efficient allocation of resources for overall economic well-being. Free marketers argue that for publicly owned enterprises, especially those in developing nations, goals such as insulation from politics, transparency, and efficiency tend not to be realized in practice. That is, they suggest that government provision of goods and services can be expensive, inefficient, and vulnerable to political overstaffing and diversion of resources to political supporters.

In recent decades, countries have mostly moved away from state ownership of all but the first category of activities noted above. In Europe, many previously state-owned enterprises in telecommunications, air transportation, energy, aircraft production, and automobile manufacturing, for example, have been privatized. Most post-Communist nations have privatized large sectors of their formerly state-owned economies. And in the developing nations, state ownership is much less common in recent decades than it was previously.

In the developed world today, most moderate left-of-center advocates support new state ownership only as an emergency move prompted by the risk of bankruptcy by a big employer or financial player. For example, in the financial crisis of 2008–2009, several governments took majority ownership of some banks that were failing. The purpose was to avoid the collapse of these and other banks that were owed money by the failing banks in a spreading contagion that could lead to the collapse of the whole financial system.

Such emergency moves are intended to be temporary to enable the banks to return to health by restructuring and disposing of their bad debts. In financial system crises, moderate left-of-center advocates and free marketers sometimes cooperate in support of such emergency actions. Once the economy has improved, the government can then sell its ownership stakes back to the private sector (as occurred in Sweden in the early 1990s and the United States in the early 2010s).

Subsidies

For governments wishing to influence a portion of the economy for national well-being, an alternative to state ownership is subsidy. Subsidies are grants, low-cost government loans, or special tax breaks for organizations and activities that serve the national interest. Most often, recipient enterprises are privately owned and run. For example, governments provide subsidies for such activities as medical education, job training, transportation improvements, production for national defense, and research and development (e.g., solar power research). A government may subsidize an enterprise in a strategic export industry, as in the case of major European governments giving aid to the European aircraft manufacturer Airbus to help it compete with American aircraft manufacturer Boeing. Or governments may provide housing subsidies for low-income people for social justice reasons and the desire to keep the nation's housing in decent condition.

Another form of subsidy comes into play during a financial crisis. It involves a government giving a large employer temporary low-interest loans to keep it from going bankrupt and increasing unemployment. Recent examples include American aid to General Motors in 2008 and 2009, and French government loans to automakers Renault and Citroen in 2009. In this period, moderate left-of-center advocates and many conservatives cooperated in supporting such temporary subsidies (again, most often in the form of low-interest loans) to banks, some other businesses, and local governments. The shared aim was to preserve bank lending, jobs, and consumer spending by preventing the recession from becoming a depression. Where state ownership of enterprises remains widespread, as in parts of China, many state-owned enterprises need ongoing government subsidies to stay afloat.

Governments can also provide subsidies less directly, by reducing taxes for businesses or consumers who are engaged in activities that the government judges to be in the public interest. Examples of these "tax subsidies" include tax cuts for companies or consumers who adopt energy-conserving technologies or pursue alternative energy development (e.g., solar or wind power), for employers providing health insurance to their employees, or for small employers struggling to comply with a law increasing the minimum wage that must be paid to workers.

Free marketers usually oppose subsidies, arguing that they distort the marketplace and contribute to inefficient resource allocation. They question the ability of government policymakers to know what the real priorities of the nation should be. In developing nations, free marketers stress that subsidies can amount to payoffs in return for political support. Again, advocates of subsidies reply that most subsidies meet real needs of large numbers of people, support public goals, and/or maintain the prosperity of communities. Here, too, at times areas of cooperation and compromise can be found between the contending sides.

Regulation

A third broad area of economic policy is **regulatory policy**: applying rules to the economy. Many economic regulations pursue such well-being values as public health, consumer safety, environmental health, and overall prosperity. Others are concerned with forms of justice such as economic or financial fairness. Regulations may protect society against financial crime and fraud, as well as against practices that can lead to overall financial collapse. Among the causes of the financial crisis of 2008 and 2009 (and deep recession that followed), for many analysts, was the failure of American regulatory agencies in the late 1990s and the 2000s to adequately regulate mortgage lending, the packaging of a variety of popular but complicated and poorly understood financial investment products, and the market for credit insurance (insuring bonds and other investments against default and loss). In effect, critics argued, there had been too much cooperation between regulators and financial enterprises, and not enough contention (see "Contention and Cooperation in Focus"). When excesses in these markets caused them to nearly collapse, the world financial system was deeply shaken.

As we saw above, in the provision of public necessities such as health insurance and electrical and water supply, if government does not own the resource it must regulate the private providers to maintain affordability and quality of service. In another example, many European governments have traditionally regulated their labor markets to protect workers against arbitrary dismissal or unfair treatment in the workplace.

Another regulatory area is environmental policy. Increasingly, moderate left-of-center advocates favor not only addressing traditional problems like pollution of the air and water, but also trying to reduce carbon emissions to slow global warming. They argue that continuing reliance on traditional energy resources such as coal, oil, and gas, which produce earth-warming greenhouse gases, can lead to widespread drought and water shortage, weather extremes, and sea level rise.

Free-market opponents of regulations regard them as often unnecessary and ineffective. They suggest that regulations often restrict the development of new products and innovative practices. Critics also question the workability of some regulations. They note that individuals and enterprises often find ingenious ways of getting around the rules. Today, a few free marketers have even challenged some of the empirical science on which regulatory arguments are based—for example, the climate science pointing to global warming (about which there is now little scientific disagreement).

CONTENTION AND COOPERATION IN FOCUS | Financial Regulation and the Crisis of 2008–2009

As the financial crisis of 2008–2009 unfolded, many observers wondered if failures of financial regulation were among its chief causes. One of the major lessons learned from the onset of the Great Depression of the 1930s was the need for strong government regulation of various investment markets to prevent deceptive practices and excesses that can lead to shocks, losses, and the possibility of spreading collapse. But this requires regulatory laws and government regulators who are willing to contend with financial businesses, and not always cooperate with them. In the period from the mid-1990s through the mid-2000s, a mood of deregulation prevailed, characterized primarily by cooperation between lawmakers, regulators, and financial enterprises wherever finance was becoming a big part of economic output (e.g., New York, London, and Dublin). Had there been more contention between government and finance, could the crisis have been averted or limited? There were four major areas of financial activity about which this question was raised.

1. **Mortgage lending.** The early and middle 2000s was a period of boom and rapidly rising values in real estate, especially in the United States. With so much money being made from home ownership and mortgage lending, governments failed to regulate mortgage lending practices. Once homeowners had signed for their "adjustable rate" mortgages, the mortgage companies immediately sold their mortgages to investment bankers at a profit. So the mortgage sellers stopped worrying about whether the homeowner could ultimately afford the mortgage payments later when, after three years or so, the interest rate zoomed upward. (If the homeowner could not afford the new payments, they could always sell the house at a profit into the booming market, yes?) Again, buyers and sellers cooperated, and the shoddy practices of "subprime" mortgage lending went under the radar of regulators.

2. **Investment bonds related to mortgages.** In turn, the investment companies buying the mortgages intended to repackage them in complex collections for resale to investors as bonds. So these investment bankers were also happy to cooperate, failing to ask tough questions of the mortgage bankers about the credit worthiness of the underlying borrowers. The government failed to require full disclosure to investors, and the new bonds and other related securities often concealed many bad mortgages under the good ones in the bundles that the investments were based on. The private agencies that rated the soundness of these investment vehicles were paid their fees by the securities' creators, who could choose the rating agency giving the most positive reviews. Not surprisingly, rating agencies were quite cooperative, regularly issuing solid ratings for the safety of the mortgage-backed securities without looking seriously into them. When the real estate bubble burst and many homeowners could not make payments, the mortgage-based investment products rapidly lost value, and investors (and banks left with unsold portfolios) suffered huge losses.

As to labor market regulation, many employers have argued that it deprives them of the flexibility they need to lay people off in response to an economic downturn. The result may be a disinclination to hire new workers when the economy turns upward. In recent years, some nations in Europe have got around those regulations through a category of "temporary workers" (or alternatively, "contract workers") who lack the full range of benefits and protections against easy layoff. In supporting the deregulation of labor markets, free marketers also highlight the aim of reducing youth and long-term unemployment.

Taxation

Government spending requires that governments collect revenue in some fashion, mainly through taxes. But who and what should be taxed? Should taxes fall

3. **Reserve requirements for financial enterprises.** Commercial and investment banks had found ways of getting around requirements to keep 10 percent or more of their assets in fairly "liquid" (quickly cashable) reserves in case of a rash of defaults (failures to repay) by their borrowers or bond issuers. And by 2008 they did much of their speculative trading with money that they themselves had borrowed. When the crisis hit and credit froze up in late 2008, many of these short-term loans were called, and the financial enterprises found themselves woefully short of capital.

4. **Insurance on loans and investments.** One of the reasons why enterprises borrowed and lent huge amounts of money without the protection of adequate reserves was that the opportunity had arisen of buying affordable *insurance* on their loans, bonds, and other investments. If a loan, bond, or other investment goes into default or otherwise loses value, the holder of the credit insurance can claim, from the issuer of the insurance, compensation for part or all of the loss.* Such credit insurance seemed to greatly reduce the risks of lending and investing. It made lenders and investors overconfident, contributing to a long-building explosion of credit worldwide. But all this turned out to be false confidence. Government had failed to regulate this obscure but large market for insuring loans, bonds, and other forms of credit/investment (the only major type of insurance not to be regulated). Consequently, the insurers, mostly big banks (and the huge insurance company, AIG) were not required to hold enough money in reserve for a rainy day of numerous credit defaults coming all at once. When the housing bubble burst and mortgage default became widespread, the insurers typically did not have the money to pay claims on the failed mortgage-based bonds and related investment securities. Thus the financial viability of these banks and other insurers was threatened. For their part, the lenders and investors were shocked to discover that the insurance they had purchased might be worthless, and pulled back from investing and lending.

To be sure, an attempt had been made in the late 1990s by a key independent regulator in the American executive branch, Brooksley Born, to initiate regulation of credit insurance. But as we shall see in chapter 14, her effort to contend with the status quo was suppressed by the chairman of the American central bank, powerful conservative lawmakers (of the Republican Party), the top American executive leadership (of the moderate left-of-center Democratic Party), and lobbyists for the financial firms. Today, regulators are continuing to struggle to make effective rules under new American legislation to address the ills that contributed to the recent Great Recession.

---

* Such an insurance policy was given an odd name; it was called a "credit default swap" (CDS). You could even buy such insurance on a bond that you did not own. In this case, the only reason for making such CDS payments was as a bet that default will occur, enabling you to profit by being compensated afterwards.

mainly on individual incomes, corporations' incomes, or wealth? Should taxes be applied to commercial transactions, whether between businesses—called **value-added taxes**—or between retail businesses and consumers, called **sales taxes**? Here the key values are (a) justice, in the form of fairness to people and enterprises, and (b) well-being, in the forms of overall economic prosperity and/or minimum household viability.

Supporters and critics of these different policy directions debate what effects they will have on those who are taxed, and on the overall performance of the economy. Moderate left-of-center advocates argue that when tax money is spent to provide for public needs, it goes back into incomes and consumer demand, and thus is not lost to the economy. Free-marketer critics of taxation maintain that high tax rates, especially on upper economic strata, withdraw money from the investment supply, distort the natural distribution of resources, and dampen incentives to work hard and produce.

TABLE 7.2	Types of Taxation	
Type of Taxation	**Characteristics**	**Examples**
Progressive	Different rates for different economic levels	Individual income taxes
Flat ("regressive")	Same rate for all	Value-added and sales taxes

A key question regarding income taxes involves different economic strata: who should be taxed, the better-off or the middle class? Moderate left-of-center advocates support **progressive taxation**, in which those who are well off pay higher percentages of their income in taxes than do the poor. Their reasoning is that poor and middle-class taxpayers spend most or all of their income on basic needs—for example, food, clothing, housing, and education for their children—and thus are less able to pay taxes than are high income earners, who earn far more than is necessary for their basic needs. Workers with extremely low incomes may not pay anything in taxes under progressive taxation. If they are parents of young children, they may even receive a subsidy for their care.

Moderate left-of-center supporters argue further that more of the income of the poor and the middle class tends to go straight into the private retail market. This supports local consumer demand, and thus private sector jobs and overall prosperity. In contrast, they suggest that for those who are better off (with plenty of surplus income beyond their basic needs), neither a tax increase nor a tax cut is likely to affect their consumer spending very much. Consequently, taxes on individuals' incomes tend to be progressive to some degree.

Free marketers generally oppose progressive taxation. They stress that maximum economic growth requires a high rate of savings to fund investment. Since higher income people are those most capable of saving, charging them higher taxes can reduce the supply of money available for banks to lend to businesses. Thus, free marketers argue, heavy progressive taxation can hold back economic growth. They often favor a **flat tax**, in which everyone—rich or poor—pays the same rate. In the United States, the tax dedicated to the government's retirement pension system (called "social security") is a flat tax, and one which is not even assessed on income above the middle-class level. Taxes on commercial transactions, whether on retail sales or on transactions between businesses, are normally all at the same rate. In practice, moderate left-of-center advocates and free marketers in many countries cooperate and compromise on a mix of mildly progressive and flat taxes (see Table 7.2).

Both the moderate left-of-center supporters and the free marketers value overall prosperity in the long run. However, they differ in their visions of overall prosperity and in their empirical beliefs about what brings it about. The moderate left-of-center supporters emphasize jobs and the well-being of the middle and lower economic strata, and desire a clear minimum floor beneath which no one should be allowed to fall. In contrast, free marketers stress protecting the incomes and wealth of the upper strata, which they see as contributing ultimately to economic improvement for all.

Interactions Among Policy Options

Policy approaches to big problems can involve combinations of policies in different policy areas. For example, environmental policy involves not only regulation but also subsidies and tax policy. Governments can use regulation to curb certain carbon-dioxide-emitting economic activities directly, while also subsidizing cleaner energy-producing technologies and providing tax cuts to companies and consumers who adopt new carbon-reducing behaviors.

Sometimes governments face a choice between tax policy and regulatory policy in addressing a problem. In trying to curb carbon emissions, for example, both European and American policymakers have largely rejected direct "carbon taxes" on all emitters of carbon dioxide in favor of a regulatory approach called "cap and trade." Government sets overall limits for carbon emissions (the "cap") and then issues permissions to various industries and corporations to emit carbon dioxide within these limits. Those emitting at levels below their permitted limit are allowed to sell ("trade") their unused emission rights to other companies who are over their limits.

This cap-and-trade approach exemplifies market-style adjustments of emission limits (as opposed to outright bans, caps, or direct taxes), and some free marketers have cooperated with moderate left-of-center advocates in support of it. Other moderate left-of-center supporters argue that cap and trade is inadequate to the challenge. Meanwhile, robust free marketers view it as too much intervention and too costly to economic growth. By the 2010s, many on both sides were pointing out that European cap-and-trade was not having much success in reducing carbon dioxide emissions there.

John Maynard Keynes, early to mid-twentieth-century British economist whose theories spearheaded modern macroeconomics.

GAINING AND MAINTAINING PROSPERITY: OVERALL APPROACHES

Beyond these particular areas of economic policy, a broader question arises: How can economic growth be best achieved or maintained? Today, there are two broad approaches to this question; in referring to them, this chapter employs labels that are commonly used in today's debates: stimulus spending and austerity.

The debate between the stimulus spending and austerity approaches centers mostly on what government should do in bad economic times when there is a downturn in commercial activity. This is when overall output of goods and services—called Gross Domestic Product, or "GDP"—is in one of two conditions. Either GDP is declining (a situation called "recession") or it is at a very low point with high unemployment and rising only very slowly. We shall call this latter phase a "slump." (Economists sometimes use the word "trough.") In recessions and slumps, moderate left-of-center people typically advocate stimulus spending by government. Austerity supporters, favoring freer markets, tend to oppose such increases in spending. As we shall see, the austerity approach has two main forms, one more moderate than the other.

Stimulus Spending and Keynesian Economics

The political contention between stimulus spending and austerity approaches began in the era of the Great Depression of the 1930s. From then up through the 1970s, the discipline of economics was heavily influenced by the theories of a prominent British economist, John Maynard Keynes (1883–1946).[4] Amid recessions and slumps, **Keynesian** approaches argue for increasing government spending to reduce unemployment and thus increase **consumer demand**—consumer spending on goods and services.

The Multiplier Effect In support of this, Keynes suggested that during economic downturns and slumps, the negative effects of layoffs on economic output are greater than just the direct loss of those workers' spending power. Imagine that a big employer in a community goes bankrupt and lays off all its workers, who sharply contract their spending in local markets. Amid this spike in unemployment, other local businesses note that sales are down and decide to contract *their* scale of operation and spending. Thus they too lay off workers. That second wave of laid-off workers, too, stop spending. This further erodes consumer demand, producing yet more business pessimism about future sales and hence more layoffs, in a vicious circle that becomes a downward spiral. Thus, with these successive waves of reduction in consumer demand, the negative effects of the first round of job losses are to some extent "multiplied."[5] Keynes called this the "multiplier effect."

Notably, the same effect can operate in reverse, positively. Government policies that lead to hiring and thus increased consumer spending have a positive multiplier effect on additional hiring to meet the additional demand for goods and services. In this case, unemployed workers are rehired, their normal spending on local goods and services is restored, and local business confidence in future sales rises, leading to added hiring, more consumer spending, and more hiring to meet that demand, etc. The key question for Keynesian economics is: How big is the multiplier effect for various types of government policy—whether stimulating consumer demand or causing it to contract?

Quantifying the Multiplier Effect: Multipliers for Various Government Policies Economists who gather data on these things have a specific quantitative measure of the strength of the multiplier effects for various policies under a given set of circumstances. This statistic for a policy change is called the **multiplier**: regarding the consequences of a change in government spending or taxation, it is the ratio of (a) the resulting change in GDP for the local or national economy to (b) the amount of money in the preceding government policy change. This single number tells us *both* (a) how much economic output increases due to a given amount of money spent by government, and (b) on the other side of the coin, how much economic output decreases due to a given amount of money cut from the government budget. That is, if the data show a rather high multiplier, say 1.5 for a policy under a specified set of conditions, it means that (a) for every euro of cuts in job-related spending or unemployment compensation, GDP contracts by an average of 1.5 euros or more, *and* (b) every euro of increase in government spending in these areas tends to produce in the neighborhood of 1.5 euros of increased output. Data has been gathered by economists (including those at the IMF; see below) related to the sharp downturn of 2008–2009 and subsequent slump in the developed nations (see Table 7.3):

TABLE 7.3	One-Year Positive $ Change in Real GDP per $ Reduction in Federal Tax Revenue or Increase in Spending		
		2008, 1st quarter[*]	2010, 4th quarter[†]
Spending Increases			
Extend Unemployment Insurance Benefits		1.64	1.55
Temporarily Increase Food Stamps		1.73	1.71
Issue General Aid to State Governments		1.36	1.37
Increase Infrastructure Spending		1.59	1.44
Tax Cuts [for the middle class]			
Payroll Tax Holiday		1.29	1.24
Across the Board Tax Cut		1.03	1.04
Permanent Tax Cuts [mostly for upper-income people and enterprises]			
Make Bush Income Tax Cuts Permanent		0.29	0.35
Make Dividend and Capital Gains Tax Cuts Permanent		0.37	0.39
Cut Corporate Tax Rate		0.3	0.32

Source: Moody's Economy.com, Moody's Analytics.
[*] Mark Zandi, testimony before the U.S. House Committee on Small Business on July 24, 2008.
[†] Mark Zandi, "At Last, the U.S. Begins a Serious Fiscal Debate," in Moody's Analytics, Dismal Scientist, April 14, 2011.

Notice that the highest multipliers—ranging from 1.3 to 1.7—show up for government spending that bolsters jobs and lower-stratum incomes, such as ramping up construction or repair of roads, bridges, and public transportation facilities, bolstering education or health care, or providing unemployment compensation or food aid to make up for part of the lost income of those out of work. Lower-stratum and middle-class people who go from unemployment to employment (or receive aid) tend to spend every new dollar, euro, pound, or yen that they get on basic consumer needs that they have been unable to meet while unemployed. This mainly supports local businesses, helping to bolster business confidence and thus private sector hiring. Here lies the biggest "bang for the buck" in government policy change.

Keep in mind, however, that such high multipliers only apply to conditions of deep recession or slump, when GDP is not affected by any other factors that, under other circumstances, might bolster consumer demand and economic output. In times of normal-to-strong economic growth, with the unemployment rate low and the economy at near-full capacity, the multiplier effect of layoffs (negative) or hiring (positive) is fairly low. Typically a laid-off worker will be able to find another job before long, with a similar income, because other positive factors are at work to support the economy, such as high business confidence, dropping interest rates for bank loans, or strong foreign demand for the country's exports. With one or more of these additional positive factors sustaining economic output when times are good, government doesn't have to think much about stimulus spending, and can even reduce spending to cut the budget deficit without worrying much about bad consequences from the layoffs for the economy. For example, in the mid-1990s, Sweden cut government spending without significant harm to economic growth, partly because her exports to the rest of Europe remained strong. Notably, in the mid-2000s period of more normal economic growth—before the economic crisis of 2008–2009—the IMF economists' analysis indicated that the multiplier for such policies was much less, around 0.5 (see below).

Tax Levels and Stimulus Another side of Keynes's analysis concerns taxes. If a government has boosted stimulus spending in a period of downturn or slump, one might be tempted to try to pay for the new spending by raising taxes. The downturn itself has reduced tax receipts, also adding to the government's **budget deficit**—the excess of spending going out over tax money coming in. But Keynes pointed out that this is the wrong time to hike taxes, especially on middle- and lower-income earners. Doing so would tend to suppress consumer demand, to some extent counteracting the positive stimulus from the government spending increase.

Keynes argued that for various reasons, government should not worry much about the level of deficit in a recession and slump. Government can fund the deficit by borrowing the money from investors at very low interest rates (see below). And later, when normal economic growth has been restored, the government can narrow the deficit through budget cuts and tax increases without harming GDP much. If policymakers in a slump want to limit the deficit increase a bit with a tax increase, it should be applied to high-income earners. They tend to earn more than they spend as consumers, so tax rate changes for them (up or down) do not affect consumer spending much. (Note the low multipliers for tax changes affecting the well-to-do in Table 7.3 above—only 0.3–0.5.)

Data recently marshaled by economists with the IMF tend to reinforce this picture.[6] As we shall see below, Germany and the European Union authorities have imposed large cuts in government spending by heavily indebted southern European nations such as Greece, Spain, and Portugal. As predicted by the data on multipliers, cuts in government spending since 2010 have indeed suppressed economic growth, contracting GDP by the expected multiplier of (on average) 1.5 times the amount of the budget cuts. Greece and Spain experience unemployment rates of over 25 percent (40–50 percent for youth unemployment), depression levels. The human toll of deprivation and widespread personal and business bankruptcy has been stunning.

Monetary Options: Money for Banks For Keynesian economics, however, there is another tool for possibly affecting economic growth. Policy on government spending and taxes are, taken together, referred to as **fiscal policy**. The remaining major category of broad economic policy involves policy actions by a nation's independent governmental "bank for the banks," called the **central bank**. A country's central bank can adjust the overall supply of money potentially

At left, Janet Yellen, chairperson of the U.S. central bank (called the Federal Reserve); at right, Italian Mario Draghi, chairperson of the European Central Bank (ECB).

available for bank lending. Such adjustments are called **monetary policy**. In a recession or slump, for example, a central bank can expand the money available for banks to lend.[7] Expanding the supply of anything usually tends to lower the price of it, so increasing the supply of money in the banking system can serve to lower interest rates. The aim of the cheaper credit is to attract businesses to borrow from banks for expansion and hiring, to help reverse the downturn.

This move by the nation's central bank can be very important in a severe downturn or slump in a particular way: saving the banking system from collapse. With very cheap money available to private banks that have been weakened by many borrowers' failures to repay, tottering banks can get capital cheaply and fast. This bolsters their balance sheets and prevents "bank runs" by fearful depositors who may want to withdraw their money from banks perceived to be failing. Runs on banks can quickly produce a cascade of actual bank failures and turn a recession into a depression. Preventing the collapse of national banking systems amid a deep recession was a major purpose of the European Central Bank's (ECB) expansionary monetary policy in the Eurozone from 2012 on, and it succeeded in that.

However, for the purpose of bringing an economy out of a slump and into sustained growth, the capacity of monetary expansion is limited. In a sharp recession or slump, businesses see no prospects for sales growth, so few of them want to borrow to expand regardless of how low interest rates drop. And the banks, for their part, are afraid to lend for fear of defaults on loans due to the slumping economy. Monetary expansion can bring interest rates all the way to their "lower bound" of zero, without increasing business borrowing. Any extra money that the banks do accept from the central bank tends to just add to their reserves (often deposited with the central bank itself) or to be used in trading activity.

So for getting an economy out of a deep downturn or slump, neither monetary expansion nor tax cuts are very effective. That leaves government stimulus spending—and thus big temporary budget deficits—as by far the most potent way of reviving growth and lowering unemployment. (This worked to produce steady improvement during the Great Depression of the 1930s in the United States, until uneasiness about deficits brought cutbacks in 1938, thrusting the economy back into depression.)

However, what about the opposite problem: when economic growth is too rapid? An overheated economy with excessive consumer demand can produce strong upward pressure on prices and wages (called high "inflation"; see below), and "bubbles" of overvalued assets. Under these circumstances, a burst of a bubble (e.g., real estate in 2008) or other shock could quickly turn boom to bust. For this situation, Keynesian economics prescribes reversing what is to be done in a slump. Government should moderately *restrain* consumer demand and business activity by reducing government spending, increasing taxes, and/or reducing the money supply (raising interest rates). Here the comparative calculus of effectiveness for the Keynesian tools is somewhat different from that of a downturn or slump. All three tools—including monetary policy—can be effective in reining in a hyperactive economy. And the tax rate increases and spending cuts both help to restore budget balance.

Austerity

Today, the main approach contending with the Keynesian one is called **austerity**. First and foremost, austerity advocates oppose government stimulus spending. If they find it going on, they want to reverse the spending as soon as possible. An "austerity budget" is one that has cut back on government outlays in such areas as unemployment compensation, health care, old age pensions, infrastructure improvements, education, and subsidies. According to austerity thinking, if tax receipts are low because the economy is bad, it only means that the government and society cannot afford the luxury of such expenditures. The government budget is viewed as just a household budget writ large.

As free marketers, in principle austerity advocates want tax rates to stay as low as possible; taxes are government intervention in the economy. But they reason that even if a government is relying on borrowing to pay for stimulus spending during a recession (to avoid raising taxes at that point), it means two things, both bad in the austerity perspective. First, sometime in the future taxes will have to go up to pay the money back. For austerity advocates, what lowers business confidence in a recession or slump is unrelated to low consumer demand; rather, it is worry about any resulting deficit in the government's budget (due to fears of future tax increases). Thus stimulus spending must be cut back as quickly as possible. A second key point in the austerity viewpoint is the contention that, regardless of the circumstances, government borrowing tends to subtract from the available investment capital. This always leaves less money available for ("crowds out") private business borrowing, which will thus face higher interest rates and be discouraged from borrowing to expand and hire. (Notably, Keynesians reply first that business confidence is low in a downturn because of low consumer demand, not speculation about possible future tax rates, and secondly that there is no scarcity of low-interest money in the banks' hands in a slump, leaving plenty of room for the government to borrow without driving up interest rates for business loans.)

To be sure, in some circumstances, reducing the budget deficit amid a slump is hard to do without tax increases. Then austerity advocates favor focusing on raising flat tax rates. The reasoning is that if businesses and individuals all still want government services, they should all pay for them at the same rate (regardless of the higher ability to pay that goes with higher incomes and more successful businesses). Examples of areas in which flat taxes might be raised are tax rates on the incomes of all businesses ("value-added taxes"), taxes on the final sales of goods and services at the register ("sales taxes"), or flat tax rates on incomes, whether "payroll taxes" to pay for benefits or general "personal income taxes."

Some austerity advocates are willing to concede the existence of drops in consumer spending during a recession. But they believe such dips to be small and brief, with recovery right around the corner if austerity is maintained. If the recession drives down wages, then the lower wages will quickly improve export competitiveness, since the cost reductions for exporters enable lower prices for the final goods, which in turn will bring more sales and greater market share in the world economy. Accordingly, austerity advocates tend to discount Keynes's multiplier effect. This was evident in the austerity approach followed in Europe by its top financial authorities in 2010 and 2011: the IMF, the European Commission (in Brussels), and the European Central Bank (ECB). Early analyses by the IMF had forecast a quick European recovery, a prediction which turned out to be wrong. When the IMF's own economists later explored the reasoning behind those early overoptimistic forecasts, they discovered that they were assuming budget cut multipliers of only around 0.5, roughly what they are under circumstances of healthy economic growth (e.g., in the mid-2000s). In fact, the IMF economists found after surveying the data from many countries, multipliers during the downturn were actually around 1.3–1.5, roughly what Keynesian analysis says they are during deep downturns.[8]

Moderate Austerity and Monetarism There are two types of austerity approach. We shall call them "moderate" and "extreme." The main difference between them concerns how they approach monetary policy: the central bank affecting the supply of money available to banks (see above). **Monetarism** as an austerity strategy contends that adjusting the money supply can do the work of (a) limiting economic downturns by adding to the money supply (mainly by having the central bank buy bonds) to make low-interest loan money available to businesses to expand and hire, and (b) if the need is to check excessive economic growth and inflation, cutting back on the money supply to raise interest rates. For monetarists, there is no need to resort to changes in government stimulus spending for these purposes (see Table 7.4). This school of thought was championed by a University of Chicago economist who was the leading American free marketer of the twentieth century, Milton Friedman (1912–2006).[9]

Notably, however, monetarism did not become popular in response to a bad economic downturn; rather, it was a prominent response to a big rise in worldwide inflation in the 1970s. A low rate of inflation—say 2–3 percent—is normal for a healthy economy. But in the 1970s higher rates of inflation had developed, largely due to huge jumps in the price of crude oil (by the new OPEC oil cartel, an alliance of oil-producing nations), then a major factor in production. Facing

TABLE 7.4	Main Schools of Market-Oriented Politico-Economic Thought	
School	**Most Common Concern**	**Main Mechanisms to Address the Concern**
Stimulus spending	Avoid recession and recover from slump	Increase government spending, cut interest rates, and cut taxes on lower economic strata
Monetarist	Avoid high inflation (or in recession or slump, achieve minimal inflation)	Raise interest rates by central bank selling of bonds and notes (or in recession or slump, lower interest rates by buying bonds and notes)

normal consumer demand, businesses tried to pass on the new energy costs to consumers through inflationary price increases. Meanwhile, the oil producers' windfall profits were being dumped on the world's banks, producing a huge jump in the money supply. The resulting extremely low interest rates fostered business activity and more inflation. Finally, a consumer psychology of "buy now, it'll only cost more next month," that inflation encourages, intensified the inflation.

To defeat the powerful inflationary forces, the American central bank (the Federal Reserve) led a massive contraction of the money supply at the beginning of the 1980s, producing huge jumps in interest rates and a brief recession that broke the back of the inflation. The mid-1980s recovery from the recession was managed in the United States largely by a steady replenishment of bank money and consequent reduction in interest rates. Money supply increase was backed up by big tax cuts and increases in defense spending in the United States, but monetary policy seemed to be leading the charge.

Subsequently, reliance primarily on monetary policy took hold in addressing mild recessions—in this case expansionary monetary policy—too. Monetarists argued that their approach also had three big *political* advantages over that of adjusting government spending. First, since monetary policy only involved the central bank buying and selling bonds and adjusting its own lending rates to banks, it did not require spending new tax dollars. Second, as unelected independent bodies, central banks are somewhat insulated from political contention and pressure. In the developed economies, at times they can even get away with harsh and politically unpopular monetary action—even causing recessions—to restrain their economies (as in the early 1980s in the United States).

Third, monetarists argue that in trying to restrain an overheated and inflationary economy, the alternatives—raising taxes and cutting government spending—are difficult to accomplish politically. Raising taxes is never popular. And regarding spending, with taxes rolling in nicely (thanks to the growing GDP) to pay for programs, many people wonder, why cut back on government spending that helps meet social needs? Under these circumstances, free-marketer critics ask a political question of Keynesian policymakers: Can those who call for stimulus spending in hard times be trusted to roll it back when the economy has been restored to vigorous growth?

To be sure, however, monetary policy seems to have little success in a deep downturn and slump. As we saw above, Keynesians point out that while monetary expansion may be needed to avoid banking collapse, it cannot effectively restore growth. Interest rates may drop to near zero with banks flush with funds, but the lack of consumer demand and poor sales prospects means little business demand for loans and little incentive for banks to lend. In Europe, monetary expansion from 2012 onward (under new ECB leadership) failed to fully counteract the contractionary impact of austerity cuts in spending. Through 2014, the Eurozone remained mired in slump. Indeed the main risk was of **deflation**, dropping prices for goods and services, due to insufficient consumer demand. Deflation can bring a ruinous consumer psychology of "don't buy now; the price will be lower next month."

Extreme Austerity Notably, there is also a second austerity approach to downturns and slumps, which takes the idea to a free-market extreme. It not only rejects government stimulus spending, but also rejects monetary policy as too much government intervention in the market. In the eyes of extreme austerity advocates, central bank additions to the money supply immediately raise the prospect of serious inflation, regardless of the circumstances. This approach is sometimes called the "Austrian school" of economics, referring to a free-marketer economic institute in Vienna that has advocated these ideas since the 1930s.

For extreme austerity advocates, there is little to criticize in any outcome produced by a completely free market. All market-set prices are assumed to reflect rational valuations at the time. This school sees no natural reason for overall inflation, and would like to see it eliminated except for price changes that reflect sudden scarcities. (Such price spikes will soon be remedied by more production stimulated by the high price, which will then come down.) Extreme austerity advocates favor completely free trade and full-scale globalization. They see the economy at all levels—world, national, and local—in the same terms of traditional supply and demand (the basis of classical "microeconomics"). If one nation's producers entirely defeat those of another in competition in world and national markets, fine; the losers do not deserve to be in those markets, and should find something else to produce that is valued by the market (something in which they have "comparative advantage").

The outlook of extreme austerity advocates regarding recessions is, if they come, so be it. Occasional economic downturns usefully clean "inefficient" producers out of the system, and get wages down low enough that employers will feel more like hiring workers. As was noted above, lower wages in exporting industries means that they can price their products lower to get an advantage in world trade. (Stimulus advocates point out, however, that empirically, wages are "sticky" in downturns; they don't go down so easily, with employers preferring layoffs to wage cuts.)

This school of thought might be dismissed as extreme—with its major empirical predictions invalidated by the data (e.g., post-2008 monetary expansion has not brought significant inflation)—but for the fact that it has been having an impact on European Union policies toward that continent's current lingering slump and depression in the south.

THE POST-2008 "GREAT RECESSION" AND THE CURRENT CHALLENGE

Starting in 2008, the contention between stimulus spending and austerity approaches found itself in a whole new context: a financial crisis and deep recession in the developed economies, followed by a long slump (see Figure 7.2). At first the crisis brought cooperation between Keynesians and moderate austerity advocates, to address the emergency. Very soon, however, contention again broke out.

The Initial Response: Emergency Cooperation between the Contending Approaches

In northern Europe and the United States, the crisis and sharp downturn of late 2008 and 2009 required dramatic interventions by governments and their central banks. Recognized emergencies that threaten near-universal disaster tend to foster cooperation among groups that normally contend with one another.

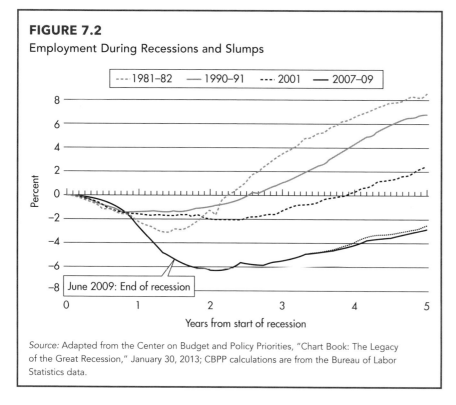

FIGURE 7.2

Employment During Recessions and Slumps

--- 1981–82   — 1990–91   ··· 2001   — 2007–09

June 2009: End of recession

Years from start of recession

Source: Adapted from the Center on Budget and Policy Priorities, "Chart Book: The Legacy of the Great Recession," January 30, 2013; CBPP calculations are from the Bureau of Labor Statistics data.

The central challenge was to avoid a new "great depression," perhaps one that could have been worse than that of the 1930s due to the far greater international interdependence that characterizes today's global economy.

The result was a comeback for Keynesian stimulus spending, alongside massive monetary intervention. To avoid an epidemic of bank failures, some governments bolstered banks' reserves directly by purchasing temporary ownership stakes in them. For example, the British government took majority ownership of the Royal Bank of Scotland and Lloyds, and the American government injected money into a large number of commercial and investment banks. For their part, national central banks made low-interest loans available to banks on a large scale and guaranteed or purchased many debts, bonds, and other securities to try to fill some of the financial hole. This bank bolstering was something that Keynesians and many monetarists could cooperate in.

However, as we saw above, monetary expansion could not by itself produce expanded lending to businesses and a momentum of recovery. Amid very weak consumer demand, banks are afraid that lenders would not be able to repay, and the poor sales prospects meant that businesses were disinclined to expand. The banks put their new money into reserves or financial trading rather than lending it out to businesses. Interest rates fell to near zero (called the "zero lower bound") without reviving lending and growth.

Thus national governments had to go beyond monetarism and turn to deficit spending to prop up consumer demand to avoid depression. There was plenty of excess capital to borrow for this stimulus spending at near-zero interest rates without "crowding out" any private demand for it (again, nearly nonexistent due to the poor business prospects). Moderate austerity advocates had to cooperate with Keynesians to address the emergency conditions. Government stimulus spending tended to focus on policies with the largest multipliers (see Table 7.3): (a) new infrastructure construction (e.g., fixing old roads and bridges) to provide jobs, (b) extending unemployment benefits, (c) providing other help such as food aid to those in need, and (d) providing subsidies to regional and local government budgets and key enterprises to limit layoffs.

Different measures were especially prominent in different countries. Resource-rich Germany, for example, led by a conservative prime minister (Christian Democrat Angela Merkel), provided subsidies for employers to shorten the work week rather than lay people off. Conservative-led France supported apprenticeship programs and self-employment opportunities. The United States boosted infrastructure spending, subsidized alternative energy efforts, extended unemployment benefits and food aid eligibility, helped state governments balance their budgets without large layoffs, and injected capital into a huge auto producer, General Motors, to avoid its bankruptcy and massive layoffs.

Especially in the United States and Britain, these measures brought a resumption of economic growth by late 2009. Where safety nets were robust (as in much of Europe), they were already providing adequate health insurance, old age pensions, housing subsidies, and other help to the unemployed; such ongoing policies helped prevent a collapse of consumer demand, and big new jobs programs were less necessary.

Contention between Stimulus Spending and Austerity Today

Soon, however, the initial emergency cooperation over economic policy succumbed to new contention between stimulus spending and monetarist approaches. Keynesians advocated continuing government spending and low interest rates until a self-sustaining recovery was assured. Amid such a deep downturn, there were no signs of significant inflation resulting from the monetary expansion and stimulus spending. There were occasional temporary rises in the volatile world prices for commodities such as oil and food grains, mainly due to Chinese demand, but in each case they soon subsided.

Austerity advocates, however, were not on board. They believed that with all the monetary and spending expansion going on, surely worldwide inflation would rear its head. It didn't, but austerity-minded policymakers nonetheless pressed for cutting back on government deficit spending as early as 2010 and 2011, despite the continuing economic slump. In addition, monetarists worried that as government levels of deficit and debt rose, outside investors might begin to demand higher interest rates because they doubted whether governments would be able to repay their mounting debts.

The answer for monetarists by 2011, with the slump still deep and recovery small and fragile, was a return to spending austerity. In the United States, for example, the conservative Republican Party won control of the lower house of Congress, and thus could block President Obama's efforts to renew the initial burst of stimulus spending. In Great Britain, the 2010 conservative election victory turned British spending policies back toward austerity. And in continental Europe, the financial straits of the southern countries brought harsh austerity as a requirement for any financial help from the EU authorities in paying southern debts to northern banks and other international financial institutions.

Again, austerity advocates suggested that if a renewed downturn did result from the spending cuts, it would be brief and mild. Wage reductions would help make exporters become more competitive in world trade. Recovery and growth, austerity advocates argued, would be right around the corner. But it wasn't; high unemployment rates and slump continued through 2014.

The Special Case of Southern Europe

In nations with their own currencies (and hence their own central banks and monetary policies), like the United States and Great Britain, monetarist advocates of austerity tended to allow their harsh antispending medicine to be accompanied by monetary expansion by the central bank (see above), to try to balance austerity's short-term contractionary effects with supportive monetary help. In those countries, only a few extreme austerity advocates wanted spending cuts without monetary support.

In the Eurozone countries of continental Europe, however, nations lack their own currencies. Thus their central banks do not have the capacity for autonomous monetary expansion. Accordingly, a nation cannot devalue the national currency to help exporters and debtors to counter spending austerity. So amid depression in some southern European countries (see Table 7.5), their governments and central banks were at the mercy of the Eurozone-wide monetary authorities in Germany and the EU executive headquarters in Brussels. The latter free-market supporters favored Austrian-style extreme austerity for the debt-pressed southern European governments and banks. In return for special aid to help Greece, Spain, and Portugal make scheduled debt payments (and thus avoid a default) to northern European banks, the German and EU authorities demanded big cuts in pensions, unemployment compensation, health care, and other spending that had helped sustain consumer demand in southern Europe.

Nor was countervailing help available from exports. With European consumer demand lagging, southern Europe was very short of exporting enterprises with sufficiently advanced technology (see below) and durable international markets to help pull their economies out of the slump. In international trade, Greece, Italy, Spain, and Portugal could not rival the likes of German high-tech industrial products (e.g., precision industrial machinery and chemicals), whose producers had markets in China regardless of the weakness of the European market. In contrast, for example, the market for Greek shipbuilding plummeted with the Western downturn.

For their part, Keynesians assessing Europe stressed that in bad economic downturns and slumps, austerity is counterproductive. The contractionary effect of spending austerity on employment, consumer spending, and output[10] will reduce government tax revenues. This, they point out, runs counter to one of

TABLE 7.5	Unemployment Rates in Selected European Countries, 2012–2013
Austria	4.9%
Germany	5.3%
France	10.6%
Portugal	17.6%
Spain	26.2%
Greece	27.0%
Source: Eurostat.	

the key goals of austerity advocates: deficit reduction. While the spending cuts tend to reduce the deficit, the consequent falloff in tax revenues due to austerity-induced economic contraction tends to increase the deficit. Consequently, with the GDP declining due to austerity, the deficit *as a percentage of GDP*—an often-used measure of deficit problems—may actually *increase* due to policies of spending austerity. With the deficit-to-GDP ratio rising rather than falling, European austerity advocates in Brussels and Germany could be expected to demand *even more austerity* of southern European governments—again, purportedly "to reduce the budget deficit"—further intensifying the vicious circle into a downward spiral. Ultimately, would-be international lenders to the distressed country's government, banks, and businesses would be wary of extending credit because of the austerity-driven recession/depression itself, which makes the country a bad risk overall.

To be sure, starting in late 2011, the ECB (under its new chairman, Italian Mario Draghi) began a new expansion of cheap credit to Europe's banks, which helped keep down interest rates for the governments of distressed economies such as Greece, Portugal, and Spain. And in late 2014, the ECB said it would authorize a limited program of buying government bonds to further boost the money supply. But this did not extend to any concrete change in policy toward Greece (see chapter 18), which by mid-2015 was in default on its debts and at risk of being expelled from the Eurozone. Through the Greek crisis of late 2014 and 2015, the ECB limited itself to just enough support for Greek banks to prevent a collapse of the Greek banking system.

Further Factors: Labor Market Regulation, Exchange Rates, Technology Advantage, and International Inequality

A discussion of the challenge of getting out of a slump would not be complete without at least brief mention of other factors that can be important in particular situations, starting with regulation of labor markets.

Labor Market Regulation A high priority for austerity advocates is loosening or removing regulatory restrictions on hiring/firing, hours, and wage cutting, to give businesses greater flexibility in responding to market conditions. In this approach, austerity advocates are contending against a key feature of the traditional continental European "variety of capitalism": government regulations (and union strength) that made it difficult for businesses to, at will, lay people off quickly or reduce their wages or hours (in contrast to Britain and the United States, for example, where employers are relatively free of such regulations). For example, basic wages and benefits might be set in sector-wide negotiations between peak union and employers' associations, rules may limit or delay layoffs, wage cutting, or reduction of hours, and substantial severance payments might be required for laid-off workers. Austerity advocates contend that such rules make it harder for businesses to adjust the scale of their activity to slumping markets, and make them reluctant to (re)hire when recovery begins.

In Europe, austerity advocates have pushed for governments to deregulate labor markets. A very prominent measure is to allow an expansion of short-term labor contracts that are exempt from key labor market regulations (as occurred in Sweden in 1993–1994 and Germany in 2004–2005, for example). Similarly, austerity advocates favor deregulation of product and service markets, to allow free entry of new competitors unencumbered by established standards and regulations. For example, quality or safety regulations may serve to protect small pharmacies from displacement by big chain (often grocery) stores, or to protect established taxi companies from Uber, an Internet company whose drivers are nominally independent contractors. The result may be lower price tags (and wages) for the service or product.

In contrast, stimulus advocates maintain that business ease in laying off workers and reducing wages and hours can intensify recessions and slumps, making conditions worse due to higher unemployment rates and lower wages for those who are still working. Even amid recovery, as GDP has begun moving up and unemployment has begun to drop, wages may stagnate or even continue to drop. In the relatively free-wheeling United States, we see a trend to outsourcing functions to various sorts of nonregular workers, such as (a) foreign enterprises not subject to labor regulations and (b) domestic "contract" workers (nominally self-employed) who are used for limited periods and projects. As in every market, the most advantaged of such functionaries can do well by freelancing, but the bulk encounter declining incomes and little income security. (Here the boundary between the "formal sector" of official enterprises and the "informal sector" of the unreported and unregulated "cash economy" begins to erode.)

Currency Exchange Rates A second major issue area is international exchange rates for currencies. The international custom of floating exchange rates that mostly prevailed in the last third of the twentieth century allowed for countries in economic crisis to experience a devaluation of their currency, whether through market forces or their country's central bank actions, or both. Amid crisis and slump, money tends to flee the suffering nation and its currency, lowering the currency's value in relation to other currencies. This has an important advantage for crisis-hit countries wishing to become more competitive in global trade: their exports become cheaper and imports more expensive. Export sector employment rises, as domestic producers get a better chance against competing imports. The country's trade deficit—imports exceeding exports—can be reduced or even replaced with a trade surplus—exports exceeding imports. These effects can be key to a national economy's recovery from a crisis and slump. Currency devaluations were important, for example, in Sweden's recovery in the late 1990s and Argentina's in the early 2000s.

The other side of this coin involves countries who are very successful contenders in international trade, with a large trade surplus and thus rapidly accumulating wealth. With freely floating exchange rates, normally such a country can expect to see its national currency *grow* in value—called currency "appreciation"—as international capital is attracted into the successful country by its investment opportunities, bidding up the value of its currency. This higher currency value tends to make the country's exports *more expensive* in world trade and thus less competitive, reducing trade imbalances and overall international inequality. Currency-related effects do not tend to reverse such international inequalities, but they do moderate them, giving the hungrier country a chance and preventing the winner from taking home all the marbles.

For a crisis-hit country, currency devaluation also has another domestic advantage: when the prices of imports all go up together, the resulting inflation tends to reduce the purchasing power of everyone's incomes. But this labor cost reduction (which helps national economic competitiveness) is relatively psychologically acceptable because it results from impersonal market forces affecting everyone at once. (Meanwhile, the inflation keeps everyone spending, supporting consumer demand.) It tends to be easier to deal with than having bosses in less successful sectors and enterprises tell their workers that their salaries or wages are being cut.

Notably, however, this currency value factor cannot be of any help in the southern European economic crisis of the 2010s. The slumping countries are in the unprecedented situation of not having their own national currencies to devalue (as well as not having central banks with the power to print money to help banks and businesses to restart growth). Hence there is little to stem the losses and enable recovery by the least successful Eurozone countries, such as Greece and Spain. Even if GDP begins to rise, as in Spain in 2014, unemployment remains well over 20 percent and wages and salaries remain extremely low. The middle class remains in the slump. The only way to lower wage costs in hopes of some export recovery is driving wages down directly, in deflation. But as was noted above, deflation's falling prices discourage consumer spending, inviting people to wait to purchase because the price will be lower later. And again, wage cuts must be done directly (and uncomfortably) by the employer, not indirectly by markets, so wages tend to be "sticky"—as economists term them—not going down as much as may be required for competitive recovery and saving jobs.

And what about the other (winning) side of the coin in Europe? Because of the single currency used by all nineteen Eurozone countries, Germany's currency cannot rise in value to increase the prices of its goods and moderate its trade surplus in Europe. Overall inequality in Europe continues to grow in Germany's favor, with little on the horizon to moderate it.

Advanced Technology and Overall Inequality A third factor affecting inequality is advanced technology or its absence. Countries such as Germany, China, Japan, South Korea, and Taiwan can produce the highest quality goods in high-return economic sectors. Moreover, their gains enable them to constantly control costs by substituting technology for labor. Whether this involves layoffs of individuals within producing units (increasing the "productivity" of the remaining labor) or outsourcing to higher-technology units elsewhere, the result is reduced demand for labor and stagnation of wages and salaries even in the successful countries themselves. The effect is similar to shifting production to lower-wage areas, such as German companies producing in neighboring East European countries and Chinese companies moving production from higher-wage eastern China to less-developed western China. Wherever the infrastructure and worker capabilities (e.g., adequate education) permit, the advanced technology can be plopped down.

Meanwhile, even as middle-class incomes may stagnate or erode within the successful exporting countries, the overall national gains from large trade surpluses bring enough money into the country to keep the service sector humming and thus keep unemployment levels low. In contrast, countries with low technology levels lose out unless they have some highly valued raw material that they can export profitably. This general tendency for technology inequality to intensify international economic inequality between nations is most intense, of course, in the special case of the single-currency Eurozone, where it is impossible for currency devaluation and central bank stimulus to come to the rescue of the less advantaged countries.

SUMMARY: CONTENTION AND COOPERATION IN POLITICAL ECONOMY

The challenge of how to distribute resources and regulate the economy remains with governments today. Through the twentieth century to the present, governments have spent money to aid disadvantaged groups, provided goods and services such as education and parks, and supported private activities that they consider in the public interest. Often the moderate left-of-center and the free-marketer approaches have contended over these forms of spending, with MLC supporters generally in favor and free marketers against them. But in practice, at critical points, opposing sides have cooperated in negotiating compromises to provide some degree of commitments along these lines.

The Keynesian and (free marketer) monetarist schools of thought disagree over the government's role in the economy. Keynes had suggested that the most effective way to avoid or escape an economic downturn was government spending to support jobs and consumer demand. Free marketers argued that such spending could not sustain recovery and could create high rates of inflation. Instead, they supported monetary policy, reducing interest rates to stimulate lending to businesses for recovery, which could (and should) quickly be turned off once recovery was underway, to avoid inflation. After Keynesians and monetarists cooperated on initial responses at the onset of the 2008–2009 financial crisis, the contention again broke out and continues today.

COUNTRY CASE STUDIES

Most of the discussion in this chapter has concerned countries of the developed world. We now turn to a post-Communist country and a developing nation. These contexts provide quite different politico-economic backdrops for economic policy contention and cooperation. However, by the 2000s, both countries seemed to be experiencing basically the same debates as the developed world regarding the role of government in the economy.

Poland: Political Economy in a Post-Communist Democracy

Under Communist Party rule from the end of World War II through the 1980s, Poland's economy was state owned (with the exception of agriculture) and controlled by the top Communist Party and government officials (see "Marxism-Leninism" in chapter 6). The leading ministers in the executive branch, all of them party members, generally made the detailed decisions. But new policy initiatives usually emerged from the council of top full-time party administrators called the secretariat. Their recommendations would then go for approval to a supreme board of directors called the "politburo," a combination of top party secretaries, leading government executive ministers, and other high officials. Informal contention could occur within the overall elite, but the appearance that the regime gave to the outside world was generally one of harmonious cooperation.

The beginning of the 1980s, however, saw the rise of a Polish union movement outside government control called Solidarity. By late 1981, Solidarity was participating in talks with the government, raising issues and proposing policies to loosen Communist Party control over labor and the economy. But in that year a top military officer, Wojciech Jaruzelski, seized control over the government, imposed martial law, and detained Solidarity leaders.

During the middle of the decade, Solidarity remained divided and shut out of politics. But by the late 1980s, the new Soviet Union leadership under Mikhail Gorbachev was encouraging the Eastern European Communist regimes to loosen the reins of centralized control. Solidarity again took the opportunity to engage in mass demonstrations. General Jaruzelski eventually released Solidarity detainees, eased restrictions on the movement's activities, and allowed talks with Solidarity. These talks led to a series of elections in 1989 that Solidarity won, clearly demonstrating that Communist Party rule had lost legitimacy. With the cooperation of many Communists, Solidarity swept peacefully to power late in the year, as similar events took place all over Eastern Europe.

Today Poland has a representative democratic political system with a parliamentary governmental structure. Voting is by proportional representation, and six or seven political parties play significant roles in the legislative assembly, known as the Sejm. Parties and interest groups freely and actively raise issues and propose policies. Until recently, the parties were aligned in two contending coalitions: a left-of-center one mainly concerned with assuring that government was guaranteeing economic protections, and a right-of-center one supporting free markets and traditional values. Typically, one or the other of these coalitions held the majority in the key lower house of parliament (the Sejm), and the coalition parties' leaders filled the cabinet positions and steered economic policymaking. Occasionally, the elected president may exert limit-setting power, since she or he has a veto power that can be overridden only by a three-fifths vote in parliament.

In practice, however, the range of economic policy options considered by Polish governments since 1991 has been constrained by external economic forces and circumstances. The new post-Communist government had inherited a large debt to international lenders that had accumulated under the last decades of Communism. Poland could not repay the debts on the terms agreed on earlier. Her creditors would ease repayment only on condition that the nation make a major break with its socialist past, along the free-market lines of "shock therapy." Shock therapy includes rapid removal of government regulations on prices and other economic practices, sweeping privatization of state-owned enterprises, encouragement of private enterprise, and strict control of government spending and budget deficits.

The changes did not go well at first. The decontrol of prices produced extremely high inflation. The newly privatized enterprises still amounted to a network of monopolies as in the former Communist period, slowing price competition. And imports were expensive due to a drop in the value of the Polish currency (the zloty). Moreover, many of the new private corporations, led by former Communist era managers, aroused suspicions of corruption.

From the mid-1990s onward, however, the Polish economy recovered and grew. Poland was eager to enter the European Union, and the requirements for entry bolstered support for Poland's market-oriented path. But Poles also remembered the hardships of the early 1990s and insisted on a strong social safety net. This included a state pension system, free health care and education, disability benefits, minimum wage guarantees, worker protections against being fired under certain circumstances, and efforts to reduce unemployment. These factors narrowed the range of policy options for the Polish government. The result was incremental policymaking and no big initiatives to address challenges such as unemployment, budget deficits, and corruption.

This ongoing situation has meant that hopes raised during election campaigns usually lead to disillusionment later on. In the successive parliamentary elections of 1993, 1997, 2001, and 2005, the governing coalition, whether left of center or right of center, was thrown out in favor of the rival coalition. The latter would then preside over a few more years of failure to solve Poland's problems before losing the next election.

After the right-of-center coalition won the 2005 election, its parties fell into sharp contention with one another, primarily over value differences, and split into two coalitions. The conservative Law and Justice Party, which emphasized cultural issues and was less free market oriented than its former coalition partner, won the presidency. At first, it led a coalition with smaller parties. In parliamentary elections in 2007, however, the other key right-of-center party, the free market-focused Civic Platform (PO), led and formed a coalition with the smaller Peasant Party.

The Civic Platform (PO—ideologically, classical liberal; see chapter 5) predictably favored cutting government spending and reducing regulation of the economy and the labor market. But the leading party's free-market-oriented program was curbed by the 2008–2009 international financial crisis. The downturn required stimulus to the economy and discouraged the further budget cuts and privatizations that the Civic Platform had wanted to pursue. Poland weathered the financial crisis well in comparison to its Eastern Europe neighbors, and the PO's public support remained stable through 2009. Poland's advantages of low debt, already relatively cheap labor, the flexible exchange rate for the zloty, and overall attractiveness to Western investors served the country well.

But with the European debt crisis starting in 2010, pressure increased on Poland to reduce government deficits and debt. After the Civic Platform-led coalition won the 2011 election, the party's leader and prime minister Donald Tusk adopted unpopular austerity spending cuts, including raising the retirement age. By late 2012, Poland's deficit-to-GDP ratio had been cut by more than half (to 3.5 percent). However, economic growth was also cut in half, and unemployment remained high at 13 percent, all contributing to a drop in the coalition's poll ratings. By late 2013, Tusk had got an unpopular increase in the retirement age (to 67 for men) and an expansion of short-term labor contracts that sidestep labor protections, and

Solidarity had led union members in large demonstrations. Law and Justice (LJ), calling for a softening of austerity, had forged ahead in the polls.

At the end of 2014, Civic Platform found a temporary end to its slide; it replaced Tusk with Ewa Kopacz as its leader and prime minister. She put further austerity on hold, and even improved a few state services, enabling PO to gain a few points in the polls. However, in 2015 the eurosceptic and increasingly ethnic-ultranationalist Law and Justice party (LJ) made a comeback. LJ won the presidency in May and parliamentary elections in November, pledging to bolster traditional Catholicism and Polish nationalism, and block absorption of refugees from the Middle East. Economically, the new government aimed to provide additional aid to families and a small tax on bank assets, while keeping the government deficit under the EU-recommended cap of 3 percent of GDP. But the LJ's sociocultural policies have proved more striking and ominous. By early 2016, LJ party leader Jaroslaw Kaczynski was dominating Polish politics, and the party and government seemed to be taking control of the security services, the bureaucracy, the judiciary, and the broadcast media, suppressing critical views. These moves drew critical notice from the EU authorities.

South Africa: Race and Political Economy

Policymaking in South Africa has until recently centered around race and ethnicity.

In the seventeenth century, Dutch-descended farmers, called Afrikaners, claimed the land and defeated and enslaved first the Hottentots and San bushmen, and later other tribes. In the eighteenth century, the English-speaking British took over and eventually outlawed slavery, to the dismay of the Afrikaner farmers. Even though the majority of South African whites were Afrikaners, English speakers (including the mixed-race "colored" and Indian minorities) reigned in industry, commerce, and such big cities as Cape Town and Johannesburg. By the middle of the twentieth century, however, an ethnic ultranationalist Afrikaner political party, called the National Party (NP), had gained the

majority in the British-style parliament and prevailed in policymaking. Afrikaners cooperated in cohesive support for the NP.

Economically, NP policy favored state intervention, but not in today's conventional left-of-center style. The NP supported subsidies and regulation to further the interests of Afrikaners. They had suffered from depressed farm prices before World War II and needed employment in the largely English-controlled urban economy, civil service, and military. More importantly, however, the NP aimed to organize and consolidate the subordination of the black majority. They did so with a set of policies known as *apartheid*. Apartheid denied the black majority citizenship and the right to vote, under the fiction that blacks were instead citizens of a handful of reservations (white-controlled) called "homelands." The majority of black people lived outside the homelands, and their residence and movement were tightly controlled. Their treatment systematically violated human rights norms in the U.N.'s Universal

Declaration of 1948. The NP held together its majority in parliament, dutifully cooperating with the prime minister and cabinet to maintain apartheid.

By the 1950s, however, black South Africans had formed an antiapartheid political party, the African National Congress (ANC). It spearheaded civil disobedience with boycotts, strikes, and mass demonstrations. After an especially violent response by the police in the early 1960 Sharpeville Massacre that killed sixty-nine people, the regime declared a state of emergency, undertook mass arrests of ANC members, and banned the party. After further incidents of police violence, the ANC formed a military wing and undertook selective sabotage. Starting in the 1960s, when the ANC's leader Nelson Mandela was captured and incarcerated, the party's determined stand against apartheid made it by far the party most favored by the black majority.

By the early 1980s, however, policymaking within the NP cabinet had become more complex, with growing contention over whether to soften some of the apartheid restrictions of blacks. The party's right wing opposed any modifications of apartheid and split off to form the Conservative Party. Meanwhile, some English-ancestry people who favored weakening apartheid had joined the NP. This more reform-oriented party, led by P. W. Botha, still held the majority. In the late 1980s and early 1990s, President F. W. de Klerk (of the NP) began informal negotiations with Nelson Mandela, the still incarcerated ANC leader, to end apartheid. Although the process was not without hesitations and violence, free elections with an enfranchised black majority were finally held in 1994, which the ANC won. Nelson Mandela became president.

In all of the postapartheid parliamentary elections (1994, 1999, 2004, and 2009), the ANC gained roughly two-thirds of the seats in the National Assembly. The presidency and the cabinet are made up entirely of the party's leadership and a few leaders from its supportive allies in the "Tripartite Alliance" (also including a trade union federation, the Congress of South African Trade Unions—COSATU—and the South African Communist Party). The leading conservative and free-market opposition party is the mainly white and middle-class Democratic Alliance (DA). The DA's supporters include many English-ancestry whites (a number of which were antiapartheid in the past), Afrikaners, and, especially in the state of Western Cape where it is strongest, many coloreds and Indians. The DA won 16 percent of the national election vote in April 2009. Support for the Zulus' Inkatha Freedom Party, mainly concentrated in the Zulu area of Kwazulu-Natal, has slipped to 4.5 percent nationally.

Politically, the ANC leadership in the government has been pulled in different policy directions. Its range of policy options is constrained in ways that require consultation with an array of key interests. On one hand, by tradition the ANC is a party on the ideological left, favoring government intervention in the economy. Poverty, inequality, housing, poor service delivery, and unemployment in the black townships remain huge problems in South Africa.

On the other hand, Mandela and his successor Thabo Mbeki recognized that the country needed a motivated white minority in both the urban and rural economies to maintain growth and prosperity. South Africa is in some ways the economic engine for most of southern Africa. ANC moderates argued that the government could not adopt big budget deficits, high taxes, and programs of new state ownership or resource redistribution without alienating many white businesspeople and farmers. Whites' departure could put the economy into a tailspin similar to what occurred in neighboring Zimbabwe. Many MLC supporters of the ANC suggested that moves to address pressing social needs must be based on a strong economy to provide the revenues for them.

The ANC finance minister from 1996 to 2009 was Trevor Manuel, a capable white financial expert respected by a wide range of groups in South Africa. While the country developed a welfare system directed mainly at the poorest 10 percent, budgetary constraints heavily restricted spending on ordinary government services. A "cost recovery" system required payment of fees for many services; consequently, the well-off areas that could afford the fees generally were best served.

Poverty and unemployment rates for blacks remain high, alongside other problems such as crime, electricity shortages, deficiencies in government services, and AIDS. Mr. Mbeki's approval ratings dropped over the mid-2000s. At a party conference in December 2007, the ANC left wing unseated Mr. Mbeki as party chief and installed Jacob Zuma at the helm. In the elections of April 2009, the ANC won 66 percent of the vote and the National Assembly chose Zuma as the new president. Before the election, some Mbeki centrist supporters had defected from the ANC to form a new centrist black party, the Congress of the People (COPE). But the new party won only 7 percent of the vote, and subsequently was weakened by internal divisions.

In 2009, the worldwide economic downturn affected South Africa as exports dropped and unemployment and poverty increased. But prudent prior government policies had avoided widespread subprime lending and questionable securities and investments, and South Africa endured the downturn more easily than many other countries in the developing world. However, high unemployment (24 percent, and over a third if one includes those who have given up looking for work), very low wages for many, and poor conditions (especially for blacks) continue. The government is known for dealing government contracts to supporters and at times trying to bend the police and courts to its purposes. Over time, the left-of-center leanings of President Zuma, many of his ANC supporters (especially the party's youth wing), and his allies in the Tripartite Alliance are likely to combine to pressure South African policies incrementally in the direction of stronger social programs to alleviate poverty and other ills.

In 2012, however, two developments dented Zuma's personal standing (beyond earlier allegations of corruption, and one of rape, that did not result in prosecution). In August 2012, the police killed thirty-four demonstrators on strike at the Marikana platinum mine, and numerous mine layoffs followed. And in the same year, a scandal arose over apparently excessive spending and diversion of state money on security improvements at Zuma's residential compound in Kwazulu-Natal. In December, however, Zuma easily retained the ANC leadership in a party vote.

Zuma then elected a new deputy and likely future successor: a wealthy businessman, Cyril Ramphosa (former ANC trade union leader but now mine owner) known for his economic management skills. This served to reassure investors, and powerful economic interests and investors will continue to press for more efficient and stable economic management. But it did not endear him to the left wing of his party.

All this set the stage for a diversification in the range of opposition contenders that persists to the present. A left-wing populist and former ANC youth league chief, Julius Malema, started a new party in 2013, the Economic Freedom Fighters (EEF). Favoring the pre-1992 ANC program of nationalization of the mines and banks, and land reform, EEF was able to get 6 percent of the vote in the 2014 parliamentary elections. Since the election, the country's metalworkers' union has dropped its support for the ANC, perhaps presaging a new left-wing labor party or a new labor wing of EEF.

To the free-market-oriented right of the ANC, the Democratic Alliance (DA) made gains in the 2014 election, receiving 22 percent (up from 17 percent in 2009). It bolstered its coalition's majority in the regions around Cape Town and reduced the ANC's majority around Johannesburg, showing more support among middle-class blacks. In early 2015, the DA replaced its long-time white leader, Helen Zille (a former anti-apartheid journalist), with a young and popular black man, Mmusi Maimane. Still, Zuma continues to hold together the ANC, which got 62 percent of the vote in 2014 (down from 65 percent in 2009) despite the emergence of the EFF, and is unlikely to relinquish power anytime soon.

PRACTICE AND REVIEW ONLINE

CRITICAL THINKING QUESTIONS

1. What case(s) can be made for and against types of government ownership in the economy? For example, should the government run schools, health insurance, or electrical utilities?

2. Are there resources whose state ownership MLC adherents and free marketers can cooperate in supporting?

3. How can different types of economic policy such as regulation and subsidy cooperate to solve a problem? Or substitute for one another?

4. Which approach, Keynesian or monetarist, do you think is most effective in restoring economic growth after a recession and why? How and when might their supporters cooperate?

KEY TERMS

bubble, 174
import substitution industrialization (ISI), 178
tariffs, 178
inflation, 178
redistribution, 182

FURTHER READING

Backhouse, Roger E., and Bradley W. Bateman. *Capitalist Revolutionary: John Maynard Keynes.* Cambridge, MA: Harvard University Press, 2011.

Bartels, Larry M. *Unequal Democracy: The Political Economy of the New Gilded Age.* Princeton, NJ: Princeton University Press, 2008.

Caparaso, James A., and David P. Levine. *Theories of Political Economy.* Cambridge, UK: Cambridge University Press, 1992.

Drazan, Allan. *Political Economy in Macroeconomics.* Princeton, N.J. Princeton University Press, 2000.

Hancke, ed. *Debating Varieties of Capitalism: A Reader.* Oxford: Oxford University Press, 2009.

Heilbroner, Robert. *Twenty-First Century Capitalism.* New York: W. W. Norton. 1994.

Krugman, Paul. *Stop This Depression Now!* New York: Norton, 2012.

Persson, Torsten, and Guido Tabellini. *Political Economics: Explaining Economic Policy.* Cambridge, MA: MIT Press, 2000.

Reinhart, Carmen M., and Kenneth S. Rogoff. *This Time is Different: Eight Centuries of Financial Folly.* Princeton, NJ: Princeton University Press, 2009.

Wapshott, Nicholas. *Keynes Hayek: The Clash That Defined Modern Economics.* New York: Norton, 2011.

Weingast, Barry R., and Donald A Wittman. *The Oxford Handbook of Political Economy.* Oxford: Oxford University Press, 2008.

Yergin, Daniel, and Joseph Stanislaw. *The Commanding Heights: The Battle Between Government and the Marketplace That is Remaking the Modern World.* New York: Simon and Schuster, 1999.

NOTES

[1] For more on the details of the decision-making process, see chapter 13.

[2] See Immanuel Wallerstein, *The Modern World-system* (New York: Academic Press, 1974).

[3] Similar consequences follow in conditions of "oligopoly," where there are only a handful of producers and they can easily cooperate to keep prices high rather than competing on price.

[4] See *General Theory of Employment, Interest and Money* (New York: Harcourt Brace, 1936). Keynes's theory has received some updating in the last half of the twentieth century; see Yale professor James Tobin, *National Economic Policy; Essays* (New Haven, CT: Yale University Press, 1966).

[5] At worst, consumer spending drops so much that it produces a general decline in the prices of goods and services. This deflation is especially damaging because those who still have incomes may be tempted to hold off on spending them because the price of whatever they want will be lower in the future. For Keynesians, history's nightmare is the Great Depression of the 1930s, when this scenario became reality across the world. This may seem like ancient history, except that the world came close to it again during the financial crisis of 2008–2009.

[6] For reports by International Monetary Fund economists showing loss of growth and jobs due to austerity budgets across a very large number of cases, see Lawrence Ball, Daniel Leigh, and Prakash Loungani, "Painful Medicine," *Finance & Development* 48, no. 3 (September 2011), and Olivier Blanchard and Daniel Leigh, "Growth Forecast Errors and Fiscal Multipliers," IMF Working Paper 13/1, IMF Research Department, January 2013.

[7] Central banks do this by (a) buying government bonds—investments that guarantee repayment plus interest,

(b) reducing the amount of money that the banks have to hold in reserve for a rainy day, and (c) lowering the rates that the central bank charges for its short-term lending to banks.

[8] See note 9.

[9] Notably, Friedman's initiative was motivated partly by a value that was supremely important in his mind: entrepreneurial freedom. For example, he opposed one of the Keynesian tools for slowing down an economy that was growing too rapidly (see below): raising taxes, in part because he saw tax increases as new constraints on business freedom.

[10] See note 9.

Political Attitudes

FOCUS QUESTIONS

- **WHAT** is political culture, where does it come from, and what are its most important consequences?

- **WHAT** can be the consequences of substantial diversity in political culture?

- **WHAT** are the consequences of contending patterns of political socialization in society?

- **WHAT** factors contribute to sharp contention within public opinion? To greater uniformity of views?

- **HOW** does the media affect political attitudes?

IMAGINE THAT YOU ARE A GERMAN CITIZEN in 2012. Most of your neighbors believe that the economic problems of other European nations such as Ireland, Greece, Spain, Portugal, and Italy are of those nations' own doing. Their banks and governments seem to have borrowed and spent beyond their means, and thus found themselves with major debt problems. Many Germans believe that their country "cleaned up its act" financially in the mid-2000s and should not have to aid errant nations with which it shares a currency (the euro). Such widespread views among German voters produce political pressure on the German government to oppose such help.

Ultimately, however, German foot-dragging on aid threatens the common currency zone itself, the Eurozone (the seventeen nations using the euro). Often financial deterioration among the hard-pressed Eurozone countries seems to be outrunning aid efforts. The latter nations are resisting German demands to immediately slash spending, which economic data suggest might produce depression there. The results might even include the break-up of the common currency zone itself, which could bring international economic instability and seriously harm Germany's own competitive position in world trade.

As you can see, political attitudes in one country can have a deep impact not only there but well beyond the nation's borders. We now turn to political attitudes as both a causal factor and a consequence in relation to political contention and cooperation.

THE TOPIC AND ITS DOMAINS

We may define **political attitudes** as values, beliefs, and preferences related to politics. Especially in representative democracies, the attitudes of people who pay attention to politics can play important roles in political contention and cooperation. Widespread political attitudes have played parts in numerous recent controversies. These include the resurgence of traditional religious values in some Muslim-majority nations, the growing alarm over global warming, and the ongoing responses to the lingering financial crisis. Starting in 2011, political attitudes contributed heavily to a new wave of democracy movements in North Africa and the Middle East, challenging authoritarian elites.

As we shall see, the impact of political attitudes involves the interplay of contention and cooperation. In the first section of this chapter, we focus on long-term aspects of countries' cultures that affect politics. Then we proceed to political socialization: how individuals develop their political attitudes. Next we consider the communications media, which supply information in ways that affect politics. Finally we discuss public opinion, the short-term sector of political attitudes that concerns the public's beliefs and preferences regarding politics, politicians, and policy issues at any given time.

POLITICAL CULTURE

A nation's **political culture** refers to the long-term, multigenerational sector of political attitudes: widespread and long-held values, beliefs, and related customs concerning what citizens expect from their government and how they relate to it. As was noted in chapter 4, political culture can be important for political legitimacy—the public's sense that their governmental system is rightful and just. Shared habits, values, and views among a country's citizens often provide informal support for, and a "comfort level" with, the rules of the game of political contention. First, however, we will get a feel for what political culture is by noting some of its sources.

Sources of Political Culture

As noted in chapter 3, typically multiple causal factors have impacts on political phenomena, and this is certainly true regarding political culture. Such factors as religion, history, ethnicity, past social structure, economic conditions, and popular literature, can all affect widely held values, customs, and beliefs.

Let's consider some historical examples of religion as a contributor to political culture. In chapter 4, we noted that for centuries the Russian Orthodox Church supported czarist authoritarian rule by teaching that kings ruled by divine right, and that it was a Christian duty to obey the czar. Thus, the legitimacy of authoritarian monarchic rule was bolstered. But religion can have other effects on political culture, as well. In Western Europe, the political sociologist Max Weber focused attention on "the Protestant ethic"—norms of hard work and frugal saving to gain prosperity and salvation, derived especially from the Calvinist brand of Protestant Christianity. The Protestant ethic, Weber contended, supported the steady rise and acceptance of capitalism in Europe. In a different sort of example, Islam considers achieving justice in the world to be part of religious duty, in contrast to Christianity, which tends to reserve worldly justice to secular government and leave ultimate moral justice to God. Hence many Muslims prefer a greater role for religion in criminal justice than Christians favor.

Another contributor to political culture can be socioeconomic circumstances. For example, historically, Japanese feudalism (along with certain Shinto and Confucian cultural views) stressed deference and respect for family and elders. Such habits surely contributed to a continued Japanese preference for group consensus and deference to the group in decision making. In another example, the American tendency toward individualism and limited government that prevailed until the Great Depression (see Country Case Studies, chapter 4) was affected by the independent, small-farm life of most settlers. If the type of government fits the political culture, the result is greater citizen cooperation with government.

Significant historical events and developments, too, can play roles in political culture. The American revolutionary experience of throwing off the rule of a distant king and parliament reinforced inclinations to limit central government power. It also fostered the cooperation between contending leaders that made possible agreement on the new constitution of 1787. In the eighteenth century, France had inherited a tradition of deference to a privileged class of landowners, but then came the French Revolution (1787–1789). The overthrow of the nobility and its privileges played a major part in instilling three things: (a) a distrust of organized group associations in politics, (b) a taste for disruptive protest when political grievances run high, and (c) a preference for a strong centralized state imposing the rule of law and equal treatment by government. These shared attitudes fostered cooperation in the subsequent structuring of French political contention. The Great Depression of the 1930s, and responses to it, deeply affected political cultures in many areas around the world. A key consequence was greater citizen cooperation with a stronger role for the government in the economy.

The Temptation to Stereotype

We have to beware, however, of oversimplifying political culture. The temptation to stereotype national, ethnic, or racial populations is probably as old as human communication. For example, Americans may be thought of as individualist, the French look to the centralized state, and Russians want a strong leader. But as Frenchman Alexis de Tocqueville pointed out in the 1830s, although such generalizations seem to give us broad understanding, they can oversimplify (see "The Philosophical Connection"). When political scientists characterize a nation's political culture, they are really only saying that certain values, beliefs, and customs exert a wide pull on many individuals there. In truth, people are subject to multiple influences, many of which are not unique to a specific national setting. And people often weigh contending values and preferences in making choices that ultimately may run counter to so-called national characteristics.

Moreover, a nation's political culture may be far from homogenous. First, cultural differences often exist between active participants in politics and government, on one hand, and the less involved general population, on the other. In long-established democracies, for example, leaders and activists in political parties, interest groups, and government institutions may be more consistently supportive of civil liberties than is the general population. Average citizens may favor freedoms of expression and association in general, but make exceptions regarding particular groups that they find especially threatening or distasteful.

In addition, one or more minority ethnic, racial, religious, regional, and/or linguistic subcultures may be significant in a society. Examples include the Muslim minority in France or Latinos and African Americans in the United States. A nation may even have no single majority ethnic or religious group, as in Lebanon. Or economic and social and inequalities might be so great as to contribute to significant cultural differences between economic strata, as in the traditional caste structure of India. Political cooperation is much more common within each subculture than between them, where contention is common.

Coinciding Versus Cross-Cutting Political Cleavages

Political subcultures often involve political cleavages, introduced in chapter 4. Political cleavages are enduring intergroup divisions in society over differences in ethnicity, religion, region, language, or socioeconomic stratum. When a society experiences "coinciding cleavages," distinct groups of people are opposed to each other in multiple issue areas, such as religious, ethnic, and economic policy. Such a pattern of political contention can divide a society into groups with distinctive values, customs, and beliefs. We saw this in northern Ireland in recent decades, where people in the lower economic strata tended to be ethnically Irish and Catholic in their religion, in contrast to the tendency of the upper socioeconomic strata to consist of Protestants and people who were ethnically Scottish or English. This situation enhances attachment to one's own political subculture and political cooperation with fellow members of it, and intensifies contention with one or more opposing groups.

In most developed nations, such lines of cleavage do *not* coincide. They do not divide society in the same way on issue after issue. Instead, we see what political scientists call "cross-cutting cleavages." For example, portions of different ethnic groups or religions find themselves allied as members of the same economic stratum or region, on economic or regional issues. That is, attachment to an ethnicity or a religion is softened by divisions within that group over other issues. Antipathy toward someone in one issue area is softened by alliance in other issue areas. Thus, political contention between groups tends not to harden into sharply contending political subcultures (see Figure 8.1).

In societies that *are* sharply divided by coinciding cleavages, the way that subcultures relate to one another can itself become an important part of the nation's political culture. This was the case in two societies that the political scientist Arend Lijphart studied in the 1950s and 1960s, Austria and the Netherlands. There, Protestant, Catholic, and secular leaders adopted a political culture of mutual accommodation that allowed each community to adopt its own approach to certain sensitive policy areas.[1] The assurance of a degree of autonomy for each group, with each getting its fair share of resources, produced a cooperative pattern of mutual accommodation which Lijphart called "consociational democracy."

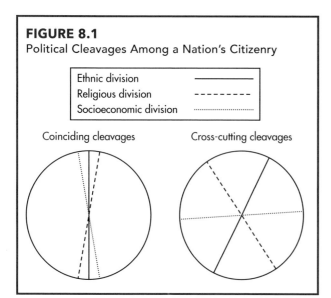

FIGURE 8.1
Political Cleavages Among a Nation's Citizenry

Ethnic division	———————
Religious division	- - - - - - - -
Socioeconomic division	··················

Coinciding cleavages   Cross-cutting cleavages

Democratic Political Culture

As was noted above, a key issue related to political culture involves political frameworks: how well a nation's governmental structure matches its political culture. The question of what types of governmental system fit what social and cultural circumstances is not new in the study of politics. It dates back as far as Aristotle in the fourth century BCE, and was raised by Baron de Montesquieu in the eighteenth century (see chapter 5). If a form of government fits well with the nation's political culture, political contention will be more likely to stay within the boundaries of procedural cooperation.

A key concern of some political thinkers has been to discover the values that support democracy. Classical political philosophers such as Plato and Aristotle (see chapter 5) linked democracy to a strong societal preference for the values of freedom and equality. But they were referring to direct or participatory democracy (as in ancient Athens), not representative democracy. In the modern world, what type of political culture most favors stable representative democracy that is accepted by the public?

The Civic Culture According to Almond and Verba's classic 1963 study,[2] a **civic culture** is present where large numbers of people (say, 50–60 percent or more) have a "participant" orientation toward politics. They tend to see themselves as competent and effective, and to see politics as important, at least enough so to vote. However, there will also be many people with a "subject" orientation. This group is aware of politics but is mainly passive and defers to government. And some people may even remain in a "parochial" orientation. For them, personal and local concerns predominate, and they have little political awareness. According to Almond and Verba, there must be portions of the population in these last two categories. If too many people participated in intense forms of political contention, the political system could become overwhelmed by demands that it could not meet. Pressures on government should be moderate enough to provide some leeway for it to make decisions and mistakes. Without this, rising mass discontent and political mobilization could bring instability, erosion of legitimacy, or even breakdown of democracy into authoritarian government.

What is the position of the civic culture in today's established democracies? The answer seems to be: fairly solid. Intensive participation in political groups and campaigns remains low (roughly 15–30 percent), but half to two-thirds or more of all citizens still vote. Political contention remains prominent, but substantial numbers of citizens fit in the subject and parochial categories. However, analysts have noticed two recent trends in democratic political culture that raise questions about it: a possible decline in "social capital" and a rise in "post-materialist" values.

Social Capital Particular factors may be found to affect democratic political culture. Political scientist Robert Putnam stressed that healthy democratic communities need a degree of self-government and related networks of voluntary social organization in civil society. Among the latter are fraternal organizations, sports leagues, women's groups, and other community organizations. In a form of cross-cutting cleavages, people of contending parties and policy preferences will thus share membership in local organizations and gain experience in working practically with each other. Participation in such local civic networks thus builds **social capital**, a fund of mutual trust and good will shared among members of otherwise contending groups. Social capital's mutual confidence and trust makes it possible for people to cooperate enough to get things done, and facilitates democratic participation.[3] Political participants can accept electoral defeat without fear that it would be disastrous.[4] (See "The Philosophical Connection").

To be sure, participation in local organizations and activities does not inevitably assure and protect democracy. In the case of the breakdown of German democracy between the world wars, widespread local civic participation in associations failed to save democracy (see chapter 9, "Concept in Context"). Civic participation in local associations can be a contributing factor to stable democracy, but it is not a sufficient condition.

Some analysts have suggested that in the United States, the trust-building networks in civil society that Robert Putnam described may have weakened in the late twentieth century. As Putnam put it in a later book, more Americans are "bowling alone," rather than in leagues, which helped link them to their neighbors.[5] He pointed to a recent decline in American civic involvement that has followed generational change over the last half of the twentieth century, and noted a correlation of this trend with the rise of television and its individualizing sociopsychological effects. Indeed, as we shall see in chapter 9, today most interest group memberships do not involve much face-to-face interaction in community groups or organizations with local chapters. Could a decline in social capital reduce participation in, and support for, democratic government?

Before we can answer this question, however, we must note two specific features of contemporary political culture. First, although face-to-face contact within groups may have declined, increased direct mail solicitation and communication, followed by the development of the Internet and other new media and their social networking capabilities, have opened new channels of participation and interaction. Second, another factor affecting democratic political culture is post-materialism.

Post-Materialism and Democratic Legitimacy In the last third of the twentieth century—among the baby boom generation born between 1946 and 1964—increasing numbers of younger and better-educated people in the developed democracies had known only high living standards and secure welfare states. They seemed less concerned than their parents with the basic economic worries about wages, jobs, working conditions, pensions, and health care, which had preoccupied the traditional political parties from the Great Depression through the postwar years. Baby boomers focused instead on **post-materialist** values, which include:

- peace, including nuclear disarmament,
- environmental well-being,
- women's rights,
- human rights,
- local autonomy and participation, and
- self-expression by cultural and lifestyle (e.g., sexual orientation) minorities.[6]

Many post-materialists distrusted the established political frameworks and parties. They preferred to participate in social movements pursuing the above-mentioned values. Unconventional expressions of "contentious politics" such as protest marches and demonstrations became more common.

As early as the 1960s and 1970s era of student protest over war and social inequality, some analysts feared these protests would undermine the legitimacy of the established political frameworks. Gains in education seemed to be bringing greater attention to government and higher expectations of it. Value-related political demands might outrun government performance and thus lead to a "crisis of democracy."[7] Meanwhile, the last decades of the twentieth century saw increasing budgetary pressures on government, reducing its capacity to address problems. Many post-materialists questioned whether they could trust the government to put long-term public values above narrow, short-term self-interest.

For their part, some political scientists wondered whether rising discontent, distrust in government, and loss of confidence in its ability to meet expectations[8] could lead to widespread alienation, cynicism, and withdrawal from politics. With membership in political parties dropping, political scientists Russell Dalton and Martin Wattenberg suggested that all this seemed to be accompanied by reduced attachment to the traditional political parties.[9] Could this situation be undermining the legitimacy of representative democratic government?

By the turn of the century, however, the answer seemed to be no. Poll respondents' approval of representative democracy has not fallen appreciably. Public respect for democracy in principle, and for the civil and political liberties enshrined in the human rights tradition, remained high during this period of rising educational levels, value-related concerns, and shrinking budgets for addressing problems. How so?

In practice, many post-materialists have found outlets in local community participation and related interest group activity. And notably, Dalton himself in more recent work has conceded that political parties have reached out to embrace voters' particular concerns (see chapter 10).[10] Both moderate left-of-center and conservative parties have absorbed, into their ideological identities, policy directions on issues from peace, environmental protection, and women's rights to worries about immigration. In addition, new parties—such as the Green parties on the left and the ethnic ultranationalist parties on the right (e.g., France's National Front)—have emerged to join in political contention. Recently, religious fundamentalist movements, and reactions against them, have found party outlets through which to engage in political contention. Protests and strikes, such as those in Greece and Spain in reaction to sharp budget cuts, often provide support for the concerns of such parties. In general, the participant orientation has remained strong in political contention in the established democracies.

Polling indications of distrust and dissatisfaction seem often to reflect unhappiness with the policies of the current leader, party, or coalition controlling government (or with the outcomes of those policies) rather than a lack of belief in democratic government itself. In Latin America, for example, opinion on how democracy "was working" dropped to very low points in 2001 when economic instability and policy failure were common, and had leaped upward by 2010. But when people are asked about democracy as a form of government, attitudes were much more stable and consistently favorable (see Figure 8.2). Dissatisfaction can make citizens determined to vote to try to fix things in the next election rather than leading them to reject the idea of democracy or withdraw into cynical passivity.

As long as partisan fervor in group contention is not too overwhelming, it may be a healthy expression of the classic participant orientation found in the

FIGURE 8.2

Latin American Views on How Democracy is Working and Whether Democracy is Preferred

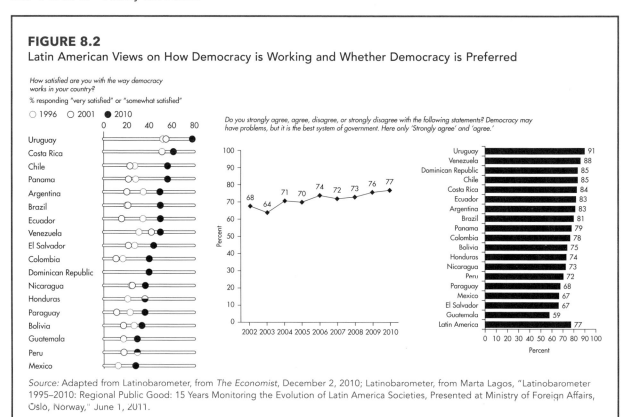

Source: Adapted from Latinobarometer, from *The Economist*, December 2, 2010; Latinobarometer, from Marta Lagos, "Latinobarometer 1995–2010: Regional Public Good: 15 Years Monitoring the Evolution of Latin America Societies, Presented at Ministry of Foreign Affairs, Oslo, Norway," June 1, 2011.

civic culture model. And distrust of opponents at the national level need not rule out cooperation and trust at the local level of politics. Although some types of involvement in civil society may be declining, other sorts of civic participation are emerging, such as local participation in social movement politics and new opinion groups formed around Internet-based social networks. The civic culture's rough balance of attitudes between participant and subject seems to remain in the established democracies. As the political scientist Ronald Inglehart put it, "postmodernization erodes respect for authority, but increases support for democracy."[11]

Political Culture and Transition to Democracy in Developing and Post-Communist Nations

How does a democracy-supporting political culture develop in the first place? How can it underpin a shift from authoritarian government to representative democracy?

According to the civic culture view, many of the developing world's political cultures are not ripe for representative democracy. The subject and parochial orientations discussed above may be dominant, and the participant orientation weak. Citizens tend to passively accept an authoritarian political process or ignore national government altogether. For example, German political culture at the turn of the twentieth century was strongly characterized by deference to authoritarian leadership, as was Russia's under the Czarist monarchy in the nineteenth century.

Under these circumstances, as we shall see in chapter 15, where regime change does occur, it tends merely to replace one authoritarian elite with another. A resurgence of ethnic solidarity or religious enthusiasm may lead to strong contention by a political movement based on reviving traditional values rather than instituting or deepening democracy. Once the movement's leaders gain power, they may foster the view that the previous authoritarian government had pursued the wrong values, not that authoritarian rule is inherently wrong. This was the case during the Iranian Revolution of 1979, when a social movement spearheaded by Shia Islamists under the personal leadership of Ayatollah Ruholla Khomeini overthrew a secular authoritarian monarchy that had ruled the country since mid-century. The revolution replaced the old regime with a new, religiously based authoritarian government of its own. What must happen so that challenges to authoritarian rule can lay the cultural foundation for democracy, rather than a different form of authoritarian regime?

Economic Factors and Modernization One key cluster of variables involves economic and social conditions. A nation with a poor, undeveloped, and uncertain economy is not fertile ground for democratization. In such circumstances, people may long for security and stability above all else. There may not be a large middle class with the education, economic resources, and confidence to engage in independent group behavior in civil society. These circumstances can discourage the mutual trust and confidence that democracy requires (in the social capital model). They may leave people vulnerable to intensely contentious social movements that operate outside ordinary democratic channels. Moreover, pervasive economic insecurity tends to raise the stakes of victory or defeat for the leaderships of ethnic nationalist or religious movements as they contend for control of government and all that it may bring (including the returns of bribery and corruption). Once in power, the new leaders may prove intolerant of future democratic challenge.

Accordingly, one approach to explaining the evolution of democracy recognizes economic improvement as important in the shift from authoritarian to democratic government. As we saw in chapter 3, the modernization school of thought stresses factors for cultural change that are broadly associated with the rise of democracy. Among these are increases in

- urbanization,
- industrialization,
- economic growth,
- literacy,
- modern communications,
- education,
- international contacts (travel, migration), and most importantly,
- the development of a sizable middle class.

Political Leadership Values A change in political culture toward the acceptance of representative democracy may also stem from the rise of political leaderships

At left, Jawaharlal Nehru, India's first prime minister after independence in 1947, and at right, Mohandas Gandhi, pacifist spiritual leader of India's anticolonial resistance before 1947, in conversation in 1946.

that are committed to democracy. This scenario allows a role for the personal leadership model of influence distribution (see chapter 3). In the early and middle twentieth century in India, for example, a major contribution was the commitment to nonviolence on the part of Mohandas Gandhi, the spiritual leader of the independence movement. Later came the commitment of Jawaharlal Nehru and his followers to an inclusive democratic vision, in the successful adoption of representative democracy after Indian independence from British rule in 1947.

Alternatively, economic factors can combine with leadership orientations to affect the development of cultural support for democracy. In Russia, following the fall of Communism, the 1990s saw a rapid introduction of multiparty democracy, with most party leaders committed to it. But economic recovery remained uneven, and a market-based middle class was still in its infancy. Party access to resources and television advertising time depended on connections, either to the government or to newly rich private businesspeople called oligarchs. New democratic institutions and parties remained shaky.

Then, in the subsequent decade of the 2000s, came booming oil and gas revenues to bolster the financial position of the government. But the political leadership of that period was not committed to a robust democracy, and pushed through various changes that ensured the dominance of the leading party, United Russia. President Vladimir Putin did seem to want whatever political legitimacy could be gained from holding elections. However, his government to some extent reflected the residual belief, inherited from Russia's traditional political culture, that order and well-being depend on centralized, controlling leadership. This pattern of "electoral authoritarian" government is even more evident in other nations of the former Soviet Union. For example, in both Belarus (see chapter 1's Country Case Study) and Kazakhstan, an authoritarian political culture remains underneath democratic formalities.

Multiparty electoral procedures have been spreading in the developing world, too, but there the development of a democratic political culture remains uneven. Conditions of economic stagnation in many developing nations probably do not help. In Islamic countries, religious pressures might also weigh in against cultural freedom. Some Islamists express the view that political practice must be rooted in a nation's culture, and that human rights and democracy are Western ideas that should not be applied as universal standards (see "The Human Rights Connection").

Do these realities mean that human rights-based pressure for electoral contention should back off because the appearance of democratic procedures can hide a still-authoritarian political culture? In the transformation from an authoritarian regime to representative democracy, the answer seems to be no. Incremental change in the political framework can facilitate the gradual development of attitudes favoring a more democratic political culture. As long as the electoral procedures of representative democracy reflect some degree of freedom and fairness, prospects remain for further incremental development toward genuine

THE HUMAN RIGHTS CONNECTION | Human Rights and Cultural Variation

A major area of human rights controversy involves cultural differences between nations. A common objection to applying human rights standards is that "our culture is different; we don't see things that way, and those rules shouldn't apply to us." This objection is prominent in the debate about the treatment of women in some political cultures. For example, Islamic fundamentalist authorities in some countries assert that to preserve the dignity of females, their hair and bodies must be covered in ways that are not form fitting and their activities outside the home such as work, movement, and education must be restricted.

In principle, the human rights tradition opposes moral relativism—the idea that moral values are all relative to the surrounding culture and not valid outside it. The abstract idea of rights seems to have originated in the West, but the call for human rights in the post–World War II era came from all parts of the world—from the surviving Jews of Eastern Europe and the Chinese of Nanking, for example, as well as from the world's national governments as they signed the U.N.'s Universal Declaration in 1948. The crux of human rights is that some human behaviors must be prohibited, and cultural variation provides no excuse. Today everyone condemns certain practices that were once accepted in some cultures, such as human sacrifice in early Indo-American kingdoms. All major religions, despite their many differences, prohibit murder. The idea of universal limits to human behavior, which local cultural differences may not legitimately transgress, is largely accepted throughout the world.

In its key texts and in practice, however, the human rights tradition is minimalist, general in language, and pragmatic. It allows for debate and local cultural variation. For example, the U.N.'s civil-political Covenant calls for free and fair elections, but it does not describe a specific arrangement. Even a right such as freedom of expression has its limits. In the United States, for example, it does not protect speech that poses a "clear and present danger" of harm to others. The human rights Covenants allow the government to make exceptions to some rights in order to preserve "public order." Interpretations of this approach differ in different countries. For example, some European nations prohibit "hate speech" that is not prohibited in the United States. Some critics of the public order exception see it as a crack through which all kinds of suppression of dissent may travel. The key point here is that the human rights tradition does accommodate local cultural differences somewhat, even as it aims to protect the rights of humans in general.

The U.N.'s economic-social Covenant has similarly loose provisions. In principle, its "cultural rights" aspects prohibit one culture from suppressing another, but does not define specifically what a culture is. Economically, the Covenant requires feasible steps toward assuring "an adequate standard of living" with regard to food, health, and so forth, requiring only progress on these fronts. In contrast, human rights provisions on nondiscrimination are much clearer: the state may not provide education to males while excluding females, for example. And the civil-political human rights Covenant presents civil-political obligations as immediate, ruling out the idea that economic development to reduce poverty permits postponing civil-political rights.

respect for contending political associations. Progress can be slow and the road long. Authoritarian limits on democratic procedures can persist for decades, as they did prior to the Arab Spring of 2011. But, once planted, the seeds of free group contention may suddenly sprout.

POLITICAL SOCIALIZATION

Political socialization affects both the long-term side of political attitudes, political culture, and the short-term side: public opinion, which we will consider later in this chapter. Through **political socialization**, people pass on to others their values, norms, and views concerning politics and policies. How are these attitudes conveyed? Political socialization can take many forms. Some sorts of political socialization are conscious and intentional, and some unconscious and unintended. Sometimes the influence comes from individuals, sometimes from groups, and sometimes from practices in society at large. Here, we will examine a series of agents of political socialization, from the family and the schools to peer groups, religion, the workplace, and political parties. (We will consider the mass media in a later section of this chapter.)

Family

The earliest influence on most children is their parents. Parents influence the values, norms, and views of children both consciously and unconsciously. They may teach norms of behavior such as self-reliance, self-assertion, cooperation, and fairness, or deference and submission. Parents also influence children in indirect and unintended ways. Children overhear parents' statements about values, politics, parties, leaders, and other social groups. They observe the example set by parent behavior in "family politics."

At the extremes, the difference between a parent who rules with an iron hand, and one who encourages children to come up with their own opinions is very important. Parent identification with an ethnic or racial group, an economic class, or a religion, cannot help but influence children. Attitudes regarding gender can affect their children's views. Role relationships that develop among siblings of different ages may also play a part.

Schools

Schools socialize children to identify with their nation and respect its system of government (see chapter 4). They teach the history of the nation, often in glowing terms, and students are often assigned to read literature related to key events in their nation's history. Schools in most nations also perform patriotic rituals, like saying a pledge of allegiance to the nation and singing the national anthem.

U.S. schoolchildren and their teacher pledging allegiance to the American flag.

In socioculturally conservative settings, such as under authoritarian regimes in Saudi Arabia and Iran, courses teaching an Islamic worldview may be compulsory. As we noted in chapter 4, family socialization may reinforce or contradict school political socialization. When family socialization opposes school socialization, the latter's effects may be considerably weakened.

Especially for students in the established democracies, higher education can have major effects. College education frequently introduces students to a greater range of alternatives on issues and politics than they had previously known. They may be exposed to critical thinking and a greater tolerance of diversity, appropriate to a political culture supporting representative democracy. Students may feel more competent to pay attention to and participate in politics. In 2011 in Egypt, young, college-educated people spearheaded the challenge of participation there to democratize their nation's politics.

Peer Groups

Peer groups, too, can influence values, norms, and beliefs related to politics, from adolescence into adulthood. Our **peers** are people in our social environment who are like us. Sometimes the term refers to a "primary group" that includes face-to-face contact, and sometimes it refers to a broader group of people with similar characteristics. Teenagers are often influenced by their peers in school, but such influence doesn't usually have much long-term bearing on their politics. However, if the group is a gang or "the wrong crowd" (in parents' eyes), its influence can foster attitudes and behaviors that defy authority. In college, where many students first consider political ideas and issues, student friendships, discussions, and group interactions can have political socialization effects.

In later life, our peers may be our neighbors, friends sharing racial or ethnic backgrounds, members of a professional organization, or members of leisure activity, religious, and community groups. Although our political values, norms, and beliefs have often taken shape by our twenties, they may still change. If you become involved with a local community as an adult, the community's expectations may influence your pursuits and attitudes. It is even possible for our fellow citizens to exert a form of regional or national peer pressure on us, as Alexis de Tocqueville suggested about early nineteenth-century America (see "The Philosophical Connection," chapter 2).

As was noted above, a nation's political culture may be diverse and include distinct religious, ethnic/racial, regional, and/or social class subcultures. In these cases, our fellow subculture members may influence our values and norms. Usually, however, the effect is to reinforce earlier political socialization. Whatever the nature of the cultural or political groups that we identify with, today's media provide us with access to information from nearby and around the world that can reinforce or alter our values, views, and norms.

Literary and Popular Culture

Literature, historical writing, and popular culture can also exert a socializing effect outside of school. A nation's historians and writers of historical fiction may vary in their viewpoints, but often they also convey elements of a shared perspective, contributing somewhat to socialization. Heroines and heroes in a nation's popular literature and television shows may represent role models and values.

The cinema has also had an important effect, especially given its wide audience. In the multicultural United States during World War II, for example, war movies often presented members of different ethnic and religious groups fighting together in a single military unit, discovering their common humanity in their shared sense of solidarity. Later, such film images as Clint Eastwood's "Dirty Harry" and Bruce Willis's "Diehard" character expressed an image of the committed individual having to go around the rules to get something done, perhaps

THE PHILOSOPHICAL CONNECTION | Marcuse and Habermas

Herbert Marcuse was a German product of the Frankfurt School of critical social theory who, before World War II, emigrated to the United States where he did most of his writing. In an early work, *Eros and Civilization* (1955),* Marcuse argued that modern industrial society's stress on what he called "the performance principle" produced psychological repression. However, he was best known for a broader work, One Dimensional Man (1964).[†]

While critical of Soviet bureaucratic socialism, Marcuse focused his fire on conformism under capitalism. He observed that peoples' lives are immersed in the productivity and technological rationality of the industrial and consumer economies. But inherent in that system, he argued, was not only waste, destruction, harm to nature, and failure to focus on people's real needs, but also manipulation of people's sense of their own needs and interests. For Marcuse, that manipulation was not only a matter of popular culture—advertising, entertainment, and news all sticking to the basic story of the successes and satisfactions of the system. Beyond that, he maintained, was a daily life in which, both in work and leisure time, the technological and economic patterns around people are psychologically absorbed into, and occupy, their inner lives. Marcuse argued that the boundary between inner and outer life erodes to yield one psychological dimension, that is, in effect, dominated by the economic/technological "establishment." In effect,

Marcuse argued, the prevailing ideology is carried into attitudes not by official propaganda, as in the totalitarian Soviet Union, but rather by the work, products, and enjoyments of daily life itself.

Under these circumstances, Marcuse argued, the prospects for human liberation seem paltry. If the operations of daily life serve to fix people's ideas about themselves and their world, how are people to step outside to take a critical or comparative look? Alternative paths are considered unworkable and/or utopian, so they will not be understood or tried. Marcuse argued that under these circumstances, rebellion could only take a vague and negative form: the diffuse "No!" of protest, without a clearly defined alternative to the status quo. On that point, Marcuse was in touch with the general approach of the student rebellion of the late 1960s and early 1970s that heralded him as its guru. What the diverse ideas and forms of contention by protesters shared in common, allowing them to cooperate to some extent, was concern framed by values: charges that the established system failed to achieve either peace or freedom.

Later in the century came a more realistic evolution of the Frankfurt School perspective, that of another German, Jurgen Habermas. A prolific writer whose thinking evolved through phases of exploration, Habermas started with a Frankfurt-style critique of the domination of modern society by instrumental (or "strategic") rationality and knowledge—using reason only to implement the prevailing goals of the system.

helping pave the way for the 1980s' resurgence of antigovernment individualism in the United States.

Religion

As we have seen, religion often influences political culture. Peers in a religious congregation are all under the same socializing influence of the minister, priest, rabbi, or imam, who may make statements with political implications. Moreover, attitudes toward politics may be affected by the method of decision making within the religion. In Christianity, the Catholic and Orthodox communities used hierarchies to decide how to interpret the Christian scriptures, whereas Protestantism left interpretation to individual believers and local ministers. To some degree, these differences in decision-making patterns may influence some of their adherents' conceptions of what was proper in public life outside religion. Religious figures' tolerance or intolerance of other religions may affect the attitudes of their congregants.

But Habermas diverged from standard Frankfurt School views in three key ways. First, he was less critical of logic and reason per se; he held out hope for what he called "emancipatory" rationality: using reason to rise above mere instrumentalism to the exploration of more desirable values and alternatives. Over time, this emphasis evolved into a focus on communication.

Second, rather than seeing a single source of domination in the prevailing system as a whole, he distinguished different sources: the strategic "discourses" of the market, the state (including social welfare bureaucracies), and political parties. Third, Habermas articulated a scenario that he called "communicative action" and the "ideal communication community." This seems to refer to any communication which (a) is free from steering by organizational hierarchies, (b) involves free discussion and debate about both the accuracy of empirical claims and the desirability of values and paths of action to address the problematic situations, (c) implicitly endeavors toward practical agreement, and (d) treats each participant as a free and equal in status. These aspects of rational communication, Habermas argued, point out a universal ethic of discourse, which can be applied to resolve any challenge.

Arguably, a limitation of Habermas's argument is his seeming rejection of key players in the political process. Government and political parties, for example, are among the "bad guys" steering communication toward manipulated strategic discourse. The only pure and transformative communication would be that of social movement politics, such as environmentalism or feminism, for example. But arguably, many actual examples of the type of communication that Habermas seems to stress occur in and around political parties and government, for example. And at least some portions of parties and government certainly seem to be attempting transformative action.

Moreover, what seem to be other empirical examples of political action by communication communities, like the Arab Spring revolutions, have ended up in new forms of oppression. This was partly because the participants engaging in the destruction of bad regimes proved unwilling or unable to engage in the sort of real-world organization (e.g., in political parties and government) that Habermas seems to disapprove of. Successful contention often requires cooperation that includes not only rational agreement but also organization.

Can you think of a situation in which you rebelled against a distasteful surrounding condition and engaged in communication to try to alter it? Did you feel a pressure to accommodate your views to those around you?

---

* Herbert Marcuse, *Eros and Civilization: A Philosophical Inquiry into Freud* (Boston: Beacon Press, 1955).

† Herbert Marcuse, *One Dimensional Man: Studies in the Ideology of Advanced Industrial Society* (Boston: Beacon Press, 1964).

Workplace

Especially for those who work for long in the same field, political socialization received in the workplace can have lasting influence. Our work consumes more of our lives than any other social activity. Management hierarchies have access to workers in offices, factories, or projects, whether private or governmental. To varying degrees, the employing organization may support a mind-set and values that employees cannot ignore, especially in their younger years. This influence can shape not only a sense of mission for employees regarding their economic role, but also a larger outlook on the political world that fits that mission.

Political Parties

As we shall see in chapter 10, political parties seek to socialize people toward the values, ideologies, and interests that they represent. This phenomenon was especially prominent in parts of Europe in the early and middle twentieth century.

For example, some of the social democratic parties there sought to organize a whole social life for their supporters. A party might sponsor sports leagues, youth groups, newspapers, women's groups, adult education, and so on, to bring together their likely supporters. To some extent, these venues facilitated political socialization to the party's values and outlook, partly through peer socialization in these activities. In a less comprehensive form of political socialization, in some large American cities in the late nineteenth and early twentieth centuries, political parties tried to socialize various new immigrant groups into American political life. For example, in return for jobs, services, opportunities for socializing and solidarity, and other help to Irish immigrants, the America's Democratic Party looked for their voting support.

In single-party governments, the state itself could take this route. In the former Soviet Union, the Communist party organized groups for this purpose, and party control of the surrounding media reinforced their messages. In the 1930s and 1940s, the Nazis organized teenagers into the "Hitler youth" to socialize them into their party's ideology. Part of the Nazis' goal was to pry young Germans loose from the restraints of family and religious socialization, and glorify the idea of dying for the fatherland. They organized competitive activities that encouraged rough treatment of weak performers to desensitize the children to violence.

Where there is significant multiparty competition under representative democracy, the public may encounter the values and ideology of each contending party. Especially in election campaigns, in the words of mid-century political scientist E. E. Schattschneider, contending parties are each trying to "mobilize bias" in favor of the values, views, and interests that the party is trying to represent.[12] But here, political culture is not likely to be dominated by any one party. Elections themselves socialize the public to respect the custom of contending views, and each party's human right (with freedom of association and expression) to present its views.

In short, the many different sources of political socialization contend with each other. Sources of socialization from childhood may be overcome by those that come later. But often multiple sources of socialization cooperate in reinforcing an underlying political culture or subculture. (Some social critics see all of these sources of socialization as woven together in a web of constraint; see "The Philosophical Connection.")

In addition, socializing factors affect people's views on the policy issues and politics of the day. An especially important factor in this context is the news media, so much so that it deserves its own section of this chapter.

THE NEWS MEDIA

Another major factor influencing political attitudes is the news media, which is especially important in the operation of representative democracy. To understand and participate in the political process, citizens need news that is accurate and informative about issues, leaders, and alternative policy proposals. How effectively do the media play this role? What changes have occurred in recent years?

The Media and Political Socialization

In chapter 4, we noticed the role of the news media as countries met the challenges of national identity and legitimacy. First newspapers, and then radio and television in the twentieth century (and now also the Internet) can inform a whole country at once about an event, which thus becomes something happening to the nation as well as to those immediately involved. This encourages people to identify with their nation beyond their own parochial locality or group. News respectfully highlighting decisions by institutions tend to reinforce the public's sense of their legitimacy.

In addition, news media coverage can shape the public's awareness of the range of alternatives for public policy and political leadership. If the news simply covers a government policy without context or critical evaluation, the media tends to socialize people to accept what they presume to be what the experts have advised the government to do.

The Development of the Mass Media

In much of Western Europe and North America, representative democracy had taken hold well before the advent of today's broadcast media technologies. Many nineteenth- and early twentieth-century newspapers were largely party mouthpieces. Each party's paper simply reflected the party's view of the world. When radio emerged in the 1920s and 1930s, a few prominent governments in Europe were turning in totalitarian directions, most notably Nazi Germany, Fascist Italy, and the Soviet Union. These regimes viewed the media's news reporting as a key tool for spreading the official ideology and its view of the world, in what we have come to call **propaganda**. In such cases, the media became an instrument of partisan political socialization. The aim was to make the dominant party's ideology central to the nation's political culture, and to enshrine the regime's top leader in the hearts of citizens. There could be no competing viewpoints.

The effectiveness of such strategies in molding minds depended partly on whether family, religious, or ethnic group socialization ran counter to it. Later in the century, some authoritarian governments—such as the many military ones in Latin America and Africa from the 1960s through the 1980s—did not try to propagate a totalitarian ideology. Instead they exercised limit-setting power over the news media—removing messages and messengers that clearly ran counter to the status quo.

As television joined radio in the post–World War II era in the representative democracies, these new broadcast media were generally not allowed to further the interests of only one party or another. In Europe, government-owned networks with independent management boards dominated television. For the most part, they engaged in even-handed news reporting. As privately owned outlets developed later in the twentieth century, government regulations banned privately purchased television advertising in the last few weeks of election campaigns. Instead, networks provided free prime airtime to the parties to get their message out.

In the United States, where the broadcast media have always been entirely privately owned, the era of the 1930s–1950s witnessed a climate of government regulation and standards aimed at the public interest. The new television networks tended toward fairly neutral and objective reporting on issues and contending parties. (Notably, neutrality toward other nations and their views, however, was viewed as much less necessary.) Networks competing for advertisers and profits wanted to reach as wide an audience as possible.

They did not want to turn off any significant portion of their potential audience by being associated with narrow political views. Similarly, as newspapers became predominantly dependent on advertising revenue for their support in the twentieth century, most of them also strove to avoid obvious partisanship in news reporting.

The Media Today

In recent decades, most people have been getting their information about politics and government from the broadcast and electronic media, especially television. Under representative democracy, most television and radio outlets are now private, but some are still owned by the government (e.g., the British Broadcasting Company (BBC)). Such media compete for the largest possible audience, mostly using programming that is entertaining and not politically controversial, while delivering the advertising that provides the income and profits. Such advertising often implies that happiness lies in pleasant consumerism rather than community or political involvement. Comedy and drama usually deal with personal concerns and occasionally social issues, but rarely include political involvement as part of a story line.

In the world of private commercial news, the coverage of each politically newsworthy event tends to be brief, partly for fear of losing the attention of the average viewer. Politically relevant news must compete for precious minutes with coverage of such events as sensational crimes and court trials that often are of greater interest to audiences.

As we noted in chapter 3, political coverage in broadcast media news tends to emphasize, for audience appeal, the drama of personal rivalry in politics. Typically, this comes at the expense of in-depth analysis of the issues and the facts related to them. Much coverage focuses on the chief executive, whether president or prime minister. Official events get the most attention, and coverage relies heavily on official sources. This media practice tends to foster the personal leadership model of the distribution of influence, which tends to portray political contention in terms of rival leaders, their followers, and who seems to be winning the "horse race" at any given time.

Another theme in broadcast news coverage is simplicity. In covering politically relevant events, broadcast news frequently offers a single simplified explanation of a development, without in-depth context and historical background. A single motive may be given for a public figure's action, with little attention to other contributing factors. On important issues, reporters typically treat their audience to little more than brief "sound bites" by spokespersons on the opposing sides. This leaves people poorly equipped to sort out what is true and what is false. Neither the broadcast media nor most print outlets have the resources to do much full-scale investigative reporting to evaluate the accuracy of the public statements that they report.

This situation can tempt some public figures to occasionally employ distortions or even outright falsehoods in what sound like statements of fact. The idea behind this tactic seems to be that the audience's first impression counts most. Any later revelation that a statement is false is likely to be mentioned only briefly in the media (if at all) and little noticed. Often the matter is left to a competing partisan sound bite that the public is similarly ill equipped to evaluate. News media may be reluctant to point out that a statement is flatly false for fear of appearing partisan themselves to advertisers (see "Concept in Context"), or of losing access to the public figure in the future.

In the end, the contention between different perspectives tends to be simplified into two gladiator viewpoints, the left and the right. Many in the audience may ask, how can the two sides be saying such different things about a single situation? The audience may end up disengaged and distrustful of much of the political content in the media.

To be sure, we can find more informative exceptions to these patterns in today's broadcast and electronic media. Television networks may offer investigative programming in a "news magazine" format that explores issues in greater depth than does the ordinary evening news. And with the growing importance of the Internet, many of the magazines, newspapers, wire services, blogs and "tweets" from the entire world are immediately available to us. Blogs and social media even allow us to comment on reports and read the comments of others.

Certainly, we can learn more from several sources providing different views than we can from any one source. But the fragmentation and abundance of information on the Internet can invite people to either suffer sensory overload and check out in confusion, or stay with outlets that match their preexisting preferences. The Internet can provide access to a stream of information from just about any group, immersing us in that group's special point of view. However, these sources may or may not be trustworthy. And for much of the public, it is still television that they have time to access. The most watched television outlets tend to stick to a mainstream range of issues and views that they believe their audience wants to hear about.

Perspectives and preferences are especially popular if they point to policy positions that seem to engage cooperation between substantial portions of both the left and the right. This may leave people unaware of what they need to know to form thoughtful views on important policy issues. For example, in the 2000s, otherwise contending groups seemed to be able to cooperate in support of "biofuels." Biofuels are components of car or truck fuel (15 percent of it at most) that come mostly from agriculture in some form, such as ethanol processed from corn or sugar cane, and biodiesel processed from palm or canola oils. Biofuels had an aura of alternative energy about them, and seemed to help achieve energy independence from oil imports. However, the biofuel enthusiasm—actively supported by farmers and plantation owners—tended to suppress or ignore several inconvenient facts: that taking corn out of the grain market and land out of food production would make food more scarce and expensive for the poor (especially in developing areas), that large forest areas might be cut for palm oil plantations (e.g., in Malaysia), that crop processing into biofuels requires almost as much energy as we get from the product, and that if the price of oil and gas were to come down (as occurred in the last half of 2014), the high cost of biofuel would be prohibitive in comparison to conventional fuels. Biofuels seem to be a bad bargain.

The overall consequence in this rapidly changing media culture is a combination of (a) some people who are well informed because they have the time, education, and interest to seek out information, (b) a number of partisans who access only information from their side, (c) some who cannot afford the latest modes of access to the news and thus are ill informed, and d) many others who become disengaged and distrustful.

Is There Bias in Media News Coverage?

The news media contribute to the shape and boundaries of the public agenda, the range of issues that enter public opinion as significant. This fact is not lost on partisan media outlets. Today some television networks and radio stations are returning to the path of the old party-mouthpiece newspapers, presenting selective and often biased portrayals of issues and facts related to them. In the United States, for example, this accusation has for some time been leveled at some conservative "talk radio" stations and at the cable television network Fox News. After many years of this, MSNBC appeared and began offering a left-of-center viewpoint to contend with Fox. On such outlets, producers and talk-show anchors select stories that shed positive light on a favored party, officeholder, candidate, or ideological direction, or that are unflattering to opposing contenders or points of view. Interviewing, analysis, and evaluative commentary may be steered in favor of certain policy directions.

If there are multiple partisan sources, people can get from them a full articulation of the major contending viewpoints. And if the reporting on matters of fact is accurate, the audience can sometimes hear more about a wider range of events and conditions than are covered by the traditional news outlets. The key here is actual accuracy in reporting on matters of fact, which can vary among partisan sources.

Within the realm of factually accurate reporting, however, two unfortunate phenomena are evident. Even a nonpartisan, neutral outlet may see its objectivity questioned by partisans if the facts that it reports are not favorable to them and their views (see "Concept in Context"). On the other hand, however, subtle bias may indeed be found amid factually accurate reporting and the appearance of neutrality. Coverage may sidestep developments favorable to the candidates, parties, or policy directions that the editors or publishers oppose, or note them only briefly in passing. Meanwhile, minor occurrences that favor one's side may be made to sound significant. (These tendencies may be found especially in local print outlets, which most people automatically assume to be politically neutral in their news reporting.) Often such low-profile partisanship in news coverage may not be noticed by many readers. Political activists can detect it, but ordinary readers are likely to assume the coverage to be neutral and objective.

This phenomenon can express itself in ways that may not be partisan in a conventional political sense, but that operate on behalf of the nation as a whole. A country's news outlets often judge significance and insignificance according to the values, interests, and widespread beliefs—in both the long-standing political culture and contemporary public opinion—of their nation. For example, American news coverage by the mainstream networks may differ in emphasis and tone from that offered on the BBC cable TV channel, or Internet access to Reuters, the most prominent British wire service. Al Jazeera, the Qatar-based television and Internet news outlet, tends to report accurately but couches coverage in a more Islamic and Arab point of view; it has had great difficulty getting access to the American cable news audience.[13] Clearly, media outlets can play a role in the political socialization of their citizens.

Whatever the partisan outlets' motivations, respect for the human right to freedom of expression allows them to do what they do. But news outlets should keep in mind democracy's need for truthful representation of the facts related to politics and policymaking. The public needs an accurate understanding of the

CONCEPT IN CONTEXT | "Balanced" Coverage in Nonpartisan Media Outlets

Media outlets that take an objective approach to political and issue-related news sometimes face accusations of having political leanings. Some partisan commentators characterize basically nonpartisan outlets as having a left-of-center bias or a conservative bias largely because the outlet's more objective coverage differs from the commentator's own orientation. Indeed, pursuing the facts of a story may not yield a "balance" between two points of view if one of the perspectives is not supported by the facts. In some situations, an in-depth analysis of an issue may be uninviting to a newspaper or network if a full and accurate exploration of the facts upsets the desired impression of "balanced" coverage. We should want full coverage of the story, but not all outlets are so courageous.

However, nonpartisan news outlets have one tendency in common with the handful of openly partisan ones—an inclination to feed the latest news appetites of their audience. Because commercial media are competing in a marketplace, they often pay attention to what interests their consumers at any given time. In the United States in 1966, for example, when the majority favored the war in Vietnam, or in 2003 when the majority of Americans favored invading Iraq, more stories appeared

covering facts that seemed to support the path of war. In these periods, one might accuse the media of "conservative" ideological bias. But by 1969 and 2006, respectively, the majority had turned against war. More coverage was directed at the problems encountered by the war strategy, which in turn invited some conservative partisans to claim that there was a left-of-center bias among the media. In fact, such skewing of coverage is not fundamentally the consequence of ideological bias. For each war, the media seemed primarily to be accommodating to changes in public opinion and reporting what their audience was eager to hear about. Still, occasionally the media's coverage may deserve critical resistance because it may not be giving the citizenry the full picture that it deserves.

One conclusion is clear: there is a relevant distinction between common-sense facts on the one hand, and subjective interpretations and normative evaluations of them, on the other. In recent years, some commentators have claimed that news reporting is generally subjective and value-laden rather than objective. However, this view contrasts sharply with our common-sense experience that there are facts that contending groups can agree on, and the public needs access to those facts.

alternative policies, issues, parties, leaders, and significant facts related to them. Just as officeholders in a representative democracy rely on accurate information to make thoughtful choices in politics and government, so, too, do the members of the public rely on fair and accurate media reporting as they try to thoughtfully form their attitudes and voting preferences.

To be sure, some matters of fact are complex and invite disagreement among informed observers pursuing scientific truth. Indeed, disagreements in analysis and interpretation are a legitimate part of politics. But outright misrepresentation of matters of fact is among the most powerful sources of distrust between political contenders. It undermines that minimal degree of procedural cooperation that keeps politics civil.

PUBLIC OPINION

Public opinion is the public's views and preferences concerning the issues, leaders, and parties of the day. Many people have the impression that polling will readily reveal the majority opinion on issues. However, people who answer poll questions vary greatly in their attention to the issues and the strength and clarity of their positions. People tend to have more knowledge and clearer preferences about issues that affect them as members of various groups. The public's views may be influenced by the media, the "experts" (some backed by accurate information, some not), or party and interest group leaders. Polling methods may vary in quality, and the results vary in their validity. Here we shall first look at how political scientists measure public opinion, and then proceed to some factors that influence public opinion and its relationship to ideology.

Measuring Public Opinion

When political scientists conduct surveys on the public's views concerning an issue, they typically want to discover peoples' relevant beliefs and preferences. This includes how they want the government to respond to the problem. But researchers first face a question: whom should they ask? Political scientists obviously cannot survey whole populations. Over many decades of experience, they have discovered how to survey a **representative sample** of the population they are interested in—a portion of the population that fairly accurately represents the array of opinions in the whole.

One requirement for this purpose is **random selection** of respondents, such as by having a computer generate random phone numbers to be called. In addition, survey researchers need to avoid overrepresenting or underrepresenting groups that are relevant to the survey topics. For example, imagine that researchers are doing a national survey on whether the national government should provide more aid to public schools. Ideally, they want to be sure that city dwellers, suburbanites, rural dwellers, parents of schoolchildren, ethnic minorities, residents of different regions, women, and so forth are sampled roughly in the same proportions as we find them in the overall population. To achieve this, in the poll, respondents are asked to identify the groups that they belong to. Then the researchers might statistically reduce the weight of the data from an oversampled group or weight more heavily the data from an underrepresented group. With these and other state-of-the-art methods, a telephone survey of no more than a thousand respondents can provide a good scientific sample of public opinion, within a 3–4 percent margin of error, for an overall population of a hundred million or more.

Recently, telephone pollsters have encountered problems with fewer people willing to answer a polling organization's call and do the survey, and more people only using cellphones or the Internet rather than traditional landline phones for communication. Some pollsters have adjusted by including some cellphone respondents. A few have even gone to the Internet, randomly sampling a large pool of Internet users who have registered to be available and adjusting to be sure demographic groups are represented in the right proportions. Despite adversity, pollsters continue to get good results. Regarding polling just prior to the American presidential election in 2012, the U.S.'s National Council on Public Polls calculated that the average error for the major polls on the national popular vote was just 1.4 percent off the final election results, in line with poll performance in past presidential elections.[14]

Another key question is just what the researchers want to know about the views of the respondents on an issue. At the outset, they might be interested in whether the respondents were *aware* of a phenomenon: for example, do they believe that global climate is warming, or do they believe that the national government is running a budget deficit? People's empirical views concerning the political issue are relevant to whether they see it as a problem that government might address. Secondly, the researchers may want to know how significant the problem is to the respondents, either by directly asking or by having respondents rank its importance alongside other issues.

In addition, the researchers are interested in what respondents want government to do about the problem—their preferences on policy. Should government act to regulate or tax fuel burning (by cars and power plants, for example) to reduce global warming, even if that increases the prices of gasoline and electric power? Should government deal with a budget deficit mainly by reducing social spending (e.g., on health care or help for the poor), or by reducing the military budget, or by raising taxes?

In asking these questions, pollsters have to be alert to two key considerations. One concern is not to distort results by asking the question in a way that encourages a particular answer. For example: "Should the government do anything about the horrific prospect of global warming?" immediately implies that global warming is a problem. Rather, ask about whether the respondent thinks there is a problem (as we saw above), and give them options about how much the government should do. A second pitfall is closely related to the first. The questions should not be too general. If the question asks "Do you believe that the government is intervening too much in people's lives," responses may point in a different direction—for example, a general ideological one—than if the question regards a specific policy area, like social security or health care. The more general the question, the less the pollster may be learning about what people think government should actually do.

Another important aspect of polling is how strongly the respondents feel about what they favor: their **preference intensity**. One way that survey researchers learn about this is by giving the respondents a statement and asking them not just whether they agree or disagree, but also whether the respondents strongly agree, agree, disagree, strongly disagree, or have no opinion.

The responses may be presented in graphic form. The vertical axis shows how many gave a specific response. The horizontal one presents the four options in the form of a spectrum from strongly agree at one extreme to strongly disagree at the other. Three patterns commonly appear, whether weakly or strongly, in such data. If the respondents mainly agree with the statement, the highest data points will be in the "strongly agree" and "agree" categories on the left of the graph, and the lowest percentages will be on the right. Where the pattern is either strong agreement or strong disagreement, with the number of respondents high on one side and low on the other, the resulting graph is called a "J" curve. If the respondents are more evenly split, there will be a **normal distribution**, or "bell-shaped curve." Here the public is not very sharply divided. With fewer people displaying intense preferences at the sides and more in the moderate categories in the middle, policy makers have more leeway to try what they think will work without worrying so much about the immediate public response.

Third, public opinion can be sharply divided, with two bulges ("modes"), one at each side. In this outcome, most people have strong views on one side or the other, and few have moderate views. Political scientists sometimes refer to this **bimodal distribution** of opinion as "polarized." Of course, many survey research results fall in between these types of curves or mix them in various ways.

Public Opinion and Voting

Public opinion isn't limited to attitudes regarding issues. The public also forms views on parties and leaders. Here there is a special, very important poll: the election. Votes cast in elections provide a uniquely large sample of the citizenry, but it is not a random sample. Those who vote generally possess a minimal level of concern and awareness of politics that has motivated them to go to the polls. This pool may somewhat overrepresent the better educated, more active, or more partisan citizens, and it may be weighted toward middle and upper socioeconomic strata.

Voting and elections form the topic of chapter 11, but here we should note a few things about preelection and "exit" (immediately post-voting) polling. Polling before elections gives political scientists an opportunity to test the ability of a poll's small random sample (again, say 1000 participants in a national telephone survey) to get results that predict accurately the election outcome. An initial challenge stems from the fact that not everyone who answers the phone will actually turn out to vote. Pollsters have developed ways of asking questions to find out whether each respondent is a likely voter, to be included in the final sample. As election day draws nearer, pollsters tend to sample only likely voters.

In addition, pollsters often want to identify any trends of change in voter support over the weeks before balloting, filtering out random day-to-day variation that does not indicate a real trend. The solution is a **tracking poll**, a survey over an extended period that samples a new batch of respondents each day, and on a daily basis releases the results only for the most recent three or four days. Despite these challenges, in the 2000 American election for president, seven of the ten major polls got the margin of victory within 2 percent of the final election outcome, and nine were within 3 percent.[15]

In addition, **exit polls** of those leaving representative polling places after voting tend to be remarkably accurate. They provide not only a check on the accuracy of vote counting (which can be important in new democracies), but also include questions about why people voted the way they did (see Country Case Studies, chapter 11).

Many polls attempt to uncover links between election outcomes and public opinion about issues or conditions in the country. For example, one frequent correlation is that between election results and perceptions about the condition of the economy.[16] If times are bad with high unemployment, throw the current leaders out! In addition, however, a governing party's policy directions may affect its popularity. In 1979, just before the Conservative Party led by Margaret Thatcher won the election of 1981, support for lower taxes versus better government services was fairly polarized, with more to the extremes than in the middle. But later, in 1997 when the Labor Party won back control of the government, opinion

Voters who chose to fill out an exit survey after voting in Albuquerque, New Mexico, USA.

APPLYING THE MODELS | Influence over Political Attitudes

For the established democracies today, three of the models we have studied—majority preference, elite, and pluralist—seem especially relevant to the distribution of influence over political attitudes.

In some ways, political culture and socialization, at least, seem to be based on majority preference. The most common factor influencing today's political culture is yesterday's political culture. Current political style and habit represent continuity with values that a majority of people accepted in the past.

Today the elite interpretation centers more on limit setting than on directive power. It suggests that an elite establishes customary ways of doing things in society and politics. Custom serves to limit the horizon of what people consider to be possible and reasonable. In the view of left-of-center writers such as Antonio Gramsci, Herbert Marcuse, and Stephen Lukes, an elite of business and wealth limits people's conceptions of their wants and needs (e.g., through advertising and consumer behavior itself) to those that they can satisfy within the prevailing market system. On the right, proponents argue that education and the media confine the available range of values and options to a "modernist," left-of-center perspective. According to both arguments, people who challenge prevailing views and customs are likely to be discouraged. Going beyond the boundaries appears to be unreasonable and self-defeating.

The pluralists do not see political attitudes primarily in terms of shared majority values. Nor do they see them in terms of limits set by a dominant elite. Rather, political attitudes result from the constant and mutual adjustment of different interests with different aims, resources, and skills. To pluralists, the values that are important to society are often the different values of its groups. Here consensus in political culture mostly concerns agreement on political procedures, alongside customs of compromise and rational accommodation to achieve realistic goals.

At times, the personal leadership model can also play a role in political attitudes. In the middle of the twentieth century, such figures as Hitler, Stalin, Mao, and charismatic leaders of anticolonial movements in developing countries possessed great influence. And in special situations, such as the mid-2010s period of occasional Islamist terrorism in Europe and North America (e.g., the attack in Paris in November 2015), ethnic ultranationalist demagogues showed that they could stoke fear and prejudice. But in recent decades overall, with a few exceptions, the nationwide impact of leaders on political culture has tended not to last. On a micro level, individual leaders no doubt contribute to political socialization in their organizational environments (e.g., in political parties). But today, few analysts see personal leadership as exercising continuing broad influence over political culture.

Which of the models of influence distribution seem to best explain political culture, socialization, and public opinion around you?

---

had shifted toward extending government services.[17] Public opinion certainly at times looks like a factor affecting political outcomes. But political culture, socialization, and the media affect both public opinion and political outcomes. What model of influence distribution best explains political attitudes overall? (See "Applying the Models").

SUMMARY: CONTENTION AND COOPERATION IN POLITICAL ATTITUDES

We have looked at four features of political attitudes. Political culture can lean in an authoritarian direction under the influence of traditional social structures and religion, or in a democratic direction due to other factors. In a democracy, civic participation and mutual trust among participants encourages cooperation among contending forces. Only at points of change, whether toward or away from democracy, does political culture fail to foster procedural cooperation and structure political contention. In the established democracies, even amid post-materialist political contention, underlying support for representative democracy continues. Enough procedural cooperation persists to structure political contention peacefully.

Political socialization concerns the transmission of political culture among people. Political culture is passed on between generations in the family and schools, as well as between peers in peer groups, religion, the workplace, and through political party involvement. Public opinion involves short-term political attitudes toward the issues of the day, parties, leaders, and policies. Polling tries to measure the beliefs, ideology, values, particular policy preferences, or interest group goals that can motivate political action.

Both political culture and public opinion are affected by the news media. News reporting in the media is important for the functioning of democracy, but it often oversimplifies and personalizes politics. The media generally can aim to be objective or can engage in selective and partisan reporting, or even outright falsehoods.

COUNTRY CASE STUDIES

Political culture, socialization, and public opinion vary widely from nation to nation. Thus, they obviously have varying consequences for the development of a democratic civic culture. We now turn to two cases, one from Western Europe and the other from Southeast Asia. Both show the evolution from primarily subject and parochial political cultures toward democracy-supporting ones in the late twentieth century.

Spain: Political Attitudes in a Delayed Democracy

Spain's modern political culture began with a crucial event: the defeat and expulsion of the Muslim Moors at the end of the fifteenth century. This occurred after seven centuries of Muslim rule over Spain's irregular terrain, with its slow and difficult transportation and communication. The Moors had tolerated other religions during the most stable periods of their rule. Spain had become a center of Arab and Jewish learning and, for medieval Europe, a window into classical Greek sources preserved and studied by the Arabs.

Military victory over the Moors by the Catholic forces enabled the unification of Spain under a Christian monarchy based in two central regions, Castile and Aragon. But with it came a harsh religious uniformity, imposed by the Spanish Inquisition, which used violence and terror to eliminate minority cultural practices, expel the Jews, and compel adherence to the Catholic faith. Centuries of authoritarian political culture followed, supported partly by gold and silver from Spain's colonial empire. Especially among the landowning nobility, the army, and the mostly illiterate peasantry, customs focused on status hierarchies, honor, and semifeudal loyalty in extended patron-client hierarchies. Conflict was often resolved by force. At the ground level, family and village were paramount in a parochial political culture.

In the nineteenth century, however, Spain lost its empire, failed to keep up with the economic development of its European neighbors to the north, and experienced the political reverberations of the French Revolution. Intellectuals and businesspeople in the cities, especially in the prosperous Basque country in the north and Catalonia in the northeast, increasingly questioned the legitimacy of centralized monarchic rule. For these areas with their distinctive regional languages and cultures, the challenge of national identity had never been overcome, and center-periphery cleavage persisted.[18] The Basque region and Catalonia allied themselves with classical liberal antimonarchist groups elsewhere who were more inclined to support their aspirations. The resulting conflicts were sometimes settled militarily, and periods of more liberal rule alternated with traditional monarchy. On the eve of the civil war of the late 1930s, the republican leaders again supported Basque and Catalonian proposals for autonomy. Regional and political-system cleavages seemed increasingly to coincide.

Beyond the reinforcing center-periphery and liberal-monarchist cleavages in Spanish political culture, there was another division over the role of the Catholic Church. Many Spaniards with republican sympathies favored greater sociocultural freedom and wanted the Church to give up its generous subsidies from the government, its broad influence over education, and other privileges. The classical liberal forces, in power at times in the nineteenth century, remained weak enough that they had to accommodate the Church. But the intensity of the conflict, perhaps reinforced by Spain's traditional custom of settling contests for honor by force, simmered under the surface. Moreover, in the early twentieth century, the development of Spanish industry brought numerous workers into urban areas, many of whom were desperately poor and radicalized by repression.

In the early 1930s, a republican government had replaced the previous military-backed dictatorship. The governing republicans moved aggressively to remove church privileges. Resulting opposition contributed to the conservatives' return to office in the middle 1930s. The tide again turned with an election victory by the left in 1936. With the clerical, regional, and political-system cleavages now largely coinciding, public opinion was sharply polarized. An extreme conservative, Francisco Franco, led a sector of the military into civil war with support from the Church. Franco's forces won, brutally suppressed their opponents, and assured the privileges of the Church in education, censorship, economic benefits, and repression of other religions. Thousands of Franco's political opponents were executed and large numbers went into exile.

The Franco regime had a heavy impact on Spanish political culture. Under the regime's threat of terror and the vivid memory of the civil war, public support for democracy and political participation fell. Spaniards again retreated into the family and private concerns of earlier centuries. Parochial and subject orientations predominated. To steer cooperation among contending economic and social interests along regime-favored lines, Franco used state-dominated corporatism in a style similar to Mussolini's (see Country Case Study, chapter 6). He organized advisory councils to represent various sectors of society on a group basis, with labor and business combined in each economic sector.

By the 1950s and early 1960s, however, Spanish political culture was shifting. Economic development picked up substantially, and modernization was gaining momentum in areas such as education, literacy, urbanization, communication, industrialization, international travel (out of the country, for labor opportunities), and tourism. These factors all indicated an expanding middle class and greater political and sociocultural freedoms. Meanwhile, migration of other Spaniards into Basque and Catalonian areas softened separatist sentiments there, moderating the center-periphery cleavage. And by the 1960s, the Church had become more ambivalent and divided over the authoritarian Franco regime, with the stirrings of liberation theology (see chapter 6) among some priests. In this context, Franco's regime somewhat loosened its cultural control over civil society.

By the mid-1970s, economic stagnation had set in, and Franco's death in 1975 revealed a major portion of his own elite favoring a transition to democracy. Between 1975 and 1978, led by Franco's own chosen successor as head of state, King Juan Carlos, and Franco's last prime minister, Adolfo Suarez, the regime negotiated a democratic transition with its republican proponents. New laws made way for the democratic order, largely preserving the legitimacy-enhancing rule of law in the process of change. By that time, a strong majority of Spaniards had come to approve of democracy. A centrist coalition controlled the executive leadership until the early 1980s, when the moderate left-of-center Socialist Workers' Party took over. It presided over an economic boom and a consolidation of democracy, with Spain joining the European Community in 1986.

In the mid-1990s, however, corruption scandals brought down the moderate left-of-center cabinet. The conservative Popular Party (PP) that took its place proved moderate and consensual in its approach, ending fears of a return to neo-Francoism. But led by Prime Minister José Aznar, the PP remained pro-Church on sociocultural issues and opposed to autonomy demands by Catalonians and Basques. After Aznar falsely blamed Basque terrorism for the bloody train bombing in Madrid in March 2004 (al-Qaeda was responsible), the PP lost that month's election to the moderate left-of-center Socialists, who won again in 2008. The government pursued a left-of-center agenda on sociocultural issues. These included approval of gay marriage in the face of sharp opposition from the Church. Spain had achieved high rates of voter turnout and had clearly emerged as a "civic culture."

Subsequent economic challenges at the end of the decade and the beginning of the next sharpened political contention. Over the 2000s, membership in the Eurozone had brought a big influx of tourism, easy credit, and a real estate boom with inflated property prices. But the worldwide economic downturn of 2009 sharply suppressed credit, investment, consumption, and tourism, and the property bubble burst.[19] Amid the contraction in overall economic output and a huge jump in unemployment, the finances of borrowers, the banks, and the government were all in trouble. In Spain's political culture, the post-materialist issues of Church influence and regional autonomy have now been largely superseded by a return of basic bread-and-butter concerns.

The moderate left-of-center cabinet pursued some government stimulus spending to support the unemployed, housing, and distressed businesses and banks. But the widening budget deficit and debt levels of both banks and government, alongside the still-declining consumer economy, undercut the willingness of outside investors to lend to Spain. By late 2011, the interest rates that Spain faced were creeping up toward unsustainable levels. Meanwhile, European authorities were demanding multiple rounds of harsh spending cuts by the government to narrow the budget deficit, as a condition for outside aid to help Spain make its debt payments. But such cuts were likely to further suppress consumer demand and contract the economy, thus reducing tax revenues and the narrowing of the budget deficit. Social unrest was inevitable, and protest demonstrations were frequent. Many were upset that so soon after Spain's democratic revolution, the country was losing control of its economic policy to European Union authorities. Nationalism was becoming a new undercurrent in Spanish political culture.

In this no-win situation, the governing coalition led by the moderate left-of-center Socialist party was defeated in the December 2011 election, in a negative retrospective judgment by the voters. But the new government, that of the conservative Popular Party led by Prime Minister Mariano Rajoy, was more supportive of the austerity approach demanded by the European Union authorities than its predecessor had been. This involved tax increases, spending reductions (including pension cuts and infrastructure investment cancellations), and continued tight credit as failing banks were restructured and investors in them took losses. All this was accompanied by the government loosening labor regulations to allow easier layoffs and wage cutting by business, and expanded use of short-term labor contracts outside the rules. Among the consequences were high unemployment (26 percent—up from 23 percent in 2011—and over half of those under 25), and suppression of consumer demand. Real estate values continued their slide (after the bursting of the real estate bubble) and tax revenues declined, again limiting the narrowing of the budget deficit.

By early 2013, public opposition to Spanish membership in the Eurozone shot up from the low single digits to over a third. Amid increasing frequency of protest demonstrations, the Rajoy government was hit in early 2013 by a corruption scandal involving cash payments in the 2000s to its party leaders (including Rajoy himself, according to a former party treasurer) from a construction company-supported slush fund. The result was the deepest "trust-in-government" crisis in Spanish political culture since democratization. Poll support for the conservative PP dropped by almost half (to 25 percent), though it continued to be a few points ahead of the moderate left-of-center Socialists, who many hold responsible (retrospectively) for the development of the crisis in 2010 when they were in power. GDP began to turn slightly upward in 2014, but Spanish public opinion remained focused on the realities of continued high unemployment and corruption. Attitudes in Spain were changing.

At first, only a small center party and the far-left coalition benefited in the polls. Spain lacked a party alternative that directly attacked austerity itself. That lack was remedied in 2014, with the formation of a new, left social democratic party, Podemos ("We can"; Spain's version of Greece's Syriza at the time). Podemos is anti-austerity and favors tax increases on the rich to bolster state services and restructuring Spain's large government debt (around 100 percent of GDP). When parliamentary elections were held in December 2015, the two anti-austerity parties by that time, Podemos and the Socialists, together won over 40 percent of the votes and seats. But differences over Catalan autonomy seemed to rule out a left-led majority coalition. Meanwhile PP, having lost some support to a new centrist party, Ciudadanos (Citizens), won only 28.7 percent of the vote. Amid such divided public opinion, a coherent majority coalition seemed unlikely.

Indonesia: Political Attitudes in a Developing Society

Indonesia is a multiethnic nation of roughly 200 million people spread over hundreds of islands in Southeast Asia. In the past, the area had exhibited a mix of Hindu, Buddhist, and animist faiths. Following the development of trade links with the Arabian Peninsula in the thirteenth century, Islam gradually came to predominate among the people of the region. Over the centuries, various empires and kingdoms held sway over its many islands and island groups, without an overall sense of national identity. The territory that now comprises Indonesia was entirely created by the Dutch colonial occupation.

The official language, Indonesian, was adapted from Malay by early Dutch traders. However, hundreds of ethnic-regional groups have their distinct languages and cultures. The Javanese of east and central Java make up almost half of the country's population and form the largest group. Javanese political culture stresses social harmony and support for the group. To some extent (though not uniformly), it teaches deference to those in authority.

Javanese are typically Muslims, along with the vast majority of Indonesians. But their traditional culture included some pre-Islamic Hindu influences and some traditional spirit-worship. Attitudes of deference to hierarchical structures of authority were also encouraged by the Dutch authorities, who enlisted the native social hierarchy to support social order. Authority and hierarchy were further bolstered after 1966 by repression and threat of terror under the military regime of General Suharto.[20]

The predominant sect of Islam in Indonesia is Sunni. However, given Indonesia's multicultural past, it is not surprising that Islam is not rigorously followed. Islam interacts with other cultural traditions and accommodates them somewhat. But the tradition of deference to authority is reinforced among the more devout Muslims, referred to in Indonesia as the "santri." The piety of the santri Muslims, who pray five times daily and attend Friday prayers at the mosque, is more prevalent among the Sundanese of western Java. But it seems to be spreading in some other parts of Java, as well.

The resulting traditional political culture of Indonesia was primarily subject and parochial. But those orientations did not go unchallenged in the twentieth century. A nationalist movement arose after 1910 to resist Dutch colonial occupation. To some extent, it saw the traditional parochial ethnic attachments and customary deference to authority as obstacles to national self-assertion and independence. When the Japanese expelled the Dutch in the early 1940s, the nationalists led by Sukarno took the opportunity to become the intermediary layer between the Japanese occupiers and the people. In that role, they were able to spread the nationalist anti-Dutch message.

The Dutch returned to Indonesia at the conclusion of World War II, but they were defeated militarily by a national independence movement in 1949 led by Sukarno. He and his political supporters nonetheless remained a minority, and his multiparty parliamentary regime was unstable. Frequent cabinet changes and regional rebellions enhanced the influence of the regime's critics. Also, the democratic regime lacked a key element of support associated with democratization, a growing native middle class. Entrepreneurship was dominated by the ethnic Chinese minority (4 percent of the Indonesian population), who led commerce and finance in the cities of Indonesia. The rest of society traditionally resented this group's economic role. Politically, the Chinese-Indonesians had to remain in the background and defer to their protectors in authority. Hence Indonesia did not possess a rising native business class to spearhead modernization and serve as a supportive and stabilizing cultural foundation for democratization.

At this point, Sukarno and the portion of the military that supported him were not comfortable with full-scale democratic political contention. They shut down the previous regime in 1960 in favor of a top-down style of leadership that they called "guided democracy." At this point, Sukarno had to depend partly on the support of the Communist Party, which had upward of 15 percent of the vote. This alliance alienated the more religious Islamic groups and much of the military. A military coup in 1966 (supported by the U.S. government) overthrew the Sukarno government. Led by General Suharto, the new government slaughtered the Communists and their associates by the hundreds of thousands, and imposed itself by terror and intimidation. Calling itself "the New Order," the Suharto military government heavily limited political expression, the press, and party formation.

Suharto ruled through a dominant party that was based on an older social organization, Golkar. Made up of professional groups, civil servants, retired military officers, and other groups, Golkar served as a ready-made complex of patron-client networks to bolster the New Order. Thus a key portion of civil society, rather than participating in autonomous middle-class pressure for modernization and democratization of political culture, instead became an informal linchpin of support for traditional authoritarian tendencies in Indonesian political culture. Economic growth after 1970 helped ease political tensions, and Suharto's authoritarian reign reinforced the traditional deference to authority and the subject and parochial attitudes.

Only in the late 1990s did a reform movement begin to gain traction, enhanced by the spectacle of corruption and enrichment by Suharto's family and friends. When the Asian financial crisis hit Indonesia in early 1998, leading segments of Suharto's support base, along with other major interests, called for his resignation. His weak successor was able to get legislation passed for a free election in mid-1999. Political parties ranged from a secular nationalist one, which did well in the 1999 elections, through moderate Islamist parties to Islamic fundamentalist ones. Indicating the anti-Suharto mood of these times of transition to democracy, the legislature-chosen president from 2001 through 2004 was Megawati Sukarnoputri, daughter of Sukarno, who led the Indonesian Democratic Party of Struggle (PDI-P). No parties proved dominant, however, and little was done about corruption.

In the next legislative election in 2004, the most successful party was the old military-Suharto support group, Golkar, with its strong following in outlying rural areas. But it won only 22 percent of the vote overall. Then for the first time, the president was elected directly, and the office was won by a non-Golkar retired general from the small Democratic Party, Susilo Bambang Yudhoyono. President Yudhoyono appointed a multiparty cabinet, and governed mainly by consensus, avoiding major new initiatives and any broad attack on corruption.

When the international financial crisis hit in late 2008, Indonesia was somewhat protected by its extensive regulation of the economy, helping to insulate it from international trade and globalization, and its continuing exports of oil, gas, coal, and palm oil to China. The nation was able to ride out the crisis fairly smoothly, and in the next parliamentary elections in April 2009, the Democratic Party emerged stronger. Yudhoyono then won a big presidential victory in mid-2009, and again put together a broad coalition, continuing to rule by consensus. Golkar remained a key part of that coalition, and was able to resist efforts by a respected financial reformer in the government, Sri Mulwati Indrawati, to pursue cases of corruption and tax evasion. (In early 2010, she was forced out as finance minister.) By the end of Yudhoyono's second term, his party's standing was plagued by corruption scandals involving its leaders.

In contrast, the mid-2010s have been the years of a new phenomenon in Indonesian politics, public opinion, and political culture. The rise of the current president, Joko Widodo ("Jokowi"), was made possible by the post-Suharto decentralization of democracy in Indonesia, which allowed local mayors to be directly elected. From a modest background and after early experience in the furniture business, Jokowi served several years as an honest and accessible mayor of a mid-sized town in central Java, and then went on to be elected governor of Jakarta, the country's capital. He was a member of Megawati's PDI-P, but his incorruptibility and folksy, everyman style proved attractive to voters beyond his party. PDI-P led in the legislative elections of 2014, but with only 19 percent, trailed by Golkar (15 percent), the Great Indonesia Movement Party (Gerindra, 12 percent), and the Democrat Party (that of Yudhoyono, 10 percent).

Attracting many young supporters of a new Indonesian politics, Jokowi became the leading contender for the presidency, with the support of both Megawati and, informally, many members of a dissident faction of Golkar led by Jokowi's vice presidential running mate. As governor of Jakarta from 2012, he was admired for focusing on practical problems such as traffic paralysis and rainy season flooding, as well as avoiding corruption scandals. Jokowi's opponent clearly represented the old politics: Prabowo Subianto, Gerindra leader and former special forces commander under Sukarno. Subianto was supported by Gerindra and by Golkar and its traditionalist leader (and business tycoon) Aburizal Bakrie. Aided by many young volunteers, Jokowi won the presidency by six points.

One strength claimed by Jokowi has been his ability to get things done despite opposing majorities in legislative assemblies, in both Solo and Jakarta. He has needed such skills as president; Subianto's coalition with its parliamentary majority has taken control of the speakership and the committee leaderships. Nonetheless, in office in 2015 Jokowi was able to eliminate the costly fuel price subsidies (with the help of the recent plunge in the world price of oil), freeing up funds for initiatives in education, health care, and infrastructure. His aggressive punishment of drug perpetrators (including capital punishment) and foreign fishing poachers has supported his law-and-order and nationalist credibility. His Corruption Eradication Commission has started some investigations (including a high police official linked to his own ally, Megawati), and Jokowi is pressing to get local governments and state-owned enterprises to become more transparent by doing business online. To be sure, to some extent patronage, deals, and getting along are part of Indonesian culture, and with decentralized democracy are unlikely to disappear soon. But high-level corruption has at least arrived on the agenda of Indonesian public opinion.

◥ PRACTICE AND REVIEW ONLINE

CRITICAL THINKING QUESTIONS

1. How can we legitimately describe the political culture of a country? How might it be inaccurate to do so?

2. Is post-materialist political contention undermining democracy? Why or why not?

3. Consider different sources of political socialization in your life. Which do you think has had the greatest effect on your views, and why?

4. How accurate are public opinion polls in gaging people's attitudes? How might poll results affect those attitudes?

5. If a news presentation has an evaluative slant, what about it can make the report still useful? When is it deceptive and not useful?

KEY TERMS

political attitudes, 214
political culture, 214
civic culture, 217
social capital, 218
post-materialism, 218
political socialization, 224
peers, 225
propaganda, 229
public opinion, 233
representative sample, 234
random selection, 234
preference intensity, 235
normal distribution, 235
bimodal distribution, 235
tracking poll, 236
exit poll, 236

FURTHER READING

Clark, Terry Nichols, and Michael Rempel, eds. *Citizen Politics in Post-Industrial Societies.* Boulder, CO: Westview Press, 1997.

Dalton, Russell J. *Citizen Politics: Public Opinion and Political Parties in Advanced Industrial*

Democracies, 2nd ed. Chatham, NJ: Chatham House, 1996.

———, and Martin P. Wattenberg, eds. *Parties Without Partisans: Political Change in Advanced Industrial Democracies.* Oxford; New York: Oxford University Press, 2000.

———, David M. Farrell, and Ian McAllister. *Political Parties and Democratic Linkage: How Parties Organize Democracy.* Oxford, UK: Oxford University Press, 2011.

Dautrich, Kenneth, and Thomas H. Hartley. *How the News Media Fail American Voters: Causes, Consequences, and Remedies.* New York: Columbia University Press, 1999.

Graber, Doris A. *Mass Media and American Politics*, 5th ed. Washington, DC: CQ Press, 1997.

Haynes, Jeffrey. *Religion in Global Politics.* London; New York: Longman, 1998.

Huntington, Samuel P. *The Clash of Civilizations and the Remaking of World Order.* New York: Simon & Schuster, 1996.

Inglehart, Ronald. *Culture Shift in Advanced Industrial Society.* Princeton, NJ: Princeton University Press, 1990.

Inglehart, Ronald, ed. *Human Values and Social Change: Findings from the Values Surveys.* Leiden; Boston: Brill, 2003.

Lane, Jan-Erik, and Svante Ersson. *Culture and Politics: A Comparative Approach.* Aldershot: Ashgate, 2002.

Lane, Robert Edwards. *Political Ideology: Why the American Common Man Believes What He Does.* New York: Free Press of Glencoe, 1962.

Norris, Pippa, ed. *Critical Citizens: Global Support for Democratic Government.* Oxford; New York: Oxford University Press, 1999.

Norris, Pippa. *A Virtuous Circle: Political Communications in Postindustrial Societies.* Cambridge, UK; New York, NY: Cambridge University Press, 2000.

Pharr, Susan J., and Robert D. Putnam, eds. *Disaffected Democracies: What's Troubling the Trilateral Countries?* Princeton, NJ: Princeton University Press, 2000.

NOTES

[1] See Arend Lijphart, *Democracy in Plural Societies: A Comparative Exploration* (New Haven: Yale University Press, 1977).

[2] Gabriel A. Almond and Sidney Verba, *The Civic Culture; Political Attitudes and Democracy in Five Nations* (Princeton, NJ: Princeton University Press, 1963).

[3] See Robert Putnam, *Making Democracy Work: Civic Traditions in Modern Italy* (Princeton, NJ: Princeton University Press, 1994).

[4] This approach is consistent with the observation by French political philosopher Alexis de Tocqueville, that at the local level in the United States, a degree of professed self-interest was quite consistent with good will and reciprocity in rational, nonthreatening democratic participation.

[5] See Robert Putnam, *Bowling Alone: The Collapse and Revival of American Community* (New York: Simon & Schuster, 2000).

[6] See Inglehart 1990.

[7] See Michael Crozier et al., *The Crisis of Democracy* (New York: New York University Press, 1975).

[8] See Pharr and Putnam (2000), chapter 1, for an overview.

[9] See Dalton and Wattenberg (2000).

[10] See Dalton, Farrell, and McAllister (2011).

[11] In Norris 1999, 236–56.

[12] See *The Semisovereign People: A Realist's View of Democracy in America* (Chicago: Holt, Rinehart and Winston, 1960).

[13] In early 2013, Al Jazeera bought a failing partisan American cable channel, Current TV (which only had partial access to the American cable audience), in hopes of getting its views heard in the United States.

[14] In Mark Blumenthal, "2012 Polling Accuracy: Right Winner, but Different Trends," *Huffington Post*, December 23, 2012.

[15] "Final National Presidential Poll Results," National Council on Public Polls, www.ncpp.org.

[16] See chapter 11.

[17] See Anthony Heath, Roger M. Jowell, and John K. Curtice, *The Rise of New Labour: Party Policies and Voter Choices* (New York: Oxford University Press, 2001).

[18] See chapter 6.

[19] See chapter 7, "Contention and Cooperation in Focus."

[20] As in this case, many Indonesians use only one name rather than adding a family name to a given one.

Interest Groups

- **WHAT** is an interest group?
- **WHAT** sorts of cooperation allow interest groups to contend in politics?
- **WHAT** are the most important types of interest groups?
- **HOW** do interest groups' differences affect their effectiveness in political contention?
- **WHAT** key resources do interest groups wield as they contend for influence?

IMAGINE THAT READING A NEWS ARTICLE leads you to be concerned about a problem you had never considered: the trash your city produces every day. Landfills are reaching full capacity, toxic waste is a problem, and little recycling is taking place in your area. What can you do? You may have done little in your life that you consider "political," but you may well hear about and join a group working for more sustainable waste disposal. In return for joining and making your contribution, the organization sends you a newsletter about the issues, politics, and policymaking affecting the group, and describing the organization's activities. In addition, when you vote on election day, you may try to match your concern about waste disposal and the environment to the preferences of a candidate or a party.

WHY INTEREST GROUPS?

From a "bottom-up" point of view, when people who share a concern want to do something about it, they soon learn that they will accomplish more if they work together to try to affect political outcomes. But there is also a top-down reason why interest groups are important. Government officials want to know more about the effects of policies on specific groups. Combine the groups' desire to affect policy with the government's desire to communicate with affected groups, and interest groups typically result. Recall from chapter 1 that an interest group is any group of people or organizations with shared concerns relevant to politics, or any association representing such a group, that tries to influence policymaking without running candidates for office under its own banner.

The Significance of Interest Groups

As was noted in chapter 1, the interest group is one of the two most pervasive types of groups involved in political contention (alongside political parties). In addition, interest groups are a key link between government and politics on the one hand, and you as an individual citizen, on the other.

Interest groups vary in shape and size. For example, local child welfare organizations in the United States have a national association to represent them in their efforts to, for example, increase funding from the government: the Child Welfare League of America. Other examples of such groups are metalworkers in France, women in Afghanistan, ethnic Yorubas in Nigeria, tenant farmers in Sierra Leone, palm oil growers in Malaysia, and the aircraft industry in Brazil. Membership in organizations that represent such groups is a widespread form of political participation. They provide a way to channel your concerns related to such things as your occupation, values, ethnic background, religion, economic stratum, gender, hobby, or any number of other classifications.

Studies of voters indicate that for large numbers of people, awareness of political issues tends to be selective and pragmatic. People tend to focus on issues that affect groups that they belong to. Thus, for any given policy issue, only a small portion of the population—the groups most directly affected by the policy—will be knowledgeable and have clear preferences. Accordingly, political scientist Robert Dahl referred to modern democracy as "minorities rule."[1]

When you enter the voting booth, you may consider how an election victory by a party or candidate might affect a group that you identify with. To be sure, this may not make your voting decision easy, since we all belong to many interest-related categories. No party or candidate will represent all of your interests. But in any given election, one or two of your group identifications, those most significant to you in relation to the issues of the day, may affect your preferences regarding who the policymakers should be. In the opening vignette above, the voter concerned about environmental issues may look for the party or candidate with the best record on them.

Some people have negative impressions of interest groups. We sometimes hear the phrase "special interest," and think of a group seeking exceptional consideration for itself. Or the phrase "pressure group" suggests officials making decisions under group pressure rather than freely and rationally. In reality, however, interest groups are a mixed lot. As we shall see below, some pursue a value or an interpretation of the public interest rather than (or in addition to) material self-interest, and most wish for modifications in laws rather than exceptions to them. And only under certain conditions can such groups apply real "pressure" on government officials. At any rate, political scientists prefer terms that do not imply a negative or positive evaluation, so they have arrived at the more neutral phrase "interest group."

In this chapter, we will examine how interest groups contend with one another to influence public policy. First we encounter the four levels at which interest groups exist: the category of people or organizations represented by the organization, the organization's formal membership, the group's officials, and its lobbyists. Next we will note some key differences among interest groups that can affect

THE PHILOSOPHICAL CONNECTION | Rousseau, Madison, and Calhoun

In the development of political thought, a focus on interest groups (as distinct from social classes or "orders") emerged rather late. The Frenchman Jean-Jacques Rousseau (see chapter 5), writing in the mid-eighteenth century, favored very small democratic states where laws could be approved by the citizens directly. In that context, he worried about the influence of group interests. Rousseau hoped that in the legislative meetings of the whole community, people would see beyond the groups to which they belonged, and instead think of themselves only as average citizens in search of the public good. Ideally, for him, such a community would be made up primarily of independent farmers who knew each other and shared more interests than they differed over. (If multiple interest groups were evident, Rousseau hoped that they would be numerous and generally equal in power.)

James Madison (1751–1836), the leading framer of the new American representative democracy, disagreed (see chapter 5). He recognized the trend toward the development of commerce and a diversity of occupations with distinct interests. Madison argued that "factions," as he called them, inevitably emerged to play a central role in democratic politics. He suggested that people's opinions are naturally affected by their self-interested passions. In Madison's view, this occurred especially among different economic interests such as those of farmers, merchants, bankers, creditors, debtors, and others, but noneconomic issues could also prompt group-interest engagement. In addition, as various issues, causes, and opinions catch people's attention, rival personalities will step forward to attract support in factional contention. Elected representatives deciding on laws must weigh the competing interests of such groups. But the officeholders themselves belong to the contending groups.

In this situation, Madison worried most about the possibility that one faction might gain the majority in a democracy and trample on the minority. His solution was twofold. First, the nation should be large enough to include numerous interest groups. Then no one group could comprise a large enough portion of the citizenry, or be sufficiently capable of coordinating its efforts over long distances, to be able to impose a majority tyranny (see chapter 5). Second, Madison recommended having two legislative houses, with each separate from the executive branch. The three independent units would "check and balance" each other, making it harder for one faction to gain overall control.

American Southerner John C. Calhoun (1782–1850) agreed with Madison on the importance of interest groups in representative democracy. But in the context of the growing contention between the North and the South about slavery in the South, he argued that having numerous groups might not by itself rule out majority tyranny. Calhoun contended that like-minded factions would form alliances to gain majority control. Such a majority alliance would then oppress the minority, taxing it heavily and steering the benefits to itself. Calhoun's proposed answer was to give every interest group in society an absolute veto over any policy proposal.

Calhoun's solution directly contradicted the democratic principle of majority rule (see chapter 1), and was unworkable. If any group could stop action in its own self-interest, government would rarely be able to make a decision about a problem. Calhoun's reply was that any group wanting change that affected others negatively would just have to offer compensating benefits to them as the price of cooperation.

Calhoun's argument was undercut in the twentieth century by the later pluralists. They pointed out that interest groups are not typically united internally, as Calhoun had assumed. Groups are often divided and weakened by cross-cutting interests (see the "Interest Group Membership" section below). And the formation of interest group alliances in political parties (see chapter 10) involves further compromise and moderation by the contending interests.

Do interest groups in your country seem to be united as they contend with each other in politics? And are they able to form alliances that dominate policymaking to serve themselves? Or are they too numerous, diverse, and moderate to be much of a threat, as Madison suggested?

how much influence they can wield. Finally, we will examine some key types of resources that interest groups use in political contention and cooperation.

The Rise of Interest Groups in Democracy

When states were very small, one or two locally prominent interests tended to prevail. But when the nation-state began to be the norm, bringing several regions under one national umbrella, more interests began to interact around government. America's leading founding father, James Madison, saw that the modern era's increase in the territorial size of political communities would bring numerous groups into contact with each other (see "The Philosophical Connection"). And for Madison, a large number of interest groups could even play a positive role in countering the risk of tyranny by a majority faction.

When agricultural economies gave way to industrialization in late nineteenth- and early twentieth-century Europe and North America, numerous new occupational interests appeared. In addition, in some countries (e.g., the United States), waves of immigration brought new ethnic groups into the political community. Then the Great Depression of the 1930s triggered a major expansion of governmental activity. Beneficiaries of the new programs and other affected groups formed associations to protect and promote their interests in those programs. For example, in many developed nations government-run old age pension programs arose or expanded during the Depression. Organizations then emerged to represent the interests of the elderly in supporting and maintaining those programs.

By the mid-twentieth century, political scientists were discovering interest groups in their great variety in democracy, contending, bargaining, and compromising.[2] In recent decades, when authoritarian governments have often yielded to democratization and its respect for the human rights to free expression and association, interest group associations tended to spring up. In the same period, some of the established democracies saw big increases in participation in interest group organizations (see Figure 9.1).

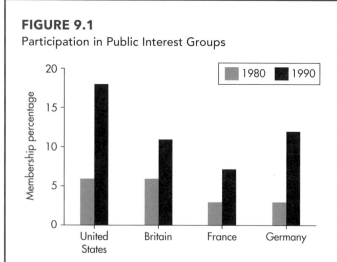

FIGURE 9.1
Participation in Public Interest Groups

Source: Adapted from Russell J. Dalton, *Citizen Politics: Public Opinion and Political Parties in Advanced Industrial Democracies* (New York: Chatham House Publishers, 2002), 46; data are from 1980–81 World Values Survey and 1990–93 World Values Survey.

LEVELS OF INTEREST GROUP ACTIVITY

The officials and lobbyists of an interest group organization usually get the most attention and participate most directly in political contention. But usually they would not be in those positions without the classification/category of people or organizations that they represent, and the cooperation and support of at least some of the category as ordinary members of the organization itself.

The Categoric Interest

The broadest level of meaning of the phrase "interest group" is the **categoric interest**: the category (classification) of people or organizations that is affected by government policy. Several types of categoric interests may be important in politics. For example, economic categoric interests include upper-income people, the poor, the middle class, workers, small business owners, taxpayers, consumers, renters, electricians, doctors, and many other occupational categories. In addition, different sectors of the economy such as banking, television, real estate, and chemical manufacturing refer to business enterprises, investors, and people working in those fields. Ethnic or racial categories include people of African, Arab, Indian, Hispanic, and Irish ancestry. Religious classifications include Catholics, Protestants, Jews, Sunni and Shia Muslims, Hindus, and Sikhs. Examples of regional interests are the American south, the Nigerian north, the Basque country of northeastern Spain, and Bavaria in Germany. Gender and age classifications include, for example, women, youth, and the elderly. Political opinion groups represent people supporting specific ideological orientations.

Members of these categories vary in their degree of awareness of the group and government's impact on it. (As we shall see below, there is great variation in how large a proportion of the category has joined in membership in an association that represents it.) Some people in a categoric interest may act directly to express their concerns, independently of any organization. Such activity can range from defending their interests in a conversation to participating in a protest demonstration. For example, in 2006, French youth spontaneously protested a law to exempt young new workers from existing labor protections. Today, coordinating street protests is much easier thanks to Internet social media such as Facebook and Twitter, which played roles in the Arab Spring demonstrations of 2011. Such actions may give rise to publicity that alerts decision makers to a category and its problems, and may spark the creation of a formal association to represent it.

Quieter forms of support for a category's interests may go largely unnoticed. People sharing ethnicity, religion, or gender may help each other in informal ways that are seldom noticed by others (see below, under "communal" interest groups). The tendencies of various "voter groups" to prefer one party or another may only become known to pollsters and political scientists doing public opinion research.

If a category is especially large and members are expressing its concerns directly, the result may be a **social movement**. Social movements often result from shared values (see below). Examples include the U.S. civil rights movement of the 1960s (see "Concept in Context"), the independence movement of Québec in Canada, democracy movements in Eastern Europe prior to the collapse of Communism, and the recent Arab Spring demonstrations in the Middle East.

The Organization's Membership

The next level of activity of interest groups is the formal **membership** in an organization. People usually become

Mass demonstration for nuclear disarmament in London, U.K., in 1982.

CONCEPT IN CONTEXT | The American Civil Rights Movement

We can usually view a social movement in two ways, depending on the context. It may comprise only the members of a large category who cooperate to contend for their shared values or interests. Alternatively, we may think of a social movement as a broader political opinion grouping that includes people or organizations beyond the category who share values as well as support for a group interest. In the civil rights movement in the United States, members of the key category (African Americans) played an important role in politics independently of the organizations representing them. Was the civil rights movement limited to the categoric interest of African Americans, or was it an even larger political opinion group, including many supportive whites?

Southern African Americans obviously had shared concerns. From the last quarter of the nineteenth century on, they had lived under segregation—isolation and inferior treatment with regard to education, employment, residence, and public facilities. After 1909, African Americans had an association in the North, the NAACP (the National Association for the Advancement of Colored People), which mainly pursued legal remedies to segregation. But in the South, African Americans were denied the right to organize or run for office. They were kept from voting by such legal devices as the literacy test and the poll tax, but the main weapon to deter African Americans from organizing to change these conditions was the threat of beatings and lynching (murder).

By mid-century, however, some prominent whites began to cooperate in the fight against segregation. President Harry Truman desegregated the armed forces in the late 1940s, and the Supreme Court outlawed segregated schools in 1954. In a few instances, Presidents Eisenhower and Kennedy used federal marshals or the National Guard to protect African Americans in the exercise of their rights, such as National Guard protection in the integration of schools in Little Rock, Arkansas, in 1958.

At the grassroots level in the South, however, brave African Americans were beginning to act independently of formal interest group organizations. The African American minister Martin Luther King, Jr., led a movement of peaceful protest marches and boycotts that gained national media attention. Over time, local groups such as the Mississippi Freedom Party began to form, and the NAACP became more of a mass organization. The Congress of Racial Equality (CORE) organized "freedom rides" of African Americans and whites from the North who cooperated to peacefully violate segregation rules in Southern bus stations and lunch counters. Their civil disobedience sometimes brought beatings by racist whites, stays in jail, and even a few killings. Later, other African American organizations emerged, ranging from the radical Student Nonviolent Coordinating Committee (SNCC) and the Black Panther Party to the more conventional Urban League. For those militant African Americans who stressed that the primary effort must be one by African Americans only, the phrase "black power movement" arose.

Most participants in these demonstrations and boycotts initially were African Americans. Increasingly over the 1960s, however, more white people supported and participated in the civil rights struggle. Starting in 1964, the passing of civil rights laws by the national government finally made racial discrimination illegal. The expression "civil rights movement" came to encompass all of its participants, including supportive whites.

As the movement achieved its most prominent goals and African American groups settled into ordinary contention for greater economic opportunity alongside other interest groups, they and their issues have somewhat receded from view. What groups and issues related to group opportunity have replaced the civil rights movement, and why?

members of an interest group association by enrolling through the mail (or e-mail) and making a yearly contribution to it. (Associations involving face-to-face participation, such as local clubs and fraternal organizations, seem less prevalent today than in decades past.) When you join, you typically get more than just membership in something greater than yourself. Periodically, the organization will inform you of its efforts, and you may have access to other benefits (e.g., for a farm organization, low-cost crop insurance).

An association's membership rarely includes the whole categoric interest that it represents. Even if you tend to be a joiner, you are unlikely to enroll in all of the organizations representing all categories into which you fall. Those in a category who don't join its association—but nonetheless benefit from its efforts—are called **free riders**. The larger the proportion of the category that joins its association (that is, the fewer the free riders), the more resources the association will possess to attempt to influence policy.

Various factors may affect how many people who are part of a category actually join an organization that represents them. One such factor is the possibility of competition from cross-cutting interests. For example, a clean air group trying to reduce air pollution in a city may have trouble gaining members if many of the city's residents are employed by the polluting companies. The companies will say that the costs of stricter air quality regulations will lead them to cut back in the city, lay off employees, and maybe even move somewhere else.

As we shall see below, a related factor affecting how much of a categoric interest joins its association is material self-interest (emphasized by "rational choice" theory; see chapter 3). For example, the members of an association of chemical manufacturers are corporations, with direct financial interests in avoiding regulations and taxes. Such "bottom line" benefits provide a powerful incentive for a company to join its trade association and pay the dues that fund the association's activities. And the comparatively small number of units in the categoric interest (again, corporations rather than individual people in this case) may also be a factor. Each enterprise's dues make a real difference to the effort, so there will be great pressure on each to join.[3]

In contrast, the members of categories such as "consumers" or women are large numbers of individual people, to whom the benefits of lobbying success may not be very noticeable. For example, for a national environmental group working for cleaner air, the tangible benefits of success may be slow in coming, incremental, and not evident to the eye. Meanwhile, the numbers of people breathing the air are huge, so each is tempted to view his or her contribution as a "drop in the bucket," not essential to the group's success. Thus, we say that such groups face a "collective action" problem. Only a small proportion of the affected categoric interest will join and pay dues, while large numbers of free riders nonetheless get the benefit of the cleaner air.

To be sure, much joining behavior cannot be explained by self-interested cost-benefit calculations, and the rational choice approach has received heavy criticism recently.[4] Other intangible factors may play roles. These include value-related concerns (see below), ideological commitment, a sense of social solidarity, satisfaction in being part of something bigger than yourself, anger at an injustice, and the desire to defeat an opposing group that you dislike.[5]

The Organization's Officials

As we move closer to actual governmental decision making, the next level of interest group activity is that of the **officials** of the association. They work for the organization in formal positions such as executive director, treasurer, or researcher. Usually most officials work in the capital cities of nations or regions, the source of government activity. They do the actual work of the interest group, including such functions as:

- conducting research
- developing strategy
- formulating positions on issues
- monitoring the behavior of government officials on relevant issues
- attending legislative committee hearings and testifying before them whenever possible
- communicating with the membership and the rest of the category
- fund-raising
- deciding how to allocate the association's information, money, and other resources
- overseeing lobbyists

Top officials wield significant influence within the interest group (see "Applying the Models").

APPLYING THE MODELS | Influence within the Interest Group Organization

Which model best explains the distribution of power within the interest group itself? Related to the elite model, usually the memberships of interest group organizations do not elect their officials democratically. The officials are either hired by higher-level officials or chosen by the group's board of directors. And officials tend to be above average in education, though not necessarily in income. One study has pictured them as entrepreneurial managers, working primarily for paycheck and position.* Some interest group organizations depend on one or a few major financial sources, and these elite "patrons" may heavily influence the organization.† All this contributes to an elite-model picture of the distribution of influence within the interest group.

Additionally, however, a case can be made for the majority preference model. The officials usually seek to represent the majority preference of the group's categoric interest, which they translate into concrete policy goals. To do so and to recruit new members, interest group officials must know what the people in the category want. (This becomes especially clear if more than one organization contends for the category's support.) Moreover, officials' positions are not particularly lucrative. Many staffers are young and work long hours for little pay, at least partly due to their commitment to the interests of the category. From this point of view, the education and information possessed by the officials enables them to be more effective representatives and instruments of the majority preference, rather than an elite.

However, minorities may exist within a categoric interest and yield a more pluralistic picture of the organization's governance. For example, a nurses' association's officials must pay attention to the interests of home care nurses as well as emergency room nurses or intensive care nurses, and so on. As we saw above in the case of urban air pollution, other cross-cutting categoric interests may result in contending opinions that may moderate a group's stances on issues.

The personal leadership model also deserves consideration. Some interest groups spring from a charismatic leader. In the United States in the 1960s, the inspiring leadership of Ralph Nader contributed to the creation of a network of consumer interest groups around his original Public Interest Research Group. These groups got consumer issues on the public and governmental agenda.

The interest group obviously involves elements of all four models of influence distribution. Think of a categoric interest that you might identify with, and an association that seeks to represent it. Which model(s) do you think best explains the distribution of influence within that group?

---

* See Robert H. Salisbury, "An Exchange Theory of Interest Groups," *Midwest Journal of Political Science* 13 (1969): 1–32.

† See Cigler and Nownes 1995.

Sometimes the officials of like-minded interest groups cooperate with each other in informal coalitions in pursuit of their goals. For example, in the United States, a key issue today is offshore tax havens, where loopholes in American tax laws allow some corporations to set up fake headquarters in certain low-tax countries (perhaps nothing more than a post office box), to avoid paying taxes in the countries where their real operations are but which have higher tax rates. A leading interest group opposing such practices is a "public interest" one (see below), the Public Interest Research Group (PIRG). But in some of its tax-related efforts, PIRG cooperates with another group, the Citizens for Tax Justice, and others in what is, in effect, a lobbying coalition on the issue.

In some cases, related interest group associations cooperate in larger umbrella organizations called **peak associations**. For example, in the national capital one or more union federations may broadly represent labor, and one or more may represent business. In Britain, for example, the Trades Union Congress speaks for labor and the Confederation of British Industry speaks for business. When a division of interest exists within some broad economic sector, there may be more than one peak association in it. In France, the National Council of French Employers represents big business, but the General Confederation of Small and Medium Enterprises has a different constituency.

Peak associations may have formal connections with government. For example, in some Northern European countries, peak associations representing employers and organized labor have seats on advisory councils in the executive branch of government. They work with government officials on matters ranging from labor market issues (e.g., wage guidelines and layoff regulations) to overall economic planning and even educational policy. However, most nations lack such formal structures for regular contact between the government and officials of interest groups. Most often, interest group officials lobby governmental officials informally, on their own.

The Lobbyists

Finally, we arrive at the level of interest group activity that is closest to actual governmental decision making. We can distinguish those interest group representatives who actually interact with government officials on behalf of the group: the **lobbyists**. This is the most direct way in which interest groups contend to influence policy in ways favorable to the group's interests. While we may think of "lobbying" as taking place in lobbies of public buildings,[6] lobbying also occurs in offices, in restaurants, at cocktail parties, on the golf course, or in the streets. It may involve talking to the most relevant staff members of the public official rather than the official directly.

One or more officials of an interest group organization may lobby as part of their jobs. But associations with ample resources may hire outside professional lobbyists. These lobbyists might be independent individuals, work for lobbying firms, or belong to law, accounting, or public relations firms. They often have worked in government in the policy area(s) that they represent. The ranks of lobbyists include former legislators and legislative staff, former bureaucrats, former interest group officials, and people with experience in multiple such roles. Many lobbyists specialize in just one or two policy areas, reflecting their experience and connections. Thus they belong to the "issue networks" that they work in.[7]

The process begins as officials of the interest group meet with their lobbyist(s) to indicate what the group's goals are, and supply them with information on the relevant issue. Then the lobbyists, armed additionally with their own political information and contacts, go to the decision makers.

Lobbyists concentrate on points in the political process where they have the greatest chances of influencing public policy. Here the structure of government has a role to play. Under parliamentary government, as we have seen, legislators tend to vote cohesively with their party. There it makes sense for a lobbyist in a particular policy area to go to the party leaders, especially those most influential on the party committee for the relevant policy area. In a presidential system, where legislators may vote more independently of their party, lobbyists typically have many people in government to approach. For example, a farm lobbyist may focus on the members of relevant subcommittee of the agriculture committee in a legislative assembly, and the most relevant sector of the bureaucracy. As we shall see in coming chapters, different parts of government matter to different policy areas.

In the American presidential system, the period of the 1970s and 1980s saw a major growth in the numbers of both interest groups and "decision points" where lobbyists can have influence. As two lobbyists noted,

> If you go back a few years ago, you would have to say that if the National Association of Realtors and the National Association of Home Builders spoke, that was the whole industry speaking. Now there are more groups, such as low income housing groups, real estate developers, residential real estate developers, etc. . . . Members of Congress have to listen to all these groups.[8]

And

> In [the early 1960s], if you could get the ear of the chairman [of a Congressional committee], you could [count on] your case as being a victory. That isn't true today. Individual congressmen contribute more. Today, other congressmen have much more influence. Before, if the committee chairman didn't like your proposal, your chances for getting it through were over.[9]

During the American Congressional debate over financial reform that followed the financial crisis of 2008–2009, interest groups fielded thousands of lobbyists representing well-funded financial firms. They focused especially on drawing individual members of the Democratic Party majorities in the House and the Senate away from support for the stronger regulatory provisions of the party leadership's bill. In the eyes of many analysts, the lobbyists successfully weakened the regulation enacted.

In authoritarian systems, usually the executive branch holds sway (see chapter 12). Interest groups focus on the appropriate agencies or offices there.

DIFFERENCES AMONG TYPES OF INTEREST GROUPS

Interest groups differ from one another in key ways that affect how much influence they may have in political contention. For each source of difference, there is a pair of opposing "types" of interest group:

- Single-issue versus multi-issue. This dimension concerns how large a range of issues a given interest group gets involved in.

- Material stake versus value related. This dimension involves the extent to which a group pursues direct tangible benefits for its category members, versus shared values.

- Communal (versus instrumental). This dimension focuses on whether the group is closely related to the personal identity of its members (communal) versus less so.

- Institutional (versus associational). This dimension addresses the extent to which the organization exists independently of politics, and its lobbying produces benefits that flow to or through the organization itself.

To be sure, we need to remember that distinctions such as these do not always refer to clearly demarcated, night-versus-day categories. Each type is really an extreme pole at each end of a spectrum of variation between the two poles. Real-world examples may not be all the way at one end or the other on the continuum. But they are likely to be in one segment or another of it, closer to one pole or the other, along one of the following dimensions of difference between interest groups. How much influence an interest group wields may depend partly on how close it is to one or the other extreme on one (or more) of these dimensions of difference.

Single-Issue Versus Multi-Issue Groups

Interest groups differ in the range of issues that the group focuses on, between single-issue and multi-issue. Most groups are **multi-issue**, starting with a specific population (e.g., teachers or veterans) and then dealing with various issues that affect it. Unions, for example, do not focus on only workers' rights and occupational health and safety laws. They are also concerned with minimum wage legislation, universal health insurance, and other issues that affect people well beyond the workplace.

In contrast, **single-issue** groups arise around only one issue or a cluster of closely related issues. For example, the American "Proposition 13" group was antitax, backing a 1970s' measure in the American state of California to drastically cut and cap local property taxes supporting education. (They were successful, resulting in large cuts in spending on public education in California.) In practice, however, groups that sound like single-issue ones often are not purely so. American "right-to-life" groups focus on opposing abortion. They are certainly in the single-issue segment of the continuum (and thus deserve the classification), but are not at the extreme end of it. They deal with a range of issues such as sex education in the schools, procedures governing protests at clinics offering abortion, and what restrictions the government may impose at which trimester of pregnancy.

If a single-issue group's particular issue disappears, it may dissolve. But multi-issue organizations are in for the long haul. They develop experience, expertise, and political connections that single-issue groups often haven't had time to build. A single-issue group may have to rely more heavily on personal leadership factors such as the enthusiasm, energy, and charisma of its leadership and activists, and the momentum that it gains while the issue is high on the public or governmental agenda. But such factors can be hard to maintain over time. Multi-issue opponents of single-issue groups sometimes outlast them. Single-issue groups survive only if they can find other related issues to take on after their initial victory, defeat, or compromise. An organization first sparked to protect a small park may discover new issues later that affect the area and transform it into a long-lived neighborhood association. The group that was originally called Proposition 13 to reduce property taxes in the American state of California still exists as the Howard Jarvis Taxpayers' Association, trying to reduce other taxes as well.

Material Versus Value-Related Concerns

As was noted above regarding factors contributing to membership in interest group associations, some groups focus primarily on a material stake that they perceive in policy issues affecting them. In contrast, however, other groups focus mainly on some public value (see chapters 1 and 3) that they consider worth pursuing in public policy.

Material Stake Groups When people think of interest groups, often what comes to mind first are economically definable groups that are affected financially by government policymaking, and thus have a material stake in outcomes. For example, a country's lumber industry may believe that growing its profits and jobs depends on expanding logging in state-owned wilderness areas. As its trade association seeks the cooperation of the logging companies in joining the association and contends for influence over policymaking, it benefits from the long-term material self-interest that drives the industry.

Some political scientists refer to such categoric interests as "sectoral," referring to sectors of the economy such as "the banks," "the television industry," or health care, with their trade associations (of businesses), professional associations, or labor unions. But other sections of the population also have tangible interests in public policy, such as the elderly, students, consumers of a good or service, or people lacking clean air or clean water. Material benefits are not limited to money alone. Another word that is sometimes used to label material stake groups, "protective," casts too wide a net. Almost all interest groups may be viewed as trying to protect something. Here I borrow from revealing ordinary language, and call them **material stake** interests.

Value-Related Groups The contrasting type of interest group exists not to further or protect a material stake, but rather to further a cause, such as environmental protection, equal opportunity, or fair criminal justice. The essential feature of this type of group is the pursuit of some sort of public value (see chapters 1 and 3). For example, the public value might be some form of well-being, such as environmental health or national security against terrorist attack. Or the goal may be some form of freedom such as civil liberties, or equality in the form of equal treatment under the law, or order in the economic form of stability in the financial system to protect it from risky investment activities that might bring it down (see chapter 8). In this book, groups that pursue such values are labeled **value-related groups**.

Some who write about interest groups use other terminology to denote these groups, such as "promotional" or "purposive." But these other terms seem to cast too wide a net. Virtually every interest group promotes its cause and has purposes. Again, the phrase "value related" gets to the heart of the matter in distinguishing this category of interest groups from others.

Think of the American logging companies' conservationist opponents, such as the Wilderness Society, the World Wildlife Fund, or the Sierra Club. They oppose allowing lumber companies to cut timber on state-owned forest preserves, or letting them use the method of "clear-cutting"—taking all trees on a mountain—in doing so. People who join and support such conservation groups are at the far end of the value-related segment of the continuum. They have no material stake at all in the issues involved (the material stake belongs to the plants and animals whose habitats are at stake). Such groups prefer wilderness preservation entirely as a public value—part of their sense of their country's well-being. Members' concerns are primarily aesthetic (nature as beautiful) or benevolent (helping otherwise defenseless animal and plant life), not self-interested.

Polar bears need the disappearing arctic ice as their base for feeding. Even in the case of global warming, among the first and most direct victims are animal and plant life.

Close to the value-related end of the continuum are **public interest groups**. They represent the interests of all people, but without a very noticeable tangible stake for most individuals. For example, American groups such as Common Cause and the above-mentioned Public Interest Research Group focus on a form of justice—having the country's institutions work fairly, humanely, and with integrity. In Mexico, Civic Alliance has played an important role in monitoring and exposing traditional patterns of fraud in Mexican elections. It helped lay the foundation for the fairer political contention that arose in Mexico in the first decades of the twenty-first century (see Country Case Studies).

Also under the public interest heading are human rights interest groups. Internationally, nongovernmental organizations (NGOs) such as Human Rights Watch and Amnesty International publicize violations of civil-political rights. In the economic-social rights area, the French organization Doctors Without Borders works to address pressing health problems in the developing world such as the Ebola crisis in West Africa in 2014 and 2015. Other NGOs work to address human rights and humanitarian problems within the borders of their countries. Officials and activists of both international and domestic groups often sacrifice heavily, and may even risk their lives for their cause. They receive little material support from the mostly poor citizens around them.

To be sure, tangible benefits from such groups' activities come in the long run to everyone.[10] But again, usually such benefits are not very direct and apparent to the citizenry in general. Public interest groups depend on conscious and voluntary attachment to public values such as particular forms of freedom, justice, and minimal well-being for the whole community.

The Spectrum and Its Consequences Material stake and value-based motivation, like most other opposing pairs of concepts for classification, can be a matter of degree. Some interest groups fall between the extremes of the continuum, where we find some overlap between value-related concerns and mild forms of material stake (see Figure 9.2). Regarding consumer issues, for example, large swathes of the population have tangible stakes, but they are typically less large and clear than for sectors of the economy. On an issue such as producer manipulation of the price of coffee, for example, the tangible impact on each consumer of coffee is small, and for non-coffee drinkers is nonexistent. For consumer groups, a key part is played by values such as justice in the form

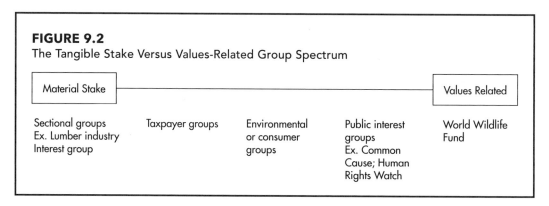

FIGURE 9.2
The Tangible Stake Versus Values-Related Group Spectrum

of fairness (in pricing, in this case), or well-being in the form of consumer safety.

Consider the situation of a national environmental group working for clean air. Its efforts pursue a particular public value, environmental health as part of the nation's well-being. But a degree of tangible stake is present, too. Over the long term, the types and amounts of pollutants in the air make a material difference for the physical health of each individual breathing it. However, as was noted above, in the short time horizon of most of the public, immediate gains in air quality are incremental and almost unnoticeable—that is, they do not seem *very* tangible. For those joining and supporting the group, the public value carries most of the weight. Thus we want to say that the categoric interest—most broadly, everyone breathing the air, or more narrowly, those supporting clean air—are mostly in the value-related segment of the continuum (though not at the extreme pole of having no material stake at all). Similarly, we may say that taxpayer groups are primarily in the material stake segment of the continuum; their main purpose is to have more money in their bank account each month. But for some of their supporters, their material stake may not be the whole story; value-related fairness arguments may also be used to justify cutting taxes.

To be sure, the value-related preferences of members of consumer, wilderness preservation, or antiabortion groups can be just as intense at times as those of their material stake rivals. But the lack of a strongly felt material stake may make momentum hard to maintain against opponents who have such a stake, such as trade associations of business enterprises.[11] A good example of this was the American health-care debate in 1993–1994.[12] Initially, a majority in polls wanted universal health insurance coverage. But most people already had adequate health insurance through their employment, so the number of uninsured would-be beneficiaries of the proposed bill was small. And the providers of drugs, patient care, health insurance, and medical devices had a big material stake in avoiding regulations and possible cost controls that might limit their incomes. They were able to marshal huge resources for media advertising against the bill as a possible threat to patient choice. In the end, nothing was achieved toward universal health insurance. Over the years since then, good employer-provided health insurance became less common. But nonetheless, when the 2008–2009 financial crisis brought high rates of unemployment, many people lost their health insurance along with their jobs. With so many more Americans uninsured or fearing loss of job and health insurance, a limited health insurance bill was able to pass.

Communal (Identity) Groups

Another distinction among interest groups centers on what unites the categoric interest. A small proportion of interest groups are united by something that touches their *personal identity*, as something that is not chosen: who you are rather than what you pursue. Racial and ethnic groups, for example, can have a sense of family-like solidarity. Political scientists refer to these as **communal groups**. For example, if you are of black African ancestry, you did not choose to be in that category. The situation is similar for some ethnic categories such as the Basques of Spain, Walloons in Belgium, Tutsis or Hutus in Rwanda, and countless other ethnic groups around the world.[13] The same can be said about women as a group.

In contrast, the vast majority of interest groups share concerns that are related to *practical choices* that people make in life, in pursuit of their goals or values. Examples are what occupation to take up, what region to live in, or whether to be concerned about environmental or consumer issues. Such groups could be labeled "instrumental," in that membership in the categoric interest is related to the goals or values that people pursue, such as successfully making a living or improving the environment.

Here too, there are group attachments that can have elements of both. Religious identification can range between the communal and instrumental types; a religion may feel like something one was born into, as part of one's identity (e.g., for many Muslims or Catholic Christians), or it may feel like something that was consciously adopted. Coinciding (or superimposed) cleavages (see chapters 4 and 8) tend to reinforce lines of ethnic or religious division and intensify the personal-identity link to the group.

As with other types of interest groups, communal categoric interests tend to form associations to serve their needs and promote their interests.[14] But the greatest political importance of the communal group is *informal*. Fellow members of an ethnic group may try to help each other out informally in ways that can be a factor in politics, such as in hiring or in steering government benefits. In many developing countries, such ethnic or racial identification can be very powerful. There, impersonal norms of merit and equal treatment often play a smaller part than in most of the developed world. Also, religious identity can be a target for an ideology seeking to recruit supporters, as in the case of militant Islamism (see chapter 6).

Institutional Groups

As we have seen, the vast majority of interest group organizations are associations that are formed for social and/or political purposes. For them, lobbying gains directly benefit the categoric interest that the association represents. For example, consumer groups try to benefit consumers, and trade associations each try to benefit its sector of business. Such interests may be called **associational groups**.

However, a limited portion of groups that behave as interest groups at times (e.g., in lobbying) depart from the most common model in two key ways. Here, the organization exists originally for some purpose *other than* socializing and/or influencing government policy, and any gains from lobbying come to or through the organization itself. Political scientists refer to these as **institutional interest groups** (because of their being somewhat "institutionalized," independently of the political process).

Governmental Institutional Groups An especially important cluster of institutional interest groups comprise portions of the executive branch of government. Cabinet ministries (or "departments") in the executive branch, such as those for finance, labor, industry, agriculture, defense, or culture, exist originally for the purpose of implementing the laws and programs relating to their specific policy areas. But at times they also act like interest groups. Sectors of the bureaucracy may lobby other government officials for purposes such as maintaining or expanding their budget, staffing, and autonomy. Sometimes, they have to contend vigorously in budget battles, especially to avoid downsizing. These types of groups may be labeled **governmental institutional groups**.

In the case of governmental institutional interests, there is a broad categoric interest that a ministry tends to benefit, such as the country's workers for a labor ministry, those involved in the arts for a culture ministry, or supporters of environmental protection for an environment ministry. But in this case, the gains from lobbying tend to pass through the ministry itself, and then on, indirectly, to the categoric interest. If an environment ministry wins a fight to avoid downsizing, successfully protecting its staff and budget, the ultimate consequence will be more effective implementation of environmental regulations and programs for the country and its supporters of environmentalism.

Governmental institutional groups can be very effective in political contention. They often have resources of organization, information, expertise, and contacts beyond those of most ordinary interest groups. In some developing countries, especially those that have experienced military rule, the armed forces can be the most important such group. In pre-2011 Egypt, for example, key officials in then President Hosni Mubarak's government came from the ranks of military officers (see Country Case Study, chapter 11). When Mubarak was driven from power after months of demonstrations in 2011, the military took power for over a year before yielding to an elected Islamist government. But when the Islamists seemed to be concentrating too much power in their own hands, the military stepped in again, taking over the government.

Institutional interests tend to be especially unified and cohesive. The membership level of the organization consists largely of the employees and management of the organization itself. They form a **primary group** with ongoing face-to-face interaction. Political socialization from both management and peers in the organization can reinforce the group's sense of its values and mission. For example, employees of the government's forest service in Kenya have negative attitudes toward the poaching of animals that are very different from the attitudes of some of their neighbors in the area who do not work in the service.

An interesting question for a governmental institutional interest has to do with whether it plays the role of a material stake group or a value-related one (see above). If we emphasize the institutional interest's pursuit of its mission, most segments of the executive branch can be considered as value related. Again, an environment ministry pursues the public's environmental well-being, the military exists for national security, a justice ministry aims at criminal justice and legal fairness, a culture ministry seeks to enhance the nation's cultural life, etc. But in a few cases, the categoric interest in society that ultimately benefits seems to be more clearly a material stake one. A nation's commerce ministry, for example, works mainly to drum up business abroad for the country's exporting enterprises.

However, what about the material stake interests of a ministry's employees themselves—the institutional interest's "membership"? For example, especially in some developing nations, a ministry or department may not appear to be pursuing its mission very avidly. It may seem more interested in patronage jobs and clientelistic benefits for its supporters (perhaps involving bribery and corruption). For example, in 2014 when much of the Iraqi military collapsed and ran in the face of a broad offensive by the radical Islamist group Islamic State, it became known than some of its soldiers saw their jobs as patronage, and some officers were skimming off money and equipment for their own private gain (e.g., by diverting and selling some of the weapons and ammunition provided by the Americans). Here material stake would be an appropriate label, applied to the organizational membership rather than an outside categoric interest represented by the membership.

Societal Institutional Groups Not all institutional interest groups are governmental. We also have the category of **societal institutional interests**. For example, a religious hierarchy (e.g., the Catholic church in Latin America) exists to organize worship by the religion's believers. It does not exist primarily for social or political reasons, as is the case for associational groups. However, it may behave at times like an interest group, such as the Latin American church's involvement in policies concerning education and abortion. Benefits tend to come through the organization (perhaps including the church's full congregations), but on behalf of the categoric interest standing behind it: the whole body of the religion's believers.

Another category of societal institutional interest is economic. One subtype is large economic enterprises that lobby independently, on their own behalf. The American energy-trading corporation Enron (before its fall in 2001) formally existed for purposes unrelated to politics or socializing: to perform a commercial service, make profits, and provide jobs and incomes for its employees and investors. But it didn't follow the usual associational path of leaving the care of its political interests to an energy-sector trade association of which it was a contributing member. Instead, Enron's lobbying attention was focused primarily on gaining benefits for itself, rather than for a separate categoric interest that it might be seen as representing. In this type of institutional interest group, in effect the categoric interest *was* the organization. In its heyday in the 1990s, Enron was one of the most powerful interest groups in Washington in its own right. (In the early 2000s, it was caught concealing its debts from American regulators and Wall Street, and more or less collapsed.)

Another economic subtype is unions. They exist primarily to represent an economic sector's workers in collective bargaining negotiations with its employers. But they also have political interests, and at times lobby on behalf of workers of a country generally (e.g., for minimum wage legislation), beyond the confines of their formal membership. Professional associations, too, exist for economic purposes that are independent of socializing or lobbying. For example, a country's doctors' association, or that of its dentists, regulates the qualifications, training, and practice of the profession to maintain standards (in effect, functions delegated to it by government).

Now that we have examined the four dimensions of difference among interest groups, note that any given group may be classified on all four of these differences (see Table 9.1).

| TABLE 9.1 | Examples of Interest Groups and Their Types |

Interest Group Example	Issue Range	Type of Motivation	Type of Linkage to Individual	Institutional or Associational
An association of chemical manufacturers	Multi-issue	Material stake	Instrumental	Associational
An antiabortion group	More single issue	Value-related	Mixed (some Religious/ communal)	Associational
The industry ministry of Germany	Multi-issue	Mixed	Instrumental	Institutional

RESOURCES AND EFFECTIVENESS IN THE POLITICAL PROCESS

The resources of interest groups can greatly affect their level of influence. A complete list of available political resources would be a long one.[16] For our purposes here, five major resources stand out: information, votes, money, formal connections with government, and connections with political parties.

Information

Sometimes an important resource for lobbyists is the *information* that they can provide to policy makers. Government officials may get from lobbyists not only substantive information about the issues, but also political information on who is supporting which side, how, and why. The information from any one lobbyist is likely to favor the side of the interest group that he or she represents. But government decision makers get a fuller picture by hearing from lobbyists on other sides of the issue. Notably, the information presented by a lobbyist must be accurate if the lobbyist and group want to be given access and be taken seriously in the future.

Moreover, interest groups often provide an especially important type of information for policymaking: specific, fleshed-out policy *alternatives*, along with their justifications. To make wise policymaking decisions, government officeholders must at least have detailed alternatives before them. Contending interest groups provide such options.

Votes

Another key resource that interest groups in representative democracies can provide (or withhold) is *votes* in the next election. Interest groups monitor how legislators vote on bills, identify the group's friends and opponents, and often endorse candidates or parties prior to election day. The association's endorsement can significantly affect the election result if:

- a sizable categoric interest exists in an election district;
- the association can reach much of the category through recommendations to its membership and advertising;
- the group's voters generally turn out to vote; and
- they consider the group's interests when voting.

At the Democratic National Convention in September of 2012 in the United States, women urging support for health-care aid for women, abortion choice, and the Democratic Party.

Just one or two of these factors may be enough to make a difference in a close election. Hence the group's preferences may carry some weight in candidates' policymaking decisions, especially when candidates lack strong views of their own on the matter at hand. In addition, a disappointed business group can have an *indirect* effect on the vote total for current officeholders seeking reelection, if it then contracts its local employment with harmful effects on the district's economy. Political scientist Charles Lindblom suggested that this situation in democracy gives business a "privileged position" in policy decision making.[16]

Money

Money is an especially important political resource for interest groups, as it is necessary for much of their activity. Money pays qualified staff, supports research to get information to use in lobbying, and pays for media advertising to mobilize public opinion. Money also funds communication with the association's membership. Well-endowed interest groups can afford to hire top-notch lobbyists with the best connections to represent their interests to public officials or party leaders.

Another important use of money is campaign contributions to friendly candidates to pay for expensive television advertising and other costs. In an important form of political cooperation, interest groups with significant financial resources can deploy more money to help the election campaigns of candidates. In the United States, for example, loopholes in the regulatory framework allow groups of any size to do this extensively (see "Contention and Cooperation in Focus").

Does this involve a form of bribery? It is difficult to show that a particular official switched issue positions due to a new campaign contribution (or a big increase over the last contribution). In the absence of concrete evidence, this comes down to a chicken-and-egg question: which came first, the idea of the policy switch, the campaign contribution, or the candidate's anticipation of the contribution? In fact, the great majority of campaign contributions by interest groups aim to help the election chances of candidates who are known to have favored the group's side of the key issue in the past. Nonetheless, it is often known to candidates that bigger campaign contributions are available from interests on one side of an issue than those on the other, which can create an unsavory atmosphere for policymaking by elected officials.

In contrast, most of Europe does not permit privately purchased campaign advertising during the later weeks of parliamentary election campaigns.

CONTENTION AND COOPERATION IN FOCUS | American Campaign Finance Regulation

The first broad attempt to regulate campaign finance in the United States came in the early and middle 1970s. New laws allowed groups such as those representing sectors of labor and corporations to cooperate in "political action committees" (PACs) to raise money and contribute to candidates' campaigns. Among other things—including public disclosure of contributions—the legislation limited PACs to contributing $5,000 per candidate per campaign (for individuals, $1,000).

Quickly, however, loopholes appeared that greatly weakened regulation of the use of interest group money in electoral contention. In 1976, the U.S. Supreme Court (in Buckley v. Valeo) struck down any limits on independent groups' spending related to policy advocacy. The Court declared, in the name of free speech, that PACs could advertise regarding an issue as long as it didn't explicitly support or oppose a candidate. The result was oppositional advertising by independent 527 PACs (named for the relevant line in the tax code) that attacked candidates for their issue stands without formally making a voting recommendation. Such ads in campaigns came to be called "sham issue ads." And in 1979, new legislation allowed unlimited contributions to political parties for "party-building" activities—called "soft money"—which soon expanded to a wide range of election help for candidates. In effect, control of cooperation between interest group money and the campaigns of contending candidates had been circumvented.

In 2003, however, new legislation took a second shot at real regulation. The McCain-Feingold law banned soft money contributions to parties, as well as independent issue advertising by groups within sixty days of national elections. However, by 2010, the U.S. Supreme Court had become sharply conservative. In its Citizens United decision, the Court struck down all limits on ad spending by corporations or unions that expressly advocate voting for or against a candidate, as long as the group did not cooperate with the favored candidate's campaign. Even disclosure requirements could be circumvented if donor groups made their contributions to PACs that passed them on to "superPACs." The superPACS could then place ads, and only be required to disclose which PACs had contributed to them, not the original contributors to the PACs. (Such PACs might have names that make them sound like interest group associations with members—for example, "Americans for Freedom"—but in fact have no membership roles, and be no more than technical conduits for money.) The superPACs who did the advertising were often run by officials who had only recently been working in candidates' and party organizations. So even the remaining restrictions on cooperation between candidate organizations and these superPACs (without spending limits or real disclosure requirements) had been, in effect, circumvented.

To what extent do groups with money distort political contention in your country? Are the rules to regulate the role of money effective?

Parties instead receive free primetime television access to appeal to voters. In addition, parties in parliament may receive government subsidies to support their activities.

As we saw in the membership section above, the clear and substantial material stake interests of small groups such as business trade associations can encourage more of their category to become dues-paying members. Thus more money will be available for the association to use to influence policymaking and elections. In addition, corporations and wealthy individuals often have easy access to cash without much transparency or accountability. Unions also have autonomous access to money, but their presence in countries' work forces has weakened greatly in recent decades—especially in the United States—and their available funds are far smaller.

However, we should not assume that the financial advantages of business trade associations or other groups funded by wealthy contributors will automatically steer policymaking in an elite-model direction. In theory at least, voters can ignore campaign advertising. And value-related groups can gain members and receive contributions because of such nonmaterial factors as a sense of social solidarity, concern for the public interest, or a sense of righting a wrong. An otherwise financially weak group may find a few wealthy backers.[17] Moreover, business may itself be divided. For example, in India, exporters wanting to reduce regulations and trade barriers contend with established domestic producers favoring trade protection and regulations that limit foreign competition. In another current example, alternative energy companies developing solar and wind technologies may battle the traditional oil, gas, and coal industries over such policy options as energy subsidies, carbon taxes, and emissions caps.

In addition, officials' skills can sometimes compensate for meager financial resources. The organizing and publicity talents of a group's leaders can be employed to gain free news media coverage. For example, in the United States in the 1970s, Ralph Nader was an effective "political entrepreneur" for the interests of consumers. And in trying to affect policymaking, groups may enlist the help of other like-minded groups. Representatives of one group may join in meetings and offer support to another related group, with the expectation that the help will be reciprocated in the future. Factors such as these emphasize the pluralist model of the situation more than money-based elite-model pictures.

To be sure, some categoric interests are at a disadvantage in terms of both money and organizational skills. Disadvantaged racial or ethnic minorities (and the poor generally) usually display low rates of voter turnout in most countries. This trend makes organizational skills among the association's officials all the more important. But such skills normally go with education, and the poorer strata tend to have lower levels of education and less knowledge of the skills necessary to organize associations effectively.

Connections with Government Institutions

Another key resource for interest groups is formal connections with government. For example, governmental institutional interests have advantages here. Ministries and governmental agencies have regular formal access to upper-echelon power centers in the executive branch and legislative committees. Their expertise and special control over information augments their influence.

In some nations, other types of interest groups formally participate in governmental decision-making processes, in a phenomenon called **neo-corporatism**. Especially in Europe, certain designated interests commonly get seats on particular councils and commissions in the executive branch (see chapter 13), related to their policy concerns. Such committees may review and discuss new ideas before they come before parliament as actual proposals. Also, key interest groups may get to perform certain quasi-governmental functions regulating their own categoric interest. For example, professional associations (e.g., medical, dental, law) often have the responsibility of licensing and regulating their own profession.

To some critics, neo-corporatism conveys an elitist atmosphere in which specific well-established interest groups—business associations, union federations, and related governmental institutional interests, for example—always get seats at the table, leaving other groups to contend on their own. Recently emerging post-materialist interests such as environmental groups, women, youth, and cultural minority interests often find themselves left out of long-established corporatist arrangements. However, those enmeshed in corporatism may find themselves constrained by these connections with government. At times they may have to cooperate more (and contend less) than they prefer regarding agreements that they are not happy with.

State-controlled corporatism may be found under authoritarian regimes, imposing an extreme degree of cooperation. Here, interest groups have formal representation in councils, but they do not participate in an autonomous way. Rather, they are in effect controlled and used by the government, to secure their cooperation with party-government initiatives and to promote the dominant party's message (see chapter 13). In Nazi Germany, Fascist Italy, and the former Soviet Union, the government controlled or screened interest group representatives to assure that the interests of the government and the dominant party would remain preeminent. Autonomous behavior by these interest groups was usually limited to jockeying to protect or expand their benefits from government.[18] Sometimes a military takeover of a government would replace largely autonomous corporatist arrangements by more state-controlled ones, as in Brazil after 1964.[19]

In systems that lack neo-corporatist patterns, key interest groups have no formal link to governmental institutions. The United States, for example, does not have councils or commissions in the executive branch of government that formally include interest groups alongside bureaucrats and parties' representatives.[20] Lobbying there is almost all informal, and interest groups contend individually. This does not mean, however, that the system lacks patterns of cooperation in lobbying. Again, related groups may also support each other's proposals, plan strategy together, and even meet jointly with public officials in lobbying, to contend more effectively than they could separately.

In addition, informal patterns of interaction can enhance cooperation. Particular policy areas (e.g., chemical waste disposal or aid to education) often have their own informal "issue networks" of experienced interest group lobbyists, executive officials, and party experts in the particular policy area. People on various sides of issues have become acquainted with one another from past interaction in their shared policy area. As they contend they may also cooperate procedurally and even compromise in adjusting policies.

To be sure, such cooperation can also take an elite-model form. In such policy areas as agricultural and energy subsidies in the United States, and government support for big industries in Japan (see Country Case Studies below), observers have noted "iron triangles" dominating policymaking. In these situations, we see cooperation and goal sharing among (1) the biggest private producers, (2) the relevant unit of the executive branch bureaucracy, and (3) the relevant legislative committees (see chapter 12). Such informal alliances frequently produce policies that may not be supported by broader groups.

Connections with Political Parties

Another key resource for interest groups seeking to influence the political process can be their relationships to political parties. Often a significant party appeals to one or more interest groups as a key portion of its "social base." For example, linkages may be close between peak labor organizations and social democratic parties, and between employers' associations and conservative parties. If multiple interest groups have connections with a party, political scientists say that it engages in **interest aggregation**—attending to the views of contending but supportive interests, to bring their cooperation around the party's election platform. We will consider further how interest groups are linked to parties in chapter 10.

SUMMARY: CONTENTION AND COOPERATION WITHIN AND BETWEEN INTEREST GROUPS

Interest groups play a key role in political contention, but they also require cooperation. Interest groups exist at four levels: (1) categories of people with politically relevant interests, (2) the memberships of actual interest group organizations, (3) the officials of those organizations, and (4) the lobbyists who contact public officials to try to influence them toward the group's aims. For interest groups to influence politics, portions of represented categories must cooperate in joining and supporting associations. Lobbyists cooperate with the group's officials as they contend to influence government officials.

A series of dimensions of difference exists among interest groups. These include how many issues the groups address, how tangible their goals are for the category members, whether identification with the group defines personal identity or just achieves practical goals, and whether or not the group exists for purposes other than influencing politics. In various ways, these differences affect a group's effectiveness in contending for policy influence.

Five key types of resources affect how, and how much, the group achieves influence: information, votes, money, formal connections with governmental institutions, and connections with political parties.

COUNTRY CASE STUDIES

In both Japan and Mexico, one party has dominated politics for a period by accommodating major interest groups. However, important differences exist between these countries. Japan since World War II has been a representative democracy with a center-right leading party and extensive cooperation between interest groups and the government. Mexico over most of the twentieth century had an electoral authoritarian government with a center-left corporatism organized partly through the dominant party and partly outside it by the executive branch. Both nations, however, became genuinely multiparty in the 1990s.

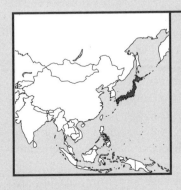

Japan: Government Coordination in a Developed Nation

Japan is an industrially developed nation with high ethnic homogeneity. Material stake groups have been prominent, particularly business groups. Their powerful peak association, the Federation of Economic Organizations (joined recently by the Japan Federation of Employers), leads business trade organizations. Japan's authoritarian past displayed loose ties between business and government in the Tokugawa period of shogun rule up to 1868, the Meiji modernization of the last third of the nineteenth century, and during the militarization of the 1930s through World War II. Habits of interest group cooperation accompanied a political culture that stressed the group over the individual. This focus deeply affected Japan's response to the challenges of economic recovery after World War II. Japanese business had to cooperate with government planning in the national interest. Japanese nationalism, stifled politically and militarily by the war's outcome, moved into the economic arena.

Large industrial groupings known as *keiretsu* integrated many enterprises, with some coordination from the center-right Liberal Democratic Party (LDP). The LDP, in cooperation with the all-powerful Ministry of International Trade and Industry, dominated the Diet (the Japanese legislature) and catered to business interests. Government consistently provided favorable protectionist policies (regulations and tariffs) against foreign imports. In addition, the government facilitated business participation in cartel-like groups for cooperative long-term research and development. Cooperative civil servants often both authored legislative proposals and presided over their application.

The LDP did not confine its attention only to big business. It also used regulation to protect local retailers against national chains. In addition, the dominant party protected agriculture. The government gave the peak association for agricultural cooperatives, Nokyo, a role regulating agriculture and helping farmers. Economic nationalists in the LDP believed in preserving domestic food production despite the high costs and inefficiencies of small-farm Japanese agriculture. The farmers got price supports, tariff and quota protection from foreign grains, and low taxes. In turn, the farmers rewarded the LDP with parliamentary seats in rural areas. Recent years, however, have seen calls for opening up Japan's food and agriculture markets, especially in light of the budding Trans-Pacific Partnership that stresses reducing trade barriers. Current prime minister Shinzo Abe, with a large parliamentary majority and thus less dependent on Nokyo's rural support, is pressing Nokyo on these matters—albeit carefully.

Organized labor remained weak throughout the twentieth century. Most Japanese unions are company based rather than industry based. Small and medium-sized enterprises are typically not unionized. This situation discourages strikes, which affect only one enterprise at a time and thus serve to help competing enterprises. Moreover, the customary lifetime job security encouraged worker loyalty. This orientation has been eroding, but even in the midst of the sharp economic downturn of 2008–2009, cost cutting by Japanese enterprises often steered clear of laying off permanent employees.

The alternative for frustrated left-of-center unionists was the Japanese Socialist Party (JSP), comprising democratic socialists and left social democrats. In the late 1980s, however, many unions from both the public and private sectors formed a more pragmatic peak labor federation, the Japan Trade Union Confederation ("Rengo"), in part to reach beyond the JSP toward the center. By the late 1990s, the JSP had lost its remaining moderate labor support and now (renamed the Social Democratic Party) is no longer a significant presence in the Diet. The proportion of the labor force that is unionized has continued to drop toward its current quarter of the work force.

By the 1970s, an environmental movement had arisen, in part because of health crises in the late 1960s such as the prevalence of asthma resulting from poor urban air quality and diseases from eating fish contaminated with chemical waste. After left-of-center parties and citizen activists won control of numerous local governments, in the 1970s the LDP adopted anti-pollution measures and reasserted its local political dominance. Conventional social welfare interests have followed a similar pattern. The LDP government paid little attention to social welfare issues until the JSP and the Communists began making gains on them in the 1970s. Then the LDP began to adopt programs to address issues such as old age pensions, and regained the political upper hand.

Religious Buddhists comprise a mainly urban organization, the Soak Gekas. Organized at the neighborhood level, it has been the foundation of the Clean Government Party, or Komeito. It is center-left ideologically, favoring such value-related concerns as peace, social welfare, and integrity in government. Komeito supports the postwar constitutional provision that Japan's military must be limited to territorial self-defense forces, leaving Japan's international defense to its alliance with the United States. With only a small presence in the Diet, the party has become more important since 2012 as the coalition partner of the current LDP government led by Prime Minister Shinzo Abe. Its peace orientation came into play especially in 2015, as Abe pressed his proposal to allow Japan's military to participate in limited roles in support of its alliance partners, especially the United States (in light of recent Chinese sea expansion).

Japanese women increasingly work outside the home (approaching 40 percent). However, they experience workplace discrimination in pay, status, and opportunity. Their most prominent representative organization is Coiffure, active mostly on consumer issues. Such issues increasingly are raised by the moderate left-of-center Democratic Party of Japan (DPJ), and there are signs of a greater role for conventional feminism among Japanese women's groups. Japanese women remain poorly represented in government. However, since the mid-1990s' advent of party-list PR voting for part of parliament, more parties have been allocating list positions to women to increase their parties' appeal to female voters. Women have material stake interests, but they are often obscured amid the low status of women in the surrounding culture.

Overall, economic nationalism in LDP policy invited interest group cooperation in its politics. This was facilitated by the unusual electoral system used by Japan until the early 1990s. The Diet was chosen in multimember districts, whose two to five representatives were those who won the largest numbers of votes as individuals (called "at large" voting). The most efficient way to be among the top vote-getters in a district was to win overwhelmingly the votes of one or two big local interest groups. Often candidates contend in a personalized way, as much against other candidates from one's own party as against those of other parties. Especially the LDP candidates would each back local spending or offer other help to a major material stake interest group in return for generous campaign contributions and local support. Thus overall the Japanese political system was considered clientelistic, and the pro-business and center-right LDP did not consistently follow a *laissez-faire* ideology. Nationally, the party was composed primarily of factions, each with a top leader and patron-client linkages to clusters of interest groups.

The LDP was able to do all this partly with the proceeds of a long period of postwar economic growth. In the early 1990s, however, two developments necessitated change. First, the economy turned stagnant in 1990, after the bursting of a real estate inflation bubble. This constrained the LDP's ability to finance its support for interest groups. By the early 2000s, the LDP faced serious economic discontent, as contention arose over now-scarce resources. Secondly, 1993 brought a major change in Japan's electoral system. After years of controversy over campaign fund-raising scandals and overrepresentation of rural areas, the LDP suffered a major bout of defections to an opposition coalition led by the new Democratic Party.

After an unusual opposition (anti-LDP) victory in a parliamentary election in 1993, in the following year a change was made in the electoral system (ultimately with LDP consent). The new electoral system combined (a) single-member district plurality voting (SMDP) in small districts filling 300 of the lower-house Diet seats, with (b) filling the 200 other seats by district-level proportional representation (PR) voting among contending party lists (called a "mixed member" system).[21]

The new system did a better job of encouraging overall contention between two large contending coalitions—an opposition coalition and one led by the LDP (with its small New Komeito coalition partner). However, the new electoral arrangements were not so successful in discouraging personalistic and clientelistic campaigning. This was because (a) individuals could run both as SMDP contenders and on the party list, and (b) SMDP losers could move up the party list according to how many votes they got individually in their losing SMDP effort. Thus the basic approach of getting into parliament by personally winning the most votes from a small area, with its personalistic and clientelistic implications, was largely preserved.

From 2001 to 2006, under the leadership of then prime minister Junichiro Koizumi, the LDP faced pressure to privatize enterprises and lessen subsidies and wasteful spending for interest groups. It evolved toward more conventional moderate free-market ideology. In addition, it faced a new moderate left-of-center party, the DPJ. In 2007, the DPJ won a majority in the upper house of parliament (the House of Councilors). The economic crisis and downturn of 2008–2009 led to a DPJ victory in the lower house as well, with broad union support. The DPJ campaigned to steer Japan away from the previous dominance of the corporation-ministry complex, and to protect Japanese jobs and consumers against the free-market policy directions of the increasingly conservative LDP. But subsequently, the DPJ suffered reverses over such issues as the U.S. military presence in Okinawa, continued high unemployment, price deflation, campaign finance scandals, and a proposal to increase the sales tax (to reduce the deficit). The DPJ lost its upper house majority to the LDP and has had to replace its leaders. Nevertheless, the old LDP-dominated pattern of interest group clientelism seems gone.

In addition, the Fukushima nuclear disaster of March 2011, involving coastal reactor meltdowns after extensive damage from a tsunami, prompted antinuclear sentiment that brought a suspension of nuclear power generation. By late 2012, however, this rise of value-related interest group influence (alongside health-related material stake concerns) was being challenged by (a) an array of material stake groups over the high cost of relying on imported oil and gas, and (b) value-related groups concerned about global warming, who see nuclear power as a necessary non-carbon-emitting part of energy responses to limit climate change, if nuclear energy can be made safe.

Recent years have been dominated by a new policy direction by the LDP, toward stimulating the Japanese economy. The party's new leader, Shinzo Abe, led it to a huge victory in late 2012, winning a lower-house majority so large (with its small coalition partner, Komeito) that its measures could not be vetoed by the upper house. Abe and the new LDP won on a promise of large Keynesian stimulus—both spending and monetary—to the economy. A raft of new infrastructure construction began, and the Bank of Japan began buying securities at a high rate, pumping money into banking and investment. The new policy direction promised to reverse deflation and its economic stagnation, and address the albatross of the yen's high exchange rate that had been holding back Japan's all-important export sector.

After strong GDP growth in early 2013 with the weaker yen (down over 20 percent in relation to the U.S. dollar), however, economic growth and the trade balance were deteriorating by the end of the year, hurt by a number of factors. Among them were the high cost of imported oil (necessary due to the post-Fukashima shutdown of Japan's nuclear plants) with the weaker yen, new international competition in consumer electronics (e.g., smart phones), and a continuation of the outsourcing trend of the pre-Abe era. Meanwhile, new job creation was primarily in nonregular, unprotected jobs with low pay, dragging down wages. Also, Japan's exporting powerhouses in consumer electronics and cars, for example, seemed to be using the lower yen not to cut prices for greater market share and export volume, but rather to pad their profits and cash stocks at home in Japan. This was to reverse past losses from the previous high-yen decades and to protect corporations against uncertainty, but it deprived the economy of much of the new export-based prosperity that the low yen was supposed to bring. In addition, the spring of 2014 brought a long-scheduled increase in the sales tax rate, from 5 percent to 8 percent (to limit the budget deficit), further holding back consumer demand.

By the beginning of 2015, however, things were looking better, including Japan's trade surplus. The huge oil price drop of late 2014 helped, along with new indications of corporations' willingness to give higher bonuses to their regular salaried workers amid a tight labor market (especially in areas where construction projects are hiring). But poverty in Japan continues to increase. The jury on "Abenomics" is still out.

Mexico: To and From Party-Government Corporatism

Mexico has always been a field for contending groups. Ethnically, the population is roughly one-third Native American, descended from the indigenous population that was devastated by the original Spanish conquest and the diseases it brought, and by subsequent forced labor and poverty. About 10 percent are white and of Spanish ancestry. They occupy most of the top economic and social stratum in Mexico. The rest of the population is mestizo, of mixed European and Amerindian blood. After Mexico gained independence from Spain in 1821, large landowners and military strongmen dominated. National politics involved the republican classical liberals, the monarchist conservatives, and the Catholic Church. The late 1800s and early 1900s dictatorship of General Porfirio Diaz saw the emergence of export-oriented mining, agricultural, and later oil interests.

In 1910, the rule of Diaz ended with a revolt by Francisco Madero, backed by an array of social reform and middle-class interests. A quarter century of periodic instability and military conflict followed, with two notable developments. In 1917, a diverse constituent assembly produced a new constitution that promised land to the peasants, rights to workers, mineral rights to the government, political freedoms, and restraints on Church power. Second, in 1929, what is now the Institutional Revolutionary Party (PRI) emerged to implement these reforms. But the party and the government it led was only firmly established when its leadership passed in the mid-1930s to Lázaro Cárdenas. As president, Cárdenas redistributed large expanses of land to peasant cooperatives, extended education, nationalized the oil sector, undertook infrastructure projects, supported industries, and encouraged urbanization and economic growth.

As party leader, Cárdenas developed a PRI-coordinated corporatist system, setting up broad "sectors" within the party. These represented three interest clusters of support for the Mexican Revolution: organized labor, the peasants, and the "popular sector" of professional, middle-class, and other groups in civil society. In addition to sponsoring numerous particular interest groups under each sector, the PRI set up a peak association for each sector: the Confederation of Mexican Workers (CTM), the National Confederation of Peasants (CNC), and the National Confederation of Popular Organizations. The PRI viewed the sectors as material stake beneficiaries of:

- the major expansion of urban jobs and labor protections that developed from the 1940s through the 1970s,

- the land reform, and

- the expansion of government services and subsidies, and trade protection via high tariffs, which fostered economic growth and the urban community.

During the subsequent decades of strong economic growth and industrial development, the PRI used this corporatist structure to communicate the government's goals and new proposals, to distribute clientelist benefits to individuals, to remind people of the source of their gains, to mobilize support for the PRI in elections, and to recruit local and regional party officials and elected officeholders.

The sectoral interest group organizations also provided outlets for the expression of complaints and demands. The government thus could limit and control these within the PRI, whether by accommodation, by co-opting critical activists into higher party positions, or by threatening persistent dissidents. Some parts of the PRI's sectoral interest group apparatus became dominated by regional and local "bosses." Open dissent was repressed, sometimes violently.

The three interest group sectors within the PRI formed only part of the regime's approach to interest groups, however. Publicly owned and private business, the military, and the Catholic Church stood outside the three PRI sectors. These interests often sidestepped party sectors and went straight to government contacts, sometimes at the highest level. The large expansion of state-owned enterprise from the 1940s to the early 1980s led to a major role for these corporations as institutional interest groups within the government. Private businesses and their trade associations participated formally in the government corporatist structure, as members of one of the state-chartered business confederations. More importantly, influential private businesses had direct connections with individual government bureaucrats. Up to the 1980s, the majority of medium and large businesses depended on the government for favorable regulatory decision making, subsidies, or trade protection by high tariffs. Ultimately the bureaucracy, overseen by the president, made the key decisions affecting business.

Patron-client relationships formed an important pattern of interest aggregation. Some relationships were with bureaucrats at various levels who remained in their positions over time, and some were with members of clientelistic clusters called *camarillas*. A camarilla followed its contending patron as he rose to higher positions, and might rise or fall with the succession of presidential terms of office. This pattern of political cooperation often involved the trade of client political support for patron favor. It provided ample opportunities for corruption.

By the last quarter of the twentieth century, however, many Mexicans were questioning the legitimacy of PRI single-party dominance. The expansion of government intervention in the 1970s was met with a rise in business opposition. Increased welfare distribution, a tripling of the number of government-owned enterprises, and a big increase in international borrowing contributed to widening budget deficits and ballooning international debt. By the early 1980s, when interest rates zoomed upward and the price of Mexico's oil exports dropped, the government neared insolvency.

Under pressure from international creditors, Presidents Miguel de la Madrid (1982–1988) and Carlos Salinas (1988–1994) reversed many of these policies. The PRI government cut back on spending, began privatizing government-owned enterprises, and opened up the economy to free trade and foreign investment. An alternative business confederation arose outside the traditional ones—the Confederation of Employers, which lobbied the government to adopt free-market reforms. The PRI became associated with the ideological center-right.

These moves brought economic growth and gains by the middle and upper economic strata. Foreign-owned factories (*maquiladoras*), with their exemptions from trade restrictions, sprang up along Mexico's northern border. But the switch to free-market policies widened inequality and hurt many in the middle and lower strata. Real wages were nearly halved, firm closings and layoffs soared, and rates of unemployment worsened.

By the end of the 1980s, public dissatisfaction had reduced support for the PRI. Its left wing broke away to become a left social democratic contender, the Party of the Democratic Revolution (PRD). Human rights groups became more vocal. Meanwhile, the free-market conservative party to the PRI's right, the National Action Party (PAN), gained strength, especially in the north. The end of the 1990s saw the end of PRI repression, vote rigging, and assassination of PRD activists, and the emergence of a genuine three-party system. The PRI lost its Congressional majority by 1997 and lost the presidential races in 2000 and 2006 to the conservative PAN, led first by Vicente Fox and then Felipe Calderón. In states won by PAN, the new leaders tried to establish more direct channels of contact between local government administrators and citizens.

In the last two decades, autonomy has increased for many interest clusters in Mexico. In the early 1990s the newly formed Civic Alliance, a federation of nongovernmental election reform groups, played a prominent role in the demise of PRI vote rigging. Membership in the peak business confederations is no longer required of companies. By the time of the Fox presidency, big business support and connections had largely gravitated toward PAN. The official union confederation, the CTM, no longer has a union monopoly and no longer enjoys the support of the government. Unions that have arisen outside the CTM have formed the National Union of Workers.

On the ideological left, an indigenous Mayan guerilla organization, the Zapatista Army of National Liberation, arose in the early 1990s in the impoverished state of Chiapas, a traditional PRI stronghold. It opposed PRI vote suppression, foreign investment, land ownership concentration, and lack of development among the indigenous Native American poor. Government control in Chiapas was restored, but negotiations with the Zapatistas continue today.

Two more groups—the drug cartels and the military engaged to fight them—play an important role today, especially along Mexico's northern border. The drug cartels are flush with money and skilled in the use of coercive violence. They intimidate and even sometimes control police in areas that are important to them as drug conduits into the United States. Drug-related murders—including those of judges, lawyers, and politicians—are rampant in the affected areas.

For its part, the Mexican military has a remarkable history of noninvolvement in politics and of subordination to the Mexican government. Since 1930, it has been called out only occasionally to deal with emergencies or disorder that the police could not handle. Some critics have accused elements in the army of deals with drug lords, but little is proven.

Most recently, contentions involving labor, business, and government have centered on developments in the economy. Through the 2000s, workers mounted opposition to free-market reforms, somewhat benefiting the left social democratic PRD. In 2006, its presidential candidate Lopez Obrador lost a disputed election by a razor-thin margin to the PAN candidate, Felipe Calderón. By mid-2009, the recession had produced high unemployment and discontent.

However, the PRD has not been the main political beneficiary. By the end of the decade, the now centrist PRI had made a broad comeback and became the main opposition party to the PAN. Along with its small Green party ally, the PRI gained a majority in the Chamber of Deputies in 2009 and remains the most successful party at the state and local levels. PAN president Calderón had to negotiate his legislative priorities with the PRI in Congress. In the 2012 elections, the PRI presidential candidate, Enrique Peña Nieto, won the presidency with 39 percent of the vote, to the PRD candidate's 32 percent and the PAN candidate's 26 percent.

Nieto had campaigned on being able to get some centrist jobs done that most Mexicans support, and that in one way or another concern key interest groups. He began by organizing an unprecedented effort at political cooperation: a pact of the three parties that dominate Congress—the centrist PRI, the conservative PAN, and the left-leaning PRI—behind his most broadly popular initiatives. These included, first, challenging the near monopoly position of the media empire of multibillionaire Carlos Slim, and education changes to the evaluation and training of teachers. These were opposed by the powerful teachers union and brought vigorous protests and strikes among southern Mexican teachers who point to resource starvation as the problem. Other

Nieto initiatives that have garnered opposition from one group or another have included:

- increasing competition and efficiency in banking and the delivery of electric power;
- allowing private partners alongside the state oil company, Pemex, in new energy ventures;
- sending troops and federal employees to the local level to coordinate local police forces and anti-gang vigilante groups in the fight against gang violence and crime;
- enabling broader and more effective tax collection;
- providing increased infrastructure spending;
- allowing greater government transparency and information access; and
- limiting election abuses by local PRI operatives.

The last item on this list, election reform, was successful enough during local election contention in mid-2013 to preserve the three-party alliance. An advantage of the Pact for the PRD was that it could demonstrate enough moderation to cement its ideological evolution from its early left social democracy into the party's current position as Mexico's moderate left-of-center party. But this cooperation has come at a price. The PRD is not entirely happy with the loosening of Pemex control over oil, or the value-added taxes on the necessities of the poor (e.g., food and medicine), and has worked to soften these initiatives. Nonetheless, the nearly half of the Mexican population experiencing poverty have an ever harder time affording the price of food. The PRD's most prominent past figure and presidential candidate, Lopex Obrador, has left the party to establish a new left social democratic one. Despite all the policy initiatives and the continued success of the export sector (especially to the United States), overall economic growth has remained low and problems of corruption and crime remain prominent. Business, for its part, resists the higher income tax rates and value-added taxation, and protests the continuing budget deficits and debt increases.

The voters have become glum. In the mid-2015 state and Congressional elections, the three major parties together dropped their vote share by over 15 percent. (Obrador's new left social democratic party, Morena, jumped in with 8 percent.) However, their coalition still easily maintains its Congressional majority, so that whatever measures they can compromise and cooperate over will pass.

⇥ PRACTICE AND REVIEW ONLINE

CRITICAL THINKING QUESTIONS

1. How do interest groups help to serve democracy? How might they run counter to the ideals of democracy?

2. Do certain features of public interest groups make them more admirable than others in interest group politics? If so, which features and how?

3. Evaluate the role of money in interest group politics. In what circumstances can money help level the playing field? How can it tilt the playing field in the direction of certain types of group?

4. How do certain interest groups benefit from relationships with government units? Could regulation help prevent such advantages? If so, how?

KEY TERMS

categoric interest, 248
social movement, 249
membership, 249
free rider, 251
officials, 251
peak association, 253
lobbyist, 253
multi-issue group, 255
single-issue group, 255
material stake group, 256
value-related group, 256
public interest group, 257
communal group, 259
associational group, 259
institutional interest group, 259

FURTHER READING

Ball, Alan R., and Frances Millard. *Pressure Politics in Industrial Societies.* Atlantic Highlands, NJ: Humanities Press International, 1987.

Baumgartner, Frank R., and Beth L. Leech. *Basic Interests: The Importance of Groups in Politics and in Political Science.* Princeton, NJ: Princeton University Press, 1998.

Berger, Suzanne D., ed. *Organizing Interests in Western Europe: Pluralism, Corporatism, and the Transformation of Politics.* New York: Cambridge University Press, 1981.

Berry, Jeffrey M. *The Interest Group Society,* 3rd ed. White Plains, NY: Longman, 1997.

Cigler, Allan J., and Burdett A. Loomis, eds. *Interest Group Politics,* 4th ed. Washington: CQ Press, 1995.

Franz, Michael M. *Choices and Changes: Interest Groups in the Electoral Process.* Philadelphia: Temple University Press, 2008.

Garson, G. David. *Group Theories of Politics.* Beverly Hills, London: Sage, 1978.

Goldstein, Kenneth M. *Interest Groups, Lobbying, and Participation in America.* New York and London: Cambridge University Press, 1999.

Grossmann, Matt. *The Not-So-Special Interests: Interest Groups, Public Representation, and American Governance.* Stanford: Stanford University Press, 2012.

Keck, Margaret E., and Kathryn Sikkink. *Activists beyond Borders: Advocacy Networks in International Politics.* Ithaca, NY and London: Cornell University Press, 1998.

Petracca, Mark P., ed. *The Politics of Interests: Interest Groups Transformed.* Boulder, CO: Westview Press, 1992.

Schlozman, Kay Lehman, Sidney Verba, and Henry E. Brady. *The Unheavenly Chorus: Unequal Political Voice and the Broken Promise of American Democracy.* Princeton, NJ: Princeton University Press, 2012.

Thomas, Clive S., ed. *First World Interest Groups: A Comparative Perspective.* Westport, CT and London: Greenwood Press, 1993.

———. *Political Parties and Interest Groups: Shaping Democratic Governance.* Boulder, CO and London: Lynne Rienner, 2001.

Walker, Jack L. *Mobilizing Interest Groups in America: Patrons, Professions and Social Movements.* Ann Arbor: University of Michigan Press, 1991.

Wilson, Graham K. *Interest Groups.* Oxford and Cambridge, MA: Blackwell, 1990.

Watts, Duncan. *Pressure Groups.* Edinburgh: Edinburgh University Press, 2007.

Zeigler, Harmon. *Pluralism, Corporatism, and Confucianism: Political Association and Conflict Regulation in the United States, Europe, and Taiwan.* Philadelphia: Temple University Press, 1988.

NOTES

[1] *Preface to Democratic Theory* (Chicago: University of Chicago Press, 1956).

[2] See David Truman, *The Governmental Process* (New York: Knopf, 1951); Robert Dahl and Charles Lindblom, *Politics, Economics, and Welfare* (New York: Harper, 1953); Dahl, *Who Governs?* (New Haven, CT: Yale University Press, 1961).

[3] See Mancur Olson, *The Logic of Collective Action: Public Goods and the Theory of Groups* (Cambridge, MA: Harvard University Press, 1971).

[4] See chapter 3, note 13.

[5] For a review of these elements, see Paul A. Sabatier, "Interest Group Membership and Organization," in Petracca, 1992.

[6] The term originated from a hotel lobby in Washington, DC, where nineteenth-century American president Ulysses S. Grant met with people. Today, however, most people think of lobbyists as waiting in the lobby outside a legislative chamber to track down legislators.

[7] See Hugh Heclo, "Issue Networks and the Executive Establishment," in *The New American Political System*, ed. Anthony King (Washington, DC: American Enterprise Institute, 1978), 87–124.

[8] Berry 1989, 180.

[9] Ibid., 183.

[10] An early pluralist, David Truman (see above), called civil-political public interest groups "rules of the game interests."

[11] In the Japanese case, consumer and environmental organizations are hardly developed at all on a national basis; see Ronald J. Hrebenar and Akira Nakamura, "Japan: Associational Politics in a Group-Oriented Society," in Thomas, 1993.

[12] For a discussion of interest group activity in this debate, see Goldstein 1999, 72–105.

[13] Focus in political science on this sort of difference began decades ago in the work on Italian politics of Joseph LaPalombara, who distinguished between pragmatic "clientela" relationships and family-like "parentela" ones. See LaPalombara, *Interest Groups in Italian Politics* (Princeton, NJ: Princeton University Press, 1964).

[14] A prominent early analyst of interest groups, Gabriel Almond, used an unfortunate and confusing label for communal groups: "non-associational." They do indeed form associations for social and political purposes.

[15] For example, see Nelson Polsby, *Community Power in Political Theory: A Further Look at Problems of Evidence and Inference*, 2nd enlarged ed. (New Haven: Yale University Press, 1980), 119–20.

[16] *Politics and Markets* (New York: Basic Books, 1977).

[17] See Allan J. Cigler and Anthony J. Nownes, "Public Interest Entrepreneurs and Group Patrons," in Cigler and Loomis 1995.

[18] See note 14 above.

[19] See Alfred Stepan, *The Military in Politics: Changing Patterns in Brazil* (Princeton, NJ: Princeton University Press, 1971).

[20] For a comparative discussion of the American pluralist case and corporatism, see Zeigler 1988.

[21] See chapter 3, "Contention and Cooperation in Focus."

Political Parties

FOCUS QUESTIONS

- **HOW** did political parties develop?

- **WHAT** activities of political parties matter most for democratic government, and why?

- **WHAT** or who do political parties represent, and how?

- **HOW** do differences among political parties affect the ways in which they contend with each other and their success in doing so?

- **WHAT** factors affect how much decision-making power party leaderships have?

- **HOW** do political parties in authoritarian systems differ from those in democratic systems?

IN 2010, A NUMBER OF IDEOLOGICALLY conservative Americans who in the past had not participated actively in politics were aroused by their fears of government deficits, debt, and a new law to support and regulate access to health insurance. Strongly opposing almost any form of economic intervention by government, including any tax increases, they called themselves the "Tea Party" movement (a reference to the Boston Tea Party protest against taxation during revolutionary times). Most thought that to affect politics, they had only one realistic option, to support and try to influence America's main conservative party, the Republicans. They proceeded to back the most economically conservative candidates to run under the Republican banner in the general elections. Tea Party support played a major role in the Republicans' winning the majority of seats in the House of Representatives in the 2010 elections.

Consequently, amid an ongoing economic slump in 2011, the direction of government economic policy changed. Since bills must pass in both houses to become law, no new legislation was possible without Republican support. Internally, the House Republicans chose cooperation over contention, to contend more effectively with the Democrats. Republican House members remained united in voting against nearly all of Obama's proposals. Thus, for example, President Obama and his fellow Democrats in Congress could no longer pass new legislation for infrastructure spending (on rebuilding roads, bridges, etc.) to create jobs and stimulate the economy.

An earlier temporary stimulus spending program expired, without replacement. Recovery from "the great recession" slowed down. The consequences of this outcome, both political and economic, continue today (see "Contention and Cooperation in Focus").

Clearly political parties, their approaches to political contention, and their capacity to cooperate internally, play a crucial role in political contention and cooperation. Imagine that you were a Tea Party member in early 2010. Would you have wanted to join the Republicans (as most did), or start your own party? Why?

ORIGINS AND ORGANIZATION

A political party is an organization that runs candidates for government office under its own banner. Parties allow political activists with similar preferences for policies and leaders to cooperate and focus their efforts. For voters, the party label can usefully indicate candidates' ideological orientations, policy preferences, and interest group support. For the democratic system as a whole, parties organize and maintain the electoral system, run election campaigns, propose policies, and help coordinate policymaking.

Many people think of political parties as cooperative enterprises, with each party united behind its policy program. In this perspective, the main political contention is between parties. As we shall see, however, parties generally have contending groups and individuals within them, too. Such internal contention affects how parties contend with one another. Groups within parties may differ over such matters as how (and how strongly) the party should pursue its ideological orientation, which values to stress, how to address different interest groups supporting the party, and how to relate to other parties. A party's government officeholders may differ with some of its supporters outside the government, experience factional division among themselves, and disagree with party leaders.

We shall begin by examining how parties began and what they do, followed by what they stand for in contention with other parties. Then we shall consider the distribution of influence within parties and the factors that affect it.

The Development of Political Parties

We can find the germ of the political party during the predemocratic era of the European monarchies. Sometimes factions (opinion groupings) arose within councils that advised the king. Typically, they were drawn from economic and social elites. Each such grouping tended to share viewpoints on issues before the court or support for a particular leader.

With the establishment of more modern legislative assemblies in the early nineteenth century, such factions founded some of the earliest political parties. They remained elite-based groups. With the vote still limited to an elite stratum by property (or literacy) requirements, legislative representatives were linked to their supporters through regional and local notables who backed the legislative grouping. Influential landowners, industrialists, and bankers might support the conservative parties of the day, while modernization-oriented journalists, lawyers, and teachers might be among those backing classical liberal parties. French political scientist Maurice Duverger referred to such groups as "caucus" parties.

The further expansion of the vote in the nineteenth century brought more of the population within reach during election campaigns. The first representative democracy to give the vote to the majority of adult males (by setting low property requirements in an increasing number of states) was the United States, in the early nineteenth century. American parties reached out to the population at large, but they were only loosely organized and were active mainly during election campaigns. Duverger called this type the "cadre" party.[1]

In contrast, the early twentieth century in Europe saw a more densely organized and continuously active party type. It aimed to mobilize a mass membership from a target group, usually defined by socioeconomic class or religion. Duverger called this phenomenon the "mass" party (later, in the work of Sigmund Neumann, it was referred to as the "mass integration" party[2]). For example, European social democratic parties targeted industrial labor. They strove to provide workers with voting rights, economic protections, and a sense of solidarity, while building a base of party members at the grassroots. The latter formally joined their local party "branches," paid dues, and attended meetings year-round, as well as campaigning prior to elections. Soon other European parties copied this approach to some extent, including some parties with a Christian religious identity.

Duverger also noted two further types of party that retain little relevance today. Communist parties, for example, were "cell" parties, extending party organization to small groups in workplaces. They were tightly and hierarchically organized, often secretive, with extreme ideologies and strategies. They sought converts rather than large numbers of votes. The early Nazi party in Germany and the early Fascist party in Italy were similar in some ways, but their grassroots units were, in effect, militias, ready to march and use violence against rivals. Duverger called these early fascists "militia parties." In today's long-established democracies—those openly democratic at least since World War II—cell and militia parties have declined to relative insignificance.

By the middle of the twentieth century in the established democracies, mass parties were reaching beyond their early class or religious bases. Meanwhile, many cadre-style parties had increased their organizational and mobilization efforts. While parties still differ somewhat in their degree of **organizational density**, most have some degree of organization at all three key levels: local, regional, and national. Thus the original mass-cadre distinction has largely lost its usefulness, and this chapter will employ a different typology of political parties related to their identity—what parties stand for.

Levels of Party Organization: Local, Regional, and National

Political parties contend with each other to win votes and influence policy at three levels: local, regional, and national. Local party units serve several functions. They provide feedback to the party leadership on issues, values, and policy ideas, supply local volunteers and funds for campaigning, and serve as a recruitment pool for future candidates and leaders. In Europe, the local **party branch** maintains its official list of party members. In contrast, American political parties do not have official membership lists. People just call themselves Democrats or Republicans. In the United States, the functional equivalent of the European local party branch is the town (or county) party committee, which does have official enrollment and can be quite large.

At the regional level, parties often have committees that include delegates from the local branches or committees. The regional committee may be led by a smaller executive committee, officers, and staff. Regional party organizations can be especially important in federal systems, which include a regional level of elected government and region-specific policy issues. Regional party organizations also have a role to play in countries in which regions constitute the electoral districts for national elections (e.g., Germany and Argentina). Here, the regional level of party organization plays a role in selecting each region's list of candidates for election.

At the national level, often two distinct sectors of each party may be found: (1) the national executive committee with its central administrative and research staff, and (2) the party's holders of legislative and executive office. A party's legislators are collectively referred to as the **party fraction** (or "caucus") in each legislative assembly. At times, the policy priorities of the national executive committee may differ somewhat from those of its legislators. And sometimes a third, more informal force can be important at the national level: the party's biggest financial donors.

Overall, the developed world has more extensive party organization than do the post-Communist and developing worlds. Nations that are newer to democracy often lack resources for much party activity. Some parties just focus on benefiting their supporters, who are client groups seeking material help such as jobs and subsidies. These are called **clientelistic parties**. But as democracy consolidates over time, parties often increase their organizational density and become more effective in their policy-oriented efforts. We have seen this especially in some post-Communist Eastern European countries, such as Poland and the Czech Republic.

In the established democracies in recent decades, party approaches in contending for votes have changed somewhat (see chapter 11). In particular, new media technologies have reduced the importance of ground-level, face-to-face campaigning in favor of broadcast and electronic appeals (e.g., television, radio, and the Internet).

PARTIES' FUNCTIONS

When we say that parties "contend" in politics, what concrete activities are we referring to? Political parties do a lot of things, but three stand out: nominating candidates, proposing policies, and making policy in government. Parties choose who is to contend for office in elections, they propose and defend contending policy directions, and they contend in government to affect governmental policy (see Figure 10.1).

Selecting Candidates

Overall, political parties serve democracy importantly by recruiting people into active roles in political life and government. The most visible form of this is parties' role as

FIGURE 10.1
Party Activities

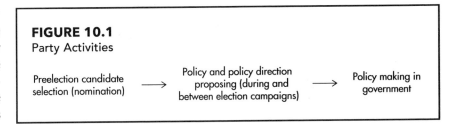

Preelection candidate selection (nomination) → Policy and policy direction proposing (during and between election campaigns) → Policy making in government

selectors of candidates. In representative democracies, political parties usually provide the candidates that voters choose from. In governmental systems with single-member district plurality (SMDP) elections (e.g., the United States and Great Britain; see chapter 4), each party puts forward one name for each legislative district. Under the proportional representation (PR) system that is prevalent in continental Europe and Latin America, districts are larger, and each sends multiple representatives to the legislature. Each party nominates a list of candidates to fill the district's legislative seats.

Parties select candidates with different goals in mind. A party may recruit and nominate candidates on the basis, for example, of:

- popularity outside the party among the electorate,
- representing important interest groups such as women, minorities, or young people,
- possession of new ideas and approaches,
- financial support for the party,
- support of the party's ideological orientation,
- long and faithful service to the party, and
- loyalty to the current party leadership.

Individual party members may contend for their party's nomination based on one or more of these advantages. As we shall see later in this chapter, the process of choosing candidates can be concentrated in the party's upper leadership strata, or may be dispersed to lower levels. Or a party may employ a mixture of the two approaches.

Proposing and Supporting Policy Directions

Parties must also decide what policy directions to support and present to the public. These choices involve identifying (1) what new issues to raise, (2) what values, interests, or ideological direction to emphasize regarding the issues, and (3) what policies to support to address those issues. Certainly, other entities besides political parties also raise issues and promote policies. Interest groups, members of the bureaucracy, and individuals (via the media) do so, too. However, because parties play such a central role in election campaigning, and their members hold office in government, they have an advantage in getting issues and policy ideas onto the political agenda.

Some observers of politics believe that contending parties should present clear and comprehensive policy programs to voters. Then voters can decide how each

A British parliamentary candidate, Karen Hamilton, campaigning in Birmingham, U.K.

party's program matches up with their own policy preferences. At the beginning of election campaigns in some of the established democracies, some parties publish detailed policy "manifestoes" or "platforms." Generally, however, parties tend to fall short of this level of specificity in their policy ideas. Often regarding one or a few issues, we may see contending interests and values among parties' potential supporters, discouraging party leaders from proposing detailed policies for fear of losing some faction's support. As for voters, research generally indicates that the average voter tends to lack clear, knowledgeable, and strong policy preferences on most issues, especially on those that don't seem to affect them very directly.

As we shall see in Chapter 11, however, on significant issues voters may have an idea of what *general direction* they would like government policy to take.[3] That direction may be along the lines of an ideology (e.g., moderate left of center or conservative), or toward a value (e.g., a healthy environment, a prosperous economy, or enhanced national security), or toward helping an interest group (e.g., farmers, small business, or retired people), as well as toward a particular policy. And voters who don't know the specifics of parties' issue positions may nonetheless have a sense of the general policy directions that parties advocate. For example, the left social democratic party in Mexico, called the Party of the Democratic Revolution (PDR), raises the issue of poverty and emphasizes the values of social justice and minimal economic well-being for ordinary Mexicans (see Country Case Studies, chapter 9). In the Netherlands, the classical liberal People's Party for Freedom and Democracy (VVD) stresses the values of business innovation and overall economic growth as it presses for particular policies that loosen regulation of businesses (see Country Case Studies). Friedrich Hayek, a classical liberal political thinker of the mid-twentieth century, in effect suggested a theory of party division by suggesting that the most fundamental modern source of political differences is the distinction between the values pursued by employers and those of employees (see "The Philosophical Connection").

Making Policy in Democratic Government

Once candidates have been nominated and elected, and alternative policy directions have been presented, government must decide what policies to adopt. Ultimately, political parties want to affect policymaking in government. As we shall see, for a contending party to be a major factor affecting legislation, its legislators must display a key form of cooperation: voting cohesively (together, in a unified way) on bills presented to them. In contrast, where fellow party members in office vote independently and sometimes contend with the party majority or its leadership, we can say that party plays less of a role in governmental decision making.

Chapters 12 and 13 will explore all this further, but at this point we can preview a key factor for party cohesiveness in voting on bills: the type of governmental structure. Cohesive voting tends to be greater and more continuous in parliamentary government. Recall that in parliamentary systems, the prime minister (PM) is chosen by a majority vote of parliament—requiring her or his party (or parties, in an alliance called the majority coalition) to be united in support. But to remain in their executive positions, the PM and her or his appointed cabinet of ministers must also *continue* to get majority parliamentary support for cabinet policy proposals. Thus does the PM demonstrate that (s)he has the

THE PHILOSOPHICAL CONNECTION | Friedrich Hayek

Friedrich Hayek (1899–1992) was a leading contributor to conservative, free-market-oriented thought. As we saw in chapter 6, the free-market orientation falls to the right of center on economic issues—favoring little government intervention in the economy. In industrial society, Hayek saw the battle lines drawn mainly between the world views of "the employed" and "the employers."* In his perspective, the employed—not just industrial workers but all employed people—were most concerned about economic stability and security. Thus, according to Hayek, the employed tend to embrace government economic planning as the path to economic security, and favor modifying economic systems to better reward "merit"—effort in work—at the expense of the free-market approach, which in principle rewards only the value of the product.

In Hayek's view, however, the human mind cannot accurately evaluate other individuals' level of effort and self-sacrifice. Moreover, for him, people are also incapable of coordinating all the elements of a complex modern economy toward ends that people can agree on. (Unable to agree on ends, he thought, societies in effect delegate the choice of ends to planning bureaucracies.) He argued that this inevitable ignorance means that people should not interfere with the production and selling of goods and services in the market. In particular, he thought that the employed cannot grasp the point of view of the employer and entrepreneur, who must face risk, take initiative, and innovate in order to succeed. In Hayek's view, the employed fail to see that a successful, growing economy has to leave entrepreneurs free in the marketplace to make new discoveries and innovations. These innovations could not be foreseen or planned by anyone, but their benefits are appreciated in the form of the available goods and services that result.

Hayek conceded that many innovative products by entrepreneurs will initially cater to the wealthy. They are the only ones able to pay the high prices that new products fetch at first, to pay for the high cost of their initial development. However, Hayek argued, these high prices also serve to fund the further development of products so that they can later become cheap and available to the masses. For Hayek, there was no value in government regulation of the economy or in redistribution to provide a minimal floor of security for the economically disadvantaged.

In the established democracies, often the two largest contending parties have taken positions on either side of Hayek's divide between the employed and the employers. Notably, moderate left-of-center parties in the last half of the twentieth century have accepted some of Hayek's arguments. They have backed away from aggressive central economic planning, in favor of more modest measures of stimulus spending (when needed), regulation, and redistribution. Many such parties continue to advocate some government intervention in the labor market, arguing that avoiding arbitrary layoffs is fairer and supports consumer spending to keep economic growth and prosperity up, as does fairly strong unemployment compensation (see chapter 7). But conservatives, on the employer side, focus on what they see as business psychology. They argue that often European-style labor restrictions on laying off workers cause enterprises to be reluctant to hire when the economy turns up, and that all government spending portends future tax increases that weaken business confidence today.

Think about the two biggest contending political parties in your country. Do they seem to be aligned in the way that Hayek would predict: the interests of employers versus those of employees? Where should they look to help to resolve their contention? Can the actual economic data help? Can the contending parties find any common ground for cooperation?

---

* See Friedrich A. von Hayek, *The Constitution of Liberty* (Chicago: University of Chicago Press, 1960).

"confidence" of parliament, so as to be able to stay in office atop the executive branch. This requires continuous party unity in voting.

In presidential government, in contrast, the chief executive is chosen directly by the voters and serves a set term of office, regardless of whether the president's bills pass in legislative assemblies. So there is less pressure for legislators of the president's party (and any other supporting parties) to all vote together for his or her bills, and for opposing parties' legislators to vote cohesively against them. Unless circumstances other than the governmental structure are at work to produce party cohesion, it will be less in presidential democracy than under parliamentary government.

As we shall see below, this key difference has consequences for how influence is distributed within political parties as they contend with each other. But first, we have to look at what parties stand for—what tends to hold parties together regardless of the type of governmental structure in which they contend.

PARTY IDENTITY

As contending alternatives for voter choice, what does each significant party stand for in the minds of the voters and their own activists? Today, there are two main aspects of the identities of parties in the minds of political participants: ideological identity and interest group support. To one degree or another, today's significant political parties each tend (a) to represent some sort of ideological orientation, whether general or specific, and (b) to be associated with (whether loosely or more tightly) one or more group interests, which tend to support the party and that the party appeals to. Most parties play both of these representative roles to some extent as they contend with one another, although they may not emphasize both equally. We'll take these two components of party identity one at a time, starting with ideological identity.

Representing Ideological Alternatives

As we saw in chapter 6, an ideology connects values, related policy preferences, and empirical perspectives on society and history, into a somewhat logical package. Usually a significant political party is linked—whether tightly or loosely—to one of the eight major ideologies that we examined in chapter 6. From left to right, the main ones today are democratic socialist, left social democratic, Green, moderate left of center, classical liberal, conservative, and ethnic ultranationalist. To be sure, some parties are ideologically centrist, or may even lack much ideological identity. But contending political parties tend to present, to the voters, alternative ideological directions in which they would like government policy to go (see below).

Linked to a party's ideological identity is attachment to associated values. For example, moderate left-of-center parties stress pursuit of social justice, while conservative parties tend to emphasize criminal justice. Democratic socialist parties may stress equality heavily, while left social democratic parties emphasize reducing inequality and moderate left-of-center parties talk most about equality of opportunity and a minimal floor of economic well-being. Conservative parties emphasize social order alongside entrepreneurial freedom, while classical liberal parties place greater stress on the latter. Conservative and ethnic ultranationalist parties tend to weigh national security heavily.

By the 1990s, political scientist Russell Dalton and some other students of parties' linkages to voters had suggested that a trend was occurring toward the erosion of linkages between party leaderships, ideological identities, and voters.[4] Formal party membership was in decline, and fluctuations in vote shares between contending parties ("volatility") was on the rise. Some saw voters leaving behind traditional ideological and party attachments in favor of new, post-materialist issues (see chapter 8), as the proportion of service sector and professional employment in economies (often included in the "middle class") was growing and the proportion of industrial workers was declining. Meanwhile, parties were leaving behind grassroots-level campaigning in favor of reliance on mass media. Subsequently, political scientists Mark Blyth and Richard Katz even saw some parties' leaderships shifting their concerns in an elite-model direction, toward just maintaining their positions and perks in a "cartel" of insider parties that (a) depended substantially on campaign finance support from the government and (b) paid less heed to the preferences of their voters.[5]

However, especially with the political contentions that have arisen since the financial crisis of 2008–2009, this picture of de-linkage between parties, ideological identities, and voters seems not to have been borne out. Dalton himself and some of his colleagues seem now to have conceded this.[6] For one thing, economic issues remain prominent and continue to prompt interparty contention. The new prominence of left social democratic parties (e.g., Syriza in Greece and Podemos in Spain) fighting against austerity, inequality, and globalization suggests new wrinkles in an old pattern. And recent issues related to post-materialism (e.g., Greens' concerns about the environment) and immigration (ethnic ultranationalist worries about losing jobs and national cultural identity to foreigners) have not altered party identities as much as many suppose. To be sure, new parties have indeed emerged. But as I suggested in chapter 6, I think the best way to view intense green and (ethnic ultranationalist) anti-immigrant views is as distinct ideological directions, one on the left and the other on the right, each with a party making the new ideological direction central to its identity.[7]

To be sure, the new issues afoot have complicated the issue mix. Obviously, the new parties have pried loose some people who traditionally would have remained in one of the older parties' tents, producing electoral volatility in the process. But this new volatility tends to represent differentiation of new parties within either the left-of-center coalition or the right-of-center one.[8] As political scientist Peter Mair put it, such "party change" does not mean that there has been a fundamental change in the "party system."[9]

Meanwhile, the traditional large parties—the moderate left-of-center one on one side and the conservative one on the other—have generally adopted positions on the new issues (usually more moderate than those of the new parties), and integrated those stances into their ideological orientations as they continue to contend for members and votes. And the conventional broad divide between the left-of-center parties—generally favoring more intervention by government to address economic problems but little in sociocultural areas (to protect individual freedom)—and the right-of-center parties (the reverse of these two orientations) remains. There was never much reason to assert that an overall de-alignment and de-linkage between parties and their voting supporters was taking place. That said, we can identify cases where a party has adjusted its ideological identity, to which we now turn.

Variation in Party Ideological Identity One challenge in understanding parties' ideologies is that a party's name (which may have originated in the distant past) may not clearly indicate its actual ideological identity at the present time. For example, today the French Socialist Party is not socialist, but rather is moderate left of center. (Or a party's name may amount to simple misrepresentation; Russia's Liberal Democratic Party is actually ethnic ultranationalist, not classical liberal.)

In addition, we often see cross-national variation in the ideological identities of parties that share the same ideological family. The ideological identities of parties in different countries can present more or less extreme versions of the same ideology. How far a party in a country wants to go in its ideological direction may evolve over time. And parties in different countries may express a given ideology differently because of distinctive features of each nation's history, political culture, and policy challenges. The democratic socialist party in Finland, for example, may differ in some ways from the one in Bulgaria. These parties share the ideological directions toward which their views point, but not exactly how far they go in those directions, and in what ways. And within a party, members and supporters can vary in how intense or extreme their views are. For example, members of a moderate left-of-center party can range from almost centrist to left social democratic in their views, and moderate right-of-center "conservatives" can vary from almost centrist to arch-conservative (perhaps extremely free-market-oriented) or even ethnic ultranationalist.

Party ideological identities help explain why large parties continue to diverge from each other ideologically as they contend, despite the often-assumed temptation of contending large moderate parties to converge on the center-leaning "swing voter" (or what political scientists call the "median voter") to win close elections. In some election cycles, the large parties do not seem to have converged at all.

Another often-cited factor tending to reduce party ideological differences is the last few decades' limitations on the available range of policy options for parties in government, such as globalization-imposed curbs on deficit spending. Certainly we can cite instances of, say, moderate left-of-center parties in governing coalitions having to go along with spending austerity measures that are imposed by past international agreements like those governing the Eurozone in Europe. But if we give credence to their leaders' protestations, such parties' cabinet ministers do not seem to be doing so enthusiastically (or even willingly). And commonly, parties whose decisions in government seem to be moving to the center tend to subsequently lose votes—sometimes heavily—to another party that stayed true to its ideology. The post-2008 left-right debate over budgetary austerity in economic slumps (see chapter 7) has displayed continuing contention over globalization and inequality, testimony that rival ideological and policy directions are alive and well in today's interparty contention.

The Electoral System and the Number of Contending Ideological Options Within national politics, a key question about ideological contention among parties is, how many options are presented to the voters? This depends on the number of significant parties contending in the party system. Recall from chapter 1 that party systems can be broadly classified as either two-party or multiparty. In a two-party system such as in the United States or Britain, small parties tend to be either absent or not significant in their capacities to affect government policy. One or the other of the two large parties typically wins enough seats to hold legislative majorities, without having to ally with a small party to do so. Thus we may say that under these circumstances, only two are **policy-significant parties**: parties whose legislators' support might be required to maintain an ongoing legislative majority, either now or sometime in a plausible future.

Recall from chapter 3 ("Contention and Cooperation in Focus") that this situation is normally linked to an SMDP electoral system. Under it, each seat is filled in its own small district, with only the biggest vote-getter winning the single seat. Thus the biggest parties tend to win the vast bulk of the seats. Many would-be voters for small parties avoid them, thinking that votes for them would be wasted (if they have a preference between the large parties). And since the large parties win many seats by moderate margins, the most successful party in an election will win a greater proportion of the seats—normally a majority—than its proportion of the votes (typically 40–45 percent). Consequently, small groups tend to combine with one of the large parties to have a chance of winning seats, rather than trying to go it alone with their own party.

As a result of all these SMDP factors, overall the two largest parties tend to prevail, normally representing the two most moderate and popular ideological directions: moderate left of center and conservative. For example, Ghana in West Africa has an SMDP voting system, and 271 of the 275 seats in its parliament are held by the two dominant parties: the moderate left-of-center National Democratic Congress and the conservative New Patriotic Party. Similarly, New Zealand had two prevailing parties until it changed its electoral system in 1993. (The exception is when a contending party's support is small nationally but concentrated in a region where it is big enough to come in first in many SMDP races, such as a party based on the interests of that particular region or its dominant ethnic group.[10])

In contrast, the other major electoral system alternative, proportional representation voting (PR), employs large, multimember districts. Parties win legislative representation in them in proportion to their shares of the district's vote, so small parties can have legislators and voices in policymaking from an array of districts, as well as large parties.[11] Since under PR typically too many parties gain representation in legislative assemblies for any one party to win the majority, a coalition of allied parties must form to build a majority to pass legislation. And that means that even small parties will be policy-significant, in that their support might be needed to complete the majority needed to pass bills.

This allows a variety of ideological directions to each have its party vehicle. On the right, such ideologies as conservative, classical liberal, and ethnic ultranationalist may each have distinct party representation. On the left, moderate left-of-center, left social democratic, Green, and democratic socialist ideologies might each have a party. And there may be ideologically centrist parties, too, perhaps leaning a bit center-left or center-right. In the Dutch lower house, for example, a substantial number of ideologies may each win party representation (see Figure 10.2 and Country Case Studies). Small parties that are mainly interest-based may get representation, too (see below).

To be sure, the number of party alternatives under PR may be limited by having small multimember districts that choose as few as five legislators each (what political scientists call a low "district magnitude"). Political scientist Gary W. Cox has referred to the "M+1" rule, that the number of contending parties might tend to be no more than the number of district seats plus one, since each party tends to hope for at least one seat.[12] But research indicates that a variety of factors other than the electoral system—including economic and social cleavage patterns, past party experience, and others—can affect how many party alternatives are presented to the voter.

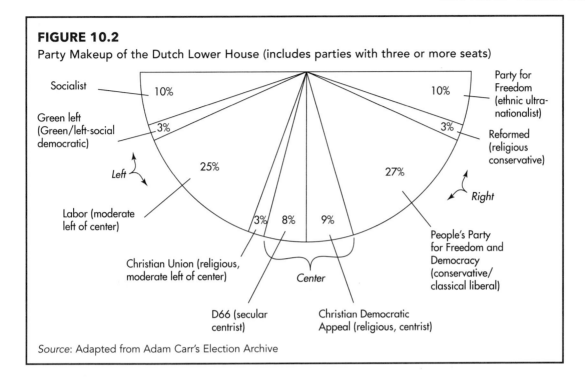

FIGURE 10.2

Party Makeup of the Dutch Lower House (includes parties with three or more seats)

Socialist — 10%

Green left (Green/left-social democratic) — 3%

Left

25%

Labor (moderate left of center)

Christian Union (religious, moderate left of center)

3% 8% 9%

Center

D66 (secular centrist)

Christian Democratic Appeal (religious, centrist)

Party for Freedom (ethnic ultra-nationalist) — 10%

Reformed (religious conservative) — 3%

Right

27%

People's Party for Freedom and Democracy (conservative/classical liberal)

Source: Adapted from Adam Carr's Election Archive

Representing and Aggregating Interests

A second aspect of parties' identities is their links, whether vague and implicit or formal and explicit, with interest groups. Most parties appeal to one or more interest groups by representing their concerns to some extent. As we saw in chapter 9, interest groups are defined by shared concerns, related to such factors as economic status, occupation, ethnicity, religion, region, gender, policy opinion, or other characteristics. For most parties, a range of interests associated with the party—whether narrow or wide—forms a portion of its "social base." For example, moderate left-of-center parties generally appeal to labor, certain minorities, and the poor and middle economic strata. Conservative parties tend to be favored by the wealthy, business interests, certain professional groups, religious traditionalists, and rural dwellers.

By representing interest groups, political parties help to link and mediate between government and interests in civil society. Recall from chapter 9 that parties tend to engage in interest aggregation: moderating and merging the aims of like-minded interests into broad policy proposals.[13] Seldom can a single interest group supporting a party get that party's support for all that it wants. In practice, a group's full aims will be inconsistent, in one way or another, with those of other groups that are linked with the same party. However, a political party may be able to hammer out enough compromises among related interest groups to form a manageable common-front party program. In performing interest aggregation, parties help tame interest group conflict.

This pattern of contention and cooperation differs from the approach of some of the original "mass parties," noted above. In early twentieth-century Europe, some prominent party organizations focused either on a social class or on members of a religion, and they worked hard to organize that base. For example, a social democratic party might offer workers a whole range of party-sponsored associations, with its own newspaper, unions, schools, soccer league, women's association, youth organization, and even burial society. Noticing such efforts, some religious and conservative parties followed suit to some extent, with their bases.[14] Thus a local community might have as many as three women's groups, each sponsored by a different political party. Or a single industry might have three party-sponsored unions (see "Concept in Context").[15] Later in the twentieth century, however, major political parties broadened their appeals beyond class and religion. Attempts by parties to sponsor their own interest group associations began to recede.

In a milder form of appeal to group interests, political parties have performed the service of integrating new groups into the political process. In the United States, for example, starting in the mid-nineteenth century, the

CONCEPT IN CONTEXT | Voter Groups, Parties, and the Breakdown of Democracy in Weimar Germany

The mid-twentieth-century political scientist William Kornhauser argued that the fabric of interest groups in the democratic German Weimar Republic (established after World War I) remained thin. In his view, German voters remained a rootless mass, vulnerable to the demagogic election campaign appeals of Hitler and the Nazis.* This "mass society" view seems to echo Tocqueville's picture of egalitarian democracy's mass of isolated individuals, vulnerable to the "tyranny of majority opinion" (see "The Philosophical Connection," chapter 7).

However, political scientists have since shown that a fabric of interest group associations did exist in Weimar Germany. The electoral rise of the Nazi party between 1928 and 1933 did not result from any lack of interest-based associations. Rather, the problem lay in the patterns of interest group cooperation with parties, which impeded groups and parties from combining their efforts in resisting the Nazis. Many party-sponsored associations focused on segments of the same categoric interest (chapter 9).[†] This duplication of local associations by parties kept Social Democrats and Catholic Center Party members, for example, from participating in the same clubs. Associations of women or young people did not bring together members of different parties. Thus, civic associations could not play their democracy-supporting role of building positive relationships between people who may have been opposed politically (see chapter 8).

To be sure, some local associations including middle- and upper-middle-class people remained outside the party-organized segments. The middle and upper classes had lost much of their wealth and security with the hyperinflation of 1922–1923, its harsh aftermath, and then the Great Depression. The government seemed to have failed them, and many lost faith in the traditional parties and politics of the Weimar Republic. Some of the supporters of the traditional middle-class parties split off into smaller associations.[‡] Leaders of choral societies, veterans' groups, and others became available for recruitment to the Nazi cause, with its abstract appeals to catch-all values (see below) like revival of national dignity and economic security for all.[§] These developments played a role in the inability of parties and groups to unite to defend the Weimar democratic system against the Nazi political onslaught.

Think about some of the local associations in your community. Do they bring together people with contending political views? Do they contribute to a basis of shared community that might soften political contention?

---

* See William Kornhauser, *The Politics of Mass Society* (New York: The Free Press, 1959).

† See Bernt Hagtvet, "The Theory of Mass Society and the Collapse of the Weimar Republic," in *Who Were the Fascists?*, ed. Steinvgelvik Larsen et al. (Oslo: Universitet Storlget, 1980), 66-117.

‡ Ibid.

§ For a more recent review of research on this, see Sheri Berman, "Civil Society and the Collapse of the Weimar Republic," *World Politics* 49, no. 3 (1997): 401–29.

Democratic Party's urban political machines encouraged the political participation of Irish immigrants. The Irish Americans got more than just a link to jobs and benefits; they got a sense of belonging in the American political system. When African Americans became more directly involved in national politics, starting with the civil rights struggle in the 1950s and 1960s, they eventually found a home in the Democratic Party. On the ideological left, various political parties embraced the causes of other social movements associated with post-materialist issues (e.g., international peace, environmental concerns, and the rights of minorities and women).

On the ideological right, America's Republican Party welcomed the country's evangelical Christians seeking a new political role in the 1970s and 1980s. Today, Europeans worried about immigration have found ethnic ultranationalist "national front" parties to support. In some Muslim-majority countries, Islamic revivalists have formed political parties to pursue their concerns. Retaining but sometimes adjusting their ideological identities, political parties still channel feelings and provide a sense of belonging for groups that identify with them.

PARTY TYPES

As political parties have contended with one another in representative democracies, different types of parties have emerged. As I noted above, older distinctions that focused on differences in the density of party organization—between (a) extensively organized "mass" or "mass integration" parties and (b) "cadre" or "individual representation" parties whose organizational hierarchy only appeared in election campaigns—have become blurred. Parties of each type have moved toward the other's methods somewhat. While degrees of organizational density still vary between parties, now they appear much more as a spectrum than as a distinction of types.

Consequently, here I distinguish types of party more with an eye to the above-noted sources of party identity as they contend with each other: what they stand for in relation to ideologies and interest group support. First I'll address large parties, which each tend to represent an ideology and supporting interests somewhat differently from how most small parties do.

Broad Parties

Large parties typically have moderate ideological identities and try to reach out to a range of interests with an eye to winning elections. In recent decades, a label commonly applied to such parties is "catchall." But this term is misleading, because it implies a vague appeal to very general values, without policy direction content. The German political scientist Otto Kirchheimer, who coined the term "catchall," actually presented this very abstract picture of the catchall party. It pandered for everyone's vote by appealing only to universally shared values, such as helping "the people," restoring the nation's past glory, strong leadership, competence in managing the economy, or general problem-solving expertise. Such appeals give little indication of what sorts of policies would actually be pursued.[16] Kirchheimer was referring to an extreme pole on a continuum (toward which some parties of his day were moving, he thought), not to today's large parties. As I noted above, large parties do tend to retain an ideological identity, and they do appeal to some groups more than others. For example, moderate left-of-center parties address a range of economic issues with proposals for government intervention, but in doing so they are hardly likely to "catch" voters who are worried most about their tax bill and what they consider excessive government regulation.

To capture today's large parties, I borrow the word "broad" from ordinary language and use the phrase **broad party** (though small parties can be broad, too; see below). As noted above, moderate left-of-center parties such as the Democratic Party in the United States, Britain's Labor Party, France's Socialist Party, and Germany's Social Democratic Party strive for the support of labor, ethnic minorities, middle and lower economic strata, and moderate environmental interests. On the right, mainstream conservative parties such as Britain's Conservative Party, America's Republican Party, France's Rally for the Republic, and Germany's Christian Democratic Party rely on the support of upper income strata and many businesses, professionals, religious traditionalists, and rural and small town areas. The key for each broad party is the appeal to a range of interests.

Choice of Policy Directions by Broad Parties Since members and supporters of broad parties can vary in the intensity of their ideological views and interest group support, such parties often advocate some fairly general policy directions during election campaigns. At times they may avoid strong and specific policy proposals that could divide the party's social base and cost the party votes. For example, a moderate left-of-center party's campaign might stress environmental health as a value, but shun specific proposals for environmental regulation in a particular local area if such rules might threaten jobs.[17] (In effect, such an approach exemplifies "interest aggregation.")

In multiparty political frameworks, however, broad parties have to be concerned that if they are *too* moderate and general in their policy direction support, they may lose some of their supporters to a smaller party that is more intense. As political scientist Angelo Panebianco pointed out, both party activists and party supporters among the electorate (whom the parties need to turn out to vote) tend to be attached to the party's core values and related policy directions.[18] Contention within a broad party can even cause the party to split and thus have less ability to contend with other large parties for votes. For example, as we shall see below, Germany's moderate left-of-center Social Democratic Party lost its far left wing in the mid-2000s over party leaders' concessions to right-of-center parties that involved weakening unemployment benefits and labor protections against layoffs.

In contrast, in SMDP-voting nations such as the United States and Great Britain, usually only two broad parties dominate the scene.[19] Minority opinion groupings generally have little choice but to join one of the large parties. The moderate left-of-center party may include some ideological greens and left social democrats, as well as various interest groups, and the conservative party will likely include some classical liberals and ethnic ultranationalists, along with other groups. In SMDP two-party countries, broad parties are especially broad. As political scientist Lorelei Moosbrugger points out, this can create problems; if the super-broad parties are competitive and the margin of victory of the most successful is small, any significant group in its range of support can threaten to abandon the party if it does not get what it wants.[20] Each of the supporting groups becomes a **veto player**. Especially since 2010, the arch-conservative wing (with its multibillionaire donors) of the American Republican Party has generally blocked the party from supporting even very moderate spending proposals by the Democratic administration.

At times, broad parties adjust their policy directions. One sort of adjustment is by addition, to address a new issue that might be grabbing voters' attention. This occurred frequently in the established democracies during the 1970s and 1980s, as new post-materialist issues (e.g., the environment, women's rights) arrived on the agenda. A different form of adjustment is related to parties' participation in coalitions in multiparty systems. Broad parties may have to adjust their policy directions in order to be able to cooperate with a coalition partner party. If a broad party needs a small center party in its coalition, it may moderate some policy positions on issues that are important to the smaller party, for the sake of coalition cooperation. Alternatively a broad and moderate left-of-center party may find itself in a coalition with a left social democratic party, and have to move a bit leftward in some of its issue positions to preserve coalition comity.

To understand broad party directional adjustments, the personal leadership model of influence distribution can sometimes help (see chapter 2). A party leader with enough personal appeal among the public to help a party's national election chances may consequently reap enough influence within the party to engineer a policy direction change. Examples from conservative parties include shifts to the right on economic issues in the 1980s under Margaret Thatcher leading the Conservative Party in Great Britain and Ronald Reagan atop America's Republicans. The 1990s saw moderate left-of-center parties move toward the center under Tony Blair of the British Labor Party, and Bill Clinton leading the Democrats in the United States.

Extremes of Breadth: Catchall and Centrist Parties Party breadth can be carried to an extreme, not far from the "catchall party" described above. Some ideologically centrist parties (see chapter 5) are especially broad. Their policy directions may remain vague, sounding like they are just advocating "splitting the difference" between left-of-center and right-of-center goals and policies, while pursuing general instrumental values such as competence in economic management.

Other centrist parties may mix very moderate left-of-center and very moderate right-of-center policies (often called "center-left" or "center-right"), and contain a diversity of factions. If such parties take specific center-leaning positions on issues, though, it is not fair to call them catchall; rather the best description is simply ideologically centrist.

In the established democracies, broad center parties usually remain small. On occasion, however, such a party can become a leading contender in its political system. The Christian Democratic Party in Italy anchored most postwar governing coalitions before its implosion amid corruption scandals in the 1990s. Other examples exist in some developing nations that have recently made transitions to democracy. There, a party that originally arose to spearhead the democratization movement may have subsequently evolved into a heterogeneous centrist party once democracy was largely secured. Prominent examples include the Brazil's Democratic Movement Party and Nigeria's People's Democratic Party. Some of these may also be classifiable as clientelistic. Again, a clientelistic party is based on patron-client relationships to particular groups, such as one or more ethnic groups or networks of followers of a personalistic leader. Such a party will use its role in government to funnel benefits to its supporting groups and networks, in return for their political support.

Italian media tycoon Silvio Berlusconi, who in the 1990s established a right-of-center party that was initially very personalistic, but subsequently evolved into Italy's largest conservative party, with a strong strand of nationalism.

Some extremely broad parties may be **personalistic**, held together to a substantial degree by the charismatic appeal of the party's leader. In relation to a party's followers, personalism suggests the personal leadership model, regarding the distribution of influence within the party. However, in decision making about the party's favored policy directions, the public impression of personal leadership may not be accurate. Behind the scenes, other individuals or groups may be most influential, with the public leader serving in effect as a "front" person.

To be sure, personalism can play a role in parties that are not fully centrist or catchall. Juan Peron's party in mid-twentieth-century Argentina combined left-of-center links to labor with ardent nationalism and ties to the military (see Country Case Studies, chapter 2), and Jean-Marie Le Pen's National Front Party in late twentieth-century France was ethnic ultranationalist. The latter two parties both survived the exit of their original founders, and remain significant today. Personalistic parties may also be heavily clientelistic, as Argentina's Peronist Party certainly was.

Focus Parties

Many smaller parties have narrower appeals than broad parties. Some stem from ideology and others emerge from an interest group of some sort. No general term is in use in political science to embrace both major types of small party. Here, to contrast them with broad parties, we will use the term **focus party**.

Focus parties play a significant role mainly where the voting system is PR, so that small parties can win seats in large multimember electoral districts in proportion to their shares of the vote (see Figure 10.3). This is not to suggest that the number of small parties will vary directly with the quantitative degree of proportionality—the number of seats in each district, which political scientists call the "district magnitude." Just how "multiple" the parties will be under PR is affected by an array of other factors, such as the pattern of ethnic, socioeconomic, and regional cleavages and interests in society, whether elections are "concurrent" (coming at the same time) in presidential systems, whether there is a minimum vote-percentage threshold for gaining PR seats, whether the governmental system is federal, etc. My point is only that, as political scientists Octavio Amorim Neto and Gary Cox put it, PR voting is "permissive" of multiple parties in general, and they do arise under it.[21]

Ideological Focus Parties An **ideological focus party** aims more to persuade people to its ideological outlook than to win large numbers of votes in elections. (Political scientist Austin Ranney referred to this type as the "missionary" party.[22]) The political attitudes of members generally focus on the party's ideology and policy programs. These usually reflect the Far Left or Far Right, in at least some policy categories.

Historically, the Nazi Party in the Weimar German democracy, the Fascist parties in Italy and Spain, and the pre-1990 Communist parties in the established democracies fit this description. Today in India, for example, small Marxist-Leninist parties still compete in democratic politics, and Maoist ones have adopted revolutionary strategies in Nepal and Peru. Other small democratic socialist parties around the world favor government ownership of key sectors of the economy and tend to oppose privatization (see chapter 7). On the right in European politics are parties with ethnic ultranationalist ideologies, from relatively moderate ones such as Le Pen's above-mentioned National Front Party in France to the much less moderate Svoboda in Ukraine.

Interest-Based Focus Parties A different type of party primarily represents just one group interest, or a cluster of closely related interests: the **interest-based focus party**. For example, Scandinavia's farmers' parties concerned themselves mostly with the material stake interests of agriculture. As small parties, they, too, are found mainly in PR-voting multiparty systems. The exception to this tendency is ethnic-regional parties, which can win seats even under SMDP electoral arrangements, as they do in India, for example. They appeal mainly to the distinctive interests of a region, or the communal interests of an ethnic group concentrated in its home region. In that region (though typically, nowhere else), the group's large numbers produce enough support to win some SMDP seats for the party. It is possible for an ethnic-regional party to also be classified as clientelistic (see above).

An interest-based focus party tends to be more pragmatic than ideological, favoring whatever serves the interests of the group that comprises its support base. Ideologically, they are often toward the center, with much variation among their members' views on issues that are unrelated to the shared interest. Supporters of an interest-based focus party may also differ in the intensity of their policy preferences.

Notably, a few focus parties blend both ideological and interest-related aspects, revealing a continuum rather than a bright line between the two types. For example, green parties focus on environmental interests as well as green ideology (see chapter 5). Norway's taxpayer-oriented Progress Party has a single-minded focus on putting more money in the hands of taxpayers, but that also puts it to the right of center on economic issues. And a focus party based on a regional interest can also have ideological leanings. The Northern League in Italy represents the country's more prosperous north, but is right of center in generally opposing

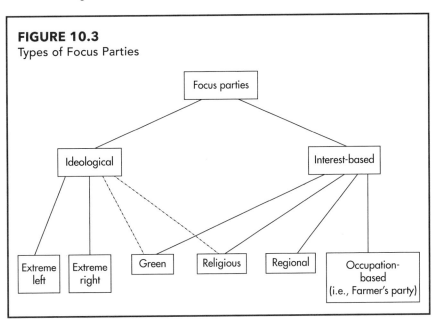

FIGURE 10.3
Types of Focus Parties

high taxes, bureaucracy, and redistribution toward the poorer south (see Country Case Studies, chapter 13).

Moreover, some cases reveal a continuum between broad and focus parties. Between World War II and the 1960s, Germany's Social Democratic Party gradually evolved from its earlier focus on democratic socialism and the interests of industrial workers into a broad, moderate left-of-center party accepting capitalism. Classical liberal parties may be intensely free-market-oriented on economic issues, like the Libertarian Party in some American states, or more mild, center leaning, and broad, as in the case of Great Britain's Liberal Democratic Party.

FACTORS AFFECTING THE CENTRALIZATION OF PARTY DECISION MAKING

We have seen that influence is an important causal factor in politics. As parties contend with each other, influence is both a tool and a goal. But within parties, influence can also play a major role in producing cooperation and coordination among party members, which in turn can be important for a party's effective contention with other parties. To understand the role of influence, however, we have to be clear about where decisions are made in the organization. With **centralized decision making**, key decisions are made at the party center, among top members of its leadership and organizational hierarchy. According to this picture, whether the party is deciding on nominations for elective office, on what policy initiatives it will propose and support, or on how members will vote on issues in government institutions, at least publicly the party as a whole tends to cooperate in implementing those decisions.

To be sure, a centralized pattern of decision making within a political party does not presuppose any particular answer to a question I presented in chapter 2 that can be posed regarding any sort of political group, institution, or processes: Which model of influence distribution—majority preference, elite, pluralist, or personal leadership—best explains the overall distribution of influence within a given political party? The idea of centralized decision making sounds like the elite model, and for some centralized parties that is indeed the best answer. The elite model was certainly at work in Frenchman Robert Michels's 1915 work, *Political Parties*.[23] Focusing mostly on the German Social Democratic Party of his day, Michels argued that the mass of average party members depended heavily on the concentrated expertise in the party's leadership, and tended to entrust decision making to an organizational elite. In his famous words, "all organization is oligarchy."

However, the top organizational leadership of a party may look in various directions for cues in making key decisions. It may have tried to take the measure of the majority preference of party members, or to strike a balance among multiple factions and interests within the party (the pluralist model), or to reflect either the top leader's preference or an agreement between two or three top leaders within the party (the personal leadership model). The idea of centralized party decision making reflects more the pattern of public cooperation that follows the decision than any prior particular pattern of contention or cooperation that went into it.

I refer to the alternative as **decentralized decision making**. Here decision making is dispersed to various groups or lower levels within the party. Again, such dispersed decision making may be heavily influenced by local leaders, interest-related factions, elites, or majorities in one region or another.

As we shall see, parties may fall somewhere on the continuum between these two poles. Moreover, a party might display centralized decision making in some of its functions and decentralized decision making in others. What factors affect these patterns?

Governmental Structure and Centralization

The surrounding governmental structure can affect whether party decision making is mainly centralized or decentralized, not only in making government policy but also in the other two key party activities: candidate selection and policy proposing (see Table 10.1).

Party Decision Making in Parliamentary Government As we noted above, under parliamentary government a party fraction (a given party's members of parliament) that participates in the parliamentary majority has to vote cohesively on bills. It is this unity in favor of the cabinet's bills that keeps the party's leaders in their positions in the cabinet, atop the executive branch. Again, opposition parties normally follow the same practice in voting against the cabinet's bills, showing their capacity to hold together in a hoped-for future majority. This high degree of cooperation within each party—at least in final votes on bills—allows it to effectively contend with other parties under parliamentary government. Such cohesion in parliamentary voting is a product of **party discipline**: a party's legislators actually following its leadership and remaining unified in legislative voting.

To some extent, a party's sense of its identity—around shared values, ideology, and interest representation—certainly contributes to cohesive voting. But whatever the type of governmental structure, differences and diversity can arise among a party's legislators over how to interpret and apply its values, ideology, and interests to the particulars of policymaking. In practice under parliamentary government, mostly it falls to the influence of the party leaders to sum up the position it will take, and assure that all of the party's legislators will be disciplined in following the party's position in final voting on bills.

TABLE 10.1	Major Factors Affecting Centralization Versus Decentralization in Internal Party Decision Making	
Factor	**Favors Centralization**	**Favors Decentralization**
Government structure	Parliamentary	Presidential
Party type	Ideological focus	Broad, interest-based focus
Electoral system	PR	SMD
Main campaign finance sources	Party	Individual candidate fund-raising

This imperative of party discipline in parliamentary systems has important consequences for the first party function discussed above: candidate selection. Normally, the organizational leadership will hold the primary influence in the nomination of candidates for election. Party leaders must be confident that if elected, the party's candidates in parliamentary elections will follow party discipline in voting on bills.

This pattern of centralized influence is consistent with a variety of formal procedures in candidate selection. The top ranks of the national party may make the final choice of candidates, as in Spain and Israel, for example. In other countries, the full local membership may participate in the final vote on nominees, as is done in Finland, Austria, and Britain. Or the formal choice may be made at the regional district level, by regional conferences of delegates from the local party organizations. But regardless of the level of party organization making the final selection, centralization is evident in narrowing the list of options; regional or national executive committees screen the list of potential candidates for the nomination choice.

This limit-setting influence by the upper ranks of the organization also occurs in the choice of party leader. Whether the final, formal selection is by the parliamentary fraction, by a national party conference, or by the whole party membership, usually the top leadership of the party controls the short list of candidates put forward for the choice of party leader.

In parliamentary systems, similar considerations apply to policy proposing: parties' choices of what policy directions to propose and support. Candidates destined to cast legislative votes under tight party discipline usually campaign in ways that are closely coordinated with their party, and stay within the range of the party's views when they make speeches in parliament. (Not surprisingly, the public tends to vote more for the party than for individual candidates; see chapter 11.) To be sure, especially in broad parties, different candidates from the same party may *emphasize* different issues, values, and policy directions, in their different districts or regions. But parties in parliamentary systems cannot allow individual candidates to publicly propose or support policies that depart significantly from the party's stance.

Again, however, this does not mean that there may not be some differences and contention informally within the party. For example, it is possible—though unusual—for leaders to adopt a policy preference that pushes the limits of ordinary party legislators' sense of the party's identity. Privately, within the confines of a caucus meeting of the party's parliamentary fraction, disagreements can arise that the leadership may have to address with adjustments to its approach. If contention becomes sharp, and opposition extends to the majority of party legislators (sometimes also involving the party organization outside parliament), the party has in reserve a type of "nuclear option": to replace the current party leaders with others (e.g., the British Conservative Party's replacement of its leader and prime minister in 1991; see "Contention and Cooperation in Focus"). Alternatively, a dissident minority may even decide to leave the party. We saw this in the departure of the left wing of Germany's Social Democratic Party in 2004 to join the former Democratic Left Party to form a new "Left Party."

These possibilities—however rarely they actually arise—may be said to give the whole parliamentary fraction a degree of *limit-setting* influence (see chapter 2) in the background, informally behind the usual directive power in the hands of the party leadership. In principle, then, in governance within parties we see a type of mixture of the elite model with the majority preference and/or the pluralist models, which was discussed in chapter 2: the "accountable elite" picture of party organizational leadership. Normally, a leadership elite makes the final determination on particular policies, but it is held accountable by the capacity of the party mass to replace their leaders (see "Applying the Models"). On occasion, the leadership may be forced to make adjustments.

Party Decision Making in Presidential Government As we have seen, under presidential government, the chief executive stays in office for a set term whether or not the cabinet's bills pass in the assembly. This means party discipline in support of the president's proposals is less necessary. Thus party leaderships will not be as consistently influential as they are in parliamentary governmental systems. To be sure, party discipline may be strong in a particular situation, such as that of Republican legislators in the U.S. Congress cohesively supporting almost all of the bills proposed by Republican president George W. Bush between 2001 and mid-2008, and opposing all of the key proposals of Democratic president Barack Obama from 2010 through 2014. But in such cases, factors other than the governmental structure will be at work (see chapter 12).

With less party discipline in government policymaking under presidential government, decision making in candidate selection can be more decentralized. At the extreme, parties' nominees can be chosen in a **primary election** process, as occurs in the United States. There, all party supporters may vote, and candidates for president or Congress typically can get on the primary ballot fairly easily, with a certain number of voter signatures on a petition. They don't have to secure permission from the top rungs of party organization. A candidate wins the presidential nomination by accumulating a sequence of victories in state-level presidential primaries. Parties in other nations with presidential systems (e.g., in Latin America) use a variety of methods to select a party's presidential candidate, ranging from behind-the-scenes negotiations among top party leaders to national conferences of delegates chosen at lower levels or even a vote by all enrolled party members.

The choice of what policies or policy directions to support is also substantially decentralized in American parties. In election campaigning, individual candidates adopt their own positions regarding ideology, values, interest group support, and specific policy ideas. They often tailor their views to the interests of the voters in their localities. American parties do adopt policy "platforms" at their national conventions every four years. However, they are not binding on candidates for Congress and the presidency. And again, party platforms often remain vague on some issues to avoid dividing the party's supporters. While contending for the presidential nomination of their party, presidential candidates tend to stay close to the views of party activists. In the general election, however, nominees' positions may range more widely to appeal to the more independent and moderate "swing" voters.

To be sure, whether the governmental structure is parliamentary or presidential is not the only factor affecting centralization or decentralization of decision making within parties as they contend with one another. Other factors may have their impacts, such as the party type, the electoral system, and the way in which campaigns are financed. Such factors may weaken or even counteract the impact of the governmental system on party centralization or decentralization of influence (see below).

Party Type and Decision Making

The type of party is another factor that can affect parties' degree of centralization of influence. Recall that broad parties must balance the concerns of their different supporting interest groups (as well as retaining an ideological identity) as they seek to expand their voting support and win elections. Since different interests may be important in different election districts, a broad party might want decisions about candidate selection to be made closer to the ground level. Local party members may know best which candidates will appeal to voters in their district. Even in a parliamentary system, where the need for party discipline in legislative voting suggests centralization, parties may want direct local input. In the case of nominations for the British Conservative Party, for example, conferences in each constituency pick their favorite to run for parliament, but the national party headquarters has the option of vetoing the local choice and substituting their own preference (though they seldom do so).

In broad parties, centralization may also be reduced by factional division within the party. Reaching out to a range of interests, a broad party may experience a degree of internal contention between groups of supporters and leaders that can weaken its capacity to control the party's candidates, legislators, and functionaries. Especially in two-party systems (with their SMDP voting), where the two parties are especially broad, a threat by a group to lessen its support for the party in the next election if it doesn't get its way can force a policy adjustment by the party and reveal a reduction in party leadership influence.[24]

One source of factional division may arise when pressure for ideological purity comes from a party's organizational headquarters outside government, while the bulk of its parliamentarians may be more moderate and willing to compromise with other parties. This occurred in the above-mentioned case of internal contention in Germany's Social Democratic party in the early 2000s over approaches to job creation. The main division was between (a) the party's top administrative apparatus outside parliament, led by the more left-leaning Oscar Lafontaine, and (b) its more moderate parliamentary fraction led by Chancellor (PM in the German system) Gerhard Schroeder.

Lafontaine and his supporters objected especially to their cabinet ministers' acceptance of two of the "Hartz reforms": cuts in long-term unemployment benefits and the exemption of some workers from traditional protections against easy layoffs. By the time of the parliamentary election of 2005, Lafontaine and some of his supporters had quit the party to join the left social democratic party. This exit of much of the left wing of the party organization affected the Social Democrats' ability to contend with other parties; the Social Democrats lost a portion of their voting support, and subsequently the Social Democrat-Green coalition has been unable to win parliamentary elections. Other examples of factional conflict within broad parties can be found in both Great Britain and the United States (see "Contention and Cooperation in Focus").

Divisions within broad parties may also stem partly from personal leadership contention. For example, Japan's conservative Liberal Democratic Party has long been characterized by contention among factions that each center on a top-level figure with patron-client ties between that leader and followers at various levels (see Country Case Studies, chapter 9).

CONTENTION AND COOPERATION IN FOCUS | Intraparty Factional Division in American and British Broad Parties

In the early 1990s, the British Conservative Party became divided between the hard right supporters of Prime Minister Margaret Thatcher and the more moderate faction supporting her finance minister, John Major. After Thatcher insisted on a tax policy that most Conservative MPs opposed, the party voted her out as leader and made Major the party leader and hence the new prime minister. Subsequently, the factional contention largely subsided into cooperation under Major's leadership.

The United Kingdom's other large broad party provides a more recent example of factional contention. In 2010, after the Labor Party's election defeat, Prime Minister Gordon Brown resigned not only as prime minister but also as party leader. A spirited contest for the Labor leadership broke out at a national party conference. David Miliband, a leader of the more moderate faction including Brown and former prime minister Tony Blair, narrowly lost to his younger brother Ed, who represented the more left-leaning and union-representing faction. Subsequently, policy proposing settled back into the usual pattern of cooperation.

In recent years, America's conservative Republican Party has experienced a powerful grassroots insurgency. Overall, the party had been evolving in an increasingly conservative direction for decades. As for the moderate left-of-center Democrats, when they won the presidency and majorities in both houses of Congress in the 2008 election amid a deep financial crisis, at key points the party cooperated internally. Democrats successfully passed spending and regulation in 2009 and 2010 to contend with the economic crisis and the problem of unaffordable health insurance for many. The response of arch-conservatives among the Republicans was the formal emergence of an angry Tea Party faction. In the 2010 Congressional election campaign, they opposed all government initiatives regarding the economy. Mobilizing heavy support in funding and votes, Tea Party candidates defeated some mainstream Republican conservatives in party primaries for state and national office. Many Tea Party candidates won their general election races, contributing to the Republican conquest of the majority in the House of Representatives (though not the Senate).

Subsequently the contention between the Tea Partiers and the more moderate Republicans became explicit. In the 2012 elections, the Republicans were able to hold onto their House majority, but the extreme Tea Party policy positions of some of their Senate candidates contributed to the Republican failure to win the Senate majority. Contention within the Republican Party ensued. By the time of the 2014 election campaign, Republican Party leaders had recovered enough influence to impose some more moderate and appealing policy positions and candidates on the Republican Senate campaigns.

Tea Party dissatisfaction over this tended to be muted amid the two factions' shared hostility to the Obama administration. Late in the campaign, pro-Republican advertising blamed Democratic president Obama for the Ebola threat, the spread of control by a militant Islamist group in Iraq and Syria (called IS, or "Islamic State"), and the slow economic recovery. In the Senate, there were more Democratic seats exposed to reelection fights than Republican seats, and pro-Republican ads trumpeted how often Democratic candidates had "voted with Obama" in Congress (often over 90 percent of Democrats' votes).

Meanwhile, the Democrats were divided. The president's poll ratings were not high, and those who wanted the Senate campaigns to stress traditional party values and what they saw as the president's positive record generally lost out in discussions of campaign strategy. In contending with Republican opponents, most Democratic Senate candidates were unwilling to produce a counter-narrative extolling the government's accomplishments, in containing the spread of Ebola, stopping the advance of IS, lowering the unemployment rate, cutting the deficit, and providing new access to affordable health insurance while reducing the rise in medical costs. To many in the electorate, most Democratic candidates' silence on the president's record sounded like a guilty plea. Many likely Democratic supporters among women, Hispanics, and young people were not inspired, and failed to turn out to vote (common in American election years when the president is not being chosen). But Republican supporters did show up, and many undecided voters went Republican. The Republicans were able to win control of the Senate.

Clearly, among both the British and American broad parties, each experienced internal contention. But they differed in their approaches to dealing with it and pursuing cooperation. These differences in turn affected their ability to contend effectively with the opposing party. What would you have advised the parties and their factions to do at key points in these sequences?

Among focus parties, ideological ones tend to be centralized in choosing candidates and policy proposing, whether in parliamentary or presidential frameworks. An ideological focus party is especially concerned to win converts to its ideological program. This encourages stress on ideological purity among candidates, encouraging centralized selection of candidates and guidance in policy proposing. In contrast, interest-based focus parties normally lack a very clear ideology. They tend to be more pragmatic and flexible in their campaign proposals for how and how much to benefit their interest group. On issues unrelated to the party's interest group focus, diversity may reign.

The Electoral System and Centralization

The electoral system, too, can have an impact on the degree of centralization of decision making regarding candidate selection and policy proposing. Recall that in PR systems, normally each party runs its ranked list of candidates in each election district. A party's share of the district's seats is determined by its proportion of the vote there, and the particular candidates taking the seats won by their party are determined by counting down, on the ranked list, the number of seats won. Thus being ranked high on the list often determines one's chances of becoming a legislator. The list tends to be drawn up by the leadership of the party organization, whether at the regional or the national level. As political scientist John M. Carey stresses,[25] all this—everything else being equal—means more leadership influence over candidates and legislators. In addition, with a list of candidates running together in party list PR elections, the party organization must coordinate a common policy platform. This, too, can strengthen a party leadership's hand somewhat.

These PR effects apply even under the presidential governmental structure, pervasive in Latin America, as political scientists Scott Mainwaring and Mathew Shugart have argued.[26] To be sure, as we have seen, presidential government otherwise allows for more decentralization of party decision making. But Latin American lower legislative houses are mostly chosen by PR voting. Thus leaders of parties and factions within them are often more able to commit their backbenchers' votes than would otherwise be the case without PR.

Party leadership influence over the list is negated, however, in the few PR systems that are **open list**, as in Brazil. There, the *voters* can pick the candidates that they favor from the list, and the party-earned seats go to those with the most votes. In this case, the electoral incentives point to each candidate to some extent leaving party discipline behind to appeal to her or his voter base in a clientelistic fashion. To be sure, however, the Brazilian case reminds us that the electoral system is just one factor at work along with others; in most of its recent history the Workers' Party has been rather disciplined in the lower house. Political scientist Herbert Kitschelt and colleagues stress that disciplined structure and ideological cohesion will be found in some parties even where electoral incentives seem to point to decentralization and clientelistic politics.[27]

In contrast, in single-member district voting, each candidate runs alone, inviting the party to go with whatever candidate can give it the best chance of winning in the particular district. In some cases, this might point to more local influence in identifying which candidates have the most local appeal (though party leaders may still want to have their say).

Party Finance and Decision Making

Another factor that can affect the degree of centralization of party decision making is the source of funds for party electoral contention. Election campaigns are becoming more media driven and expensive, raising the importance of money. Not surprisingly, in the American presidential system with its SMDP voting and decentralized party decision making, candidates usually do much of their own fund-raising, with the rest coming from independent outside groups.[28] Under this pattern of campaign finance, candidates owe less to the party organization, contributing to their independence of the party leadership (though their dependence on outside campaign contributors may increase).

In contrast, in parliamentary systems, it is the party that primarily conducts fund-raising and allocates money for campaigns. This adds to the influence of the upper levels of party organization. To be sure, campaigns in Europe face significantly lower costs than do those in the United States. Again, most European countries ban or tightly limit the purchase of television advertising by parties in the last weeks of election campaigns. Instead, they offer the parties free prime airtime on the public television networks. In managing their costs, today European parties depend much less on member dues than previously, and more on party organization fund-raising and government subsidies. The funds are distributed through the party organization, further contributing to the influence of the party leadership over policy proposing.

Trends in the Influence of Organizational Levels

Yet another factor affecting the degree of centralization and cooperation is the amount of influence held by lower levels of party organization. In recent decades in many of the European democracies, the local units of party organization seem to have declined in vitality. Reductions in local branch membership may partly reflect a decline in "solidary" motives to join parties (to socialize with like-minded people). A related factor may be declines in the traditional class-based and religion-related subcultures that had previously supported major parties. Today, local face-to-face campaigning is less important in parties' election strategies; media-oriented campaigning and its media consultants have become more prominent.[29] These trends seem mainly to encourage more centralized control over policy proposing in election campaigns.

However, those who remain active at the local branch level may have greater ideological commitment and policy interest. They press to be heard, often through informal networks of policy discussion and feedback,[30] including on the Internet. Ground-level concerns cannot be wholly ignored. Certainly, the parties still need local efforts to turn out their voters on election day, and need recruits from the local level to serve in higher party positions and run for legislative office.

PARTY TYPES IN AUTHORITARIAN AND SEMI-DEMOCRATIC FRAMEWORKS

Political parties are most comfortable in democratic political frameworks. There they form spontaneously and do not face official constraints on their activity. Some authoritarian regimes, however, do employ political parties. In chapters

15 and 16, we will consider authoritarian and semi-democratic regimes in detail. This section limits itself to brief looks at two additional party types that have been important in authoritarian frameworks. The dominant political party in an authoritarian regime may be an ideological focus party, as in the case of the former Communist regimes. Or it may be just a "government party," kept together mainly by the shared goal of keeping control of government.

Ruling Communist Parties

As we saw in chapter 6, ruling Communist parties have an explicit Marxist-Leninist ideological orientation and an elaborate organization outside government. At its height, the Soviet Union's Communist Party operated at national, regional, and local levels. Each level of the party organization had its own large committee (called the "central committee" at the national level), and specialized administrative chiefs called "secretaries" who supervised party department heads. The top leader of the party at each level was called the "first secretary" (at the national level, "general secretary").

Overseeing the party apparatus at each level was a board of directors called the "bureau" ("Politburo" at the national level). It brought together (a) the top party secretaries such as those in overall charge of ideology, the economy, and the lower territorial party units, (b) a few key lower-level first secretaries, and (c) a handful of top government figures. The main jobs of this apparatus were to:

- oversee (but not directly make) appointments in government and economic management,

- monitor the economy and the performance of other governmental units,

- determine the general directions to be taken by national government policy, and

- guide the politically relevant views expressed by the schools and media.

Government officials were always party members, and the top government figures at each level usually belonged to its party bureau. Since the government owned and ran virtually the whole economy, a party office existed for (parallel to) almost every significant subdivision of every ministry in the executive branch of government. Job histories of top figures in party and government always included stints in both party administrative work and government.[31] In different ways, ruling Communist parties were both broad and ideological focus, simultaneously.

The most apt model of influence distribution in such parties is the elite one, with some mixing of pluralist and personal leadership elements. For example, internal contention might involve limited contest between different sectors of the economy, among different patron-client groups and their leaders, and between the party and its ideological directions and the government with its established methods and practices.

In the last half of the twentieth century, China's Communist Party fit this model, with the exception of the Cultural Revolution period of the late 1960s when normal party operation was suspended. But while China is politically still under single-party Communist rule, the party's role in the economy has greatly receded. In the broad swath of eastern China that is primarily capitalist, there are far fewer state-owned enterprises to oversee. In the big state-owned enterprises of the Chinese hinterland, however, and in the state banking system, party influence remains strong. In this ideologically and politically mixed situation, the Communists look much like a "government party," to which we now turn.

Government Parties and Clientelism

In some minimally democratic, semi-democratic, and authoritarian nations, a single political party without a clear ideological identity prevails in government. Typically centrist and catchall in nature, such a **government party** tends to be held together mainly by its desire to stay in power. In a semi-democratic or minimally democratic state such as Nigeria until 2015, the government party dominates patronage in ways that tend to assure victory in every election. In single-party-dominant authoritarian states, other parties either are outlawed or face restrictions that prevent them from contending seriously in elections.

Goodluck Jonathan, until 2015 the President of Nigeria and leader of the country's government party, the Peoples Democratic Party (PDP); Jonathan and his party finally suffered electoral defeat in early 2015 amid an oil price collapse that strained government finances and a perception of a weak fight against a militant Islamist rebellion in the Northeast.

Government parties may tout their past populist or nationalist achievements in order to keep popular support. For example, in the 1970s, Zambia's United National Independence Party stressed its role in the earlier struggle to end British colonial rule (see Country Case Studies, chapter 13). In Mexico, prior to the end of single-party rule, the Institutional Revolution Party (PRI) highlighted its successful land reform program of the 1930s (see Country Case Studies, chapter 9). But those past glories often bear little relation to present conditions. Alternatively, a government party may serve partly as a political vehicle to support control by (and cooperation with) another political force, such as the armed forces. For example, this was the role played under military rule from the late 1960s through the 1980s in Brazil by ARENA (the National Renovation Alliance party; see Country Case Studies, chapter 4) and in Indonesia by Golkar (see Country Case Studies, chapter 8).

A government party may once have had an ideological identity that has since largely faded. For example, the parties ruling post-Communist Belarus, Kazakhstan, Turkmenistan, and Uzbekistan no longer embrace the Marxism-Leninism of their Soviet past, but still employ authoritarian control of the government. Today a government party will stress its experience in government and its capacity to induce cooperation within government and between the government and society.

Government parties typically involve patron-client networks in the various levels of party and government and between government and society. Through them, the party dispenses governmental jobs and other favors, and mobilizes voters for less-than-meaningful "elections." Political contention arises between patron-client complexes as well as between different sectors of the economy and society that party leaders may be linked to. Where the government allows limited electoral competition, it usually favors SMDP ("winner take all") elections. Such arrangements allow the ruling party, typically organized throughout the country, to win many seats by limited margins. This can turn plurality support among the voters into majority dominance in the legislature, and thus keep the party in power.

A clientelist party may be in a similar position. Such a party aims to funnel benefits through patron-client networks to a particular economic sector, personalistic group, ethnic group, and/or region, for example. (Government parties are often substantially clientelist, as well.) In the many multiparty systems that we see in the developing world, the most significant parties each anchor a coalition, which may include smaller, clientelist parties. The winner in an election is not just its biggest party (often a broad one), but also its smaller coalition partners, who expect to benefit from their connections to, and within, the cabinet and relevant ministries.

SUMMARY: CONTENTION AND COOPERATION IN POLITICAL PARTIES

The political party is a key vehicle for contention and cooperation in the political process. Political parties perform functions such as nominating candidates for office, proposing and defending directions for government policy to take, and making policy in government. In those activities, a contending political party tends to represent both an ideological direction and one or more group interests, though often not stressing both roles equally. Political parties may be broad (representing a range of interests), ideologically focused, or interest group focused. These different party types tend to achieve internal cooperation in different ways and to different degrees, and experience different degrees and types of internal factional contention within the party.

Influence over decision making in party candidate selection, policy proposing, and policymaking may be centralized, decentralized, or something in between. Parliamentary government encourages elite-model centralization of party decision making, while presidential government allows more decentralization. In addition, party type, the electoral system, the pattern of party financing, and the roles of different levels of party organization also affect the distribution of influence and patterns of contention and cooperation within political parties.

Distinctive types of political parties play dominant roles under authoritarian and semi-democratic political frameworks: the twentieth-century Communist model and the currently more common government party type.

COUNTRY CASE STUDIES

These country case studies contrast political parties in two multiparty democracies. The Netherlands has a long-established parliamentary system. In contrast, Peru's party development suffered from the recurring threat (and reality) of military intervention and rule in the twentieth century. In both cases, interparty alliances affect political contention. However, Peru generally lacks the degree of strong party organization and formal coalitions that mark Dutch politics.

The Netherlands: Fragmentation in a Multiparty Parliamentary Framework

The Netherlands has a multiparty parliamentary framework. Its legislature includes a directly elected, 150-seat lower house, the House of Representatives, and an indirectly elected, much less important upper house. In characteristic parliamentary fashion, Dutch legislators support their party leaders in voting. The Dutch PR electoral system uses the whole country as a single election district, allowing a wide array of ideologies to have party expression. In the absence of a significant minimum vote threshold for gaining proportional representation, even very small parties can win seats and play significant roles. We would expect these circumstances to foster all key types of parties: broad, interest-based focus, and ideological focus. That is indeed what we see in Dutch party politics.

In the early twentieth century, Dutch parties were partly a product of cross-cutting religious and economic cleavages. Regarding religion, four groupings were significant: Calvinist Protestants, non-Calvinist (Dutch Reform) Protestants, Catholics, and a major secular population. But the economic division between labor and business cut across the religious cleavages. A given religious identity might be linked to two parties, each with its class-related identity. Similarly, the secular-oriented population was divided into two parties. One was a free-market classical liberal party on the right, the People's Party for Freedom and Democracy (VVD) whose sociocultural views were center-left. The other was a moderate left-of-center party, Labor. Each of the most important parties developed its own social organizations, such as union federations, schools, newspapers, women's clubs, youth organizations, and football leagues. In effect, they produced their own distinct political subcultures, referred to as the "pillars."

In the 1960s and 1970s, however, the political picture changed. Economic success boosted the service sector and blurred class lines, while the strength of religious attachments began to ebb. Also, people raised new post-materialist issues such as the environment, international peace, local democracy, and rights for women and minorities (see chapter 8). The Labor Party

left behind its early socialism and became a moderate left-of-center party. Alongside it on the left were the ideologically focused Socialist Party and the Green Left Party. The centrist Democracy 66 (D66) was concerned with some post-materialist issues.

On the right, the political influence of religion was weakening. In the mid-1970s, prominent faith-based parties combined into a single broad party, the Christian Democratic Alliance (CDA). As a moderate conservative party, it took its place alongside the other broad right-of-center party, the classical liberal VVD. After Labor-led governments in the 1970s expanded socioeconomic protections, CDA-led governments in the 1980s cut back on the public sector and reduced spending and wage increases. The left-of-center Labor Party usually receives about 20–30 percent of the votes and parliamentary seats, with the Green Left and the Socialists earning 5–10 percent each. On the right, the moderately conservative CDA usually gained 25–30 percent of the votes and seats, but has dropped off to 14 percent and 9 percent in the parliamentary elections of the early 2010s. The free-market-oriented and secular VVD tends to win 15–25 percent.

Strikingly, in the early 2010s a new ethnic ultra-nationalist party popped up, the Party for Freedom (PVV). It won 16 percent and 10 percent, respectively, in the 2010 and 2012 elections. Somewhat personalistic, the PVV is identified with its leader, Geert Wilders. While Wilders otherwise supports a free-market economy, he combines centrist positions in economic areas such as pensions and health care with far-right sociocultural views; he is extremely nationalistic, anti-immigration, pro law and order, against European integration, and hostile to Islam. In particular, he sees Islam as a threat to the mainstream Dutch Christian and secular culture (carrying on the tradition of the politician Pim Fortuyn of the early 2000s).

The main features of Dutch parties are evident in the three broad parties. In the VVD, candidate selection has remained largely centralized. In the 1970s, Labor and the CDA gave their rank-and-file membership the final selection of parliamentary candidates. However, members chose from short lists approved by the central party organizations. By the 1990s, party leaders were using their influence over candidate selection to include more women and youth candidates. Dutch parties generally have the parliamentary fraction select the party leader. Thus influence over candidate selection and policy proposing in the main Dutch parties is mostly centralized, though leaders are sensitive to the need to galvanize their voting supporters.

The party leaderships of Labor, the CDA, and the classical liberal VVD have been mostly moderate and pragmatic over the last twenty years. Indeed, each party has cooperated with each of the other two parties in majority coalitions at one time or another (see below), despite having to compromise some of their policy preferences along the way. To be sure, the more natural coalition alignments along left-versus-right economic lines have prevailed at times, such as in the 1980s when CDA-VVD coalitions governed. And in the middle 2000s, the two parties formed a center-right coalition that gained a parliamentary majority after the 2003 elections by including D66, the small centrist party. CDA prime minister Balkenende pursued limited cutbacks in the Dutch welfare state.

Labor had led in establishing a robust social welfare system by the late 1970s. But under its subsequent leader, Wim Kok, Labor largely refrained from pushing for further gains despite the wishes of many rank-and-file members. In 1991, Labor prime minister Kok, in coalition with the moderately conservative CDA, agreed to cut state pensions. His party chairman resigned, and Labor suffered heavy losses in the 1994 elections. Another Labor-CDA coalition arose to deal with the economic crisis of 2008–2009 and its recession. The emergency conditions (see chapter 7) prompted the CDA, with its humanitarian Christian heritage, to cooperate with Labor in support of emergency state interventions in the economy to:

1. stabilize the banking system with nationalizations and capital injections,

2. aid the unemployed and homeowners, and

3. support employment with stimulus spending, especially in construction.

But the CDA got an agreement that policy would turn rightward toward budget cuts as soon as possible. In a common phenomenon, the party making most of the concessions, the CDA in this case, lost a lot of its voter support and did poorly in the next election.

Such a governing coalition that spans the left-right divide, between a moderate left-of-center party and either a classical liberal or a conservative party, is referred to as a "grand coalition."[32] Grand coalitions tend to arise when (a) neither conventional coalition holds a parliamentary majority, and/or (b) there are serious policy challenges that need addressing, around which the available smaller parties are uncooperative as coalition partners. The 2008–2009 economic crisis was such a situation, with its Labor-CDA coalition. Even a Labor-VVD grand coalition can arise. In the late 1990s, these two secular parties found enough common ground to govern together in coalition, excluding the Christian-affiliated parties.

Perhaps the most striking example of such a grand coalition was the Labor-VVD coalition that governed from 2012 through 2015. This grand coalition began its life in a period when, paradoxically, the electorate and the parties seemed to be settling into a traditional pattern of contention between the natural left coalition (The left social democratic Socialists and the PVD) and the conservative one (the DVD and CDA). This return to traditional European patterns of coalition contention and cooperation arose from, not surprisingly, a battle over austerity policies being pressed by the European Union authorities (especially the Germans).

Prior to the election of late 2012, a minority DVD CDA government (kept in office by informal parliamentary support from Wilders's PVV) was in office, trying to carry out a program of austerity to rapidly reduce the Dutch budget deficit to the 3 percent of GDP required by the EU commission. Despite the stagnant Dutch economy (also hurt by the earlier burst of a housing bubble), the austerity measures included, for example, cuts in government pensions, health care, and housing support that affected the middle class and the poor, along with value-added tax increases. In the spring of 2012, a week before the EU deadline, the Eurosceptic PVV declared its opposition to the austerity cuts and the submissiveness to the European authorities that the cuts symbolized to many. This required the government to fall, but as it continued in a caretaker capacity (until new parliamentary elections could be held), it immediately put together majority support—from all parties other than the left-leaning ones, the Socialists and the PVD—for an austerity plan that met the EU authorities' demands. Public dissatisfaction with austerity continued through the summer, and the parliamentary election in September produced a big majority for the parties that had been unwilling to vote for the austerity plan approved the preceding April. Of course, though, Wilders's PVV could not join a left-of-center coalition, and without the PVV seats the left finished almost even with the conservative coalition of the VVD and CDA.

In contrast to what seemed to be clear battle lines between left and right over austerity, after the election the moderate left-of-center PVD chose to enter into a grand coalition with the VVD. The coalition continued its pursuit of austerity and spending cuts (with the PVD seeking to distribute austerity's impacts as "fairly" as possible). In 2013, GDP growth went positive, exports improved, and the government's borrowing costs remained low, but unemployment stayed high and anti-austerity sentiment continued its growth (including among PVD supporters). Both the local elections of 2014 and the regional assembly elections of 2015 left Labor with only around 10 percent of the votes and seats, and the VVD with roughly

15 percent. The government does not hold a majority in the Senate, which reflects regional and local outcomes, so it must bargain with the other parties to pass legislation there. Anti-austerity sentiment continues to run high.

Notably, after periods of left-right grand coalition, the junior partner party may appear to many of its voters to have sacrificed its principles, and it does poorly in the next election. Labor lost big in 2002, and the CDA suffered large losses in 2010. To be sure, contending parties may need to cooperate at times to provide compromise solutions to policy challenges. But each party also needs to preserve its capacity to contend effectively with other parties, which requires cooperation with its mass membership and voter support. There is no automatic recipe for resolving the tensions that can arise between these contending imperatives.

Peru: Evolution in Party Types and Systems

Peru has a multiparty presidential political framework, as do most Latin American countries. The one-house, 150-member Congress is chosen by PR voting. Party lists contend in regional units called departments, filling seats ranging from a few to nearly thirty for Lima, the capital. Multiple candidates run for the presidency, which has a five-year term. The presidential election includes two rounds, with the second a runoff between the top two first-round finishers. With multiple parties filling Congressional seats, the president's party seldom has a majority in Congress. Although informal coalitions form, the presidential governmental structure discourages strong party and coalition discipline.

Prior to the 1930s, literacy and property requirements for voting excluded most citizens. Patron parties associated with the landed oligarchy dominated politics. Within the landed elite, the owners of export-oriented sugar and cotton plantations and mines had the most influence. By the 1930s, urbanization, modernization, and economic growth had led to significant increases in the laboring population and in literacy rates. Property requirements for

voting were dropped, and modern Peruvian politics emerged.

Peru's significant parties since World War II reflect different degrees of (1) ideological focus, (2) durable party organization, and (3) personalism. Most small ideological focus parties have been on the left, ranging from socialist to left social democratic. Their supporters come from such groups as indigenous Andean peasants of the Sierra, radical workers, and left-oriented intellectuals. In 1980, most such parties joined in an alliance called the United Left. But in 1989, this grouping split up, mostly into left social democratic and socialist clusters. In the same era, a revolutionary Maoist group called the Shining Path arose. It waged a persistent rural insurgency with much violence until it was largely suppressed in the 1990s.

Peru also has had broad parties with durable organization and fairly clear ideological identities. Over the years, the American Popular Revolutionary Alliance (APRA) provides the most prominent example. Traditionally, APRA's ideological identity combined populism and nationalist anticolonialism with left social democracy. Sharply opposed to the landowning and mining elites, its strongest interest base was industrial and plantation labor, together with reform-minded and nationalist middle-class intellectuals who opposed the economic oligarchy and foreign investment.

This orientation, together with incidents of violence, made APRA an enemy of the armed forces. The military banned and at times brutally suppressed the party in the 1930s and 1940s and again from 1948 to 1962, after which it was re-legalized. However, APRA's organization had enabled it to persist and at times to support election victories by left-of-center alliances. In 1985, APRA won an election outright, and its leader, Alan Garcia, became president. Garcia turned government policy in a left social democratic direction, including nationalizing the banks. However, economic problems and violence by the insurgent Shining Path led to APRA's defeat in the 1990 election.

When APRA reappeared in the 2000s, Garcia had moved the party toward the center. Admitting past mistakes and committed to fiscal prudence, APRA did well in the 2006 election and Garcia became president again. Economic growth helped Peru weather the late 2000s' financial storm. But Garcia's centrist (some would say center-right) government was judged to have achieved little redistribution, and APRA did poorly in the 2011 election.

To the right of center, the Christian People's Party (PPC) is a broad party with a clear ideological identity and a fairly durable organization. It began as a conservative, free-market-oriented splinter from the earlier Christian Democrats. But the PPC retained elements of Catholic social thought allowing for moderate social spending for the poor. During the period of military rule from 1968 to 1980 and the authoritarian Fujimori era of the 1990s described below, the PPC remained organized and vigorously pro-democracy. PPC-led conservative coalitions won 15 percent of the Congressional vote in both 2006 and 2011.

Another type of Peruvian party is broad and moderate left of center, while featuring personalism and weak organization. An early example was the National Democratic Front of the 1940s, whose leader, Jose Bustamante y Rivero won the presidency in 1945 with the informal support of APRA. Bustamante pursued trade protectionist tariffs, active government support for domestic industries, and government spending in such areas as public works, education, and housing until he was removed by the military in 1948. Later, favoring similar policies, Fernando Belaunde Terry of the moderate left-of-center Popular Action (AP) won the presidency in the 1960s. But amid inflation, widening budget deficits, and an emerging rural leftist insurgency, the military took power in 1968 and ruled for a decade.

A present-day example of a personalistic party is the Peruvian National Party. It is led by Ollanta Humala, a former military officer, whose ideology has migrated. In the early 2000s, Humala and his thinly organized party seemed to be left social democratic ideologically, focusing on Andean ethnic ultranationalism and leftist populism. He called for revival of Peru's ancient Inca heritage, hostility to foreign ownership of mines, and redistribution to the native poor. However, by the time of the 2011 election, Humala had moved into moderate left-of-center territory, proposing only to increase taxes on mining and energy companies. Since then, as president he has become center-right ideologically, accommodating the foreign-owned mining interests that he previously opposed. In response to protests at a mine, he sent troops to restore order, and removed several left-of-center allies from his cabinet. Now with a center-right technocratic cabinet, few seem sure just where Humala stands.

Broad personalistic parties with distinct ideological identities also exist on the right. In the late 1970s, Popular Action (AP) reemerged, having shifted its ideological orientation to moderate classical liberal. When the AP leader Belaunde was again elected president in 1980, he opposed substantial government spending and economic regulation. Further to the right, with a conservative ideology but a personalistic bent, lies Force 2011, a party of Fujimori sympathizers, now led by his daughter, Keiko. In the 2011 elections, she narrowly lost (to Humala) in the second round for the presidency.

Another sort of Peruvian party is personalistic but ideologically centrist and pro-democracy. Peru Possible (PP), led by Alejandro Toledo, exemplifies this type. After helping to lead the pro-democracy movement against Alberto Fujimori in the late 1990s, Toledo became president and pursued center-right policies until mounting problems led to his resounding defeat in the 2006 elections. A coalition of the PP with the now centrist AP received 15 percent of the vote in the 2011 Congressional elections.

Other Peruvian parties have been personalistic, authoritarian, and free-market conservative, while linked to the military and to conservative business interests. In the early twentieth century, this orientation was exemplified by personal autocrats who ruled without a party.[33] In the post–World War II era, however, such leaders recognized that they needed a party to win often-manipulated elections. After leading a military coup in 1948, General Manuel Arturo

Odria reversed most of Bustamante's policies, suppressed the unions, and banned APRA. But General Odria also targeted a limited amount of welfare and public works spending for the poorly educated urban informal sector in the shantytowns (accompanied by populist rhetoric) to build clientelistic support among them.

The most prominent recent example of the personalistic and authoritarian conservative party came in 1990. Alberto Fujimori came to power amid a major economic crisis and a serious security threat from the Shining Path. Using a personalistic party vehicle called "Change 90," Fujimori campaigned successfully as a moderate centrist. But once elected, he adopted vigorous free-market-oriented policies, removing economic regulations and privatizing many state-owned enterprises. Having fought and defeated the Shining Path, Fujimori proceeded in the mid-1990s to dissolve Congress in a so-called "self-coup." He then used his personalistic and national security appeal to win a majority for his supporters in a constituent assembly, which wrote a new constitution to his liking.

Through 2000 Fujimori manipulated elections, intimidated and smeared rivals, took control of the judiciary and the top military leadership, and dominated the media. In addition, following Odria's earlier playbook, he targeted limited aid to the urban informal sector to gain clientelist support there. After his 2000 election "victory," however, a large scandal revealed the whole range of Fujimori tactics, and he was removed. In 2009, Fujimori was convicted of human rights abuses, embezzlement, bribery, and phone tapping.

The post-Fujimori return of fair elections after 2000 brought a proliferation of new parties. The establishment of regional government and elections in 2002 invited regional parties to form as well. However, a minimum vote threshold of 5 percent has been set for gaining proportional representation in Congressional elections. Now small holdovers from the past can win seats in Congress only if they join together in coalition units. Hence a pattern of party contention and cooperation seems established: a few major party contenders, each leading its coalition of smaller groups.

The 2010s has proved to be the era of Ollanta Humala. As was noted above, as president he began with some small programs to help the poor, child care, and students, raised the minimum wage, and moderately increased taxes on mine profits. But later in 2011, after protests over a new mining project, Humala removed his leftist ministers (of his Peruvian National Party, PNP, and its support coalition, Gana Peru) from the cabinet, along with those of his ally PP (led by former president Toledo). They were replaced with technocrats and, in the security area, former military friends of Ollanta. Since then he has basically jettisoned both his party and most of its previous left-of-center themes, and governed from the center-right. Humala hoped to continue the record of prosperity and income gains of the preceding (Garcia) years.

Peru's comparatively rapid economic growth, based on exports of commodities with rising world prices during the 2000s and the early 2010s, has provided the government with the resources for supporting widely popular infrastructure projects. These include new roads in the poor Andean highlands, in turn enabling growth in both trade and agriculture there. But crime, corruption, and scandals continue to plague Peru. The mining tax money that has flowed into regional administrations may be attracting organized crime in some areas. And many suspect that connections remain between Humala's military people in security positions and the oppressive and discredited military-security people of the Fujimori era of the 1990s.

The downturn in mineral and other commodity prices from 2014 on has weakened growth and slowed new projects. Peruvian employment remains bifurcated, into the two-thirds in the informal sector (cash) economy with no benefit programs and protections, and the third in the formal sector with fairly rigid labor regulations. As prosperity has weakened in the mid-2010s, especially the informal sector workers will suffer declines.

Politically, Humala's position is increasingly weak. His job approval has dropped into the 20s, and the number of legislators in his Gana Peru coalition has dropped into the mid-30s (of 130 in Congress). Under Peru's semi-presidential arrangements, Humala has frequently had to replace his prime minister (who requires Congressional approval). Most importantly, the hollowing out of Humala's already personalistic party does not help with Peru's perennial challenge of strengthening its political parties. The twenty-five locally powerful regional presidents are predominantly independents. The now centrist APRA still possesses something of a national organization, and the center-right PPC and right-wing Fujimorists remain on the scene with prominent leaders willing to run for the presidency. But if Peru is to resurrect a pattern of coherent electoral contention between left-of-center and right-of-center parties and coalitions, it needs a more coherent left-of-center alternative for the space vacated by Humala's rightward shift. If an economic downturn coincides with pressures for major austerity, the public reaction may produce that alternative.

Peru's long history of periodic authoritarianism seems to be over. But the consequences of that history, in relatively weak party organization and unstable patterns of party contention, remain.

⌇ PRACTICE AND REVIEW ONLINE

CRITICAL THINKING QUESTIONS

1. When and how might a party's emphasis on its ideology contend with its role in representing certain interest groups? Under what circumstances might the two roles cooperate more harmoniously?

2. What types of political parties do not seem to fit clearly into either the broad or the focus categories? Into either the ideological or the interest-based focus categories? Why might this be so?

3. Which pattern of party decision making seems to be most effective in political contention: centralized or decentralized? Why? If your answer depends on the circumstances, what circumstances affect it?

4. Why do parties in authoritarian countries often fall short in performing the functions and playing the representative roles that parties in democracies do?

KEY TERMS

organizational density, 278
party branch, 278
party fraction, 279
clientelistic party, 279
policy-significant party, 285
broad party, 290
veto player, 290
personalistic party, 292
focus party, 292
ideological focus party, 292
interest-based focus party, 293

centralized decision making, 294
decentralized decision making, 294
party discipline, 295
primary election, 297
open list proportional representation, 300
government party, 303

FURTHER READING

Dalton, Russell J. *Citizen Politics: Public Opinion and Political Parties in Advanced Industrial Democracies*, 4th ed. Washington, DC: CQ Press, 2006.

Dalton, Russell J., and Martin P. Wattenberg, eds. *Parties Without Partisans: Political Change in Advanced Industrial Democracies*. Oxford: Oxford University Press, 2000.

Dalton, Russell J., David Farrell, and Ian McAllister. *Political Parties and Democratic Linkage: How Parties Organize Democracy*. Oxford: Oxford University Press, 2011.

Day, Alan J. *Political Parties of the World*, 5th ed. London: John Harper Publishing, 2002.

Diamond, Larry, and Richard Gunther, eds. *Political Parties and Democracy*. Baltimore and London: Johns Hopkins University Press, 2001.

Gunther, Richard, Jose Ramon-Montero, and Juan J. Linz, eds. *Political Parties: Old Concepts and New Challenges*. Oxford: Oxford University Press, 2002.

Lawson, Kay, ed. *How Political Parties Work: Perspectives from Within*. Westport, CT and London: Praeger, 1994.

Lewis, Paul G. *Political Parties in Post-Communist Eastern Europe*. London and New York: Routledge, 2000.

Mair, Peter, Wolfgang C. Muller, and Fritz Plasser, eds. *Political Parties and Electoral Change: Party Responses to Electoral Markets*. London, New Delhi, and Thousand Oaks, CA: Sage Publications, 2004.

Rommele, Andrea, David M. Farrell, and Piero Ignazi, eds. *Political Parties and Political Systems: the Concept of Linkage Revisited*. Westport, CT: Praeger Publishers, 2005.

Thomas, Clive S., ed. *Political Parties and Interest Groups: Shaping Democratic Governance*. Boulder, CO and London: Lynne Rienner, 2001.

Webb, Paul, David M. Farrell, and Ian Holliday, eds. *Political Parties in Advanced Industrial Democracies*. Oxford: Oxford University Press, 2002.

Yesilada, Birol A., ed. *Comparative Political Parties and Party Elites*. Ann Arbor, MI: University of Michigan Press, 1999.

NOTES

[1] See *Political Parties: Their Organization and Activity in the Modern State*, trans. Barbara and Robert North (London: Methuen; New York: Wiley, 1954).

[2] See Sigmund Neumann, "Toward a Comparative Study of Political Parties," in *Modern Political Parties; Approaches to Comparative Politics*, ed. Sigmund Neumann (Chicago: University of Chicago Press, 1956), 395–421

[3] For the work of some political scientists on directionality in voter policy preferences, see Chapter 11, note 7.

[4] See Dalton (1996) and Dalton and Wattenberg (2000).

[5] See Mark Blyth and Richard Katz, "From Catch-all politics to Cartelisation: the Political Economy of the Cartel Party," *West European Politics* 28, no. 1 (2005), 33–60.

[6] See Dalton, Farrell, and McAllister (2011).

[7] For steps in this analytical direction, see Herbert Kitschelt's discussions of the new "left-libertarian" tendencies versus the "new radical right"; *The Transformation of European Social Democracy* (Cambridge, UK: Cambridge University Press, 1994) and *The Radical Right in Western Europe: A Comparative Analysis* (Ann Arbor: University of Michagan Press, 1995).

[8] See Stefano Bartolini and Peter Mair, *Identity, Competition and Electoral Availability: the Stability of European Electorates 1885–1985* (Cambridge, UK: Cambridge University Press, 1990).

[9] See Peter Mair, *Party System Change* (Oxford, UK: Oxford University Press, 1997).

[10] In India, for example, there are many such regional interest-based parties, to the point that India has a multiparty system despite its SMDP electoral system.

[11] As we saw in chapter 4, when the continental European systems were extending the right to vote and forming their democracies, multiple contending groups wanted a voice and most smaller ones knew they would be excluded by the sort of two-party system that SMDP had produced in the United States and Britain.

[12] See Gary W. Cox, *Making Votes Count: Strategic Coordination in the World's Electoral Systems* (Cambridge, UK: Cambridge University Press, 1997).

[13] See Gabriel A. Almond and James S. Coleman, eds., *Politics of the Developing Areas* (Princeton, NJ: Princeton University Press, 1960).

[14] This aspect of mass parties played a large part in Sigmund Neumann's elaboration of the "mass integration" party type (note 2 above).

[15] In this early period in Europe, the party system could be complicated by a cross-cutting pattern between two major cleavages. For example, workers might be divided by the secular versus religious cleavage, so that a Social Democratic Party might focus on secular workers while a Catholic Social Party might go after the more religious workers.

[16] See Otto Kirchheimer, "The Transformation of the Western European Party System," in *Political Parties and Political Development*, ed. Joseph LaPalombara and Myron Weiner (Princeton, NJ: Princeton University Press, 1966), 177–200. Some of today's political scientists refer to these vague instrumental values as "valence issues."

[17] See chapter 9 regarding possible difficulties in bringing categoric interests into membership in associations to represent them.

[18] See Angelo Panebianco, *Political Parties: Organization and Power* (Cambridge, UK: Cambridge University Press, 1988).

[19] Because of exceptional circumstances surrounding the 2010 election, the resulting British parliamentary majority comprised a coalition between the broad Conservative Party and a small centrist party (the Liberal Democrats); see Country Case Studies, chapter 1.

[20] See Lorelei Moosbrugger, *The Vulnerability Thesis: Interest Group Influence and Institutional Design* (New Haven, CT: Yale University Press, 2012).

[21] See Octavio Amorim Neto and Gary C. Cox, "Electoral Institutions, Cleavage Structures, and the Number of Parties," *American Journal of Political Science* 41, no. 1 (1997): 149–74.

[22] *Governing* (Saddle River, NJ: Prentice-Hall, 2000).

[23] See note 1 above.

[24] See Moosbrugger (2012, note 20 above).

[25] See "Competing Principals, Political Institutions, and Party Unity in legislative voting," *American Journal of Political Science* 51, no. 1 (2007): 92–107.

[26] See "Presidentialism and the Party System" in *Presidentialism and Democracy in Latin America*, ed. Mainwaring and Shugart (New York: Cambridge University Press, 1997).

[27] See Herbert Kitschelt, Kirk A. Hawkins, Juan Pablo Luna, Guillermo Rosas, and Elizabeth J. Zechmeister, *Latin American Party Systems* (Cambridge, UK: Cambridge University Press, 2010); and Kitschelt and Steven I. Wilkinson, eds., "Citizen-politician Linkages: an Introduction" in Kitschelt and Wilkinson, *Patrons, Clients, and Policies, Patterns of Democratic Accountability and Political Competition* (New York: Cambridge University Press, 2007), 1–49

[28] The only exception to this was a period in the 1990s and early 2000s when legal limits on contributions could only be circumvented by giving "soft money" to parties, whose organizations then decided how to allocate the money to candidates (see chapter 9, "Contention and Cooperation in Focus").

[29] For this trend in Europe, see David M. Farrell and Paul Webb, "Political Parties as Campaign Organizations," in Dalton and Wattenberg, 2000, 102–28.

[30] See the discussion of these questions, and citation of particular sources, in Gallagher et al. 2005, 330–35.

[31] See Jerry Hough and Merle Fainsod, *How the Soviet Union is Governed* (Cambridge, MA: Harvard University Press, 1979).

[32] See chapters 12 and 13.

[33] For example, President Augusto Leguia of the 1920s and Generals Sanchez Cerro of the early 1930s and Oscar Benvenides of the middle and late 1930s.

Voting and Elections

FOCUS QUESTIONS

- **HOW** do voters think about contending alternatives when they are voting?

- **HOW** does the number of alternatives affect voting?

- **WHAT** considerations contend for attention in the minds of voters? How might they cooperate to support a particular choice?

- **HOW** does voters' identification with a political party affect voting?

- **HOW** do parties and candidates maneuver to gain votes?

- **WHAT** does it mean for voter choice to be meaningful?

IMAGINE THAT YOU WERE A FRENCH VOTER during the presidential and national assembly elections of April–June 2012. What issues would you have considered as you cast your vote? The presidential race was developing into a contest mainly between François Hollande, the leader of the moderate left-of-center Socialist Party (PS), and the incumbent, President Nicholas Sarkozy, leader of the conservative Union for a Popular Movement (UMP). But the leaders of the smaller ethnic ultranationalist National Front, the left social democratic Left Front, and the centrist Centre for France were also getting some attention. The personalities of leading candidates can be a factor, but neither Sarkozy nor Hollande stood out here.

The country's economic performance surely would play a role. Conditions in France were not favorable, with high unemployment and problems with the budget and economic growth. Especially during the last weeks of the campaign amid the widening European financial crisis, an important consideration was the directions that the candidates and their parties wanted the government to take regarding deficits, debt, and growth. Hollande supported stronger growth-stimulating policies, whereas Sarkozy and the UMP seemed to favor the Germany-backed path of austerity (see chapter 7).

In the election results, the candidates of all the above-noted parties won significant portions of the votes for the presidency and the assembly (except for a poor assembly showing for the Centre). But Hollande and his PS won by about 3 percent, and together with its smaller coalition allies won a clear majority in the National Assembly.

France is one of the two most important countries in the Eurozone (with Germany), and this election result seems undeniably significant. Why did the voters vote the way they did? That is a question that political scientists try to answer, and the one we shall consider here.

In elections in representative democracies, average citizens participate in the political process and influence government. They do so by choosing office-holders and holding them accountable for their past performance. Voters make their selections mainly from a range of contending individuals and political parties.

We begin this chapter with a brief look at the contending options facing the voter on election day. We then turn to the various motivations that can be at work as the ballot is cast. These, too, contend or cooperate with one another in voters' minds. Later in this chapter, we will take an overall look at how parties contend in elections, building on what we learned about parties in chapter 10. We will conclude with a discussion of how and when election outcomes allow for voter choice to be more or less meaningful.

ALTERNATIVES FOR VOTER CHOICE

Voters select from an array of contending alternative candidates and parties. What sorts of choices must the voters make on election day, and how many alternatives are before them as they choose? How does the array of options affect how voters perceive their choices in the voting booth?

The Number of Alternatives: The Electoral System Factor

One major feature of the democratic voting situation is the number of significant alternatives before voters. There may be very few important options for choice, or many. Since political parties usually nominate the candidates, the number of significant contending parties is an important factor determining the range of significant alternatives before the voters on election day. What makes a party important enough for its candidates to be significant alternatives for voter choice? An important factor here is whether or not a party may realistically have a hand in government policymaking. As we saw in Chapter 10, a policy-significant party may be defined as any political party whose legislators' votes might be needed to regularly pass policy proposals into law, either now or in the not-too-distant future.

Recall from earlier chapters that concerning the number of significant parties in a democracy, the main categories are two-party and multiparty. In a two-party system, only two large, policy-significant parties prevail and contend with one another. In a given legislative assembly, one or the other will hold the majority. Coalitions are unnecessary, and the other parties are too small to make a difference in policy outcomes. (Since such small parties may hold a few seats each, perhaps a more specific title for this pattern would be the "two prevailing party" system.)

Two-party systems tend to be present where the electoral system is SMDP (single-member district plurality), under which each district is small and sends only one representative to parliament: the candidate that got the most votes (see chapters 3 and 10). Again, here only large parties can be victorious in very many districts, so (a) voters tend to vote for one of them rather than "wasting their votes" on small parties, and (b) small groups—with virtually no chance of having their candidates come in first—tend to join with other groups, often the largest parties, to get bigger and have a chance of holding office.[1] As was noted in chapter 10, only where there are regional interest-based focus parties (or others with regionally concentrated support) that are big enough in their home bases of strength to win seats there, might we fail to see one or the other of the two biggest broad parties win a legislative majority in its own hands (see British Country Case Study, chapter 1).

Alternatively, in a multiparty situation a voter can choose from among several parties (say four, five, or more) that each have the potential, either now or in a plausible future, to be a necessary part of a majority coalition. As we saw in chapters 3, 4, and 10, multiparty systems normally occur with PR voting. Legislative seats are allocated to parties according to the share of the vote that each has won in large multimember districts (each district usually filling five seats or more), allowing small parties to win seats. Too many parties end up with seats for any one of them to have the majority by itself. So a coalition of two or more parties must form to make up a majority and be assured of passing legislation. Thus even small parties may be necessary parts of majority coalitions, giving voters several policy-significant alternatives on the ballot.[2]

Votes must be cast for a favored party or candidate, but the main impetus may be against another party or candidate. SMDP voting, with its two significant contending alternatives, may contribute to a substantial amount of **oppositional voting**. Under SMDP, if you strongly oppose a candidate or party, you have only one other significant choice. This situation encourages parties and candidates to engage in negative campaigning against their opponents, because they know that if their oppositional approach is persuasive, the voter has only one alternative, theirs. In contrast to SMDP, PR's multiparty elections tend to produce less oppositional voting. You may oppose a party strongly, but you still have a decision to make among several remaining significant alternatives. This reduces the incentives somewhat for parties to rely on negative campaigning, because it may not produce votes for them.

Voting for Candidate or Party: The Governmental Structure Factor

Another question to consider is: What types of alternatives do the voters see before them? They may view their choice in two contending ways, as either (a) picking individual candidates, or (b) selecting political parties, guided more by the candidates' party labels than by the individual names on the ballot. In the case of party-focused voting, I assume that the voter's preference can change from election to election according to the motivation and criteria at work at the time. Only in the special case of "party identification"—considering oneself a "member" of a party (see below)—does party voting remain fairly constant over successive elections.

Parliamentary candidate John Prescott campaigns in his district in Great Britain; there, voters tend to vote by party and pay less attention to the name of the candidate, whereas in the United States, more voters focus on the individual candidates.

Of course, emphasis on party or individual candidate depends partly on personal inclination. But other factors can also encourage one approach or the other. A major one is the type of governmental structure. We have already seen that under parliamentary government, the party or coalition holding the majority must vote cohesively (in a unified way) in favor of the policy proposals of its leaders in the cabinet to retain control of the executive branch. By the same token, opposition parties tend to vote cohesively against cabinet bills. Voters and officeholders alike expect each party's legislators to display party discipline. Consequently, it is the relative success of the contending *parties* in an election—reflected in their seat strengths in parliament—that indicates whose policy preferences will become law. Understanding this, voters tend to consider their vote as the choice of a party more than the choice of particular candidates for parliamentary seats. In fact, many pay little attention to the individual names on the ballot.

In contrast, recall that under presidential government, the chief executive stays in office for a set term, regardless of whether her or his policy proposals pass in the legislature (see chapters 1 and 10). Thus, the legislators of the president's party or coalition do not necessarily have to vote in a unified way in favor of the president's policy proposals. And opposition-party legislators don't have to vote cohesively against them. As a consequence, the voting records of individual candidates matter, and fewer voters who know much about the candidates will be guided solely by party.

Another variable, the electoral system, can also have some effect on whether voters focus on party or on individual candidates. SMDP, by definition, formally involves picking an individual candidate's name (though as we have seen, voters in parliamentary systems tend to pay more attention to the party label). In contrast, PR asks the voters to choose between party lists—slates of candidates organized on the ballot by party. That formal feature of PR voting, which can occur in presidential governmental systems as well as parliamentary ones, encourages voters to focus on the party as they cast their votes.

Voter Turnout and the Option of Not Voting

In addition to the alternatives in casting votes, a further option is not to vote at all. Some voters may not have enough positive or oppositional interest in the options to draw them to the polls.

Countries and elections can vary in their rates of **voter turnout**—the percentage of eligible voters who actually come out to vote on election day. For example, American voter turnout tends to be between 50 percent and 65 percent of registered voters in presidential election years, and less in the alternating Congress-only elections. In contrast, European turnouts typically range from 65 percent to 90 percent. The type of governmental structure may be a factor affecting such a difference. In parliamentary systems, more voters may believe that their votes will make a difference in government policy decisions. Another factor may be that continental Europe's multiparty frameworks offer more parties to choose from, improving the chance of matches between voter preferences and the alternatives.

Other practical differences in voting may also contribute. In Europe, elections usually occur on convenient weekend days, and there are few or no voter registration requirements to discourage voters. Some European nations even legally require citizens to vote (sometimes with nonvoters charged a small fine). In contrast, in the United States, elections occur on a work day during the week (Tuesday), and require cumbersome registration procedures for would-be voters.

In a single nation, turnout may rise and fall from election to election. Different election years may present sharper or fuzzier contrasts between the parties and candidates, making voter choice seem more or less meaningful (see below). Surrounding events can arouse controversy and draw larger numbers to the polls. In the United States in November 2008, for example, the combination of a historic candidacy of an African American Democratic candidate and an erupting financial crisis boosted turnout to 62 percent, a comparatively high level for the United States (see Country Case Studies below).

Notably, in a wide swath of established democracies, average voter turnout dropped by between 5 percent and 15 percent over the last half of the twentieth century. However, in the twenty-first century, turnout seems to have turned the corner and is rising in many nations.

In some countries, procedures allow a **referendum** item to be on the ballot that stimulates special interest and a higher voter turnout in a given election. A referendum is an example of direct rather than representative democracy; citizens vote directly on whether a policy proposal will become law. A referendum measure may be put on the ballot by a party's activists or officeholders to turn out more of its voters on election day, as in the case of a socioculturally conservative party getting an abortion-related or gay marriage referendum question included in an election. In a few countries allowing referenda, a measure can get on the ballot with no more than a certain number of signatures on a petition. (The required number of signatures may be easily gained with enough money to pay enough canvassers to go door to door getting signatures.) In some countries, this approach may be used to call a special election on whether to **recall**—remove from office—an officeholder.

Other factors affecting turnout have to do with portions of the electorate rather than with the surrounding framework or the events of the day. For example, suburban dwellers typically vote at higher rates than rural dwellers. (Perhaps the greater distance that rural people have to travel to get to a polling place makes a difference.) And research shows that more education, higher income, and age are each associated with a higher probability of voting. Less-educated, lower-income, and younger people may follow political events less regularly and intensively.

CRITERIA FOR VOTER CHOICE

Whether a citizen voted for individual candidates or their parties, or their motivation was positive or oppositional, a key question remains: why did the voter choose to vote the way (s)he did? Voters make their choices for a variety of reasons, but we can classify voter motivations under three general headings:

1. Affective voting: personal (gut-level) feelings about the alternatives.

2. Retrospective voting: a desire to hold leaders accountable for the impact of past policymaking on society.

3. Policy direction voting: preferences regarding what general directions government policies should take, such as toward (or away from) a value, an ideology, help for an interest group, or a particular policy on an issue (see below).

Very commonly, more than one of these six categories of voter motivation are at work in a given voter's choice at the polls. We should think of them more as components of voter choice, such that often two (or even three) of them work together to affect how a voter casts her or his ballot. But just as in chemistry we need to understand atoms before studying molecules, we shall look first at each in isolation before examining how they combine.

Affective Voting

Whether a voter focuses on an individual candidate or a party, the choice may follow largely from personal feelings about the alternatives. Political scientists don't agree on a general term to describe such voting as it applies to both individual candidate and party. Here, I borrow the term "affect" from social psychology in referring to gut-level motivation. **Affective voting** can be oppositional as well as positive; that is, one's vote can follow from gut-level feelings of disapproval toward a rival candidate or party, as well as a positive attraction to the chosen alternative.

Affective Voting for an Individual Candidate Political scientists do have a phrase for affective voting by individual candidate: **candidate orientation voting**. One form of such motivation lies in a shared social identity between voter and candidate. In South Africa, for example, a Zulu voter may choose the Zulu candidate based on ethnic identification that creates a comfort level with the candidate. Alternatively, voters may be attracted to something admirable that they perceive in the personal character or qualities of a candidate, apart from the candidate's favored policy directions. An American example is a 1950s' voter who agreed with the ad slogan, "I like Ike" (President Dwight Eisenhower, the former supreme commander of the allied forces in World War II). Another example is a 1960s' French voter who voted for Charles de Gaulle because the voter considered him to be "a great man." The voter may feel that a candidate is honest, displays strong leadership, or has shown integrity in sticking to campaign promises.

Alternatively, the voter may be drawn to a candidate as simply having an attractive personality—or charisma. For example, many Americans were drawn to the personal appeal of John F. Kennedy and his brother Robert in the 1960s, and of Ronald Reagan in the 1980s. Affective attachment to candidates can play a role in nominations by parties. In France in the 1970s, as the right-of-center coalition looked for a presidential candidate, it passed over the leaders of its largest party, the conservative Gaullists. Instead, the right-of-center coalition parties chose Guiscard d'Estaing, the head of the small Union for French Democracy (a vaguely classical liberal group of small parties), primarily because of his personal popularity in the nation. Indeed, he won the election on behalf of the conservative coalition.

Affective voting by individual candidate can also be primarily oppositional. Voters may perceive a candidate as dull, weak, indecisive, slick, untrustworthy, or arrogant. Voters with such perceptions tend to avoid voting for that candidate.

Affective support for a leader can be influenced by events and circumstances. For example, a crisis or emergency can produce a jump in the approval ratings of the chief executive. He or she may give a rousing speech showing determination to battle the challenge, causing people to rally around their chief's "leadership" in the crisis. Such support benefited British prime minister Margaret Thatcher following the invasion of the Falkland Islands by Argentine forces in 1982, and American president George W. Bush after the 9/11 terrorist attacks in the United States in 2001.

Affective Voting for a Party A voter may also choose to vote for a political party out of affective motivation. Childhood socialization at home can create a sense of personal connection with a particular party that lasts into adulthood. The result can be a comfort level with the party without thinking much about its record or policy direction preferences. Or the party may appear to represent a group with which a voter identifies. An example is identifying a party with one's religion or social class (common in early twentieth-century Europe), or with one's ethnicity or region, or both, as in India (see Country Case Studies below). Another factor in purely affective attachment can be associating a party with an instrumental value, such as competent economic management or forceful foreign policy, without reference to the particular policies and goals pursued by such management. (Such instrumental values can be closely linked to "retrospective voting" based on judgments of past success or failure while the party was in power; see below.)

An affective linkage to a party is a major contributing factor to what political scientists call "party identification." But most often, pure affect is not the only factor behind a person's party identification (see below). Note also that affective voting by party can be primarily oppositional. For example, a major corruption scandal may disillusion many voters with a party, as occurred in the early 1990s in Italy regarding the center-right Christian Democratic Party and the center-left Socialist Party, culminating in both parties' dissolution.

Retrospective Voting: How Have Things Been Going?

In another style of voting, the voter holds officeholders responsible for positive or negative outcomes in the country. If things seem to be going well, especially for the economy, some voters will vote positively for the incumbents; if things are going poorly, such voters will cast oppositional votes for the challengers. Political scientists tend to refer to this sort of voting as "retrospective," in the sense of "looking back." **Retrospective voting** assumes that the currently governing party is responsible for the present situation, usually without thinking much about *how* politicians' past policies may have caused a prosperous or weak economy, or a successful or unsuccessful war.[3]

For example, support levels for American president George W. Bush in the 2000s illustrate retrospective concerns. In the months and years after 9/11, further terrorist attacks on American soil failed to materialize. Many Americans credited the Bush administration with protecting them, probably contributing to Bush's reelection in 2004. After 2004, however, things didn't go well in other policy areas. By 2006, the American public perceived the intervention in Iraq to have gone poorly and to have been costly in both money and lives. American approval of the Republican administration's handling of the war went from the 50–60 percent range to 25–35 percent, and President Bush's overall job approval rating showed a similar drop. The Congressional elections of November 2006 reflected a degree of oppositional retrospective voting against the president's party, as many Republicans lost their seats to Democrats. And in 2008, the Republicans lost the presidency (and the Senate) to the Democrats, partially due to an economic crisis that was frightening many voters at the time.

Retrospective voting is often related to economic conditions at the time of the election, regarding what is happening to such indicators as the rates of unemployment, inflation, or economic growth (growth in "gross domestic product," or GDP). Where we see such "economic voting," it tends to affect the electoral support for the party of the chief executive, especially where external factors do not seem evident and one party seems responsible for economic policy[4]; attributing responsibility to individual parties in cases of coalition government is harder.[5]

To be sure, cross-national studies of economic voting have shown little dependence of electoral success on actual economic conditions at the time of voting.[6] One complication regarding retrospective voting is that it is affected by voters' *beliefs* about whether things are going well or poorly. But at times, objective and accurate answers to this question may be hard to come by among ordinary voters, and different perceptions may contend with one another. For example, during the American election campaign in the fall of 2012, were things going well because a depression had been avoided and the economy was gradually recovering, or were things going badly because the unemployment rate, the government budget deficit, and the American national debt all still seemed high? And even where the outcome and reasons for it are identifiable, often retrospective voters make errors regarding these things, blame or praise incumbents for outcomes beyond their control, and are affected by their own partisan sympathies.

Among the factors influencing this perception, the news media's presentation of events looms large. Does television news coverage present the situation hopefully and optimistically, or the opposite? And during election campaigns, the contending messages of the parties about the economy, for example, may fight for center stage. The amount of money spent on television advertising can be a major factor in what messages the voters see. If a party can dominate the "ad wars" and swing poll results in its direction, the news media reports of such poll results tend to further boost the bandwagon.

Policy Direction Voting

Finally, voter attitudes toward candidates and parties may result in **policy direction voting**: support for, or opposition to, directions that the candidates and parties would like government policy to take on important issues. As was noted in chapter 8, there is much reason to question whether many people cast votes based on the specific policy preferences that they hold, and how such preferences match up with parties' official policy positions (what political scientists call "proximity voting"). More often, however, average voters have at least vague notions about what general directions they want government policy to take, regarding issue areas that seem important to them. This notion extends the idea of **directional** voter and party preferences that was first introduced by political scientists George Rabinowitz, Stuart Elaine MacDonald, and Ola Listhaug, more than two decades ago.[7] They focused on preferences in the direction of (or away from) particular policies to address issues; here I expand the scope of the directional concept to include other sorts of policy direction, as well. At least four major types of policy direction contend for the voter's attention and support:

- toward a value, such as some particular form of well-being or freedom (see chapters 1 and 3),
- toward an ideological orientation,
- toward helping an interest group that the voter supports, or
- toward a particular policy to deal with an issue.

As we shall see below, I am not suggesting that the majority of policy direction voters fall into only one or another of these categories. We tend to see combinations of two or more of them in voting decisions. But again, like someone beginning the study of chemistry, we need an acquaintance with the elements before we get to the compounds and how they interact and combine with one another.

Value-Related Voting In voting for a candidate or party due to policy direction preference, one possible focus is the candidate's or party's perceived commitment to pursue one or more values. (For an ancient Greek view of this factor, see "The Philosophical Connection.") Some voters may know little of the policy approaches that are contending in a campaign, but are attracted to candidates or parties based on the values that they espouse. For example, a voter may want government policy to move in the direction of some form of national well-being, such as relieving economic insecurity, strengthening national security against foreign threats, or bolstering the traditional family. Candidate and party appeals to such values are often related to their ideological orientations (e.g., moderate left-of-center parties tend to support social justice), but value appeals can sometimes stand on their own in ways that may resonate with voters.

Ideological Direction Voting Voters may also cast their ballots along ideological lines. A voter may want government policy to move more in the direction of a particular ideology, such as classical liberal or moderate left of center, or a broader ideological direction, such as right of center or left of center. Multiparty systems with PR voting tend to present more ideological options, whereas two-party SMDP settings tend to present just a broad moderate left-of-center party contending with a broad right-of-center party.

In multiparty frameworks, the choice between two broad ideological directions comes into play in how parties contend and cooperate in coalitions. For example, commonly a left-of-center coalition contends with a right-of-center one. Because many voters know of the probable coalition alignments, their support for a party may also express indirect support for its coalition and its broad ideological direction.[8]

THE PHILOSOPHICAL CONNECTION | Aristotle on Elections

In the fourth century BCE, the Greek philosopher Aristotle (see chapter 5) wrote about values and voting. For him, a state might pursue one of three key values: individual freedom, wealth/property, and personal moral goodness. For Aristotle, the democratic form of government holds freedom as its key value. The logic of democracy was that since all citizens were equal in being free (not slaves), everyone should have an equal chance to serve in government. Ancient Greece practiced direct democracy. Policymaking was done by the whole citizenry—in practice, whoever came to the public square on the day for making a decision. The few government officials were not elected; instead, their names were drawn "by lot." In practice, Aristotle argued, direct democracy was one of the bad forms of government in that it usually pursued the self-interest of the ruling group—in this case, the poor majority—rather than the common good.

For Aristotle, a government with property or wealth as its key underlying value was an oligarchy. Oligarchy, too, was a bad form of government because its ruling group—here, the wealthy—governed in its own self-interest. Oligarchy set a minimum property requirement for holding political rights. The oligarchic way of filling government offices was by voting in elections. In practice, election winners tended to be those with enough property and wealth to have time for public service, and financially secure "gentlemen" were assumed to be less tempted to engage in financial wrongdoing than the poor.

To Aristotle, the third main value was another interpretation of well-being: personal moral goodness. For him, this was the focus of the aristocracy, or rule by the few for the common good. Participation in the perfect aristocracy included only those who fully possessed moral goodness (including wisdom) and had the material means to provide the leisure for the "good life." Perfect aristocracy's main governmental job was educating the citizenry to goodness. The problem with this form for Aristotle was that it was a perfectionist extreme. That all citizens would be fully moral and wise was too much to expect of the real world (much as it is implausible, in Aristotle's view, for the mind of a king never to be overcome by passion).

For Aristotle, the most practical acceptable regime was something else: a mixture of oligarchy and democracy. He called this mixture *polity*, the rule of the many in the common interest. In its choice of officeholders, polity employed oligarchy's method of election. From democracy came the practice of allowing all citizens to vote. Aristotle suggested that the different contributions of "the many" to decision making could add up to a richer sum of good judgment than could anyone or a few alone. Thus, the many—including the best alongside everyone else—was qualified to appoint government officials and judge them at the end of their term of office. Here we have an idealized articulation of our own idea of representative democracy.

Aristotle also mentioned certain types of personal goodness in connection with polity. He stressed that stable polities had a large middle class with attitudes that involved certain forms of justice: fairness, impartiality, and law-abidingness. Most important for polity, however, was a point that he also made about less-than-perfect forms of aristocracy: those that fall short of full-scale, ideal aristocracy but are achievable in the real world. If a regime respects all three values—freedom, property, and personal goodness—and employs personal goodness among its criteria for electing officeholders, it could be equally described as both a lesser aristocracy and a polity. Thus, for common real-world circumstances, Aristotle favored a polity with a strong middle class that votes for candidates with personal goodness in mind.

How many voters are ideologically consistent across a range of issue areas and look for candidates and parties to match their views? Certainly the parties' candidates tend to represent their party's ideological identity on the left-right scale, as has been stressed by political scientists Herbert Kitschelt, Michael Laver, and others.[9] Only exceptionally do we see party leaderships depart from ideological consistency, as in the case of moderate left-of-center party leaders accepting harsh austerity in southern Europe—and losing many of their traditional voters in the process. (This case seemed to be an example of parties' earlier commitments to pro-Europe rules that had unforeseen consequences later, when applied under the very different circumstances of the five-year European economic slump and debt crisis of 2009–2014.)

Regarding voters, in a study of Europe in the 1990s, political scientists Herman Schmitt and Jacques Thomassen found a strong degree of fit between party candidates' ideologically connected positions and those of their voters on a range of perennially important issues.[10] But this is not true for all issues. For example, many voters were less enthusiastic on closer European integration (e.g., easy migration and the Euro) than were the candidates of the parties they voted for.

As was noted in chapter 6, the reality appears to be a continuum, from voters who are fairly consistent ideologically across issue areas and party choice, through a larger number who lean in some ideological direction in most issue areas but not all, to others who are fairly nonideological.

Voting to Support an Interest Group Another sort of policy direction is toward promoting the interests of one or more groups in society. Many people are most interested in (and knowledgeable about) policy issues that affect groups that they are part of. As we saw at the beginning of chapter 9, an important role for interest groups in politics stems from the tendency of many voters to look for a match between the preferences of a party or candidate and the concerns of one or more important groups with which the voter identifies. And chapter 10 noted that one of the main representative roles of political parties is representation of groups. Consequently, "voter groups" that comprise substantial categories of people are especially important in elections.

One important category of such groups is broad economic strata (upper, middle, and lower income levels). Recall from chapter 10, for example, that middle and lower economic strata tend to support moderate left-of-center parties, while more people associated with business and wealth tend to lean toward conservative or classical liberal parties. To be sure, the last third of the twentieth century saw a gradual decline in voting according to economic stratum. Many people were becoming interested in new, less economic "post-materialist" concerns, such as women's rights, the environment, peace, lifestyle, minority rights, and local democracy (see chapter 8). However, under the impact of today's globalization, economic stress, and increased budgetary pressures, the concerns of economic strata may again be rising on the public agenda and affecting voting more.

Ethnic or racial groups can also be prominent. In France, for example, people of West African ancestry are a distinct group, as are those of North African Arab ancestry, alert to the representation of their interests as they vote in French elections. In the United States, African Americans and Hispanics are important voter categories who lean toward the moderate left-of-center Democratic Party.

Gender can play a role, too. Recent American elections have displayed a "gender gap," a pattern of more women voting Democratic and men tending to vote Republican. Similarly, the urban and rural sectors, regional differences, and religion can affect voting. And smaller interest groups such as particular occupational categories can also be important. We need to remember, though, that these sorts of differences emerge more as mild statistical tendencies rather than solid blocs voting for one party or another. Interest group support is, after all, only one of the types of policy direction voting.

Interest group-oriented voting is roughly in line with the pluralist model of influence distribution. Recall from chapter 2 that this model places interest groups and their contention and bargaining at the center of policymaking (see "Applying the Models"). Those who vote based on their group interests may find more opportunities to do so under presidential than parliamentary frameworks. With less pressure on lawmakers for party cohesion, each officeholder may be more open to the appeals of interest groups in making decisions.

Voting to Support Particular Policies Some voters may want the government to move in the direction of a particular policy to solve a problem or achieve a goal. For example, an American voter concerned about the abortion issue may support a candidate or party who favors restricting abortion. Similarly, a European voter concerned about climate change will favor a party pushing for more restrictions on carbon burning.

The purest form of this sort of policy direction voting is the rational and public-spirited citizen who identifies the policy issues that are most important to him or her and asks what specific policy will best secure the common good on that issue. The voter would examine each issue on a case-by-case basis, without attachment to any one value, ideology, or interest group. But such citizens usually represent only a small minority. More commonly, in any given election campaign, some voters focus especially on one or a few prominent issues, and the candidates' or parties' favored directions that policy should take on those issues.[11]

For votes that are cast with a policy focus, a common style is oppositional. Here the policy direction that the voter favors is *away from* a policy. A voter who lacks a clear solution for an issue may still oppose a certain policy that seems to the voter to be failing. As we have discussed, many Americans who had supported the invasion of Iraq in 2003 concluded by 2006 that its aims could not be achieved and its costs were too high. Many Democrats won office pledging to move government policy toward departure from Iraq.

Combining the Factors

Typically, multiple factors contribute to a given political decision (see chapter 2). Voting is no exception. Two or three factors can cooperate to produce a preference for one alternative over another.

Common Patterns of Factor Cooperation For example, two commonly interwoven motivations are retrospective voting and value-oriented policy direction voting. When voters seek to oust a party that presides over a weak economy, their retrospective vote also rests implicitly on a value—overall prosperity (an economic interpretation of well-being)—as well as an empirical judgment that the economy is doing poorly. Another common link is between support for a particular policy and support for the value it pursues. An opponent of a war policy may also generally support international peace. In addition, values often link with ideological preference. For example, conservative ideology includes support for well-being in the form of national security against military attack. Yet another common association is that between support for an interest group and support for a policy favoring that group. For example, organized labor in the

APPLYING THE MODELS | Voting

Voting can reflect the various models of the distribution of influence: majority preference, elite, pluralist, and personal leadership. In the majority preference model, the political process translates the policy preferences of the citizen majority into government policy. In this picture, the voters' issue preferences are primary in how they vote, as they match them with those of candidates and parties. The candidates who most effectively express the majority's policy views and receive broad press coverage will win. This model seems relevant if we refer to the voters' preferred policy *directions* (because most voters do not seem to have clear and strong views on specific policies), and if we see the voters as picking a legislative majority of some sort—either between parties in a two-party system or between coalitions in a multiparty system.

The elite model seems to fit less well with voting and elections. Those supporting the elite model might stress the limited range of alternative candidates on the ballot, and suggest that this selection of nominees leaves room for limit-setting influence:

- by officials of the political parties over their own nominations,
- by the willingness of campaign donors to give enough money for a campaign to be viable, and/or
- by the willingness of media to give accurate and fair attention to candidates.

Elite-model supporters may also suggest that in the final electoral competition, voter perceptions may be constrained if one side has much more money available to buy campaign advertising. At worst, a financial elite group favoring one side can flood the media and drown out the other side's message (perhaps by driving up the advertising rates to the point of unaffordability for the less advantaged candidate).

The milder elite-model view by Joseph Schumpeter (see chapter 2) presents contending party organizations themselves as would-be elites pursuing majority support. It integrates the elite perspective with a mild form of the majority preference model. Schumpeter saw many voters as voting retrospectively, primarily based on how things have been going for the country or their district. If things are going well, voters tend to support the current leadership; if not, they vote in the opposing party-elite. In Schumpeter's perspective, voters leave policymaking to an elite, but it is an elite they choose in competitive elections.

In the personal leadership model, the voter supports a candidate or party because the voter likes the candidate or party leader. In a way, the voter adopts the candidate or party leader(s) as his or her leader(s).

The pluralist model does not see voting as reflecting either a majority preference or the sway of an elite (or elites). Here voters pay attention to whether parties and candidates are generally favorable or unfavorable toward particular interest groups that they identify with or otherwise support. Does the candidate or party have one's interests at heart as, for example, a working person, a member of a racial or ethnic minority, or a southerner? In particular, significant voter groups in a district or nation may have limit-setting influence; alienating one or more of them may doom a candidate's chances.

It is possible to suggest a combination of two models—for example, the personal leadership model and the majority preference. We may consider democracy as needing attractive leaders to present policy alternatives to voters in search of majority support. However, this combination can yield an unpleasant result. Consider the charismatic demagogue who whips up and manipulates popular passions by oversimplifying emotional issues. Alternatively, the combination of personal leadership with majority preference factors can have positive results. A candidate may have her own view of the public interest on a tough issue and try to persuade voters to reject a shortsighted or irrational view. In a more pessimistic picture, one may combine the elite with the pluralist models. Multiple interest groups contend, but those with the strongest financial backing are able to give their favored candidates and parties the advantage in campaigning.

Think about a recent national election. Which model (or models) of influence distribution seems to best explain the outcome? What do you think about this situation?

In the United States, a campaign worker handing a partisan voter guide card to a voter on the way into a polling place on election day.

United States supported government aid to the ailing American auto industry during the post-2008 downturn.

Another example combines affective support for a candidate with support for one or more policy directions. Consider the example of a candidate-oriented American voter who favored Robert Kennedy for president in 1968. Kennedy declared himself a candidate late in the nominating process but immediately became a leading contender for the Democratic Party nomination. His perceived charisma helped him. However, so did his most prominent policy direction preferences. These included concern for social justice (a value) aimed especially at ethnic-racial minorities (interest groups), and his newly declared opposition to a specific policy, the war in Vietnam.

Party Identification An important example of cooperation of multiple factors is **party identification**—considering oneself a member of a party, and thus voting regularly for that party over time.

As we noted above, one factor that is fairly consistently in the mix for party identification is affective attachment to a party. But the affective factor often appears alongside other reinforcing factors. A common combination is affective attachment cooperating with interest group identification. Broad interests and the political cleavages that define some of them (see chapter 4) can affect a voter's party choice. We have already noted that in the first half of the twentieth century in Europe, for example, political cleavages along religious, class, and sometimes regional lines heavily structured party identification. Even today, a German worker may vote habitually for candidates of the Social Democratic Party as "the party of the workingman," not only because of gut-level identification but in association with appreciation for worker-supporting policies in the past and future. Or a French businessman may vote consistently for the Republican Party (until recently called the "Union for a Popular Movement"), the main French conservative party, out of both affective attachment and a belief that the party will promote his business interests.

Other policy direction factors can also play roles in party identification. One is ideology. A voter may start out with an ethnic ultranationalist ideological viewpoint, and come to identify over time with a particular party as the best long-term representative of that ideological policy direction. Retrospective voting can play a role, too, as pointed out by political scientist Morris Fiorina.[12] For example, a mid-twentieth-century Mexican farmer may have felt grateful to the Institutional Revolutionary Party because of a policy that it had pursued in the past: the 1930s' land reform program that provided his family's forbears with land (see Country Case Studies, chapter 9). Such an example can be multifaceted: an (a) affective tie entwined with (b) positive retrospective voting related to (c) an outcome for an interest group.

Survey research over the last quarter century shows a decline in party identification related to social class and religion in the established democracies. As Figure 11.1 shows for nine European nations, however, the really significant declines between 1976 and 1992 seem to have occurred among the weaker party supporters ("sympathizers," but not members), dropping from over 40 percent in 1976 to just under 30 percent in 1992. The numbers without any party identification correspondingly increased from 30 percent to 40 percent. The data for those who were "fairly" or "very" involved in politics, however, showed only slight declines.

What might explain this? In many countries during the 1970s and 1980s, successive governmental leaderships of contending parties failed to solve difficult and persistent economic problems (see chapter 7). Perhaps many of those weaker party identifiers whose attachments were linked to policy direction preferences lost their party leanings due to these negative retrospective factors. In any case, party identification remained

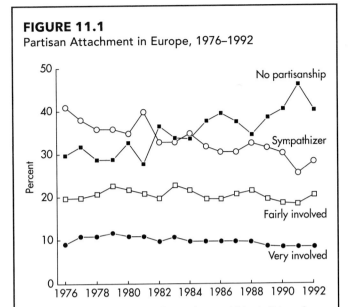

FIGURE 11.1
Partisan Attachment in Europe, 1976–1992

Source: Adapted from Russell J. Dalton and Martin Wattenberg, eds., *Parties Without Partisans: Political Change in Advanced Industrial Democracies* (Oxford: Oxford University Press, 2000), 27; data are from 1972–96 Eurobarometer cumulative file.

remarkably stable among those who were most involved in politics. During such trying times for policymakers, voters do not seem to have become generally disconnected from parties, as suggested by political scientists Mark Blyth and Richard Katz.[13] Rather, as Herbert Kitschelt argues, for some voters party identification seems at times subject to shift in response to new issues and consequent party strategy adjustments,[14] usually within the overall left-of-center and right-of-center coalitions.[15]

Sometimes expected patterns of party identification do not occur, given cross-cutting lines of intergroup division. In developing nations, many of the poor live in rural areas, have little education, find themselves in patron-client dependencies on landowners, and are heavily influenced by a traditional religion. Thus, rather than favoring left-of-center parties, they might back a conservative party with traditionalist sociocultural views. And new democracies emerging in developing nations can experience volatility among voters and parties as they try to connect with one another, as political scientists Scott Mainwaring and Timothoy Scully have pointed out regarding Latin America.[16]

A category that is relevant to party identification is the **independent voter**. This is a voter who not only fails to identify as a member of a party, but also does not regularly lean toward support for one party or another as a voter. Another voter category is the **independent leaner**, who inclines to support a party but does not identify with it as a member. Most political scientists who study election-related attitudes see independent voting, party leaning, and party identification as subject to change over time, rather than frozen. Even over the final weeks of a single election campaign, polling can show momentum in a party's direction increasing the numbers of its identifiers and leaners, and reducing the number of "independents." Accordingly, the independent or "swing" voter gets a lot of attention from both contending parties and political analysts.

Especially in studies of two-party systems, the availability of the independent voter has been presented as driving contending parties toward convergence in the moderate middle in policy proposing. However, true independents often have little interest or knowledge regarding politics and policy, and many other independents, when pressed by pollsters, turn out to be party leaners rather than true independents. The importance of the independent voter remains open to debate.

CAMPAIGNS AND ELECTIONS

Now we turn from the voters to a focus on how candidates and parties contend for votes. As they campaign, parties and candidates take advantage of opportunities, offered by the circumstances, to influence voter motivations.

Party Self-Definition

At times, a major factor in elections is parties redefining themselves and their images to face new electoral circumstances. For example, in the early 1990s in Italy, a scandal that caused the collapse of major center-leaning parties led to the creation of two new broad parties: (a) the conservative Party of Liberty, led by media magnate Silvio Berlusconi, and (b) the Democratic Party, with the merging of several left-leaning groups. In the late 1990s and 2000s, the Workers' Party of Brazil shed its former left social democratic ideology and in effect became a moderate left-of-center party with wide electoral appeal, though it included substantial ideological diversity (see Country Case Studies, chapter 4).

In multiparty countries with PR, some parties may have to adjust their appeals to voters because the parties must cooperate with other parties in coalitions. Numerous European countries have enduring left-of-center coalitions among the moderate left-of-center, left social democratic, and green parties. Right-of-center coalitions form among conservative and classical liberal parties, perhaps joined by a moderate ethnic ultranationalist party. More extreme parties may have to moderate their policy positions, and moderate and center-leaning parties must sometimes sharpen their policy differences with the opposing coalition.

A third aspect of party self-definition concerns the timing of the electoral cycle, especially for broad parties. At party nominating conferences early in campaigns, large parties tend to emphasize their ideological identities to their "base" of strong identifiers. But as election day approaches, their positions often move toward the center to attract "swing voters" and relatively pragmatic interest groups. In addition, events during the campaign may raise issues that force parties to refine their policy stances. In Latin America in the 2000s, voters increasingly perceived free-market ("neoliberal") policies and globalization as having failed to produce benefits for the middle and lower classes. As a result, moderate left-of-center parties won elections by sharpening their differences with free-market opponents. They advocated more government spending to help the poor and resist globalization, while continuing to favor keeping budget deficits under control.

Parties may respond to unusual circumstances with departures from one or two facets of their normal ideological orientations. Recall from chapter 10 that in the mid-2000s Germany faced unemployment and deficit problems; the Social Democratic Party agreed with the Christian Democrats in support of reductions in long-term unemployment benefits and in some labor market regulations. And when the financial crisis hit Europe in 2008–2009, some conservative parties in power shifted to favoring government intervention to bolster the banks and stimulate consumer spending. They were then rewarded with success at the polls by voters grateful for their flexibility.

Parties' capacity to redefine their policy directions in response to events is enhanced by today's mass media-oriented campaigning. In the early twentieth century when campaigning relied primarily on local activists mobilizing traditional support groups on the ground with face-to-face appeals, quick party responses to new issues were hard to manage. Today, however, advertising and news coverage in the broadcast and electronic media allow candidates and party leaders to quickly shift gears to emphasize a new issue or take a new stand on an older one. They can thus not only reach voters fast with something new, but also quickly communicate the adjustment to their local supporters. To be sure, responses using the mass media can be glib, opportunistic, and even manipulative. But they can also be serious responses to voters' desires for action on pressing new issues.

Electoral Realignment

Certain elections and policy-related developments, or a series of them alongside a changing electorate, can yield longer-term change in patterns of party support. Political scientists call such a change a **realignment**. A traditional twentieth-century view of European party-group relationships was the "freezing hypothesis": European party systems appeared locked into patterns based on ethnic, religious, and regional cleavages that lasted from the 1920s through mid-century.[17] However, changes in group-party alignment do sometimes occur, based on parties' campaigning choices as well as changes among groups in society.[18] When the Great Depression hit the United States in the early 1930s, the Democratic Party became a moderate left-of-center one by proposing a range of government actions on the economy that were unprecedented in American history. Groups suffering from the depression such as farmers, labor, and minorities lined up substantially with the Democrats.

Sometimes more gradual developments provide opportunities for contending parties to lead realignments. In the 1960s, America's Democratic Party, in line with its ideology and its history of representing the interests of disadvantaged minorities, pursued civil rights for African Americans. This weakened the party's traditional support among Southern whites. The election campaigns of 1968–1994 saw the Republican Party strike hard to win white southerners away from their traditional Democratic allegiance. During the same period, new activism arose among Protestant religious fundamentalists in the West and Midwest, allowing the Republicans to draw many farmers and small-town voters into the conservative Republican fold.

The Role of Personal Leadership in Election Campaigns

Personal leadership has often been a major factor in party breakthroughs and realignments. Democratic president Franklin Roosevelt's charisma in his radio "fireside chats" contributed to the above-mentioned party realignment that the 1936 landslide election confirmed. In recent decades, parties seem to have placed even more emphasis on the name and face of their leader during election campaigns. Wherever possible they turn to leaders with widespread name recognition and personal appeal. For example, in the early 2000s the Peruvian APRA Party turned to its widely known past leader Alan Garcia to spearhead its comeback efforts as a centrist party (see Country Case Study on Peru in chapter 10), despite Garcia's past association with the now unpopular left social democratic policies of the 1980s.

Presidential systems of government forefront the names of the would-be chief executives of contending parties in elections and provide an individual to hold responsible for a government's policies and performance. Today, however, even parties in parliamentary systems highlight their party leader in campaigning. As long as it stops short of catchall personalism, this approach can provide an advantage in political contention. If a party's policy directions fail, it may be able to limit the negative fallout by switching leaders. This option is a strength of semi-presidential governmental systems, as we shall see in chapter 13.

Party Identification and District Design

In some systems, legislative district boundaries are periodically redrawn in a process called **reapportionment**, which adjusts representation to changing population distribution. Party reapportionment strategies can affect elections and thus become a factor in electoral contention. For example, in the case of districts in the American House of Representatives, reapportionment occurs at the regional (state) level every ten years, following the U.S. Census. The stronger party in the state government can then redraw the state's Congressional district boundaries in ways that maximize the number of seats that it can win. In an area where opposition-supporting voter groups are fairly strong, they may be redistributed to multiple districts, just thinly enough that the opponent will lose many seats by moderate margins (say, by 53–47 percent). Where the opposing party's support is too heavy to be effectively divided this way, it can be concentrated in just one or two districts that the opponent will win by huge margins (say 90–10), yielding very few seat victories. The result is that the opposing party can have the majority of voting support overall but win very few seats despite its large numbers of voting supporters. In the state of Pennsylvania in 2012, where the Republicans controlled the state legislature and drew the boundaries for the state's districts for national House of Representatives elections, Democrats won a majority of the overall Congressional vote but only a third of the state's seats in the House of Representatives.

In some nations where districts are not periodically adjusted, migrations of people over time have led to imbalances in district populations. Districts with declining populations may end up overrepresented, with the same representation as those with far greater populations. An example is the overrepresentation of conservative rural voters that exists in some Latin American and African countries, as district boundaries have remained largely unchanged despite decades of migration from rural areas to big cities. Supporters of city-based parties may find themselves underrepresented by being confined to a few urban districts with large populations.

Thus party and candidate self-definition and electoral system features also contribute to voter choice and election outcomes, alongside the types of voter motivation discussed earlier in this chapter (see Figure 11.2).

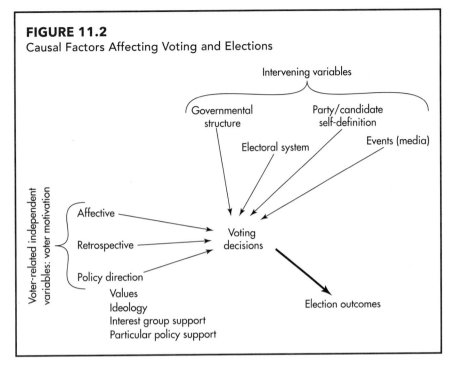

FIGURE 11.2
Causal Factors Affecting Voting and Elections

CHALLENGES TO MEANINGFUL VOTER CHOICE

Elections allow voters to try to influence politics and policymaking. In that effort, however, voters sometimes contend (or cooperate) with other causal factors such as elites, new issues that come along after the election, and money.

Some commentators favor what can be called "deepening" democracy, in search of a closer link between (a) citizens' concerns and (b) governmental policymaking and its outcomes. As we have seen, however, voters have diverse motivations. And most voters lack clear knowledge or preferences on very many policy issues. At most, we can say that many voters, in one or a few policy areas that are important to them, would like policy to move in general directions that they favor. The most realistic goal that we can hope for may be **meaningful voter choice**: voting whose results make a difference to subsequent policymaking in directions favored by voters who supported the most successful candidates and parties. But how much of a difference, and how? As with many other concepts related to politics, meaningful voter choice involves a continuum between extremes, rather than a clear-cut classification.

Difficulties arise in connecting voter intentions to election outcomes and desired policy directions. As we have seen in this chapter, voter choice can be motivated by affective attachment, retrospective concerns, policy direction concerns of various sorts, or some combination of these types of motivation. The voter hopes that if her or his favored candidate(s) or party wins, more effective policymaking will result. What factors affect the degree to which voter choice will be meaningful in this way?

Procedures

We should immediately note a factor that is often taken for granted: the need for the largest number of votes to in fact determine the winner. Rigging of the vote count, or intervention by an institution such as the military or a court to declare a winner at the expense of the vote count, is generally a mark of semi-democratic

CONTENTION AND COOPERATION IN FOCUS | The Electoral College System in the United States

In the American two-party presidential system, the election of the president is filtered through the Electoral College system. Voters in each state cast their votes for a slate of "electors" pledged to support their favored presidential candidate. (Normally, the plurality-winning slate will later attend a purely ceremonial meeting to cast all of the state's electoral votes for the candidate who won the state.) The Electoral College (EC) votes are allocated to states based largely on population—the state's number of House seats, plus two for each Senate seat. The elected president must have won the majority of these EC votes overall. This system, which evolved from EC provisions in the American constitution, is one which the contending parties and voters cooperate in observing.

The EC winner usually has also won the majority of the national popular vote. But the electoral vote victor—the new president—may fail to gain a majority of the national popular vote. In 1992, Democrat Bill Clinton won a clear majority of the Electoral College votes, and hence the presidency. However, his popular vote plurality fell short of a majority. It is even possible for the EC victor to fail to gain the national *plurality* of the popular vote (more votes than any other candidate). This occurred in the 2000 election. Democrat Al Gore won the national plurality by a few hundred thousand votes but lost to George W. Bush in the electoral vote total.

This occurred under unusual circumstances. One populous state, Florida, tipped the electoral vote balance in Bush's favor. In the official Florida vote tally, Bush had a tiny plurality of a few hundred votes out of millions. One key factor in this outcome was that to the left of center ideologically, some left social democrats chose to contend rather than cooperate with the moderate left-of-center Democrats by supporting a third-party presidential

campaign by the well-known consumer advocate Ralph Nader. Nader ran and took tens of thousands of votes in Florida that would no doubt have otherwise gone to Gore.

In addition, irregularities appear to have prevented many members of core Democratic-supporting groups from voting or having their votes counted as they intended. Such irregularities included the false voter instructions published in the heavily African American city of Jacksonville, the misleading "butterfly ballot" in heavily Jewish Palm Beach County, false disqualifications of many African American voters who came to the polls, and technical problems with the physical voting process that left some votes unrecorded. In the weeks after the election, lawyers for the Democrats contended sharply in state courts for pursuing potential remedies for these problems, while Republican lawyers argued for sticking to the original official vote tally with its Republican victory.

Eventually a hand recount of the votes was mandated by the Florida Supreme Court to try to deal with some of these problems and get at voters' intent. But the U.S. Supreme Court intervened to stop the recount, and declared the earlier official tally to be final, resulting in a Bush victory. If the Florida irregularities could have magically been addressed and corrected, the Florida popular vote result may have basically replicated the national one—a narrow victory by Gore. Thus, the electoral vote outcome would have coincided with, rather than contended with, the national popular vote result. Gore, not Bush, would have become president. Notably, under the American Electoral College system for presidential elections, special difficulties or irregularities in just one important state such as Florida or Ohio can determine the overall outcome. This may contribute to subsequent political distrust and contention.

or authoritarian systems rather than established democracies. And among democratic systems, complicated ways of getting from vote counts to winners, such as the American **Electoral College** system, can sometimes reduce voters' sense of meaningful choice (see "Contention and Cooperation in Focus").

A given procedural approach may have both advantages and disadvantages. For example, two-stage SMDM elections such as those for the presidency in

France and Latin American nations can enhance the sense that the final winner has majority voter support. In the first phase in these multiparty systems, voters choose among several presidential candidates. But the ultimate winner is determined by a second **runoff election** between the top two vote-getters from the first round, inevitably giving the victor a majority of the votes. Nevertheless, voters whose first-round favorites did not qualify for the second round must ultimately pick between alternatives that they did not support. This lesser-evil choice can affect government's policy directions, but perhaps less meaningfully than a purely positive choice.

Governmental Structure

A nation's particular type of democratic governmental structure affects voting and elections. Might either presidential or parliamentary government have advantages with regard to meaningful voter choice?

Presidential Government Ultimately it is individual people who directly make policy decisions in government. Since more voters in presidential systems tend to pay attention to the individual candidates, presidential government may have an advantage for meaningful voter choice. Officeholders in presidential systems can act more independently of their party, so the personal records of individual candidates may matter to voters.

However, this candidate focus is subject to two limitations, one coming before election day and the other coming after. The preelection question is: How can voters tell what candidates will do in office? The media and voters often do not do much to critically examine what candidates say about what they and their opponents have done and will do. Campaign advertising and rhetoric fill this vacuum to some extent, but they may misrepresent or conceal the actual records of candidates. Critics argue that often the candidate supported by the most money, and thus the most media coverage, may determine much of what voters think.

Moreover, even if the voters have accurate information about what the candidates will do in office, the reality of decision making after election day can be another factor limiting meaningfulness of voter choice. We have seen that presidential government encourages the independence of individual officeholders from their party. And there are multiple decision points at which policy proposals may be blocked. Consequently, the victory of a voter's favored candidate(s) or party may not guarantee what policy decisions will be made by the government after an election. Contention and bargaining among individual officeholders must occur to pass legislation, and the voters cannot foresee the future course of such interactions.

Parliamentary Government In contrast, a parliamentary government is essentially party government. As we have seen, voters don't pay much attention to individual candidates because what counts are the resulting strengths of the contending parties in parliament. Normally, the parliamentary majority can pass the bills of its leadership in the cabinet at will. This adds to the meaningfulness of retrospective voting, because such voters can observe the results and hold the majority party or parties responsible in the next election. Policy direction voters can review the past record of each significant party, and can observe whether a parliamentary majority's postelection policies match its campaign promises. The main risk from campaigning is parties' exaggerated claims of national gains following their electoral victory, and of the dangers attending the opponents' victory.[19]

However, recall that at times in two-party systems, political scientists have seen parties appeal to centrist "swing voters." They are up for grabs between the two broad parties and can determine the winner in a close election.[20] Appeals to the swing voter, more evident in campaigning as election day approaches, could reduce the meaningfulness of voter choice if differences between the parties' policy directions diminish. Voters may decide that the election results will not make much difference for subsequent government policy.

On this count, multiparty parliamentary systems present a wider range of options, perhaps increasing the voters' sense of finding a match that will make a difference in subsequent policies and outcomes. But what ultimately matters here is which *coalition* has won the most seats. And retrospective voters can judge only the coalition's performance in office. Most voters know of the coalition alignments, and thus recognize that votes for a party are in effect votes for its coalition. They are also likely to know who would be prime minister for each coalition if it were victorious (normally the leader of its largest party), and whether a given coalition is broadly left of center ideologically, right of center, or center-right or center-left.

However, in these multiparty parliamentary settings, voters typically cannot predict the particular policy directions that will follow in government after an election. Contention, cooperation, and compromise must take place among the parties in the majority coalition and their leaders in the cabinet. It has been argued that such "inside information" must not be open to the public if parties in a coalition are to be free to cooperate and compromise with each other.[21] Others argue that keeping such information private is not good for democracy.[22]

In addition, the makeup of the majority coalition may change between elections, and at times even coalition accountability can be a challenge.[23] If voters cannot tell what coalitions will form after an election, policy decision making passes largely into the hands of interparty negotiation, and voter choice becomes less meaningful. Notably, however, today such changes usually replace one small (often center) party with another, without a major shift in the coalition's key policy directions.

ELECTIONS UNDER NONDEMOCRATIC CONDITIONS

Do elections play any significant role in nondemocratic political frameworks? If so, what is it? Under authoritarian government, either elections are not held or they are not meaningful. For one reason or another, the regime and its favored policy directions will prevail, regardless of voting outcomes. Nonetheless, many authoritarian rulers like the ceremonial appearance of elections. They provide an excuse to mobilize the regime's supporters and try to generate a sense of legitimacy among them (see "The Human Rights Connection").

In the 1960s–1980s' heyday of authoritarian regimes (see chapter 15), the ways in which different sorts of authoritarian governments used elections were variations on the theme of controlled voting alternatives to choose a powerless

THE HUMAN RIGHTS CONNECTION | Can Elections Be Partly Free but Not Fair?

We know that the U.N.'s civil-political Covenant of human rights requires that elections be "free and fair." The freedom of elections primarily means freedom of association and assembly for political parties, freedom of expression for them and their candidates, freedom of information access for the voters, free and equal access to voting without discrimination, and the secret ballot. One of these rights can be curbed only to protect another of them, or to protect public safety or order, such as when one party threatens or conducts violence against another.

In addition, elections must be fair. Examples of fairness requirements are roughly equal representation of voters per elected representative ("one person/one vote"), unbiased administration of the process, guarantees against corruption and fraud in voting and vote counting, and fair access to the media by competing parties and candidates.

A useful example to examine regarding the relationship of freedom to fairness in elections is the recent one in Belarus (see Country Case Studies, chapter 1). In the presidential election campaign of February and March 2006, the government of incumbent president Alexander Lukashenko allowed opposition organizations to field candidates, including two significant rivals: Aleksandr Milinkevich, supported by a cluster of opposition groups, and Aleksandr Kozulin, party leader of the Belarusian Social Democratic Party and former chief of the Belarusian State University. (This contrasts with, for example, the late 1990s Nigerian military ruler Sani Abacha's registration of only parties willing to declare him to be their presidential candidate.) Opposition candidates were each allowed an hour of television time. There was no overt violence or intimidation at polling places on election day.

These minimal concessions toward a free election, however, coincided with Lukashenko's unwillingness to allow the elections to be fair. There is a past record of unsolved disappearances—assumed to be murders—of opposition leaders, suspected to be at the hands of government security forces or supportive death squads. According to a report by the Long-Term Observation Mission of the OSCE Office for Democratic Institutions and Human Rights, the campaign saw harassment and detention of campaign workers, and detention and beatings of leading opposition figures. The government also used criminal prosecutions, reportedly arbitrarily, to hinder opposition activity, assured that national broadcast media covered only Lukashenko and his campaign, suppressed independent media outlets including seizure of newspapers, and had security services claim that opposition groups were really terrorists and intended to seize power by force.

In addition, vote counting was under the control of the government and closed to outside monitors. Finally, the hour of television campaign footage granted to each party was aired at rush hour when the minimum number of people would be able to watch. Clearly, a fair and level playing field was missing for this election. Despite the formalities of free election, the surrounding climate of fear and intimidation robbed the electorate of the substance of freedom. If you lived in such a country, would you be inclined to vote? If not, what minimal changes would you require to become involved?

legislature. Communist Party-run regimes traditionally offered one Communist candidate to the voters, and the "winners" occupied seats in merely ceremonial legislatures. Non-Communist single-party regimes might allow multiple candidates to contend and represent local interests under the one-party umbrella (e.g., 1970s' Zambia), but overall policymaking remained under the control of the party-government leadership. Military regimes often created their own military-supporting party vehicle and manipulated elections to assure its victory and its compliance with the generals' wishes.

Under the single-party-dominant political framework, multiparty elections are held, but only one party regularly wins large victories and controls the government (e.g., pre-2011 Egypt). The government and its dominant party control the electoral system, and election officials often falsify the vote count. Party control over the media and harassment of opposition parties suppress their campaigns. The latter can take the form of arrest, detention, and prosecution of opposition leaders and activists, or informal bullying or intimidation, or both. The ruling party typically controls the flow of government benefits through some form of patron-client system. If governments with single-party dominance avoid repressive tactics, we can consider them semi-democratic rather than electoral authoritarian.

SUMMARY: CONTENTION AND COOPERATION IN VOTING AND ELECTIONS

Voters cast their ballots with one or more orientations in mind. They can have more or fewer alternatives to choose from, and may vote positively for one option or oppositionally against another. Voters may think of themselves as choosing either among parties or among individual candidates. Various motivations may contend in voters' minds. They may decide based on affective motives, or in pursuit of retrospective accountability. Or voters may look for candidates or parties who seem likely to move government policy in the directions that they favor: whether toward one or more values, toward an ideology, toward help for an interest group that the voter identifies with or is concerned about, or toward a specific policy (or oppositionally, in a direction contrary to one of these policy directions). Multiple motivations may cooperate or contend with one another to reinforce a voter's choice. Party identification commonly involves multiple voter motivations working together to produce a vote.

Parties and candidates respond to the opportunities presented by these voter motivations. Most often they contend with one another, sometimes partially redefining themselves in response to new policy challenges, changes in the pattern of interparty contention, or changes among the voters. Sometimes parties cooperate in multiparty coalitions, such that coalitions become contenders as well as individual parties and their candidates. Many voters want their votes to make a difference for government policy in some way. However, challenges to this aspiration exist, some of them related to differences among political frameworks. Elections in authoritarian regimes are formal rituals that have no chance of affecting government policy.

COUNTRY CASE STUDIES

The following country cases serve different purposes. The first focuses on particular presidential elections in the United States, with its two-party presidential framework. The second case surveys electoral contention in India, with its multiparty parliamentary political framework.

The United States: Voting in Recent Presidential Elections

The United States has a two-party presidential political framework with SMDP elections. This means much voting by individual candidate as well as by party, and some oppositional voting. Third parties cannot make much impact, and two broad parties contend: the moderate left-of-center Democratic Party and the conservative Republican Party. Ideologically, classical liberals tend to support the Republicans, given their shared free-market economic policy direction, and green-inclined voters tend to support the Democrats.

Nearly all of the types of voter motivation discussed in this chapter can be found in American elections. This country case study will focus on the presidential elections of 2004, 2008, and 2012, with the most emphasis on 2008 in comparison with 2004. Surveys of voters can indicate which characteristics of the candidate and party appeal to which voters. There were four likely key factors in the 2008 election result:

- oppositional retrospective voting due to an economic crisis under a Republican president,
- policy direction voting related to economic values and ideology,
- policy direction preference for helping certain group interests, and
- affective voting regarding the presidential candidates' personal qualities.

Oppositional retrospective voting by party. Exit polling showed that by election day in 2008, the economy had replaced the Iraq war by a wide margin as voters' main concern (62 percent to 10 percent). The previous eight years had seen little improvement for the middle and lower strata. Most importantly, late 2008 saw a precipitous financial and economic decline, including a sharp fall in home prices, a threat of international financial breakdown, a dive in the stock market and hence in many voters' retirement accounts, and a possible depression. Most voters didn't have an answer to the economic crisis, but they did know that the Republican Party had been in power for eight years,

and John McCain was its candidate (in the Senate he had voted for Bush's proposals 90 percent of the time).

Policy direction voting based on values and ideology. Retrospective accountability was accompanied by policy direction support for pursuing a value: economic security, a form of well-being. People wanted the government to act to stem the crisis. (McCain's own identification with a value, national security and its 9/11-related concerns, had become much less relevant for the voters than it was for George W. Bush in 2004.) Economic value-related concern was entwined with policy direction along ideological lines. When the financial crisis hit only weeks before election day, many experts agreed that it had resulted in part from inadequate government regulation of Wall Street and the mortgage industry. But this view went against a core stance of Republican free-market ideology: its belief that government regulation stifled economic growth and should be avoided. Until the crisis, McCain had consistently campaigned against economic regulation, and he continued to oppose government spending to boost jobs. McCain had been fully associated with conservatism's opposition to government intervention in the economy.

Policy direction voting related to group interests. Barack Obama seemed to have benefited from voting by policy direction toward help for certain categoric interests. How much of the 10 percent swing toward the Democratic candidate (from Democratic candidate John Kerry's 3 percent loss in 2004 to Obama's 7 percent victory in 2008), might be explained by Obama's gains among particular voter groups? The following categoric interests among the voters stand out as supporting Obama more than they had supported Kerry in 2004:

- White voters—75 percent of the total—where Obama's gains (especially among the young) amounted to nearly a third of his overall improvement over Kerry (perhaps 3 of the 10 percentage points of overall improvement).
- Latinos—10 percent of voters—where Obama's gains (especially young Latinos) over Kerry amounted to nearly another third of his overall improvement (perhaps 3 of the 10 points of improvement).

- African Americans—13 percent—voted heavily for Obama (1–2 of the 10-point gain).

- Younger voters—18 percent under 30—whose higher turnout and heavier support for Obama (66 percent) amounted to almost half of Obama's improvement over Kerry (perhaps 4 of the 10 points of overall improvement), distributed across white, Latino, and African American populations.

Why did Obama's results improve over those of Kerry among these groups? White voters included not only workers who feared for their jobs amid the economic crisis, but also people with retirement savings invested in financial markets. These categories included many in the upper income and education brackets who turn out to vote. Many favored assertive government action to stabilize the country's financial situation.

Many Latinos, two-thirds of whom voted for Obama, tended to favor government action on the economy and noted McCain's backing away from a path to legal status for immigrants. African Americans, already traditionally Democratic voters, may have assumed that the African American in the race, Obama, would be better for them. And across these groups, many pro-choice women feared that Republican appointments to the Supreme Court might restrict or reverse a woman's right to abortion. Finally, many young people favored a new, more idealistic style of politics as well as an exit from Iraq and greater government help for education.

Related to all this is party identification, which involves more than just an affective link to a party; other factors can also contribute, such as voting by party related to retrospective accountability, values, ideology, and group-interest support. Probably several of the above-discussed factors in the 2008 election contributed to the fact that the party identification percentages for the parties went from even (at 37 percent each) in 2004 to a 7 percent spread in favor of the Democrats by election day in 2008 (39 percent Democrat to 32 percent Republican).

Affective voting by candidate. At the outset, Obama had potential affective negatives. He was relatively new to national politics, and being an African American seemed to pose risks for him among some whites. But affective help for Obama came from young people. Many found him charismatic and liked his desire for a new style of politics and his frankness in describing the country's problems. Not only did young people vote in increased numbers, but they also provided an army of ground-level campaign workers to identify and turn out voters from other groups. And African Americans felt a strong identity link to their fellow African American and his historic candidacy, voting extremely heavily (95 percent) for Obama.

Affective factors among white voters may also have played a part. Despite his short political résumé, many white voters found Obama to be intelligent and steady through the financial crisis. McCain's attacks on Obama's past associations with a former anti-Vietnam radical and a controversial African American pastor did not seem to affect many swing voters. Obama received significantly greater support among white men than had Kerry in the 2004 election (though still not a majority of them). Exit polling revealed little oppositional affective voting against Obama on racial grounds.

Perhaps more important, however, were oppositional affective reactions against the McCain-Palin ticket. In McCain's favor, he was respected for his years as a prisoner of war (POW) in North Vietnam, his long experience in Congress, and his past willingness to vote against the party line on certain issues. However, McCain's reversals of some past policy positions (as he turned right to get the Republican nomination) and some vacillation on the financial crisis may have hurt perceptions of his judgment. In addition, concerns about McCain's age (seventy-two) and health (having experienced past bouts with cancer) had elevated the importance of the Republicans' vice presidential candidate in this election, Alaska governor Sarah Palin, who would succeed him if he were to die in office. To many she seemed unprepared and ideologically extreme.

The results of the 2012 presidential election will take time to digest, but it is instructive to compare its exit polls with those of 2008. Obama defeated Romney by 4 percent in the popular vote (51–47), but this represented a 3 percent Republican improvement over McCain's 7 percent loss in 2008. How might we explain this narrowing of Obama's margin? We saw virtually no change in the party identification gap (6 percent in favor of the Democrats), or in the huge group-interest advantage for Obama among Blacks and Latinos, who again turned out fairly strongly as they had in 2008. But a significant improvement for Romney over McCain did occur among white voters (72 percent of those voting). Among them, Romney won by 8 points more than had McCain in 2008 (a 20 percent margin versus 12 percent in 2008). Some of this difference may overlap with Romney's significant improvement over McCain among voters with incomes above $50,000. Romney's white upper-income gains may have driven his smaller improvements by age and gender over McCain's 2008 performance.

Probably a significant difference in voter motivation in 2012, at least among nonminority voters, was in oppositional retrospective accountability. The year 2008 had greatly favored Obama, with McCain inheriting the Bush economy in full-blown crisis. In contrast, the economy in 2012 was mixed, with still high unemployment, slow recovery, and notably larger deficits and national debt. To be sure, most voters still considered the economic downturn overall to be Bush's fault. But others held Obama responsible for the slow rate of job growth, which Romney's campaign rhetoric hit hard. (No doubt many voters were unaware that Obama had not been able to advance his jobs proposals since 2010, when Republican victories in Congressional elections had enabled them to block his jobs initiatives.) Regarding ideological policy directions, by 2012 there was little sense of economic crisis and no pervasive call for government action. Also Romney

was helped by some better-off white voters responding negatively to Obama's stated preference for raising taxes on higher incomes.

Regarding affective voting, probably the main difference between 2008 and 2012 was that Obama's persona had gone from being a dynamic face of "change" to humdrum (though still sympathetic to ordinary people) in 2012. Notably, Obama's margin among young white voters flipped from positive to negative between the two elections. Romney, for his part, presented a mixed persona. He sounded confident and assertive (but not detailed) in debates, though in ways that for some people seemed aggressive and arrogant. And even more than McCain, Romney had a reputation for reversing past issue positions. Finally, Romney presented contrasting portraits as a businessman: decisive fixer versus takeover artist offloading jobs and workers' benefits.

As this discussion makes clear, many different types of voter motivation led to Barack Obama's victories in 2008 and 2012. For numerous individual voters, undoubtedly two or more sorts of voter motivation probably contributed to their decision.

India: Electoral Democracy in a Huge Nation

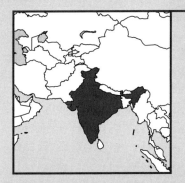

India is the world's largest well-established representative democracy. After India gained independence from British colonial rule in 1947, the victory was marred by religious division and secession of a large Muslim minority to form the nation of Pakistan (part of which later became Bangladesh). Today India has 1.1 billion people, twice the combined population of the United States and all of Western and Central Europe. Only in India does representative democracy operate on such a large scale. This fact alone makes the nation and its political experience very important on the world scene.

The 1950 Indian constitution adopted British-style parliamentary government with SMDP elections. But India is much larger and more diverse than Great Britain, with patterns of political cleavage along ethnic, religious, economic, and social caste lines that

vary by region. Not surprisingly, the nation adopted federalism, with an elected parliamentary government in each state as well as at the national level. Thus a regional interest-based focus party can be large in its home state and win numerous seats there, while lacking a presence elsewhere and remaining small nationally.

At independence, the dominant political force was the Indian National Congress. Led originally by Mohandas Gandhi, this party had spearheaded the struggle for independence by organizing people for Gandhi's "civil disobedience"—peaceful protest and resistance contrary to the official rules, while accepting the legal penalties that may follow. This effort required extensive political organization by Congress across the country. But after independence, coinciding cleavages at the regional level gave rise to significant regional parties pressing local interests. To hold the country together, above all Congress had to maintain its widespread organization and win elections. India's electoral history has evolved in three main stages:

- From independence into the 1970s, Congress won big victories and remained the dominant party.

- From the early 1970s to 1991, the Congress Party faced serious challenges in both national and regional elections. It occasionally lost to some alliances of smaller parties united by opposition to Congress leaders' authoritarian style and left-leaning policies.

- From about 1991 to the present, three coalitions emerged, one to the left, one in the center led by Congress, and a third to the right.

As it led the struggle for independence, Congress's leadership had adopted an inclusive approach toward all significant groups. This approach fit well with the cultural diversity of India as a whole. Economically, the party pursued left social democratic and nationalist policies—for example, favoring strong economic regulation to protect domestic industry, government ownership of parts of the economy, and heavy spending on schools and health clinics.

Congress's organizational machine existed in nearly all states. Under SMDP electoral arrangements, a large party can win many seats by small margins, giving it a much larger percentage of the legislative seats than of the popular vote. Congress's initial 40–50 percent of the national vote translated into clear majorities in the lower house, the Lok Sabha. Early on, opposing parties were too small, diverse, and disorganized to seriously challenge Congress.

National decision making within the Congress Party was especially responsive to top leaders—"the syndicate"—backed by regional and caste power bases and patron-client networks. In 1964, Prime Minister Jawaharlal Nehru was succeeded by his daughter, Indira Gandhi (unrelated to Mohandas Gandhi). As late as 1971, Congress maintained its national dominance. No other party or coalition could win national parliamentary majorities.

From 1971 to the early 1990s, however, India's electoral pattern followed a second mode, which included more open contention within the Congress Party. After winning a dispute with the syndicate leaders in 1969, Indira Gandhi's faction responded to pressure from the left by moving government policy leftward (including nationalizing banks). Also facing stronger contention from regional parties, Gandhi centralized party and government control around her and her son Sanjay, filling party positions with family loyalists. This personal leadership pattern of influence distribution in the Congress Party continued under Rajiv Gandhi, after the death of his brother Sanjay in 1980 and his mother's assassination in 1984.

During this period, opposition to Congress increased at the state level. Protests were partly directed at Indira Gandhi's authoritarian style, which occasionally involved emergency rule, suspended civil liberties, and arrests of opponents. At times, resentment over these tactics gave rise to opposing coalitions, which rose and dissolved with the issue of the day. Electoral swings occurred between affective attraction to Gandhi family leaders and sympathy over their assassinations on one hand, and oppositional responses to the family's authoritarian tendencies on the other. Voter ambivalence and electoral volatility featured heavily in the second phase of Indian electoral politics.

The third era in India's elections began in 1991 and continues today. The multiparty parliamentary framework now displays more stable contending coalitions, with each roughly occupying a segment of the ideological spectrum. Electoral volatility and personal leadership dominance have been reduced.

Benefiting from sympathy over Rajiv Gandhi's assassination in 1991, Congress won the most seats that year, but it failed to gain a majority. An elderly Congress veteran, Narasimha Rao, became prime minister in a Congress-led coalition. Rao rejected centralized control of the party, and revived elections within it. Ideologically, Rao moved Congress policies toward the center, and its coalition began introducing some free-market-oriented reforms. But after Hindu-Muslim rioting in 1992, later accusations of corruption, and a poor showing in the 1996 elections, Congress became an outside support party propping up a centrist government that lacked a formal majority. After further pro-market reforms, Congress withdrew its support and forced new elections in 1998.

The 1998 election confirmed the rise of a new right-of-center coalition. It was led by a broad party based on Hindu nationalism: the Bharatiya Janata Party (BJP). In many ways, it first emerged as the political arm of a Hindu revivalist social organization, the Rashtriya Swayam Sevak Sangh (RSS), stressing traditional Hindu religious values and expressing hostility to minorities of other faiths. The BJP had gained support by opposing a mosque that had been built on a sacred Hindu site, spawning bloody anti-Muslim riots. The party also embraced free-market-oriented measures of deregulation, privatization, and opposition to affirmative action for lower-caste people. It has been able to govern only as the leading party in a coalition with several small regional parties. When this coalition gained a parliamentary majority in 1999, the BJP's conservative preferences were constrained by its more moderate coalition partners.

Thus we may say that ideological policy direction voters in India have three coalition alternatives to choose from: left, center, and conservative. The center and conservative coalitions are each led by a broad party, while the left coalition is led by the Communist Party (Marxist), or CP(M), an ideological focus party.

The 2004 elections followed a period of overall economic growth, and the BJP-led coalition government expected another victory on a surge of positive retrospective voting. Its slogan was "India shining." But India did not "shine" for many middle-class and lower-strata voters. By stressing their plight, the centrist Congress-led coalition defeated its rivals but fell short of a parliamentary majority. Its cabinet relied on outside support from the left-of-center coalition, dominated by the CP(M), the third largest party in the lower house. Prime Minister Manmohan Singh's preference for more free-market reforms was blocked by the left front.

In the elections of May 2009, however, the centrist electoral coalition of Congress and its allies—called the United Progressive Alliance—unexpectedly won a much larger victory than in 2004, giving it a near majority in the Lok Sabha. Favorable retrospective voting played a key role. India's regulated economy had helped to insulate the nation from the world economic downturn of 2008–2009. In addition, the government's program of debt relief and jobs for hard-pressed farmers had fostered support from the nation's huge agricultural sector. And Congress's top leaders, such as (now former) Prime Minister Dr. Manmohan Singh, party chairman Sonia Gandhi, and her son Rahul, tend to be well regarded personally—a favorable affective factor that the BJP-dominated coalition and the left front largely lacked at the time. Enough small parties and independents then joined the coalition to give it a clear majority. (Congress had also won some state elections.) Without having to rely on support from either the left front coalition or significant regional parties, Congress and its coalition allies could pursue their mixed agenda of help for the rural poor alongside some privatizations and reductions in subsidies, and the banning of an insurgent Maoist party.

Each of the two national broad parties is to some extent a collection of regional leaders with their followings. Meanwhile, regional interest-oriented voters have alternatives in the regional parties. Such parties in the main coalitions can often influence the party leading the coalition, while other regional parties are fully independent. Some of the most important states in India have each been controlled by a regional party whose leader serves as the state's chief minister. When Congress or the BJP is in control in a state, it tends to be in coalition with the state's most important regional-interest party.

After 2009, however, Congress's star began to wane. Corruption scandals sullied the party's affective support, deficits rose, and Prime Minister Singh had difficulty getting measures through parliament. He seemed at times to be a weak leader, with key decisions taken by the party leader, Sonia Gandhi. In 2012, Congress was soundly defeated by a regional party in the state assembly election in an especially important state, Uttar Pradesh. Meanwhile, attention from television and social media (the Internet, Facebook, and Twitter) was increasing the importance of retrospective accountability for governmental performance, not only in economic growth, jobs, and corruption, but also in such policy areas as roads, education, health care, electric power, law and order, provision of rations for the food-insecure poor, and checking the Maoist insurgency.

For the parliamentary election of May 2014, the BJP found a popular leader, Narendra Modi, and a powerful retrospective line of attack on weak Congress performance in virtually all of the above-mentioned issue areas. Modi stressed his past record of economic growth and development in Gujarat state, where he had served as chief minister for more than a decade. A lifelong member of the Hindu-nationalist association RSS, Modi seemed to be backing away publicly from his earlier close association with the Hindu nationalists. (Over a decade had passed since, in 2002 in Gujarat, the police seem to have passively stood by as Hindu zealots killed up to a thousand Muslims.)

Tactically, Modi ran an efficient, modern campaign with broad influence over the media. And given the seat advantage accruing to big parties under India's SMDP voting system, the BJP's large 31 percent vote share was spread in such a way as to swamp not only Congress but many regional parties. The BJP won 282 seats for an unheard-of majority in parliament in its own hands, so that it need not depend on smaller coalition allies. Later in 2014, the Indian economy was helped by rapidly falling oil prices, and the BJP won big victories in some important state elections.

We need to remember, however, that even such massive electoral success may not last. Whatever the inspiring talk about development, over time India's huge numbers of retrospective voters will look for improvement in outcomes that they can see around them, such as job availability, corruption, the prices of food, power, and water, and the condition of infrastructure such as roads, electricity, clean water, sanitation, and flood control. Changing these outcomes in a country of over a billion people can at best be a slow process. And in India, attempts at free-market-oriented changes such as deregulation run into opposition from groups that still have strength in the upper house, the Rajya Sabha, with its limit-setting capacity to veto or amend initiatives.

India's upper house represents the state governments, and thus reflects state-level power relationships determined by state elections that are staggered over the years between national parliamentary elections. It would take years of winning control of state governments one at a time for the BJP to gain a majority in the upper house. BJP did well in a few states that elected their governments in the last half of 2014, but lost big in Delhi in early 2015, when opponents seem to have cooperated around the anti-corruption "common man" party (AAP), which won a big victory. This can occur elsewhere, especially since at times, Modi's RSS base continues to show its Hindu zeal (not disavowed by Modi) against other religious minorities. Opposing parties may become alarmed to the point of their cooperation to contend more effectively against the BJP. This occurred in late 2015 in the elections in Bihar, in which an anti-BJP coalition won a landslide victory.

PRACTICE AND REVIEW ONLINE

CRITICAL THINKING QUESTIONS

1. Which is a more effective way of voting, by individual candidate or by party, and why? How might the answer depend on circumstances? Give examples.

2. Give an example of two or three types of motivation affecting peoples' votes in a recent past election. Which motivations seem most valid?

3. Do you tend to vote for a specific party? Why or why not? Has your allegiance changed over your lifetime, and if so, why? What types of experiences can alter voters' party identification?

4. Which country has more meaningful voter choice: India or the United States? Explain your answer.

KEY TERMS

oppositional voting, 315
voter turnout, 316
referendum, 317
recall, 317
affective voting, 318
candidate orientation voting, 318
retrospective voting, 319
policy direction voting, 320
party identification, 326
independent voter, 327
independent leaner, 327
realignment, 329
reapportionment, 330
meaningful voter choice, 331
Electoral College, 332
runoff election, 333

FURTHER READING

Dahl, Robert A., Ian Shapiro, and José Antonio Cheibub, eds. *Democracy Sourcebook.* Cambridge, MA; London: MIT Press, 2003.

Downs, Anthony. *An Economic Theory of Democracy.* New York: Harper and Row, 1957.

Duverger, Maurice. *Political Parties.* New York: Wiley, 1954.

Farrell, David M. *Electoral Systems: A Comparative Introduction.* New York: Palgrave, 2001.

Gallagher, Michael, Michael Laver, and Peter Mair. *Representative Government in Modern Europe,* 4th ed. New York: McGraw-Hill, 2006.

LeDuc, Lawrence, Richard G. Niemi, and Pippa Norris, eds. *Comparing Democracies: Elections and Voting in Global Perspective*. Thousand Oaks, CA: Sage Publications, 1996.

Mayhew, David R. *Electoral Realignments: A Critique of an American Genre*. New Haven, CT: Yale University Press, 2002.

Norris, Pippa. *Electoral Engineering: Voting Rules and Political Behavior*. Cambridge, UK: Cambridge University Press, 2004.

Powell, C. Bingham. *Elections as Instruments of Democracy: Majoritarian and Proportional Versions*. New Haven, CT: Yale University Press, 2000.

Rokkan, Stein. *Citizens, Elections, Parties: Approaches to the Comparative Study of the Processes of Development*. New York: McKay, 1970.

Shugart, Matthew S., and John M. Carey. *Presidents and Assemblies: Constitutional Design and Electoral Dynamics*. Cambridge, UK; New York: Cambridge University Press, 1992.

Taagepera, Rein, and Matthew S. Shugart. *Seats and Votes: The Effects and Determinants of Electoral Systems*. New Haven, CT: Yale University Press, 1989.

NOTES

[1] The main exception to this is where we find regional-interest parties, which are small nationally but very big in their home regions, such as the Scottish National Party. Where there are many such parties, as in India, we may even see a multiparty system despite SMDP voting.

[2] Again, this "Duverger's law" application is only meant to refer to the basic difference between two-party and multiparty outcomes (e.g., four policy-significant parties or more). Within the multiparty segment of the continuum, political scientists have not found the number of parties to be quantitatively proportional to the number of seats in a multimember district (called the "district magnitude"). See Gary W. Cox, *Making Votes Count: Strategic Coordination in the World's Electoral Systems* (Cambridge, UK: Cambridge University Press, 1997). Within the multiparty category, just how many parties will be policy-significant is affected by factors other than the electoral system, especially the number and nature of political cleavages in society (see chapter 4).

[3] See Morris Fiorina, *Retrospective Voting in American Elections* (New Haven, CT: Yale University Press, 1981).

[4] See Raymond M. Duch and Randolph T. Sevenson, *The Economic Vote: How Political and Economic Institutions Condition Election Results* (New York: Cambridge University Press, 2008).

[5] See Ignacio Urquizu-Sancho, *The Political Consequences of Coalition Governments: Multiparty Cabinets and Accountability* (Madrid: Juan March Institute, 2008).

[6] See G. Bingham Powell, Jr. and Guy D. Whitten, "A Cross-National Analysis of Economic Voting: Taking Account of the Political Context," *American Journal of Political Science* 37, no. 2 (May 1993): 391–414; José Antonio Cheibub and Adam Przeworski, "Democracy, elections, and accountability for economic outcomes," in *Democracy, Accountability, and Representation*, ed. Przeworski, Susan C. Stokes, and Bernard Manin (Cambridge, UK: Cambridge University Press, 1999), 222–49.

[7] See George Rabinowitz and Stuart Elaine MacDonald, "A Directional Theory of Issue Voting," *American Political Science Review* 83: 93–121 (1989); regarding multiparty systems, see Macdonald, Olla Listhaug and Rabinowitz, "Issues and Party Support in Multiparty Systems," *American Political Science Review* 85, no. 4 (December 1991): 1107–1131; regarding parliamentary contexts, see Macdonald, Rabinowitz, and Listhaug, "Political Sophistication and Models of Issue Voting," *British Journal of Political Science* 25, no. 4 (October 1995): 453–483.

[8] For a somewhat technical discussion of this, see Raymond M. Duch, Jeff May, and David A. Armstrong II, "Coalition-directed Voting in Multiparty Democracies," *American Political Science Review* 104, no. 3 (November 2010): 698–719. Indeed, the authors go on to suggest that many voters employ a form of what political scientists call "strategic voting," supporting a party more extreme than their own overall preference in hopes that a bigger vote for that party will help pull the coalition in a voter-favored policy direction.

[9] See, Herbert Kitschelt, "Linkages Between Citizens and Politicians in Democratic Polities," *Comparative Political Studies* 33 (2000): 845–79; Kenneth Benoit and Michael Laver, *Party Policy in Modern Democracies* (London: Routledge, 2005).

[10] See Herman Schmitt and Jacques Thomassen, *Political Representation and Legitimacy in the European Union* (Oxford: Oxford University Press, 1999).

[11] See note 7 above.

[12] See Morris Fiorina, "Voting Behavior," in *Perspectives on Public Choice: A Handbook*, ed. Dennis C. Mueller (Cambridge, UK: Cambridge University Press, 1997), 391–414.

[13] See chapter 10, note 4.

14 See Herbert Kitschelt, "Citizens, Politicians, and Party Cartellization: Political Representation and State Failure in Post-industrial Democracies," *European Journal of Political Research* 37 (2000): 149–79.

15 Bartolini and Mair (1990); see chapter 10 above, note 7.

16 Scott Mainwaring and Timothy Scully, "Introduction: Party Systems in Latin America," in Mainwaring and Scully, *Building Democratic Institutions: Party Systems in Latin America* (Stanford, CA: Stanford University Press, 1995), 1-34.

17 A classic representation of this view is Seymour Martin Lipset and Stein Rokkan, "Cleavage Structures, Party Systems, and Voter Alignments: an Introduction," in Lipset and Rokkan, *Party Systems and Voter Alignments: Cross-national Perspectives* (New York: Free Press, 1967), 1–64.

18 For a contrasting perspective emphasizing party choices in the development of party linkages to society, see Giovanni Sartori, "From the sociology of politics to political sociology," in *Politics and the Social Sciences*, ed. Seymour Martin Lipset (Oxford: Oxford University Press, 1969), 65–95.

19 For a broad review of this literature as of the mid-2000s, see G. Bingham Powell, "Political Representation in Comparative Politics," *Annual Review of Political Science* 7 (2004): 273–96.

20 This approach largely originated with Anthony Downs, *An Economic Theory of Democracy* (New York: Harper and Row, 1957).

21 See Juan Linz, "Presidential or Parliamentary Democracy: Does It Make a Difference?" in *The Failure of Presidential Democracy*, ed. Juan Linz and Arturo Valenzuela (Baltimore and London: Johns Hopkins University Press, 1994), 3–87.

22 See Shugart and Carey 1992, 44.

23 See G. Bingham Powell, "Constitutional Design and Citizen Electoral Control," *Journal of Theoretical Politics* 1 (1989): 107–30.

POLITICS AND GOVERNMENT INSTITUTIONS

I — PART

II — PART

III — PART

IV — PART

V — PART

Legislative Assemblies

FOCUS QUESTIONS

- **WHICH** sorts of groups are involved in the legislative process, and how do these groups contend and cooperate?

- **WHICH** groups obtain the most influence in legislative assemblies, and why?

- **WHEN** do legislative assemblies have great influence in contention with the executive, and when little, with the legislature mainly cooperating with executive initiatives?

- **HOW** does the overall political framework in which the legislative institution functions affect group interaction and the distribution of legislative influence?

IN 2011 AND EARLY 2012, the Brazilian Chamber of Deputies and Senate negotiated and finally passed a new version of the country's Forest Code, which loosened regulations aimed at combating deforestation. This was a setback for the global environment as the Amazon is the world's largest remaining rainforest, home to some of the most diverse plant and animal life on earth.

The existing law had required 80 percent of Amazon farms to be protected as forest. But it was poorly enforced. Landowners had often "clearcut" forest (cutting down all trees in an area), ignoring regulations and occasionally using money and violence against anyone who resisted their efforts. When penalties for deforestation began in the 1990s and were increased in 2004, deforestation rates began to decline (partly due to declining world prices for beef and soybeans). Between 2008 and mid-2011, more intense aerial monitoring and enforcement contributed to a further reduction in deforestation.

However, cattle ranchers, soybean farmers, loggers, and mining interests, having already deforested roughly 20 percent of the Amazon over recent decades, pressed legislators to weaken the Forest Code. Most importantly, they remain powerful lobbies and campaign contributors for legislators in Brazil's multiparty presidential system. Contention over existing regulations and enforcement patterns was sharpening. In 2011, on its own initiative, the lower-house Chamber of Deputies had weakened the requirements and granted amnesty to deforesters prior to 2008. Conservationist legislators in the Senate faced off against not only big farmers and ranchers but also land-hungry peasants, and the Senate did little to change the legislation.

When the bill reached the desk of President Dilma Roussef of the Workers Party (which held less than 20 percent of the legislative seats), public opinion polls showed that a majority of people wanted her to reject it. But due to pressures from peasant groups, among others, she vetoed only portions of the legislation (which Brazilian presidents are allowed to do)—most prominently its grant of amnesty for non-smallholder farmers—and proceeded over the summer to negotiate other parts of the bill with the legislative bodies. Viewed alongside the delegation of much Forest Code enforcement from the national to the state and local levels that had occurred in 2011 (in effect weakening enforcement), the key consequence seems to be that deforestation will continue. Clearly, the nature of the legislative process in Brazil had a big impact on this outcome.

BACKGROUND AND FUNCTIONS

A **legislative assembly** is a governmental body that is made up of many elected members who are equal in voting power, and that approves (or disapproves) policy proposals by majority vote. I use the word "approve" in this definition because in practice, while legislators may modify bills, usually the most important proposals that pass into law come originally from the executive branch.

Background

Of the branches of representative government, the legislative assembly is perhaps the most fully "representative" of you, the citizen. In most democracies, each member of the legislative body comes from an election district, with its own distinctive features.

Prior to the late nineteenth century, most of the world's governments didn't see much need for a legislature as we know it. The king made the key governmental decisions, consulting with a few advisors and perhaps a council of elders. Societies were governed primarily by fairly stable custom, with little need for new laws. Cooperation prevailed.

To be sure, there were some exceptions. In the middle ages in some parts of Europe, a monarch in need of new tax revenues (usually for a war) would call together representatives of the major social orders—principally the nobility, the clergy, and the leading commoners of the towns—to explain the need and get their support. But it was only much later, as democratic ideals began to spread in the eighteenth century, that the idea began to catch on that representative assemblies should meet on a regular basis, continue over time, and play roles in lawmaking generally. In the case of the earliest assemblies, the king merely consulted with the body at his or her discretion. But eventually the practice arose of the legislature formally approving a wide range of new policies as an independent check on the king (see "The Philosophical Connection" below).

When modern legislatures began to develop in the eighteenth century in the United States and Britain, questions arose as to how elected legislators ought to serve the voters. One answer focused on the goal of directly representing the voters' views: the **delegate model** (sometimes called the "mandate model") of

THE PHILOSOPHICAL CONNECTION | John Locke

The first political thinker to focus systematically on a legislative branch of government to both check the king and deliver citizen consent was John Locke, in the late seventeenth century in England. As we saw in chapter 4, Locke belonged to the power-checking current of philosophical thought. He saw government as efficiently applying natural law—for him, the obligation to refrain from arbitrary taking of life, liberty, and property. Government was to enforce natural law through known laws, applied with strength and impartiality, for the public good. Locke suggested that to accomplish this, government must not be left only to the monarch and his or her agents. Pure monarchy might lead to an arbitrary and abusive king, thus taking the citizenry back into the state of nature. A separate legislative power was needed.

Interestingly, however, Locke's idea of a legislative branch did not require that it generally represent the people's views. His main concern was that the people or their representatives have some share in approving tax bills. Protecting property was a key part of government's job of implementing natural law, so the government itself may take citizen property in taxes only with some sort of expression of voluntary citizen consent to the tax laws. To be sure, Locke did write favorably about the idea of elected representatives making up a regular part of the legislature generally, especially if the assembly periodically went out of office for periods of time to live under the laws that they had helped make (so the representatives would not start to think of their own interests, distinct from those of the people). If the legislature was "always in being" (e.g., the House of Lords in office for life, not periodically chosen through elections), then some special procedure would have to be employed to allow the citizens or some chosen representatives of them to give (or withhold) their consent to tax measures—most likely in a special assembly called for that purpose. If any legislature pursued its own interests in a way that clearly threatened the life, liberty, and property of the people, in principle the people could rise up and change the legislature—the same option they have in relation to the executive.

Notably, Locke even allowed as legitimate an arrangement that gave the king a veto power over laws. He admitted that in this case, in practice, the king would be "supreme" in the government, since no legislation passed without his favor. Locke's only comment on this situation was that the king would not be supreme formally *as executive chief*, but only supreme via his veto share in the legislative function. (The American framers in 1787 rejected the idea of a chief executive for life with an absolute veto, in favor of an elected, fixed-term chief executive whose veto could be overridden by a two-third legislative vote.) In short, there is little in Locke's writings to suggest that the law of the land must be the product solely of the will of a legislature elected by the people.

representation. It suggested that the representatives' main duty in the assembly should be to support policies that are favored by the majority of the voters back home in their districts. This conception is in line with the majority preference model of influence distribution (see chapter 3) applied to the election district; according to it, the job of government is to translate the majority's preferences into policy. For a legislator, this approach to the job would have an advantage related to political contention: it would enhance the representative's chances of being reelected next time, at least if following public opinion doesn't turn out disastrously.

An alternative model was articulated by the late eighteenth-century British thinker Edmund Burke (see chapter 5): the **trustee model**. According to it, a territorial representative should act on her or his own judgment on behalf of the nation, rather than trying to follow opinions in the district. In this picture, legislators are members of an elite (or an arena for contending elites), though with an element of democracy in that members of the political elite are accountable to the voters in the next election. The trustee model serves to focus attention on the particular backgrounds of the elected legislators, as indicators of their outlook that may predict how they will vote on bills (see Table 12.1).

In practice, legislative behavior mixes aspects of these two conceptions of representation, along with other related factors and activities. We begin with the functions of legislatures, and how they are set up. Then we examine legislative committees, where much of the real work of legislatures is done. Then we ask, how influential are legislatures in different types of political framework as they contend and/or cooperate with the executive branch leadership?

Functions

The formal work of assemblies centers on approving, rejecting, or modifying policy proposals, the most important of which were first presented by the executive branch leadership. Along the way, however, legislators also do other useful things. Most of these display party contention.

One is *debating* issues, which can help educate the public. Members and parties state their positions on policy issues, justify them, and try to poke holes in the arguments of opposing members and parties. But legislative debate is televised in only a few countries (e.g., in the United States on the C-SPAN channels). When it reaches people, it is generally through the news media's coverage of assembly debates. Unfortunately, however, such coverage by television and radio news and most print and Internet outlets is thin. It tends to be limited to a few short video or audio clips, or "sound bites," often of particularly contentious rhetoric by the leading legislative spokespersons of the main contending parties. Debate does culminate, however, in *voting* on the bill. Voting by members and parties provides a more lasting record of their positions on issues, which can make it difficult for them to run away from unpopular policy stands in the next election campaign.

In addition, assemblies monitor and investigate the executive branch. This function may produce contention between the branches. In parliamentary systems, MPs (members of parliament) may easily question ministers and their deputies directly because they are also fellow members of the key legislative assembly. In presidential systems, legislative committees often monitor the performance of executive ministries (or departments), and may request documents and testimony from executive officials. This can be a source of contention between a specialized committee (e.g., an assembly's labor committee) and its parallel executive agency (e.g., the labor ministry or department).

In presidential systems, contention is especially sharp when an assembly's majority is in the hands of a party or coalition that stands in opposition to that of the chief executive and the cabinet. This was the case in the Republican-majority House versus Democratic president Obama and his cabinet after 2010, and in the Senate after 2014. Typically, the majority party can mount a

In the British House of Commons, the two main parties' legislators face each other, emphasizing the contention between them in parliamentary debate, rather than having each speaker stand at a podium before the whole assembly.

TABLE 12.1 | Occupations of Legislators in Select Nations, 1987–1992

	Total	Australia	Canada	France	Greece	Israel	Japan
Lawmaking professions							
Legal profession	18	11	19	6	38	18	6
Civil servants and administrators	11	8	10	20		5	33
Politicians and party officials	10	11	1				33
Business and finance							
Commercial and business	17	22	22	6		18	13
Accountants/financial consultants	1		3				
Chattering professions							
Educational profession	14	18	15	26	11	14	2
Journalism/media/writers	3	2	5	3		3	1
Social scientists	2		2		6	10	
Literary and artistic	1			2		4	
Other professions							
Medical profession	5	4	4	12	14	1	1
Agriculture and farmers	3		5	3		8	3
Engineering/architects	3	2	1	2	10	4	
Other white collar	3	10	3	13			
Armed forces	1	1			3		
Clergy			1			4	
Manual trades							
Manual workers	3	5		3			
Trade unionists	1	5					
Not available	6		10	4	20	12	7
Total	100	100	100	100	100	100	100
Election year		1987	1988	1986	1990	1992	1990

TABLE 12.1 | (Continued)

	Malta	New Zealand	Portugal	Switzerland	United States	United Kingdom
Lawmaking professions						
Legal profession	27	14	21	17	35	13
Civil servants and administrators	6		8			11
Politicians and party officials			1	30	11	7
Business and finance						
Commercial and business	4	20	15	12	30	24
Accountants/financial consultants	4	6				2
Chattering professions						
Educational profession	4	12	19	13	11	16
Journalism/media/writers	3		1	7	5	7
Social scientists	3		6			1
Literary and artistic				3		
Other professions						
Medical profession	20	3	6		1	1
Agriculture and farmers		15		13	4	2
Engineering/architects	13	3	10	7	1	1
Other white collar	6					
Armed forces			1			2
Clergy						
Manual trades						
Manual workers			4			10
Trade unionists		5			1	
Not available	10	21	8		1	1
Total	100	100	100	100	100	100
Election year	1992	1990	1987	1991	1990	1992

Source: Pippa Norris and Joni Lovenduski, *Political Recruitment. Gender, Race and Class in the British Parliament* (Cambridge: Cambridge University Press, 1995), 185; data are from the *Chronicle of Parliamentary Elections and Developments*, Geneva, Inter Parliamentary Union, 1990–1992.

committee investigation of almost any executive action that it disagrees with. In parliamentary systems, the minority opposition may use committee deliberations to get information about what the executive is doing.

However, legislative assemblies vary in how much power they have to pry loose information that the executive does not want to give up, and how much staff they have for examining that information. In the United Kingdom, for example, the "Official Secrets Act" gives broad protection for government agencies from having to give up information; American executive agencies have less protection, and typically must respond to a legislative subpoena (official demand for information or testimony). And American legislators have generous budgets with which to hire staff, to help them investigate issues and perform their other functions.

Occasionally, assemblies may also perform *judicial* functions concerning possible wrongdoing by government officials in the course of their public duties. Ultimately, they can decide whether the target of the investigation shall be removed from office, or merely be censured (reprimanded) for their behavior while remaining in office. In the United States, for example, in 1999 the House of Representatives voted to accuse (in a process called impeachment) President Bill Clinton of allegedly misrepresenting, under oath, his relationship with a young female intern in the White House. Following the U.S. Constitution, the case was tried in the Senate. It was questionable whether the president's conduct constituted "high crimes and misdemeanors" as required by the constitution for conviction, and the senators as jurors voted not to remove President Clinton.

Legislators are also centers of a key form of cooperation: helping citizens who live in the representative's district with particular problems they may be facing with government. Political scientists call this **constituent service**. It can range from trying to get a senior citizen's government pension payments unblocked, to helping a business get a needed license, relief from a regulation, or even a government contract. Constituent service is often done quite independently of legislators' policy preferences concerning laws or programs overall. For example, a legislator who opposed the adoption of a new weapons system for the military may nonetheless try to help a local defense manufacturer secure part of a government contract to produce the weapon.

Structure: Unicameral and Bicameral

The legislative branch may have just one assembly or two. **Unicameral** ("one-house") **legislatures** are common among smaller nations. Great Britain, for example, in practice has a unicameral legislature, the House of Commons. (The unelected "House of Lords" does not play a significant role in British policymaking.) **Bicameral legislatures**, with two houses, are particularly common among large nations with federal forms of government (see below). Unicameral legislatures can move proposals through more quickly. Bicameral legislatures introduce opportunities for institutional contention that may add to, and reinforce, contention between parties.

Where the legislative branch is bicameral, the two houses may have roughly equal power, as in the United States and Italy. Much more common, however, is for one house to be more powerful than the other, sometimes much more powerful. Why do many governmental systems include a second house?

The earliest bicameral legislatures at ancient Rome and in England had an "upper" house in the sense of representing the upper class *socioeconomically*. The ancient Roman Senate and the British House of Lords embodied the elite model of influence distribution, mainly representing a "nobility" of wealthy landowners. Supporters of the upper house suggested that an assembly of leading nobles was necessary to check the influence of the common people. As we saw in chapter 5, the nobles tended to view the commoners as uneducated, shortsighted, and vulnerable to being caught up in the passion of the moment or being manipulated by deceptive orators called demagogues, perhaps even into taking the property of the wealthy. The landowning nobles also suggested, on their own behalf, that they had a permanent stake in the community, the wealth to educate themselves and their children, time available for public service, and consequently, a capacity for calm and wise deliberation in making decisions.

With economic development and the spread of education from the late eighteenth century on, however, these arguments became less persuasive. And when the Americans set to work on the first truly democratic constitution in the late 1780s (in the sense of giving the vote to the great majority of male adults), the new nation largely lacked a nobility. The majority of people were small farmers who were already inclined to protect basic property rights, and often able to read and write. Moreover, they had some prior experience of self-government in the legislative houses of the colonial governments, with a record of responsible behavior. Nonetheless, some of the nation's founders still desired a second house to help restrain the passions of popular majorities. But without a nobility to represent, what would be the representational basis for such an upper house?

The Americans found the answer in the idea of special equal representation of distinct *regions*. Right after independence, in the mid-1780s the Articles of Confederation had left sovereignty pretty much in the hands of the independent states, giving them equal representation—one vote each—in the weak Continental Congress. But under the new constitution being drawn up in 1787, there was to be a powerful national House of Representatives with equal representation *by population*. This embodied today's principle of formal political equality (see chapter 1), but it worried the small states. States with large populations such as Massachusetts and Virginia would have far more legislators than smaller states such as Rhode Island and Connecticut. The founders compromised by setting up a second house along the lines of the equal regional representation (two senators per state, regardless of population inequalities between states) that had prevailed under the earlier Articles of Confederation. That assembly was given roughly equal power with the House.

Moreover, this upper house was insulated somewhat from electoral pressures in two ways. First, the senators were given longer terms in office (six years vs. two years for House members). Second, Senate seats were at first filled by **indirect election**—having the legislators of each state government choose the state's senators, rather than giving the choice to the people directly. Only later, following reform movements in some states in the late nineteenth century, did senators begin to be elected by the citizens directly. The direct election of senators finally became the national rule when a constitutional amendment establishing it was passed early in the twentieth century.

As democracy developed in other nations in the twentieth century, bicameral legislatures tended to follow the American example of having a lower house represent people equally by population and the upper house represent regions

TABLE 12.2	Legislative Houses and Their Characteristics		
Legislative House	**Emphasizes Equal Representation By**	**Democratic Legitimacy**	**Formal Legislative Power**
Lower	Population	Higher (especially if district boundaries are drawn impartially)	Normally higher
Upper	Region	Lower (due to unequal populations in regions equally represented)	Normally lower

equally (or more equally). However, this latter pattern, by failing to reflect regional inequalities in population, violates the principle of political equality. Hence such upper houses tend to enjoy less democratic legitimacy, and normally are given less power than the lower house (see Table 12.2). Often in bicameral systems, the lower house can easily override efforts by the upper house to defeat legislation. Moreover, in bicameral parliamentary democracies, it is usually the lower house that has the special role of electing the prime minister from its own ranks.

LEGISLATIVE COMMITTEES: CAN THEY CONTEND IN POLICYMAKING?

A key factor in the distribution of influence in the legislative process is the role and strength of legislative committees. After a bill is presented to an assembly by the relevant cabinet minister, it will go to a committee. The committee (or one of its more focused subcommittees) may hold hearings on the bill. At those times, experts and interest group representatives can have their say, and individual committee members can get their questions answered and float ideas for changes in the bill. Where committees are strong, they may actually modify the bill significantly before it goes before the whole house for a vote.

Procedures

One indication of the strength of committees in a particular legislative assembly may be found in the procedure for handling bills when they are first proposed. Do they go straight to the committee for first consideration, as in the U.S. presidential system with its strong committees? Or are bills voted on in a general way by the whole house first? This latter option assures the bill's passage before going to committee, as in the British parliamentary House of Commons, which has much weaker committees.

Even in a parliamentary system, where the overall majority in favor of the bill is normally assured, the bill's details will be examined in committee. Amendments may be suggested, but generally the cabinet decides whether to accept them. In some nations' parliamentary legislatures, opposition MPs might participate in modifying details, though in the final formal vote on the bill, party discipline will normally require them to vote against it. Most parliaments assign committee chairmanships to only members of the majority party or parties, but there are exceptions to this (see the Germany country case study below).

In presidential systems, the more lax party discipline makes a strong committee system more likely. There, committees may contend sharply with the chief executive. They can not only amend bills on their own, but also stop them. When President Jimmy Carter presented his energy conservation bill in the late 1970s, and when President Bill Clinton presented his universal health insurance proposal in the early 1990s, key features of the bills were stopped in committee despite their party's majorities in Congress. When President Barack Obama presented his health insurance proposal to Congress in 2009, it went to two or three committees in each house of Congress, and each of them amended the bill and reported out its own version. When the bill finally passed in March 2010, it contained moderate provisions added in Senate committee proceedings that the president did not favor.

Specialization and Expertise

One factor contributing to the strength of legislative committees is having them *specialized* for the basic handling of bills: one committee for agriculture proposals, one for commerce, one for labor, one for foreign relations, and so on. These permanently established units are often called **standing committees**, in contrast to the **ad hoc committees** that are occasionally created to investigate a particular scandal, for example. Each standing committee tends to parallel a ministry or department in the executive branch. (In the United States, each committee is divided further into smaller subcommittees, which are even more specialized.) The sense that committee consideration of a bill involves special expertise makes it more likely that the whole assembly will defer to the committee's judgment on most features of the bill, in the final voting on it.

In contrast, in Britain the committees that take up legislation are generic (labeled A, B, and so on) and very large. Following alphabetical order, each unspecialized committee takes up the next bill in succession. (The British also have a system of smaller committees to parallel the executive departments, but they function only to monitor departments' performance and do not handle major bills.) The French National Assembly also follows this approach.

Individual members of committees or subcommittees may build up expertise over time. In the United States, once a member of Congress gets on a committee, usually the legislator may stay as long as (s)he wants. Rank within each party on each committee is

Members of the U.S. House of Representatives' Foreign Affairs Committee (seated, facing the camera) question Secretary of State John Kerry and other top cabinet officials (backs to the camera, front row) about the proposed Iran Nuclear Agreement, in a hearing in mid-2015.

usually determined by seniority.[1] The overall emphasis on seniority allows experience and knowledge to accumulate over time, adding to the deference that the whole legislative house will give to the committee's judgments and decisions. To be sure, though, this is not always the case. In the 2014 Congressional elections, the Republican Party won control of the Senate, which meant that its most senior member of the environment committee, James Inhofe, became its chairman. Inhofe is ideologically an arch-conservative who denies the accuracy of the data gathered by the world's climate scientists regarding global warming.

Thirdly, there is the critical factor of staff resources. For example, American Congressional committees (as well as individual members) have substantial staff, including very capable people working long hours with knowledge and expertise in their own right. Staffers are typically qualified by their past experience in the bureaucracy, interest groups, university training, prior staff roles, or all of these sorts of experience. Congressional committees can also get help from bipartisan offices that are available to Congress as a whole, such as the Congressional Budget Office, the Congressional Research Service, and the Government Accountability Office. In parliamentary systems, committees typically have far less staff resources to do their work.

Might the American legislative branch be weakened by contention between its two houses, each with its strong committee on each bill? Here the remedy to promote cooperation is a committee one, as well. Where versions of a bill differ between the two houses, normally a **conference committee** is formed from leading members of both houses' relevant committees to iron out the differences. Once the conference committee has done its work, institutional custom requires that its supporting majorities in each house cooperate in passing the same compromise version.

Consequences for Influence

In the United States, when you combine staff and member expertise with (a) separation of powers and (b) the more lax party discipline in the American legislative branch, the result is Congressional experience and independence that can often contend effectively with the executive's expertise and knowledge. Committees and subcommittees may actively and substantially shape policy-making by rewriting (marking up, as it is called) bills that come from the president's cabinet. This fact provides opportunities for American legislators to build a record of policy achievements and votes that can be satisfying in itself, as well as useful to advertise to the district's voters in the next election campaign.

However, members' legislative independence also attracts the attention of interest groups with major stakes in policies that affect them. In making campaign contributions, interest groups (see chapter 9) are keen to focus on legislators who are on the appropriate committees for their policy areas. They want at least to gain access to the legislator (or his or her key staff) to make the group's case, if not more (see "Applying the Models" below). For example, the volume of contributions by Wall Street firms to the campaigns of members of Congressional committees handling financial regulation is legendary.

This situation contrasts with the general pattern in most parliamentary systems, where legislators and their committees have less staff and limited capacity to make significant amendments to government bills unless the government approves of their suggestions. To be sure, in committees opposition MPs may

APPLYING THE MODELS | Iron Triangles and Policy Networks

We may think of votes for candidates as, in part, support for the most prominent policy directions that the candidates or parties support. If so, when individuals or parties in legislative committee work anticipate the reactions of voters, the model that seems to be at work might be the majority preference one. Alternatively, though, we can think of voters in terms of the interest groups into which they may be divided. If legislators on committees are anticipating the reactions of such voters, the pluralist model comes to mind.

However, a pluralist-flavored form of the elite model also contends for the explanatory prize. That is the idea of "iron triangles" with heavy influence over policy decisions. Here the "triangle" includes (a) the most powerful interest group organizations in a given policy area, (b) the related executive bureaucratic unit, and (c) the relevant legislative committee itself. For example, many observers of the Japanese system have an elite-model impression of influence in legislative committees: policy dominance by large corporations and cooperating bureaucratic leaders from the executive branch, steering the decisions of the Japanese Diet. On this model, both limit setting and, at times, directive influence tends to stem from the most powerful interest groups.

A milder and more refined form of the elite model also contends in explaining legislative committee behavior for some political scientists: the idea of influence by an informal "policy network" (or "issue network") for each issue area (e.g., tax policy or environmental policy). Such networks includes legislators, committee staffers, bureaucrats in the executive branch, and interest group representatives, including many who have past experience in more than one of these roles related to the policy area. People in the same policy network tend to circulate from job to job within the policy area over time, and get to know each other. Policy network mates often come to share common experience, knowledge, institutional memory, and personal connections. This can invite a degree of cooperation despite their associations with contending parties, interests, values, and policy goals. According to the policy network view, the main impact of shared perspectives within a policy network is limit setting. A shared sense of what is and is not workable in the relevant issue area may tend to limit the policy agenda to a conventional range of alternatives, and discourage really new initiatives that think "out of the box."

try to get information about a bill or its implementation, and those from the majority party or parties can share ideas that they may be suggesting to their leaders in the cabinet. If there are tensions between the parties in the majority coalition over an issue, they may emerge in committee discussions.[2] But in the end, strong party discipline and usually weak committees assure that the parties' seat strengths (which reflect the outcome of the last election) and their leaders normally determine how bills fare in parliament, not its legislative committees.

Consequently, a member of parliament who wants to build expertise and achievements in a policy area will do more than just participate in its legislative committee. Well-organized parties each have their informal party committees for each major policy area. A policy-ambitious MP will want to participate in her or his party's committee for the favorite policy area, do his or her homework for it, contribute ideas to the party's policy direction in the issue area, and make speeches in parliamentary debate about it. (For parties in opposition, each policy area committee tends to be chaired by the party's leading expert in the area, the would-be minister if the party were to gain that ministry in the future as part of a parliamentary majority.[3])

CAN LEGISLATIVE ASSEMBLIES CONTEND EFFECTIVELY WITH THE EXECUTIVE BRANCH?

How powerful are the key legislative assemblies in the contention and cooperation between the legislative and executive branches of democratic government? As we have noted, the executive branch tends to originate the most important policy proposals. But the legislative branch can also exert influence. When and how? Answers to these questions have a lot to do with policy outcomes in democratic systems. In the United States (with its strong legislative houses even in budgetary matters), the conservative Republican Party took majority control of the House of Representatives in 2010, which allowed it subsequently to block President Obama's stimulus spending proposals aimed at keeping the economic recovery going. When the economy faltered, Republicans blamed the continuing high unemployment and absence of wage growth on Obama and the Democrats. This helped boost Republican gains in the Congressional election of 2014, when they took majority control of the Senate, as well. In democratic systems, we need to remember that assembly influence depends partly on the type of political framework. As we have noted, assembly influence is much less in parliamentary systems.

Ongoing Assembly Influence in Presidential Systems

As we have seen, in presidential systems the fixed term for the chief executive means that executive control does not change hands if the president loses a Congressional vote on a bill. Thus legislators of the president's party (and its informal coalition partner parties, if any) do not have to always cooperate cohesively in supporting administration bills to keep their leader in the presidency. Nor do opposition party legislators always have to all vote against a president's bill. Thus limit-setting legislative influence is common in policymaking. But the operation of this legislative influence may differ somewhat according to whether the party system is two-party or multiparty.

Legislative Influence in the Two-Party Presidential Framework In a two-party presidential system like that of the United States, uneven party discipline and the possibility of opposition majority control of legislative assemblies have important consequences for contention and cooperation. For bills to pass and become law, often there must be bargaining and compromise within and between parties and the branches of government.

Where the opposition party holds a majority in a legislative assembly, its members might refuse to cooperate even with executive proposals that are widely recognized as needed unless it gets concessions for its agenda in other policy areas.[4] Under these circumstances, in practice, the U.S. president's influence may be reduced to the limit-setting form of a veto: negating a bill passed by the legislative assemblies unless they can repass it into law—override the veto—by an extraordinary **supermajority** vote (e.g., a two-thirds majority in the United States.).

Under a two-party presidential political framework, uneven party discipline runs up against the need of each party to cooperate internally to be able to contend effectively with its rival. Party leadership structures are needed to try to unify the party's legislators in voting on bills. In both the U.S. House of

Representatives and the Senate, each party has a top leader, his or her deputy, one or more high-ranking members called "whips" (whose job it is to round up available votes for bills), a legislative strategy committee sometimes called the party's "steering committee," a committee for allocating slots on legislative committees (the committee on committees), and officers who lead the "conference" (caucus meetings). Amid these intraparty structures, leaders contend with the fact that at least at times, legislators can go their own way.

However, the relative independence of individual legislators from party control under this type of political framework does not always mean they can exercise influence with full autonomy. They also have to keep the support of voters on election day to stay in office. In chapter 2, we noted what some political scientists call power by "anticipated reaction"; in this case, the *voters* may have some influence over legislators' position taking on issues because the officeholder may do what he or she anticipates will bring a favorable voter reaction.

This requires more than just visiting the district frequently and meeting with individual constituents and interest groups. A legislator who faces significant electoral competition must also raise funds independently for expensive election campaigns to be able to advertise his or her legislative record, positions on issues, and claimed shortcomings of the opponent. This opens the door for potential influence by financial donors. Our assessment of this comes down to a question about cooperation amid contention: does the cooperation between individual and interest group donors on one hand, and candidates/officeholders on the other, extend to policymaking after the election?

As we saw in chapter 9, most campaign contributions go to candidates whose issue positions have not changed and are already known to be favorable to the views of the donor group (or individual). Here the contribution is just backing the donor's favorite horse. When policy position change does occur, particular contributions can rarely be *proven* to have changed a legislator's decision on a

In American government, even popular policies such as universal background checks for gun buyers (aimed at reducing the frequency of mass shootings in public places) can be frustrated by opposition from a minority of legislators who receive financial support from the National Rifle Association for their election campaigns.

bill. To begin with, we cannot see inside the psyches of candidates and contributors (except on the rare occasion of a documented quid pro quo). To be sure, if a big campaign contribution was immediately accompanied by a policy position change, things don't look good. But what if the policy-related request by the interest group or individual donor comes later?

And often there is a chicken-and-egg problem: which came first, the policy change decision or the knowledge of the contribution? If the decision to change policy positions came first, again, the donor's contribution may just be backing its new horse. On the other hand, donor influence over candidate policy positions may have operated by anticipated reaction

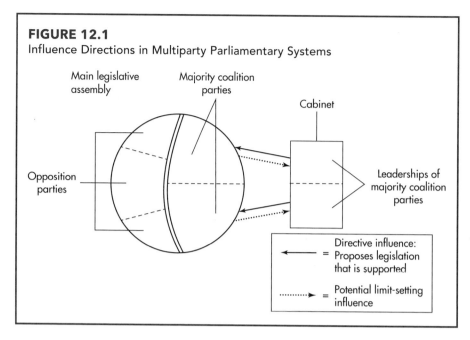

FIGURE 12.1
Influence Directions in Multiparty Parliamentary Systems

Main legislative assembly

Majority coalition parties

Cabinet

Opposition parties

Leaderships of majority coalition parties

Directive influence:
⟵ = Proposes legislation that is supported

·········▸ = Potential limit-setting influence

(see chapter 2). That is, the legislator's (or candidate's) policy position change may have occurred in anticipation of the expected new contribution by the donor, reflecting donor influence.

To be sure, the voters have the final say. But certainly a bad atmosphere lurks where legislators know that big campaign contributions are at stake—whether to themselves or to their opponents—if they adhere to certain issue positions (see "Applying the Models" below).

Legislative Influence in the Multiparty Presidential Framework Under the multiparty presidential framework—prevalent in Latin America, for example—the legislature may be even stronger. There, PR elections in the lower house produce the same multiparty result that we find in PR parliamentary systems. Typically no one party, not even that of the presidential winner, gains a majority of the legislative seats. Thus the president must try to put together informal legislative coalitions of parties or factions of them to support bills.

This may be done either ad hoc for each bill, or on a more regular basis by building an informal multiparty coalition. Such coalitions are similar to, but looser than, those in multiparty parliamentary democracies. For example, in the late 1990s in Brazil, then president Fernando Henrique Cardoso's centrist Social Democratic Party had fewer seats in the Chamber of Deputies than either the Democratic Movement Party (PMD, also centrist) or the Liberal Front Party (moderate conservative). Consequently, when Cardoso sought support for his initiative to cut back on regional government spending (by limiting spending on state payrolls to 60 percent of each state's overall budget), he had to try to maintain a coalition of his own party with the conservative Liberal Front and a large portion (one or more factions) of the centrist and diverse PMD. By 2000, Cardoso had succeeded.

To build and maintain a multiparty coalition, a president typically has to appoint a few leaders of allied parties to cabinet posts, make significant compromises on bills, and at times offer particular clientelistic benefits (called "pork barrel" spending in the United States) for supporting parties, factions within parties, regions, and even individual deputies in Congress (see "Contention and Cooperation" below). This applies in most cases in which, to achieve her or his goals, the president must pass legislation.[5]

In the face of such strong legislative influence, many multiparty presidential systems grant the president special powers in the legislative process that are not enjoyed by the president in the American two-party system. For example, the president may be given the capacities (a) to exercise a "line item veto" (of only

CONTENTION AND COOPERATION IN FOCUS | Party Cohesiveness in Multiparty Presidential Systems

When policy outcomes in multiparty presidential systems aren't going well and presidential approval ratings are down, parties in the legislative assemblies are more inclined to distance themselves from the president. Contention may replace cooperation within the informal support coalition, and passing legislation becomes especially difficult. Individual legislators and factions within parties will tend to look even more than usual to the interests of their home regions or districts. Some commentators have concluded that multiparty presidential government tends to produce generally poor legislative-executive relations.*

At times, though, this process can also yield significant cooperation. For one thing, party-list PR elections tend to enhance party cohesiveness in voting on bills. Since party leaders control the rankings on the party lists for the next election (see chapter 10), they can elevate cooperative deputies (and demote uncooperative ones), into (or out of) the top range of seats that the party expects to win. So if a deputy wants to be among those returning to the chamber after the next election, legislative cooperation with the party leadership is a good idea. The resulting higher degree of party discipline may allow leaders

of parties (or of factions within them) to be able to speak more for their whole supporting delegations, as they bargain with the president's office. In some situations, this can help the president by allowing executive bargaining efforts to focus mainly on party leaders, rather than having to bargain separately with numerous individual legislators, small factions, or regions. (Notably, however, where party lists for multimembered districts are "open"—as in Brazil—with voters choosing individual names rather than only picking ranked lists, this sort of limit-setting influence by party leaderships is removed.)

This doesn't guarantee that presidential bargaining with other parties will be successful in bringing their support. In the mid-2000s, top staff of Brazilian president Lula da Silva got into trouble for making cash payments to other small parties to get them to support Workers' Party bills. And where a president would like to pick off some legislators from an opposing party, its party cohesiveness can get in the way.

---

* For example, see Scott Mainwaring, "Presidentialism in Latin America," in Lijphart 1992.

part of a bill), (b) to restrict Congressional amendment power under certain circumstances, (c) to force rapid consideration of certain bills in the congress ("insistence powers"), and even (d) to issue decrees with the force of law without prior legislative vote, subject only to Congressional veto within a month or two. Such provisions can help the president in the constant struggle to get bills through the legislative process of multiparty presidential systems.

Occasional Assembly Influence in Parliamentary Government

The general tendency of parliamentary government is to give the prime minister and cabinet the prevailing influence over the parliamentary majority.[6] To be sure, in parliamentary systems the elected assembly chooses the chief executive by majority vote, and maintains this "prime minister" (and her or his appointed cabinet) in executive office by majority support for their major bills. In practice, however, this gives the cabinet the main directive influence over parliament. This is because the parliamentary majority—whether composed of one party or a coalition of parties— wants above all to keep the control of the executive branch in the hands of its leaders. This can be achieved only if, in parliamentary voting by such parties, the whole party fraction—all of a party's legislators holding seats in the assembly—remains cohesive in support of the proposals of their leadership (see chapter 10).[7] The **backbenchers**—ordinary members of parliament—of the majority party or parties must follow party discipline by voting "yes" on the cabinet's bills.

Party discipline under parliamentary government is also encouraged by another factor. Parties' leaders in the cabinet generally control the selection of some of their party mates in parliament to serve as their deputies in the political executive. Hopes of gaining such a position as deputy minister or assistant deputy minister further encourage cooperation by the rank and file with their leadership. Finally, as we shall see in chapter 13, ministers framing bills have access to the technical knowledge provided by the nonpartisan career civil servants under them, expertise which typically cannot be matched by parliamentary backbenchers or their committees. All of these factors contribute to the normal parliamentary situation: cooperation by the parliamentary majority with the initiatives of the political executive.

However, this is not the whole story. Occasionally, a party (or faction within a party) included in the parliamentary majority becomes very uncomfortable with the direction that cabinet policies seem to be taking.[8] A policy idea may stretch the limits of the party's ideological identity, values, or traditional patterns of interest group support (see chapter 10). Under these circumstances, the unhappy portion of parliament may exercise a degree of limit-setting influence—keeping decisions within certain boundaries (see chapter 3)—over the executive.

Influence in Two-Party Versus Multiparty Parliamentary Frameworks

Again, under two-party parliamentary frameworks, the cabinet is filled by the leaders of just the one party that holds the majority on its own. Parliamentary rebellions are rare, and when they occur they are dealt with in a way that does not sacrifice the party's majority control. In 1991 in Great Britain, a majority of the Conservative Party fraction opposed Conservative prime minister Margaret Thatcher's tax plan. Thatcher insisted on her proposal, and in the end, was forced to resign as party leader and prime minister. She was replaced in both jobs by her finance minister (in Britain called the Chancellor of the Exchequer), John Major. Similarly in 2007, Labor prime minister Tony Blair had come under increasing criticism from his own party as his Iraq war policy was going badly (among other things). He was replaced as both party leader and prime minister by his Chancellor of the Exchequer, Gordon Brown.

Parliamentary backbenchers can exert more frequent influence under multiparty parliamentary frameworks. Again, in that case it takes two or more parties, allied in a coalition, to hold the parliamentary majority and fill the cabinet with the coalition parties' leaders. This means that at times coalition partner parties will have to cooperate with each other's policy priorities (reciprocally influencing each other; see chapter 2). Under these circumstances, contention might arise within one of the parties over how far it can go in such cooperation and compromise with other coalition partner parties. In this situation, influence is no longer concentrated in the cabinet; at least a portion of the legislative assembly has significant influence, too (see Table 12.3).

Influence Between Elections in Multiparty Parliamentary Systems

The first occurrence of influence by whole party fractions might come just after an election, in the initial formation of the majority coalition (prior to the installation of a cabinet). To be sure, often in multiparty parliamentary systems there is

TABLE 12.3	When Is the Legislative Branch Influence High?
Political Framework	**High Legislative Branch Influence**
Two-party presidential	Usually
Multiparty presidential	Always
Two-party parliamentary	Rarely
Multiparty parliamentary	Occasionally

little to decide at this point. The coalition alignments are known before the election, based on natural ideological affinities—a left-of-center coalition contending against a right-of-center coalition. And the broad outlines of policy cooperation within each coalition may already be understood. The voters have determined which coalition has won, so it is the voters who have exerted the primary influence. For example, in Germany it is known that the (moderate left-of-center) Social Democrats and the Greens are ready to form a left-of-center coalition if their seats add up to a majority in the lower house, the Bundestag (see Country Case Studies below). Similarly, it is understood that the (conservative) Christian Democrats[9] and (classical liberal) Free Democrats are ready to form a right-of-center coalition if, taken together, they win a majority.

However, even with these broad understandings in place, the winning coalition's leaders will still have postelection meetings to decide how to allocate control of the various ministries among the coalition partner parties, and what the major policy priorities of the cabinet will be.[10] Normally the result is a coalition agreement—usually formalized and public but not always—which incorporates any policy compromises that are necessary between the coalition partner parties. As political scientists Michael Laver and Kenneth Shepsle (1996) stress, the resulting pact will set the guidelines of their subsequent cooperation.[11] Since it is arrived at before a cabinet is in place, we can say that this is a high point of parliamentary influence.

Once the cabinet has been formed and its parties' leaders are ensconced there, parliamentary influence usually subsides considerably. Again, the majority coalition's party fractions in parliament tend to rather automatically support cabinet proposals, to maintain their leaders' control of the executive branch. Differences between the coalition partner parties over policy are usually limited by the coalition agreement itself, to which the parties are committed.[12]

However, legislative influence might spike briefly later. First, a new issue might arise that was not foreseen at the time of the initial coalition agreement. In response, the cabinet ministers of one of the parties in the majority coalition might contend for a policy that makes another coalition partner party uncomfortable. Dealing with such contention may require the unsettled party's cabinet ministers to call a special **caucus**—a meeting of the full party fraction—to discuss the issue and suggest how far the party should go in the controversial (for that party) direction. This represents limit-setting influence by at least a portion of the legislative assembly.

At the extreme of such contention, backbencher unhappiness may even pressure the party's leaders in the cabinet to *threaten withdrawal* from the majority coalition. If this came to pass it could cause the cabinet to lose its parliamentary majority and it would have to either resign or find a replacement party in its coalition. Such a threat may force further negotiation in the cabinet about the troublesome proposal, perhaps leading to compromise or even dropping the idea altogether.

What Happens When There Is No Parliamentary Majority? Multiparty parliamentary democracies may even encounter a situation in which no conventional majority coalition can be found to assure passage of bills. For example, an election result may not clearly yield a winning coalition, and the most successful coalition may prove unable to find another party to join it to put it over 50 percent of the seats.

A key parliamentary option under these circumstances is **minority government**. In this scenario, parliament has agreed to allow one party or a small coalition to form a cabinet to administer the executive branch ministries, but without holding a majority of the parliamentary seats. This situation runs counter to the logic of parliamentary government, and usually few new policies are passed. To pass legislation, the cabinet must get the support of one or more other parties in parliament that stand outside the cabinet party or coalition. In recent decades, Sweden, for example, has experienced periods of minority government (see "Contention and Cooperation" below). Here, obviously the level of parliamentary influence remains high.

If a minority government wants to pass legislation regularly in one or a few policy areas, it must find an informal **support party** outside the cabinet that is willing to approve its initiatives in those policy areas. For example, Sweden's (left social democratic) Left Party or a centrist party may be willing to support some of the bills of a (moderate left-of-center) Social Democratic Party cabinet, without actually serving in it. This may require negotiation and compromise with the outside support party, suggesting a spike in parliamentary influence.

If a minority cabinet lacks such a support party in parliament, very few of its bills will receive parliamentary approval. We may see merely a **caretaker government**, which refrains from proposing new measures to parliament. It will only administer the executive departments under existing law until a new majority coalition or support party emerges later, either from a new election or when a new issue alters the political landscape.

Notably, a situation similar to minority government can arise in those exceptional parliamentary systems in which the upper house must approve most or all bills proposed by the lower house for them to become law. The upper house thus possesses a veto power. Election outcomes in Germany and Italy, for example, can result in a situation in which the lower house majority coalition fails to hold the upper house majority. When this happens in Germany, in trying to pass legislation the cabinet supported by the Bundestag majority must behave, for all practical purposes, like a minority government. It has to contend and negotiate compromises with the opposition party or parties in the Bundesrat to gain passage of key bills (see Germany Country Case Study below). As in minority government, here the influence of parts of the legislative branch rises substantially.

Another option for when no conventional coalition can hold the overall parliamentary majority is a **grand coalition**. It especially empowers the executive, and will be explored in chapter 13. Here I will only note what it is: an unusual coalition of a broad left-of-center party with a broad conservative party. They tend to be large parties, and together they can hold a majority of the parliamentary seats without having to deal with pesky small parties to their left, right, or center. A grand coalition can come into play if either (a) no coalition has won a parliamentary majority in a par-

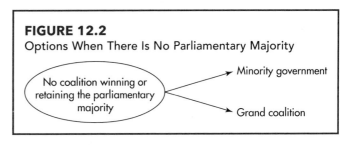

FIGURE 12.2
Options When There Is No Parliamentary Majority

No coalition winning or retaining the parliamentary majority

Minority government

Grand coalition

liamentary election, and/or (b) a pressing, sensitive issue or emergency demands action, but cuts across the usual coalition alignments and thus rules out conventional parliamentary majorities. In either situation a grand coalition may be the only way to forge controversial but necessary measures to address an important policy challenge. This option has been pursued after Germany's Bundestag elections in 2005 and 2013 (see Country Case Studies below), in Israel to conduct its withdrawal from occupied Gaza in 2005, and in Italy in 2013 and 2014 (see Country Case Studies, chapter 13).

Multiparty "Fractionalization" and Its Remedies

Difficulties in keeping conventional majority coalitions cooperating tend to arise more frequently in proportion to the number of parties contending in the system overall. A parliament's overall number of parties is referred to by political scientists as its degree of **fractionalization**. The greater the number of party fractions in parliament—that is, the greater the fractionalization—the larger the number of parties that it takes to form a parliamentary majority. The larger the number of party leaderships in the cabinet, the harder it is to find policy positions around which they can all cooperate. It is usually easier for two coalition partner parties to cooperate behind policy proposals than three, four, or five.

High fractionalization could be found, for example, in Weimar Germany in the 1920s and early 1930s, in France in the 1950s, and commonly in postwar Italy.[13] High fractionalization and occasional cabinet instability may still be found today in Israel and India, for example.

In these situations, majority coalitions frequently break down. Here the influence of the legislative branch continues to be high relative to the executive. The influence of the voters over the government's general policy directions (via the party and coalition strengths after the most recent election), for its part, declines. Cabinet resignations come much too frequently to hold new parliamentary elections each time.

In each of the above-cited European cases, changes were made to the electoral system. The aim was to reduce fractionalization, and thus to reduce the number of parties in majority coalitions and lessen cabinet instability. One option is to set a minimum vote threshold—say, of 4 or 5 percent—for a party to get its proportional representation in parliament. Once this change has been made, very small parties can't get across the hurdle and into parliament, reducing the total number of parties (e.g., as occurred in Germany in 1949).

Alternatively, a nation may decide to fill *a portion* of the legislative seats by single-member district (SMD) election, alongside the other portion filled solely by PR voting. This option, sometimes referred to as "parallel" voting, was adopted in Italy in the 1990s, and is also found in Mexico, Japan, and South Korea.

Since SMD favors large broad parties over small focus parties (see chapters 10 and 11), this change will reduce the overall seat strengths of small parties. Yet another approach to the same goal is what France did in 1958: switch to SMD elections, but with a second "runoff" vote between the top two vote-winners in the first stage. Some of the small parties rarely see their candidates make it to the second round, and even more rarely win the seat (unless coalition agreements gain them the support of a large party in the district).

Again, in most of today's established multiparty parliamentary democracies, fractionalization is limited and coalitions are generally stable and internally cooperative (at least publicly). The majority coalition tends to be held together by ideological kinship among the member parties, as each coalition shares a segment of the ideological spectrum. Shared values, too, help hold coalitions together. If a small party at the ideological extreme of the governing coalition leaves the cabinet, another small party toward the center might be found to replace it (or vice versa), without too much change in the government's overall policy directions. In Sweden, for example (see Table 12.4), a substantial number of parties coexist with a quite stable government.

TABLE 12.4 | **Swedish Elections and Legislative Composition, 1991–2002**

Party	1991 % of Votes	1991 Seats	1994 % of Votes	1994 Seats	1998 % of Votes	1998 Seats	2002 % of Votes	2002 Seats
Social Democrats	37.7	138	45.2	161	36.6	131	39.9	144
Left Party/Communists	4.5	16	6.2	22	12.0	43	8.3	30
Ecology Party	3.4	–	5.0	18	4.5	16	4.5	17
Liberal Party	9.1	33	7.2	26	4.7	17	13.3	48
Center Party	8.5	31	7.7	27	5.1	18	6.2	22
Christian Democrats	7.1	26	4.1	15	11.8	42	9.1	33
Moderates (Conservatives)	21.9	80	22.4	80	22.7	82	15.1	55
New Democracy	6.7	25	1.2	–	–	–	–	–
Others	1.0	–	1.0	–	2.6	–	3.6	–
All	100	349	100	349	100	349	100	349

Source: Gallagher, Laver, and Mair (2006), 192.

TABLE 12.5	Variation in Legislative Influence in Presidential and Parliamentary Systems	
	Presidential	**Parliamentary**
Legislature's main source of influence	Independent election; autonomous capacity to reject president's proposals and originate its own legislation	Limit-setting capacity to replace prime minister or withdraw from majority coalition
Degree of party discipline	Somewhat lax, allowing individual legislators to change, modify, or oppose executive branch proposals	Generally strict, ensures passage of executive branch proposals
Importance of a minority party or coalition outside cabinet	Partial support often necessary to pass legislation	Support unnecessary except under minority government
Strength of legislative committees	Generally strong, well resourced, expert, and capable of demanding testimony or information	Weaker, with fewer resources and powers to demand information

To be sure, coalition instability can still be found under two sets of circumstances. One concerns brand-new multiparty democracies, where party formation is just beginning. This was evident in post-Communist Eastern Europe in the 1990s. But since then, coalition instability there has been reduced by the strengthening of parties' organizations, ideological identities, party discipline, and linkages to portions of the population. Also, stability has been aided by legislative institutionalization: stabilization of the legislative branch's powers, structures, procedures, and professionalism.[14] One factor contributing to this progress has been an international one: the requirements for joining the European Union, which include improving organization and efficiency in doing legislative business.

Secondly, a country may be going through difficult, wrenching policy challenges with no attractive alternatives. Public frustration may run high, new protest parties may spring up, and factional conflict within broad parties may become sharp. We saw this, for example, in Italy in 2012 and 2013. Unpopular economic austerity policies were forced on the government from outside the country amid deepening recession and high joblessness, especially among the young (see chapter 7). In 2013, a protest party arose, led by an Italian comedian Beppe Grillo, that took enough of the vote to block either of the conventional coalitions from forming a majority (see Country Case Study on Italy, chapter 13). The result has been fragile grand coalitions that span the left-right divide and continue to struggle with unpopular European Commission demands for budget austerity. Still, aside from these exceptional situations, generally legislative branch influence is lower in parliamentary than in presidential systems (see Table 12.5).

Assembly Influence and Meaningful Voter Choice

What difference might the political framework make for the quality of democracy? In chapter 11, I suggested a picture of minimal democratic quality that

THE HUMAN RIGHTS CONNECTION | The Iranian Legislature

If an authoritarian regime permits a legislature with competing candidates, it may prove to be the germ of political reform over time in the direction of human rights respect and democratization (as in Brazil, for example; see Country Case Studies, chapter 4). In Iran, some early promise seems to have been recently extinguished.

A radical Islamist revolution in 1979 led by Ayatollah Ruhollah Khomeini established a Shia Muslim theocracy in Iran. But the regime has a legislative assembly, the 290-member **Majlis**, chosen by two-stage SMDM elections with competing candidates. A couple of times Majlis elections have involved fairly open competition for legislative seats, resulting in a relatively fair hearing for ideological and policy alternatives. As recently as the 2000 election, Iranians voted heavily for candidates who would have expanded human rights if the Majlis's views were followed, and who supported a moderately reformist president who had been elected in 1997. However, the other institutions and conditions surrounding the Majlis have repeatedly allowed unelected clerical groups to actually make policy. Such groups are ready and able to remove their rivals and reverse opposing policies at will, rendering illusory any appearances of civil and political rights respect.

A key feature of the political environment surrounding the Majlis is the separate twelve-person Guardian Council dominated by Supreme Leader (the chief spiritual guide for Iranian Shia Islam) Ayatollah Ali Khamenei. It has veto power over the membership and legislation of the Majlis, pursuant to Ayatollah Khomeini's doctrine of Islamic "juris guardianship" over the "public interest." That veto is presented as a judgment on whether the membership and legislation of the Majlis is in accord with Sharia Law based on the Koran, and with the constitution. However, Iranian Shia Islam allows a range of interpretation regarding economic and sociocultural policy issues, leaving some scope for diversity of expression, association, and political rights.

In the first few years of the Islamic regime, some left-of-center groups and leaders were removed from the political scene by the dominant clerical faction. But from 1980 through 1991, the voters elected Majlises displaying a range of ideological and policy views among their members. Conservative groups continued to use their government advantages to ban some secular opponents and do well in elections, but some left-of-center Islamists remained, and some legislation that they favored was allowed to pass. Ayatollah Khomeini's handpicked Expediency Council, an advisory body of high clerical and executive government officials, at first intervened for compromise in a few instances concerning moderate

I called "meaningful voter choice." This was defined as the voter's sense that the electoral success of the favored candidates(s) or party would make a difference in government policymaking. Some might consider voter choice to be more meaningful in parliamentary systems where the elected majority coalition holds together, and the cabinet can count on its bills passing due to party discipline and cohesion in the assembly. Thus the executive leadership and the elected assembly can respond together to policy challenges and be held accountable at once (a) for moving government policies in the directions promised in the election campaign, and (b) for the outcomes of those policies (retrospectively) whether in success or failure (see chapter 11). (However, in parliamentary cases where conventional majority coalitions fail to form and/or when party fractionalization render coalitions unstable, the requirements of meaningful voter choice would not be met; policy directions would be set by the negotiations among the parties, with uncertain linkage to voter preferences in the last election.)

In presidential frameworks, where the legislative assemblies and their committees are more independent and strong, and they negotiate with the executive economic legislation, including a minimum wage and job protections for workers.

However, it became clear early on that the Guardian Council represented conservative ideology, and it proceeded to veto a range of Majlis legislation from labor and trade regulation to a progressive income tax. After Khomeini's death in 1989, his replacement Ayatollah Ali Khamenei was a conservative, both economically and socioculturally. He basically favored a market economy, though with subsidies and protections of national business against foreign investment. During the 1990s, the supreme leader allowed the Guardian Council to intervene more heavily than before, to deny candidacy and office to more secular and left-of-center aspirants to legislative office.

By the end of the 1990s, reformers had shifted their main efforts to expanding sociocultural freedom, winning election of a reform-oriented president in 1997 and a majority in the 2000 Majlis elections. However, there was nothing in the regime's governmental structure to assure democracy and human rights respect. The 2004 Majlis elections saw the Guardian Council ban thousands of reform-oriented candidates. The result was few opponents running, a partial opposition boycott, a low voter turnout, and a big victory for the conservatives. The subsequent presidential election of January 2005 was won by a strong cultural conservative, Mahmoud Ahmadinejad, running on a pledge to redistribute oil wealth to alleviate high unemployment. In office, however, Ahmadinejad replaced reformers with conservatives in governor posts and banned western music from radio and television. His rivals, who had protested the election as fraudulent, were arrested, and many of their supporters detained. The 2008 Majlis election was similarly characterized by large-scale vetoes of candidates by the Guardian Council. Contention in the Majlis was increasingly between conservative factions, supporters of Ahmadinejad and those of the Supreme Leader Khameni, who were experiencing a rift. The 2012 Majlis elections saw victory by Khameni's supporters, this time with reformers boycotting the election. In 2013, however, the presidential election was won by a moderate, Hassan Rouhani.

Ultimately, the Guardian Council's huge limit-setting power enables it to interpret Islam in its preferred way and enforce that interpretation under the supervision of the supreme leader and his Expediency Council. The additional manipulation of candidate lists rules out truly free and fair elections to the Majlis. The backup threat of detention and imprisonment of regime opponents (with even some cases of unsolved assassination) completes the authoritarian picture.

on a regular basis, the picture looks murkier. Legislative election outcomes may not tell the voter much about what policy directions will be pursued by the government overall. Meaningful voter choice is harder to realize.

However, others might view the electorate differently. Voters may be seen as typically very diverse and divided in their views, undercutting the idea of a majority opinion even on the general directions that policies should take on the most prominent issues of the day. For example, some voters just want to see representatives elected who can produce benefits to their local district and its interest groups. Alternatively, a particular voter may view meaningful voting in terms of trying to elect more *opposition* representatives who can check policy directions that the voter dislikes. Certainly, most Republican "Tea Party" voters in American House races in 2010 and 2014 were aware that victories by their favored legislative candidates could make a difference in blocking policy initiatives by the Democrats and their leader, President Obama. For someone with this outlook, presidential government and its independent legislative assemblies provides at least some meaningful voter choice.

LEGISLATURES IN AUTHORITARIAN REGIMES

Legislatures are far less significant in authoritarian regimes than they are in representative democracies. Assemblies may be permitted, but do not function in the ways that we are familiar with in representative democracies. In various ways, the dominant power in the regime so heavily constrains what the legislature may do that real policymaking is simply not found in the legislative branch.

In the former Communist regimes, members of the assembly had to be members of the Communist Party, and some other single-party regimes had a similar requirement. By patrolling the boundaries of party membership, the regime could exercise limit-setting power over the legislature, or even go further to engage in directive power over it, as in the Communist regimes.

In another limit-setting approach, the theocratic regime in Iran has a religious body, the Guardian Council, screen all candidates for parliament, denying nomination or office to anyone it deems too secular in political orientation (see "The Human Rights Connection"). Military regimes and personal autocracies often display a third limit-setting approach, declaring major policy areas to be off limits to legislative jurisdiction. In the early 1990s, under military rule in Nigeria, an elected legislative branch was only allowed to decide on minor symbolic matters, like the design of the national flag.

In single-party-dominant authoritarian regimes, the dominant party uses its position in controlling the government to radically disadvantage any opponents who might have a chance of posing a serious electoral threat. Opposition leaders might be accused of criminal offenses and arrested, and opposition rallies prevented by denial of permission from the police. (Weak, nonthreatening parties might not be hindered at all.)

SUMMARY: CONTENTION AND COOPERATION IN THE LEGISLATIVE PROCESS

As we have seen, legislative assemblies differ substantially in how they operate, how much influence they have in relation to the political executive, and how influence is distributed within them. A major factor contributing to these differences is the political framework. Presidential government tends to produce less party-based cooperation, allowing for (a) more contention and cooperation among individuals independently of their party and its leaders and (b) more influence for the legislature as a whole in contention with the executive. Parliamentary government tends to give the political executive heavy influence over the legislative assembly, usually enhancing overall legislative cooperation.

Under the multiparty (usually PR) parliamentary framework, however, at times a party fraction within the governing coalition can have an important say in the course that the government will take. If this occurs too often—usually related to high fractionalization (numerous parties)—contention threatens to overtake cooperation in the majority coalition. In this case, either (a) certain changes in the electoral system may be adopted to reduce the number of parties and ease the task of coalition cooperation (e.g., a minimum vote threshold or filling some seats by SMDP), or (b) the system might temporarily adopt a minority government or a left-right "grand coalition" of the two big moderate parties. Regardless of the type of political framework, contention in legislative assemblies requires the lubrication of some party members who work to facilitate cooperation, whether within or among the parties or the legislative institutions.

To understand more fully the impact of these factors related to political frameworks, power, and values, though, we must move on to the executive branch.

COUNTRY CASE STUDIES

Our two country cases below represent a contrast between legislative assemblies in an established democracy (Germany) and that in a traditionally authoritarian government that is now in a process of change (Egypt). Germany's legislative branch of government illustrates occasionally strong legislative influence in patterns of contention and cooperation among individuals and parties in a multiparty parliamentary system. Prior to the 2011 Arab Spring, Egypt employed single-party dominant electoral authoritarian rule in which the executive leadership imposed cooperation on the legislature. The subsequent Islamist-majority legislators were allies of the Muslim Brotherhood president, but were removed (with him) in the 2013 military coup.

Germany: A Complex Parliament

The German political framework is multiparty parliamentary. The legislative branch is bicameral, including the 598-member Bundestag, the lower house, and the 69-member Bundesrat, the upper house. The most important unit is the Bundestag, which elects the chancellor (the German title for the prime minister) by majority vote. In typical parliamentary fashion, the parliamentary majority's leadership supplies the cabinet ministers appointed by the chancellor. In the PR voting that establishes the parties' seat strengths in the Bundestag, the sixteen "lands" serve as multimember electoral districts. With small parties present as well as large ones, no one party is able to win a majority on its own. Hence the parliamentary majority must be composed of a coalition (alliance) of two or more parties, whose party discipline in passing cabinet-proposed bills keeps the majority coalition's leaders in their cabinet minister positions supervising the ministries of the executive branch.

Notably, the German legislative branch has three distinctive features. First, in the PR voting for the Bundestag, Germany has a high minimum vote threshold for a party to get any PR representation from the states: 5 percent of the national vote. (The only exception to this requirement is the case where a sub-5 percent party wins at least 3 SMDP seats; see below.) This reduces fractionalization—the number of parties overall—in the German party system. Thus typically, no more than two parties are necessary to comprise a majority coalition in the Bundestag.

Second, Germany's lower-house Bundestag has an unusual way of filling many of parties' PR-won seats. In addition to the party preference (PR) ballot, each voter makes a second choice in her or his small single-member district. For about half of the Bundestag's seats, this second, SMDP balloting determines which *particular individuals* will fill slots won by her or his party in the PR voting. In effect, every SMDP winner automatically jumps to the top of her or his party's list in filling the seats that the party has won in party preference (PR) vote. This adds a dash of local personal responsibility in representation. But the SMDP voting does not alter the dominance of the PR vote in establishing the relative seat strengths of the parties.

As we know, it is large broad parties that do best in the SMDP races—in the German case, the moderate left-of-center Social Democratic Party (SPD) and the conservative Christian Democratic Union (CDU).[15] Accordingly, most of these two parties' PR-won slots are filled by their SMDP winners. The smaller parties—the Left Party, the Greens, and the Free Democrats (FDP)—are too small to win SMDP races, and tend to fill their seats in the usual party list fashion, from their lists in each state's PR voting.

Since the 1970s, the most common coalition alignment in the Bundestag has displayed the left-of-center coalition—of the moderate left-of-center SPD and the Greens—opposing the right-of-center coalition, of the conservative CDU and the classical liberal FDP. (Exceptions were the SPD-CDU grand coalitions of 2005–2009 and 2013–present; see below.)

As usual under parliamentary government, party discipline assures that the cabinet's bills will ultimately pass in the lower house. But a few special features of the Bundestag provide scope for more independent legislative behavior *prior* to final votes on bills, making for a bit stronger legislative branch than is usual for parliamentary systems. First, Germany has specialized committees. Also, by custom all parties in the Bundestag receive committee chairmanships in proportion to their seat strengths, rather than having only members of the majority coalition's parties chair committees. In addition, there is a council of elders, which also represents all parties in proportion to their seat strengths, that serves as a steering committee deciding on the Bundestag agenda and the amount of time for considering each bill.

Moreover, normally committee meetings do not record their internal votes. This tends to shield committee deliberations from outside attention, allowing parties' legislators to act more independently of party leaders in that setting. Limited cross-party cooperation and even opposition input is possible there. Finally, a substantial percentage of Bundestag members tend to come from economic sectors such as the national- or state-level bureaucracy (on leave for the period of their legislative service), unions, professions, and other backgrounds, that give them expertise to make technical adjustments in cabinet bills. These factors leave room for more technical tinkering with bills in German legislative committees than is usual in parliamentary committee work.

Yet another distinctive feature of the German legislative branch is the upper house Bundesrat, which may wield serious influence in the process of passing some bills. The Bundesrat represents the land (regional or "state") governments: 3–6 members per land, with each land's delegation drawn from its cabinet and led by the land chief minister (chosen by the unicameral land parliament majority). For legislative proposals that are judged to affect the states—over half the bills nowadays—the upper house Bundesrat has a veto power. (If a bill is classified as not affecting the states and vetoed by the Bundesrat, the Bundestag may simply repass the bill to make it law.) This Bundesrat veto doesn't make much difference if state elections have mostly gone the same way as the Bundestag election; with the same disciplined majority coalition prevailing in both houses, the two will cooperate.

However, state assembly elections are not **concurrent** (occurring at the same time) with the four-year schedule of national Bundestag elections; they are staggered over time. So if national policymaking has become unpopular for some reason, over time the state-level election results can trend toward victories by the opposition coalition. Eventually, enough state assembly elections may have gone against the cabinet coalition that the opposition coalition gains the Bundesrat majority. When this has happened, cooperation between the two legislative houses is likely to be replaced by contention and bargaining, with the opposition coalition in the Bundesrat influencing key legislation. (Procedurally, differences between the two assemblies over a bill are referred to a conference committee called the Mediation Committee, drawn from both houses; there, Bundesrat representatives are not bound to vote as instructed by their state cabinets, and a compromise may be worked out.) This was the situation in the years leading up to the elections of 1998 and 2005, and after mid-2010.

Such divided government was important in the early-mid-2000s when Social Democratic chancellor Gerhard Schroeder had to negotiate on his jobs program with the Bundesrat majority, which was held by the opposition right-of-center CDU/FDP coalition. This led to the controversial Hartz reforms of 2003–2004, which included cutting long-term unemployment benefits substantially and expanding temporary employment contracts that are exempt from traditional German labor protections. Later, in mid-2010, the governing right-of-center coalition (following its 2009 Bundestag election victory) had to negotiate with the Bundesrat's left-of-center majority over the government's proposals for spending cuts to try to reduce the budget deficit (see below).

It is possible—though rare until recently—for neither of the two main coalitions to win a Bundestag majority. In the elections of both 2005 and 2013, the conservative CDU's leader, Angela Merkel, became chancellor due to her coalition's winning more seats than the Social Democrats and their coalition (with the Greens). But overall in both elections, the most successful coalition failed to win a majority in the Bundestag. If we count the seats won by the left social democratic Left Party—which remains outside the conventional SPD-Green coalition—the parties on the left side of the ideological spectrum had actually won more Bundestag seats than did the right-of-center coalition.

In both of these cases, the two broad parties chose to form a center-leaning, left-right "grand coalition"— of the moderate left-of-center Social Democrats and the conservative Christian Democrats. Their usual smaller coalition partners, the Greens on the left, and the classical liberal FDP on the right, were left out. The resulting grand coalitions ended up dividing the cabinet fairly equally between the CDU- and SPD-controlled ministries, with the SPD gaining important minister positions. Thus between 2005 and 2009, and from 2013 on, left-right contention was muted amid greater cooperation; bargaining and compromise shifted to within the cabinet itself. On issues where the two parties could not find common ground, the cabinet simply refrained from proposing legislation.

The 2009 parliamentary election was won by a conventional right-of-center CDU-FDP coalition. It came at the end of the first of the above-noted grand coalition periods, and illustrates how the party not holding the Chancellorship can suffer from its grand coalition participation. In the months prior to the election, it was clear that Germany had weathered the financial and economic crisis and recession of 2008–2009 comparatively well. This was largely thanks to the Social Democrat-inspired emergency policies such as injecting funds into stressed financial institutions, extending low-interest credit to banks, nationalizing important banks where necessary to reduce risk to the system, guaranteeing commercial loans, and providing moderate stimulus spending to support consumer demand. Germany's preexisting guarantees of universal health insurance, housing assistance, and unemployment benefits had also helped to steady consumer demand. In addition, the unemployment rate was kept down with the help of a new government subsidy (the "short work" program) to employers to keep workers on the payroll with reduced hours rather than laying them off.

While these moderate left-of-center policies were in line with the Social Democrats' approach to the economy, conservative Angela Merkel, as chancellor,

got much of the credit for the CDU's reasonableness. Meanwhile, in the 2009 election campaign, the SPD could not contend sharply against a party with which it shared the government (and might continue to do so afterward). But due to its recent coziness with the CDU, the SPD lost a portion of its left-leaning voter support to the Left Party. This situation played a major part in the CDU-FDP victory in 2009 election.

Subsequently, the Merkel government was pressed especially by her classical liberal coalition partner, the FDP, toward austerity-oriented policies. To reduce the deficit, the cabinet backed spending cuts but refused to raise taxes on high incomes. This approach proved increasingly unpopular. Subsequently, the chancellor had to support limited bailout measures to save the Eurozone from the threat of southern European defaults,[16] another stance that was unpopular among many Germans. Soon the right-of-center CDU-FDP coalition had lost its majority in the Bundesrat due to losses in state elections, and the system went back to divided government.

However, when Europe reentered recession in 2012–2013, again Germany weathered the storm fairly well, anchored especially by its continuing exports (e.g., of industrial machinery and chemicals) to China. In the elections of September 2013, Merkel's Christian Democrats again won more seats than any other single party. But her coalition partner, the Free Democrats, failed to make the 5-percent minimum for PR seats in the Bundestag. Meanwhile, all of the significant parties on the left—the Social Democrats (SPD), the Greens, and the Left Party—succeeded in making the cut. As in 2005, the left-of-center parties' seat strengths were sufficient to prevent the CDU from gaining a majority. Again, the answer was a grand coalition of the Social Democrats and the Christian Democrats.

To be sure, at the outset the moderate left-of-center SPD was not eager to form such a cabinet. After serving in a grand coalition from 2005 to 2009, the party had suffered big losses in the parliamentary election of 2009 as many of its supporters wondered about its identity and relevance. A faction of the SPD, led by Ms. Hannelore Kraft (chief minister in Germany's most populous state, North Rhine/Westphalia, and SPD leader of the opposition majority coalition in the Bundesrat), opposed joining the grand coalition. She argued that the SPD could remain outside the cabinet and still be able to force compromise or defeat on the cabinet's initiatives when proposals arrived in the upper house with its left-of-center majority.

The leaders of the pro-grand coalition faction, SPD party chairman Sigmar Gabriel and parliamentary party leader Frank-Walter Steinmeier, argued that the party could get important policy concessions from the Christian Democrats within a grand coalition. (They were right.) They put the detailed coalition policy agreement (with the CDU) to an unusual referendum of all SPD party members on the question, and prevailed: the SPD joined.

Among other things, Chancellor Merkel had to agree to SPD demands for a minimum wage, improvements in pensions (and in some cases, retirement age reductions) for certain vulnerable groups such as homemakers and the disabled, labor law changes that tighten the requirements for employers' use of short-term contracts (that skirt job security protections) for their workers, rent controls, and increases in infrastructure spending. And SPD chair Gabriel would serve not only as deputy chancellor but also as minister for the economy generally and the sectors of energy and the environment. However, the SPD did not get the increases in some tax rates that it wanted, and has had to live with finance minister Schauble's target of a balanced budget by 2016. And especially important, Gabriel had to back Chancellor Merkel's hard line demanding austerity from Greece amid the latter's twin crises of depression and unpayable government debt.

The German economy continues to perform well, with very high trade surpluses and unemployment rates under 7 percent, even as the rest of Europe stagnates economically. Again, people tend to give the credit for coalition policies to Chancellor Merkel, and the SPD support level in polls seems stuck at around 25 percent. Consequently, many in the SPD are looking at the idea of returning to a left-of-center coalition in the future, perhaps even one including the left social democratic Left Party.

Egypt: A Weak Legislature

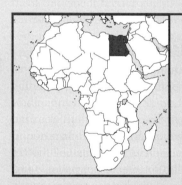

Prior to the 2011 Arab Spring uprising, Egypt had a legislature with many of the formal traits of a representative democratic one. According to the constitution, it had a directly elected lower house that could freely debate and reject government proposals and decrees, propose its own laws and override presidential vetoes with a two-thirds vote. It could monitor and investigate the government, including questioning government ministers. Yet Egyptian government overall was authoritarian, fully under the control of the president, his government party, the bureaucracy he headed, and the military with which he was closely aligned. Egypt's institutional arrangements needed to be viewed in the context of the underlying realities of imposed political cooperation.

Egypt's legislature was bicameral. The upper house, the Consultative Assembly or Majlis al-Shura, had a third of its 264 members appointed by the president, with the rest elected for six-year terms, half every three years. In political reality, however, the upper house was insignificant. It reviewed certain issues and some laws, but its views were only advisory. More relevant was the lower house, the People's Assembly, or Majlis al-Shaab. It had 444 elected members, plus 10 appointed by the president. They served for five years unless the body was dissolved earlier by the president (following a referendum). Under Hosni Mubarak, president from 1981 to 2011, over a dozen parties were legally allowed to compete for Assembly seats. How, then, did Egypt arrive at a situation in which no more than 14 seats in the lower house were won by opposing parties in each of the elections of 1995 and 2000? The answer had to do with the electoral system, heavy government control of the electoral process, and the underlying position of the National Democratic Party (NDP) as a dominant government party.

In the 1960s, the Egyptian state had a one-party authoritarian regime run by the Arab Socialist Union Party under the tight control of its leader, Gamal Abdul Nasser. In the 1970s, its new chief Anwar Sadat released many detained Islamic activists and took steps in a multiparty direction. He allowed three different platforms (and eventually parties) to contend, but they were actually three wings of the former controlling party. The center-right faction under Sadat's own control proved to be dominant, took over the former party's organization, won overwhelmingly in the 1976 assembly elections, and was renamed the NDP. It became the dominant "government party"[17] of Egypt.

Hosni Mubarak took over the NDP and the presidency in 1981 after Sadat's assassination. When the new 1983 constitution set up PR voting, it was unclear how comfortable Mubarak would be with an authentic multiparty system. After a scare in the parliamentary election of 1987 (with Islamists and a free-market-oriented party winning 38 and 35 seats, respectively), the NDP government reinforced its control. Government intervention to favor the NDP intensified, with party dominance of state TV and radio, mobilization of rural client groups benefiting from government programs, local NDP intimidation of opposing candidates, and ultimately "correction" of undesired election results. Under these conditions, the opposing parties decided to boycott the 1990 election, which drew a turnout of only 15 percent and gave the NDP an overwhelming victory. Subsequently, the Supreme Court nullified the PR election system, and it was replaced with one based on individual candidates running against each other in two-seat districts. This favored large parties in SMDP style, and in the subsequent elections of 1995 and 2000, no more than a handful of opposition party candidates were able to win seats in the lower house. The voter turnout remained dismally low, in the 15–20 percent range.

Confident again by the mid-2000s, the NDP government once again loosened controls in the run-up to the 2005 parliamentary elections. For the first time, rival candidates could run for the presidency instead of the choice being merely a referendum on the parliament-approved (NDP) nominee, as had been the case in the past. For parliament, the regime allowed contention by members of the Muslim Brotherhood—a long-standing nonviolent Islamist group favoring governmental adoption of Sharia Law (see chapter 4)—as long as they ran formally as independents. In another scare for the government, the Brotherhood won 88 seats in the People's Assembly, fully a fifth of the lower house's membership.

Seemingly stunned, the NDP government cracked down on the Brotherhood in 2006. A number of its leading members were arrested and prosecuted for alleged financial misdeeds to keep them behind bars. In 2007, new amendments to the constitution were passed to make life more difficult for competing parties. The Brotherhood was formally outlawed as a religious party. And special governmental powers under the state of emergency that remained since the assassination of Sadat in 1981 (such as detention without trial) were enacted as law. Candidates had to be members of a political party, but all parties based on religion, region, or class were banned. Some small parties could get a few Assembly seats, and parliament saw debate and criticism of government bills (along with an independent press). But significant opposition was unviable.

The NDP dominated voting in the Assembly, permeated by patron-client networks coming together in the president at the top. Mubarak periodically switched PMs and reshuffled ministers at will. The NDP-chosen speaker decided how long debate could proceed before voting on a bill, and sometimes allowed only brief periods of discussion on matters that the government considered sensitive, from the quality of imported food to the extension of the government's emergency powers such as detention without trial. The Assembly could remove parliamentary immunity from individual legislators, leaving them at the mercy of politically motivated prosecution and detention, as well as ordinary law enforcement. The NDP hierarchy continued to control the two-thirds supermajority required to limit debate and investigations, and was able to dictate outcomes. Inevitably, any amendments were minor and the government's bills were overwhelmingly approved.

By 2008, the government increasingly favored reduced government intervention in the economy. It wanted to reduce subsidies that had kept the prices of food and fuel low, but had to postpone such plans in the face of demonstrations over rising prices. Then came the international credit and economic crisis of 2008–2009, which forced the government to maintain its existing policies of strong intervention in banking and regulation, mount an economic stimulus plan to support hard-pressed ordinary Egyptians, and temporarily shelve some privatization plans. All this increased the budget deficit. But with the beginning of recovery in 2009, the government resumed market-oriented reforms, such as allowing private participation in some public projects, partially privatizing energy, reducing energy subsidies, and consolidating welfare aid into a single payment for the poor. Despite some traditionalist resistance to such moves from both within and outside the ruling party, again the government's dominance over the Assembly assured that its proposals would not be slowed down by bargaining with legislators.

Meanwhile, however, opposition was mounting over media bias, government restrictions on elections, and the continued state of emergency. Brotherhood members continued to run (as independents) in the 2010 elections, and won a significant presence in the Majlis. By 2011, Mubarak and the NDP government faced real challenges. Internet-publicized incidents in both Tunisia and Egypt helped ignite protests over police repression, regime corruption, and lack of democracy, in the context of high youth unemployment and rapidly rising prices for food, fuel, and other commodities. The protests exploded into a mass movement in which young secular protesters were soon joined by Islamists. President Mubarak was eventually forced to resign. The military took power transitionally and negotiated for elections—partly PR and partly SMDM—of a new Majlis assembly as well as a new president.

At this critical juncture, the secular-leaning young people and civil society groups that had been so eager earlier to take to the streets to bring down Mubarak did not seem willing to put in the hard work of cooperating with each other to contend against the Islamists. The well-organized Muslim Brotherhood's party won the parliamentary elections with 47 percent of the seats, and other more extreme Islamic parties added another 25 percent of the seats to make a substantial Islamist majority. The support of the Islamic clerics in the mosques and the organizational skills of the Brotherhood seemed to guarantee that for the foreseeable future, non-Islamist groups and leaders of the early demonstrations would be marginalized. A new assembly chosen to write a new constitution was dominated by the Islamists. Then in mid-2012, the courts (filled by old regime figures) found a rule violation in the lower-house election procedures: multiparty election authorities had permitted "independent" candidates to be party-identified. The courts annulled the results and the People's Assembly was suspended. Legislative power was subsequently claimed first by the top military council, and then by the remaining Islamist-dominated upper house—the Shura Council (elected with a turnout of around 10 percent of eligible Egyptians).

In the mid-2012 presidential election, the anti-Mubarak secularist groups were unable to cooperate in support of a candidate. The second round of voting saw Muhammad Morsi, the candidate of the Brotherhood's party, Peace and Justice, win a narrow victory over a Mubarak-associated leader with limited appeal, who nonetheless was able to get 48 percent of the vote. Later in 2012, Morsi decreed the elimination of judicial review, and began replacing top officials across the government. At the end of November, the new Islamist-dominated Constitutional Assembly (most of its small secularist minority had resigned in protest) passed a constitution including Sharia Law for the country and legislative oversight by religious authorities. Morsi ordered a referendum on it to be held only three weeks later, again giving the advantage to the mobilization capacities of the Brotherhood's strong organization and the Salafists' use of the mosques.

However, the referendum brought a turnout of only a third of the electorate, and passed by only 64 percent, indicating the possibility of deep division and trouble ahead. The new constitution gave legislative power temporarily to the Islamist-dominated Shura council, which began passing laws. Like the Mubarak regime before him, President Morsi seemed willing to use all available institutional advantages to exercise control. The formation of a new, secular-leaning National Salvation Front to compete in the parliamentary elections of April 2013 was too little, too late. Within a month, by late January 2013, anti-Morsi demonstrations were occurring, which in a few cases led to police firing into the crowds and killing protesters. The protests spread and enlarged. In July, the military intervened forcefully to disband the Islamist-controlled government, citing the popular uprising against it.

The new military government banned the Brotherhood, arrested numerous Brotherhood leaders and activists, and repressed their protests with force. Led by army leader Abdel Fattah al-Sisi, the regime brooks no significant opposition, whether by Islamists or secular democracy advocates. By early 2014, Sisi had proposed his own constitution, whose referendum was approved by 98 percent of a turnout that was a bit higher than that for the Islamist referendum a year earlier. In June, Sisi was elected president after a campaign in which critics—including those among the press and NGOs—were intimidated and otherwise suppressed. When a new legislature was finally chosen in late 2015, it had roughly 80 percent chosen by single-member district voting, and 20 percent by winner-take-all lists in larger districts. Sisi-allied candidates and parties dominated, as repression of critics of the regime continued. Transition to democracy remains an agenda item, not yet a reality.

⚐ **PRACTICE AND REVIEW ONLINE**

CRITICAL THINKING QUESTIONS

1. Compare the advantages and disadvantages of bicameral and unicameral legislatures. How do they differ in the forms of cooperation that they might require or the opportunities for contention that they might present?

2. Compare the operation of legislative assemblies under (a) multiparty presidential government and (b) minority parliamentary government? What sorts of cooperation are required by both?

3. What are the advantages and disadvantages of committee work for legislators? How does it provide opportunities for cooperation as well as contention between parties?

4. Does the unusually strong upper house in the German legislative branch weaken the advantages of parliamentary government? Why or why not? How does it foster contention? Cooperation?

5. Why might institutional pragmatist legislators prove to be very important in the new Egyptian parliament? Which contending groups might have to cooperate with each other?

KEY TERMS

legislative assembly, 347
delegate model, 347
trustee model, 348
constituent service, 352
unicameral legislature, 352
bicameral legislature, 352
indirect election, 353
standing committee, 355
ad hoc committee, 355
conference committee, 356
supermajority, 358
backbencher, 362
caucus, 363
minority government, 364
support party, 364
caretaker government, 364

grand coalition, 364
fractionalization, 365
concurrent, 372

FURTHER READING

Baaklini, Abdo I., Guilain Denoeux, and Robert Springborg. *Legislative Politics in the Arab World: The Resurgence of Democratic Institutions*. Boulder, CO and London: Lynne Rienner, 1999.

Gallagher, Michael, Michael Laver, and Peter Mair. *Representative Government in Modern Europe*, 4th ed. New York: McGraw-Hill, 2006.

Kurian, George T. *World Encyclopedia of Parliaments and Legislatures*. Washington, DC: Congressional Quarterly Books, 1997.

Lijphart, Arend, ed. *Parliamentary versus Presidential Government*. Oxford: Oxford University Press, 1992.

Loewenberg, Gerhard, Peverill Squire, and D. Roderick Kiewit, eds. *Legislatures: Comparative Perspectives on Representative Assemblies*. Ann Arbor: University of Michigan Press, 2002.

Longley, Lawrence D., and Roger H. Davidson, eds. *The New Roles of Parliamentary Committees*. London: Frank Cass, 1998.

Mayhew, David R. *Congress: The Electoral Connection*, 2nd ed. New Haven, CT: Yale University Press, 2004.

Mezey, Michael L. *Comparative Legislatures*. Durham, NC: Duke University Press, 1979.

Morgenstern, Scott, and Benito Nacif, eds. *Legislative Politics in Latin America*. Cambridge and New York: Cambridge University Press, 2002.

Norton, Philip, ed. *Parliaments and Governments in Western Europe*. London and Portland, OR: Frank Cass, 1998.

———, and Ahmed Nizam, eds. *Parliaments in Asia*. London and Portland, OR: Frank Cass, 1999.

Olson, David M. *Democratic Legislative Institutions: A Comparative View*. Armonk, NY: M.E. Sharpe, 1994.

———, and Michael L. Mezey. *Legislatures in the Policy Process: The Dilemmas of Economic Policy*. Cambridge: Cambridge University Press, 1991.

————, and Philip Norton, eds. *The New Parliaments of Central and Eastern Europe*. London: Frank Cass, 1996.

Remington, Thomas F., ed. *Parliaments in Transition: The New Legislative Politics in the Former USSR and Eastern Europe*. Boulder, CO: Westview Press, 1994.

Shugart, Matthew Soberg, and John M. Carey. *Presidents and Assemblies: Constitutional Design and Electoral Dynamics*. New York: Cambridge University Press, 1992.

NOTES

[1] The occasional exception is the choice of committee chairmen (of the majority party), whose choice by party caucus may depart from seniority.

[2] See Lanny W. Martin and Georg Vanberg, "Policing the Bargain: Coalition Government and Parliamentary Scrutiny," *American Journal of Political Science* 48 (2004): 13–27.

[3] The collection of all such policy area leaders in a party is sometimes referred to as its "shadow cabinet."

[4] In the United States, the Congress must approve increases in the permissible amount of overall national government debt, to allow the government to borrow money.

[5] See Octavio Avorim Neto, "The Presidential Calculus: Executive Policy Making and Cabinet Formation in the Americas," *Comparative Political Studies* 39, no. 4 (2006): 415–40.

[6] See Michael Laver and Kenneth Shepsle, *Making and Breaking Government: Cabinets and legislatures in Parliamentary Democracies* (Cambridge, UK: Cambridge University Press, 1996).

[7] See also chapter 10.

[8] For more on this, see Michael Laver, "Divided Parties, Divided Government," *Legislative Studies Quarterly* 24 (1999): 5–29.

[9] Including the Christian Social Union, which functions as the CDU in Bavaria.

[10] This is a high point of parliamentary influence. Such discussions will be especially necessary if the most successful coalition has fallen short of a majority and has to pick up another party to get over the top. The leading coalition may find that new coalition partner either toward the more extreme end of its ideological range or in the center.

[11] See note 5 above.

[12] See Wolfgang C. Muller and Kaare Strom, "Coalition Agreements and Cabinet Governance," in *Cabinets and Coalition Bargaining: The Democratic Life Cycle in Western Europe*, eds. Strom, Muller, and Torbjorn Bergman (Oxford, UK: Oxford University Press, 2008), 159–99.

[13] See chapter 13. To be sure, factors other than the raw number of parties could contribute to frequent coalition breakdown. For example, Italy allowed secret ballot voting on bills, making party discipline harder to enforce, and its largest party at the time, the Christian Democrats, was a centrist party that was exceptionally divided into multiple factions.

[14] See Michael Gallagher, Michael Laver, and Peter Mair, *Representative Government in Modern Europe*, 4th ed. (New York: McGraw-Hill, 2006).

[15] Here the label "CDU" is also meant to include the Bavarian branch of the party, which calls itself the "Christian Social Union."

[16] See chapter 7.

[17] See chapter 10.

The Democratic Political Executive

FOCUS QUESTIONS

- **WHY** is the political executive important?
- **HOW** does a presidential framework affect how the political executive is organized?
- **HOW** do groups contend and cooperate in and around the political executive in various frameworks?
- **HOW** does semi-presidentialism modify parliamentary government?
- **HOW** does the lack of significant legislative assemblies affect the authoritarian political executive?

OFTEN THE POLITICAL SKILL AND JUDGMENT of the individual occupying the position of chief executive in a country matters. In April 2012 in South Korea, Park Geun-hye, of the conservative Grand National Party (GNP), led her party to an unexpected victory in parliamentary elections. Then the following December she won the presidency, narrowly defeating the candidate of the moderate left-of-center Democratic Union Party (DUP), Moon Jae-in. These were significant accomplishments because they kept her party in control of both branches of government despite the fact that the previous president, also of the GNP, had become unpopular (South Korean presidents are limited to one five-year term). There was much discontent in the country at the time, especially over the GNP's traditional closeness to the big industrial conglomerates (the "Chaebol"), the weakness of South Korea's welfare state, growing household debt, and the lack of good jobs for the young. In early 2012, it appeared that the DUP had a good chance of winning both elections and substantially changing the direction of the country.

Park led the GNP to these victories by distancing herself from her predecessor and shifting her party's campaigning on economic policy toward the center (or even center-left at times) on some issues. Renaming her party Saenuri (or "new frontier"), she joined Moon in calling for "economic democracy"—reduction in the power of the chaebol—and jobs. And she proposed expanding the traditionally thin welfare state in ways tailored to South Korea. Thus the DUP was left with a primarily backward-looking campaign strategy of criticizing the perceived failures of the prior administration. Meanwhile, in the presidential race, a center-left candidate who would normally have been aligned with the DUP, Ahn Cheol-soo, ran as an independent against the perceived "old politics" of both of the two main parties. After thus sullying the DUP (as well as the GNP) through most of the campaign, the personally popular Ahn finally quit the race to support Moon. But he did so rather late in the campaign, and seemingly reluctantly at first.

As President Park has sought to aid the disadvantaged selectively, in limited ways such as increasing the social security budget and helping the poorest South Koreans deal with debt and college costs. She has also backed proposals to help women, such as aid for childcare needs and stronger protection from domestic and sexual violence. For the most part, she has been able to bring her free-market-oriented party around to support her proposals. This is partly because of the authority and influence associated with the position of the president in South Korean politics.

South Korea has a "semi-presidential" political framework style (see below). The popularly elected president appoints the prime minister and cabinet (a presidential feature), but only with the approval of the key legislative assembly (a parliamentary feature). In South Korea, these opposed features pose no problem because normally the legislative majority is in the hands of the party whose leader holds the presidency. One or the other of the two large broad parties can win the assembly majority on its own (or control it with a small coalition partner) because over 80 percent of the seats are chosen by single-member districts, yielding dominance by the contention between the two big parties. The party that has won the assembly majority leadership usually has the voting strength to also win the presidency for its leader. Thus as party leader, the president can normally get majority support in assembly voting for her or his most important proposals through party discipline. Carefully backing limited and targeted reforms, Park has successfully (from her conservative party's point of view) warded off bigger change for South Korea.

THE FUNCTIONS AND DEVELOPMENT OF THE EXECUTIVE BRANCH

In politics, the leadership of the executive branch of government is exercised by what is called the **political executive**. Chosen through a political process of some sort, this cluster of official positions tends to be the center of attention and the most prominent prize of political contention. The political executive gives overall direction to the professional civil service (see chapter 14) that makes up the great bulk of the executive branch of government. The political executive includes:

1. The chief executive,
2. An office under the direct personal control of the chief executive,
3. The cabinet, made up of the 15–25 appointed heads of the ministries or departments (e.g., agriculture, defense, finance, and labor),
4. The ministers' deputies and their assistants, and
5. Any committees or commissions set up to advise the PM or the cabinet ministers.

The executive leadership's responsibilities extend beyond simply carrying out the will of the legislative branch. The political executive is the source of important new policy initiatives presented to the legislative assemblies, and normally possesses a limit-setting veto power over legislation. In effect, the political executive is a participant in the legislative process. The chief executive is usually considered the overall leader of the nation.

However, we need to be wary of viewing the political executive as a single unit under the directive power of the chief executive at the top. In fact, the political executive contains within it various forms of contention—whether among organizational subunits, contending leaders (alongside their supporters), multiple party leaderships and factions within parties, interest groups that may be influential in parts of the political executive, or combinations of these. Especially important is the pattern of party contention and cooperation in the political executive, which is heavily affected by the type of political framework in which it functions.

Before the advent of representative democracy, authoritarian monarchies united legislation and administration in one unit, the king (or queen) with his or her advisors. Up through the nineteenth century, the monarch's court was the center of politics in most countries. Notably, however, authoritarian government was opposed by most of the leading modern political thinkers (see chapter 4); even Niccoló Machiavelli, who was known mostly for his book *The Prince,* saw it as useful only in initially establishing law and order, as a prelude to a transition to a republican government (see "The Philosophical Connection").

When representative democracy emerged in parts of Europe and North America, it was initially unclear who would take the lead in the new system. The voters? The legislature? The executive chiefs? As the twentieth century unfolded, it was the political executive that took the lead. How did this situation come about?

One factor was economic and technological: the century saw larger areas of trade and economic interdependence than before, brought on by industrialization, new technologies, and a greater overall complexity of society. Accordingly, there was an uptick in the scope of the challenges that governments faced. Problems such as war, the threat of recession, harm to public health and safety, and damage to the environment, for example, often crossed the boundaries of local and regional units and called for national solutions. Legislative assemblies, for their part, tended to heavily represent the local and regional interests of the small territories that elect their members, sometimes making it difficult for legislators to lift their sights to the nation as a whole.

Times of national emergency seemed to drive this point home. The two world wars and the Great Depression of the 1930s demanded fast and comprehensive action rather than long and difficult negotiations among different local and regional interests. The executive branch was the only centralized and hierarchical structure that represented the country as a whole and could act quickly on its problems. Moreover, national executives were able to concentrate key resources, both material and in human talent and expertise, that legislatures or regional levels of government could not match. How all this plays out for the modern political executive, however, is much affected by the surrounding political framework, including both its governmental structure and party system components.

THE PHILOSOPHICAL CONNECTION | Niccolò Machiavelli

An early defense of authoritarian rule in certain circumstances may be found in Machiavelli's *The Prince*. On the strength of this book, many have considered Machiavelli to have favored monarchic government, dominated by the executive branch. However, as we saw in chapter 5, Machiavelli's *Discourses* make clear that he ultimately supported a mixed republic on roughly the pattern of ancient Roman republican government, with representation of the common people, a senate, and an executive hierarchy. How are the two books' arguments to be reconciled?

Apparently for Machiavelli, a situation of disorder and license among the nobles (large landowners) and the people was not an appropriate setting for republican government because it usually led to the nobles oppressing the people. Such a situation seemed to require a "new man" to seize power with loyal troops under his own control, forcefully put down any rebellions that serve to bring out enemies and discontents among his early supporters, and most importantly, introduce new laws and institutions backed by harsh force against lawbreakers. However, Machiavelli's focus on executive power in *The Prince*, and the harsh measures to be taken there against nobles resisting the prince's new order, seemed related to the early stages in the establishment of what he considered to be good government. Subsequently, he argued, the king must turn primarily to kind and useful measures and establishing institutions to apply law for him, so that most of the time, he may present a magnanimous appearance. If the king must occasionally return to harshness in enforcing the law (or have subordinates do it for him), he must do it only to maintain the state and must justify it in terms of protecting the people.

In *The Prince*, Machiavelli praised the French practice of having a parliament to allow the people to check the nobles according to law, while the king seemed to recede into a benign distance. The *Discourses'* mixed republic seems consistent with a subsequent evolution of the prince's regime into one in which the monarch might become a merely ceremonial figurehead like the Queen of England. In a mixed republic, representatives of the people could use their numbers in parliament to contend successfully with the nobles' representatives. Leaders chosen by parliament would take the day-to-day helm of the executive branch.

Why was republican rule ultimately so important to Machiavelli? In his republican work, the *Discourses*, Machiavelli made a remarkable comparison of rule by the people with rule by a prince. Both were acceptable when each remained within the bounds of the rule of law. But it seemed easier to keep the people within the law than a prince, who could be overcome by passion (as Aristotle had argued). And when the people transgressed the boundaries of law, they were much easier to bring back to order than princes are. The people were capable of being drawn back by a good leader with oratorical skill, whereas out-of-control princes, according to Machiavelli, are not capable of such reorientation, and can only be reversed by "cold steel." The key quality of the people was its capacity, when hearing orators, to recognize which was best for the state. This comes close to justifying election of the government's top leaders.

This apparent preference for popular choice of executive leadership in Machiavelli's *Discourses*, however, presupposes that the people be kept within the bounds of law. He did argue that the best laws tend to emerge from the contentions between the nobles and the people, but he also maintained that respect for the law required periodic examples of vigorous law enforcement by a leader. Every so often, Machiavelli argued, the nobles and the people must be brought to "take stock," and return to first principles, by viewing a harsh example of punishment of a lawbreaker. For Machiavelli, popular choice of government must coexist with firm exercise of executive power in law enforcement. Today, lack of this is a shortcoming of many governments in the developing world.

THE PRESIDENTIAL POLITICAL EXECUTIVE

As we have seen, presidential systems display a political executive that is independent of the legislative branch. The popularly elected president serves a set term of office regardless of the fate of policy proposals presented to assemblies. Thus party discipline in assemblies is not necessary to keep the president in office, and he or she cannot count on it to pass the president's policy program. And yet, the chief executive (or his or her party) normally wants a record of policy achievement to address the country's problems and to run on in the next election. All of this has consequences for the form and operation of the political executive itself.

The Two-Party American Case

With **separation of personnel** between the two branches—allowing no one to serve in both branches at once—there is no need for the American president, for example, to select cabinet members from the ranks of his party's leading legislators. American cabinet secretaries often come from outside of politics. While those picked to lead cabinet departments must be approved by Congress's upper house, the Senate, the president may remove them at will.

However, the autonomy of the political executive has a downside. Without tight party discipline and assured legislative majorities, the president has no ready-made recipe for securing legislative cooperation to get bills and the budget passed. The American Congress is not even required to vote on the president's proposals. In the fall of 2011, Democratic president Obama's jobs proposal was not even considered by the Republican-majority lower house of Congress, thus denying it any chance of passage.

The American president's clearest power over Congress is limit setting, the capacity to veto a bill. A presidential veto can only be defeated in Congress by a 2/3 vote in each house to override, which is very hard to achieve with competitive parties. However, often a president's veto decision is not an easy one. The only veto option is to nix the whole bill; if a president wants most of a bill to pass, but objects only to some part of it, he or she is in a tough position. Some American presidents have wished for a **line item veto**, the power to veto only one part of a bill (which most Latin American presidents have). However, in recent decades, the American president has been allowed a less formal, limited form of line item veto by making a "signing statement" upon signing the bill. A **signing statement** indicates that the executive branch will not carry out a part of the bill that the president considers to be somehow contrary to the Constitution.

George W. Bush, president from 2001 to 2009, used this power far more extensively than his predecessors, widely stretching constitutional interpretation. In July 2006, a report by the American Bar Association (the association of American attorneys) stated what many in Congress believe, that signing statements unconstitutionally encroach on legislative power. To be sure, many signing statements have aimed at nullifying legislative veto provisions in bills, in which legislators try to influence how a law is to be applied—something that presidents tend to consider unconstitutional legislative encroachment on executive power. In theory, such constitutional questions in the U.S. system should be resolved by the Supreme Court, but the latter has been unwilling to intervene, leaving the signing statement option in place.

Organizational Units and Influence Within the Presidential Executive

Presidential limit-setting power over Congress, however, does not help much to build the President's *directive* capacity to get a favored policy through the legislative branch. To help increase support in the legislature and enhance control over units of the bureaucracy, presidents have developed additional offices and structures that are separate from the cabinet departments. These units enrich the range of policy ideas and advice for the president and marshal extra expertise and resources to influence the policymaking process overall.

For example, the American president is surrounded by two major staff complexes. The **executive office** is a cluster of agencies that help coordinate governmental functions that cut across departmental boundaries. The executive office includes such units as a budget office to prepare budget proposals, the National Security Agency, and a three-member council of prominent economists for economic policy research and advice. These units are well institutionalized, continuing from one presidency to another, and their chiefs require Senate confirmation just as cabinet secretaries do.

A second major sector is less formally institutionalized and politically closer to the president: the White House Staff. It contains hundreds of functionaries who do not need Senate confirmation and serve at the pleasure of the president. The structure of the White House Staff may vary from president to president, but it typically includes units for such purposes as policy research and planning, relations with Congress, public relations and the press, and relations with the president's party in the states. Today, the White House Staff also houses important councils that bring various key administration figures together to deliberate, such as the National Economic Council and the Domestic Policy Council.

Who are the most influential people in the American political executive? Often a powerful role is played by the president personally. Presidents Franklin Roosevelt, Jimmy Carter and Bill Clinton, for example, seem to have played direct, active roles in at least some policymaking. If a president is a key policymaking leader in the administration, he or she tends to communicate with numerous people one-on-one, and to have more people reporting directly to him or her. On the other hand, some presidents were not leading forces in actual decision making about policies. Such presidents appointed officials who they knew would go in the general directions that the president wanted a policy to take. In the United States, Presidents Dwight D. Eisenhower, Richard Nixon, Ronald Reagan, and George W. Bush tended not to be very personally involved in most policy decisions. They relied heavily on the staff hierarchy (especially the chief of staff), who may insulate the president somewhat from outside influences.

A variety of other figures in the political executive might also be very influential. Sometimes the head of the budget office exerts strong influence, and the national security advisor can greatly affect foreign and defense policy. But normally, the leading White House Staff figures are the most influential ones: the president's chief of staff, the chairman of the National Economic Council, the chief of the Domestic Policy Council, the director of communications (who supervises the president's press secretary), and the top counselor for political strategy (e.g., Karl Rove under George W. Bush). In addition, leading roles may be played by one or two cabinet secretaries who happen to be particularly close politically to the president (for example, Attorney General Robert Kennedy for his brother John F. Kennedy), or to have great expertise and prestige in their jurisdictions, such as Treasury Secretary Robert Rubin under Bill Clinton.

However, most American cabinet secretaries tend to be rather distant from the center of influence on important matters. Meetings of the whole cabinet occur rarely and only for ceremonial purposes. Most secretaries administer their departments rather independently and testify before Congressional committees when required, but rarely meet with the president. In their interactions with rest of the political executive, they commonly deal with the most relevant functionary of the policy/planning apparatus of the White House Staff, or with the budget office regarding budget matters. Cabinet secretaries may be picked based on their specialized credentials or expertise in their area, their willingness to go along with White House policy preferences, to please a key party-supporting interest group, or to help present a favorable picture of the administration to the voters.

The Special Case of National Security Policymaking Sometimes a particular cluster of figures might play the leading role in a policy area. For example, such a group was the circle for defense policy in the early 2000s under George W. Bush: Vice President Dick Cheney, his national security advisor David Addington, Defense Secretary Donald Rumsfeld, Defense Undersecretary Paul Wolfowitz, and the president's national security advisor Condoleezza Rice. Some or all of these people might have met as a group or in informal subgroups. The secretary of state (in other nations referred to as the "foreign minister"), the intelligence chief, and the top military chief of staff were involved at times, but apparently most often played implementing roles (see "Contention and Cooperation in Focus").

To be sure, there is a second approach to all this that focuses more on the organizational units that these active participants represent. Recall from chapter 9 that units within the bureaucracy can function as institutional interest groups. In political scientist Graham Allison's examination of the 1962 Cuban missile crisis, he referred to this aspect of decision making as the **bureaucratic politics model** (later renamed "governmental politics model").[1] In this pattern, contending leaders of different executive units make recommendations related to the various missions and other concerns of the structures that they head. For example, a nation's foreign minister normally may urge diplomacy and multilateralism more than the defense minister, who may be more inclined toward projecting national power. However, a defense minister may also reflect a different aspect of the armed forces point of view; he might object to proposed military missions that may strain the capabilities and budgets of the military, placing soldiers in roles that they are ill-qualified and poorly resourced to carry out.

And interested groups outside the executive may also want to have input. In the summer before 9/11 when general reports of terrorist threats were afoot among Western intelligence agencies, the airlines were likely to have lobbied the Federal Aviation Administration and the White House to avoid imposing major new security measures (e.g., removing all blades from carry-on bags) that might alarm and inconvenience the flying public during the busiest and most profitable flying season, in the absence of knowledge of specific security threats (date, time, place).

Moreover, government officials may indirectly reflect the concerns of outside interests. If the decision involves whether to intervene in a foreign humanitarian disaster such as state terror in the Darfur region of Sudan in the 2000s or Mali in 2012, American or French legislators of African ancestry may be especially sensitive to the potential high human cost of *inaction*, and apply pressure on

CONTENTION AND COOPERATION IN FOCUS | The American "War on Terror" and the Iraq Invasion

The group of officials involved in a chief executive's decision making on important defense or foreign policy decisions can display various patterns of contention and cooperation, even varying from one decision to another. The inside story of high-level decision making is seldom evident at the time, but from official investigations, participants' memoirs, declassified documents (allowing public access to documents previously kept secret by the government), and other sources, we can reach consensus at least about the broad lines of contention and cooperation in key decision making. This generalization is true for the two most consequential events for American foreign policy in the early 2000s: the 9/11 attack on New York's World Trade Center and the Pentagon in Washington, and the decision to invade Iraq in early 2003.

In the period before 9/11, there seems to have been a majority and a minority among the active participants in decision making regarding these events. In the summer of 2001, the White House Staff included a chief antiterrorism officer, Richard Clarke. By that summer, Clarke and the head of the Central Intelligence Agency (CIA), George Tenet, had become alarmed about foreign intelligence traffic indicating an immediate threat of major terrorism on American soil. (Both were holdovers from the prior Clinton administration.) In the late 1990s,

the threat of hijacking a plane and flying it into a target had been indicated in a circulated intelligence report on the future plans of the jihadists who were behind the first World Trade Center bombing in 1993 (one of whom, captured in the Philippines, divulged the information). In addition, local FBI officials in two states had noticed indications of possible jihadists taking flying lessons without apparent interest in learning how to take off or land. These and other reports, alongside intercepted messages and information from foreign intelligence services, seem to have contributed to the concerns of Clarke, Tenet, and others. Clarke testified subsequently that in 2001 prior to 9/11, however, the top security people around President Bush were not willing to have high-level meetings with Clarke to discuss the threat.

By late August 2001, Clarke and Tenet seemed still to be in the minority in their sense of alarm. No prominent preventive measures were taken to step up airline security, such as removing from carry-on bags any items that could be effective in hand-to-hand combat, or bolstering cockpit door locks to protect pilots—actions that were taken only after 9/11. (To be sure, these measures would have inconvenienced and alarmed travelers, perhaps dampening passenger airline business in a heavy travel period.)

the political executive to intervene. Regarding the American invasion of Iraq in 2003, President Bush and Vice President Cheney, both with backgrounds in the oil industry, may have been particularly attuned to the problem of partial Western dependence on the oil of the uncooperative Saddam Hussein, and the benefits of post-invasion access to Iraqi oil by American oil companies. Particularly when we consider the range of interest groups beyond the bureaucracy who seek to influence security and foreign policy from outside the top decision-making group, the pluralist model clearly comes into play alongside elite and personal leadership factors.

The Role of Political Attitudes in Foreign and Defense Policymaking

Among domestic factors that contribute to foreign policymaking in democracies is the role of public opinion. Average citizens typically have very incomplete knowledge of international affairs. As Tocqueville pointed out, modern life is busy, leaving ordinary citizens little time to investigate things for themselves, and attracted to oversimplifying "general ideas" (see chapter 8,

Before 9/11, instead of stressing preventive physical measures to generally deter hijacking, the majority of relevant Bush administration officials seemed to adhere to a conventional criminal-pursuit approach, focused primarily on trying to identify and catch would-be perpetrators before the crime. After 9/11, the Bush administration did adopt the prevention-oriented measures mentioned above, but it also continued to emphasize perpetrator pursuit, focusing on overcoming pre-9/11 procedural barriers to communication between security agencies about possible suspects, and on bolstering police powers generally.

A related case is the decision to invade Iraq. Again, the information indicates that a strong majority of the top circle favored invasion. Public statements by President Bush, Vice President Cheney, and national security advisor Rice at the time suggested near unanimous support at least among the top 10–12 policymaking participants. Shortly after 9/11, Cheney and Rumsfeld seem to have called for attacking Iraq first. But at the time they were overruled in favor of attacking Afghanistan where al-Qaeda's bases were. When their preferred targeting of Iraq finally won out in late 2002 and early 2003, Cheney, Addington, Rumsfeld, Wolfowitz, and Bush again seemed to have dominated decision making.

The most prominent possible opponent (as indicated by his apparent opposition to the idea several months earlier) was then secretary of state Colin Powell, a former general who had earlier served as the military's chairman of the Joint Chiefs of Staff during the first war in Iraq in 1991. But on the eve of the 2003 attack, Powell made a very public expression of support for invasion in an address to the United Nations Security Council.

Since 2003, however, information has emerged indicating that there were serious doubters at lower levels. Particularly in the state department's intelligence section and parts of the CIA, skepticism existed regarding the reliability of the sources and the content of claims of Iraqi weapons of mass destruction programs and links between Saddam and al-Qaeda. Apparently, some people feared the possibility of a troublesome post-invasion insurgency in Iraq against the Americans and whatever new government they set up there. However, the doubters worked primarily at lower levels and were decidedly in the minority. Cheney and Rumsfeld were able to impose cooperation on the whole executive branch, forbidding any public airing of contention over the invasion or the case for it. As to the public's perceptions of who was calling the shots, again the picture available through the media at the time was of personal leadership by a resolute president Bush, determined to invade Iraq unless, as he put it, Saddam "disarms."

"The Philosophical Connection"). People are especially vulnerable to the selective release of information from sources with an aura of authority, ranging from broadcast media news figures to officials in government press conferences, and the chief executive can use the press to influence the public mood.

For one thing, the government can usually control most of the key information regarding national security and foreign policy issues (although this is not always the case, as American media coverage of the Vietnam War showed). Chief executives may release information only partially, and in a way that puts their actions and policies in the most favorable light. In mass media news, the audience appeal of the leader's personality and celebrity is an advantage for the chief executive, personifying the nation (see chapter 2). And the broadcast media's inclination to simplify complex decision making for their audience also helps the chief executive to get the message out. For example, the chief executive can use these advantages to arouse nationalist sentiment to support foreign intervention.

All this can work out well if the decision by the prevailing group in the political executive is sound. If not, however, one of the advantages of full-scale representative democracy is that press freedom at least allows for the possibility of the chief executive's advantages being overcome by an avalanche of adverse facts. This occurred in the United States, for example, over the course of the Vietnam War in the late 1960s. And in presidential democracies, a legislative assembly may have a majority opposed to the party or coalition of the president, and its committees on foreign relations, defense, or intelligence may hold hearings to question the president's foreign policy. When developments in other countries go badly, opposing parties may blame the political executive, perhaps affecting the next election.

Factors Affecting Whether the President Gets Legislation Passed With no guarantee of legislative support for the American president's agenda, what factors enable presidents to contend successfully with opponents, gain cooperation in the legislative branch, and get important policy proposals adopted? From the mid-twentieth century onward, we can identify some presidents who pursued big new initiatives in policy, and among them, a few who succeeded in getting them through Congress and enacted (see Table 13.1).

There are many possible factors involved in the president's success or failure to turn a signature policy proposal into law. Some are specific to the particular situation, but others may span multiple presidencies. For example, presidential observers often mention presidential **charisma** (personal appeal on camera), effectiveness in trading benefits or penalties with individual legislators ("wheeler-dealer" skill), and the size of the president's most recent election victory margin.

With all the media attention that presidents receive, the appeal of the leader's personality on camera (related to the personal leadership model)—his or her charisma—can be important in influencing public opinion to build generalized public pressure on legislators to support key presidential proposals. Franklin Roosevelt rallied the nation in his radio "fireside chats" in support of his New Deal policies during the Great Depression of the 1930s, and Ronald Reagan used his charisma on camera in the 1980s to help get Congress to adopt his program of lower taxes, reduced government regulation, and military buildup. But charisma has its limits. In the 1960s, John F. Kennedy was considered by many to be charismatic, but failed in his efforts to enact domestic changes; in contrast, his successor Lyndon Johnson largely lacked charisma but was very successful with his domestic program in Congress (see below).

Another factor is skill in persuading individual legislators, either one-on-one or in small groups, to support presidential initiatives. Such efforts may address the substantive merits of the proposal, but may also involve other aspects of the politics of the situation. This includes what scholars of the American presidency call "wheeling and dealing" or "horse-trading" with legislators: offering rewards for cooperation and threatening penalties for noncooperation. Wheeling and dealing can include giving or denying things valued by the legislator, such as campaign money from the party for the next election, support for the legislator's pet proposals for his or her local district or region (called earmarks when inserted into bills), or future opportunity to rise to a higher position of some sort.

Lyndon Johnson, who served as the U.S. president from 1963 through 1968, was a master of wheeling and dealing and was immensely influential in getting policies through the Congress. Ronald Reagan had Congressional liaison people in his White House Staff who were very effective as wheelers and dealers on

TABLE 13.1	Factors Contributing to Presidents' Legislative Success				
President and Relevant Period	Prominent Initiative(s)	Success?	Significant Charisma?	Big Election Majority?	Wheeler-Dealer Skill?
Franklin D. Roosevelt (1933–1944)	Jobs, retiree pensions, regulation, World War II	Yes	Yes	Yes	Yes
John F. Kennedy (1961–1963)	Civil rights, poverty alleviation	No	Yes	No	No
Lyndon B. Johnson (1963–1968)	Civil rights, Medicare, Medicaid, food aid	Yes	No	Yes	Yes
Ronald Reagan (1981–1988)	Tax cuts, military expansion, deregulation	Yes	Yes	Yes	Yes (staff)
Bill Clinton (1993–2000)	Universal health insurance	No	Yes	No	Medium
Jimmy Carter (1977–1980)	Energy conservation	No	No	No	No
George W. Bush (2001–2008)	Tax cuts, wars on terror and Iraq	Yes	No	No	Yes (Leaders in Congress)
Barack Obama (2009–2016)	Health insurance, economic stimulus, financial regulation	Yes	No	Yes	Medium

his behalf. In the early and mid-2000s, George W. Bush also had very effective agents within Congress to wheel and deal for him, such as Tom DeLay, a top House Republican leader. DeLay (known as "the hammer") was especially effective at threatening punishments for noncooperation (e.g., threatening to back opponents in future primary elections). And Bush had outside help from the influential Republican lobbyist Jack Abramoff, who could steer campaign contributions effectively toward or away from particular Republicans in Congress.[2]

Another favorable factor can be a big initial election victory by a president and/or his or her party in the legislative branch. Lyndon Johnson was successful in getting passed such programs as desegregation for African Americans, Medicare for the elderly, and Medicaid and food aid for the poor partly because of his huge electoral landslide victory in 1964. Barack Obama led a broad election victory for the Democrats in Congress in 2008, which played a large part in his 2009–2010 legislative achievements in economic stimulus, universalizing health insurance access, and financial regulation. In contrast, Presidents Kennedy, Carter, and Clinton (in his first election) all enjoyed Democratic Congressional majorities but had not won their elections by significant voter majorities. They failed to get their signature proposals enacted.

Certainly, however, the election margin variable has its limits. George W. Bush won a razor-thin (and disputed) election victory in 2000, but succeeded in getting passed his most important proposals concerning tax cuts, military spending increases, and war.

Multiparty Presidential Systems

Most of the world's presidential democracies are multiparty. Latin American nations, for example, generally use PR voting for the lower legislative house, leading to multiparty systems. Facing four or more parties in the chamber of deputies and senate, typically the president's party will not hold majorities in the legislative branch. Nor do presidential winners typically gain a majority "mandate" in the first round of the presidential election, when all of the significant parties run their presidential candidates. Put these factors together with the familiar institutional fact that presidential proposals don't need to pass to keep the president in office (reducing the need for party discipline), and the frequent result is difficulties getting the president's bills through the legislative branch.

Presidents in multiparty systems respond to these challenges by trying to put together informal coalitions of parties in the legislature. This is done partly by offering benefits to other parties and their constituencies, such as administration jobs, support for their favored policies and programs, and aid to party-supporting local areas. The president may appoint a multiparty cabinet that includes leaders of other parties in the informal coalition, in a looser and more informal version of what happens under multiparty parliamentary government. Such cabinet posts, in turn, can bring numerous patronage appointments for their parties or party factions.

Political scientist Octavio Amorim Neto has suggested that presidents in multiparty systems can go in one of two directions. If a president's strategy focuses more on what can be achieved by autonomous executive orders or decrees rather than legislation, there will likely be more technocrats in the cabinet, fewer partisans from other parties in the cabinet, less proportionality between coalition parties' numbers of cabinet seats and their legislative strengths, and less legislative success; but if a president is oriented more toward legislative achievements, she or he will allocate more cabinet seats to the coalition partner parties, and do so more proportionally to their legislative seat strengths, with the consequences of stronger party discipline and more legislative success.[3]

However, a president may not be able to secure the cooperation of a coalition encompassing a legislative majority. Incentives for other parties to join a president's cabinet are limited by the fact that cabinet seats do not guarantee control over their ministries; since coalition partners in the cabinet are not necessary to keep the president in office (as in parliamentary systems), ultimately the president holds the power over both policy and cabinet membership.[4]

In the common case of minority cabinets in multiparty presidential systems, the most we can say is that they can help build a regular pattern of coalition legislative cooperation, at least in some policy areas, as a base from which to try to build further legislative support, ad hoc, to put bills over the top.[5] For the latter purpose, the president may offer particular benefits (e.g., new local spending on jobs, projects, or subsidies) to other parties, factions within them, regions, or individuals.

This wheeling and dealing is simplified where party discipline is stronger. If most ordinary legislators follow party discipline, the president can try to work out deals with only the leaderships of the parties and their major factions, increasing the chances of success. As we have seen, party-list PR voting enhances party discipline, thanks to leaders' control over the election list rankings that determine whether a candidate of a party has a real chance to become a legislator. However, in the unusual case where an "open list" system is used (e.g., in Brazil)—allowing the *voters* to pick who they want to get in from each list— party leaders are denied this advantage for party discipline, and they cannot bargain so effectively with the president.

Dilma Roussef, president of Brazil.

As was noted in chapter 12, some multiparty presidential systems have given presidents special procedural powers in the legislative process to compensate for difficulties in gaining legislative cooperation. These include (a) the line item veto (see above) and high percentages required to override presidential vetoes, (b) **insistence powers** to force assemblies to vote on legislation within a certain time period or without amendment, (c) a monopoly over proposing certain kinds of legislation (e.g., the budget), or (d) the capacity to rule by decree on certain matters for limited periods of time, subject to Congressional veto after the fact. By periodically renewing decrees with small amendments—called decree "rollover"—presidents of Brazil, for example, could turn temporary decrees into long-term policy.

THE PARLIAMENTARY POLITICAL EXECUTIVE

Normally in parliamentary systems, the chief executive is much more assured of getting his or her program through the legislative process than in presidential systems. The party or parties making up the parliamentary majority, to keep their leaders in their positions atop the executive branch, must show disciplined support for the proposals of the prime minister and cabinet. However, *informal* contention may still arise within the political executive, especially between the PM's office on one hand, and other party (or party faction) leaders in the cabinet, on the other.

The Cabinet in Parliamentary Systems

Under parliamentary government, prime ministers (PMs) must work much more closely with their cabinet ministers than presidents do with theirs. The cabinet, containing the other leaders of the party or parties that hold the parliamentary majority, forms a key link between the PM and parliament. Correspondingly, the PM's own staff office normally plays a less prominent role than, for example, the White House Staff does in the U.S. presidential government.

A key factor here is who the prime minister chooses to fill the cabinet minister positions. In practice, the PM cannot fill all the cabinet slots with just anybody he or she wants from the majority party fraction(s). At least in part,[6] the PM must draw on the other leading members of the parliamentary majority. This is based on the desirability of ministerial positions. In practice, directing one of the ministries is the highest position that a politician can realistically aspire to under parliamentary government. It gives a direct hand in policymaking, together with high prestige, influence, and perks. Virtually all of those in the upper ranks of leadership in the majority party or coalition will aspire to and contend for these positions. Thus, while an appointed minister often was the chairperson of the party's informal committee for that policy area, in practice ministers do not have to have technical background or credentials in the ministry's policy area; on-the-job training is common. With the ministers' party leadership roles to give them clout, the cabinet cannot be so easily controlled by staffers in the PM's office as they may be in presidential systems.

In multiparty parliamentary systems, the prime minister's cabinet appointments must also accommodate the leaders of the *other parties* in the majority coalition. For example, in Social Democratic PM Gerhard Schroeder's initial cabinet in the late 1990s in Germany, three ministries were allocated to his coalition partner, the Green Party: environment, health, and foreign relations. These ministries were headed by the top Green leaders—in effect chosen by the Green Party, not by Schroeder. A party given a ministerial appointment usually fills most of its subordinate positions, too, such as the deputy ministers and assistant deputy ministers, who supervise the various subdivisions of each ministry. So appointing a minister amounts to allocating control of that ministry to the minister's party.

Nonetheless, the working principle of parliamentary cabinets is **collective responsibility**: the rule that if you are a minister, you must publicly support all bills proposed by the cabinet to parliament. Any misgivings that a minister expresses privately about a cabinet policy cannot get in the way of her or his public support for it. If you are a minister and cannot go along publicly and formally with the cabinet's proposals, you are expected to resign. For example, this was the only option for British Labor Party foreign minister Robin Cook in 2003 when he felt compelled to publicly dissent from Britain's participation in the invasion of Iraq. (If it is just the minister personally who cannot go along, as in Cook's case, (s)he will be replaced by someone else from the same party; if it is the minister's party that objects, it must quit the coalition if it cannot get the proposal acceptably modified.) Thus the collective responsibility requirement imposes formal cooperation on ministers who may be informally contending with one another in the cabinet.

The politically appointed top levels of management of each ministry supervise a large structure of career civil servants. These professional bureaucrats are in principle nonpartisan and duty bound to impartially carry out the directives of their superiors and the existing laws and rules. However, such cooperation is not always as smooth as this model indicates. Existing laws, rules, and bureaucratic procedures can restrain cabinet-inspired attempts at rapid policy change. The top professional bureaucrats of a ministry, with their experience, expertise, and sense of the mission of their units, can sometimes contend informally with the political executive (see chapter 14).

Inter-Ministry Relations and the Prime Minister's Office

When a new policy initiative arises in a particular ministry's policy area, the minister will typically take the lead in presenting it to the cabinet and parliament. If a proposal involves more than one ministry, it may first be considered by a portion of the cabinet, a committee made up of the ministers in related policy areas. For example, an economic policy committee may bring together the ministers of finance, industry, labor, and planning. Or for environmental matters, an informal committee might include the ministers of health, environment, industry, and energy. For a policy idea to build momentum, it may need to gain the support of the relevant cabinet committee, with approval by the whole cabinet normally following. In addition, there may be an "inner cabinet" that includes ministers who are especially close to the prime minister, and with whom the PM will consult on the most politically sensitive initiatives.

The PM is responsible for chairing cabinet meetings and preparing the agenda. If a ministry's work is important to the PM's overall policy priorities and strategy, the PM may become involved to some degree in the decisions and proposals of the minister. Also, PMs may become involved when ministers find themselves in informal contention with each other over policy proposals. A new policy or program that affects several ministers' jurisdictions may require delicate negotiations, especially when they involve ministries run by different parties in the governing coalition.

To help coordinate and sometimes direct the cabinet, the PM normally has an office of his or her own, which may vary in size. Its role is to forge cooperation behind significant new initiatives before a cabinet meeting, as well as monitor what the ministers are doing. Where the prime minister's office is large, it may contain officers or advisors paralleling each of the ministries and their policy areas, as in the office of Germany's chancellor (as the prime minister is called in Germany).

Forming and Maintaining a Multiparty Cabinet

After a multiparty parliamentary election, political attention is usually focused on the outcome: How many seats has each party won, and which coalition of parties holds the most seats? As we saw in chapter 12, usually the party leader of the winning coalition's biggest party fraction takes the lead in negotiations to form a cabinet. (He or she may be formally requested to do so by a ceremonial **head of state**, who often holds the title of president.[7]) To some degree, this winning coalition and its leaders may be said to represent the majority of voters (see "Applying the Models").

As we saw in chapter 12, the winning coalition partner parties usually start by negotiating a coalition pact, whether formal or informal. The coalition partner parties have to agree on two key things that are interrelated: which ministries will be allocated to which party, and what policy directions the coalition and its cabinet will pursue. The *number* of ministries allocated to the coalition partner parties is usually in rough proportion to their party fractions' relative seat strengths within the parliamentary majority. Which particular ministries will fill out a party's quota depends on its most important policy priorities and how they fit into the priorities of the other party or parties in the cabinet. How detailed the coalition pact will be depends not only on how much the coalition partner

APPLYING THE MODELS | The Distribution of Influence in Multiparty Parliamentary Systems

In the two-party parliamentary framework, where normally one of the two significant parties gets the most votes and wins the parliamentary majority (see the British case study, chapter 1), the majority preference model looks good. In contrast, under a multiparty parliamentary framework the main policymaking group is a coalition of party leaderships in a multiparty cabinet. But the voters cast ballots directly for particular political parties. Thus the coalition's party fractions or its cabinet of party leaders may look like an elite that stands above the voters' party choices.

However, the cabinet does lead the parties that, taken together, won the majority of votes. And in the next election within a few years, the voters will hold it accountable for the consequences of its policies. To some extent, then, the majority coalition and its leaders in the cabinet may be seen as representing the voter majority's preferences, at a very general level, regarding the policy directions that the government should take on the most widely discussed issues. Voters tend to be aware that one coalition tends to be generally left of center, while the other is right of center. If the contending coalitions are fairly stable, voters can know which coalition their favored party normally joins. Thus voters know which coalition they are supporting, in effect, when they vote for a party. Moreover, each coalition contains a largest party with a well-known party leader, who is likely to be its prime minister if the coalition wins the election. Here we can say that in the election, a majority voter preference is being followed to some extent, at least regarding who the leading policymakers will be.

However, it is less clear to voters which particular policies will result from the postelection compromises made within the cabinet. Here the cabinet's elite aspect comes back into view, especially under conditions of high fractionalization and instability in the majority coalition and cabinet. If coalition patterns frequently change, on election day the voters have no way of knowing which combination of parties will ally with one another after the election to form a majority coalition. Here the chief policymaking group emerges not from the voters' will but rather primarily from a process of negotiations among party leaderships. Recall that parties may represent not only ideological directions but also interest groups. Here the pluralist model may have a hand in a good explanation.

The personal leadership model may also play a part when we remember that some voters are oriented toward the leaders of the parties. One coalition may be said to have won partly because it had one or more attractive leaders. Again, many voters seem at least to be aware of who are the leaders of the two largest parties, which tend to be the broad moderate left-of-center one and the broad conservative one. These two leaders are widely known to be the rival candidates for the prime minister slot, depending on which coalition wins. As you can see, depending on your point of view, elements of all four models of influence distribution come into play in the phenomenon of multiparty parliamentary elections.

In your country, which model of influence distribution seems to best explain the patterns of executive leadership in relation to the inclinations of the citizens? How much does your answer depend on the sort of political framework in your nation?

parties contend over policy and ministry allocation, but also how certain they feel about each other's intentions and about how they think their participation may affect the next election outcome.[8]

Once the interparty negotiations within the majority coalition are complete and the ministry allocations have been set, many nations require that the lower house of parliament formally pass a "vote of confidence" or an "investiture" vote approving the prime minister and, perhaps, the whole cabinet.

One cluster of motivations for a party to join and stay in a governing coalition is **office seeking**: simply to share in the influence and status brought by holding positions in the political executive. Here the main objective of each coalition partner party would be to gain the maximum number of ministerial positions for its leaders. The explanatory model that best expresses the office-seeking motivation is called the **minimum winning coalition** model of coalition formation.[9] According to this model, cabinets will represent no more parties and seats than are necessary to assure a bare majority of votes for the cabinet's bills in parliament. The fewer the parties in the majority, the larger the number of ministerial positions that are available for each party. This explanatory approach is in line with the rational choice style of analysis, which tends to assume that contending actors are motivated primarily by self-interest and that they have high levels of knowledge and certainty about each other's intentions.[10]

This explanation, however, doesn't reflect the realities of many coalition cabinets. It doesn't say much about which *particular* parties will join, and fails to account for the third or more of postwar European cabinets that have been either larger than the minimum majority size, or smaller.[11]

An alternative explanation that tries to address these difficulties is the **policy-seeking** approach.[12] It assumes that as parties join or leave cabinets, they mainly pursue their favored policy directions. Parties are acutely aware of the above-noted principle of collective cabinet responsibility: their ministers must pledge to support all of the cabinet's policy proposals to parliament. They will join coalitions in which their favored policy directions find a comfortable home. (Again, I define policy direction expansively, including pursuit of values, ideological orientation, and interest group support, as well as favored particular policies.)

Policy-seeking concerns broadly fit what we saw in chapter 12: that most often we find a degree of ideological kinship among parties in the majority coalition. Usually each major contending coalition occupies a segment of the left-right continuum and shares related values. Typically, the most prominent contending coalitions—whether formally allied in the campaign or likely to form after the election—are a left-of-center coalition arrayed against a right-of-center one.[13] If a coalition is rather moderate ideologically and includes one or more center parties, it may be referred to as center-left or center-right.

Most often, one of the coalitions will have won a majority in the last parliamentary election. Or the most successful coalition will have done well enough to be able to gain the parliamentary majority by adding a small party in postelection negotiations. The resulting governing coalition tends to include all parties within its segment of the ideological spectrum.[14]

This can lead to more parties in the cabinet than the bare minimum necessary for a parliamentary majority, called a **surplus majority cabinet**. Surplus majority coalitions have made up over a third of the majority-backed cabinets in postwar Europe.[15] With an extra party or two, such a coalition has the advantage of being able to ride out the withdrawal of a small party (due to contention within the cabinet), without losing the cabinet's majority support in parliament.[16] In contrast, in a minimum winning coalition cabinet, the exit of a small party could cause the PM and cabinet to resign if they lose the parliamentary majority. Thus in a minimum winning coalition cabinet, the coalition partner parties may at times be able to play the role of "veto players," stressed by political scientist George Tsebelis (2002).[17]

The Policy Trade-Off in Cabinet Participation

A party in the cabinet has made some office-seeking gains—control of one or more ministries. But again, there is a policy-related price to be paid, due to the above-mentioned principle of collective responsibility. That price is that you will

TABLE 13.2	Party Goals and Theories of Coalition Building
Theoretical Approach	**Predicted Outcome** (number of parties in the parliamentary majority)
Office seeking	Minimum winning coalition
Policy seeking	Minimum ideological range

have to publicly subscribe to all cabinet proposals to parliament, including those of the *other* parties' leaders atop *their* ministries.[18] A party's ministers may be pressed to go along with a cabinet measure that is uncomfortable for their party. If they do so, their party may risk (a) being divided by internal contention over whether the measure is consistent with its values, ideological identity, or interest group support, and/or (b) externally, losing some of its voter base, who may be put off by the compromise.

As we saw in chapter 12, this situation may at times give influence to the whole parliamentary fraction of the uncomfortable party, including the backbenchers. They may be called in to help their leaders decide whether to (a) go along with the proposal, (b) threaten to leave the cabinet, in order to force an amendment or the withdrawal of the proposal, or (c) to actually exit the cabinet, perhaps leading to the cabinet's resignation.

Due to such phenomena, majority coalitions are not likely to extend any further than necessary toward an ideological extreme or toward the center. This is to avoid having to deal with unpalatable policy demands from parties at either end of the coalition's ideological range. In France, for example, right-of-center coalitions have tended to exclude the far-right (ethnic ultranationalist) National Front. And Germany's left-of-center cabinets tend to exclude the Left Party, which is left social democratic ideologically. Hence, while multiparty coalition governments are not necessarily minimum winning ones, they do often seem to follow a "minimum ideological range" approach[19] (see Table 13.2).

As we saw in chapter 12, if the system suffers from having too many parties—high "fractionalization"—as many as three or more parties may have to join to achieve a majority coalition. In this case, pleasing all the ministers in the cabinet may be too tough, and cabinets may not last long (see "Contention and Cooperation in Focus"). Germany in 1949, France in 1958, and Italy in 1993 all changed their electoral systems to reduce the number of small parties in parliament and thus reduce the number of parties in cabinets. They moved either to require a minimum vote percentage to get proportional representation in parliament (e.g., 4 percent in Italy[20] or 5 percent in Germany), or to have part or all of parliament elected by some form of SMD voting (France in 1958 and Italy in 1993).

The Minority Government and Grand Coalition Options

Thus there are potential costs of a party's participation in the cabinet. In the exceptional case where policy challenges are multiple and sensitive, those costs may be widespread.[21] Especially after an election in which neither traditional coalition has been able to win a majority, no conventional majority coalition may be possible.

Multiparty parliamentary systems have two options for this situation. As we saw in chapter 12, especially if the circumstances do not require much new policymaking, the system may carry on with a minority government—a cabinet without majority legislative support. To pass bills, it must look for help among the opposition. Where there is one very large party in parliament (especially if it is not far from holding a parliamentary majority on its own) that is center-leaning, a single-party minority government will be likely to form, and be able to pass some bills by shopping for support from moderate parties outside the cabinet.[22] Otherwise, a minority coalition will form. Either way, the outcome tends to empower the legislative assembly (see chapter 12).

Alternatively, if a serious policy challenge or emergency requires a new policy, the two contending broad parties may form a left-right "grand coalition"—excluding nearly all of the small parties—to get the job done. In Israel in 2005, for example, the challenge was circumstances requiring Israeli forces to withdraw from the occupied territory of Gaza. But the existing right-of-center majority coalition, led by the Likud Party, included small religious parties that were hostile to concessions to the Palestinians and could not agree on the withdrawal. The moderate left-of-center Labor Party allied temporarily with conservative Likud to conduct the withdrawal from Gaza.[23]

Where the main left-of-center and conservative parties are accustomed to cooperating with each other at times,[24] grand coalition may be an alternative to minority government in situations where neither of their coalitions has won a parliamentary majority in elections. In German parliamentary elections in 2005 and again in 2013, the most successful party—the moderately conservative Christian Democrats led by Angela Merkel—was not part of a majority-winning coalition. In both cases, the moderate left-of-center Social Democrats formed a majority grand coalition with the Christian Democrats, without participation by either of the smaller party allies (the Greens on the left and the classical liberal Free Democrats on the right).

Notably, however, periods of grand coalition can have consequences. If the left-right cabinet has a lot of difficulty accommodating one or more disaffected factions among their parliamentary backbenchers, the broad parties involved in a grand coalition may pay a high price for their cooperation in a grand coalition. The resulting compromises may cost one of them at the ballot box in the next election if a partisan portion of its voter base abandons them. The middle policy course adopted by the grand coalition may even lead to a split in one of the broad parties in it. In Israel, the moderate faction of Likud that had supported the evacuation of Gaza split off from the rest of Likud to form a new smaller center party called Kadima.

THE POLITICAL EXECUTIVE IN SEMI-PRESIDENTIAL SYSTEMS

Up to now, our consideration of democratic governmental systems has focused mainly on presidential and parliamentary ones. But there is also a hybrid option that most political scientists call **semi-presidential**. A semi-presidential system has a popularly elected president with significant powers, who appoints a prime minister. But the PM must also be approved (parliamentary-style) by the lower house of parliament. While semi-presidential democracy remains more parliamentary than presidential in its fundamental nature, in the operation of its political executive, the multiparty semi-presidential system has distinctive features.

France After 1958

France is the earliest prominent example of a semi-presidential political framework. Up through the middle 1950s, the French had a PR-elected parliamentary system with no minimum vote threshold, very high fractionalization, and cabinet instability. In the late 1950s, the country was faced with crisis and national contention over whether to withdraw from its rebellious North African colony Algeria. General Charles de Gaulle, the prestigious leader of the French government-in-exile during World War II, agreed to come out of retirement to resolve the crisis only if the nation restructured and stabilized its political system. In two steps in 1958 and 1962, France established a popularly elected president with a fixed term of office. The president was given significant powers: to appoint and remove the prime minister, approve the PM's choice of cabinet ministers, chair cabinet meetings, call for new parliamentary elections when necessary, and exercise veto power regarding certain government procedures and key aspects of foreign and defense policy. The idea was for the president to be able to change PMs if the prior policies were faring badly, without always having to hold a new election or change the governing coalition.[25] In effect, the president could shift the general policy directions taken by the PM and cabinet.

Strikingly, however, there was also an important *parliamentary* feature in the semi-presidential system: the PM *could be removed by the majority of the members of the National Assembly* (via a vote of censure), regardless of the president's wishes. French semi-presidential government involved multiple lines of influence (see Figure 13.1). What if poor policy outcomes and a new parliamentary election put the National Assembly majority in the hands of the *opposing* coalition (or party)? This could easily happen—and it did in 1986, and again in 1993 and 1997—because the National Assembly's term was capped at five years, in contrast to the president's seven-year term.

In each case, the president wisely deferred to the voters' most recent choice and took the path of cooperation with the new parliamentary majority rather than contention. First left-of-center president François Mitterrand, and then right-of-center president Chirac chose to merely sign off, pro forma, on the opposing coalition's choice of PM, the PM's cabinet appointments, and implicitly, the policy directions taken by the cabinet. Thus "cohabitation" of the opposing

FIGURE 13.1

Lines of Influence in the French Semi-Presidential System

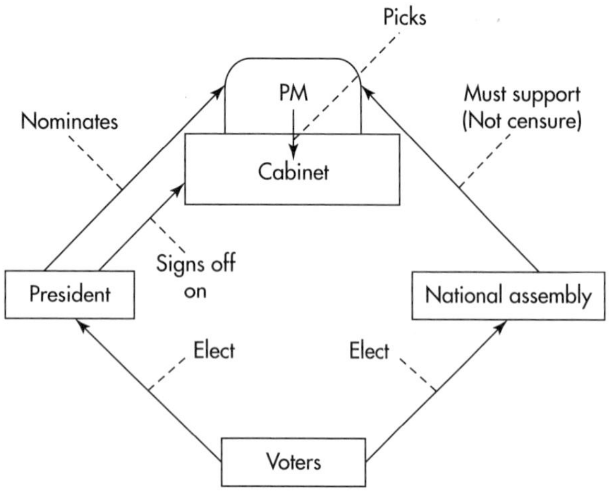

parties in practice meant that the PM and cabinet representing the opposing National Assembly majority proceeded to run the government, parliamentary-style, without having to pay much attention to the president (except under certain circumstances in foreign and defense policy).

The French, however, never seemed wholly comfortable with seeing the choice of PM switch back and forth between the president and the Assembly with election outcomes. To avoid this, in 2000 France changed the president's term of office from seven years to five, the same as the maximum term for the National Assembly. The now concurrent elections of both president and National Assembly—normally occurring at the same time—meant that henceforth the president will likely come from the same coalition that emerged victorious in the parliamentary election. The 2012 election outcome followed this pattern. François Hollande, leader of the moderate left-of-center Socialist Party, won the presidential election as his party won the National Assembly majority. Hollande chose the PM, Jean-Marc Ayrault, from the ranks of his own party. By early 2014, Hollande and his cabinet's popularity had declined due to continued economic stagnation, and his party suffered a big defeat in local elections. Hollande then chose a new PM from his party, the more center-leaning Manuel Valls.

French president François Hollande (right) with PM Manuel Valls (left).

Russia in the 1990s

The multiparty semi-presidential political framework was adopted in several former French colonies as they became independent in the 1960s. A version of it was also adopted in the post-Communist system in Russia (and some of the other post-Communist governments).

However, in Russia the president was given even stronger powers than in France. These included the capacity to dissolve parliament if it repeatedly (three times) rejected his choice for PM. This was partly related to the fact that in the 1990s, the political parties of post-Communist Russia were mostly new, often poorly disciplined, and unable to form stable coalitions. President Boris Yeltsin, who had led the 1991 removal of the old Soviet Union and Communist rule, was the only prominent leader in this precarious new democratic situation even though his supporting party was small.

In this fragmented context, Yeltsin was able to try different PMs in an uneven pursuit of a market economy and the privatization of state-owned enterprises. Only once, briefly, in the midst of an international financial crisis affecting Russia in 1998, did an opposition coalition coalesce in the State Duma (the lower house of the Russian Assembly) and impose a prime minister with policy aims different from those of the president (Yevgeny Primakov, leading a left-leaning coalition of his Fatherland-All Russia Party with the Communist Party).

However, democracy in Russia did not last beyond the 1990s. As we shall see in chapter 15, Yeltsin's successor, Vladimir Putin, greatly boosted presidential dominance in ways that led to a transition back to authoritarian government. By using prosecutions in the courts, media dominance, and other means, Putin suppressed any significant rivals and established a single-party-dominant authoritarian system. As leader of the dominant party, United Russia, Putin could control and manipulate both the legislative branch and the judiciary.

THE POLITICAL EXECUTIVE IN AUTHORITARIAN SYSTEMS

As we saw in chapter 1, under authoritarian government the main outlines of policy are *not* set by officials who are freely and fairly elected. A dominant group—whether it be a single party, the military, a religious hierarchy, or simply the supporters of a particular leader—controls government, usually primarily through control of the executive leadership.

If "elections" are held under authoritarian frameworks, they are not meaningfully competitive. If there is a legislative branch of government, it is not freely and fairly chosen and/or does not have a significant policymaking role. The judiciary has little independence. The government may gain control of the main media outlets to manage press coverage in its favor. With nothing to check the group that dominates the executive leadership, essentially it *is* the government, from which policy initiatives come. Any political contention that occurs proceeds informally, whether within the dominant group or among groups supporting the government. The basic features of the different types of authoritarian regime, along with how they arise and decline, will be examined in chapter 15.

SUMMARY: CONTENTION AND COOPERATION IN THE DEMOCRATIC POLITICAL EXECUTIVE

As we have seen, the distribution of influence in representative democracy, both between branches and within the executive branch, varies partly in response to the political framework. Presidential executives normally have much more of a struggle getting their policy proposals through the legislative process than do parliamentary executives. Presidents work more with staff around them, partly to help influence the legislature, while parliamentary chief executives must rely more heavily on their cabinets. Under the multiparty parliamentary framework (as in the great majority of parliamentary governments), occasional difficulties in maintaining the majority coalition and its multiparty cabinet tend to disperse influence to the leaderships (and sometimes backbenchers, too) of the parties in the cabinet, and lead to various strategies to form and maintain coalitions. Under authoritarian frameworks, the political executive is the center of the action, and influence is often concentrated in the hands of the executive chief.

COUNTRY CASE STUDIES

Here we turn to two contrasting cases: Italy, an established parliamentary democracy in a developed country, and Argentina, a presidential democracy in a developing nation with past experience with military rule.

Italy: A Multiparty Parliamentary Political Executive in Transition

Italy has an unusually complex multiparty parliamentary framework. In the decades after World War II, the country's two legislative houses were highly fractionalized by the PR electoral system with no minimum percentage of the vote required for parties to gain representation. Among the many parties, characteristics of the biggest ones ruled out the formation of two main contending coalitions. The largest party on the left, the Communist Party, was excluded from cabinets due partly to NATO security concerns (despite its "Euro-communist" independence from Soviet direction). The largest broad party, the Christian Democrats (DC), was usually the main anchor for majority coalitions. It was ideologically centrist and catchall, containing several factions, some leaning left and some right in various policy areas.

In addition to the linchpin DC, the majority coalition's cabinet would include a couple of small centrist parties along with either (a) the moderate, classical liberal, and pro-business Liberal Party—a common coalition in the 1950s—or (b) the moderate left-of-center Socialist Party, common in the 1960s and 1970s, or both, during much of the 1980s. The DC was itself held together partly by an extensive patron-client system, whereby portions of the bureaucracy tended to be staffed to satisfy party-supporting interests. Subsidies, contracts, jobs, pensions, and various kinds of welfare benefits were delivered in return for political support. These clientelist aspects also enveloped other coalition partner parties to some extent. Italy failed to provide the voters with a meaningful choice between contending coalitions representing alternative ideological and policy directions.

In Italy's multiparty, center-leaning cabinets during these decades, contention among the leaderships of the small parties and the large party factions was common, and cabinet breakups and reorganizations were frequent. Cabinet instability was enhanced by electoral rules that made it hard for party leaders to maintain party discipline (and hence cohesive party cooperation in voting on bills) in parliament. Voters could pick individual candidates from the favored party's list ("open list" PR, as in Brazil), rather than only choosing between the parties' ranked lists. Thus party leaders could not effectively use the list rankings to maintain party discipline. In addition, voting in parliament was normally secret, so party leaders could not systematically monitor whether their members were voting with their party.

Moreover, committees in parliament were strong and large, sometimes acting like mini-parliaments in making the key decisions on the cabinet's bills. Thus the majority coalition might break down in the midst of committee action on a cabinet bill. Finally, the Italian parliament is unusual in that its upper house, the Senate, is nearly equal in power to the Chamber of Deputies. Defeat of a cabinet bill in the Senate could also bring down a government. All of these features encouraged contention rather than cooperation by individuals, factions within parties, and parties within coalitions.

After a huge corruption scandal (uncovering Mafia involvement) in 1993 that brought the dissolution of the DC and the Socialist Party, Italy seemed fed up. The electoral system was reformed to reduce the number and seat strengths of the small parties and to encourage cooperation in more coherent electoral coalitions. The new system had 75 percent of the 630-member Chamber of Deputies elected in single-member districts, and set a 4 percent threshold for parties or coalitions to win representation in the PR-chosen quarter of the assembly. The SMD element and the threshold did reduce the number of small parties and their seat strengths in the parliament somewhat, though not by as much as reformers desired. Parties winning less than 4 percent of the vote could still win PR seats if they joined a viable coalition before the election, and could even run candidates for SMD seats under the coalition label. But the new electoral arrangements did foster electoral coalitions, and resulted in a pattern of contention between two more stable coalitions, one to the left of center ideologically and the other to the right of center.

On the ideological right, out of the ruins of the old DC and its factions emerged a new broad party of moderate conservatives called Forza Italia ("Go, Italy"). It was led by Silvio Berlusconi, an extremely wealthy media magnate. At first Forza was little more than Berlusconi's personalistic and media-driven vehicle, as he used his heavy influence over Italian broadcast news to assure favorable coverage for himself and his party. After briefly leading Italy's first cabinet after the 1994 election, Berlusconi and Forza remained out of office through the late 1990s. During that intervening period, however, Forza built up its organization and profile to become the leading party on the right. By the 2000s it was able to get 20–30 percent of the votes and seats in Parliament.

In 2001, Berlusconi led to victory a right-of-center coalition called House of Liberty, which also included (a) the National Alliance (a moderate vestige of an old neofascist party), (b) the regionally based and economically conservative Northern League (LN),[26] and (c) a couple of small centrist groups that later combined into the Union of Christian and Center Democrats (UDC). With small variations and sometimes additional allies, that coalition remained largely intact and occupied the cabinet from 2001 through 2005 and from 2008 through 2012. For most of this period Berlusconi was a center-right PM, championing economic growth through both tax cuts and job creation efforts. Over the last twenty years since the 1993 reforms, the PM's office has gradually expanded and exercised increased influence over the cabinet, especially regarding the budget and the planning process.

On the left, after Communism fell in Eastern Europe and Russia in 1989–1991, the Italian Communist Party reorganized and shed its Communist traditionalists (who formed the small Communist Refounding Party). The result was the Democratic Party of the Left. It was initially a mix of democratic socialists and left social democrats, but it has since reached out to include some other small parties (in 1998) and has evolved into a broad moderate left-of-center party. It was the largest single party in the various center-left "Olive Tree" coalitions (including small parties of former left-leaning DCers) that won elections and governed Italy between 1996 and 2001. Despite occasional reshuffles of Olive Tree cabinets and periods of minority government, they were able to pass reforms in the areas of health, education, criminal justice, immigration, governmental decentralization, and regional elections. Notably, this moderate coalition was willing to implement the budget cuts and tax increases that allowed Italy to meet the requirements for admission to the single-currency Eurozone at its birth in 1999.

By the mid-2000s, however, the Italian political system was under great pressure from the small parties (especially on the fragmented left) to return to some form of all PR voting. But Italians still wanted to keep incentives for coalition formation. The electoral reform of 2005 restored all PR, but with a threshold of 2 percent for parties that joined electoral coalitions. This might have led to multiple small coalitions and a return to something like pre-1993 cabinet instability, but for a second major feature of the 2005 reform, aimed at encouraging large coalitions. It awarded to the plurality-winning coalition enough bonus seats in the lower house to give it an automatic clear majority, 54 percent of the Chamber's seats. However, there was a catch, which could lead to less stable control of the executive. For partisan reasons the leader of the Northern League (LN), the author of the election bill, demanded that in the Senate, bonus seats be granted only at the level of the regional election district. Thus different regions' majorities could go to different coalitions, and the Chamber winner might not carry enough Senate regions to secure the majority there.

Sure enough, subsequent cabinets did not last long. The 2006 elections were narrowly won by the center-left Union coalition, spearheaded by the Democrats of the Left. That party then merged with a group of former left-leaning DCers and some other smaller groups to form today's moderate left-of-center Democratic Party. In 2008, the Democratic Party and its fractionalized coalition lost a key vote in the Senate and resigned, leading to new elections. The center-right People of Liberty coalition led by Forza won the 2008 elections and Berlusconi became PM until his resignation in late 2011. His replacement in 2012, technocrat Mario Monti, aimed primarily to accommodate EU pressures for austerity, which made him very unpopular due to the continuing economic slump.

This set the stage for the election of 2013. Berlusconi continued to favor tax cuts and infrastructure spending, and to criticize EU demands for austerity. Thus both the left-of-center and the conservative coalitions shared a dissatisfaction with austerity under Italy's conditions of continuing slump and high unemployment. In addition, a new and somewhat chaotic protest party (that wanted Italy out of the Eurozone), the Five Star Movement led by a comedian, Beppe Grillo, did well with 20 percent of the vote.

In the voting results, the left-leaning coalition led by the Democrats won the Chamber bonus by only a third of a percent, but failed to prevail in the Senate. The only alternative was a left-right grand coalition including the Democrats, Forza, and Monti's small party. This grand coalition was led by a Democrat as PM, Enrico Letta. That cabinet survived a late 2013 split within Forza over parliament's expulsion of Berlusconi due to his tax convictions in the courts; Forza's anti-Berlusconi cabinet ministers formed a new small party calling itself the new center-right and stayed in the governing coalition.

As this left-right grand coalition cabinet continued the struggle to accommodate to EU pressures for austerity, overall dissatisfaction—and yearning for a way to break out of the situation—was reaching a boiling point. To complicate matters further, in late 2013 a Supreme Court decision invalidated the 2005 electoral system because of what the court saw as two failures: (a) to sufficiently provide individual names for the voters to consider (as had the 1993–2005 electoral system), and (b) to yield a single overall parliamentary majority for a stable cabinet.

Into this situation of public frustration strode a new figure who was nationally popular but something of an outsider in his Democratic Party (PD): former Florence mayor Matteo Renzi. Pledging political reforms and policy changes to address several major problems at once, Renzi became PD leader in a vote of the whole party membership at the end of 2013, and thus replaced Letta as PM leading the grand coalition cabinet. In it Renzi began by replacing the PD ministers—mostly older party leaders—with people in their 30s and 40s whom he saw as more in tune with the national sentiment for change.

The Italian economy of 2014 was basically stagnant (along with the Eurozone generally), with unemployment at around 14 percent and southern economic conditions much worse than in the north. To address the economy, Renzi produced a long list of proposals. In the face of EU austerity pressures related to Italy's large debt of 135 percent of GDP, Renzi declared that economic growth had to be the foundation of any solution, and stimulus spending must temporarily become the order of the day. Taxes were cut for lower-income individuals and some businesses, a range of job-creating infrastructure projects were begun (especially to rebuild schools) and the government would pay off its unpaid debts to private contractors. Renzi argued that despite his spending proposals, the government budget deficit would not exceed the EU target of 3 percent.

Another important economic policy area for Renzi was labor market regulation. Regarding private sector employment, Renzi sought a compromise between (a) the traditional job protections (with their assured pensions) that made layoffs very difficult, and (b) the newer employer-favored "temporary" contracts that were exempt from the protections and pension assurance. The bill (passed in 2015) offered new hires a single three-year contract with gradually increasing job protection over the period, which would culminate in permanent employment. But employers would be able to lay off permanent employees (unless discrimination could be proven) if those dismissed were compensated, with payments (of over a thousand Euros a month, gradually declining) lasting up to two years. These measures were sufficiently center-leaning that even Berlusconi and Forza would support many of them, while the unions and some left-leaning PD groups grumbled publicly. Traditionally, on such a controversial issue dividing his party, Renzi would lift the requirement of party discipline and its cohesive party voting, and allow legislators to vote their conscience. But fearing too many defections on the bill, Renzi publicly made it a "confidence" measure—if it failed, the PD cabinet would have to resign.

Another set of proposals addressed Italy's political framework. These were aimed at satisfying the court's critique of the current system (see above), and assuring a parliamentary majority in the future. Renzi proposed that (a) in the electoral system, the minimum thresholds for small parties to get into the Chamber of Deputies were to be doubled, to 4 percent, (b) the PR districts would be made small (4–6 seats each, in effect reducing the proportionality of the voting system) to forefront candidates' names for the voters to see, (c) the Senate would be much reduced in size (to 100 members), become indirectly elected, and lose its prominent role in legislation, so that only the majority of the lower-house Chamber of Deputies would matter for control of the cabinet, and (d) if no coalition got over 37 percent in the first round of voting for the lower house, there would be a second, runoff vote between the top two vote-getting coalitions to award a majority bonus of 15 percent. On this point, a subsequent revision of the proposal in late 2014 made it the leading *party*—rather than coalition—that would get the seat bonus and the parliamentary majority.

This last change would reduce the role of smaller parties as coalition partners, an especially big problem for the right of center in Italy, which does not have a single large party like the PD on the left. And with the party leaderships continuing to choose their candidates, these reforms would lead to more influence for the governing party's leader (the prime minister) over its backbenchers. In all, the political framework changes will mean much more influence for the Italian prime minister than the position has had in the past.

The constitutional changes diminishing the size and role of the Senate must await a referendum vote in late 2016 to become final. Meanwhile, mid-2015 saw indications of a surge in popularity for the Northern League, which is becoming more ethnic ultranationalist, antiimmigrant, and Eurosceptic than in the past, and is trying to surpass the now split Forza as the leading party on the right. But for the moment in Italy's still fragmented political system, cooperative coalition politics seems to be prevailing in the passage of Renzi's reforms.

Argentina: The Political Executive in a Multiparty Presidential System

The Argentine governmental system is presidential. The chief executive, the president, is elected directly by the people and serves a fixed term of office, whether or not her or his proposals pass in the Chamber of Deputies (the lower legislative house) and the Senate to become law. Thus, unlike parliamentary systems, there is no overwhelming pressure for the president's own party's legislators to vote in favor of the policies (s)he proposes. With each branch of government relatively autonomous and capable of limiting the other, the president can have a hard time getting a policy program through—but again, failure to do so does not threaten the chief executive's tenure in office.

Argentina's proportional representation (PR) voting system for the Chamber of Deputies is a major factor behind its multiparty politics. Voting districts are large with multiple representatives each, and parties win seats according to their proportion of the votes. Thus small parties can win seats and numerous parties gain representation in the Chamber. The usual result is that there are too many parties in the legislature for the president's own party to possess majorities in the legislative assemblies. To pass bills regularly, a president must form an informal support coalition to back her or his proposals. (Similarly to parliamentary government, this means that leaders of coalition partner parties must be given seats in the cabinet.) Such coalition support is not airtight, since presidential government lacks the imperative party discipline that parliamentary government enjoys. And a presidential coalition may not encompass majorities in Congress.

So to get bills approved, Argentine presidents typically cannot get around having to engage in at least some negotiating, on a case-by-case basis, with other parties, factions within them, or individual legislators with their followings. As you can see, the strength of the political executive in Argentina is very much a matter of the political parties and their relationships and interactions.

To be sure, other factors can still make it possible for two major parties to significantly surpass the others and contend with each other to lead the government, on occasion allowing one of them to possess legislative majorities. One factor was the repetition of military intervention and dominance (1943–1944, 1955–1958, 1962–1963, 1966–1973, and 1976–1983), during which open party contention was shut down. This recurring phenomenon hindered the development of a range of parties other than the two long-distance runners discussed below. Another major factor concerned the characteristics of one very large and long-lasting party, the Judicialist Party, whose members are informally known as the "Peronists" after the charismatic Juan Peron who founded the party in the mid-twentieth century.

Especially early in his political career, Peron pursued policies that were strongly left of center and activist with respect to the economy. He actively supported industrialization, jobs, urbanization, and social welfare, in contrast to the relatively free-market agricultural export economy that had preceded him. For example, Peron's policies included government ownership of some enterprises, financial support for others, strong job-protecting regulation of labor markets, pensions for the elderly, government spending to keep food and transportation costs low, financial support for regional and local government, and high tariffs (taxes on imports). But on sociocultural issues, Peron had a conservative streak; originally a military man and a nationalist, at times he favored law-and-order policies that were considered right of center. Meanwhile, the Peronist party was always partially a sprawling alliance of regional and ideological factions, which sought to represent a significant array of sectors of the Argentine economy and its political society. They contended informally with each other for advantage and benefits under the Peronist umbrella, even as they cooperated partly due to shared allegiance to the charismatic Peron himself. In periods when the military allowed the Peronists to contend in politics, and their left-of-center and center-right factions could cooperate, the party might win Chamber majorities, as they did in the late 1950s and mid-1970s.

Peron died in 1974. Twenty years later, the Peronist leadership took a sharp turn in its favored policy directions for the economy. The party's center-right faction took control of its economic policies and turned most of them in a free-market direction. Under the leadership of then president Carlos Menem, the Peronist government adopted measures such as reducing economic regulation and tariffs and selling off state-owned enterprises to the private sector. Notably, Menem got much support because he stopped rapid inflation by tying Argentina's currency to the dollar. But disaffection among the Peronist left did not result in a party split. In addition to its ideological factions, the Peronists included interest groups and regional factions, as well. Amid a fast-recovering economy in the early and middle 1990s, the Menem government was able to continue to provide a minimum of spending, jobs, and support for grateful regional and lower-stratum groups. Again, a party like the Peronists involves cooperation among a wide range of groups which at times contend with each other, too.

However, the party lost power at the end of the 1990s amid a severe economic downturn and a consequent government budget crisis. Sharp contention then broke out between the two major Peronist factions. In 2003, control of most of the party shifted back to its left-of-center wing, with the rise of President Nestor Kirchner. The Peronists again began to win legislative majorities. By the end of the decade, however, came the culmination of a trend long in the making: the formal emergence of its two major factions as parties in their own right: (a) the left-of-center Kirchner wing called Front for Victory (FPV), subsequently (after Kirchner's death in 2010) led by his wife, then president Christina Fernandez Kirchner, and (b) the center-right faction now called Federal Peronism, led mostly by Eduardo Duhalde.

The other historically prominent party is the center-leaning Radical Civic Union (UCR). The UCR led Argentina during its first years of universal-suffrage democracy, between 1916 and 1932. But at times it, too, was divided into contending factions, with a center-left wing that was relatively friendly with other parties on the left ideologically, and a center-right wing that could work better with conservatives. Prior to the 1980s, the UCR could win legislative majorities only during periods when the Peronist party was banned by the military. In the early 1980s, however, the UCR recaptured its old heritage as a pro-democracy movement by spearheading the rejection of military rule and the popular reestablishment of democracy. Under the leadership of President Raul Alfonsin, the party won majorities in the Chamber of Deputies in the mid-1980s until it lost power amid an economic crisis in the late 1980s. In the late 1990s, however, when another economic crisis sank the Peronists, the UCR's center-left wing led an alliance with a group of leftist parties to victory. But that victory proved to be short lived, as unrelenting economic deterioration and debt burdens proved unmanageable for UCR president Fernando de la Rua.

In the last decade, the UCR has been fragmenting. In 2003 its center-left wing became what is now called the Civic Coalition, led by Elisa Carrio, who has links to center-left Catholicism. The UCR's center-right wing, more free-market-oriented, became Recreate for Growth, led by Lopez Murphy, which has allied with other small free-market-oriented groups (some regional) in a coalition called Republican Proposal (PRO). Between these two wings of the old party is its most consistently centrist group that still claims the UCR name (led today by Ricardo Alfonsin, son of Raul), leading a centrist coalition called the Union for Social Development.

At times, an alliance of parties on the left has also made its presence felt, either on its own or in a coalition with part or all of the UCR. The left alliance is now called the Progressive Ample Front, led by the Socialist Party. And roles are also played by the numerous other small parties (many of them regional, based in just one province) that PR voting allows to gain representation. Today, the principal parties—each formerly a faction of one of the earlier era's large parties, the Peronists and the UCR—each tend to lead a coalition with one or more smaller supporting parties. Despite their complicated and fluctuating past histories, though, the most prominent parties today display an ideological range, at identifiable locations on the left-right spectrum: ample on the far-left, Front for Victory (FPV) as the mainstream left-of-center representative, Civic Coalition at the center-left, Alfonsin's remaining UCR in the center, Federal Peronism at the center-right, and Republican Proposal/Recreate representing full-scale, free-market conservatism.

Today's presidential situation is framed by the country's recovery from its debt-and-deficit crisis of 1999–2001, during which Argentina defaulted on its debt and suffered terrible economic conditions with unemployment shooting to over 20 percent. In the subsequent years, Argentina's devaluation of its peso allowed a resurgence of agricultural and manufacturing exports (especially to neighboring Brazil), which the government taxed to help balance its books. Under Kirchner since 2003, continuing government spending stimulus (e.g., energy and other subsidies, infrastructure investment, wage increases, and a child allowance to poor families) further spurred jobs and recovery, with GDP growth over 6 percent. Barred by a regional trade agreement from hiking tariffs, the government has recently used an import licensing scheme to limit imports and favor domestic production. Kirchner's FPV held legislative majorities during most of the 2000s and again since 2011 (following Kirchner's resignation as president in 2008 and death in 2010), led by his wife, Christina Fernandez de Kirchner as president.

However, attending all this has been continuing high inflation. By the early 2010s, inflation was running above 25 percent a year, the nation's trade surplus was much reduced, some unions were striking over wages trailing inflation, and crime was increasingly perceived as a problem. In the late 2013 Congressional elections, FPV kept its majority but in a few strongholds (including Buenos Aires) lost to an FPV breakaway group called Front for Renovation (FR), led by the charismatic mayor of a town near Buenos Aires, Sergio Massa. (Massa's policies are nearly identical to those of FPV, except for his more aggressive stance on crime and his criticism of taxes on agricultural exports.)

By late 2015 a long list of problems plagued the Fernandez government: a large fall in the price of a key export, soybeans, repeated devaluations and the need for more, rising unemployment, dropping real wages, inflation continuing at around 30 percent, shortages of imported inputs for manufacturing, the economy at times in mild recession, and an unresolved international lawsuit over unpaid Argentine debt. The president's approval rating dropped to only around 30 percent. Fernandez's successor as FPV leader and presidential candidate for the October 2015 elections, Daniel Scioli (recent governor of Buenos Aires province), was perceived as more moderate and attractive than Fernandez. But to the surprise of many, Scioli was defeated by the moderate conservative Mauricio Macri (mayor of Buenos Aires) of the PRO (Republican Proposal). While pledging to retain existing policies aiding the poorest, Macri otherwise sought to move the government toward austerity.

✈ **PRACTICE AND REVIEW ONLINE**

CRITICAL THINKING QUESTIONS

1. In two-party presidential systems, what parts of the political executive seem to you to be most influential most often, and why?

2. In multiparty presidential political executives, how does the presence of several parties complicate the efforts of the political executive to turn its policy proposals into law, in comparison to two-party situations? What are the advantages and disadvantages of each?

3. Which seems to be the most important motivation for parties' leaders in parliamentary cabinets, office seeking or policy seeking, and why?

KEY TERMS

political executive, 380
separation of personnel, 383
line item veto, 383
signing statement, 383
executive office, 384

FURTHER READING

Dahl, Robert A. *On Democracy*. New Haven, CT: Yale University Press, 1998.

Dahl, Robert A., Ian Shapiro, and José Antonio Cheibub, eds. *Democracy Sourcebook*. Cambridge, MA; London: MIT Press, 2003.

Elgie, Robert. *Semi-Presidentialism: Sub-Types and Democratic Performance*. Oxford: Oxford University Press, 2011.

Gallagher, Michael, Michael Laver, and Peter Mair. *Representative Government in Modern Europe*, 4th ed. New York: McGraw-Hill, 2006.

Haynes, Jeff. *Democracy in the Developing World: Africa, Asia, Latin America, and the Middle East*. Cambridge, England; Malden, MA: Polity Press, 2001.

Helms, Ludger. *Presidents, Prime Ministers, and Chancellors: Executive Leadership in Western Democracies*. New York Palgrave, 2005.

Lijphart, Arend. *Democracies; Patterns of Majoritarian and Consensus Government in Twenty-one Countries*. New Haven, CT: Yale University Press, 1984.

Poguntke, Thomas, and Paul Webb, eds. *The Presidentialization of Politics: A Comparative Study of Modern Democracies*. New York: Oxford University Press, 2005.

Shugart, Matthew Soberg, and John M. Carey. *Presidents and Assemblies: Constitutional Design and Electoral Dynamics*. Cambridge, England; New York: Cambridge University Press, 1992.

Strom, Kaare, Wolfgang Muller, and Torbjorn Bergman. *Delegation and Accountability in Parliamentary Democracies*. New York: Oxford University Press, 2004.

NOTES

[1] See Graham Allison, "Conceptual Models and the Cuban Missile Crisis," *American Political Science Review* 63, no. 3 (1969): 689–718, and *Essence of Decision: Explaining the Cuban Missile Crisis* (New York: Little Brown, 1971).

[2] By the mid-2000s, both DeLay and Abromoff had run afoul of ethics investigations that led to their removal from the scene.

[3] See Octavio Avorim Neto, "The Presidential Calculus: Executive Policy Making and Cabinet Formation in the Americas," *Comparative Political Studies* 39, no. 4 (2006): 415–40. For an extension of these perspectives to democratic governments in general, see Amorim Neto and David Samuels, "Democratic Regimes and Cabinet Politics: A Global Perspective," *Revista Ibero-Americana de Estudos Legislativos* 1, no. 1 (2010): 10–23.

[4] See David Samuels, "Presidentialized Parties: the Separation of Powers and Party Organization and Behavior," *Comparative Political Studies* 35, no. 4 (2002): 461–83.

[5] See Jose Antonio Cheibub and Fernando Limongi, "Modes of Government Formation and the Survival of Democratic Regimes: Presidentialism and Parliamentarism Reconsidered," *Annual Review of Political Science* 5 (2002): 151–79.

[6] In some countries, such as France, the Netherlands, and Sweden, some cabinet posts may be filled by former civil servants.

[7] A country's head of state is usually its top ceremonial figure (e.g., the queen of England), for example, representing the nation formally in signing treaties, formally designating a new prime minister (in parliamentary systems), or attending the funerals of high-prestige foreign leaders. In presidential and semi-presidential systems, the president is also the head of state; in parliamentary systems, the head of state is separate from the PM and has no significant political role.

[8] See Kaare Strom, Wolfgang C. Muller, and Torbjorn Bergman, eds., *Cabinets and Coalition Bargaining: The Democratic Life Cycle in Western Europe* (Oxford, UK: Oxford University Press, 2008).

[9] See William H. Riker, *The Theory of Political Coalitions* (New Haven, CT: Yale University Press, 1962).

[10] See Paul Mitchell and Benjamin Nyblade, "Government Formation and Cabinet Type in Parliamentary Democracies," in *Cabinets and Coalition Bargaining: The Democractic Life Cycle in Western Europe. Comparative Politics*, ed. Kaare Strøm, Wolfgang Müller, and Torbjörn Bergman (Oxford, UK: Oxford University Press, 2008), 201–36.

[11] See Gallagher, Laver, and Mair (2006).

[12] An early example of this view was Abram de Swan, *Coalition Theories and Cabinet Formations* (Amsterdam: Elsevier Scientific Publications, 1973).

[13] See chapter 6.

[14] See Gallagher, Laver, and Mair (2006), 387.

[15] See Gallagher, Laver, and Mair (2006), 401.

[16] For circumstantial factors encouraging surplus majority cabinets, see Mitchell and Nyblade (2008; note 10 above).

[17] See George Tsebelis, *Veto Players: How Political Institutions Work* (New York: Russell Sage Foundation and Princeton University Press, 2002).

[18] Partly due to such concerns, some European political executives place a junior minister of one party in a ministry being run by another party, to monitor what is happening. See Luca Verzichelli, "Portfolio allocation," in *Cabinets and Coalition Bargaining: The Democratic Life Cycle in Western Europe*, ed. Kaare Strom, Wolfgang C. Muller, and Torbjorn Bergman (Oxford, UK: Oxford University Press, 2008), 237–67.

[19] See Gallagher, Laver, and Mair (2006), 387. These authors refer to such coalitions as "minimal connected winning" ones.

[20] See Country Case Study below.

[21] Political scientists have identified several factors that can affect coalition joining and leaving. See Wolfgang Muller and Kaare Strom, eds., *How Political Parties in Western Europe Make Hard Decisions* (Cambridge, UK: Cambridge University Press, 1999), and Strom, Muller, and Bergman, eds (2008, see note 18 above).

[22] See chapter 12, note 5.

[23] A personal leadership factor weighed in here; then Likud leader and PM Ariel Sharon exercised his wide personal influence to push through the policy of withdrawal from Gaza.

[24] See the section in chapter 12 on upper-house vetoes.

[25] For example, in the early 1980s the president was François Mitterrand and the PM was Pierre Mauroy, both of the moderate left-of-center Socialist Party that was in coalition with the Communist Party. Mauroy pursued left social democratic policies that were producing big budget deficits and inflation, reducing the popularity of the government and contributing to sharp contention within the majority coalition. In 1984, President Mitterrand replaced Mauroy with the more center-leaning Laurent Fabius as PM, who halted the leftward policy tilt.

[26] The Northern League is anti-bureaucracy, antiimmigration, and opposed to redistribution from Italy's more prosperous north to the poorer and less developed south. This puts it in some tension with the National Alliance, which defends aid and patronage for Italy's poorer south, the party's base.

Applying the Law
Public Administration and the Courts

IN THE EVENTS LEADING UP to the financial crisis of 2008–2009 in the United States, questionable practices in mortgage lending and foreclosures played a major role. In response to the crisis, the U.S. Congress passed the Dodd-Frank financial regulation law in 2010. Among its many provisions was the establishment, in the executive branch of government, of a Consumer Financial Protection Bureau (CFPB) to protect consumers in their interactions with any individuals and companies that are involved, directly or indirectly, in lending to consumers. The bureau was to combine, coordinate, and strengthen, under one independent agency, regulatory activities that were previously located in various points in the executive branch.

However, as is common practice in legislation, the U.S. Congress did not specify what new regulations would be applied by the CFPB as it tried to assure financial transparency for consumers. The law only stated that regulations would aim to prevent "unfair, deceptive, or abusive" acts, products, or services that consumers might encounter, with general definitions of those terms. This laid out a particular direction for government policy to take, but the job of defining just how and how far policy will go in that direction was left to the **bureaucracy**, the nonpartisan, professional civil service workers who carry out laws and programs.

The conservative, anti-regulation Republican leadership in Congress had lost the fight over the law. But as the statute was worded regarding the CFPB, only the director could issue the crucial rules. Accordingly, the Republicans in the Senate (alongside lobbying by financial businesses) fought a long, vigorous battle to block Senate confirmation of a director. The Obama administration had to give up its first choice for the post (Elizabeth Warren, former Harvard professor and the early champion of the idea of such an agency) as too controversial. Instead Obama nominated Richard Cordray, who had a substantial record as former state treasurer and attorney general in Ohio. Through 2012, the Republicans refused to allow confirmation of any nominee, hoping to paralyze the agency. Finally, in mid-2013 they yielded and approved Cordray. The long fight underlined the importance of rule-making in the bureaucracy, in the application of the law.

As sites for policymaking, the bureaucracy and the courts are quite different from legislative assemblies and the political executive. In general, the bureaucracy applies laws that it receives from elsewhere, and courts handle disputes about that application. Thus in both the bureaucracy and the courts, action is far more circumscribed by decisions made elsewhere (and in the past), than is the case with the political executive and the legislative assemblies.

A rough sequence of policy application:

Legislation → political executive → bureaucracy → courts

However, this does not mean that cooperation prevails and contention is absent in and around the bureaucracy and the courts. Bills' lack of specificity at key points means that contention can arise within the institutions for policy application, as well as between them and affected groups in society and between those affected groups. But this scope for administrative and judicial discretion and contention is narrower than we have found in examining such political sites as parties, elections, the legislative branch, and the political executive. In effect, the formal statutes often serve to exercise limit-setting power (see chapter 3), establishing hedges around the detailed policymaking of administrative and judicial bodies. As we shall see, between those hedges bureaucrats and judges must act on their sense of the letter and spirit of the legislation, other existing laws and practices, and related public values. We shall first take a look at the bureaucracy, and then move on to the courts.

THE BUREAUCRACY

As was noted in chapter 13, the bureaucracy is another name for the civil service—the body of professional, career functionaries who carry out laws and programs, free of party partisanship. In addition to fleshing out the rules that give specific content to legislation, they provide technical information and advice to the other policymakers, and actually implement government policies.

Max Weber, a political sociologist of the early twentieth century, wrote extensively about bureaucracy after studying the administrative workings of the late nineteenth-century Prussian army. Weber stressed that as much as possible, modern bureaucracy should

- be organized in hierarchies of authority;
- operate impartially, according to fixed written rules and set procedures;
- be made up of officers who are specialized in their functions;
- be made up of officers who are hired and promoted according to merit, in the form of appropriate qualifications of education, experience, past performance, and/or testing, for their roles; and
- be protected from political pressure, usually by assuring bureaucrats of tenure in their jobs.[1]

The bureaucracy is divided into broad ministries (called "departments" in some countries with a British colonial history), such as those for labor, commerce, foreign relations, the environment, or defense, and smaller independent agencies, boards, commissions, or government corporations for specific purposes.

The top professional administrators in the civil service are positioned just below the political executive in authority. In each ministry, these senior civil servants may or may not have their own chief bureaucrat, in Britain called the **permanent secretary**. Below this top level, a typical ministry is divided into several departments or bureaus, each with its own chief and his or her deputies. And each of these units may be further subdivided into divisions, sections, and so on. At the base are the clerical workers, inspectors, analysts, etc., who implement the detail of administrative work. As we shall see, in some units the main lines of hierarchical authority have staff attached (sometimes established by the political executive with its priorities in mind) to advise or provide services. And in some cases, external watchdog agencies have been attached to root out perceived bad practices.

The Development of Modern Bureaucracy

Some of the elements of bureaucratic patterns are evident as early as ancient Egypt, and in the Confucian bureaucracy in China, the Roman and Byzantine empires in Europe, and the hierarchy of the Roman Catholic Church. But in the kingdoms of medieval Europe, the monarch's agents were, in effect, part of her or his household, with patron-client connections to lower-level agents. In some places, particular administrative positions (and their salaries) were bought and sold.

Later, more modern bureaucratic development arose under the French and Prussian courts in the eighteenth century. A further boost to the spread of modern bureaucratic methods came with Napoleon's early nineteenth-century establishment of a legal code across his French Empire in Europe, with local prefects serving as agents of the central bureaucracy. By 1815, Napoleon's empire had fallen, but its administrative style remained in many areas. However, prior to the late nineteenth century, few government bureaucracies matched Weber's image of a fully impartial and professional civil service.

In American democracy through most of the nineteenth century, norms of impartial expertise were largely lacking. In the style of President Andrew Jackson's **spoils system** that arose in the 1830s, each new American president swept out most of the current executive employees and replaced them with his followers. Thus administrative officers didn't much need qualifications appropriate for their roles as their job was to be responsive to the democratic majority at the time.

Some totalitarian and authoritarian states of the first half of the twentieth century took this idea of bureaucracy as political spoils to extremes. As we saw in chapter 5, in the bureaucratic socialism of the Soviet Union, the government bureaucracy included the management of the whole economy and most key social organizations. The ruling Communist party had a list of all of the significant managerial positions related to the economy and society, called the **nomenklatura**, for which it could review and potentially veto appointment decisions. In Nazi Germany in the 1930s, the Nazis planted advocates for Hitler in the bureaucracy, social organizations, and some corporations, partly to patrol units' ranks for political opponents to be removed.

In the late nineteenth century, however, in North America and Europe, the bureaucracy began to become a civil service. Positions were increasingly filled by impartially considering the candidate's competence for the job, often relying heavily on performance on a standardized test. If officials were adequately competent, their jobs became secure from political removal. In principle, promotion in the bureaucracies of the established democracies came to be based on efficiency of performance and length of experience, not political criteria.

Specialization of Function and Qualifications

As was noted above, a feature of bureaucratic roles is specialization of function. We find variation, however, in how specialized must be the *prior backgrounds* and credentials of bureaucrats for their particular high-level positions. One idea is that they should be first hired as talented generalists, valued for their overall educational achievement and skills of judgment. These factors may be measured in part by performance on a standardized test or in special schools that serve as feeders for the civil service. For example, the upper ranks of the civil service in Britain tend to recruit from graduates of Oxford and Cambridge Universities, in France from the prestigious *École Nationale d'Administration* and *École Polytechnique*, and in Germany mostly from undergraduate training in law. Such recruits are viewed as capable of serving in any of a variety of departments, where they can learn their specialized functions, call on the relevant expertise of others as needed, and later perhaps move on to another ministry. National bureaucracies using this approach tend to employ centralized recruitment and placement.

By contrast, in the United States and Latin America, for example, each department hires its own officials, with a greater focus on prior specialized expertise and credentials in the department's particular field. In this case, officials are more likely to stay in one department or one of its divisions throughout their executive branch careers.

Nations also vary in how much status and income are accorded to the professional career civil service. In France and Germany, upper-level civil servants are well regarded and compensated, whereas in the United States and Britain since the 1980s, critiques of state intervention have served to reduce their status and privileges somewhat.

In the developing and post-Communist nations, the status and pay of government functionaries are often quite low today. Salaries may have been decimated by past inflation (though sometimes fringe benefits such as bribe taking and a future pension may still be attractive). The backgrounds and standards for recruitment of bureaucrats may vary widely, and patron-client connections may prevail over impartial assessment of qualifications. Political supporters or people sharing an ethnic background may have the advantage. Many of the developing and post-Communist nations are still struggling in the direction of modern Weberian standards for their bureaucracies.

Hierarchies and Levels of Authority

Within units of the bureaucracy, the general pattern is hierarchy of authority. Higher-level civil servants make key decisions, which are carried out by lower-level ones via set chains of command. This **line authority** is the main one that steers results on the ground. But again, especially at higher levels in these hierarchies we also see **staff** units attached to key decision makers in the line of authority. Staff units may provide advice, planning, or specialized information to line decision makers. We also find secondary staff units that provide such support services as accounting, clerical work, personnel functions, and purchasing and distribution of resources.

The hierarchy of line officials generally forms the core within ministries and other agencies in public administration. However, the relations between higher and lower levels can vary somewhat. In some systems, administration is largely decentralized to the regional level, with the national ministry providing only general policymaking and supervision. In the federal systems of Germany and India, for example, most implementation of programs and regulations is done at the regional/provincial level.

Moreover, in some nations, certain regular functions are carried out by semi-autonomous boards, regulatory agencies, offices, and commissions. For example, the Social Security Administration manages Americans' old-age pensions and the Federal Employment Service helps Germans find jobs. Food safety is monitored by the Food Standards Agency in Britain or the Food and Drug Administration in the United States. Sweden favors a system in which semiautonomous boards (often using corporatist representation of key affected interests) balance the interests involved in major government programs. The independent national Board of Health and Welfare and the National Nuclear Energy Inspection Board were established to assure the insulation of their work from interventions by the political executive. Where the Swedish government owns enterprises in economic sectors such as the railroads, telecommunications, or energy (e.g., electricity, oil, and gas), independent boards try to operate their public corporations on business principles.

In some nations we also find corporatist committees attached to ministries, on which seats are allocated to key affected interests and the political parties, to represent them.[2] These committees contribute their information, views, and sometimes influence to policymaking. For example, in northern Europe corporatist boards oversee labor market protections, and such councils include representatives of not only peak employers' associations and labor federations, but also party experts and relevant bureaucrats. Other units may be less autonomous, such as temporary advisory councils that are set up by the political executive to address selected policies. They may include appointed outsiders alongside (or even instead of) career bureaucrats.

With or without such formal units, influence may be exerted in a particular policy area by an informal "policy network" of experienced experts—including representatives of affected interest groups, party members or staffers from the relevant legislative committee, and bureaucrats from related units—who may help steer the application of laws and rules. Patterns of contention and cooperation among these different types of units greatly affect how policies will be implemented.

What Bureaucracies Do

One of the major functions of professional civil servants is to provide services, which may be administered at different levels. Fire and police protection and road building, for example, tend to be administered locally. However, regional and national units also deal with some aspects of these services. Federal police units handle crimes that cross boundaries, and regional and national road construction departments manage key regional or national highway arteries. Control of education may vary, ranging from primarily local (as in the United States) to national (e.g., in France; see Table 14.1).

Another key focus for administration is subsidies: grants, low-interest loans, or tax cuts for activities that are judged to be in the public interest. For example, many nations grant money to support the housing costs of the poor or alternative energy research and development (e.g., solar or wind power). In some developing nations, a state-owned marketing organization may apply subsidies in the sale of bread, rice, or fuel, to keep prices affordable for the urban population. These subsidies must be administered and overseen by units of the bureaucracy.

A significant portion of the government bureaucracy today is involved in law enforcement and regulation aimed at preventing or reducing such ills as fraud, abuse, cheating, and outright harm to people or the environment. Here the public administrators patrol such things as building codes, sanitation requirements, electricity rates, and rules for financial transactions involving stocks and bonds. The subsidies referred to above are often accompanied by **regulatory strings** that may be attached to the program. For example, if national money is made available for after-school child care, local school systems that undertake the activity and accept the subsidy have to set up a program that meets certain minimal requirements and standards (e.g., having at least a certain number of supervisory personnel watching a certain maximum number of kids in the after-school programs). To assure that such standards are met, regulatory administrators must gather a lot of information. This often requires getting those who are regulated to fill out forms, which they are not always happy to do.

Licensing is another important regulatory activity for some units of the bureaucracy. When an activity is judged to have important consequences for the public interest or welfare, government may claim a role in approving those who are allowed to practice it. However, licensing may be done at various bureaucratic levels. Broadcast television licensing may be done by a national level agency, but

People at the Visa Section of the German Embassy in Ankara, Turkey, seeking visas (permits) to enter Germany. Immigration is one area of life that every government regulates.

| TABLE 14.1 | Percentage of Decisions Taken at Each Level of Government in Public Secondary Education, 1998 |

	Central	State	Provincial-Regional	Sub-Regional	Local	School
Austria	35	18			22	25
Belgium (French community)	6	10	2	61		26
Denmark	26				43	31
Finland					64	36
France	32		11	27		29
Germany	4	28	15		16	37
Ireland	47					53
Italy	39		25		3	33
The Netherlands	24				3	73
New Zealand	34					66
Norway	35				55	9
Sweden	13				22	66
United Kingdom (England)	20				18	62
United Kingdom (Scotland)	9				51	40
United States				2	69	20

Source: Christopher Ansell and Jane Gingrich, "Trends in Decentralization," in *Democracy Transformed? Expanding Political Opportunities in Advanced Industrial Democracies*, ed. Bruce B. Cain, Russell J. Dalton, and Susan E. Scarrow (New York: Oxford University Press, 2003), 158; data are from OECD (1998).

restaurants, for example, may be approved by local governments' administrators. And licensing may be delegated to professional associations of practitioners, as in the cases of doctors and lawyers in the United States.

Some regulatory units also perform judicial functions, giving affected groups the opportunity to contest bureaucratic rulings in administrative courts. In a well-functioning bureaucracy, often affected interests can expect to get greater expertise and less uncertainty from these specialized administrative law proceedings than they could from ordinary judges and juries.

Bureaucratic Influence and Problems

Again, where bureaucrats have influence it is often because legislation is worded in general terms that have not been fleshed out with specific rules and practices. Legislators either don't have the expertise to specify the technical means to achieve their goals, or they can't agree on the details of what they want to accomplish, or both. In addition, complex legislation may include inconsistences and even errors, which the bureaucracy is tasked to fix (see "Contention and Cooperation in Focus" below).

Complaints About Bureaucracy Bureaucratic discretion and influence can stimulate various types of contention and criticism. One line of critique is that a given bureaucracy might have too much scope for autonomous decision making. This could allow the regulator to either act arbitrarily or yield too easily to those seeking to avoid regulation. If a troublesome circumstance arises frequently enough, upper-level civil servants may need to create more detailed rules to handle particular situations. Such specific rule making, however, may prompt another sort of criticism of bureaucracy: that a unit is too restrained by these **standard operating procedures** (SOPs) to be able to respond with sensitivity and flexibility to the complexity of local circumstances.

The possibility of such criticism is inherent in the situation in which bureaucracies find themselves. Sometimes, criticism is actually motivated by political opposition to the legislation being implemented. The critics may come from regulated groups (who prefer not to be regulated), beneficiary groups calling for stronger government action in favored programs, or just ideological opponents of the type of legislation involved. Normally, the combination of rules and SOPs works just fine, enhances a unit's cooperation, and helps avoid bias or corruption. In principle, an administrator who attempts to follow his or her understanding of the rules and their legislative intent should not be faulted for the inherent challenges presented by occasional difficult situations.

How Bureaucratic Influence Becomes Political Nonetheless, units of the bureaucracy may at times engage in the interplay of contention and cooperation that we call politics. For example, administrators may at times use special information and expertise that may not be easily accessible to outsiders. Upper-level bureaucrats may, in support of the unit's sense of its mission and priorities, filter information as it passes upward to the political executive and legislative bodies. Alternatively, administrators can flood outsiders with unfiltered information, making it difficult for the latter to sort out what is important to them. Such actions by an administrative unit might be portrayed as selfish political efforts to enhance its power or budget.[3] But such portrayals often simply assume such selfish motivations, rather than clearly establishing what the unit's aims ultimately are.

On Weber's model, the bureaucracy only refines and effectuates whatever policy direction comes from the existing legislation itself, to make the law effective. If the political leadership at the top of a ministry does not like a preexisting

CONTENTION AND COOPERATION IN FOCUS | The Bureaucracy in the Obama Administration

The executive branch in the United States during President Barack Obama's administration yields good examples of contention and cooperation in and around the bureaucracy. As we saw at the beginning of this chapter, President Obama began his presidency in 2009 amid a financial crisis. In 2010, Congress passed a large and complex financial regulation bill to provide federal oversight and limitation of some of the practices that had contributed to the financial crisis of 2008–2009. Important parts of it were crafted in general terms, leaving the bureaucracy to specify the key rules. A long process of first deciding what rules to propose, followed by a period for public comment, and finally the writing of the ultimate rule, allowed for much input by the financial enterprises affected by the law. A huge effort by thousands of lobbyists for the financial industry did weaken some parts of the law, especially the "Volker rule" that tried to separate banks' deposits and lending business from their financial trading activities.

In other areas, President Obama directed the bureaucracy to modify the application of laws. Regarding clean water policy, in 2015 President Obama ordered the Environmental Protection Agency to extend the coverage of a clean water law beyond the major rivers that it had previously covered. In expanding the scope of regulation to protect small tributaries and streams that feed the rivers used for drinking water, the President harked back to the expansive wording of the original 1972 legislation.

Similarly, the Obama administration expanded the application of clean air legislation to include carbon dioxide as a pollutant that can be regulated (due to its contribution to global warming), a move that has been approved by the U.S. Supreme Court. The administration then followed up this reclassification by declaring in mid-2014 that it would initiate a "cap and trade" approach to controlling carbon emissions from electric power plants (setting overall emission caps and issuing tradable permits for enterprises to emit under those limits; see chapter 7). This plan is expected to have its greatest impact on coal-burning power plants—the worst emitters. But even the political executive cannot specify the details of such a plan, such as the number of permits to be issued, their prices, etc. It is the bureaucracy's job to apply science, special technical knowledge, and detailed understanding of particular circumstances to make the specific rules for achieving the goals embodied in legislation and rule making.

An example of the bureaucracy fixing possible inconsistencies or errors in legislative wording has arisen in the application of the Affordable Care Act, the large and complex health insurance law passed in 2010. It aimed in part to set up health insurance exchanges—whether at the state level, if a state wishes, or a federal exchange, if not—and within them, to provide subsidies to lower-income people to buy health insurance. However, the legislation contains a few words affirming that eligible people in state exchanges would receive federal subsidies, and outside opponents of the bill have tried to interpret those words as ruling out subsidies under the federal exchange (used by states that chose not to set up their own exchanges). But that interpretation is contrary to the overall intent of the bill, and is contradicted by a requirement elsewhere in the legislation that the federal exchange report on its own disbursement of subsidies. The bureaucracy has followed the intent of the bill and the latter provision by providing federal-exchange subsidies. In mid-2015, the U.S. Supreme Court declared, by a 6-3 vote, that the federal exchange could indeed provide subsidies, enabling the program to go forward.

Finally, the bureaucracy can also issue new rules related to practical difficulties and fairness issues in applying legislation. In immigration law, the Obama administration has ruled that the children and certain relatives of illegal immigrants can be protected from deportation and given a path to citizenship. Opponents object that in this case, the exclusions from deportation are contrary to the intent of the law—to contend against illegal immigration.

law, but has been unwilling or unable to get it rescinded legislatively, it may try to contend with the policy by directing the relevant bureaucratic unit to soften or drop its implementation. If the unit resists or drags its feet, its contention may stem from its cooperation with the law or program itself, undergirded by the unit's sense of its overall mission and of the program or law's target value(s). The bureaucratic unit is exerting autonomous influence, but as the agent of its "principal," the law itself. When instead a unit appears to display a strained or odd interpretation of legislation, taking a stance that departs from the wording and spirit of the law (e.g., backing off from penalizing pollution or financial abuses), most often it is acting under the influence of either the political executive or affected interests, or both.

Often a key factor is affected interests groups and their lobbying. For example, regulated economic enterprises not only lobby to weaken regulation; they also press bureaucracies to hire people with experience in the regulated enterprises, and often offer lucrative posts to individual regulators after they leave the bureaucracy (this migration of officials back and forth between regulated bodies and the regulated companies is known as the "revolving door"). Or beneficiary groups lobby administrators to keep programs strong, such as senior citizens who might try to influence old-age pension administrations, in particular to avoid pension cuts.

Another source of group contention may be the bureaucracy itself. It is divided into multiple ministries, and any given ministry has multiple units. Units may contend with each other over budgets or jurisdiction over problems, as institutional interests (see chapter 9) in carrying out a policy. In Graham Allison's "bureaucratic politics" model (later labeled the "governmental politics" model by him), bargaining may have to proceed between different but related administrative units and their contending objectives.[4] As in any pluralist pattern of political contention, bureaucrats' political skills and resources can be key to successful strategy in intra-bureaucratic contention.[5] There can be winners and losers among bureaucratic units as well as cooperation and compromise.

In such contention, control of information can be an important strategic tool, as we saw in chapter 13 regarding the American invasion of Iraq in 2003. Before the invasion, the political executive chiefs at the top of the defense department outmaneuvered some of the intelligence analysts of the state department and the C.I.A. by successfully concealing the contention going on within relevant units of these departments over (a) whether Iraq was known to have ongoing weapons of mass destruction (WMD) programs, and (b) what challenges the United States might face following a successful invasion.

Finally, personal leadership can also be important in such patterns of contention and cooperation. In the late 1990s, the American central bank chairman Alan Greenspan, a vigorous free-market advocate, played a key personal role in defeating an effort within the bureaucracy to regulate certain financial products that subsequently turned out to be dangerous to the world's financial system.[6] Greenspan, supported by big financial interests and certain key Congressional leaders (e.g., Republican senator Phil Gramm of Texas), successfully gained the cooperation of the leaders of the Treasury department, Robert Rubin and Lawrence Summers. They were able to suppress the efforts of Brooksley Born, the chairperson of the Commodity Futures Trading Commission, who had pressed for greater oversight of risky financial products (see chapter 7).

APPLYING THE MODELS | Is the Bureaucracy an Elite?

The debate about whether and how the bureaucracy exercises power may be viewed in terms of the models that we have called on periodically through this book to explain the distribution of influence: the majority preference model, the elite model (a top group ruling), the pluralist model (interest groups bargaining), and the personal leadership model. Suppose that an election has led to a right-of-center cabinet with a plan to weaken environmental law enforcement. The ministry's career bureaucrats, with their sense of mission in applying existing environmental laws, resist. The contending groups may have different perspectives on the situation, which each implicitly calls on one or two of the models.

The political executive leaders, for their part, may claim to represent the current majority preference as expressed in the last election, which, they may say, favors budget cuts and reduced regulation. The ministry's political leadership may perceive the career bureaucrats' resistance as the reaction of an unelected elite that is out to selfishly protect its power and budget. The bureaucrats, for their part, might have their own way of applying the majority preference model: the existing environmental laws were duly passed by legislative majorities, are still on the books, and should continue to be fully enforced until they are rescinded legislatively or clearly supplanted by new legislation on the same topic. The bureaucrats may see their resistance not as an autonomous exercise of political power, but rather as an instrument of the authority of the law of the land and the democratic system of government

that produced it. They might portray the political executive as an elite trying to put itself above that system.

The pluralist model would modify this picture. As was noted above, any bureaucratic unit might be viewed as an institutional interest group trying to exercise influence in pluralistic politics, on behalf of its mission and budget. Such a group finds itself in interdependent, reciprocal relationships with the political executive leadership, groups in the legislature, and outside interest groups involved in the issue. The latter include both (a) environmental interest groups supporting the existing regulatory law or program, and (b) the regulated enterprises, which weigh in on the opposite side in support of the political executive and its plans to cut back environmental enforcement.

As for the personal leadership model, we saw above that individuals such as the chairperson of a nation's central bank can exert significant influence. In addition, the formal organization of the bureaucracy can provide for individual influence. In the British administrative style (see Country Case Studies below), each ministry's career professionals are headed by a "permanent secretary." In other systems, there may be an informal leader, perhaps largely behind the scenes, who similarly finds himself or herself in a personal confrontation with the minister or his or her leading deputy for environmental issues. If such personal leadership is a major part of the process, then the personal leadership model may operate together with one of the other models.

All this makes it tougher to explain the distribution of influence within the executive branch with only a single model (see "Applying the Models" below).

Responses to Bureaucratic Influence and Problems

In recent decades, a number of tools and trends have developed to address the problems raised by critics who perceive undue influence by, or over, bureaucratic units. These efforts have opened up bureaucratic units more to diverse influences, such as the political executive itself, various affected interests, and sometimes outside watchdog groups that seek greater transparency, efficiency, and fairness in the administrative process.

The Budgetary Power Ministers have always had a potent weapon for dealing with what they may consider an uncooperative bureaucracy: the budgetary power. If the political executive finds it too difficult or politically sensitive to get the legislature to change a law or program, it may weaken the policy's implementation by capping, cutting back, or redirecting funds for units applying the policy. This may leave key portions of the bureaucracy with the same amount of work but far fewer hands to do it. Performance may falter, and complaints about units' inefficiency or uneven impact may increase. The very opponents who supported the cuts may then claim that the regulation or program is not working, and perhaps ought to be scrapped altogether.

Alternatively, a law's bureaucratic ineffectiveness may be intended in the original legislation. In the United States, the Environmental Protection Agency has units to assure the safety of chemicals in the environment and can ban or regulate toxic chemicals. But when the regulatory legislation was first passed, it "grandfathered" (exempted) hundreds of potentially toxic chemicals already in use at the time. And in order to initiate a ban, the law required that new chemicals be *proven unsafe*, rather than requiring the producer to show that they are safe. The government has neither the money nor the capacity to test thousands of new chemicals, so the regulatory legislation was largely toothless from the start.

Decentralization A trend in recent decades has been toward decentralization of decision making in public administration. This "**new public management**" approach[7] suggested that greater autonomy for lower-level units could bring some of the benefits of flexibility and entrepreneurship that are often attributed to small private enterprises.

In some cases, such semiautonomous agencies have helped the political executive in its efforts to influence the bureaucracy. The minister might be able to appoint such agencies' chiefs from outside the regular civil service process, perhaps to be friendlier to the political executive's aims than are the central bureaucrats. In addition, in some countries, elective regional and local councils have been created to advise and work with local units of public administration for greater responsiveness, such as in France and Italy.

Such decentralizations may work as planned. But in other cases, they may only increase the influence (often already substantial) of important affected interest groups over the programs and regulatory agencies that impact them. Regulated or client groups can often be counted on to support agencies' approaches that seem to favor their interests, and oppose efforts that they see as affecting them adversely.

Another widespread trend has been toward the privatization of state-owned enterprises. Here government managing boards are replaced by a private enterprise(s) that is monitored by regulatory agencies. Sometimes, the result is increased efficiency and reduced costs, particularly where there is robust private competition for the government contract and close regulatory monitoring of the performance of the winning company. But privatization can also weaken the program or regulatory effort, or increase its costs, or both. In any case, privatization often appears tempting to budget-cutters because the government no longer bears the cost of managing the enterprise. In countries where units of government provide health and pension benefits to their employees, as in the United States, some governments want to transfer governmental functions to the private sector mainly to avoid having to pay the costs of employee health insurance and pensions.

New Appointed Positions A trend close to the top of the executive branch is toward strengthening the minister's staff for influencing the bureaucracy. For example, ministers have been supplemented by numerous "special advisors" in Britain and expanded "cabinets" in France (see Country Case Studies below), or the planning staffs of ministries have been bolstered in other countries. Such staff officials can be picked from parliament, from some specialized fields outside of government, or from the civil service itself. They tend to be selected for their willingness to support the minister's priorities and their effectiveness in furthering them in the ministry.

In addition, the political executives in some countries have attempted to more effectively steer their ministries by extending the range of top positions in the bureaucratic hierarchy that are subject to political appointment. These moves typically do not go so far as to reinstitute the old "spoils system" (see above), but some observers have characterized this trend as the "politicization" of the bureaucracy.[8]

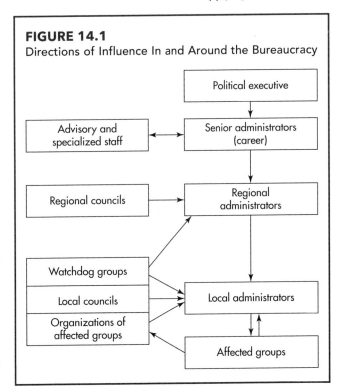

FIGURE 14.1
Directions of Influence In and Around the Bureaucracy

In a different approach, external offices or committees may be created for such purposes as financial monitoring, accounting, inspection, ombudsman services, and legislative or political executive oversight.[9] These units, alongside lobbyists from affected interest groups, can bring increased transparency and broader accountability to the work of the bureaucratic units that they monitor. But the influence of such external offices may also run counter to units' traditional institutional missions of regulation or program function, which are stressed by the regular ministerial hierarchy.

When we consider all of the different sorts of units that have been added to the bureaucratic mix in some countries, the result can be a complex web of interacting influences (see Figure 14.1).

Bureaucracy in the Developing and Post-Communist Worlds

In parts of southern Europe and in the post-Communist and developing worlds, the most prominent bureaucratic challenges concern the failure to develop the basic tenets of a modern Weberian bureaucracy, with its effective hierarchy, efficiency, and impartiality. Major sectors of a nation's bureaucracy may be filled by patronage rather than those with appropriate skills. Such staffing may favor political parties, their factions, people from the same ethnic background as powerful leaders, or regional, business, or family connections. Holding onto positions may be more important than the effective programs and impartial rule enforcement that political scientists refer to as state capacity.

In some developing countries during parts of the twentieth century, authoritarian leaders focused on the bureaucracy as a modernizing force. Leaders from President Gamal Nasser in Egypt in the 1950s to General Suharto in Indonesia and the Latin American "bureaucratic-authoritarian" military regimes that held power in the 1960s and 1970s all made efforts toward modernization. But economic scarcity continued to contribute to clientelism and weak bureaucratic performance.

Scarce Resources, Politics, and Bureaucracy in the Developing World

Especially in parts of bureaucracies in developing nations, the resources and skills available for the provision of government services can vary greatly. In the schools or health facilities, for example, the central administration rarely has sufficient resources to offer at the ground level. There may be only a few old books or medical devices, providing little incentive to attract qualified teachers or medical functionaries. Consequently, school systems and government health clinics may be understaffed and undersupplied, with little modern bureaucratic management. Often government employees' pay has been eroded by past inflation, forcing them to spend less time in official duties and more time in supplementing their incomes to support their families.

Where services are delivered adequately, they may go to areas and groups that support those in power. Authoritarian rulers in single-party-dominant regimes might also use portions of the bureaucracy to weaken would-be rivals for power. Media regulation is often geared to guaranteeing, through intimidation, favorable news coverage for the ruling party and trashing its opponents. In addition, in authoritarian post-Communist countries such as Russia in the 2000s, prosecutors would be directed to go after potentially serious rivals for the presidency and their financial backers, often accusing them of financial infractions in murky and questionable cases. Weak and ineffective opponents, and oligarchs who cooperated with the regime and the dominant party, are left alone.

In regulatory policy areas in developing and post-Communist nations, these circumstances may invite widespread bribery and corruption. If regulatory rules are not applied consistently, their application appears selective, at the discretion of the official. Before long, either enforcement of a regulation or lack of enforcement may be purchased with a bribe. Business licenses can be bought or denied regardless of the applicant's qualifications.

Across the developing world, there can be tremendous pressure to expand the bureaucracy to increase employment or reward supporters of the party in power. Those with positions are often expected to try to help relatives, friends, and people from the same ethnic background to gain positions as well. Where past economic development strategies have led to numerous state-owned enterprises protected from real competition, some of them may be bloated, inefficient, and wasteful. In turn, popular resentment against "privileged" public-sector employees may build up, encouraging calls for privatization or outright abandonment of programs that don't seem to be accomplishing their goals.

Efforts to Improve: The Example of Mexico

The long-running single-party dominance of the Institutional Revolutionary Party (PRI) in Mexico operated in the bureaucracy as well as the legislative branch. Patron-client relationships prevailed in the style of a political machine, somewhat blurring the distinction between the political executive and the bureaucracy. The political executive made large numbers of appointments both directly and indirectly, with the president at its apex. Party connections heavily influenced benefits and protections for labor, peasants, and various occupational associations. The bureaucracy and the political executive cooperated extensively.

But the rule that presidents could not serve a second six-year term produced a certain fluidity in upper-level positions. Each new president could reshuffle the deck to some extent. This provided opportunities for rising officials to move up, along with their clienteles (traditionally called *camarillas*). In effect, these patron-client groups engaged in a degree of contention within the apparatus as a whole as they jockeyed for position.

By the 1980s, the PRI had turned more toward free-market policies, along with a greater emphasis on technical expertise in administration. Better-educated *technicos* rose within such ministries as finance, planning, and energy, and privatization helped reduce the number of administrative jobs. But the economy hit snags at times (including a few financial crises), and to hang onto power the party had to continue its traditional methods—patronage, corruption, and at times, electoral fraud—amid challenges on the left and right (see Country Case Studies, chapter 9).

Such methods, however, seemed to assure fewer positive electoral results over time. By 2000, a smaller party to the PRI's right, the more conservative, business-oriented PAN had won the presidency under the charismatic Vicente Fox (though not a Congressional majority). But Fox's pledge to hire by merit and reform the bureaucracy seemed to operate only at the top levels, and made little real progress down through the bureaucracy. With PAN's popularity declining later in the decade, the PRI again won the presidency in 2012, with Enrique Peña Nieto presented as a reformer. But without a majority in Congress favoring reforms, or full control over the PRI and its traditional supporting groups (e.g., the unions), it is unlikely that Nieto will do much better at bureaucratic reform than the slow trajectory of improvement that has occurred over recent decades.

THE COURTS

Most often, those who are affected by government's laws and programs cooperate with them voluntarily. Or if not, they cooperate with the response of the relevant executive branch agency. But if an executive action is contested, in principle the affected person or group may take the matter to court.

In some ways, the role of the courts in applying rules and laws resembles that of the bureaucracy. Statutes and rules for applying them are often abstract, and the judicial process has to develop its own ways to apply them to particular cases, including those with unusual circumstances. But in practice, judges must take into account an array of other factors. In applying the law they are bound not only by the primary law in question, but also by other laws, by the nation's constitution and its principles, and by relevant past court decisions. Courts must judge how particular executive practices fit within the larger context of laws and rights. A difficult case may find different constitutional principles contending with one another, each amounting to an important value represented by groups of judges who defend it.

Types of Law

When we think of law, the form that often comes to mind first is criminal law. Criminal law bans serious crimes that threaten society as a whole, such as murder or theft. The idea is to stop wrongdoing when it occurs, and deter wrongdoers in the future with the threat of certain punishment such as imprisonment, a fine, or in a few countries, even death. The party pursuing the case is the citizenry itself, represented by a prosecutor who is an employee of the executive branch of government. In criminal law, typically a high standard of proof is required, showing conclusively the defendant's willful responsibility for the harmful conduct, especially if the accused might be imprisoned if convicted of the crime.

Civil law, in contrast, aims to address wrongs committed by citizens against each other and requires the wrongdoer to compensate his or her victims. Cases in civil law are pursued by the aggrieved party, referred to as the **plaintiff**, rather than by the people as a whole. If the accused loses the case, he or she is normally required to pay damages to the plaintiff, or otherwise restore the victim to their prior condition where possible. For example, if an employee was improperly dismissed from a job, a civil court may determine that they can regain their position with back pay. Or if negligent handling of chemicals led to a fire, the guilty party may have to pay for the entire loss to the owner of the building—not only the cost of rebuilding but also any loss of income during the time that the building is being restored. Here the goal of the judicial proceedings is not to prove guilt "beyond a reasonable doubt" (as in criminal law), but rather to discover primary responsibility by the accused for the harm to the plaintiff, by a "preponderance of the evidence."

A third major area of law is **constitutional law**. This field of law pertains to the powers of units of government in relation to each other and to the rights of citizens under the constitution. An example is the American controversy in the 2000s over the Bush administration's use of wiretapping of people's phones without a warrant from a judge in an effort to combat terrorism. The courts had to decide whether the executive had encroached on legislative power by ignoring statutes passed by Congress, or had usurped judicial power by sidestepping the role for judges prescribed in the statute.

The Court Structure

In these areas of law, there are different levels of national courts: lower, appellate, and highest. The lowest court, normally presided over by a single judge, hears all basic elements of the case, and the jury or judge renders a verdict. This court has what is called "original jurisdiction," in that it is where a case begins. Intermediate-level **appellate courts** (called "circuit courts of appeals" in the United States) are panels of judges who take a second look if the lower-level judgment is appealed by a party to the case. The highest court of a nation, commonly called the "supreme" or "high" court, mainly reexamines a small number of appeals court verdicts that touch on some particularly important point of law or precedent. (As we shall see below, in some countries, cases involving constitutional law are handled by a special tribunal that is separate from the highest court.)

In federal systems, the regional level of government may have its own court system, with local, intermediate, and high court jurisdiction to adjudicate regional laws. Federal systems normally allocate most criminal and civil lawmaking and adjudication to the regional government and its courts. In this situation, the national court system focuses on cases involving national laws.

Judicial Styles

National judicial systems are usually classified into one of two broad categories: common law and code law. The two approaches differ somewhat in their philosophy and origins. Common law emerged partly from the interaction between judges and society, while code law stems directly from the state's lawmaking. In part, this distinction echoes the old debate between "natural law" and "positive law" (see "The Philosophical Connection"). However, as with many of the concepts discussed in this book, today these two categories are best understood as segments of a continuum, rather than sharply distinguished types (see Table 14.2).

Common Law The term "common law" originated in Britain, where it emerged from an effort during the Middle Ages, to identify common elements in customary dispute resolution across the nation. The formal laws promulgated by the king (called "statutes") were few and general, leaving many gaps in their application to particular circumstances. Those gaps were filled by **common law**: principles and practices that emerged in specific judicial decisions taken by higher-level courts in classic cases.

Such key past decisions are called **precedents**. They emerge especially when appellate and high courts review important cases from lower courts. The principles and practices implicit in this fund of past precedents command respect from present and future judges on the principle of *stare decisis*, a Latin phrase meaning "let the decision stand." Collectively, such precedents are referred to as **case law**.

In effect, the common law tradition sometimes left some leeway for judges to interpret the law as it applies to the particular circumstances of a case, and to search out the precedents that are most relevant to the case at hand. As times and circumstances change, precedents can evolve and new ones emerge. Over time, the customary maxims of judges might lay the foundation for new statutes adopted by the king and/or the legislators.

As to court procedures, in common law countries the contending attorneys, and not the judge, spearhead the case. In criminal cases, it is the state's attorney

TABLE 14.2	Differences Between Common Law and Code Law Approaches	
	Common Law	**Code Law**
Main task of courts	Consistency with previous cases	Application of a code of laws
Evidence brought out by	Contending attorneys	The judge
Judges trained in	General legal knowledge	First general education, then a specialized area of law
Rights of defendants	Strong	Less strong
Judicial review	Sometimes strong	Less strong

who first develops the evidence and conducts the questioning of witnesses. After that, the defense proceeds to present its side of the case and witnesses. In civil cases, where someone is accusing someone else of wrongful behavior and seeking damages, the contending attorneys also bring in their own experts to help them persuade the jury. Thus the common law system is referred to as "adversarial," substantially driven by the contending parties. The judge mainly presides over court procedure, and at the end instructs the jury about the law as it relates to the case. Juries are employed in civil as well as criminal cases.

Under Great Britain's parliamentary governmental system, parliament is viewed as the ultimate authority on the content of law. But as the common law process evolved in Britain (see Country Case Studies below), the judges and lawyers developed a strong sense of their independence in applying the law. (Traditionally, the courts were overseen not by the king or the House of Commons, but rather by a special committee of the House of Lords called the "law lords").

Along the way, there developed practices of respect for the "fair trial" rights of criminal defendants, such as **habeas corpus** (protection against detention without being confronted with charges and accusers), the presumption of a defendant's innocence until proven guilty, and protection against self-incrimination—rights which in those days were unlikely to be promulgated by a monarch on his or her own. This strong concern for rights and fairness can make cases rather complex affairs, consuming much time and resources. Where the outcome is predictable, many cases are settled without going to trial, through negotiations between the parties in civil cases or between prosecutors and defendants in criminal cases. In the latter, the agreement is called a plea bargain, in which a defendant agrees to plead guilty to a particular charge (usually of less severity) in return for some type of concession from the prosecutor that affects the sentence, with the penalty to be paid by the alleged perpetrator.

Common law created an extensive network of principles, rules, and practices that was not straightforward and easy to master. Over time, the case law of interrelated precedents became the subject of extensive study in law schools. Attorneys and judges shared the required legal training, but the king and his administrators generally did not.

Code Law Traditional continental European judicial practice is associated with the **code law** approach. It applies a more or less elaborate written code of laws and rules to the case at hand. This approach, too, is not new. The ancient Romans identified strongly with their famed "twelve tables" of the law, and much later (in the sixth century ACE) with the eastern empire's extensive Justinian code of law. In the Middle Ages, the European Christian church augmented the Ten Commandments with the tradition of Canon law. Later the Renaissance revived enthusiasm for Roman law.

Following the French Revolution, Napoleon fostered the development of universal codes of law, partly derived from the Justinian code of the ancient Romans. The Napoleonic code, carried across Europe with the expansion of Napoleon's empire in the early nineteenth century, stressed the independence of law from religious and local custom, and the equal treatment of everyone under the law (see Country Case Studies below). As was noted above, the code's impact long outlasted the empire that spread it.

Using code law, judges are not bound to review and use past decisions by higher courts in applying the law. Instead, they are charged with investigating the facts of the case and applying the code of written rules directly to the reality of the case.

Here law may be spelled out in more detail by legislative statute, subjecting court practice to clearer limit setting than the British common law model allows. The code law approach allows judges, armed with only a fairly general prior education, to receive a specialized code-based training that is targeted to the particular area of their judicial practice, rather than the broad, extensive legal training required for attorneys in common law systems.

In handling cases under the code law approach, it is the judge(s) who takes the lead in discovering the facts and interviewing witnesses. In civil cases, experts are brought in as neutral officers of the court, rather than in support of one of the contending parties. Civil cases tend to be decided by judges rather than juries.

Each of these approaches has its advantages, but also vulnerabilities if they are pursued too single-mindedly under unfavorable circumstances. In principle, the code law approach makes it easier to achieve the rule of law quickly where it did not exist before. But an extreme code law approach may not be as open to local custom or wisdom, or to broad principles of equity and fairness, as the common law style can be. For most of its historical development, the code law tradition did not formalize the rights of defendants as the common law tradition had done. And it did not require as high a standard of proof for criminal convictions as the common law tradition required (i.e., "beyond a reasonable doubt"). In the wrong hands, code law can more easily render the judicial branch as just another arm of whichever group dominates the state.

Overlaps in Common Law and Code Law The distinction between code law and common law approaches is less strict today than in the past. Nations that were traditionally common law ones seem to be embracing more elements of the code approach, and code countries' courts seem to be exercising greater independence from the executive branch and incorporating rights.

In some common law countries, key human rights have been codified into law, from the American Bill of Rights in 1791 to the British acceptance in 1998 of the European Convention on Human Rights. Moreover, legislatures in some common law countries are increasingly passing laws that narrow judicial discretion in some areas of law (most notably in sentencing) to a degree reminiscent of code law countries.

For their part, code law countries' judges are increasingly employing what amounts to case law in their actual practice, particularly in areas involving government administration. In addition, in recent years they have been strongly incorporating human rights protection into their jurisprudence, and in other ways adopting some forms of judicial review of statures for their consistency with the constitution.

Do the Courts Have Autonomous Power?

Much critical commentary about the role of the court system circles around questions about judicial influence that are similar to those raised above regarding the bureaucracy. The eighteenth-century British jurist William Blackstone famously articulated the view that the judges do not make law; rather, they are only the mouthpiece of the law. But as we have already noted, laws are not always as precise as we would like them to be. Legislators cannot remove all difficulties in how laws are to be applied to each new case, particularly if surrounding circumstances have changed since the statute was enacted.

To be sure, constitutions and the statutes passed by legislatures and executives certainly exercise strong limit-setting power over what the judiciary can do. When the courts are asked to interpret a law for a case before them (perhaps requiring reviewing how the bureaucracy or the police have been interpreting and applying the law), normally their discretion is limited to a range of options that are consistent with not only the wording and intent of the statute but also other legal principles (some constitutional), laws, and past precedents that may be relevant.

Judicial Review in Common Law Countries In what is called **judicial review**—court judgments on the consistency of legislation and bureaucratic rules with the constitution—we get the strongest impression of the courts having a political impact. In such cases, a country's highest court does address the content of a statute, and may strike it down or, in effect, modify it. The first clear emergence of judicial review in common law circumstances occurred in the United States in a Supreme Court ruling in 1803 that struck down a law concerning the legality of an administrative appointment.

The broadest impact of judicial review has been in the realm of protecting citizens' rights. Originally, the American constitutional amendments protecting freedom of speech, assembly, and religion applied only against the national government. They did not allow the federal Supreme Court to strike down (regional level) *state* laws infringing those rights. Notably, however, in the twentieth century, the American Supreme Court refocused on the implications of the post–civil war Fourteenth amendment to the constitution, which in 1868 had guaranteed personal freedom (especially for the former slaves) against state government. Beginning in the 1920s, the Court began "incorporating" the Bill of Rights under the 14th amendment, asserting that key civil liberties in the Bill of Rights—most notably freedom of expression and assembly—were to be protected against state government infringement as well as against national government infringement. This allowed the U.S. Supreme Court to strike down state laws in these areas. It was through this exercise of judicial review that key civil-political human rights were finally incorporated fully into American law.

In another key act of judicial review, the Court declared the segregation of schools in the American south to be unconstitutional (*Brown versus Board of Education of Topeka*, 1954). Such segregation was judged to violate the principle of "equal protection of the laws," but not primarily because black schools were typically run down, with worn out (or absent) books and poorly trained teachers. Rather, the main point was that psychological research had shown that separate education inevitably delivered a message of inferiority to African American schoolchildren that they were not good enough for white education. Other rulings have ranged widely, for example, requiring equal populations for Congressional districts (1962), protecting a woman's right to abortion (1973), and recently, striking down campaign finance limitations. Such cases exemplify what some have called **judicial activism**—the top court stepping in to resolve key issues where the regular democratic process is unwilling to do so.

To be sure, in practice judicial review in the United States has not always served to protect rights. In the 1950s, the Supreme Court watched in silence as the human rights of free expression and association were regularly trampled on in a phenomenon called McCarthyism: a witch hunt led by Wisconsin senator Joseph McCarthy in pursuit of alleged Communists and their "fellow travelers." McCarthy's persecution of those on the left who had exercised their rights of ordinary free speech and association continued until Senator McCarthy was defeated politically. This occurred not by judicial review,

The U.S. Supreme Court in 2015: Seated from left are: Associate Justices Clarence Thomas, Antonin Scalia (now deceased), Chief Justice John Roberts, Associate Justices Anthony M. Kennedy and Ruth Bader Ginsburg. Standing, from left are: Associate Justices Sonia Sotomayor, Stephen Breyer, Samuel Alito Jr., and Elena Kagan.

but instead through presidential rebuke (by President Eisenhower), Congressional censure, and finally in society, when, for example, the entertainment industry resumed hiring previously "blacklisted" writers, directors, and actors who had been denied work for their alleged Communist sympathies. By the 1960s, however, the U.S. Supreme Court was again active in judicial review (e.g., in the 1973 Roe v. Wade decision upholding a woman's right to an abortion), and it continues to be so today, as in a series of rulings in the 2010s striking down campaign finance restrictions.

Where a common law country has a parliamentary system, as in the United Kingdom where a single constitutional document doesn't even exist, the spirit of parliamentary government seems to rule out judicial review of legislation for constitutionality. But when Britain entered the European Union it meant accepting, for British legal purposes, the human rights framework articulated by the European Convention on Human Rights (ECHR), and applied by the Council of Europe's European Court of Human Rights and the EU's European Court of Justice. This was formally declared in 1998. In 2004, the "law lords" (a committee of the House of Lords that traditionally served as the judiciary's highest court of appeals) declared that a law passed amid the fight against terrorism by the Irish Republican Army was inconsistent with the ECHR. The next year, the Labor government proceeded to replace the Law Lords with a new, independent Supreme Court. Britain, too, seems to be on the road to judicial review.

India, by far the largest parliamentary common law country in the developing world, started its independent life with a Supreme Court. But traditionally it lacked the authority to declare acts of parliament unconstitutional. Only in the late 1960s did the Court begin to assert that the fundamental rights in the constitution must be respected by parliament. After contention with parliament over the legislators' authority to amend the constitution, in the 1970s the Court's position became that the constitution's fundamental structure cannot be changed or infringed. This premise seems to function as a basis for limited judicial review. Notably, the Indian Supreme Court allows any citizen to initiate public interest litigation to get the government to do a better job of enforcing laws and protecting the public. But the Court faces a huge backlog of cases with long waits for resolution.

THE PHILOSOPHICAL CONNECTION | Consequentialism, Hart, and Dworkin

A key question in political philosophy related to law and the courts is, what can help judges deal with "hard cases"—cases where the straightforward application of the wording of the law runs into problems, either due to complicated or new circumstances not envisioned by the statute, or to conflicting laws or principles regarding it, or both?

An important traditional approach to resolving such difficulties looked to consequences for key values. From the ancient "natural law" thinking of the Stoics and Cicero through the thought of Englishman John Stuart Mill in the nineteenth century (see chapter 5), this approach emphasized certain general principles that seem to be common to flourishing societies, such as the ancient maxim of "no harming." Mill stressed that laws curbing behavior were only justified if they prevented harm to other people (harm solely to oneself was not sufficient warrant). Moreover, Mill argued that good defined as "utility" should include not only pleasure (versus pain), but also the free development of individual minds and personalities short of harm to others.

Back in seventeenth-century England, however, Thomas Hobbes had rejected appealing to consequences in this way. He stressed that people may contend sharply about such fundamental maxims, and the resulting disagreement could upset social order and produce the worst outcome in his view: violent civil war (e.g., the sixteenth-century European Wars of Religion and the mid-seventeenth-century English Civil War). Hobbes argued that peace and safety could be assured only by simply defining justice as whatever the all-powerful sovereign body (be it a king or an assembly) declared to be law, pure and simple (see chapter 5). He considered legal rules to be thoroughly conventional, "posited" by human decision and cooperation rather than drawn from human nature, natural law, or divine will.

This "legal positivism" took a more contemporary form in the mid-twentieth-century writings of British legal philosopher H. L. A. Hart.* Hart believed that law is primarily the system of rules that has been passed following the authorized procedures, and that people should follow them without much thought to the consequences. He distinguished between (a) what he called the "primary rules" of criminal and civil law and (b) the "secondary rules" governing how law is to be arrived at and applied. Especially important among the latter was the part of constitutional law that designated the proper source of laws, which Hart called the rule of recognition. It tells the judges where to look to find (and "recognize") the valid rules. Whatever law comes out of the officially designated body is to be applied straightforwardly to cases.

Can a Judicial System Be Political? Can common law judges simply act on their personal policy preferences? In 1955, American political scientist Jack Peltason seemed to argue that since interest groups are involved in court decision making, and since judicial outcomes have favorable or unfavorable consequences for interest groups and their concerns (involving the pluralist model of influence distribution), the judicial system is flatly political.[10] However, in chapter 3, we noted that political scientists tend to reject the "benefit fallacy," the idea that if a group benefits from a decision it must have been involved in making that decision. To answer such questions, we have to study the particular decision-making process at hand. It is certainly possible to find cases in which a judge seemed to be motivated by a personally favored policy direction, such as support for a contending interest group, an ideology, or a particular policy. Alternatively, a particular judge might be motivated simply to find a point of compromise between the contending interests that would satisfy them.

In developed countries with independent judiciaries, however, the situation is usually more complex. When confronted with hard cases, judges tend to view the

However, what if a law confronts a new situation that was not envisioned by the legislature, or that seems to conflict with another law, or simply produces unacceptable consequences? Here, Hart suggested, the judge must be "creative," coming up with a new rule or decision that is (a) as much as possible in the spirit of the inherited one (the contemporary spirit, not necessarily the law's original intent), and (b) satisfactory to the legislature and the parties to the case. Such creativity did open up substantial scope for judicial discretion, but new rules are still subject to review by the lawmakers (e.g., by amending the law). At any rate, for Hart hard cases were only a small wrinkle in a much larger framework of simple rule following.

In the latter third of the twentieth century, however, a major line of criticism of Hart's legal positivism arose. American legal scholar Ronald Dworkin argued that Hart's account left out a lot of what goes into real-life judicial decision making. Dworkin suggested that hard cases are the key to the real architecture of judicial application of law. For him, they invoke not only legislation but also valued moral and legal principles that are embedded in existing law (especially constitutional law) and precedent, such as due process of law. (For example, the old common law maxim that the law should not benefit a criminal for his crime means that a grandson who murders his grandfather to claim his legally willed inheritance will not be granted that inheritance by the court.) In Dworkin's view, decision making in hard cases calls especially for careful attention to rights. Those rights include not just those explicitly enumerated in constitutions, but also those implied in the language of constitutional and other laws and in past precedents.

For Dworkin, this means that a good judge must weigh all of these factors as the parts of a potentially coherent whole—what he called "law as integrity." This can be a challenge, since the various principles and their moral values are not arranged in an automatic hierarchy of priority (though Dworkin does cite what he calls "equal concern and respect" as an especially crucial overall principle). But despite this complexity, he argued, a judge should aspire to be a "judge Hercules" who can find the "right answer" to how the ideal moral and legal community would want to decide the case. Hopefully, success will be reflected in support by higher courts and judicial peers. Dworkin believed that this combination of shared laws, values, and principles served to constrain judicial discretion in hard cases more effectively than had Hart's combination of legislation and judicial "creativity."

---

* *The Concept of Law* (Oxford, UK: Clarendon Press, 1961).

statutes and the facts of the case alongside constitutional provisions, principles, and values embedded in them, which must also be taken seriously. A serious commitment to weigh these factors and strike the right balance among them may not seem to leave a wide range of political discretion for him or her; rather, it may seem to require a particular decision. This style of judicial decision making, evident in the model of Ronald Dworkin (see "The Philosophical Connection"), displays an institutional loyalty to the role that judges are ideally supposed to play. Certainly individual judges may disregard this norm, but nonetheless they are under pressure not to.

Judicial Review and Human Rights in Code Law Countries In European code law countries in recent decades, judicial review has become much more common through the creation of special constitutional courts.[11] In some countries, these courts have the power to judge the constitutionality of laws when they are passed (a process known as **abstract review**), in contrast to common law's practice of judging a law only after it is in place and has prompted a court case (known as **concrete review**). Only a few code law countries, including the Netherlands and Sweden, still have no clearly identifiable unit for judicial review.

The judges of these constitutional courts tend to have limited terms of office (e.g., from six to nine years). They are picked in various ways, often involving the head of state, legislators, and/or legal experts. So at any given time, such courts mix elder statesmen from the political parties with people with particularly strong legal credentials, and include figures from several past governments and their contending parties and coalitions.

Increasingly, these constitutional courts' interpretations and applications of rights provisions are binding on regular courts and administrative actions, and complaints by individuals on rights issues can be brought to constitutional courts. In 2014, for example, Greek and Portuguese courts struck down their governments' austerity measures in such areas as layoffs of public workers and cuts to their salaries and pensions. Some observers see these developments as part of a general increase in judicial power in the world.[12]

As constitutional courts have emerged, there has also been a heightened focus on human rights law and jurisprudence. European governments' acceptance of the European Convention on Human Rights has moved them well into the realm of rights protection, and the number of cases brought before Europe's human rights court has increased greatly since 1980 (see Table 14.3). The case law that has developed in the European Court of Human Rights has to some extent empowered national judiciaries within countries (see "The Human Rights Connection"). With national courts' roles as intermediaries between European and national law, judicial independence from the executive branch has become much more firmly established in Europe.

Special Types of Courts

Separate from the regular court system and constitutional courts are two special types of court that deserve comment: administrative law courts and Sharia courts (where they exist).

Administrative Law Several nations now use specialized tribunals of judges for particular categories of cases, alongside the regular civil and criminal courts. As we saw in the section on the bureaucracy above, some administrative units have special courts attached to them to decide on whether administrative behavior is legal, which fall under the heading of **administrative law**. Such courts are always easier to set up in nations that follow code law practices, with their specialized training of judges. There, training of administrative law judges could be less extensive than the broad training of ordinary attorneys because it is based on the particular area of administration and its distinctive code. Again, in common-law countries, the judging of bureaucratic practice is generally done in the regular court system. But even there, a few specialized courts may operate to deal with particular legal areas (or appeals in them) such as commercial transactions, labor arbitration, old-age pension cases, tax matters, and the military. In administrative law courts, judges may be joined on a judicial panel by experts in the particular field to ensure that judicial decisions are informed by practical expertise in that field.

TABLE 14.3	Number of Rights Claims Brought Before the European Court of Human Rights, by Country: 1961–1997				
Country	1961–1969	1970–1979	1980–1989	1990–1997	Total
Austria	3	4	17	48	72
Belgium	3	5	21	20	49
Denmark	0	1	4	11	16
Finland	0	0	0	6	6
France	0	0	6	77	83
Germany	1	3	20	10	34
Ireland	3	0	3	4	10
Italy	0	0	17	130	147
The Netherlands	0	2	10	30	42
Norway	0	0	0	3	3
Sweden	0	2	13	22	37
United Kingdom	0	5	42	53	100
Total	10	22	153	414	

Source: Data compiled by Rachel A. Cichowski and Alec Stone Sweet from Council of Europe (1996; 1997) and Gomien (1995) and originally published in "Participation, Representative Democracy, and the Courts," in *Democracy Transformed? Expanding Political Opportunities in Advanced Industrial Democracies*, ed. Bruce B. Cain, Russell J. Dalton, and Susan E. Scarrow (New York: Oxford University Press, 2003), 206.

Islamic Sharia Law A different sort of judicial practice is found in some Muslim nations that turn to early Islamic texts for legal principles and practices. **Sharia law** is derived from the Koran itself and the hadith, reports of Mohammed's life and actions and commentaries on them. Sharia lays out not only specific prohibitions and penalties such as cutting off the hand of a thief or stoning an adulterer to death, but also general recommendations such as to avoid drinking and gambling, to act with compassion toward the poor, and for women to dress modestly.

Using Sharia fully means employing the nation's Islamic clerics to serve as its judges, courts, and legal experts, at least for Muslims. In fact, however, there is a range of degrees of use of Sharia and Islamic courts. Saudi Arabia and Iran use it

THE HUMAN RIGHTS CONNECTION | The International Impact in Europe

Probably the most direct international impact of human rights standards is to be found in contemporary Europe. In 1950, the post–World War II Council of Europe (made up of the European nations' heads of government) signed the European Convention of Human Rights. The Convention included the key civil-political rights that are now elaborated in the U.N.'s international civil-political Covenant: (a) protection of the person, such as the right to life and protection from torture, inhuman and degrading treatment, slavery, and forced labor, (b) fair trial rights, and (c) civil liberties such as rights to freedom of conscience, expression, and association, protection against discrimination, and the right to privacy.

By 1960, the European Court of Human Rights (ECHR, located in Strasbourg, France) had been formed to implement respect for the Convention. With one judge from each member state, at first the court's authority was limited. Member states could decide whether to permit the practice of appealing to the ECHR, and cases had to be accepted by the European Commission of Human Rights first. Still, the court did hear some high-profile cases, including a 1977 judgment that Britain was guilty of "inhuman and degrading" treatment of interned prisoners from the conflict in Northern Ireland.

Since the fall of Communism in Eastern Europe in 1990, the Council of Europe has enlarged from twenty-five to forty-seven members. The number of ECHR cases grew rapidly, and subsequent protocols strengthened the tribunal. Now member states have almost all accepted the Convention into national law. Individuals may bring cases directly to the ECHR after remedies in national courts have been exhausted, and cases are screened only by committees of the court's own judges. Indicating the court's increased stature, in October 2006 the ECHR held the Russian government responsible for the deaths of five Chechens among those allegedly massacred by Russian police units in Grozny in 2000. It assessed nearly $300,000 in damages to be paid by Russia to the relatives of the victims.

However, difficulties still remained for the ECHR. If a state resists a decision, the ECHR has no formal means to enforce it. And the number of cases submitted for the court's consideration has ballooned to over 10,000 a year, with a huge unprocessed backlog. A new series of reforms was proposed in 2004 to streamline the process and give new tools to the Council of Ministers (which supervises enforcement) in getting resisting governments to accept ECHR rulings. But these proposals had to await the unanimous approval of all forty-seven governments that is required for the proposed changes to go into effect.

However, the smaller twenty-eight-member European Union (EU) requires all of its member states to comply with the decisions of the ECHR. Some member states formally incorporated the Convention into their own law, allowing national judiciaries to apply it and its ECHR case law directly, rather than requiring claimants to go to the ECHR for a decision. And the EU's own court, the European Court of Justice (ECJ, whose decisions are binding on EU member states) has explicitly applied the ECHR case law in its own decisions in human rights-related issues and cases. In addition, the ECJ is willing to give preliminary rulings on how international human rights law applies to cases during national judicial proceedings. In effect, all this tends to bring the ECHR case law right into the decision making of the national courts of EU member states, helping to empower national court efforts to exercise judicial review of statutes.

To be sure, the ECJ still depends on national courts and governments to enforce its judgments. And national courts may still avoid referring a matter to the ECJ, or dispute the consistency of an ECJ judgment with the national constitution. In light of this, the ECJ has been reluctant to reject clear national policy objectives without a very strong case for doing so. Generally, however, national courts have respected ECJ judgments.

In 2000, EU bodies approved a new Charter of Fundamental Rights for the EU, which includes not only the traditional civil liberties and fair trial rights in the European Convention, but also incorporates key elements from the economic/social Covenant of human rights, including protections regarding working and dismissal conditions, social assistance, health care, environmental and consumer protections, and rights of minorities. But until the Charter was formally incorporated into the controlling EU treaty, it was not legally binding on member nations. This incorporation finally came when the EU's new Treaty of Lisbon (a set of reforms of the founding EU treaties, the 1958 Treaty of Rome and the 1993 Maastricht Treaty) was finally ratified by all member states in 2009, making the Charter binding on EU nations.

for criminal law as well as civil and family law. But other nations only ask regular judges to use Sharia to supplement secular law where the latter is inexact, or to use Sharia only for family matters.

In nations that are religiously mixed but want to use Sharia, Islamic courts typically apply only to Muslims. In a northern Nigerian state, for example, an expert Mufti cannot issue a fatwa to settle an issue between Christians. In some areas of life, the medieval origins of strict Islamic law make it unworkable, as in Muhammad's prohibition of charging interest on loans. In these areas, adjustments are made.

One difficulty for Sharia courts is that they can yield punishments that from a human rights perspective seem cruel and unusual (e.g., those for thieves and adulterers noted above). Some applications, such as public flogging of someone caught drunk or smoking, or of a woman caught in public with a man who is not her relative, may be controversial even in some countries using Islamic law. Another major problem is that Sharia courts' proceedings provide few explicit rights for defendants.

For many of Sharia's supporters, this is just the point: to provide swift and sure justice to strike fear into would-be wrongdoers. Sharia is attractive to some in parts of the developing world where existing secular law enforcement is weak, street crime is out of control, and judicial and police decisions can be bought. In practice, however, application of Sharia law seems in some places to be most preoccupied with women's dress, independence, and relations with men in ways that constrain women's ability to live freely and develop themselves. Meanwhile, it often treads lightly regarding corruption and other crimes by men (which the Koran also condemns).

Judicial Power and Politics in the Developing and Post-Communist Worlds

In the developing world, judiciaries tend to be both weaker and more political than in the developed world.[13] Typically, past authoritarian governments had kept judiciaries compliant with the preferences of either the national political executive or lower-level power-holders. In most of the twentieth century in Mexico, for example, the president and the ruling party (the PRI) assured that constitutional provisions for judicial review were not meaningful; for example, by custom the Supreme Court resigned and was replaced with each new president. In Iran, the judiciary is in effect controlled by the supreme leader and the Guardian Council.

Reversing such a political-cultural hold on judges is an uphill climb. In the 1980s and 1990s, new democracies in common law countries lacked a fund of impartial case law, and code law countries' courts did not have to follow precedents from prior high courts' rulings. (Only in 2004 did a constitutional amendment allow Brazil's Supreme Federal Court to impose its rulings on lower courts.) Also, sometimes the constitutions of new democracies have enshrined special protections from ordinary legal process for members of previous elites (e.g., military officers), included as part of the bargain of transition to democracy (see chapter 16). In cases of more chaotic regime change, the judges, inherited from the prior governments who appointed them, may embrace judicial review to try to limit the rate and scope of change (e.g., Egypt in 2012 and 2013 and Thailand in 2014).

Judges in these circumstances are often poorly paid and vulnerable to bribery, threats, and other political pressure. Legal processes can grind on slowly and inefficiently, with huge backlogs of unprocessed cases. Consequently, the public may generally perceive the courts as corrupt. People may be unwilling to testify where the rule of law and police protection are weak. Local power-holders may be able to protect individuals from legal accountability, sometimes including members of such illegal forces as drug gangs in Columbia or Mexico.

Some of the post-Communist nations of central Europe have made significant progress toward modern roles for their judiciaries, partly out of their eagerness to qualify for inclusion in the European Union, which sets high standards for the rule of law. In the states of the former Soviet Union, however, progress has been uneven. In the most prominent case, in Russia we have seen government resources (from past high oil prices) used to modernize ordinary judicial processes, but a pattern has also emerged of using the courts to selectively prosecute the regime's most serious political opponents.

SUMMARY

Decision making in the bureaucracy and the judiciary does not allow for the same broad scope for politics that we find in sites such as political parties, elections, the legislature, and the political executive. In principle, the bureaucracy and the judiciary are limited to applying the law, which directs what they are to do and exercises strong limit-setting power where administrators and judges do make decisions. Still, laws cannot specify every detail, so bureaucracies and judiciaries must make rules and adopt precedents that flesh out the laws so they can be effective in particular cases.

As we have seen regarding the developed nations, the bureaucracy is undergoing change. Pressures toward decentralization and fragmentation into more autonomous agencies may render bureaucratic units more flexible, responsive, efficient and accountable to political forces outside the bureaucracy. But they may also weaken its capacity to resist the efforts of the political executive or affected interests to steer administration away from the intent of existing legislation.

The judiciary is in a bit different situation, but also undergoing change. Increasingly it is *expected* to exercise autonomous influence on behalf of not only the laws but also constitutional rules, principles, and the values behind them. Particularly in common law presidential systems such as the United States, we don't consider this sort of judicial independence to be especially political; we think of it only as judges doing their jobs under the democratic political framework. In contrast, in traditionally parliamentary systems, judiciaries mostly defer to their legislatures (in common law systems) or their political executives (in code law systems). As we have noted, however, in recent decades the established parliamentary systems have seen significant change in the direction of autonomous influence by the judiciary. Under the influence of human rights law's values and rules, both common law parliamentary systems (e.g., Britain) and European code law ones (e.g., France and continental Europe)—particularly within the European Union—have strengthened the independence of their judiciaries from both legislative and political executive influence. Thus we may say that values have had a major impact on the distribution of influence at work in the judicial sector of political frameworks.

COUNTRY CASE STUDIES

Great Britain and France are the two classic cases that define the contrasting types of both bureaucracy and judiciary.

Great Britain: A Common Law Country

As we have seen, the top positions in British ministries (called "departments" in the United Kingdom) are occupied by members of parliament from the majority party's leadership. The minister of each department, in Britain called its secretary, is typically a generalist politician rather than an expert with formal credentials in the department's field. The same can be said of his or her immediate subordinates in the managerial line of the political executive: the undersecretaries, junior ministers, and parliamentary private secretaries.

In contrast, the permanent secretary and the other senior career bureaucrats typically have gained real expertise in the field of their department's activity. They have access to all of its privileged information, know its "institutional history" regarding what seems to work and what doesn't, and may share a strong sense of departmental mission. In a long-running British television comedy called "Yes Minister" (later "Yes, Prime Minister")—no doubt with an element of comic exaggeration—the minister was presented as a vain, bumbling fool who seldom seriously got in the way of the sly and expert permanent secretary, who really ran the department. Again, the career administrators often have developed a point of view and sense of mission that carries great weight in advising the minister and his political aides.

In the British bureaucratic tradition, high-level civil servants are recruited from the country's top universities (most notably, Oxford and Cambridge) and usually come from upper or upper-middle-class socioeconomic backgrounds. (But their common background does not necessarily translate into shared ideological or class-related attitudes among the upper bureaucracy.) Rising bureaucrats may then get experience in various departments and positions before settling into the top levels of a department, where they deepen their expertise in its affairs over time. British administrators are imbued with the ideals of political neutrality, obedience to their political superiors, and strict confidentiality regarding departmental business. However, when the administrators feel that an initiative from the political executive must be modified to be workable, the departmental point of view can be a formidable force.

The conservative governments of Prime Ministers Margaret Thatcher (1980s) and John Major (early 1990s) tried to reduce the policy impact of the career bureaucracy. They adopted the "Next Steps" program, which devolved program implementation to hundreds of local and regional agencies with varying degrees of autonomy, whose heads were often picked by the minister from outside the traditional civil service recruitment process. The program reduced the size of the central department bureaucracies, and reduced their role to that of supervising the new agencies to assure their responsiveness to the goals of Parliament and the government. Some viewed the appointment of agency heads by the political executive and the addition of special advisors to ministers' staff as helpful in increasing flexibility, efficiency, and responsiveness to the voters and consumers. Others saw these moves as steps toward administrative politicization, patronage, and influence by outside interests.

Alongside this general decentralization, the Thatcher and Major governments pursued the privatization of public corporations that had owned and run such industries as rail, road, and air transportation, coal, gas, electricity, and telecommunications. Particularly where the new private enterprises remained de facto monopolies, new government agencies had to be created to regulate them and their rates, agencies that were also run in a semiautonomous fashion. The Labor government led by Tony Blair starting in 1997 (and Gordon Brown from 2007 to 2010) focused on pressuring the local authorities and agencies to improve the quality of operations and services, especially the National Health Service.

To improve infrastructure for economic development, the Labor government of the 2000s organized autonomous regional organizations called "quangos," short for quasi-nongovernmental organizations. They also sought to involve the private sector in decision making at the regional level and foster private-public partnerships (though most of the support went to public projects and services). When the Labor government was replaced by the coalition of the Conservatives and Liberal Democrats in May 2010 (see Country Case Studies, chapter 1), the conservatives criticized the regional quangos as too expensive and public-sector oriented, and not sufficiently supportive of local private enterprise. Each was replaced by a single regional fund with roughly half the previous budget for regional development. This move was presented as further decentralization of decision making and as a financial benefit to local businesspeople and councilors, though some critics saw it as a recentralization of influence into the hands of the administrators of the fund.

In financial regulation, the new government of David Cameron (2010–present) removed regulatory responsibility from the Labor-established Financial Services Authority and placed it in the hands of the central bank, the Bank of England. And the responsibility for public financial monitoring and forecasting was removed from the treasury and placed in a new Office of Budget Responsibility, with the stated intention of making financial reporting more complete and better insulated from politics. In practice, however, some of these examples of bureaucratic change seem also to further the political aims of the largely classical liberal cabinet. The dismantling of the regional quangos smoothed the way for big cuts in public investment and the public sector at the regional level. And the new budget office has served to publicize and emphasize the levels of deficit and debt, thus providing ammunition for larger spending cutbacks. Again, the Cameron government seemed to be shifting regulatory influence away from traditional public-sector bureaucracies and into separate units, which may prove to be more responsive to cabinet priorities.

The most extreme case of this was the mid-2010 cabinet proposal to reorganize and decentralize the National Health Service. Labor had already decentralized health decision making to 150 local units and had recently halted the spending increases that had characterized the quality improvement campaign of the 2000s. The new conservative Cameron government then reorganized health care again, dismantling and eliminating much of the current public management of the health service. Hospitals became autonomous quasi-commercial units, weakening the existing rules aimed at assuring quality and reducing patient wait times. The new model gave most decision making over care and spending to primary doctors, whose regional associations would negotiate prices with hospitals and specialists (no doubt increasingly with private practitioners). Only time will tell what the results will be.

British judicial practice, true to its common law roots, developed on the basis of broad experience with law and society rather than specialized training in a particular set of rules. In medieval Britain, Saxon law tended to follow local custom until the Norman kings arrived in 1066 and called for common principles of law across the realm. But these common elements were not formulated by the king and his agents. Rather, they were drawn up by the judges themselves from aspects of customary dispute resolution, Roman law, church law, and their own reasoning. The resulting "common law" approach relied on the understandings and customs of judges and barristers, at least somewhat independently of the king and his agents. In deciding cases, they called on respected past precedent as well as traditional legal rules.

The British courts also traditionally respected the administrative norm of obedience to the king or Parliament when its will was explicit. Britain never officially wrote a constitution to reign over Parliament, and Britain's highest appellate court, the "Law Lords" committee of the House of Lords, never had the formal authority to strike down acts of Parliament as inconsistent with the informal British constitution.

However, this situation is now beginning to change. Britain's membership in the Council of Europe mandates British respect for the European Convention of Human Rights (ECHR) and the case law of the Council's European Court of Human Rights. Moreover, the EU's European Court of Justice (ECJ) has made national court systems the watchdogs over national law's adherence to European Community law, and the ECJ's case law (which in turn recognizes and incorporates the ECHR case law).

With regard to human rights protection in particular, the British parliament has formalized this approach by passing the Human Rights Act of 1998. In effect, this law incorporated the European Convention into British law. It allowed individuals to challenge executive actions, and permitted the courts to hold executive actions to recognized human rights standards. More generally, the courts may issue "writs" questioning whether government actions are *ultra vires*, or beyond statutory authority. As we have seen, the Law Lords has been replaced as Britain's highest court by a new Supreme Court, which began operating in 2009. At least regarding human rights, judicial review seems to be developing.

France: A Code Law Country

The professional bureaucracy is also a powerful force in French government. There are upwards of a million permanent civil service employees at all levels of the ministries, apart from such categories as soldiers, schoolteachers, and employees of state-owned enterprises. France has extensive state regulation, and the National Assembly has often left the specifics of legislation to the civil servants to craft.

France's post–World War II strategy of state-led reconstruction and national economic planning included numerous nationalized industries up to the 1980s. Public corporations existed in such areas as energy, transport, banking, and insurance, and even included an automobile manufacturer, Renault. The new left-of-center government of the early 1980s at first expanded state ownership in the economy, especially in banking and insurance. Within a couple of years, however, President François Mitterrand reversed course amid rising inflation and large public budget deficits. Subsequent governments privatized many of these economic enterprises, and the last decade has seen further privatization in such areas as military-supporting industry, transportation, and telecommunications.

Like those in the top levels of the British bureaucracy, those high in the French civil service tend to share a similar educational background. In France, they come mostly from one of the two highly selective universities dedicated to preparing administrators: the *École Nationale d'Administration (ENA) and the École Polytechnique.* Lower-level civil servants are prepared by regional administration institutes.

The units within the bureaucracy (over a thousand) are called corps. The most important sector of the bureaucracy is what is called the grand corps—including the highest professional levels in such ministries

as finance, foreign affairs, and interior, and interior's hierarchy of prefects at the regional (*department*) level and the local district (*arrondissement*) level. As in Great Britain, most of these high-level administrators come from well-to-do backgrounds, but do not necessarily share common ideological views. Perspectives may differ significantly from one ministry to the next, often in line with the ministry's particular role in recent decades—for example, between the free-market-oriented finance ministry officials presiding over privatization, and the labor ministry officials seeking to protect job security for workers, or environment ministry officials concerned about reducing pollution and fighting global warming.

ENA-educated administrators may also play strong roles in the French political executive. French law does not require ministers to be members of parliament, which allows civil servants to be appointed to the position. The French bureaucracy has no equivalent to the British permanent secretary in each ministry. Rather, a cabinet of ten or more advisory staff helps the minister coordinate the ministry. Many of these staffers are policy supporters selected from the ranks of the civil service. They are coordinated by a staff chief and a principal political advisor. This group tends to stay with a particular minister if he or she moves on to another ministry.

Civil servants also play prominent roles in the commissions set up periodically to study particular problems and recommend policy changes, such as the 2004 Stasi Commission on the secular character of the French polity. The Council of State, part of the grand corps, scrutinizes draft legislation to ensure that it conforms to existing law, and handles cases when citizens challenge bureaucratic behavior.

Past parliamentary initiatives have sometimes been checked or redirected later by the upper bureaucracy. In policy areas such as education, prison reform, and discrimination by race, religion, and immigration status, at times bureaucratic units have either failed to implement rules or have crafted them in ways that run counter to the legislation's intent. When this occurs, however, most often it is under the direction of the political executive, rather than in opposition to it. For example, under Presidents Charles de Gaulle and Georges Pompidou up through the early 1970s, and in the first two years under Mitterrand in the early 1980s, the National Planning Commission and its committees played a strong role in government spending and labor policies. Subsequently, however, free-market policies in the finance and industry ministries increasingly prevailed, and the commission has been relegated to the role of economic monitoring.

The unitary character of French government means that in principle, no significant areas of policymaking are delegated to regions. However, a limited degree of administrative decentralization has been introduced in recent decades. The Mitterrand government of the 1980s opened new opportunities for local participation, responsiveness, and experimentation in policy areas such as education, culture, health, welfare, roads, and housing. In these cases, the regional or departmental prefect and his or her specialist advisors are accompanied by popularly elected councils. These councils pass on budgets and taxes (subject to prefectural veto) to cover activities not directly under the jurisdiction of national law and administration. Such decentralization has generally been welcomed by localities. But where it is accompanied by the transfer of some financial obligations to regional departments and local districts, often wealthier areas have proven better equipped to shoulder the costs than poorer ones.

In its judiciary, traditionally French practice has also been more centralized than in Britain. France is a classic example of a code law system. In making their decisions, French courts are not expected to scour the record for the most relevant precedents. Instead, they simply apply the detailed code of laws developed by the executive branch to the case at hand. In contrast with common law systems, French judicial practice does not have the plaintiff's attorney (in a civil case) or the ministry of justice's prosecutor (in a criminal case) take the lead in investigating and developing the evidence. Instead, the French system has a special independent category of judge, the *judge d'instruction*, to interview witnesses, compile evidence, decide whether to bring the case to court, and recommend a verdict to the regular judge and jury. This leaves the contending attorneys with a far less significant role than they play in the adversarial system of common law in countries such as Britain and the United States.

Partly as a consequence of this approach, traditional French legal practice did not develop defendants' rights nearly as formally and firmly as in common law countries. In recent decades, however, most elements of fair judicial process have been incorporated into French justice. In line with human rights standards, legislation has assured habeas corpus protections, pretrial detention periods have been reduced, the presumption of innocence has been assured, indigents have been guaranteed legal representation, resident aliens' rights now approach those of citizens, and police powers have been increasingly limited. French courts accept ECHR and EU human rights guarantees and have the standing to protect them.

The French bureaucracy faces judicial limits as well. Within the executive branch, France has an elaborate structure of thirty administrative courts to oversee the ministries and their practices. This structure is independent of the rest of the executive, and culminates in the very prestigious Council of State, one of the most important of the *grands corps* and made up predominantly of leading graduates of the ENA. The Council serves as a kind of supreme court for citizens' complaints against administrative actions, and advises parliament on the constitutionality and legality of proposed legislation. In 1992, it was the Council of State that formally recognized the supremacy of European Union law over domestic national law where the two conflict.

Finally, France has developed a form of judicial review. The nine-member Constitutional Council is made up of elder jurists and politicians of the highest rank, sometimes including former presidents. They are selected by the presidents of the National Assembly, the Senate, and the nation (each selecting three). This constitutional court is entirely separate from the regular and administrative court systems. Its members serve staggered nine-year terms, and each may only serve one term. Often past leaders of opposing coalitions coexist on it.

Today the Constitutional Council may consider the constitutionality of any part of a bill at the request of only sixty Assembly deputies or sixty senators. Since the parliamentary opposition to a bill can regularly get these numbers to seek review of majority-passed legislation, now important legislation commonly receives judicial review. On most bills the government at least consults with the Constitutional Council. Thus the Council exercises abstract review—direct judicial review of bills at the point of their passage, without waiting for a case concerning a law to arise in the courts. However, the Constitutional Council may not take up past legislation as a court case arises involving a challenge to a law, as in the American common law system.

In both the bureaucracy and the judiciary, then, authority in applying French law is substantially centralized, but it finds checks to keep it within the bounds of human rights standards.

◁ PRACTICE AND REVIEW ONLINE

CRITICAL THINKING QUESTIONS

1. When and how does the bureaucracy exercise autonomous influence, and does it serve the purposes of democracy in doing so?

2. How has centralization of influence within the bureaucracy been reduced in recent decades, and how has that change affected the effectiveness of bureaucracies?

3. How might increased political executive control be good for bureaucracy? What negative effects might it have?

4. When and how do the courts exercise autonomous influence, and do they serve the purposes of democracy in doing so?

5. How might the courts be viewed as political? How not? Who do judges contend with, and for what purposes?

KEY TERMS

bureaucracy, 409
permanent secretary, 411
spoils system, 411
nomenklatura, 412
line authority, 413
staff, 413
regulatory strings, 414
standard operating procedures, 416
new public management, 420
plaintiff, 424
constitutional law, 424
appellate court, 424
common law, 425
precedent, 425
case law, 425

habeas corpus, 426
code law, 426
judicial review, 428
judicial activism, 428
abstract review, 431
concrete review, 432
administrative law, 432
Sharia law, 433

FURTHER READING

Aberbach, Joel D., Robert D. Putnam, and Bert A. Rockman (with the collaboration of Thomas J. Anton, Samuel J. Eldersveld, Ronald Inglehart). *Bureaucrats and Politicians in Western Democracies.* Cambridge, MA: Harvard University Press, 1981.

Abraham, Henry J. *The Judicial Process: An Introductory Analysis of the Courts of the United States, England, and France.* New York: Oxford University Press, 1998.

Cappelletti, Mauro. *The Judicial Process in a Comparative Perspective.* New York: Oxford University Press, 1989.

Crozier, Michel. *The Bureaucratic Phenomenon.* Chicago: University of Chicago Press, 1987.

Geddes, Barbara. *Politician's Dilemma: Building State Capacity in Latin America.* Berkeley, Los Angeles, London: University of California Press, 1994.

Guarnieri, Carlo, and Patrizia Pederzoli. *The Power of Judges: A Comparative Study of Courts and Democracy.* Oxford: Oxford University Press, 2002.

Heady, Ferrel. *Public Administration: A Comparative Perspective.* New York: Marcel Dekker, 2001.

Katz, Alan M., ed. *Legal Traditions and Systems: An International Handbook*. Westport, CT: Greenwood Press, 1986.

Koopmans, Tim. *Courts and Political Institutions: A Comparative View*. New York: Cambridge University Press, 2003.

Page, Edward C., and Vincent Wright. *Bureaucratic Elites in Western European States*. New York: Oxford University Press, 1999.

Peters, B. Guy. *The Politics of Bureaucracy: A Comparative Perspective*, 6th ed. London and New York: Routledge, 2000.

Pierre, Jon., ed. *Bureaucracy in the Modern State: An Introduction to Comparative Public Administration*. Aldershot, Hants, England; Brookfield, VT, USA: E. Elgar Pub. Co., 1995.

NOTES

[1] See Max Weber, "Bureaucracy," in *From Max Weber*, ed. Hans Gerth and C. Wright Mills (New York: Oxford University Press, 1946), 196–244.

[2] For more on this, see chapter 9.

[3] See W. A. Niskanen, *Bureaucracy and Representative Government* (Chicago: Aldine Atherton, 1971).

[4] See Graham Allison, *Essence of Decision: Explaining the Cuban Missile Crisis* (New York: Longman, 1999).

[5] For a survey of political aspects of administration in the United States, see James W. Fesler and Donald F. Kettl, *The Politics of the Administrative Process*, 2nd ed. (Chatham, NJ: Chatham House, 1996).

[6] These were credit default swaps, a form of insurance to compensate lenders, bondholders, or other investors in case of default (failure of repayment) on their loans or investments; see chapter 7.

[7] For a defense of this strategy, see David Osborne and Ted Gaebler, *Reinventing Government: How the Entrepreneurial Spirit is Transforming the Public Sector* (New York and London: Penguin, 1992).

[8] See Guy Peters and Jon Pierre, *The Politicization of the Civil Service in Comparative Perspective* (New York: Routledge, 2004).

[9] See Christopher Hood et al., *Regulation Inside Government: Waste-Watchers, Quality Police and Sleaze-Busters* (Oxford and New York: Oxford University Press, 1999).

[10] Jack W. Peltason, *Federal Courts in the Political Process* (Garden City, NY: Doubleday, 1955).

[11] See Alec Stone Sweet, *Governing with Judges: Constitutional Politics in Europe* (Oxford; New York: Oxford University Press, 2000).

[12] See C. Neal Tate and Torbjorn Vallinder, eds., *The Global Expansion of Judicial Power* (New York: New York University Press, 1995).

[13] For a look at judicial independence in the new democracies, see Tom Ginsburg, *Judicial Review in New Democracies* (New York: Cambridge University Press, 2003).

Authoritarian Regimes and Revolution

FOCUS QUESTIONS

- **WHAT** are the main types of authoritarian political frameworks?

- **WHAT** are the key differences between single-party rule and single-party-dominant, electoral authoritarian rule?

- **WHAT** do they have in common?

- **WHAT** factors have tended to undermine military regimes? Single-party regimes?

- **WHAT** factors contribute to their endurance?

- **WHAT** makes the overthrow of an authoritarian regime a revolution?

IN MAY 2014, A MILITARY COUP (a takeover of the government by military officers) in Thailand overthrew the elected government of Prime Minister Yingluck Shinawatra and installed a military-run authoritarian regime that remains in power today. Military coups have been frequent in Thailand since the beginning of the constitutional monarchy in 1932. The current military government is related to a deep political cleavage in Thailand between the poor, mainly rural, but very populous north and northeast of the country, and the much more developed and better-off capital city of Bangkok, the south, and the southeast.

Personal leadership has played a role in this cleavage. Yingluck's very wealthy brother, Thaksin Shinawatra, is now in exile after being convicted of corruption. Since the 2000s, Thaksin has been viewed as the informal leader of first the People's Power Party and now the (renamed) Pheu Thai Party. The Thaksin-led government of the mid-2000s brought much-needed help and government services, from roads to education and health care, to the neglected rural areas of Thailand. When fair elections have been held recently, the northern majority tends to reward the Shinawatras with parliamentary majorities for whatever coalition they lead. But Thaksin has sometimes used his wealth and power in corrupt and even abusive ways.

This has fueled support for the southern Democratic Party and its allies, who see themselves as representing the more prosperous, educated, and industrially developed (with much Japanese investment over recent decades) areas of the south and Bangkok. Allied with the latter are key elites: the military itself, the courts, and the king's followers. With the support of politically active portions of the urban middle class, amid Thailand's traditions of street demonstrations and military intervention to "rescue" the country from disorder, this combustible combination has at times resulted in the removal of properly elected democratic governments. Of course, the rescue tends to empower one side of the north-south cleavage, in this case the south over the north. In one form or another in Thailand, authoritarian rule—whether directly or using a manipulated constitution—is likely to be in place for some time. We need to understand authoritarian forms of contention and imposed cooperation.

DEFINITIONS AND DISTINCTIONS

The center of attention on regime change over the last century has been transitions to and from authoritarian rule and representative democracy. In this chapter, we start with the various types of authoritarian regime and their characteristic forms of destabilization. We begin by distinguishing authoritarian regimes both from representative democracy and from a more intense form of nondemocratic rule, totalitarian government.

In chapter 1, authoritarian political frameworks were distinguished by the enduring dominance of politics by some top group and its allies, in contrast to having political leaders selected in free and fair elections. If so-called "elections" are held under authoritarian frameworks, they are not meaningful. If there is a legislative branch, it is not freely and fairly chosen and/or does not have a significant policymaking role. The judiciary is not fully independent. And under authoritarian government, there is no guarantee of related features of democracy: the protection of human rights such as the right to free expression and association, autonomy for groups such as interest groups and political parties, political accountability, and formal political equality. Within the top group and its allies, contention and cooperation are informal, while overall, the top group imposes cooperation on the rest of political society.

As was noted in chapter 3, when political scientists apply pairs of contrasting concepts to the real world, they do not always distinguish cases in a clear night-versus-day, "bright line" fashion. We tend to find a continuum or spectrum between extreme poles. Some comparative political scientists suggest a middle category that mixes democratic and authoritarian features, using terms such as "semi-authoritarian" or "hybrid" government. However, most empirical cases of such mixture can be placed somewhere in either the democratic-leaning segment of the continuum (which I call "minimally democratic") or the authoritarian-leaning segment. Thus I will not use terms that suggest a midpoint.

We also face the question of terminology for the various types of authoritarian rule. The thoughtful and sophisticated typology of political scientist Juan Linz, for example, includes a rather long list of authoritarian types, including characteristics such as whether the regime relies on bureaucracy, pursues modernization, employs corporatist arrangements (see chapter 9), or has recently evolved from a totalitarian system.[1] This chapter's approach to terminology starts with a simpler set of broader categories.[2] These are based on (a) the distribution of influence—who is the top group—and (b) the type of formal political framework. These authoritarian types are personal autocracy, single-party rule, military government, theocracy, and **single-party-dominant**, **electoral authoritarian** governance—authoritarian rule in which the dominant party permits multi-party elections, but aggressively disadvantages other contending parties to the point that they are not really competitive in those elections. Then, within each category, I note possible variations related to such aspects as the regime's policy pursuit (e.g., modernization), structural reliance (e.g., on bureaucracy or corporatism), degree of personalism, ethnic-exclusionary behavior, or post-totalitarian status continuing certain totalitarian elements (e.g., Soviet Communism from the 1960s on).

Authoritarian regimes must also be distinguished from the more intense control that characterizes totalitarian rule. In chapter 1, I defined totalitarian rule mainly in terms of (a) the top group's imposition of an ideology on the media, education, and culture, (b) its requirement that top managers in the system be members of the dominant political party or sect, and (c) systematic infringement of the human rights of actual or suspected dissenters, via detention, torture, and/or murder. Historical examples are the Nazi single-party regime and Japanese military rule before and during World War II, and Communist single-party government in the Soviet Union from the 1930s until Joseph Stalin's death in 1953 and Pol Pot's regime in Cambodia in the 1970s. More recent examples are today's North Korea under Kim Jung Un, the Taliban theocratic regime in Afghanistan prior to 2003, and Islamic State rule in parts of Syria and Iraq after mid-2014.

After examining the types of authoritarian political frameworks, the chapter discusses revolution, the bluntest form of replacement of authoritarian regimes, which often tends to replace one authoritarian form with another.

PERSONAL AUTOCRACY

Personal autocracy is a form of rule in which the chief executive is also the chief lawmaker, without an explicit role for other institutions or organizations. If the leader is formally associated with a political party, that party is merely an insignificant personalistic vehicle for the leader. Personal autocracy comes in two main forms: traditional monarchy and personal dictatorship.

Traditional Monarchy

Until the late nineteenth century, the chief form of personal autocracy was **traditional monarchy**, in which personal rule was a formalized system. At most, kings might consult with informal councils. The "bureaucracy" was, in effect, an extension of the king's private household management. Loyalty was crucial, and the king or queen often relied on patron-client connections downward into society. In these clientelistic networks, regional and local notables (usually large landowners) could be a key rung. This landowning nobility might be closely integrated into the king's and his army's administration (as in Russia), or more independent (as in France). The kingship typically passed from father to son in a royal family. The system overall was often supported by religion as well as tradition.

Today where monarchs exist outside the Middle East, they are mostly ceremonial and symbolic figures with no real political role; cases where a monarch has taken significant action have been rare.[3] In the Middle East, however, there

The new Saudi king Salman, who succeeded King Abdullah upon his death in 2015.

remain a few monarchies with small citizenries but big oil reserves, usually called emirates. The large Saudi royal family, for example, which practices an austere form of Islam called Wahhabism, sits atop an extensive patron-client system. Oil wealth funds the health, education, and other needs of the mainly leisured Saudi citizens. The work is mostly done by noncitizen guest workers, including many from South Asia.

Personal Dictatorship

Other forms of personal autocracy tend to be called dictatorships. **Personal dictatorship** is a form of personal autocracy that lacks both institutions and traditional legitimacy. It relies on force and personal loyalty, and permits rather arbitrary rule by the top leader.[4] African examples included the reigns of Mobutu Sese Seko in the Congo during most of the last third of the twentieth century, and Emperor Bokassa in the Central African Republic from 1966 to 1979. Examples in Latin America include the Somozas who ruled Nicaragua from 1936 to 1979, Alberto Stroessner, who led Paraguay from 1954 to 1989, and "Papa Doc" Duvalier who ruled Haiti in the 1960s.

In those states, the leader may have first gained personal control as head of an insurgent party or military coup. But subsequently, the dictator successfully concentrated power to such an extent that he always had the last word and did not depend heavily on any party or military structure to rule. Personal dominance was bolstered especially by control of police power, and by wealth gained through family members' and their associates' businesses and financial connections. But the threat of force is seldom sufficient by itself to maintain the dictator's position. He may also have to rely to some degree on cooperation from supportive actors such as military officers, large landowners, leaders of the prevailing religion, or key economic interests such as mine owners. These actors get security in their pursuits in return for their support for the regime. Patron-client networks, bribery, and corruption often play key roles in maintaining these relationships.

Within the government administration, top officials know that as clients of the leader, their individual positions depend on his favor. Discovery of client disloyalty could lead to loss of everything (including liberty, in the case of imprisonment). In addition, high officials may be periodically reshuffled to prevent them from building their own power bases and possibly becoming rivals of the chief. Typically, the whole regime depends on the often glorified leader, and his removal could lead to collapse of the regime and the removal of most or all of his officials. Thus the officials are unlikely to cooperate to try to overthrow the leader.[5]

One theoretical hypothesis regarding this situation is that personal dictators suffer from what could be called the **dictator's dilemma**. Their regimes rely heavily on repressive force and fear, and lack institutions such as political parties and (weak) legislative assemblies—along with the political interactions in and around them—to provide reliable information on how much support they actually have. Thus, the theory goes, personal dictators have a hard time knowing how much they should spend on attracting the support of potential opponents and providing clientelistic benefits to their groups.[6] Both overshooting and falling short in these efforts pose risks for the leader and the regime.

Many of these personal autocracies have yielded to change, as we shall see below. When personal autocracies fall, they may do so in various ways, ranging from assassination or defeat in war to crises that lead to peaceful transition. When the ruler dies, the line of succession may be unclear or the successor may have difficulty filling the former leader's shoes. Or an economic crisis may coincide with the rise of a challenging group (e.g., ethnic, regional, or military) or a democracy movement. In such situations, the personalistic basis of the regime may leave the ruler with few powerful friends or institutional supports.

In many ways, personal dictatorship is the epitome of the personal leadership model of the distribution of influence, applied to the political framework overall. But as we shall see below, more limited degrees of personalism may also play roles in other political frameworks such as military and single-party regimes.

MILITARY REGIMES

Military regimes were widespread in the developing world between the middle 1960s and the early 1980s, more numerous then than either personal autocracies or single-party regimes. During this period, the armed forces were not intervening temporarily, just to arrange new elections or replace one civilian regime with another; they were there to stay. Many military governments maintained control through military force and civilian bureaucrats, but without political parties or legislative institutions. Thus, in some ways, military rule was similar to the sort of colonial rule that in many cases had preceded it by only a few years (see "Concept in Context" below).

Triggers for Military Takeover

Such governments typically begin with a **military coup**. Possible triggers of military takeover of the government—often interrelated—include:

- A young and poorly institutionalized prior regime, losing legitimacy due to its immersion in clientelism, corruption, inefficiency, and/or weak law enforcement (the "weak state" syndrome).
- Unmet economic challenges, such as growing government budget deficits, economic stagnation, high inflation, and widespread strikes.
- Protest by those left behind by the prior government's policies (perhaps including the military itself), by its patterns of clientelist favoritism, or by the termination of either.
- Ideological opposition in the military to the prior regime's heavy government intervention in the economy (or rarely, the lack of it, as in Egypt in 1952).
- Perceived threats to the key interests of established elites (e.g. business, landowning, mining), whether from disadvantaged groups, an insurgency, or government itself.
- Ethnic, religious, and/or regional tensions (perhaps over a new civilian group gaining power).

CONCEPT IN CONTEXT | Military Coup Triggers in Chile

The setting for the 1973 military coup in Chile was in some ways similar to those of other Latin American coups of the preceding period, but in other ways different. Chile was unusual in Latin America at the time in having a comparatively stable democratic system, with well established political parties, a settled presidential governmental structure, and a military that had remained largely professional and isolated from politics in the prior few decades.

Among the common triggers that were present, however, were threats to established interests. Inequality was a longstanding source of tension and polarization, especially in the rural sector. Land was very unequally owned, with large estates ("latifundia") and numerous hungry landless and smallholding peasants. Prior proposals of land reform had not gone far until the presidency of Socialist Party leader (and Marxist) Salvador Allende Gossens in 1970. Allende carried out a significant expansion of land reform, redistributing latifundia land to its laborers to be run as cooperatives. This not only made enemies of the powerful local oligarchies, but also left many of the rural poor still land-hungry and frustrated. In the early 1970s, some poor peasants simply seized land and occupied it without government authorization. (Some workers also took over their factories.) Among the upper strata, this situation sparked Cold War-style fears of revolution and Communism.

As to the political parties, four significant ones competed in the multiparty PR elections: the conservative National Party (PN) to the right, the Christian Democrats (PDC, sympathetic to moderate land reform) in the center with its center-left and center-right factions, and on the left, a "Popular Unity" coalition (UP) of two far-left, ideological focus parties: the larger Socialist Party led by Allende (PS, democratic socialist), and the smaller Marxist-Leninist Communist Party (PCCh). (Revolutionary and right-wing groups at the extremes were very small.)

Here a key factor was Chile's presidential governmental structure, with its frequent legislative-executive contention and deadlock. Some political scientists consider this "divided legitimacy" to be a recipe for democratic breakdown under circumstances of sharp polarization (see chapter 16). According to Chile's (1925) constitution, whenever the presidential vote did not yield a majority winner—which happens regularly, given the multiparty PR system—the final choice would be made by the Chamber of deputies. In the 1970 presidential election, veteran Socialist leader Allende had just barely won the plurality with 36 percent (to 35 for the PN candidate and 27 for the PDC leader), and his leftist UP coalition held only around

As this list indicates, military coup leaders' stated goals often vary, including (for example) to address a crisis in the economy, to control ethnic, religious, or regional tension or conflict, to clean up corruption, to speed up the modernization of their country, to suppress a leftist threat, or to just replace another poorly performing military regime. Overall, militaries tend to argue that the challenges of modernization and social peace require greater unity and a firmer hand—more cooperation and less contention—than the prior democratic or authoritarian government can offer.

In line with the variety of triggers for military intervention, political scientists have suggested various motivations for military coups. Some tend to accept the generals' above-noted account about the national need for modernization, unity, and order, viewing the military favorably as a patriotic actor. Another explanatory option centers on the military itself as an institution, stressing officers' worries about the prior regime's underfunding of, or interference in, the armed forces. Other observers stress the common phenomenon of coups' support for the interests of elites such as big businesses and landowners, at risk from populist unrest or economic instability, or both at once.

40% of the Chamber seats. At the last minute, the centrist, swing-vote PDC chose to adhere to past custom and supported the plurality winner, allowing Allende to take office as yet another "minority president."

Initially Congress approved Allende's takeover of the copper mines from U.S. companies, but subsequently the PDC's conservative wing balked at supporting Allende's overall program of state takeover of industries and large agricultural properties. Both business and agricultural elites were alarmed by it, and the PDC joined the PN to form a majority opposition to Allende in the Chamber. To proceed with his nationalization plan, Allende retrieved from obscurity an old emergency law (from the short-lived "socialist republic" period in the early 1930s) permitting takeovers without Congressional approval. The Chamber majority opposition challenged the constitutionality of what they considered presidential overreach in Allende's signature program.

Economically, big mandated wage increases, government spending, and other economic stimulus measures got the economy going early. But by the time of the March 1973 Congressional elections the economy was contracting, with zooming budget deficits, inflation, and strikes creating an atmosphere of economic crisis (another coup trigger). The UP coalition was able to win only 43% of the Chamber

seats, not enough to rescue political legitimacy for Allende's controversial pursuit of socialism.

Amid the Cold War atmosphere of widespread fear of Communism, by mid-1973 Chile was one of the few Latin American nations that was not (yet) under military rule. Some among the Congressional opposition deputies were openly calling for a military takeover (apparently also supported by the American CIA). In September the military intervened decisively, led by its new army chief of staff, Augusto Pinochet Duarte. Pinochet replaced hesitant officers with cooperative ones, disbanded parties and democratic institutions, and installed military men in key positions in the executive. The security agencies hunted down, arrested, and tortured thousands of UP activists and other leftists who were not able to escape into exile (with hundreds "disappeared"—murdered in obscurity).

Ultimately, the ideology of the military was revealed to be yet another factor. Pinochet not only restored taken properties to their prior owners, but also entirely replaced decades of past economic policies with a thoroughly free market regime: privatizing pensions and other government functions, heavily cutting or eliminating government aid to education and health care, disbanding many unions, prohibiting strikes and collective bargaining, cutting tariffs, and welcoming foreign investment.

However, a prominent early analyst of military intervention, Eric Nordlinger, stressed the military's relative autonomy of societal interests.[7] Some intervening military leaderships have been partly motivated by an ideology and the values related to it, such as (a) the 1970s' Peruvian military's moderate left-of-center pursuit of limited land reform as necessary for successful modernization (as in post–World War II South Korea and Taiwan, for example), (b) Augusto Pinochet's pursuit of free-market ideology in Chile in the 1970s and 1980s, and (c) Egyptian Gamal Abdel Nasser and the support of his Free Officers Movement for Arab nationalism and socialism in the 1950s and 1960s.

These approaches to understanding military coups tend to see the military as a single elite group when it intervenes to take control of the government. However, close studies of intervening militaries tend to reveal a more complex picture within the military itself. For example, the armed forces may be divided by their formal segments (e.g., the different services—army, navy, and air force, some of which may be viewed as, to some extent, institutional interests; see chapter 9), and even into informal political factions (see below). Within the military, we may discover some of the same ethnic, regional, religious, and economic cleavages

Two prominent military rulers of the 1970s and 1980s: Augusto Pinochet of Chile (left), and Suharto of Indonesia (right).

and tensions that exist in the surrounding society. In this case, military intervention may actually aim to redress a pattern of influence distribution in the civilian government that is opposed by the leading group(s) within the officer corps, or to bolster a pattern that is favored by the leading military faction.

Characteristics of Military Government

During the heyday of military rule in developing countries in the 1960s–1980s, most such regimes were ideologically conservative. They tended to share the U.S. Cold War aims of contending with the threat of Communism by suppressing the left.[8] But many officers were also nationalistic, wanting to maintain national unity, public support, and sociopolitical order. Thus many chose to continue at least some state ownership, socioeconomic programs, and regulation in the economy; they merely installed their own supporters and patronage in governmental structures.

In their approach to potential political opposition, militaries in power have tended to be authoritarian but not totalitarian. They censored the press to suppress criticism of military rule, but did not try to directly take over the management of the media. But having come into power by force and lacking ordinary legitimacy, military governments did tend, at least at times, to employ one characteristic totalitarian tactic: substantial state (or state-sponsored) terror. When confronted by serious opposition, the regime might declare a national emergency and use detention, torture, and assassination to silence political opposition.

Whether directly in military or police operations, or indirectly by supporting informal "death squads," sometimes their goal was outright murder of their opponents. A particular group might be targeted, as in the mass slaughters of Communists by Generalissimo Chang Kai-shek in China in 1927 and by General Suharto in Indonesia in 1966. Or individual leftists might be the victims, as in the 1970s "dirty wars" in Chile, Argentina, Guatemala, and El Salvador. Or the regime might instead focus primarily on detaining and torturing suspected dissidents for intimidation and information (the main focus in Brazil in the late 1960s and early 1970s). Notably, in such cases of systematic human rights abuse, there is little that the U.N. or other international organizations could do (see "The Human Rights Connection").

The original military coup might be led by top-ranking generals or by a group of lower-level officers, say at the rank of major or colonel. Usually the new government sets up some sort of supreme military council to make or approve policies. The distribution of influence within the supreme military council might vary, from leadership by a leading individual officer to dominance by a small group (e.g., 3–5) of generals called a **junta**, or even more collective decision making, by the full committee.

Path-breaking work on the Brazilian military regime of the 1960s and 1970s by political scientists Alfred Stepan[9] and Guillermo O'Donnell,[10] for example, revealed a highly institutionalized military, with regular procedures of periodic collective choice of which general shall serve as Brazilian president. This suggests rule by an established elite whose decisions are loyally supported by subordinate officers. Military officers normally occupied the top ministerial positions in the executive branch, but might employ civilian technocrats from there on down in the bureaucracy. O'Donnell referred to the Brazilian pattern as **bureaucratic authoritarian** rule, in which the generals relied on an institutionalized bureaucracy to make many policy decisions.

The personal leadership model of influence distribution (see chapter 2) helps explain some cases of military rule, where influence seems to be concentrated in the hands of a single top officer. Indeed, the military as an institution, with its traditions of disciplined hierarchy, loyalty of subordinates to their commanding officers, and top position of "supreme commander," may be viewed as particularly vulnerable to strong leadership by its top-ranking officer. For example, personal leadership within the officer corps played a key role in the regime of Nigerian military ruler Sani Abacha in the middle and late 1990s. Abacha had risen through the ranks, participated in earlier military coups, and built a network of loyal supporters in the army.

Indeed, one might be tempted to classify such cases as personal dictatorships rather than military regimes.[11] However, especially when the regime leader is suddenly removed by another officer—a not-infrequent occurrence in such cases—we are reminded that ultimately this is still a form of military government, and the leader still relies fundamentally on the cooperation of the officer corps with its special possession of, and training in, the means of violence. Second, personal leadership may be accompanied by elite-model factors such as the overall dominance of officers who belong to the leader's ethnic group. Abacha kept influence generally in the hands of officers who were Hausa-Fulani, Muslim, and northern Nigerian in origin as well as, more specifically, his cronies and family members. General Idi Amin, ruler of Uganda in the 1970s, surrounded himself with people who were fellow members of his Kakwa tribe, allied West Nile region tribes, and fellow Muslims. (He removed and harassed people from the Acholi and Lango tribes.)

Most importantly, with regard to personal leadership by the top military officer, political scientists need to keep in mind the limits of what we know. These regimes tend to be secretive. Behind the scenes of seeming personal dictatorship, the public leader may in fact depend heavily on other leaders and groups whose identities we do not know. Despite a vigorous public relations effort to make the

THE HUMAN RIGHTS CONNECTION | International Intervention to End Human Rights Abuse?

Almost all cases of governmental human rights abuse have occurred in authoritarian states where the executive leadership has unchallenged power within the country. Where can people turn to remedy such a situation?

In principle, the United Nations should be a source of help. The U.N. was born after World War II on the wings of victory over totalitarian states that had no respect for human rights. The 1948 Universal Declaration declared the U.N.'s intention to pursue the observance of human rights, and the governments of Germany, Japan, and Italy were replaced by democratic ones observing such rights. As we saw in chapter 2, the subsequent U.N. civil-political Covenant (completed in 1966, in force for signatories in 1976) is a treaty obligating member states to respect human rights and allow free and fair elections. However, how are these rights to be implemented? Does the close linkage of human rights respect with democracy justify outside human rights-based intervention in the government of an authoritarian nation to install a democratic government?

In this context, we have to remember that the war against the German and Japanese forces was also fought to protect national self-determination. It was followed over time by the 1960s dismantling of the European empires in the developing world. Not surprisingly, both of the human rights Covenants start out with the same Article 1 preamble, providing for a fundamental national "right of self-determination." This would seem to rule out invasion to change a form of government.

In practice, U.N. interventions seem to focus primarily on ending ongoing violations of human rights rather than installing democratic regimes. Faced with genocidal repression within a country, for example, U.N. activity tends to focus on imposing economic sanctions on the perpetrator government, helping refugees, and if possible, stationing peacekeeping troops to help stabilize the situation and end human rights abuses. Direct military action by the U.N. might be supported only in the case of outright invasion of one country by another (as in Korea in the early 1950s). And even then, any of the five permanent member nations on the Security Council—the United States, Britain, France, Russia, and China—may prevent action by vetoing the resolution.*

To be sure, concern to end severe human rights abuse has sometimes played a role in regime change. But when this has happened in recent decades, it has not been done under U.N. auspices and has occurred only under a narrow list of circumstances.

top leader seem all-powerful and not to be crossed, he may even be little more than a "front man" for the dominance of one or more groups in the background.

Another aspect of military government is its interaction with civilians. Especially in Latin America, the generals were likely to set up their own supportive (and dutifully compliant) political party, while making it clear that military officers are in charge. If there is a formal legislative branch (e.g., Brazil in the mid-1960s and mid-to-late 1970s), it is controlled by the military via its support party, or lacks real influence, or both. People in government positions are typically screened by the military or their supporters to ensure their cooperation with the regime.

Why might a military government go to the trouble of setting up a military-supporting party and permitting a heavily constrained legislature, perhaps even including a weak opposition party? (Few are persuaded that these moves bring real democratic legitimacy, so that cannot be the reason.) First, the regime may face daunting policy challenges and significant opposition in society. A party vehicle helps it get the leadership's message out, co-opt mid-level civilian leaders, and manage the distribution of clientelistic benefits. Second, a military-supporting party can facilitate limited communication with diverse groups whose support for the regime may vary. As political scientist Jennifer Gandhi points out,[12] safe

When other nations have intervened to defeat an armed force engaged in human rights violation, the burden of ending genocide has fallen on neighboring countries or on former colonial occupiers (e.g., French interventions in Mali and the Central African Republic in 2013). Examples are the late 1960s' invasion by Tanzania to depose the bloodthirsty regime of Idi Amin in neighboring Uganda, the mid-1970s' Vietnamese invasion to remove the genocidal Pol Pot regime in neighboring Cambodia, and in the mid-1990s, the NATO military action to end genocide in Bosnia and Kosovo, and the invasion of Ruanda by a Uganda-backed force to end genocide there. In each case, the U.N. played no part other than aiding refugees.

In contrast, there was a worldwide outcry (also within U.N. bodies) against the American-British invasion of Iraq in 2003. Several of the above-mentioned conditions commonly at work in accepted interventions had not been met. Certainly the Saddam Hussein regime had engaged in serious human rights violations in the past, both before and after the first Gulf War in 1991, but patterns of systematic abuse of identifiable groups seemed to have ended by the middle 1990s (partly with the help of American air patrols keeping Iraqi aircraft out of certain opposition-oriented areas to the north and the south). The invasion of Iraq was not led by neighboring nations, but rather by outside actors whose interests seemed not to be directly at stake. Claims of a direct security threat against the West by Saddam's "weapons of mass destruction" were not borne out by the facts.

As for U.N. intervention to protect human rights, the nation-state remains the sovereign unit in the world, not any broader union. To be sure, the spectacle of the few and poorly armed Dutch "peacekeepers" in Bosnia abandoning the Muslims in the town of Srebrenica prior to the massacre there, and that of the United Nations abandoning its offices in Rwanda in the middle of the Hutu genocide against Tutsis there, are, to us all, haunting images of failure. But, in practice, military intervention to halt ongoing genocidal repression is left to the moral force of human rights obligation rather than to formal U.N. military action.

---

* The U.S.-led Korea intervention under U.N. auspices proceeded only because Russia was boycotting the Security Council at the time.

(harmless to the regime) arenas for exchange of views—to be sure, with clear limits on the scope of permissible criticism of the regime—may facilitate policy compromises that put the regime in a good light, and enable it and its critics to better understand each other's political capacities and aims. (This applies to single-party and single-party-dominant, electoral authoritarian regimes, too; see below).

The Decline of Military Rule

With weak claims to political legitimacy on other grounds, military governments had only performance-based support to fall back on: their ability to solve the above-listed economic and cultural problems and conflicts that they had cited in seizing power. But the generals were not in power long before they were hit with a new challenge in the early 1970s: a spike in oil prices imposed by the new cartel of oil-producing nations. The results often included waves of inflation, economic stagnation, and budget and debt problems that lasted through the decade. By the beginning of the 1980s, inflation was raging across the globe, and the world's monetary authorities (led by the American central bank, called the Federal Reserve) felt that they had to respond. They raised interest rates sharply (constricting credit) to tame inflation by suppressing consumer demand. The skyrocketing interest rates made developing nations' debt problems much worse. Typically, authoritarian regimes had to turn toward budgetary austerity, intensifying the pain of the consequent recessions.

Many of the problems that had dogged the pre-military governments of the 1960s reemerged on the generals' own watch. The armed forces in particular had presented their intervention as partly aimed at modernization, efficiency, and cleaning up corruption; however, over time, military regimes tended to produce their own forms of waste, inefficiency, misguided projects, padded military budgets, cronyism, and corruption.

As the military elite lost support, internal contention tended to arise over whether to stay in power. Notably, the armed forces have a secure professional position and role to retreat to if they give up political control. (Single-party and dominant-party leaderships do not have that option, and thus have more to fear from losing power.[13]) Retiring to the barracks can allow the army to restore its institutional unity after the divisions that arise from running government. Toward the end of military rule in some countries in Africa, for example, the military faction that wanted to stay in power might have been united by little more than its shared desire to continue plundering the country until the end, and to forestall prosecution for its misdeeds (e.g., Nigeria's Abacha regime in the mid-late 1990s). Meanwhile, opposition groups found that they could tap into public discontent and cooperate under the umbrella of a movement for democracy.

The 1980s and early 1990s saw a trend of transition toward at least formal democratic procedures. Where the generals are still in control of the government today, they often prefer to take off their military caps (by formally retiring from the armed forces) before becoming presidents or ministers (e.g., Egypt and Myanmar).

SINGLE-PARTY RULE

Single-party government does not permit other political parties to operate in the system. Its forms in the first half of the twentieth century included, prominently, the totalitarian Fascist and Marxist-Leninist regimes. In the second half of the century, the forms of single-party rule diversified and tended to be authoritarian rather than totalitarian. A major division of single-party authoritarian rule is between (a) the post-totalitarian Communist regimes of the 1960s through the 1980s and (b) the various non-Communist single-party regimes.

The Marxist-Leninist Single-Party Regime

Among single-party authoritarian regimes, at the high end of central control were those in which the ruling party adhered to Marxist-Leninist ideology (see chapter 5). Such regimes were commonly referred to as Communist. Until the fall of Communism in most such nations in 1989–1991, they covered territory from Eastern Europe to East Asia. Mid- to late-twentieth-century African examples that roughly paralleled this model included Benin, Guinea, Congo-Brazzaville, Angola, Zimbabwe, Ethiopia, and Mozambique. In these systems, the state aggressively pursued industrialization and state ownership of productive enterprises.

At least until the death of Soviet leader Joseph Stalin in 1953, Communist regimes employed the full gamut of totalitarian means of dominance, including Communist Party control of the media, education, and culture, and state terror (from detention and imprisonment to death in prison labor camps as in Stalin's purges of the mid-late 1930s). At times, force was used against whole groups of perceived opponents, as in the case of Stalin's post-collectivization use of famine in 1932–1933 to punish the Ukrainians for their prior resistance to collectivization, and the mass deaths in Siberian prison labor camps during the "great purge" of the late 1930s. The regime of Pol Pot emptied Cambodia's cities in the mid-1970s, sending numerous educated Cambodians to their deaths (by murder or malnutrition-related health problems) in remote rural areas. However, following Soviet leader Nikita Khrushchev's policy in the mid-1950s known as "de-Stalinization," the use of totalitarian controls was reduced somewhat in the Soviet-controlled regimes. The Communist Party maintained ideological control of the media, education, and culture, but otherwise the regime settled into authoritarian styles of rule.

In Soviet-type government, the one-party legislative Supreme Soviet was purely ceremonial and held no power. But the regime's executive branch was huge. Every sector of the economy and society had its ministry or state committee in Moscow to run it. At the top was a cabinet with over a hundred members called the Council of Ministers. In addition to the prime minister and two or three first deputy prime ministers, this cabinet included ten deputy prime ministers, sixty-odd ministers, and up to thirty heads of state committees.

The legislative function in this system was performed substantially by the Communist Party. Managers in the executive branch bureaucracy had to be members of the Communist Party, and their units were monitored by parallel units of the Communist Party. At the top of the party's structure was the **politburo**, led by the party general secretary. It functioned as a supervisory board of directors for the regime, in which the top party secretaries (e.g., for the economy, ideology, and party organization) met with the most important ministers to set any new directions for policy to take. In operational management, however, managers followed the directives of the executive branch hierarchy up toward the relevant ministry in Moscow, not the parallel party units.[14]

As we saw in chapter 7, the whole mechanism was supposed to follow "the plan" handed down by the planning ministry. As a network of interdependent monopolies, the system left managers with no alternatives in case of supply-chain failures. Resulting shortfalls could grind their portion of the machine to a halt. Usually reports on problems got passed up the managerial or party hierarchies to be shelved at some higher level, rather than acted on. There was little real incentive for innovation, which would require disruption of enterprise operations and thus failure to satisfy the plan. Especially amid the increased contact with the West that came with "detente" (a reduction of Cold War hostilities in the 1970s and 1980s), growing numbers of Russians became aware that Soviet technology was falling behind that of its western rivals.

Meanwhile, by the 1980s, a steep decline in the price of exported oil deprived the Soviet Union of its main supply of hard currency to keep it and its client states going. This intensified shortages and produced long lines at official stores that contributed to consumer frustration. The bureaucratic-socialist economies were increasingly perceived as failing to "deliver the goods," leaving them few supporters at the ground level when they faced uprisings in 1989–1991.

Among the few remaining regimes governed by Communist parties today (e.g., China, North Korea, Vietnam, Laos, and Cuba), the most significant is China. In China, the Communist single-party authoritarian framework still governs the population, which comprises over 20 percent of the world's population (see Country Case Studies, chapter 3). Economically, however, capitalism is prevalent in the more developed eastern parts of the country, and the central executive bureaucracy is proportionally far smaller than in the old Soviet model. However, numerous state-owned enterprises remain, with special government-supported powers, privileges, subsidies, and access to cheap government-supplied credit.

Non-Communist Single-Party Governments

Non-Communist single-party governments ranged from the Fascist cases of Mussolini's Italy after 1922 and Nazi Germany after 1933, to the single-party regimes of the 1960s and 1970s that emerged from anticolonial national independence movements in Africa and Asia. As we saw in chapter 6, Fascism relied on ideology propagated by the ruling party, but also blended in a strong element of personal leadership by Hitler and Mussolini.[15] (In Italy, the party had an especially reduced profile as Mussolini's regime developed.) In the postcolonial era of the 1960s in the developing world, some of the new nations began with multiparty democracy led by the party that had earlier spearheaded the independence movement. But as policy challenges, public criticism, and intergroup contention intensified, often the leading party banned opposition parties and declared authoritarian one-party rule (see the Zambia Country Case Study, chapter 3).

Characteristics of Non-Communist Single-Party Governments In most of these post–World War II cases, the controlling party's ideology was not very specific, and was not imposed in totalitarian fashion. Rather, the ruling party pursued economic development and sociopolitical cooperation around nationalism and some leading slogan or idea. In Tanzania, for example, regime leader Julius Nyerere talked about adapting traditional African village practices of cooperation and consensus to the task of national development. In parts of Asia such as South Korea, Taiwan, and Singapore, the Confucian theme of guided social harmony (see chapter 4) was stressed.

New governments often followed some variation of the strategy of import substitution industrialization (ISI). Under ISI programs, the state became involved in running and/or subsidizing new industries, protecting them with tariffs, building modern infrastructure, and even (in government-owned "parastatal" organizations) distributing key resources such as food grains, electricity, and transportation. All this ISI-related state activity provided many positions to be filled by the leadership of the dominant party/government. Patron-client networks and related corruption tended to proliferate. Even where the government was rather market oriented, as in Kenya, the Ivory Coast, and Botswana, for example, the government still owned some enterprises and the bureaucracy could be large, partly to maintain clientelistic support.

Leaders of the party in control would staff the cabinet and the rest of the political executive. Typically the party leader also held the governmental title of president, perhaps assisted by a handpicked prime minister to manage the cabinet, following semi-presidential formalities. The president could be the actual leader (on the personal leadership model), or just preside over a collective leadership. Or the president might in effect be only a powerless "front man" for a small group, an informal leader, or a few powerful interests that were most influential behind the scenes. The party might maintain a substantial organizational structure of its own, separate from the government, or instead might be little more than a personalistic vehicle for the leader and the patron-client networks under him (at the extreme, blending with personal dictatorship). Over time the single party often became a classic "government party" (see chapter 10), primarily a vehicle for hanging onto all the perks that attend positions in the government executive, and drumming up participation in the occasional one-party "elections."

Single-party rule might be harsh and dictatorial, as in the Ba'ath party cases of Syria under the leader of the Assad family (now Bashar al-Assad), and Iraq under Saddam Hussein (overthrown in 2003). Or the regime could be much gentler and more inclusive. In the cases of Zambia and Tanzania in East Africa, the single-party regimes invited everyone into the government party, allowing multicandidate legislative elections (to assemblies without real influence) and a degree of intraparty factional contention.

Toward potential rivals, the president often employed **co-optation**— incorporating would-be contenders into the regime's structure by offering party or government positions and other attractive inducements in return for cooperation. Detention or exile might be reserved only for intransigent critics of the regime, partly to set an example for others. In addition, setting up a one-party legislature with contending candidates for seats helped the regime to gain other advantages of the sort noted above under military government: perhaps most importantly, safe arenas for exchange of views among the regime's leadership, more or less supportive groups, and critics (again, within regime-set limits on the scope of permissible criticism of the party and government). This helps the ruling group, its allies, and its critics to better understand each other's intentions and capabilities, and even arrive at compromises that might defuse potentially troublesome issues.[16] Meanwhile, the periodic one-party election campaigns provide occasions for the regime to trumpet the benefits that it delivers to the people and to demonstrate its popular support.[17]

In countries that were socially divided along ethnic, regional, and/or cultural lines, often one ethnic group dominated the top leadership of the ruling party. Its leader would confine the upper rungs of the system to his own trusted ethnic group and its allies, as did Jomo Kenyatta of Kenya's Kikuyu tribe in the 1960s and 1970s. Other groups might be included in a second tier of the system, by co-optation. But open oppositional activity would be greeted with harsh suppression. Because dominance by an ethnic group normally operates through a political party representing it, I classify this pattern as a variant of single-party rule rather than as a separate authoritarian type.

The Decline of Non-Communist Single-Party Governments Of course, all this requires regime access to resources. Such advantages as a growing economy or a lucrative natural resource for export (either via state ownership or royalties from private operators) certainly help fuel the regime's clientelism and its consequent popular support. But in 1970s many African and Asian single-party regimes faced declining export earnings, expensive failures in industrial and infrastructure projects, rising energy costs, weak domestic tax revenues, and thus increasing budget and trade deficits. Unless the regime could get significant international development aid, often it could not pay for spending programs without simply printing money that spurred high rates of inflation.

Ultimately regimes with high debt and deficits could be forced by the IMF to cut their budgets and reduce regulation (see chapter 7). In this situation, contention grew between groups over the dwindling distribution of resources. The top group in the ruling party tended to take care of itself first, with much less left over to keep client groups happy. Lower-level officials who still had their government jobs often found their real incomes greatly reduced by inflation, inviting corruption to bolster income (or many no-show days while scrambling for other opportunities to try to feed their families), further reducing popular support.

Meanwhile, increasingly over the 1980s and 1990s, aid from foreign donors became conditional on steps toward democratization (see chapter 16). These steps in turn allowed dissatisfied groups to apply greater pressure in politics. Here the picture begins to look more like one presented by political scientist Milan Svolik[18]: powerful groups around the single party that appear less like clients of the regime and more like its necessary allies, in a "balance of power" within a dominant coalition. If the contending allies can cooperate sufficiently with each other to oppose the ruling party leadership, the regime could be forced to admit at least the forms of multiparty government. Alternatively, especially if support for the military is jeopardized by resource scarcity, military intervention may be the outcome.[19]

The days of single-party regimes were numbered. Some continued to resist democratization and responded with increased repression (e.g., Moi in Kenya and later Mugabe in Zimbabwe), while most began the journey of democratization that we examine in chapter 16. The former single party might lose power in the first multiparty election, or it might find ways to continue its dominant role despite multiparty elections. Especially if the ruling party thinks it can continue to be dominant after adopting multiparty elections, by constraining the chances of opposition victory in various ways, single-party authoritarian rule may yield to the formalities of democracy without its substance: our next authoritarian regime type.

SINGLE-PARTY-DOMINANT, ELECTORAL AUTHORITARIAN RULE

In single-party-dominant governments with authoritarian characteristics, the dominant party permits multiparty elections, but aggressively disadvantages other contending parties to the point that they are not really competitive in those elections. Thus the dominant party's role tends to bear a strong resemblance to that of the ruling party in a single-party regime.[20] Another useful way of designating this type is "electoral authoritarian."

In these regimes today, presidential or semi-presidential formalities are most common. Typically, a strong president controls a handpicked cabinet. This executive branch is formally independent of a weak legislative branch, whose compliant majority is in the hands of the government party headed by the president. Such governments tend to favor SMDP elections to maximize the dominant party's legislative majority, though an especially dominant party may employ PR elections of the legislature (e.g. Russia).

In these cases, typically the president and his administrative apparatus heavily influence the implementation of projects and programs, economic regulation, licensing, government contracting, and many jobs in government and in state-owned enterprises. These prodigious clientelistic advantages might be enough to assure electoral victory, but in this regime the dominant party takes no chances. For example, any protest demonstrations are broken up by force and their leaders detained. But most importantly, during election campaigns any serious rivals are harassed and denied full freedom of assembly and expression (See Country Case Study on Belarus, chapter 1, and Russia below).

The means of repression are many and varied. The dominant party may use the requirements and procedures for registering parties and candidates either to deny eligibility to viable opponents or to encourage a proliferation of harmless small parties to divide the opposition. Voter registration lists may be manipulated. As the election campaign gets under way, opposition leaders may be imprisoned on spurious charges. The campaigns of vigorous challengers may be denied the permits required to hold rallies (while the activities of small, harmless parties may be left untouched). The media, controlled by the dominant party, typically gives either negative or no coverage to sharply contending parties' events, and opposition press outlets may be intimidated or closed. On election day, ballot boxes may be stuffed or lost, or votes miscounted. On the continuum of political frameworks between the fully democratic and the harshly authoritarian poles, such single-party-dominant regimes have clearly tipped over into authoritarian territory (e.g., the current regimes in Belarus, Russia, and Zimbabwe).

If the resulting legislature is obviously not the result of free and fair elections, in effect the regime is denied the democratic legitimacy that elected assemblies are supposed to confer. So it is fair to ask, what purposes do they serve for the regime? The answer amounts to a richer and more elaborate form of the advantages noted above for a party and legislature under military or single-party rule. First, as political scientist Jennifer Gandhi stresses, subordinate assemblies and elections of them have some direct benefits for the dominant-party leadership such as

- increased knowledge of where opposition may be emerging and what it wants, to better know who to repress or to conciliate with benefits;[21]

- more paid positions for the dominant party to use to co-opt critics or would-be opponents; and

- opportunities for explicit exchange with other groups to give the public the occasional impression of magnanimous compromise by the dominant party.[22]

In addition, subordinate legislative bodies have indirect benefits for the leadership of the regime. Legislative election campaigns help the dominant party and its legislators to manage and bolster the top leadership's relations with its most important allies and its other patronage beneficiaries. The regime does this through communication about goals, conferring clientelistic benefits in return for electoral support (and sometimes penalties for lack of support), and reassuring cooperative allies that they will not be abused by the top regime leaders.[23] In addition, the electoral process demonstrates the overwhelming capacity of the dominant party to mobilize support and suppress any serious opposition, thereby demoralizing and discouraging the latter.[24]

Notably, if a leading party *refrains from* suppressing opponents' efforts, and wins elections repeatedly through such positive advantages as satisfactory policies (e.g., delivering economic growth and development), clientelism, and/or plentiful resources for campaigning, the political framework may be classified as at least minimally democratic. Examples are Botswana's dominant National Democratic Party, and India's Congress Party during its early decades of dominance (1947–1980). Ideologically, such parties often position themselves somewhere toward the center between smaller parties on the left and the right, and come close to being what we call "catchall" government parties.

As we shall see in chapter 16 on democratic transitions, various factors can contribute to the end of the electoral authoritarian regime and its dominant-party harassment and suppression of serious contenders. Among such factors are economic policy challenges, a mass democracy movement that forces free and fair elections, and international pressures. However, the new regime that succeeds it may not be a representative democracy. For example, once the Arab Spring uprising in Egypt in 2011 had removed the prior authoritarian regime, many in secular groups began to worry that the ultimate outcome might be theocracy rather than democracy, and the military stepped in to take power.

THEOCRACY

Theocracy is rule by a religious order of some sort. It is rather rare today, found only in authoritarian form in Iran (after the overthrow of a pro-Western monarchy in 1979), and in totalitarian form in Afghanistan during the years of Taliban rule and in radical Islamist-controlled regions in such countries as Pakistan, Syria, Iraq, Yemen, Somalia, and Libya.[25]

In Iran, the dominant form of Islam is Shia, which is more hierarchical in its religious authority than the Sunni form that is more prevalent among Muslims elsewhere. A few Iranian religious leaders called Ayatollahs have some authority over other imams. Supreme Leader Ayatollah Khamenei controls the Guardian Council, which must approve parliamentary decisions and controls elections and nominations in Iran (see "The Human Rights Connection," chapter 12). The Guardian Council often denies potential candidates the right to run for office and decides who may run for the Assembly of Experts, a body of senior clergymen that is formally the highest ranking one because it chooses the supreme leader. The Iranian government exercises substantial influence over culture and education, and at times practices selective terror against democracy activists. Arbitrary detention and punishment of dissenters was traditionally coordinated through the interior ministry, but today a major force is the Revolutionary Guard Corps, a heavily Islamized sector of the armed forces.

To be sure, there are moderate and extreme factions within the religious elite of Iran. Elected presidents perceived as comparatively moderate have held office as recently as 1997–2005 (Muhammad Khatami) and 2013 to the present (Hassan Rouhani). But they operate under the watchful eye of the supreme leader and within the religious boundaries set by the other units noted above.

While Iran is best described as authoritarian with a few totalitarian traits, recent radical Sunni Islamist regimes imposing strict Sharia law (e.g., Taliban Afghanistan up to 2003 and Islamic State-run sectors of Syria and Iraq today) seem to be fully totalitarian. The Islamic State (IS) has used murder as a policy toward opponents and dissenters from its views, whether Muslim or non-Muslim. IS focuses on holding and administering territory as well as fighting to gain more. For resources, it relies on selling oil and crudely refined oil products, smuggling, kidnapping for ransom, and taxation of commerce. It says that it is ruled by a top "caliph"—a label taken from the heads of the medieval Islamic empires—named Abu Bakr al-Baghdadi. But at the same time, IS remains a fighting force, and former Iraqi Baathist officers play important command roles. Alongside its violent enforcement of strict Sharia law, IS attempts to keep some state services going where possible. Reportedly its officials do not take or demand bribes.

Where theocratic regimes have fallen, the most common determining factor has been military defeat. The Taliban regime in Afghanistan fell to military invasion by the American and British forces in 2003, and radical Islamist forces in Mali and the Central African Republic were removed from power by French intervention in 2012 and 2013.

REVOLUTION

Some of the most prominent authoritarian regimes have met their demise in revolution. We may define a **revolution** as a decisive and thorough replacement of the prior regime that occurs over a limited timeframe, is spurred at least partly by unconventional, contentious participation by some sort of mass movement, and has a major and enduring impact on government and society.

In this definition, the word "decisive" suggests that the regime change sticks; actors from the old regime do not subsequently get power back.[26] By the phrase "limited timeframe" I suggest that while there may have been a long buildup of factors contributing to a revolution (e.g., of modernization in the economy or the government), we can identify an interval of time—usually from a few days or weeks to a few years, in which the struggle was openly fought to its conclusion. Historical examples with fairly short timeframes include the defeat of King James's forces in England and the collapse of his regime in November 1688, the French king's acceptance of the supreme authority of the National Assembly and the storming of the Bastille in June and July 1789, and the defeats of former dictators Fulgencio Batista in Cuba in 1959 and Anastasio Samoza in Nicaragua in 1979.

However, revolutions can take years to play out, especially if a **civil war**—a war between contending forces within a single country—is involved. The initial seizure of power may prompt continued counterrevolutionary efforts that must be overcome for the revolution to succeed. The American revolutionary war continued from 1775 into 1783. After the onset of the revolution in November 1917, the Bolsheviks in Russia had to fight a three-year civil war to assure their hold on power. A few revolutions including civil war have taken quite a while to finish. Arguably the Vietnamese revolution that started during World War II took over a decade to complete in the north, and much longer if we include the southern part of the country.

In other cases, there may be a period of some uncertainty between the removal of the old regime and the establishment of the new power structure that has an enduring impact on society. The Iranian overthrow of the Shah's forces in late January and February of 1979 began nearly a year of political jockeying before Ayatollah Khomeini was able to achieve his referendum supporting an Islamic republic. The Mexican revolution that began in 1910 took over a decade to sort out control, and the first Chinese revolution of 1912 required an even longer period—until the massacre of the urban Communists in 1927—to establish the full dominance of Chiang Kai-shek and his Nationalist (Kuomintang) Party.

Two Contributing Factors: Social Movements and Policy Challenges

While a revolutionary leadership is normally required, a revolution must be propelled substantially by the support of a contentious social movement. To be called a revolution under this definition, the regime replacement cannot arise wholly "from above"—as in a takeover by an elite group. Movements boosting the transformation may be diverse or fairly homogenous, may or may not embrace the majority, and can take various forms. In Russia over the course of 1917, for example, urban protests over World War I's economic privations at home, soldiers abandoning the failed western front, and peasants opposing land inequality and domination by landlords, all played key roles during the ten-month period between the abdication of the czar and the Bolshevik seizure of power. During the subsequent civil war of 1918–1920, ultimately a necessary factor in the Bolshevik victory was large numbers of Russian peasants joining the Red Army (comprising the bulk of its foot-soldiers), due to the land reform that the Bolsheviks pledged and delivered. In the 1989–1991 removal of Communist rule in Eastern Europe and Russia—sometimes portrayed as "revolution from above"—the democracy movements and their mass protest demonstrations were crucial at key junctures in propelling the transformation.

Much discussion about revolutions concerns the political attitudes underlying and boosting the successful social movement. Karl Marx, for his part, stressed economic class and, in the overthrow of capitalism, material distress among workers. Social scientist Ted Gurr emphasized frustration and anger over a sense of relative deprivation.[27] Alexis de Tocqueville pointed to periods of improvement just before the revolution that gave disadvantaged groups their first real hope for economic and social change.[28]

Comparing diverse revolutions, one pervasive factor among these social movements that contribute to revolutions seems to be a concern about values—most often forms of justice[29] and well-being. From anger over the killings and detentions of demonstrators and political opponents (criminal justice) to peasant resentment at handing over half the crop to the landlord at harvest time (social justice or fairness), some sort of response to injustice seems to be at work. Regarding well-being, a common factor is mass insecurity regarding regime failures to handle economic challenges—for example, acute shortages and/or inflation in food and fuel prices. Ultimately the only common thread among the various motivations behind such social movements may be intense preferences that the government more effectively pursue certain values.

In this context, revolution is often sparked by particular policy challenges related to these values, that the regime cannot handle, whether economic, international, or both,[30] such as a failed war (e.g., Russia in 1917), economic crisis, or dramatic examples in the press and social media of rampant corruption or police brutality in the face

Portrayal of a mob of revolutionaries storming the Bastille at the beginning of the French Revolution in July 1789.

of peaceful demonstrations. The chances of revolution increase if the existing regime is perceived as failing to make serious efforts to address the key challenges. This latter condition is more likely if the existing regime has displayed a prior pattern of state weakness and selective clientelism, and has resisted demands for expanded participation.[31]

Organizing a Revolution

A further requirement for a revolution is some sort of organization.[32] For a movement with grievances to arise and actually gain power it must have leadership. But here two phases are relevant: the coordination of the initial onslaught that removes the old regime, and the subsequent consolidation of the new order that ultimately has the impact on society. If at the outset the movement shares little more than concern for key values at a moment of intense distress, the leadership in the first phase only needs to mobilize the movement to feel its outrage or anxiety at events, and take contentious action. But since the first goal is simply limit setting and negative—removing the old regime—the tight coordination and cooperation offered by a single-leadership organization may not be necessary. One group may take the lead, with other groups and their leaderships also contending against the old regime, whether independently or in loose coordination with each other.

However, the contentious social movement's initial success in overturning the prior order is only a first step. Movements sharing value-related concerns are rarely unified regarding what structures and policies they want to install in place of the status quo. The consolidation of the revolution in a new order over subsequent months is another story. Here strong organization is key. If the opposition movement is diverse, but includes a portion with strong organization and vision, including effectiveness in establishing linkages to supportive groups in civil society, it will rise to the top and steer the outcome. Examples are the Bolsheviks building their membership and gaining majorities in the soviet councils in St. Petersburg and Moscow over the course of 1917 in Russia, the Iranian Islamists led by Khomeini outmaneuvering secular groups in 1979, and the Afghan take-over by the Taliban in the late 1990s. Prospects for the leading group's dominance are enhanced if it has an ideological vision and values, articulated by leaders and embraced by followers, to motivate the risk taking, sacrifices, and persistence needed to make and defend the revolution (see "The Philosophical Connection"). This is a key reason why revolutions usually end up replacing one authoritarian regime with another.

When a contentious movement for change lacks a leadership willing and able to cooperate internally and dive into party organization after the overthrow, the would-be revolution may fizzle into unintended outcomes. The Egyptian Arab Spring of 2011 does not qualify as a revolution, not only because it didn't stick (it was reversed in a military coup in 2013), but also because the secular groups that originally spearheaded it failed to cooperate sufficiently to be able to contend effectively against the Islamists.

Consequences for Society

A further requirement for a revolution is that it must have important and enduring *consequences* for politics and society. Here some students of revolutions have contrasted merely "political" revolutions that are focused mostly on replacing the state structure, with more far-reaching "social revolutions" that deeply transform social structure. This is a valid distinction. But as with other such distinctions, there is a continuum between its poles. Revolutions that were primarily political ones, such as the English and American revolutions, did have impact on society. For example, the English Glorious Revolution of 1688 not only established the enduring influence of parliament but also reinforced the ongoing shift toward commercialized agriculture and business, and permanently removed the threat of Catholic religious dominance and the attendant risk of civil war over religion. And the American Revolution reinforced the ongoing American spirit of individualism, meritocratic opportunity, and skepticism toward government. To be sure, slavery remained in the south for more than half a century. But arguably, the rights asserted in the Declaration of Independence and the Bill of Rights planted the seeds of the later "new birth of liberty" (in the words of Abraham Lincoln) that came with the Civil War's abolition of slavery.

However, what we call social revolutions went further, leading to the direct transformation of social structure in ways that the American and English revolutions did not. Clearly in the social revolution territory is the French Revolution of 1789, which not only removed the old monarchy, nobility, and church from political power but also broke up the old landed estates. To be sure, a revolution's full impact on society may take time to play out. Thorough state ownership and control over the economy came to the Soviet Union only in the 1930s, and was established in urban China only in the mid-1950s, in each case several years after the initial overthrow of the prior regime.

SUMMARY: CONTENTION AND COOPERATION IN AUTHORITARIAN REGIMES AND REVOLUTION

In authoritarian regimes, contention and cooperation mostly occurs within the confines of the ruling group and any others that are closely associated with it.

THE PHILOSOPHICAL CONNECTION | Ibn Khaldun

Ibn Khaldun (1332–1406), a Muslim thinker of the middle ages, seemed to suggest that stable governance could persist—at least for a while—if the aristocratic ruling group held tenaciously to a sense of its solidarity and its traditional values. Khaldun saw himself as a student of the rise and fall of states and empires in an era in which trade, cities, and the production of luxuries and wealth were growing in importance. For him, states and empires usually decline eventually due to their ruling groups' attachment to material comforts and status. Facing contention for power, they ultimately succumb to invasion by rustic tribes from the surrounding wilderness. For example, the western Roman Empire fell to the Goths and Vandals, nomadic Arabs conquered the Byzantine and Persian empires, and the Mongols overcame the Islamic civilization of the Middle East.

Khaldun argued that the conquering tribe could maintain its position as long as it kept strong its "group feeling" and hardy vigor from its past life in the wild. Cooperation around its traditional values was key. However, he suggested, such groups tend over time to adopt the habits and pursuits of those whom they conquered. Khaldun was an early student of what is today called microeconomics, noting how profit from the production of new luxuries supported demand for further labor and growing urban populations. The wealth and soft life of luxury offered by the city would win out, and the dominant group would end up raising taxes to support its lifestyle. Taxes would eventually reach a level that discouraged entrepreneurship.

As to government, it was assumed that the tribal group would hold power by force, without any mention of elections. It would recognize at its head a ruling family, as a dynasty. Khaldun observed that the dominant group would become attached to status, borrowed from the nobility of the ruling family. Thus the ruling group would inevitably lose sight of the cohesion and vigor that had originally enabled it to arrive at power. Cooperation would succumb to contention, and a new, vigorous group from the outside would come in and start the cycle all over again.

For Khaldun, the only thing that could avert the tendency to decline would be a religious ideology, which could revitalize and maintain the cohesion of the ruling group. For him, this seemed to be a factor in the expansion and persistence of Islamic civilization in the Middle East and North Africa. Regarding taxation, note that while Islamic teaching affirms private property and inequality, it also requires aiding those in need (zakat). Apparently the early caliphs (Muslim rulers) did impose taxes to provide for the poor. Note that when Khaldun worried about the dominant group raising taxes too high, they were raised to enrich the ruler. Insofar as Muslims disdain ostentatious consumerism, Islam seems to fit Khaldun's idea of a religion that can help strengthen the leading group's position and hinder tendencies toward decline.

Personal autocracy involves dominance by a monarch or a personal dictator. Marxist-Leninist single-party regimes, with their pervasive ideology, were tightly controlled, operating under a plan that came down from above. Noncommunist single-party regimes banned other parties, but typically relied more on clientelism. Single-party-dominant, electoral authoritarian regimes behaved much like single-party ones, but permitted elections in which they harassed and obstructed other parties to keep them weak. Military regimes resulting from coups were typically dominated by a supreme military council professing to assure order in society, and theocratic regimes seek to impose a religious vision on society. In a revolution, such an authoritarian regime is entirely and decisively replaced, a transformation substantially spearheaded by a social movement and resulting in deep and lasting change.

COUNTRY CASE STUDIES

Here we consider two very different cases of authoritarian rule in the last century. Russia has experienced revolution and different types of authoritarian rule over the last century: first single-party Communist and now single-party-dominant, electoral authoritarian. Myanmar (formerly Burma) experienced a long stretch of military rule over the last half century, followed more recently by a military-dominated form of single-party-dominant, electoral authoritarian rule.

Russia: Change in Authoritarian Rule

Prior to the revolution of November 1917, the Russian Empire displayed a monarchy with entrenched authoritarian habits, a dominant landed oligarchy entwined with the army, and no experience with real multiparty contention for power. The new legislative Duma setup in 1906 was weak and ultimately ignored by the monarch, called the czar. Apart from a few pockets of industry and mining, in 1917 the country still largely lacked such modernization factors as widespread industrialization, urbanization, education, and a middle class. Deference to the czar, backed by the Russian Orthodox Church, ran deep and his secret police was aggressive.

At the beginning of 1917, however, the czar's regime fell due to factors such as Russia's disastrous World War I defeats at the hands of the German army on the empire's western border, war-related economic distress including punishing inflation and food and fuel shortages, and ever-growing protest demonstrations in St. Petersburg and Moscow. The provisional government that followed the czar's abdication (resignation) was weak, with no real middle class to rely on. Its PM, Alexander Kerensky, continued to pursue the failing war policy, as numerous soldiers simply abandoned the front and economic conditions at home got worse. By the late summer of 1917, the Bolsheviks, campaigning for "bread and peace" and land to the peasants, proved to be the most successful party in organizing opposition to the government in the new urban councils that they had spearheaded, called the "Soviets." The Bolsheviks' long-time chief was Vladimir I. Lenin, author of a politicized offshoot of Marxism,[33] but its public leader in the key St. Petersburg Soviet was a rapidly rising new entrant to the party, the charismatic Leon Trotsky.

In the fall of 1917, the Bolsheviks seized power and canceled the government's plans for an assembly to write a democratic constitution. To fight what became a three-year civil war, they took over the urban economy, redistributed land to the peasants, rebuilt the railroads, and organized an army under Trotsky's leadership. Peasant families provided most of the foot-soldiers for the Red Army and, less happily, the grain that was confiscated to feed them. Coerced former Czarist army officers led their military training.

After victory in the civil war, the next important point of regime change occurred in the spring and summer of 1921. On the policy side, the Bolsheviks accepted a market economy and free private agriculture to accommodate the peasantry and consolidate their shaky position amid very harsh economic conditions. In politics, a debate within the party over trade union policy led to the removal of the Trotsky-led group that had overseen the seizure of power, the civil war, and the big expansion of the party's membership that accompanied both. The victor (with Lenin's support) was Joseph Stalin, leader of the party's now small portion of pre-1917 Bolsheviks who had been largely sidelined during the war years. By mid-1921, Stalin had de facto control of the party organization, and in 1922 formally took the position of its general secretary. Following Lenin's series of strokes and his death in 1924, Stalin again defeated Trotsky and other leaders politically. Acting under the authority of the "party unity resolution" (spearheaded by Lenin in 1921), Stalin ended the practice of allowing group contention within the party over policy. Everywhere Stalin's people made positions and income in the party and government dependent on political support for him.

By 1930, Stalin was in a position to dictate new policy at will, and he did. The regime removed market coordination in the economy with a huge, centrally planned and controlled industrialization push, employing forced labor. To get the resources for this, Stalin forcibly "collectivized" peasant agriculture to get food for the cities at very low cost. The resulting "command economy" was run by Stalin as prime minister and his other ministers in Moscow. By 1935, the regime had made big industrial gains, but they were accompanied by much hardship and grumbling. Stalin's answer in the mid to late 1930s was his Great Purge, which added state terror to the totalitarian mix. He used the secret police to arrest all former rivals and their followers, anyone else who had ever shown independent thought, and many more, sending them to prison labor in the most challenging projects in Siberia, referred to by historians as "the Gulag."

Under the worst imaginable conditions of cold, malnutrition, and lack of medical care in Siberia, the average survival period for the millions in the gulag was little more than a year. Thus a continuing supply of new victims was required to handle the attrition and keep the projects going. (Back home, the managerial ranks were replenished with new trainees from technical institutes who knew little of politics other than obedience.) The loss of most military officers to the purges contributed to the Soviet Union's early lack of preparedness and defeats in World War II. But the ultimate victory over Germany (including conquest of Eastern Europe) only bolstered Stalin's confidence in his methods. Change could come only with Stalin's death, which occurred in 1953.

Stalin's replacement as general secretary, Nikita Khrushchev, ended systematic state terror and largely allowed freedom of private speech (though public speech and publication continued to be supervised by the party). Khrushchev also rebuilt the Communist party organization, which had been decimated by Stalin's purges. The party was to help monitor the economy and suggest new initiatives.[34] Under Khrushchev's successor in 1964, Leonid Brezhnev, the soviet party-state system was expanded and deepened. Eventually, the cabinet, called the Council of Ministers, contained more than a hundred ministers, chairpersons of inter-ministerial state committees, and other officials.

As we have seen, however, the centralized bureaucratic-socialist economy was encountering mounting problems by the mid-1980s[35]: the central plan's implicit discouragement of innovation, the lack of alternatives for enterprises (under the monopoly conditions) when supply-chain breakdowns occurred, shortages of consumer goods amid the priority of heavy industry and the military, the 1980s' decline in the price of Russia's most lucrative export, oil, and three deaths of elderly general secretaries (by natural causes) in quick succession.

Finally a younger man, Mikhail Gorbachev, was chosen as general secretary to try to address these problems. First, his 1987 policy of *glasnost* ("opening"), actually instituted free speech—both public and private—and freedom of association in Russia. But his contemporaneous proposal of *perestroika* ("restructuring") made little real progress in incorporating market elements such as competition and private property into the economy. And its new political institutions (e.g., the Congress of People's Deputies with competitive two-candidate SMD elections) operated under conditions that allowed the party traditionalists to retain overall control of the Soviet Union. By the late summer of 1990, the traditionalists, spearheaded by the security-related sectors of the party and government, had basically shut down *perestroika*.

Nonetheless, real regime change was to come in 1991. In the Baltic republic of Lithuania, the traditionalists overplayed their hand. A paramilitary attempt to shut down the region's new institutions was defeated by mass peaceful resistance in February. Next, a springtime coal miners' strike in Russia led to loss of overall Soviet jurisdiction over that crucial energy resource, in favor of its control by the government of the Russian Republic. That government was led at the time by a well-known reformer who had quit the party, Boris Yeltsin. In July 1991, Yeltsin won the first presidential election in the Russian Republic, which comprised the bulk of the Soviet Union. By then the traditionalists were back on their heels and worried.

Finally in August, traditionalists attempted a coup to dissolve the new institutional structure throughout the Soviet Union in favor of rule by "committees of national salvation." This clumsy effort received cooperation by the bulk of the Soviet executive structure and the Communist Party, but within days was defeated by mass popular resistance in Moscow and Leningrad (formerly St. Petersburg). With most of the Soviet Union government implicated in the failed coup, the Yeltsin-led Russian republic government took over. By the end of 1991, the Union had been disbanded, its component republics became independent nations, and President Yeltsin temporarily banned the

Communist Party due to its widespread cooperation with the failed coup attempt.

The dramatic collapse of the Communist-run Soviet government seemed much like democratization by sudden rupture (see chapter 16). But beneath the surface were many elements of a step-by-step transition. First, Russia did not have to come up with a whole new system right away; the removal of the old Soviet overlay left in place, in each republic, its own Congress of Peoples' Deputies (in the Russian republic, with 1000 members), elected president, and bureaucracy. But while these institutions provided transitional stability, they had developed under the previous system without clear rules adapted to real representative democracy, and were mostly populated by former Communists who had merely dropped their party affiliation. In 1992, Russian president Yeltsin vigorously asserted presidential power to move toward a market economy, with measures such as price deregulation and gradual privatization. However, legal uncertainty, the presence of many traditionalists in the holdover Russian Congress of Peoples' Deputies, and public suffering from high inflation and economic decline, all contributed to sharp contention over Yeltsin's policies. Impatient to move economic reform faster, in 1993 Yeltsin got a favorable referendum result on his policies, disbanded Russia's holdover Congress of Peoples' Deputies, and quickly appointed a commission to write a new constitution. The voters ratified the constitution at the time of the first parliamentary election under it, at the end of the year.

The new system was multiparty semi-presidential (formally similar to France[36]). The directly elected president nominated a prime minister, who must be approved by the lower house of parliament, the State Duma. But the Yeltsin constitution gave the Russian president stronger powers than the French one had, including presidential rights (a) to dissolve the parliament and call new elections if the Duma repeatedly rejects the president's PM nominee, and (b) to rule by decree subject only to a two-thirds legislative veto.

The Duma was elected half by SMD and half by PR (with a 5 percent party threshold), producing at least six significant parties.[37] But apart from the Communists (reregistered in 1993), the other parties were largely undisciplined and poorly organized. They had voting support only in certain localities, and had difficulty forming majority coalitions with each other. Yeltsin's own party, Our Home is Russia, typically got only 10–15 percent of the votes and seats. Nonetheless, Yeltsin was usually able to get the PM he wanted, and with some negotiation and compromise, to get some of his policies through. Only during part of 1998, amid a financial crisis, did Yeltsin face an opposition majority in the Duma and have to temporarily live with a PM that he did not want (a leader of the Fatherland-All Russia Party, or FAR).

Yeltsin was able to keep his position and get reelected in 1996 despite a long list of problems. These included deep public mistrust over corruption in the privatization process and the rise of oligarchs (newly rich private entrepreneurs) who contributed to the president's campaign, Yeltsin's own shaky health, a bad economy with low prices for Russia's oil exports and deteriorating government finances, weakening central power over Russia's regional governments, and a Muslim insurgency in the region of Chechnya.

In 2000, however, came Russia's exit from democratic transition. In 1999 Yeltsin picked from obscurity a new PM, Vladimir Putin. His background was in intelligence and security, but he displayed strong public relations skills and a much more effective political operation (drawing heavily on his old secret police comrades) than had Yeltsin. While PM in 1999, Putin and his staff organized a new, seemingly centrist and nationalist party called Unity, which was remarkably successful in the parliamentary elections late that year. When Yeltsin resigned at the end of 1999 (citing ill health), he was succeeded by the PM (according to the constitution), Putin. As the incumbent, Putin then won the presidential election in early 2000 with the help of criminal accusations and media attacks directed against his main opponent, the popular mayor of Moscow, Yuri Luzhkin of FAR (who ended up quitting the race a few weeks before election day).

Subsequently, Putin got FAR to merge with Unity in a new dominant party, United Russia (UR). Instead of two large and moderate parties, now there was only one. Since then, Putin has reliably (a) used his control of the prosecutors and courts to effectively destroy any would-be serious rival (along with the rival's financial backers, often with obscure tax-related prosecutions), (b) used the government's control of the media to back up his judicial attacks, and (c) employed the security apparatus to arrest and detain critics. The lack of an independent judiciary and the absence a free press contribute substantially to the authoritarian nature of Russia's current single-party-dominant, electoral authoritarian regime. Putin used UR's majority in parliament to pass changes in the electoral rules (e.g., increasing the PR threshold to an astronomically high 7 percent) that serve to eliminate or disable any new parties that might seriously contend with UR.

Putin is perceived as bringing stability and economic gains to Russia after the hardships and seeming disorder of the 1990s. He benefited politically from a turnaround in government finances that resulted from steadily rising world-market prices in the 2000s for Russia's huge oil exports. Putin used new laws and bureaucratic structures to assert central control over the regions, and in 2005 he abolished the election of regional governors in favor of de facto presidential appointment. Putin won the support of many nationalists by brutally suppressing the insurgency in the rebellious Muslim region of Chechnya, and by blocking foreign ownership in key resources. He has reasserted the government's majority ownership in such sectors as oil, gas, minerals, and manufacturing of cars, aircraft, and armaments. Regarding aid for the poor, Putin has removed the old direct subsidies for housing, transportation, etc. in favor of a single monetary subsidy, a move sharply opposed by the Communist Party. Again, Russia's democratic transition has failed, yielding a single-party-dominant, electoral authoritarian regime.

To be sure, the regime faces challenges. Most importantly, the mid-2010s drop in the price of oil imposed budgetary stress on the government and recession on the economy, and a Putin ally was expelled from control of neighboring Ukraine. While intervening with troops and equipment in Eastern Ukraine and annexing its province of Crimea (bringing Western economic sanctions and further economic stress on Russia), however, Putin mounted an intense campaign of nationalism and militarization of the country. These moves were followed in 2015 by heavy Russian air attacks in Syria, mostly to defend the hard-pressed government of Putin's ally Bashar al-Assad. As yet, Puntin's domestic dominance remains unchallenged.

Myanmar: Colonial, Then Military, Now Under Challenge

Myanmar's national boundaries are largely a product of British colonial boundary drawing. A core area is dominated by ethnic Burmans, who make up two-thirds of the country's population, surrounded by less-populated regions of other ethnicities (e.g., the Shan, Karen, Chin, Mon, and Kachin people) that speak other languages and were independent before the colonial era that began in 1824. The military governments that have run Myanmar for the last half century have clung to control of the non-Burman periphery, while suppressing and excluding the other ethnicities. This policy has led to frontier rebellions and human rights infringements, as some groups have been driven from their lands into internal displacement or external exile.

After gaining independence in 1948, Burma (the country's name before it was changed to Myanmar in 1989) was governed by a British-style parliamentary system. The independence-leading party, led by Prime Minister U Nu, was dominant until factional division split it up in 1958. Burma's top military commander, Ne Win, then took over until civilian rule returned in 1960. But amid growing intergroup tensions and security challenges, in 1962 General Ne Win led a formal military coup, this time to stay. The military's governing Revolutionary Council nationalized privately owned enterprises and set up a supporting political party, the Burma Socialist Program Party (BSPP). Ne Win served as both party chair and state president. Pro-democracy protests arose in the mid-1970s, but were brutally suppressed. A new constitution and legislative assembly in 1974 made little real difference, as it was fully under BSPP (and military junta) control. In 1981, Ne Win handed over the presidency but kept the party chairmanship, and thus overall dominance.

In 1988–1990, however (a high water-mark period for democratization around the world), there was a new rise in pro-democracy activity in Myanmar. In 1988, a new round of protest began, first by students and then by much larger numbers in Yangon (formerly Rangoon), the capital. After first reshuffling associates of Ne Win in top leadership positions, the military again formally took over. It renamed its junta the State Law and Order Restoration Council (SLORC), and violently suppressed the protests. Clearly, the cabinet was subordinate to SLORC.

But despite this, the regime then seemed to turn to allowing a transition to democracy. SLORC renamed its support party the National Unity Party (NUP), and in 1989 a multiparty election campaign began, aimed at a legislative assembly vote in 1990. A leading opposition party emerged, the National League for Democracy (NLD). The party was led by a former U.N.

official, Aung Sang Suu Kyi (the daughter of Aung San, leader of the Burmese independence movement until his assassination in 1947). In the May 1990 election, the NLD swept to a huge victory, winning four-fifths of the seats.

In fact, however, all was not well with democracy in Myanmar. Suu Kyi had been held in house arrest since mid-1989, and SLORC declared that the new legislature would not be seated until a new constitution was drawn up, which, not surprisingly, would be long in coming. In effect, the election that had revealed such broad antimilitary and pro-democracy support was nullified. When Suu Kyi received the Nobel Peace Prize in 1991 and demonstrators protested her continued detention, they were suppressed with mass arrests. In 1992, Than Shwe took over the posts of SLORC chair and PM, and subsequently a new military-support vehicle was organized, the Union Solidarity and Development Association (USDA). Over the following years, opposition parties were de-registered, numerous NLD activists were imprisoned (though Suu Kyi was released in 1995), and the army drove dissident ethnic rebel forces out of the frontier areas. In 1997, the junta renamed itself the State Peace and Development Council (SPDC) and, once more, reshuffled the cabinet.

The 2000s in Myanmar saw more stops and starts for democratization. In 2001, after a decade of spreading economic boycotts of Burmese goods by Western retailers, again the regime loosened political controls a bit. It allowed the NLD to set up offices throughout the country. But in 2002, the regime resumed the house arrest of Suu Kyi, and by 2004 had resumed its suppression of the NLD. When fuel price increases in 2007 sparked mass protests led by Buddhist monks, they were again suppressed violently, with thirteen deaths and thousands of arrests.

In 2008, though, again under pressure from international economic and U.N. sanctions, the regime announced, and secured referendum approval for, a new constitution in which it allowed an elected parliament (while reserving 25 percent of the parliamentary seats for military appointment). But in its first election campaign in 2010, Suu Kyi remained under house arrest. Rejecting this and other detentions of NLD activists, and demanding democratic reforms, the NLD leadership chose to boycott the election. The military had formally turned its supporting USDA into a political party, the USDP, which without competition from the NLD, won over three-fourths of the seats. But irregularities were widespread and Western observers proclaimed

the election to be fraudulent. Nonetheless, the lower house proceeded to choose a civilian prime minister and cabinet—composed primarily of retired generals. The regime had become a single-party-dominant, electoral authoritarian one, with the military still the dominant influence behind the scenes.

Starting in 2011, however, a real change in the style of military dominance seemed to have occurred. Long-time junta chief Than Shwe was replaced as president by his most recent PM, Thein Sein. By the time of the by-elections (to fill legislative vacancies) of April 2012, Suu Kyi had been released from house arrest, and the NLD was reregistered and allowed to contend freely. It won 43 of the 44 seats that it contested (out of 46 in all—one of them by Suu Kyi herself), foreshadowing NLD victory in any future free and fair election. The cabinet was reshuffled to replace several hardliners with figures more open to reform.

However, the cabinet remained full of former generals. By 2014, the military and its USDP were pushing Buddhist nationalism (amid anti-Muslim riots), and cracking down on minority ethnic nationalities, especially the Muslim Rohingyas of Rakhine state who became refugees in large numbers. But by 2015, factional contention had broken out within the dominant military-supporting party, the USDP. President Thein Sein, seemingly favoring a slow and reluctant transition to democracy, faced a rival, another former general, Shwe Mann, USDP chairman and speaker of the lower house of parliament. Shwe Mann seemed to support more rapid democratization; he maintained contacts with Suu Kyi, favored a change in the constitution to alter the military appointment of a quarter of parliament, and seemed to have opposed having large numbers of former officers run for parliament under the USDP banner. In August, the president finally used police to oust Shwe Mann from his party post, seemingly assuring that the USDP would be running in the November elections as a solidly military-supporting party.

However, neither this imposed party cooperation nor the pro-Buddhist nationalism campaign proved to be of help to the USDP in the November 2015 parliamentary elections. The contest was allowed to be free and fair overall, and the NLD won roughly 80 percent of the vote and 60 percent of the seats. (To be sure, back in 1993 the military had refused to recognize a big NLD victory in a parliamentary election, but in 2012 international sanctions against Myanmar had been suspended only on condition that democratic transition proceed.) The NLD's parliamentary strength is enough to allow it to choose the president but not enough to amend the constitution (which has 20 percent of parliament appointed by the military). According to the constitution, Suu Kyi is barred from serving as president (since her late husband was not a citizen), but as party leader she will likely be the main influence over an NLD president and the party's parliamentary majority. Nonetheless, the military retains special powers in security policy, and thus will likely continue to claim some cabinet seats. As you can see, transition away from military rule need not be either swift or sure.

◀ PRACTICE AND REVIEW ONLINE

CRITICAL THINKING QUESTIONS

1. How might personal autocracy blend with military rule?

2. How might the triggering factors behind a military coup (for example, see Concept in Context: Military Coup Triggers in Chile) affect the sort of military regime that ensues?

3. What similarities exist between Marxist-Leninist single-party rule and theocracy? What are the biggest differences between the two?

4. Why have some authoritarian regimes fallen to revolution?

KEY TERMS

single-party-dominant, electoral authoritarian rule, 445
personal autocracy, 445
traditional monarchy, 445
personal dictatorship, 446
dictator's dilemma, 446
military coup, 447
junta, 451
bureaucratic authoritarian, 451
politburo, 455
co-optation, 457
revolution, 461
civil war, 461

FURTHER READING

Ayittey, George B. *Defeating Dictators: Fighting Tyranny in Africa and Around the World*. New York: Palgrave, 2012.

Brownlee, Jason. *Authoritarianism in an Age of Democratization*. Cambridge, UK: Cambridge University Press, 2007.

Gandhi, Jennifer. *Political Institutions under Dictatorship*. Cambridge, UK: Cambridge University Press, 2008.

Goodwin, Jeff. *No Other Way Out: States and Revolutionary Movements, 1945–1991*. Cambridge, UK: Cambridge University Press, 2001.

Gurr, Ted. *Why Men Rebel*. Princeton, NJ: Princeton University Press, 1970.

Levitsky, Steven, and Lucan Way. *Competitive Authoritarianism: Hybrid Regimes after the Cold War*. New York: Cambridge University Press, 2010.

Linz, Juan. *Totalitarian and Authoritarian Regimes*. Boulder, CO: Lynne Rienner, 2000.

Sanderson, Stephen K. *Revolutions: A Worldwide Introduction to Political and Social Change*. Boulder, CO: Paradigm Publishers, 2005.

Shedler, Andreas, ed. *Electoral Authoritarianism: The Dynamics of Unfree Competition*. Boulder, CO: Lynne Rienner, 2006.

Skocpol, Theda. *States and Social Revolutions: A Comparative Analysis of France, Russia, and China*. New York and Cambridge, UK: Cambridge University Press, 1979.

Svolik, Milan W. *The Politics of Authoritarian Rule*. Cambridge, UK: Cambridge University Press, 2012.

Wintrobe, Ronald. *The Political Economy of Dictatorship*. Cambridge, UK: Cambridge University Press, 1998.

NOTES

[1] See Juan J. Linz, *Totalitarian and Authoritarian Regimes* (Boulder, CO: Lynne Rienner Publishers, 2000).

[2] This is the sort of approach taken by, for example, political scientist Barbara Geddes; see "What do We Know about Democratization after Twenty Years?" *Annual Review of Political Science* 2 (1999): 115–44.

[3] In Spain in the mid-1970s, the king moderated tensions in the transition to democracy; in Nepal in early 2005, the king temporarily took back control of government to fight a Maoist rebellion; and in Thailand in 2014, the king lent support to the Bangkok elite in its fight against the elected government, which resulted in a military coup.

[4] This is the category of political framework that Linz termed "Sultanistic." See H. E. Chehabi and Juan J. Linz, eds., *Sultanistic Regimes* (Baltimore: Johns Hopkins University Press, 1998).

[5] See Erica Frantz and Natasha Ezrow, *The Politics of Dictatorship: Institutions and Outcomes in Authoritarian Regimes* (Boulder, CO: Lynne Rienner, 2008).

[6] See Ronald Wintrobe, *The Political Economy of Dictatorship* (Cambridge, UK: Cambridge University Press, 1998).

[7] See Eric A. Nordlinger, *Soldiers in Politics: Military Coups and Governments* (Englewood Cliffs, NJ: Prentice-Hall, 1977).

[8] Much of the comparative research into military rule during this period focused on Latin America; see Alfred Stapan, *Rethinking Military Politics: Brazil and the Southern Cone* (Princeton, NJ: Princeton University Press, 1988).

[9] See *The Military in Politics: Changing Patterns in Brazil* (Princeton, NJ: Princeton University Press, 1971).

[10] See *Modernization and Bureaucratic Authoritarianism* (Berkeley, CA: University of California Institute for International Studies, 1973).

[11] This approach has been taken by political scientist Barbara Geddes, who stresses division within authoritarian regimes; see *Paradigms and Sand Castles: Theory Building and Research Design in Comparative Politics* (Ann Arbor: University of Michigan Press, 2003) and "Military Rule," *Annual Review of Political Science* 17 (2014): 147–62.

[12] See Jennifer Gandhi, *Political Institutions under Dictatorship* (Cambridge, UK: Cambridge University Press, 2008).

[13] See Barbara Geddes (1999; note 2 above).

[14] See Jerry F. Hough and Merle Fainsod, *How the Soviet Union is Governed* (Cambridge, MA: Harvard University Press, 1979).

[15] See Country Case Studies, chapter 5.

[16] See Gandhi (2008).

[17] See two conference papers by Barbara Geddes: "Why Parties and Elections in Authoritarian Regimes" (Washington, DC: Annual meeting of the American Political Science Association, 2006) and "Party Creation as an Autocratic Survival Strategy" (Princeton, NJ: Princeton

University conference on Dictatorships: Their Governance and Social Consequences, 2008).

[18] See Milan Swolik, *The Politics of Authoritarian Rule* (Cambridge, UK: Cambridge University Press, 2012).

[19] The risk of military intervention is stressed by Geddes (2006, 2008; see note 13 above).

[20] For the influence of prior authoritarian rule on attempts to establish democracy, see Gretchen Casper, *Fragile Democracies: the Legacies of Authoritarian rule* (Pittsburgh: University of Pittsburgh Press, 1995).

[21] See Beatriz Magaloni, "Credible Power-Sharing and the Longevity of Authoritarian Rule," *Comparative Political Studies* 41, no. 4–5 (April 2008): 715–41.

[22] See Gandhi (2008), note 7 above.

[23] See note 18 above.

[24] See Magaloni (2008), note 17 above.

[25] For the complex relationship of Islam to democracy, see Larry Diamond, Marc F. Plattner, and Daniel Brumberg, eds., *Islam and Democracy in the Middle East* (Baltimore: Johns Hopkins University Press, 2003).

[26] This is why at this writing it remains problematic to refer to the Egyptian Revolution of 2011; in the subsequent three years, power twice reverted to the military, which was a mainstay of the old regime.

[27] See *Why Men Rebel* (Princeton, NJ: Princeton University Press, 1970).

[28] See Alexis de Tocqueville, *The Ancient Regime and the French Revolution*, trans. Arthur Goldhammer, ed. with introduction by Jon Elster (New York, NY: Cambridge University Press, 2011).

[29] See Charles Tilly, *From Mobilization to Revolution* (New York: McGraw Hill, 1978).

[30] See Theda Skocpol, *States and Social Revolutions: A Comparative Analysis of France, Russia, and China* (New York: Cambridge University Press, 1979).

[31] See Jeff Goodwin, *No Other Way Out: States and Revolutionary Movements, 1945–1991* (Cambridge, UK: Cambridge University Press, 2001).

[32] This was stressed by Tilly (1978).

[33] See section on Marxism-Leninism in chapter 5.

[34] See also chapter 6.

[35] See chapters 6 and 13.

[36] See chapter 13.

[37] These included an aggressively pro-market party called Union of Right Forces, a more moderate pro-market one called Yabloko, the above-mentioned Yeltsin-supporting centrist group called Our Home Is Russia, a more oppositional center-left party called Fatherland-All Russia (FAR), the reregistered Communist Party further to the left, and a pro-Russian ethnic ultranationalist party named (misleadingly) the "Liberal Democratic Party."

Democratization

FOCUS QUESTIONS

- **WHAT** are the main types of democratic transitions?

- **WHAT** roles might economic developments play in the initiation of democratic transition? In the prospects for the democracy taking hold and lasting?

- **HOW** might experience with political contention prior to democratization affect the prospects for democratic survival?

- **WHAT** sorts of political parties contribute to transitions to democracy?

- **HOW** might democratic transitions break down?

IN AUGUST 1991, at the time of the fall of Communism in Russia, Ukraine declared its independence and proceeded toward democratization. Would we see democratic **consolidation**—representative democracy taking hold and persisting—in Ukraine, as it did subsequently in Poland and the Czech Republic, for example, or would it succumb to single-party-dominant, electoral authoritarian rule, as it had in Russia, Belarus, and several other former Soviet republics?

The new nation was divided. Most western and central Ukrainians were attracted to Europe and the EU, while many in eastern Ukraine, with its heavy industry, strong ethnic Russian minority, and widespread use of the Russian language, looked to its historical ties to Russia and the Russian economy. And during the 1990s, economic policy contention arose mainly between traditionalists, who favored continued heavy state involvement in the economy, and economic reformers, who wanted to pursue privatization and a market economy. In other ways, too, democratization in Ukraine is not a simple transformation. A good way to start an examination of democratization is to get a feel for the complexity of the raw events in this one case.

By the last half of the 1990s, a reform-oriented coalition had largely won out in Ukraine, by maintaining cooperation between (a) economic and political reformers, (b) the new economic oligarchs who had gained control over former state enterprises, and (c) the leader of the informal coalition, President Leonid Kuchma, whose strongest support came from eastern Russian-leaning Ukraine, and who at the time tended to follow the policies of reform-leaning Russian president Boris Yeltsin. But at the end of the decade, this coalition started to break down when the oligarchs opposed further reform. By mid-2001, Kuchma had dismissed two prominent market reformers—deputy prime minister Yulia Tymoshenko and prime minister Viktor Yushchenko—from the cabinet. The newly appointed prime minister, Viktor Yanukovich from eastern Ukraine, led the broad Party of Regions, which favored closer economic ties to Russia, which under its new president, Vladimir Putin, was turning away from reform.

However, opposition to Yanukovich remained vigorous in the legislative assembly, the 450-member Supreme Council (SC). In 2004, after the announcement of a Yanukovich victory in presidential elections apparently marred by irregularities and fraud, the Supreme Council ordered a revote. In what came to be called the Orange Revolution, reformer Yushchenko won the revote and he appointed Tymoshenko as prime minister. The forces of democracy and economic reform seemed to have won. Legislative elections were changed from a mixture of half the SC seats elected by SMD and half by PR voting, to all party-list proportional. If the two reform-oriented leaders—Yushchenko and Tymoshenko—and their parties and allies had been able to cooperate, the consolidation of democracy might have begun at that point.

However, Ukraine's semi-presidential system seemed to invite a power struggle between the president and prime minister. Constitutional changes had given the SC majority the power of approval and dismissal of cabinet ministers beyond the PM (except for the foreign and defense ministers). By the end of 2005, Yushchenko had dismissed Tymoshenko. Having thus lost the support of her party and allies in the SC, Yushchenko needed to rely on the Yanukovich-led Party of Regions to install a new prime minister. The next two years saw a tug of war and see-sawing back and forth in legislative elections and coalition formation in the SC. When the two reformers could compromise and cooperate, they could win the SC majority; when they could not—which was most of the time—they would lose the majority.

In 2010, Yanukovych won a disputed presidential election over Tymoshenko. By then in a stronger position in the SC, he was able to regain presidential appointment of the cabinet, and get permission for individual SC members to ignore party discipline in approving PMs. Yanukovich began suppressing opponents (often by judicial prosecutions) in a manner that resembled the authoritarian governing style of Russian leader Vladimir Putin. Tymoshenko and others were imprisoned.

In 2014, Yanukovich reversed his earlier outreach toward Europe, and employed violence to suppress demonstrations protesting this reversal. Consequently, he lost some of his Party of Regions support in the SC, and was removed from the presidency by the SC for allegedly having ordered the violence against protesters. The Donetsk and Luhansk regions in the east rebelled (with help from troops and weapons from Russia), and the war continues. The only bright side for democratization is the fact that the main authoritarian party and leader have been removed, and a new president, Petro Poroshenko, has been elected in what appears to have been a free and fair election in 2014. The message is, democratization can be a matter of twists and turns.

CONCEPTIONS OF DEMOCRATIZATION

Most regime changes that removed authoritarian governments during the twentieth century were *not* referred to as revolutions. They primarily affected the political system, tended to occur over more indefinite timeframes, normally involved at least an attempt to transition to democracy, and were sometimes reversed or changed. Political scientist Samuel Huntington has grouped transitions to representative democracy into three historical waves: those that occurred (a) roughly pre–World War II, (b) between 1945 and the mid-1970s, and (c) from then to the present.[1] But in classifying transitions to democracy, political scientists have also made distinctions among transitions to democracy that cut across these waves.

The discussion below begins with the ways in which democratization has been broadly conceptualized, and then focuses on some causal factors that have affected democratic transitions in all three waves. We may first distinguish between democratic transitions that occur fairly rapidly, over a period of weeks to a few months, and those that are more drawn out—perhaps taking years—and involve groups jockeying for influence, with more or less temporary agreements among them along the way.

Rupture

Democratization took center stage with the sudden fall of numerous authoritarian regimes in the 1980s and 1990s, in both the developing world and the former Soviet bloc. For many observers, a simplified picture of democratic transition emerged: what some have called the **rupture** model. First, the authoritarian regime is confronted by one or more unmet challenges such as those noted in chapter 15 (e.g, economic downturn, socioeconomic tension, international crisis, or ethnic-regional or religious conflict) at a time when modernization has awakened new social groups. The authoritarian political elite faces mass protests demanding democracy and is forced to yield, retaining little influence over what comes next. Democracy movement leaders get together to sketch the contours of the new democratic regime, elections are held, and democracy proceeds. Examples of this pattern were the removals of the German imperial government in 1918–1919, of the remains of the Salazar regime in Portugal in 1974, of military rule in Argentina in 1983, of the Marcos dictatorship in the Philippines in 1986, and of Communist rule in Czechoslovakia in 1989. Indeed, mass popular protest has certainly been a common causal factor in initiating democratic transitions.

However, even in these cases, unconventional mass contention was often not the only factor. In Eastern Europe in 1989, for example, Gorbachev's announcement that the Soviet Union would not intervene militarily in Eastern Europe in response to the uprisings was certainly important. And notably, some transitions that began with rupture have not ended in genuine representative democracy.

Some scholars have distinguished the transition period as the interval from the first protests up to the first national election. After that, the new democracy could be viewed as engaged in consolidation (e.g., with the stronger institutionalization of political parties and legislative rules). However, important turning points could come within each of these two periods, including interruptions in the trajectory of democratization. As we shall see below, some factors affecting democratization may intervene almost anytime from the start of the transition—which we shall call "transition initiation"—to the endpoint of full consolidation that is desired by many participants. Empirically, democratization seems more like a train trip toward a destination. You can get off at an intermediate stop and take an excursion to check out the countryside. You may settle in somewhere offtrack, or end up going backward, perhaps eventually getting back on the train at a station that you had already passed in your journey. As the old baseball saying goes, the game "isn't over until it's over."

Advantaged Groups and Pacts

Most transitions to democracy are more complex than the rupture model indicates. They proceed in stages, perhaps including multiple elections that take different forms. In the process, groups associated with the former elite may exert continuing influence over the transition process, alongside more bottom-up influence by groups in civil society.

This step-by-step picture of democratic transition views it as punctuated and guided by formal or informal **pacts** among traditional elite groups and democracy supporters. These agreements often protect the prior elites in important ways as democratization proceeds, giving them enough of a sense of security, trust, and confidence in the process to enable further procedural cooperation among the contending groups. In transitions away from military rule, for example, members of the armed forces might receive amnesty for their prior repressive activities, protection of the military's future autonomy, control over certain security-related policy areas, and special enhancements of the electoral chances of the military-supporting party.

For example, in 1974, the Brazilian military government began a slow democratic transition led by elite groups in power. The first step was a degree of liberalization of authoritarian politics (as in "classical liberal"), loosening controls on political expression and association. Under General Ernesto Geisel's presidency in the mid-1970s, the new policy of "decompressao" reduced the frequency of detention and torture, and permitted a pro-democracy political movement to organize and compete for office. However, this limited political competition arose under a manipulated political framework in which the military-supporting party, ARENA, was assured of retaining the leading positions in government. In this phase, opposition groups that otherwise would be contending with each other had no choice but to cooperate in a single democracy-supporting coalition. They had to go along with whatever arrangements for participation were on offer. It was not until 1979 that full freedom of expression and association returned to Brazil with the end of political detention and the safe return of exiles. Civilian government came officially only with the selection of a civilian president (by an Electoral College) in 1985 and free and fair legislative elections in 1986.

Other prominent elites might also receive assurances, such as of the protection of the property of businesses and landowners. Some assurances concerned economic policy. Many transitions took place in the 1980s and 1990s, after the developing world's debt crisis had forced many governments to rely more heavily on taxing their domestic private economies to raise revenue. At this time, some free-market-oriented elite groups (including the IMF) were able to exercise limit-setting influence on these democratizing nations, rolling back earlier ISI-style government spending and tariffs.

A focus on pacts in the study of democratic transitions tends to highlight a style of analysis called **agency theory**: an explanatory approach that emphasizes the strategies, policy preferences, and decisions of leaders of elite groups and parties seeking to protect or further their interests in democratic transitions. Factions, splits, and contention within the previously dominant elites tend to play key roles in transition negotiations.[2] In this process, a regime's **softliners**—those who are more flexible and willing to deal with challengers—often help to moderate the regime's **hardliners** (those who are less flexible). The softliners bargain with pro-democracy reformers who, in turn, helped to moderate the movement's advocates of radical rupture. Even where official pacts did not result, informal provisional ones might play key roles in facilitating cooperation among contending groups. These sorts of transitions present much less of an impression of mass contentious politics and rupture (see "Applying the Models").

Pacts at various points reflected different degrees and kinds of bargaining leverage and influence in the hands of elites and challengers in different situations. Some of the assurances that informal pacts provided to elite groups proved to be only short term; they could be overturned by subsequent events that rendered the early assurances unrealistic or unnecessary.

In these sequences, a mid-transition election could have an impact. On one hand, the first election outcome might serve to demonstrate to elites that the voters could be trusted to be moderate in their choices (e.g., in Portugal and Spain in the mid-970s, where moderate parties won in early elections). Or an election might demonstrate that the previous regime's party had little support among the public, and could not credibly hang on to special privileges and advantages in new governing bodies (e.g., as in Poland in 1989–1990, when the ruling party did very poorly in elections).

In reality, many cases fell between the rupture and pact extremes. Groups' leverage in pact formation could be affected by contentious politics outside negotiations over pacts, such as protest demonstrations and strikes. Diverse groups in civil society such as labor unions, professional associations, unemployed youth, small informal-sector entrepreneurs, community organizations, nongovernmental social service and humanitarian groups, supporters of suppressed political parties, personalistic groups and parties, and religious zealots might play parts in the "mass" side of the equation. They tended to share in at least a short-term tactical preference for democracy, but some also had their own longer-term agendas that might or might not be consistent with democratic consolidation. For example, militant Islamist groups have been important in such cases as the 2011–2013 "Arab Spring" events in Egypt and Syria.

Constitutions: A Special Kind of Pact

Often an important point in a country's transition to democracy is the drawing up of the new democratic constitution. In the African case of Benin in 1990, the contours of the new democratic system were determined by a conference of virtually all relevant interests and leaders. Earlier, in the Latin American cases of Peru in 1978–1979 and Brazil in 1987–1988, new constitutions were drawn up by elected constituent assemblies in which diverse groups had voices. These are examples of the **social pact** approach to constitution making.

Alternatively, new constitutions could be drawn up in a more elite-model fashion, by commissions appointed by the group in control at that particular

Egyptian general and current president Abdel Fattah el-Sisi (at left) and former president Mohammad Morsi (at right), deposed after mass protest demonstrations and military intervention in 2013.

point in the transition. For example, in Russia the new constitution of 1993 was formulated by a commission handpicked by then president Boris Yeltsin. Egypt's first new constitution following the Arab Spring uprisings in 2011 was drawn up by an assembly picked and dominated by an Islamist coalition, and its next constitution was prepared under the control of the military and its leader, General Abdel Fatah el-Sisi.

A subsequent referendum on the new constitution tends to approve it, perhaps because it is the only thing on offer or because of heavy organizational mobilization of interests associated with the leading group, or both. Egypt's Islamist-leaning constitution of 2013 was approved by a referendum in which the Imams and well-organized Islamist parties cooperated in urging approval, but secular groups remained disorganized and disaffected. Less than a third of the electorate voted and only 60 percent of those who voted supported the constitution. In 2014, the Egyptian generals who had seized power created a new constitution, which they put to the voters for approval. Under conditions of heavy repression of the leading Islamist party, the referendum election drew a 38.6 percent voter turnout, with over 95 percent of those voting approving the revised constitution.

FACTORS AFFECTING DEMOCRATIC TRANSITIONS

We now turn to a few of the causal factors affecting transition initiation and democratic consolidation. We start with factors that were especially prominent in the first representative democracies, which arose in Western Europe and North America: economic development, democratic values, and pre-democratic experience (or lack of it) with party contention and cooperation. Then we consider two other factors that have been important in democratic transitions in the last hundred years: economic crisis/dislocation and the relative strengths of extremist and moderate parties.

Economic Development, Modernization, and Inequality

Prior to the 1990s, many political scientists generally linked democracy to economic development. One rationale for this concerned attitudes toward political contention and distribution. Economic development tends to produce a growing pie of resources available to government. This allows a variety of contending groups to make gains if they are willing to compromise under democratic procedures. Conversely, low economic development and a poor, stagnant economy means that few can do well, and a lot is at stake in winning or losing control over government. This encourages sharp contention among groups over access to resources and struggle to control government, hindering chances for democracy.

However, this general difference between poor economies and growing ones sheds little light on how and why democratic transition gets started. For this purpose, we turn to two particular aspects of economic development that may be linked to democratization: (a) modernization and (b) reduced levels of economic inequality.

Modernization and Democratic Transition As we saw in chapter 4, the concept of modernization refers to the complex of factors that tend to accompany economic development: urbanization, industrialization, rising GDP, widening education, increased use of modern communication technologies, and a growing middle class. Spurts of economic development tend to be accompanied by at least some modernization. This, in turn, gives rise to new urban groups such as professional associations (e.g., of teachers, doctors, or lawyers), labor unions, small manufacturing and service businesses, community groups, and religious congregations, often collectively referred to as **civil society**. These groups each have a stake in the conditions around them. They naturally tend to form organizations, want (and feel they deserve) a political voice, and press for democratization. All this tends to be linked to economic growth and higher GDP.

Notably, however, economic development and modernization are not confined to high levels of overall GDP per capita. More specifically, overall indicators of national economic development such as GDP per capita may mask big urban-rural differences in economic growth. Development and modernization may be proceeding in a few urban areas of a country where much of the politics of transition initiation occurs, while large portions of the nation's population still live in poor and undeveloped rural areas that drag down overall national measures of GDP per capita. The result can be urban modernization and democratic transition occurring at a lower threshold of overall national GDP per capita than previously thought.

For example, several Latin American countries experienced urban growth from the 1920s on, and by the 1930s had brief periods of attempted democratic transition (that didn't last long, which I shall call "brushes with democracy") despite (still) low levels of overall national wealth. Similarly, the occurrence of post-1990 democratizations in some lower and middle-income countries does not rule out economic development as a factor favoring democratization. Nonetheless, careful comparative analysis has shown that (at least in countries other than Communist regimes and oil sheikdoms like Saudi Arabia and the

United Arab Emirates) both transition initiation and democratic consolidation are significantly correlated with economic development.[3]

Still, however, as political scientist Michael K. Miller has argued, economic development may strengthen stable single party or military regimes (by providing enhanced resources); he suggests that it is mainly in cases of inter-elite conflict (e.g., coups, assassinations or revolutions), destabilizing and weakening the top leadership, that the urban modernization factors noted above can kick in to start democratic transition when policy challenges hit.[4] On Miller's view, in the absence of such conflict between elite groups at the top, the most change that we can expect from other challenging factors—such as international pressure for democratization or economic downturns that mobilize discontent—is the ruling party's shift to electoral authoritarian rule, in which it continues to dominate in a merely formal multiparty system (see chapter 15).

Inequality A related factor that might affect democratization is the degree of inequality in a society, the size of the gap between rich and poor. Less developed economies traditionally displayed high levels of inequality between rich elites and the lower strata. In contrast, more developed economies show middle-class growth that tends to be associated with a reduction in overall inequality. Notably, political scientist Carles Boix[5] and the team of Daren Acemoglu and James Robinson[6] have suggested that high inequality is linked to authoritarian rule, while lower degrees of inequality are associated with democratization (see "Concept in Context" below). But more systematic examination shows, especially in the last third of the twentieth century, many cases of democratic transition amid high degrees of inequality. Clearly, in many cases wealthy elites in very unequal societies have judged that they will be able to protect their interests (including property rights) effectively under democratic arrangements, and may not be particularly afraid of transition to democracy.

Democracy-Supporting Values

The diversification of civil society groups that comes with economic development tends to be accompanied by the spread of democracy-linked *values*, especially those related to freedom, including (a) the civil liberties of expression, association, movement, etc. that are required for genuinely free and fair elections, and (b) political freedom in the sense of having a government led by people chosen in free and fair elections.

Again, in a country experiencing economic development and modernization, new civil society groups (including professional and business groups as well as unions, religious groups, and other community groups) tend to (a) want to pursue opportunity autonomously, and (b) feel a growing stake in what the government does, and thus want to have a voice in its decisions. Political scientists Christian Welzel and Ronald Inglehart, assessing a number of surveys of comparative values, have identified a key list of correlated indicators of what they call "emancipative" or "self-expression" values linked to support for democracy: aspiration to liberty, participation in petitions, tolerance of nonconformists, trust in people, and life satisfaction.[7] These center mostly around the freedom category of values—particular forms of free self-expression, their exercise, and acceptance of the freedom exercised by others—that is, freedoms as public values enjoyed by the whole community, not just oneself.[8]

CONCEPT IN CONTEXT | Real-World Limitations of the Acemoglu/Robinson Model

The view of Boix and Acemoglu/Robinson (AR) centers on the financial concerns of the rich elite. In their view, where the gap between rich and poor is wide and a crisis leads to social unrest, the elite is inclined to repress the unrest (perhaps while offering aid to the poor) rather than allowing democratization. This is due to elite fears that a democratic majority would substantially redistribute wealth (e.g., through land redistribution or high taxes on the rich to aid the poor). According to AR, only if the economic crisis (recession) is severe, the wave of unrest is very powerful, and the rich elite fears that repression might fail and risk revolution, might the economic elite allow some democratization. But as soon as a new recession challenges the democracy, the rich will take the opportunity to conduct a coup and reverse the democratization, returning to elite authoritarian rule.

When there is less inequality, according to Boix and AR, with a smaller income gap between rich and poor, the would-be democratic majority would be likely to want *less* additional taxation and redistribution. This reduces the elite's financial fears and enhances the chances of an elite offer of democratic transition to avoid any risk of revolution. This idea seems to fit cases where the proposed transition is limited to extending voting rights incrementally, to include middle-class strata (as Britain did in stages in the nineteenth century, for example). Then, at each expansion of the electorate, the new voters are not that much less well off than the lower reaches of the prior electorate, so the new electoral majority will not be likely to demand much more distribution. The elite's fears of redistribution will be low, and the elite will be more likely to concede to the proposed democratization. This picture does seem to fit some aspects of nineteenth-century democratizations in places like Britain and France, and some other European and Latin American cases up through the mid-twentieth century.

However, the AR model's predictions tend not to fare well in the last quarter of the century. For example, democratizations of military regimes in Latin America in the 1980s and 1990s occurred and consolidated despite high levels of economic inequality and universal voting rights at the outset of democratization. The AR model has a very narrow view of political motivation, financial self-interest. But in the real world, political actions may also be motivated by such factors as public values, public policy concerns, ideologies, and social solidarities, operating in addition to, and even sometimes instead of, material self-interest (see chapter 3).

Moreover, the AR model greatly oversimplifies the contending groups involved in democratization, mainly considering only a rich elite and a nonelite majority. But such complex processes as democratization involve multiple groups, with often diverse goals and strategies, some more irrational than rational and some short term rather than long term. For example, often the actions of a small radical portion of the mass, like starting an insurrection or insurgency, can provoke interactions that heavily affect the trajectory of democratization (see the Country Case Study on El Salvador, below). And authoritarian regimes can be of very different types (including militaries and other regimes that are somewhat independent of elites of business and wealth), and can experience contention between different elites and factions within them.[*] And by the late twentieth century, both industrial elites and landed oligarchies had reason to believe that they could do well in protecting their interests under democracy,[†] while avoiding the uncertainties (including the risk of resource confiscation) of authoritarian rule.

---

[*] See Geddes (2003).

[†] Even Boix himself (who otherwise subscribes to the inequality thesis) observes that the owners of mobile capital (financial or commercial, vs. land) know that the new democratic government will be very unlikely to undertake heavy taxation due to the majority's fear of the negative economic consequences that follow from capital flight.

In what may be a first step toward a country's democratic transition, an authoritarian regime may choose to loosen repression. It may grant a degree of respect for civil liberties in what many political scientists call political liberalization (as in "classical liberal"). But amid economic development, many in new civil society groups can see a difference between exercising human rights at government discretion, which can easily be taken away, and *guaranteeing* those rights. The latter requires the next step, assuring minimal *political* freedom granted by the free and fair election of leading policymakers in representative democracy.

To be sure, correlations between transition initiation and consolidation, on one hand, and national measures of the prevalence of democracy-related freedom values, on the other, are likely to be ragged. For one thing, with economic development usually proceeding first in urban areas (as noted above), freedom values are likely to emerge there first, helping spur transition initiation. But national surveys of values tend to also include large populations in rural and small-town areas that remain poor, undeveloped, and culturally conservative (e.g., large portions of Iran today). Thus we may see some urban-spearheaded transition initiation in countries that rank low in their overall national indices of freedom values and economic growth. Also, as political scientist Nancy Bermeo stresses, even where democracy-supporting values are widespread, elites may have different ideas and may prevent transition initiation or democratic consolidation.[9]

In some democratic transitions, religion can be a relevant factor. To be sure, support for the key freedom values—and support for representative democracy—can spread independently of a country's majority religion. The clearest relevant difference among religions may lie in a much narrower question: does a religion's sacred book(s) include passages that seem to support theocratic imposition of religious law? (For example, for Christianity and Buddhism the answer is no, whereas for Islam it is yes; see chapter 5). If so, such passages may serve periodically to encourage a minority of religious literalists to try to stir up the faithful to establish theocracy rather than democracy. But support for theocracy among a portion of a religion's believers does not mean that it will determine the outcome, as is demonstrated by such large-population, majority-Muslim democracies as Indonesia and Turkey.

Pre-Democratic Experiences

Another factor affecting democratic transitions is the nature of the prior authoritarian system. As political scientist Barbara Geddes stresses, for example, when military regimes face economic crises and public discontent, they seem to be more ready to negotiate their exit from government. This is partly because they have a secure place to go—back into their traditional professional military role—and partly to heal the factional divisions that may have arisen within the armed forces over the thorny economic problems facing government.[10] As they exit, military leaderships tend to protect themselves with pacts that at least insulate them from retribution for their deeds while in power.

Single-party and single-party-dominant, electoral authoritarian regimes do not have the legitimate exit haven that militaries have. So they tend to hang onto power longer, sometimes by replacing an unpopular leader and claiming to be renewed. But they do have a potential life after transition if they can secure a future role with pacts that enable them to contend in subsequent multiparty politics.

Third, Geddes emphasizes, personal dictatorships are the least likely to leave power voluntarily. They have no institutional foundation to lean on, and no place to go if the leader is removed. Personal dictatorships tend to fight to the end, and be replaced by rupture of some sort, by popular opposition contention or coercive international pressure.

The most seamless democratic transitions seem to come when the pre-democratic experience is the competitive exclusionary type of authoritarian rule (see chapter 15). This pattern was common among the earliest democracies of North America and Western Europe, for example, which had pre-transition experience with open elite-level party contention. In these cases, the actual transition to democracy tended to come by either (a) the extension of the right to vote to virtually all adult males (and by the early twentieth century, including females), primarily by eliminating or reducing property qualifications and/or literacy requirements for voting, or (b) gaining national independence from colonial rule, or both. Examples of the former are Great Britain, France, Sweden, Denmark, and the Netherlands. Examples of the latter are Australia, New Zealand, Canada, and India (all formerly under the British Empire), Finland under the Russian Empire, Norway under Swedish rule, and the Czech lands under the Hapsburg Empire.

In these cases, once democracy was initiated, it stuck and consolidated. (Only intervention by external force, as occurred in the postwar occupation of Czechoslovakia by the Soviet Army, could interfere with this path.) The reasons for this seem to be rooted in political culture and habit. These pre-democratic experiences involved open, peaceful political contention, procedural cooperation in observing the rules and norms of that contention, and mutual respect (at least among the participating parties) for the human rights to freedom of expression and association that such contention requires. Moreover, at least in some policy areas at times, contending elite-based parties had to shoulder responsibility for some policymaking. This required cooperation, exchanges of policy support, and compromise within governing bodies to agree on policies for governmental action. As contending pre-democratic leaders and parties gained familiarity with each other, a degree of mutual trust (that today's electoral or policy defeat does not spell ultimate disaster) could arise, along with pragmatic experience in forming coalitions and other alliances in the pursuit of high-priority goals. They discovered the benefits of occasional temporary coalitions to secure limited objectives, often related to shared values between parties that might nonetheless be long-term contenders. In contrast, in prominent post–World War I cases of new democracies that *lacked* prior experience with real party contention, such as Russia, Italy, Germany, Spain, and Portugal, their first brushes with democracy ended in failure (see "Contention and Cooperation in Focus").

Notably, many countries in pre-Depression Latin America had also experienced a degree of elite-level party contention prior to the full extension of the franchise. On one side, classical liberal modernizers tended to be supported by middle-class, professional, and intellectual elements in civil society. Such parties tended to be secular and sought new freedoms and economic improvements such as roads, railroads, and port facilities. They tended to favor extending central government authority to integrate their countries' regions into a single national market. Contending with them were traditionalist conservative parties, often influenced by large landowners and the Catholic Church. They sought to restrain the spirit of liberation and reform. With their private power in society, these groups mainly wanted to be left alone by the central government. Alongside these contenders might be smaller personalistic parties, some led by military strongmen with regional power bases.

CONTENTION AND COOPERATION IN FOCUS | Failures of Democratic Consolidation in the Absence of Pre-Democratic Contention

Notably, regarding the interwar (between World War I and World War II) cases of Russia, Italy, Germany, Spain, and Portugal, the prewar (and pre-democratization) periods displayed some of the formalities of open political contention. But in practice, the legislative assemblies prior to full democracy remained under the control of a political elite that permanently dominated the executive branch of government.

For example, in Russia after the 1905 revolt, the czar permitted the creation of a legislative Duma, but never allowed it to stay in session or exercise any real governmental power. In Italy's *transformismo* period from the early 1880s on, the assembly was dominated by the Liberal Party leadership controlling the executive. It used clientelistic benefits to co-opt the support of would-be parliamentary contenders, and parties' ideological identities remained weak. In the late nineteenth century in both Spain and Portugal, parliament was dominated by a moderate classical liberal elite with a superficial two-party veneer (the parties had few policy differences), and a custom of periodic military intervention to reinforce the rules (in Spain called *pronunciamiento*). In Germany, in reality the Reichstag (parliament) was

weak and subject to dominance by the Kaiser (king) and his handpicked chancellor (prime minister; at first, Otto von Bismarck). The political parties were never able to contend seriously, or allowed a role in government policymaking.

In all of these cases, democratic consolidation failed and authoritarian rule ensued. Russia's brief brush with democracy in 1917 ended late in the year with a takeover by the Bolsheviks, which by then had become the largest and best organized party. Italy's democracy (following the 1912 extension of the franchise) fell to Mussolini's "black shirt" militia, mass marches, and manipulation of parliament in 1924. Portugal's democracy ceded to military takeover in 1926 (soon becoming a personal dictatorship under Salazar), Germany fell to Hitler and the Nazis in 1933, and Spain surrendered to Generalissimo Franco's victorious army in 1939. While this record suggests a correlation (with some causal impact) between (a) genuine pre-democratic contention between elite-based parties and (b) subsequent democratic consolidation, it focuses on just one of several factors that contribute to whether transitions succeed or fail.

However, this Latin American pre-democratic experience with open political contention was limited by periodic interventions by the armed forces, often to replace one party with another at the head of government. The military might step in for various reasons, such as when it considered the contention between the parties or regions to have become too sharp, or when officers thought policymaking was failing or threatening elites. The risk of military intervention hanging over politics tended to limit the contending parties' experience of responsibility for government, both before and after Latin America's mid-century brushes with democracy.

Notably, there is a small-scale analogue for pre-democratic elite-level contention: experiences of extended informal (usually secret), personal interaction among contending leaders before, or early in, transition initiation. For example, at key points of pre-democratic conflict in both Northern Ireland and South Africa, American political scientist William Foltz spearheaded private retreats at which key leaders of contending groups could interact out of the public eye, exploring areas of possible accommodation and fostering mutual trust. In a more recent example noted by Alfred Stepan, in the years prior to the Tunisian Arab Spring of 2011, leaders of opposition groups had been meeting secretly in Europe.[11] By late 2014, Tunisia appeared to be one of the few Arab Spring transitions that seemed to be headed for democratic consolidation.

Economic Dislocation and Crisis

As we have seen, when an economic crisis hits a nondemocratic regime, it can contribute to democratic transition. Such crises are usually ones of recession or depression,[12] but galloping inflation (especially of basic staples) can also play a key role. Economic crisis can bring other public values into play—beyond the freedom ones discussed above—such as support for particular forms of justice and well-being. But if economic dislocation and crisis hits *during* a democratic transition, it can derail consolidation. Historically, the first prominent impact of economic crisis on democratization was the role of the Great Depression in the breakdown of fledgling democracies in Central Europe, to which we now turn.

The European Past and Transition Breakdown When an economic crisis arrives during a democratic transition, it might disrupt democratization and lead to a new authoritarian regime rather than democratic consolidation. Pre-World War II Europe provides examples of economic crises that were not successfully addressed by fledgling democratic governments, and thus contributed to authoritarian takeover. In Russia, World War I had decimated the economy and produced urban desperation, particularly food and fuel shortages and sky-rocketing inflation. But during the brief period of open political contention in 1917 after the collapse of the monarchy, the provisional government led by Alexander Kerensky made the fateful decision to continue the losing war with Germany rather than negotiate an end to Russia's participation. Hence the economic dislocations attending the war continued. Under the slogan "bread and peace," the antiwar Bolsheviks became the strongest of the contending parties (see Country Case Study below), and seized power at the end of the year. Italy's post–World War I economic dislocations, inflation, unemployment, and strikes contributed to the early 1920s' rise of Mussolini.

In Germany, two sources of economic dislocation contributed to the 1930s' breakdown of democracy: the aftermath of World War I and the Great Depression. First, the heavy war reparations, imposed on Germany by the punishing Treaty of Versailles, continued the post–World War I economic disarray and privations that had originally contributed to the fall of Germany's Imperial regime in 1918. Then came the shock of runaway inflation in the early 1920s, followed by severe austerity and its suppression of the economy later in the decade. The German economy had hardly had a chance to catch its breath when it was hit by the Great Depression in the early 1930s. Beyond the immediate widespread unemployment and hardships, the depression undermined the sense of economic security of the middle class. The Weimar democratic government that led Germany from 1919 to 1933 seemed unable to take

A line for a homeless shelter in Berlin, Germany in 1929, prompted by massive unemployment and a housing crisis at the beginning of the Great Depression.

substantive policy action as a terrible deflation took its toll. All this encouraged middle-class disaffection and invited a search for a savior. Spain and Portugal were similarly affected by the Great Depression in the 1930s.

Russia also experienced an ongoing economic crisis during its transition to democracy in the 1990s. The top leaders in the new multiparty democracy were trying to rapidly introduce market coordination into a Soviet-style, monopoly-based economy where habits of entrepreneurial competition were largely missing. With the end of most price controls in 1992 came a punishing inflation that deprived many Russians of their life savings. GDP plunged and racketeering became common. Some private entrepreneurs gained control of formerly state-owned enterprises, got rich fast, and were widely resented as "oligarchs." But low oil prices ruled out substantial help from the government and dissatisfaction was widespread. Not surprisingly, by the end of the decade, a new party was rising to dominance, promising a strong hand and economic security just as oil prices were recovering to provide the government with resources. In the 2000s, this new party, renamed United Russia under its leader, Vladimir Putin, snuffed out serious opposition and imposed a single-party-dominant, electoral authoritarian regime (see Country Case Studies, chapter 15).

Where economic conditions were more favorable in the early years of democratization, democracy's chances were better. After World War II, as the victorious Allies were imposing new democracies on Germany and Japan, they took no chances and infused huge amounts of aid into both countries to speed the recovery of their collapsed economies. And in the 1990s, some new post-Communist democracies had shorter periods of adjustment and recession and quicker recoveries, due partly to Western investment that accompanied economic integration with Europe (e.g., German investment in Poland and the Czech Republic).

Economic Dislocations in Developing Nations In the early twentieth century, some countries in Latin America were experiencing urban modernization, middle-class growth, and the emergence of civil-society groups. Growing numbers were meeting the property and/or literacy requirements for voting. But economic growth depended partly on exports of raw-material commodities, whose world prices could fluctuate. When prices for a nation's key export commodity took a dive, the economy could be thrown into distress. Civil-society groups might protest and press for relief and a greater voice in government. Especially with the Great Depression of the 1930s when world trade basically broke down, early brushes with democracy occurred in countries such as Brazil, Argentina, Chile, and Peru. In explaining these pro-democracy responses to economic distress, both the pluralist model of influence distribution (various civil-society groups contending with regime-associated ones) and the majority preference model (widely shared pressures to pursue civil-political freedom, social and criminal justice, and economic well-being) seem to play roles (see "Applying the Models" below).

In these settings, parties could rally around the development strategy of Import Substitution Industrialization (ISI; see chapter 7). Aiming to develop the nation's own industrial capacity rather than depending on imported goods, ISI favored (a) high tariffs against foreign manufactured goods, (b) government support for—and in some cases, ownership of—domestic industrial enterprises to replace the imports, (c) building modern infrastructure (roads, rails, electric power), and (d) subsidizing low urban prices for food, fuel, energy, and

APPLYING THE MODELS | Democratization, Civil Society, and Values

Some commentators on democratization stress the distinction between the state and civil society. Here the above-noted phrase "civil society" refers to groups and their organizations that are thought to be close to the ground or the grass roots, such as labor unions, community organizations, professional associations, women's groups, student groups, ethnic-cultural minority groups, etc. This implies a somewhat pluralistic model of participation. Civil society is contrasted with "the state" and "political society," which includes "elites" such as the bureaucracy, the military, big business where it is closely associated with the state, the formal legislative and executive units of government, and often the established political parties and their organizations. The latter realm suggests the idea of "plural elites" (see chapter 2). When mass demonstrations in response to acute economic crisis yield to pact making over time, on this view elites appear to be largely taking over the political field to the exclusion of civil-society groups.*

This picture tends to use the elite model of influence distribution empirically, to explain most pact-driven transitions. To be sure, often those who use elite-model empirical analysis would prefer, normatively, to see a greater role for majority preferences and pluralist patterns of influence distribution in democratic transitions. On this perspective, involving the popular majority more directly can give transitions more democratic legitimacy. Civil-society advocates often support a "deepening" of democracy to include listening more to average members of all groups (including economic enterprises) and giving "popular sector" organizations more influence in democratization and in policymaking generally.

While civil society's diverse groups tend to be suggestive of the pluralist model, are there factors that might add a majority preference aspect to mass pressures for democratic transition? One such factor that may be shared among diverse groups to the point of embracing a majority is heightened concern for certain public *values* that authoritarian governments did not seem to be pursuing effectively. One of these is economic well-being. Especially economic slumps and the attending high unemployment

and underemployment tend to elevate economic well-being among the concerns of groups pressing for democratization, and contribute to erosion in public support for the authoritarian regimes.[†]

Other shared values in this context come under the heading of justice. From the poor to educated university graduates (who may also be poor), norms of social justice may be perceived to be violated by the absence of decently paying jobs for those working hard or wishing to do so. Regarding criminal justice, abuse of police power against dissidents and demonstrators, and abuse of prosecutorial power after detention, can dovetail with bribery and other judicial corruption as factors contributing to a widespread sense of the need to change the system. The recent Arab Spring uprisings in Tunisia and Egypt illustrate this, with the treatment of protesters both before and after they are detained becoming human rights causes. At the same time, the above-discussed public value of freedom in its civil and political forms also spurs discontent with authoritarian rule, with democracy promising to allow popular frustrations to be freely articulated in free and safe expression, organization, and political opportunity to replace the governmental leadership through free and fair elections.

The surrounding atmosphere of values-related pressure, coming from an otherwise diverse and pluralistic majority, can help drive authoritarian elite hardliners to become softliners, and softliners to enter into pacts that further the process of democratization. (In addition, values had an international impact in the direction of democratization; increasingly from the 1970s on, international donors and lenders were including progress toward human rights and democratization among the conditions required for extending development aid.) If we ask what factor seems to be common to majorities in the transition process, it may be shared values.

_____

* See Grugel (2002).

† For a view of democratic transitions against the backdrop of economic conditions, see Haggard and Kaufman (1995).

transportation—all in support of jobs and economic development generally. The result was reduced unemployment and steadier, self-sufficient national economies, at least for a while. Public support for this strategy could contribute strongly to transition initiation to assure the citizens that ISI would be pursued by the government.

However, economic crises and dislocations could also hit fledgling democratic regimes in the developing world. In the new postindependence democracies of Africa and Asia in the 1960s, typically each was led by the party that had spearheaded the country's independence struggle. But economic challenges such as budget deficit crises, inflation, strikes, and shortfalls in development efforts could lead to mounting dissatisfaction and sharp political challenges to the governing party. A common outcome was authoritarian takeover, either by the ruling party itself (usually backed by the army) or by the military directly. In the 1960s, in such early Latin American democracies as Brazil, Argentina, Chile, and Peru, government budget crises, high inflation, and strikes, alarmed elites. Meanwhile, Cold War ideological tensions and occasional incidents of poor peasants seizing and occupying unused land, heightened fear of socialism among landowning and business elites and conservative factions in the armed forces. Military coups brought Latin American democratic consolidation to an end.

International Pressure In addition to internal conditions, international relationships can also create or threaten to create an economic crisis. As political scientists Steven Levitsky and Lucan Way have shown,[13] regular connections with the international sector and economic vulnerability to it are related to democratization. The economy of a developing nation under authoritarian rule may be financially dependent on outside actors for aid, such as a developed-country donor (e.g., France in western and northern Africa) or an international agency such as the IMF or the World Bank. International dependency can even be on buyers for its exports who might boycott its products. Examples include the boycott of South African goods in the early 1990s to protest South Africa's racist policy of apartheid and the boycott of goods from Myanmar in the late 1990s to protest that country's oppressive military rule. If necessary aid or export success is made conditional upon democratization, the donors or buyers gain influence by anticipated reaction (see chapter 3); the regime takes steps toward democratization out of concern about how donors or buyers will react if the steps are not taken.

The Number of Large Non-Extreme Parties Versus Significant Extreme Ones

Among the many factors that are discussed by political scientists regarding transitions, one that is often overlooked was prominent in earlier studies of the above-mentioned interwar democratic breakdowns in central and southern Europe. This is the relationship between moderate and extreme parties.

In chapter 10, we saw that political parties have two representative roles: representing ideological orientations (typically one per party) and representing categoric interests in society. Today's established democratic systems (e.g., in the Americas and Europe) are mostly multiparty, in that normally there are four or more "significant parties"—that is, parties that have a plausible chance of becoming necessary parts of legislative majorities (see chapter 10). In such fully consolidated systems, the largest significant parties tend to have at least some organization across the country, and display identifiable ideological directions that are not extreme in the sense of not calling for radical transformation of the system. Such non-extreme parties tend to range ideologically from left social democratic through green, moderate left-of-center, centrist, classical liberal, and conservative, to arch-conservative (see chapter 5). In these countries, parties that are ideologically extreme and anti-system, such as Marxist-Leninist, Fascist, or militant Islamist ones, tend to be smaller, to vary in their density of organization, and not to be significant.

As we survey transitions that succeeded in consolidating democracy, we tend to find two or more significant parties that are not ideologically anti-system, are at least somewhat organized, and are of substantial size. And we tend to find no more than one significant party that is extreme. But where we find only one party (or none) that is large, at least somewhat organized, and *not* extreme—especially if it is flanked by two or more extreme parties—transition seems to run risks of being halted or derailed.

Early and Middle Twentieth-Century Examples In the above-noted post–World War I cases when democracy broke down, there were many parties (high fractionalization). But only three types had significant organization, numerous members, ideological identities that were relevant to the policy issues of the day, and developed linkages to supporting interests.[14] Among them, only the Social Democrats were large, organized, and moderate by the standards of the day. Notably, the other two types were ideologically extreme and anti-system: Communist parties at the far-left, and to the far-right, ethnic ultranationalist parties (e.g., the Nazis and the Fascists) filled with fear that the Russian Revolution might spread.

Notably, both of these extreme party types were critical of the democratic system itself; hence political scientists call them **anti-system parties**. (It is unusual for such extreme parties to be members of coalitions, even temporary ones.) This very polarized state of party contention—to some extent related to the severe challenge presented by the Great Depression and its very high unemployment—tended to hinder the formation of a broad coalition capable of blocking Hitler's ascendency to the PM position (after his Nazi party received 37 percent and 33 percent of the vote, respectively, in the two parliamentary elections of 1932).

In the Latin American mid-century transitions, on the other hand, the early success of ISI development helped bolster the moderate parties that supported it. Among contending political parties, the ISI policy approach was likely to be championed by a labor-based left-of-center party, such as the Peronists in Argentina or the Brazilian Labor Party. But ISI could also be supported by more moderate center or center-left parties, such as the Radicals in Chile, Popular Action in Peru, or the Social Democratic Party in Brazil. (Socialist or Communist parties at the far left tended to remain small, extreme, and marginalized.)

In these countries during the middle third of the century, moderation was to some extent imposed by the militaries, which at times might intervene temporarily to enforce it. Following the Iberian custom (in Spain called *pronunciamiento*), the armed forces might step in, or threaten to do so, usually to ban a party or replace one party or leader with another at the helm of the government. This tended to exert limit-setting influence over the democracies' pursuit of ISI.[15]

Especially after the onset of the Cold War at mid-century, military-set requirements included refraining from serious land reform and from major seizures of private businesses and property, and the exclusion of socialist or Communist parties from cabinets.

By the period of the 1960s through the 1980s, however, aggressive ISI had come to be associated with economic crises related to mounting budget deficits, high inflation, and numerous strikes. Some center parties shifted rightward away from ISI, and the weakened moderate parties on the left had to move further left to get far-left support. Often far-right parties reflecting the views of alarmed business and landowning elites became extreme, demanding sharp change, and the military itself became an extreme party in the sense of demanding system change. As we saw in the 1960s and 1970s in Latin America, militaries intervened not just temporarily, but to stay.

Post-1974 Democratic Transitions The trend of military rule throughout the developing world began to reverse in the post-1974 wave of transition initiations. In these cases, democratization often stabilized when large, moderate parties on the left and right emerged to lead contending coalitions. Portugal's transition found its footing when its first election saw moderate parties in the lead. In Latin America, by the end of the century, moderate left-of-center parties had dropped their previous strong support for ISI, and instead focused on targeted education, food aid, and health care for the poor, alongside defense of the public sector against sharp cutbacks, aiming to remedy the economic shortcomings of austerity. Typically, they contended with a broad and moderate conservative party (and smaller ones), with either one or no significant extreme parties on the horizon.

What about transitions in which there is only one moderate, organized, large party running the government? To be sure, a vaguely nationalist and centrist catchall party[16] may remain the top government party without declining into electoral authoritarian rule. It may use its organization and control of the state for clientelist purposes,[17] especially if it has lucrative resources to draw on (e.g., diamonds in Botswana and oil in Nigeria; see Country Case Studies below). Thus such a party may be able to repeatedly win elections *without* openly suppressing other contenders, who remain weak. In this case, the system is minimally democratic in our sense of free and fair elections and respect for human rights (at least in most electoral districts). But while secure democratic consolidation may still occur, it is postponed and not assured.

The arrival of a crisis involving the economy or ethnic or sectarian tensions may bring an antielite movement that challenges the government party in the streets and/or at the polls. Accustomed to dominance, an impatient government party may start abusing judicial and police power to suppress opposition, thus becoming single-party-dominant, electoral authoritarian and thus derailing democratic consolidation. Or the opposition may end up spearheaded by an organized extreme party whose occasional engagement in democratic contention may be only tactical (e.g., much of the Islamic Brotherhood and other Sharia-focused Islamist parties in Egypt, or in Syria, Jabhat al Nusra or Ahrar al-Sham). If such an opposition party wins, its ideological zeal or sense of insecurity, or both, may prompt it to take the same electoral authoritarian route (or indeed, a single-party one).

Once single-party-dominant electoral authoritarianism has set in (e.g., in Russia in 2000), democrats can only hope that subsequently, other factors might force the regime to back off from suppressing potential rivals. Examples of such factors are an economic crisis, the rise of a rival large party with a popular ideological direction despite suppression, and pressure from spreading democracy-supporting freedom values that stand in opposition to the regime's oppressive tactics toward popular demonstrations and potential political rivals. And again, where the regime has links to other countries on whose aid its budget depends, international pressure might press the regime back to at least minimal democracy.

Breakdown in the Politics of Democratization: Civil War

Political contention in the democratization process can break down into civil war. **War** may be defined as the application of physical force to defeat an enemy and gain control over territory. Civil war takes place between contending forces within a single country. We often think of civil wars as struggles to control the whole state. Civil wars can occur outside the context of democratization, as in the revolutionary civil war fought in China in the late 1940s. Where a country has a lucrative resource (e.g., oil) that can enrich those in power, material gain may be part of the impetus to civil war.

Alternatively, a civil war may be fought over whether a particular region will be allowed to secede and form its own nation. The Biafran civil war in Nigeria in the late 1960s is an example of such a **separatist war**. It was fought to determine whether the ethnically Ibo and Christian southeast would be allowed to be its own independent nation (see Country Case Studies below). Until the end of the nineteenth century, the American Civil War (1861–1865), prompted by the secession of southern states over the issue of slavery, had been the bloodiest war in world history (in terms of numbers of deaths).

Today civil war or the threat of civil war may be connected to the politics of democratization. In the recent case of Syria, what began in 2011 as pro-democracy protests against an authoritarian regime has turned into all-out civil war. By mid-2014 in neighboring Iraq, too, open civil war had broken out. It was forced by an extreme Sunni Islamist party, the Islamic State (IS), which

Kurds in a refugee camp in Turkey just across the border from their town in Syria, Kobani, that had been besieged by IS militants.

had also seized significant territory in Syria. IS had allied with—and often coerced into cooperation—some Sunni tribal leaders and factions and former Saddam Hussein (the prior dictator) loyalists, in parts of central and western Iraq that were hostile to the Shia-dominated government in Baghdad.

In itself, war is not a form of politics. It represents the failure of politics to resolve contention. In war, contention has intensified to the extreme point of direct conflict of physical force, ruling out even the most minimal forms of cooperation between the contending groups. Civil wars are the source of terrible human suffering, both directly and indirectly through the disruption of the economy. They typically generate large numbers of refugees who flee for their lives to avoid violence, starvation, and malnutrition-related health threats. These situations violate human rights on a large scale, and often prompt the United Nations and other humanitarian organizations to assist the refugees created by war (see "The Human Rights Connection").

Within each contending force, we may see politics, but normally factions tend to cooperate heavily due to the necessities of the war effort. Where one side in a civil war is a minority insurgency, groups on the other side may cooperate and centralize to neutralize the threat, as in the case of Peru's 1990s' defeat of the Maoist Shining Path guerillas in the hills. Once the enemy is defeated, the pressure for cooperation may ease, helping pave the way for the emergence of open political contention and re-democratization, as it did in Peru in the 2000s.

THE HUMAN RIGHTS CONNECTION | Civil War, Refugees, and the U.N.

Civil wars generate large numbers of refugees partly because of how they are fought, especially in cities and towns. Usually one side is associated with the incumbent government, and often neighborhoods are controlled by either rebel or government forces. If troops or firing positions for mortars or rocket-propelled grenades, for example, are placed in residential neighborhoods, any attempt by the other side to fight the war must strike against those firing positions and forces. Unless those strikes are done with detailed intelligence and small, high-tech, precision-guided weapons (e.g., today's American or Israeli drone strikes), which developing nations do not have, the strikes will inevitably involve numerous civilian casualties. They may even completely miss the targeted locations. (If the casualties are in rebel-held areas, their public relations outlets will trumpet the message: "See, the regime is attacking its own people!"). Sometimes indiscriminate terror is used, perhaps including murder and rape, such as by Serb forces at times in Bosnia and Kosovo in the 1990s, and by the Sudanese regime-supported Janjaweed militia in Darfur in the 2000s. In a different example, in Syria and Iraq, the Islamic State (IS) has used religiously motivated murder as a tool of terror. For many in the affected areas, the only option is to flee (except for those who are too poor to do so). Whether intentional or not, inevitably large numbers of refugees result from today's civil wars.

The U.N.'s prevailing international Covenants of human rights seek to assure these rights by obligating signatory nation-state governments to, for example, (a) protect civil-political rights such as those to physical security and civil liberties, and (b) cooperate, within the limits of available resources, to provide minimal food, shelter, and health care. The U.N. cannot directly enforce its human rights law within nations, but it can act directly to care for refugees fleeing human rights abuse.

Refugee assistance falls under the jurisdiction of the U.N. High Commissioner for Refugees (UNHCR). Cross-border refugees from wars, persecution, or natural disasters are housed in refugee camps, created and supported by the UNHCR, host governments, and humanitarian nongovernmental organizations (NGOs). Refugees typically live in tents in camps in available open areas in neighboring nations where the U.N. and other aid agencies try to supply food and minimal health services. For example, Turkey and Lebanon now have over a million Syrian refugees each, with over half a million each in Jordan and Iraq. Not all of these people can be housed in camps; in Lebanon, for example, refugees must simply move into available space alongside other residents. In addition, there are over 6 million internally displaced people within Syria's borders, many trying to survive in open spaces without even minimal shelter. The U.N. tries to organize relief convoys to help these people, but they are often obstructed by the surrounding war. Such efforts by the U.N. and other donors require financial support from member nations.

The Framework Factor: Presidential Versus Parliamentary Government

Regarding the political framework of the new democracy, recent transitions have tended to favor either (a) presidential systems (especially in Latin America, where they were traditional) or (b) semi-presidential frameworks in some variation of the French model (see chapter 13), as in most post-Communist arrangements. Once elected, a president can officiate at key points in the transition, coordinating the implementation of pacts in ways that can calm the apprehensions of groups that supported the prior authoritarian regime. In the Brazilian case in the 1980s, for example, the concerns of some military officers about handing over power were no doubt reduced by having Jose Sarney as the first civilian president (1985–1989) because only a few years earlier he had been a leader in the military-supporting party, ARENA.

However, these presidential features do not always work out well, and presidentialism has been challenged as a political framework for democratic transition. For example, political scientist Juan Linz and others[18] argue that presidential government is less stable and more subject to breakdown than the parliamentary option. They point to the "divided legitimacy" of an elected president who faces an independently elected legislative assembly. The bulk of the world's presidential democracies are multiparty, and in Latin America, for example, typically the president's party holds only a minority of the legislative seats. Without a stable support coalition amid the uncertain party discipline that is characteristic of presidential government (see chapters 12 and 13), deadlock may arise. A frustrated president whose program is obstructed by the legislative assembly may then claim a nationwide mandate from the presidential election results, and be tempted to lead a breakdown of democracy. (S)he may try to weaken legislative powers, strengthen presidential ones, and manipulate the rules to greatly weaken the chances of opposition parties (e.g., the actions of Presidents Alberto Fujimori in 1990s Peru, and in the 2000s, those of Hugo Chavez in Venezuela and Vladimir Putin in post-Communist Russia). Some in Egypt have argued that former president Morsi's actions of this sort contributed to the military coup that overthrew him in 2013.

Linz and others suggest that in contrast, under parliamentary democracy a group pursuing breakdown must interfere in obvious and major ways with the basic operation of policymaking; tinkering won't do the job. Parliamentarism, its advocates argue, offers a single source of legitimacy, the majority coalition in parliament. It encourages governments to address the problems that they were elected to resolve, while still requiring consent among the coalition partner parties and voter approval in the next election.

Defenders of presidentialism respond that the matter is complex, and a presidential framework need not result in deadlock.[19] Presidents have advantages in dealing with the legislature—including a degree of control over the flow of clientelistic benefits to legislators' constituents—that often allow elements of the president's program to pass despite the independent behavior of legislators inside and outside the president's support coalition. And again, presidential priorities can be supported by special presidential powers over the agenda, such as "insistence" powers to push rapid consideration of certain sorts of presidential initiatives and temporary decree powers to implement legislation first, subject to congressional vote within a month or two (see chapters 12 and 13).

In addition, leaders of parties in the president's legislative coalition can bolster party discipline to support presidential proposals. They may be able to direct clientelistic benefits in ways that reward disciplined legislators, as well as control the rankings on the PR party lists. Also, defenders of presidential government suggest that certain adjustments in the institutional and electoral features of presidential democracy (e.g., having presidential and legislative elections occur concurrently) can provide incentives for parties to form more stable coalitions to steady the process. Recently, numerous presidential governments in Latin America have hung on without breakdown, and Peru's 1992 "self-coup," in which President Fujimori dissolved Congress, has since been reversed with the return of Peruvian presidential democracy in the 2000s.

Overall, by the 2010s a range of new democracies seemed to be consolidating fairly well. Particularly in Latin America and parts of post-Communist central Europe, peaceful transitions of power have occurred and key parties and coalitions on the left and right seem to be solidifying to provide voters with the option of meaningful choice. Outside these areas, however, presidentialism is faring less well in consolidating democracy, and a number of cases of single-party dominance have emerged from presidential forms. The outcomes of the recent Arab Spring transitions remain uncertain, and the debate over presidentialism goes on.

SUMMARY: CONTENTION AND COOPERATION IN DEMOCRATIZATION

Democratization tends to be a step-by-step form of regime change that involves elite groups and their interactions and agreements as well as pro-democracy mass demonstrations. Factors that tend to support democratization include economic development and the spread of democracy-supporting values such as forms of civil and political freedom, social justice, and minimal economic well-being. Pre-democratic experience with peaceful political contention also favors democratization. Economic dislocation and crisis can prompt the initiation of a democratic transition, but it can also, later in the process, threaten democracy's subsequent consolidation. Another factor affecting democratic consolidation is the number of moderate parties (the more the better) versus the number of ideologically extreme ones (the fewer the better). If this balance is unfavorable, democratization might derail into single-party-dominant, electoral authoritarian rule. If the prior authoritarian regime had been keeping the lid on sharp societal cleavages along ethnic, religious, and/or regional lines, transition politics might break down into civil war.

COUNTRY CASE STUDIES

Here we consider two developing countries whose somewhat complicated, pact-driven democratizations have included reversals. In Nigeria, ethnic-regional contention has been a primary factor, while El Salvador mainly faced socioeconomic contention.

Nigeria: Ethnic-Regional Contention and Democratization

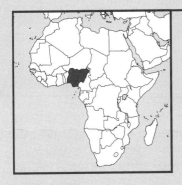

Nigeria first experienced colonial rule (see "Concept in Context," chapter 7) and then mostly long periods of military government, interrupted by brief democratic phases, followed by democracy after 1998. Nigerian politics has been preoccupied with contention between groups with distinct ethnic, regional, and religious identities, and often plagued by corruption and inefficiency in government performance.

The British colonial authorities ruled Nigeria in an authoritarian style that included Africans only in local government (under "indirect rule") and the lower rungs of the civil service. Most importantly, the British colonial authorities divided the colony into three large regions, each marked by its most important ethnic group and religious complexion. The Hausa-Fulani Muslims were the principal group in the north, the Ibo Christians in the southeast, and the Yoruba, who followed a mixture of Christianity and traditional religions, in the southwest. Thus, each major ethnic-religious identity in Nigeria had its own home region of dominance. Most Nigerians identified more strongly with their home region and tribe than with the colony of Nigeria as a whole.

When Nigeria became independent in the mid-1960s, political parties emerged along ethnic-regional lines. Each of the three key regional ethnicities was represented by its party, yielding a reinforcing coincidence of no less than five types of cleavage: ethnicity, religion, language, region, and political party identification. Thus members of a group always have the same allies and the same opponents across a wide range of issues. This tends to reinforce and intensify both antipathy toward the opposing group and identification with one's own.[20] As we saw in chapter 4, especially where region is one of the cleavages, with each of the three key groups possessing its home area of dominance, one or more of them may even want to be its own nation.

This past colonial experience tended to focus politics on getting advantages from a distant government that was often perceived as an alien elite. During the First Republic period of 1960–1966, the majoritarian parliamentary political framework left by the British exacerbated the situation. It invited sharp conflict among the parties to gain the parliamentary majority, allowing the majority party to call the shots and steer projects, contracts, spending, and favors to its own region. Only the Hausa-Fulani and their Muslim-dominated northern party had a chance to gain this advantage since the northern region contained a near majority of the population.

This regional conflict had historical roots. In colonial times, partly as a matter of convenience, the British had favored the two southern regions with regard to investments, projects, and settlement, as they were near the seacoast and its harbors. So in the view of the north, the era of independence and democracy was the time to reverse such past favoritism. Seeing this tendency developing during the First Republic of the mid-1960s, a group of Ibo military officers took over the government in a coup in 1966. (This was a peak period for military coups all over the developing world.) They declared their intention to abolish the regions and nationalize Nigerian politics. But the north had a warrior tradition related to the region's nomadic cattle-herding way of life and the nineteenth-century Holy War that brought Islam to the northern savannah. Many of the country's military officers were Muslim northerners. A group of them conducted a counter-coup, producing a northern-dominated military government. The Ibo responded by seceding, declaring their region the new nation of Biafra. In response, using Nigeria's growing oil revenues, the army expanded vastly (from roughly 10,000 to over 250,000 troops) over the course of the civil war (1967–1970). Eventually it was able to besiege and defeat Biafra. In the process, the military extended the central government's authority across the territory of Nigeria.

However, as corruption mounted under military rule, demands by civil-society groups for a return to democracy intensified. After General Yakubu Gowon's regime refused to allow a return to civilian rule, a new military coup occurred in 1975, followed by the assassination of its leader and the accession of his deputy, the Yoruba Christian general Olesegun Obasanjo. Obasanjo brought about the civilian Second Republic by 1979 (he was later elected the first president in the current democratic period). This new democracy rejected the previous parliamentary political framework in favor of presidential government, with SMDP-elected legislative assemblies separate from the elected president. And the old three-region federal system was replaced with a nineteen-state division of the country.

Nonetheless, a key political problem had not been solved: the three major political parties continued to be based on the same three-region division as before. The northerners won again in 1979, led by President Shehu Shugari. Four years later, Shugari, accused of clientelism and corruption, was unpopular and expected to lose, but surprisingly won the official vote count. After widespread protest over alleged vote rigging, a new military coup was led by an anticorruption northern general, Muhammadu Buhari (who later became a perennial presidential candidate and was finally elected president in 2015). But Buhari's harsh discipline and economic austerity led to a faltering economy and made him important enemies.

In 1985, yet another military coup replaced Buhari with northern general Ibrahim Babangida. He extended central patronage and influence further into the states, cronyism and corruption continued, and northerners became even more dominant in the officer corps of the military. The government owned the oil business, commodity marketing, and numerous other enterprises. With Nigeria's large oil revenues, Babangida could resist pressures from the International Monetary Fund to significantly reduce the state's role in the economy.

Sensitive to public opinion, this regime, too, promised a return to civilian rule. After several delays, in the early 1990s the generals allowed regional and legislative elections. The number of states was again increased, from nineteen to thirty (though states still lacked their own taxing powers and remained financially dependent on the central government). The presidential system was kept, but Babangida imposed a new party system: only two moderate, nationally based parties could contend: a center-left one and a center-right one. However, the old north-south division was not entirely overcome. The left-leaning Social Democratic Party was mostly led by Yoruba, not likely to please northern generals, while the conservative National Republicans were led by northerners.

The Social Democratic Party won the regional and legislative elections in 1992, and, apparently its presidential candidate in 1993, a Yoruba Muslim businessman, won as well (public voting was used to combat ballot stuffing). But the northern generals rejected this result; they claimed irregularities and nullified the election. By the end of 1993, a new military dictatorship had emerged under General Sani Abacha,

the most oppressive of Nigeria's past military leaders. Abacha arrested critics, imprisoned some military officers whom he accused of conspiring against him (including Obasanjo), allowed oil-refining facilities to fall into disrepair, and stole billions from the public coffers for his family and cronies.

The last of Nigeria's regime changes came at the end of the 1990s. Abacha began orchestrating a manipulated, fake democratization in 1997 that would crown him president (by requiring parties to name him as their candidate as a condition for their registration). In response, a groundswell of respected Nigerian figures signed a public letter condemning it. Suddenly, in mid-1998, Abacha died. Swiftly, an anti-Abacha military coup (rumored to have been led by Babangida) freed Abacha's political prisoners, began prosecuting top-level corruption cases from Abacha's era, initiated efforts to retrieve money looted by Abacha, and set up a quick sequence of new elections to move to civilian rule.

This time, a genuinely national political party was organized by the non-Yoruba leaders of the civilian resistance to Abacha: the Peoples' Democratic Party (PDP). A center-right catchall party, it won roughly 60 percent of the votes, governorships, and parliamentary seats in the elections of 1999, 2003, 2007, and 2011. Each presidential election until the most recent one has been won by the PDP leader: Obasanjo twice (1999 and 2003), then Umaru Yar Adua in 2007 and Goodluck Jonathan in 2011. But the party's elected officials in the House of Representatives and Senate tend to lack party discipline and to be focused on local interests. Some of the governors rule their states with an iron hand, and corruption seems to be widespread.

The PDP is to some extent a typical African clientelist party, which has not successfully addressed Nigeria's greatest problems. The economy remains a mess, with rampant corruption, poor transportation and energy infrastructure (despite continuing oil revenues), double-digit inflation, expensive and unproductive state-owned enterprises, and high levels of violence and crime generally. The education, health, electricity, and water supply sectors are in poor condition. Militias and gangs in the Niger River delta steal oil and engage in kidnapping and piracy for ransom, often disrupting oil production there.

In the 2000s, tensions continued, especially around northern states' adoption of Islamic Sharia law for criminal justice involving Muslims, and their attempts to ban alcohol, gambling, and mixing of the sexes. (The twelve northern states with Sharia have been reluctant, however, to apply Sharia's most extreme penalties for crimes.) Ethnic and communal riots, attacks, and other clashes between Muslims and Christians—occurring especially in "middle belt" states with their mixed populations—claimed thousands of lives in this period. And in recent years, the north has suffered from the rise of Boko Haram, an extremist Sunni Islamist group that employs murder and kidnapping widely to terrorize communities and to enforce strict Sharia law. Only in 2015 have the Nigerian armed forces, with important help from units from neighboring Chad, Cameroun, and Niger, begun to significantly curb this lethal insurgency.

From the return to civilian rule in 1999 through the elections of 2011 Nigeria lacked the alternation of parties in power that for many political scientists is a marker of successful democratic consolidation. But in this period, Nigeria did maintain a free, lively press and a fairly independent judiciary (though often corrupt). Election irregularities seem not to have been sufficiently widespread to determine national outcomes. And we have not seen the sort of systematic suppression of key opposition parties' activities, manipulation of parties and electoral rules, political use of criminal prosecutions, and media control by the party in power, that tend to characterize electoral authoritarian single-party dominance. Nonetheless, the PDP remained a catchall, centrist government party that used its dominant influence to monopolize political credit for the provision of government benefits, and lacked a serious broad-party competitor. So until 2015, we could classify Nigeria as a single-party-led minimal democracy at best, not yet fully consolidated.

However, the seeds of change were planted some years earlier. By 2007, the other prominent parties were (a) the All Nigeria People's Party (ANPP), which is more northern based and conservative, and (b) the Action Congress, which resulted from a merger of an earlier left-leaning Yoruba party (the Alliance for Democracy) with some smaller parties and recent defectors from the PDP. By the time of the 2011 elections, however, the former ANPP presidential candidate, Muhammadu Buhari (military regime chief from 1983 to 1985) had split off from the ANPP. Along with his supporters he formed a center-left party, the Congress for Progressive Change (CPC), and as its presidential candidate, Buhari again came in second for the presidency in 2011. Then in 2013, the CPC and other also-ran parties accomplished a remarkable feat of cooperation: the CPC, the Action Congress, and the ANPP rose above their previous regional patterns of support and merged into a broad center-left party, the All Progressives Congress (APC), led by Buhari. (As we have seen, SMDP elections tend to encourage such joining of forces.) By the time of the 2015 elections, Nigeria finally had, in the APC, a national, head-to-head rival to the PDP.

Meanwhile the PDP, for its part, was hindered by the perception that the Jonathan administration had failed to curb problems such as corruption, infrastructure failures, and the Boko Haram insurgency. The APC won a decisive victory in the election, gaining the presidency for Buhari and clear APC majorities in both the House of Representatives and the Senate. A key question remains: in the coming years, will the APC—with its diverse component parts that have recently contended with each other as individual parties—be able to cooperate sufficiently internally to actually become a single political party? Or will it become at most a coalition, in the legislative process and in coming election campaigns? At any rate, Nigeria seems to be consolidating as a democracy.

El Salvador: Contention along Economic Lines

The long process of democratization in El Salvador illustrates the difficulties that states encounter when socioeconomic tensions play a major role amid a diversity of contending groups. The process has included elite groups worried about potential redistribution (especially of land), active military factions, ideological passions, lower-strata protests, international influences, and temporary pacts that failed to hold. Patterns established early in El Salvador's history showed remarkable persistence in recent decades (though often in shadowy ways).

In Central America, El Salvador has often been referred to as a "coffee republic." Indeed, following the mid-nineteenth-century decline of the indigo trade, coffee production gradually took over in this mainly agricultural country. The Native American population provided the bulk of the peasant labor on the coffee plantations. (They were descendants of the Pipil tribal nation, whose resistance had required three military expeditions in the early 1500s to complete the Spanish conquest of the area.) As was characteristic down the Pacific coast of Latin America, people of Spanish and mestizo (mixed blood) origin dominated the region economically, socially, and politically. Through the last half of the nineteenth century and the early decades of the twentieth, free trade ideology, the coffee landowning elite, and allied military leaders deeply influenced Salvadoran government policies. The government and the military worked closely with landowners who provided financial support. National Guard units were posted at coffee plantations to preserve order there.

As in the rest of Latin America in the nineteenth century, periodically elections were held among the small elite who had the right to vote. El Salvador was an example of the competitive exclusionary form of authoritarian rule (see chapter 15), which political scientist Robert Dahl referred to as "competitive oligarchy." Political contention was primarily between the Liberals, who favored free trade and development of modern infrastructure, and the conservatives, supported by traditionalist landowners and the Catholic Church. In El Salvador, most often the Liberals won. But often there was little practical difference between the parties' favored policy directions. And most importantly, leadership change was frequently punctuated by military intervention. Often a general might seize control of the government and then get himself voted in as president in the next presidential election, or a general from neighboring Guatemala might intervene to impose his favorite candidate in the Salvadoran presidency. So amid such periodic interference in party contention and cooperation, El Salvador's pre-democratic experience with elite-level electoral contention was a weaker positive factor for later democratic transition that it would have been without such military interventions.

From 1930 to the 1970s, the Salvadoran politics of democratization saw a repeating pattern, in a context of elite anti-Communist and anti-land reform fears. Every so often, a softliner military faction would take control and allow a somewhat free election. The official results would show a victory by the right-of-center, military-supported party, but substantial support for a left-of-center party or coalition. Then the dominant army-backed party would use fraud and/or disqualifications to settle into a single-party-dominant, electoral authoritarian rule for several years, often a decade or more. This pattern was repeated, with the formal names changing but the underlying pattern persisting, after elections held in 1931–1932, 1950, 1961, 1966, and 1972. Periodically, the military-backed presidents would follow the lead of Hernandez Martinez (president from 1931 to 1944), who started limited reform initiatives such as small social welfare programs, some trade protection for the urban informal sector, and a small export tax.

Over the course of this era spanning the middle third of the twentieth century in El Salvador, the most notable particular developments involved the treatment of the far-left opposition. At the beginning in 1932, legislative elections were held in which, surprisingly, the Communists were allowed to participate. But in retrospect this seemed to be aimed at identifying who and where their supporters were. After the Communists won a few seats, their winners were denied office. They then started a local insurrection in a few towns that was suppressed, followed by a brutal campaign of state terror by the military, killing something like 20,000 peasants (versus some thirty deaths in the original insurrection) and producing a coerced calm in the rural areas that would last for decades. In the 1950 election, the only left-of-center opposition was a broad center-left party (the Party of Renovating Action, or PAR), which for the rest of the decade declined to contest elections because of large-scale vote fraud guaranteeing victory by the dominant party.

A couple of significant new factors, however, emerged in the mid-1960s. First, President Julio Rivera approved a change to proportional representation (PR) elections in the fifty-two-member Legislative Assembly. This allowed smaller parties to get a foothold in the regional districts' legislative representation, rather than nothing in the previous party winner-take-all format. It also made possible contention by opposition coalitions (see below). Second, a new Christian Democratic Party (PDC) had been born (founded first in 1961). The PDC was then a center-left pro-democracy group seeking to apply moral principles to government while avoiding the extremes of right-wing repression and left-wing anticapitalism. It soon became the opposition acceptable to the military; PAR was accused of being Communist-infiltrated, and banned.

By the 1972 election, the PDC had adopted land reform as a cause, and allied with some smaller left-wing parties under a moderate platform, in what was called the United National Opposition (UNO). But again, the left-of-center opposition was gaining a level of support that frightened the regime. At a time of heightened Cold War tensions and fears among the coffee elite, the 1972 PDC presidential candidate, San Salvador mayor Jose Napoleon Duarte, seemed to have won a narrow victory. But the dominant party in control apparently manipulated the presidential vote count in favor of its own candidate. In the ensuing tumult, a coup attempt by a group of Duarte-supporting (softliner) military officers failed, culminating in Duarte's exile to Venezuela.

These developments cemented single-party-dominant, electoral authoritarian rule by the Party of National Conciliation (PCN), backed by the military and the coffee oligarchy. Expecting electoral fraud, the mainstream opposition boycotted the next elections. For all practical purposes, peaceful transition initiation in El Salvador was over for the decade of the 1970s. Radical groups—the most prominent of which was the Farabundo Marti Popular Liberation Forces (FPL)—organized supportive "mass organizations" (some officially led by radical priests). But they also increasingly adopted full-scale urban insurgent tactics such as bombing government offices, assassinations, and kidnappings for ransom. Apparently, the radicals' goal in these provocative actions was to create chaos which, they seemed to hope, would open the way for a popular revolution along the lines of the Sandinista revolution that proved victorious in Nicaragua in 1979.

The regime's approach in the 1970s was to increase repression. In the rural areas, the National Guard—aided by intelligence work by the paramilitary peasant cells of the shadowy Nationalist Democratic Organization (Orden)—helped coordinate widespread assassinations and "disappearances" by death squads, largely composed of retired and off-duty military officers. Meanwhile, the coffee elite vetoed weak formal gestures in the direction of land reform.

Amid this pattern of left-right political polarization and conflict, a softliner military coup occurred in 1979, whose junta included a couple of civilian PDC figures. However, the new junta's reform decrees—including democratic transition, the disbanding of Orden, and land reform—were frustrated by the conservative faction of the military (led by Roberto D'Aubuisson) and never really implemented. Moreover, repression

and death squad activity continued unabated. Anyone associated with opposition from the left could suffer assassination or disappearance at the hands of the death squads. Victims included the Catholic archbishop of San Salvador, four American churchwomen, and two American land reform advisors.

The various leftist organizations at that time included both (a) broader anti-regime groups trying to engage in demonstrations and strikes, associated in the Revolutionary Democratic Front (FDR), and (b) the smaller revolutionary parties in their Farabundo Marti National Liberation Front (FMLN). Ultimately the two forces consolidated their efforts in pursuit of armed insurrection. A big offensive in 1981 failed to arouse the Salvadoran population overall, and was suppressed. The FMLN settled in for a long insurgency, trying to get the upper hand in a few towns and areas, mostly unsuccessfully.

In the early mid-1980s, a pact-driven transition effort, in which international influence played a part, fell short of democratic consolidation. Under pressure from the United States, the military's chief aid provider, the government agreed to allow PDC leader Duarte to serve as temporary president while holding elections to a constituent assembly to write a democratic constitution and pick a provisional president. The elections featured three parties, the pro-democracy centrist PDC, the military softliner PCN, and the military hardliner party, the Nationalist Republican Alliance (ARENA), led by D'Aubuisson. While the PDC won a plurality, gaining over a third of the votes and seats (under PR voting), they were still opposed by the alliance of the two military-supporting parties, PCN and ARENA.

Negotiations produced a timetable for presidential elections in 1984 and legislative and local elections a year later. The main presidential contenders were the PDC's Duarte and the military hardliners' candidate D'Aubuisson (signaling the beginning of the decline of the military softliner PCN). Apparently, fraud did not play a major role in the vote count; Duarte won the runoff, and in 1985 his centrist PDC gained a legislative majority. This bolstered the influence of donors such as the United States (aiding the military) and the IMF (aiding the economy and business), who both pressed for peace negotiations.

This situation, however, made Duarte and the PDC government responsible for economic policy, wherein the IMF demanded austerity. In 1986, budget cuts, tax increases, fuel price increases (due to subsidy reductions), devaluation of the currency, and consequent inflation were unpopular with both business and labor. Protest marches increased. The PDC government had lost popularity, and legislative elections in early 1988 resulted in a narrow ARENA majority, followed by ARENA leader D'Aubisson winning the presidency in 1989.

Meanwhile, over the previous years, peace talks with the FMLN-FDR insurgency leaderships had occurred occasionally. But the talks had foundered over insurgent demands that their fighters be integrated into the army, and military demands that the insurgents lay down their arms. Amid the transfer of power from the PDC to ARENA, the FMLN-FDR no longer had reason to postpone peace negotiations in hopes of getting a more sympathetic government to negotiate with. On the right, the collapse of Communism in Eastern Europe was lessening ideological fears of revolution, and suspicion about FMLN intentions was receding. Both sides seemed willing to negotiate, and to accept the idea of the insurgency transforming itself into a peaceful political party. In mid-1991, a U.N. human rights observer mission arrived in El Salvador to monitor the behavior of both sides. By the end of 1991, they had agreed to a ceasefire, and within a year both the insurgency and key anti-insurgent units had disarmed.

The FMLN subsequently led a coalition of parties on the left, which was usually outvoted by the collective strength of ARENA plus the more moderate small parties, the center-right PCN and centrist PDC. But in the wake of the 2008–2009 financial crisis, the candidates of the FMLN-led left coalition won legislative and presidential victories. President Mauricio Funes, who served from 2009 to 2014, pursued moderate left-of-center policies similar to those of President Lula da Silva in Brazil in the 2000s. Alternation in power, a key indicator of consolidation, had finally been achieved. Notably, the small Grand Alliance for National Unity (GANA) and the PCN remain minor but significant parties in the ideological center/center-right—potentially needed to form majority legislative coalitions. Each tends to win 6–10 percent of the vote, and in the 2014 presidential election they formed a coalition called the Unity Movement, whose candidate, Antonio Sacca, won 11 percent of the first round votes. In the 2014 presidential election, the FMLN candidate Salvador Sanchez Ceren eked out an extremely narrow 50–49 percent second-round win over ARENA's Norman Quijano (with the bulk of Sacca's voters apparently going to Quijano). The early 2015 legislative elections were similarly tight, with ARENA slightly edging out the FMLN by 1.5 percent, and GANA and PCN together winning 16 percent.

Thus the two broad parties are likely to continue to be the major contenders, with the smaller center-leaning parties often holding the balance. The Salvadoran parties seem well on their way to institutionalization, and Salvadoran democracy virtually consolidated. A major remaining policy challenge is gang-related crime. President Cerén has pledged an all-out security push, and in early 2015 a new truce seemed to be holding between the two major Salvadoran gangs (MS-13 and Barrio 18). But the gangs' predatory impact on ordinary Salvadorans continues, contributing to the flow of desperate young illegal immigrants crossing the U.S. border.

◁ **PRACTICE AND REVIEW ONLINE**

CRITICAL THINKING QUESTIONS

1. What are the key differences between revolutions and democratic transitions?

2. What sorts of democratic transition exemplify a plural-elites model of influence distribution? Which exemplify a majority preference model?

3. How and when is sharp contention essential to democratic transition? How and when is cooperation also essential?

4. Which is best for democratic consolidation, presidential, semi-presidential, or parliamentary government?

KEY TERMS

consolidation, 473
rupture, 475
pacts, 476
agency theory, 477

FURTHER READING

Anderson, Lisa, ed. *Transitions to Democracy.* New York: Columbia University Press, 1999.

Boix, Charles. *Democracy and Redistribution.* Cambridge, UK: Cambridge University Press, 2003.

Bratton, Michael, and Nicolas van de Walle. *Democratic Experiments in Africa: Regime Transitions in Comparative Perspective.* New York: Cambridge University Press, 1997.

Cheibub, Jose Antonio. *Presidentialism, Parliamentarism, and Democracy.* New York, NY: Cambridge University Press, 2007.

Diamond, Larry, and Leonardo Morlino, eds. *Assessing the Quality of Democracy.* Baltimore: Johns Hopkins University Press, 2005.

Diamond, Larry, Juan Linz, and Seymour Martin Lipset, eds. *Democracy in Developing Countries,* 4 vols. Boulder, CO: Lynne Rienner; London: Adamantine Press, 1988.

Geddes, Barbara. *Paradigms and Sand Castles: Theory Building and Research Design in Comparative Politics.* Ann Arbor, MI: University of Michigan Press, 2003.

Grugel, Jean. *Democratization: A Critical Introduction.* London and New York: Palgrave Macmillan, 2002.

Haggard, Stephan, and Robert R. Kaufman. *Political Economy of Democratic Transitions.* Princeton, NJ: Princeton University Press, 1995.

Huntington, Samuel P. *The Third Wave: Democratization in the Late Twentieth Century.* Norman: the University of Oklahoma Press, 1991.

Lindberg, Staffan I., ed. *Democratization by Elections: A New Mode of Transition.* Baltimore, MD: Johns Hopkins University Press, 2009.

Linz, Juan J., and Alfred Stepan. *Problems of Democratic Transition and Consolidation: Southern Europe, South America, and Post-Communist Europe.* Baltimore: John Hopkins University Press, 1996.

Linz, Juan J., and Alfred Stepan, eds. *Breakdown of Democratic Regimes.* Baltimore: John Hopkins University Press, 1978.

Linz, Juan J., and Arturo Valenzuela, eds. *Failure of Presidential Democracy.* Baltimore, MD: Johns Hopkins University Press, 1994.

Moore, Barrington. *Social Origins of Dictatorship and Democracy: Lord and Peasant in the Making of the Modern World.* Boston: Beacon Press, 1966.

O'Donnell, Guillermo, Philippe C. Schmitter, and Laurence Whitehead, eds. *Transitions from Authoritarian Rule: Comparative Perspectives.* Baltimore: Johns Hopkins University Press, 1986.

Przeworski, Adam, Michael E. Alvarez, Jose Antonio Cheibub, and Fernando Limongi. *Democracy and Development: Political Institutions and Well-Being in the World, 1950–1990.* New York: Cambridge University Press, 2000.

NOTES

[1] See Samuel P. Huntington, *The Third Wave: Democratization in the Late Twentieth Century* (Norman: University of Oklahoma Press, 1991).

[2] A classic example of this sort of analysis is Guillermo O'Donnell and Philippe Schmitter, "Tentative Conclusions about Uncertain Democracies," in O'Donnell, Schmitter, and Whitehead (1986). For an early version, see Dankwart Rustow, "Transitions to Democracy: Toward a Dynamic Model," *Comparative Politics* 2 (April 1970): 337–63.

[3] See Carles Boix and Susan Stokes, "Endogenous Democratization," *World Politics* 55, no. 4 (2003): 517–49. This tends to weaken the contention of Przeworski et al. (2000) that while economic development is correlated with democratic consolidation, it is not so with transition initiation.

[4] See Michael K. Miller, "Economic Development, Violent Leader Removal, and Democratization," *American Journal of Political Science* 56, no. 4 (October 2012): 1002–20.

[5] See Boix (2003).

[6] See Daren Acemoglu and James Robinson, "A Theory of Political Transitions," *American Economic Review* 91 (2001): 938–63.

[7] See Christian Welzel and Ronald Inglehart, "Emancipative Values and Democracy," *Studies in Comparative International Development* 41, no. 2 (2006): 74–94 and Inglehart and Welzel, *Modernization, Cultural Change, and Democracy: the Human Development Sequence* (New York: Cambridge University Press, 2005).

[8] Again, in this book I have defined public values as particular forms of broad value categories such as freedom, order, justice, well-being, and equality—particular forms that people pursue on behalf of the whole community as well as for themselves or for a particular group that they identify with. Contending civil-society groups soon discover that they cannot gain civil and political freedom for themselves without assuring it for all.

[9] See Nancy Bermeo, *Ordinary People in Extraordinary Times: The Citizenry and the Breakdown of Democracy* (Princeton, NJ: Princeton University Press, 2003).

[10] See Geddes (1999, 2003).

[11] See Alfred Stepan, "Tunisia's Transition and the Twin Tolerations," *Journal of Democracy* 23, no. 2 (2012): 89–103.

[12] Recession is stressed in the model of Acemoglu and Robinson.

[13] See Levitsky and Way (2010); Huntington (1991) also stressed international pressure in "third wave" democratizations.

[14] The Catholic Centre Party got significant numbers of votes (11–12 percent), but was not well organized, targeted only the Catholic minority, and had little by way of clear ideological orientation.

[15] This pattern was most explicit in the Brazilian "moderator model"; see Alfred C. Stepan, *Rethinking Military Politics: Brazil and the Southern Cone* (Princeton, NJ: Princeton University Press, 1988).

[16] For the potential role of nationalism in single-party dominance, see Jack L. Snyder, *Democratization and Nationalist Conflict* (New York: Norton, 2000).

[17] For the general problem of such "neo-patrimonial" parties, see Bratton and van de Walle (1997), who suggest that the prevalence of such parties in Africa hinders the pacts that are needed for democratic consolidation.

[18] See "Presidential or Parliamentary Democracy: Does It Make a Difference?" in Linz and Valenzuela (1994), 3–87.

[19] For example, see Jose Antonio Cheibub and Fernando Limongi, "Democratic Institutions and Regime Survival: Parliamentary and Presidential Democracies Reconsidered," *Annual Review of Political Science* 5 (2002): 151–79.

[20] Occasionally the terms "superimposed" and "reinforcing" have been used to refer to this cleavage pattern.

INTERNATIONAL POLITICS

International Politics and Its Classic Models

FOCUS QUESTIONS

- **WHAT** are the main objectives of the international institutionalist approach to foreign policy?

- **WHAT** are the main types of institutions that structure international interactions?

- **WHY** might nations want to expand their power beyond their borders?

- **HOW** and why is national power checked in international relations?

- **WHAT** happens when balance of power patterns fail?

BY 2015, YEMEN, LOCATED ON THE SOUTHERN TIP of the Arabian Peninsula, was engulfed in all-out civil war. In many ways, the conflict appeared to be a domestic one that stemmed from deep internal political cleavages. Yemen had long been divided between its northern and southern regions. By the mid-nineteenth century, the British had colonized the south, but the north remained a traditional emirate dominated by the Zaidi sect of Shia Islam. (Today, the Zaidis comprise some 30 percent of the Yemeni population, centered in the northernmost and poorest Yemeni province, Sadah.) After the British withdrew from Yemen in the early 1960s, two Yemens formed: the Zaidi-dominated Yemen Arab Republic in the north, and the anticolonialist, left-wing People's Democratic Republic of Yemen in the south.

By 1990, the East European Communist regimes had fallen, and the decline of Marxism-Leninism in the south had paved the way for Yemini unification. The government was initially led by President Ali Abdallah Saleh and his General People's Congress party (GPC), which had formerly controlled only the north. Soon, however, a new form of north-south contention was emerging. South of the Zaidi heartland, Sunni religious orthodoxy was spreading and a Sunni Islamist party called Islah was organizing. Islah was linked to the Muslim Brotherhood, the Egyptian underground party, and among its top figures were tribal leaders of the Ahmar clan.

Among Islah's supporters, Sunni Salafist sentiment seemed to be growing. Salafism favors strict Sharia law based on a literal reading of the Koran and the early Sunni hadith (see chapter 6), as directives to be enforced—as many Salafists envision—by the state in a theocratic Islamic regime. By the end of the 1990s, a branch of the militant Sunni terrorist group al-Qaeda had sprouted in a few parts of the south. Under the name al-Qaeda in the Arabian Peninsula (AQAP), this offshoot pursued theocracy through military jihad and terror.

Many Salafists consider all Shias to be apostates (guilty of abandoning the true Muslim faith) and thus punishable by death according to the Sunni hadith. The spread of Salafism among Yemeni Sunnis created insecurity among the northern Zaidis. In the 1990s, a moderate Zaidi religious revivalist movement arose, called Believing Youth (BY), which sponsored clubs and summer camps for young people. By 2004, some Zaidi BYers were expressing themselves politically, chanting anti-U.S. and anti-Israel slogans outside mosques in the Yemeni capital, Sanaa. The Saleh government cracked down, arresting hundreds and pursuing (and ultimately killing) a leader of Zaidi revivalism, Hussein al-Houthi. Soon the "Houthi" insurgency was born among the Zaidis of the north.

Starting in 2005, the regime launched several military offensives (led by a top Islah leader, General Ali Mohsen al-Ahmar) against the Houthis, which at times brought widespread destruction to the already impoverished Zaidi heartland. These offensives persisted until a peace agreement was finally signed in 2010. Meanwhile, formidable economic problems continued, including water shortages and corruption in the government. By 2011, the Arab Spring protest movement had spread to Yemen, where protesters, backed by Islah and Mohsen's troops, ousted Saleh in 2012. But Saleh's less assertive replacement, his former vice president Abd Rabbuh Mansur Hadi, also of the GPC party, could not reunite the contending groups. His initial transitional government did not include Houthi representation, corruption and economic challenges continued, and the northern Houthis revived their resistance. Both the Houthis in the north and AQAP in the south gained territory at the expense of the government.

Finally, in 2014, Hadi removed the government subsidies that had kept fuel prices low, prompting widespread protests against the resulting skyrocketing price of fuel. The protests, supported by the Houthis, also demanded that the government address corruption, shortages, and high costs for other basic goods (including water), and Yemeni poverty generally. Former president Saleh (himself a Zaidi)—along with much of his GPC party and the large portion of the army that was still loyal to him—was still powerful, and Saleh shared the Houthis' opposition to the idea of Sunni theocratic rule that was being pressed by the Salafists. Finally the Houthis, with the support of many non-Zaidis concerned about the nation's corruption and poverty, and of major Saleh-loyal military units, were able to overrun much of the country. Military units loyal to Mohsen and the Islamist Islah party failed to stem the tide, although some tribal and Islah-affiliated groups continued to fight in local areas. By 2015, AQAP, recovering from an earlier loss of territory in the southwest, had established a new foothold in the southeast, and was conducting suicide bombings in Houthi-controlled areas.

These domestic developments, however, explain only part of the Yemen tragedy. International forces played a role as well. The original spread of Salafism in Yemen in the 1990s was partly the result of a concerted policy of Saudi Arabia's Sunni Wahhabist clerics, who follow the ultra-orthodox

Shafi'i school of Sunni Islam. They sought to export Salafism to Muslims everywhere, spreading the idea of using the state to enforce strict Sharia law. Moreover, Saudi financial backing has played a key role in the rise of the Islah party in the last two decades, General Mohsen's military campaigns of 2005–2010 against the Houthis in the north, and ultimately the Salah-backed removal of president Saleh. In addition, al-Qaeda exiles from Saudi Arabia (driven out of the kingdom when the monarchy turned against AQ jihadists after the end of the anti-Soviet Afghan war in the early 1990s) make up a substantial portion of AQAP in Yemen.

Among the Shia Zaidis, the Believing Youth religious movement of the 1990s itself had some international stimuli, being inspired partly by Shia clerics from Lebanon and Iran. Even the discontent that undermined the Hadi government in 2014 was not without international contribution: Hadi's fateful decision to abandon fuel subsidies (thus producing skyrocketing fuel prices) was largely a product of IMF pressure. By 2015, as the Houthis pushed their offensive southward, the Saudi military intervened with an air war against the Houthis. And the Saudis cut off funds to Houthi-controlled areas. While Iran does not seem to directly control the Houthis (who claim they are not receiving weapons or money from Iran), nonetheless Yemen is considered by some observers to be part of a larger power struggle in the Middle East between (a) Saudi Arabia and its Sunni allies and (b) Iran and its Shia allies. As you can see, the tragedy in Yemen cannot be fully understood without an awareness of the many international factors affecting the country.

POLITICS AMONG NATIONS

With this chapter, we move from politics within nation-states to politics between them. How does international politics differ from domestic politics? One key difference concerns political frameworks. In domestic politics, as we have seen, factors such as political parties, interest groups, and trends in public opinion contend and cooperate in the context of an overall governmental structure. In contrast, international relations is largely a matter of nation-states contending or cooperating with one another in an international environment with *no* sovereign authority structure over it.

This chapter examines two main theoretical approaches to how nations interact. Recall from chapter 3 that in political science, a theory tends to emphasize a particular independent variable or cluster of related variables, which are presented as usually the most important causal factors affecting politics generally, or some sector of the political world. In an international example, one major analytical approach starts from the absence of any overarching sovereign power over the world as a whole. In this context, many observers have traditionally stressed that countries primarily pursue their own national self-interest, using whatever advantages they have. This approach, called **realism** (explored below), suggests that concerns about national security drive nations' foreign policies. It pictures nations as preoccupied with military capacity and political and economic influence, relative to that of other nations. Thus internationally, realism stresses contention over cooperation. Where international cooperation occurs, realism views it as the result of the influence of one or more "great powers" coordinating their alliances to acquire more influence and security.

A contrasting analytical approach to international politics focuses more on cooperation than contention. It suggests that the world is becoming more cooperative over time, and stresses the role of international treaties, institutions, and diplomacy to ensure peace, security, and prosperity through formal international bodies such as the United Nations, the World Trade Organization, and the European Union. It is this aspect of international politics—the political framework aspect, if you will—that tends to come to mind first when students think of foreign relations. For this reason, we begin with this more recent approach to analyzing international politics (most international institutions developed only in the last century). Then, against this institutional backdrop, we will turn to the realist model and indications that it still plays a role in today's international relations.

INTERNATIONAL INSTITUTIONALISM

In the aftermath of the brutality and destruction of World Wars I and II, people across the world were hopeful about the potential for international cooperation and organization. They were motivated by a desire to prevent further wars and to promote internationally shared well-being values such as peace, security, and economic progress. A key result was a model of international behavior that I call **international institutionalism**. This explanatory approach focuses on diplomacy, negotiation, and rule following in international interactions. It emphasizes ways in which contentions between nations are structured by international institutions and customary cooperative practices as they pursue their national interests. Often the result is compromises that achieve some gains for all, but with no group getting everything it wants. Thus international institutionalism is partly an extension, onto the world stage, of ideas rooted in domestic representative democracy.[1]

International institutionalism in international relations focuses primarily on cooperation in two ways: through procedures and structures, and through shared values. A key form of cooperation that is evident in most national political processes is procedural: in their interactions, contending groups tend to comply with the rules and procedures of surrounding organizational frameworks. Such cooperation helps to structure political contention. But again, in international arenas there is no overall authority to enforce procedures and collective decisions as there is in domestic national politics, so cooperation among nations remains largely voluntary. Nonetheless, cooperation with international institutions—either formal or informal (I include established customary practices in my broad definition of "institutions")—is widespread in international relations. Nations' foreign policymakers know that their disregard of past commitments and institutional decisions can lead to retaliation by other nations, and cooperative behavior will be rewarded with reciprocal cooperation by other countries.

This perspective on international politics also points toward a second form of cooperation that centers on values. One or more values shared between contending groups can encourage them to explore, pragmatically, the empirical facts of the issues they are dealing with (perhaps with the help of the social and natural sciences) regarding how those values may be pursued most effectively. The international institutionalist perspective views interactions between nations as directed, at least partially, toward public values that seem to be nearly universally recognized as important internationally.

These public values can be classified under various broad value headings (see chapters 1 and 3). The most prominent are national and international well-being, in the form of peace and prosperity. Another relevant value category is freedom as it relates to national self-determination and universal respect for civil and political rights. A third relevant broad value is order, in the form of stability in the ways that nations interact politically and economically. More specifically, this means regular procedures and structures for resolving disputes. And recently, a role is emerging for justice. First, this refers to holding accountable those who violate internationally recognized norms, especially respect for, and observance of, civil and political human rights. Ideally, this includes appropriate judicial procedures and penalties for human rights abuse. Secondly, social justice is implicit in the (as yet very limited) pursuit of economic and social rights such as the rights to food and to health-care access.

These aims have led nations to establish specialized structures and roles for dealing with other nations, arriving at agreements with them, and adhering to international law. The fact that there is no world government—with the kind of authority over nations that national governments have over their citizenries—does not prevent people from having confidence that agreements, structures, norms, and stable processes can enable nations to resolve sharp contentions and achieve shared goals without resorting to force or war.

International Institutionalism and The National Interest

Within the international institutionalism model, contending nations are analogous to the citizens of a representative democracy. (Indeed, some observers see this perspective as naturally spearheaded by democracies because it reflects their political culture.) National governments interested in security are viewed more or less as equals. They are basically inclined toward cooperation and mutual respect, since they are "all in this together." From this perspective, national governments are capable of interacting rationally with other nations to avert disasters such as war and economic disruption. They are seen as inclined to pursue mutually beneficial objectives such as increased trade, prosperity, and protection of human rights. This pursuit of national security and other values can be viewed as a cooperative enterprise of many nations with diverse values and traditions, under the overall rubric of enhanced authority for international political frameworks. **Collective security**—in which all members come to the aid of a victim of violation—supported by all is considered more effective than trying to go it alone.

The spirit of international institutionalism was captured early by the eighteenth-century German philosopher Immanuel Kant (1724–1804), in an influential essay in 1795 entitled "Perpetual Peace" (see "The Philosophical Connection" below). After making a series of practical recommendations for avoiding war, Kant proceeded to make broader suggestions that he called "definitive articles" of peace. In addition to adopting representative government internally and accepting visitors from other countries with hospitality, Kant recommended the formation of a "federation" of "free states" to help resolve disputes between nations and regulate international commerce under international law.

THE PHILOSOPHICAL CONNECTION | Immanuel Kant

Kant's theory of international peace was founded on his general approach to philosophy and ethics. In his philosophy of knowledge,* Kant concluded that we do not know the "thing in itself" ("noumenal" reality). We only see the world as it appears, as "phenomena" already processed through certain categories (taken from Aristotle) such as space and time, that seem to be permanently programmed into our minds. But for Kant, there is one entity that we can be directly aware of: our own mind and its capacity for reason.

To be sure, we are partly physical beings, like animals, sometimes just pursuing our natural inclinations for good or ill. But for Kant, more deeply we are rational beings, capable of "practical reason." In our social behavior, we are capable of treating each other morally, as defined by what he called the "categorical imperative." Taking his cue from certain aspects of Rousseau's thought about the social contract (see chapter 5), Kant defined the categorical imperative as acting according to maxims that we would wish to be universal laws—a kind of "golden rule." Another key theme of Kant's ethics was treating other persons as ends—respecting their autonomy and consent—rather than trying to use them merely as means.

If we follow these practices, Kant argued, we will act with what he called "good will," and will refrain from pursuing purely utilitarian strategies that may sacrifice some for the benefit of others. To be sure, Kant did not seek to bar people from pursuing natural inclinations, such as material gain or the happiness of others. He only wanted such pursuits to be governed and moderated by maxims that were applicable universally and valuable in their own right, rather than for their utilitarian value. Kant argued that if nations try to use each other as means to achieve their "natural inclinations," they will not treat other nations the way they would want to be treated under the same circumstances, and there will be endless wars. But if nations follow the categorical imperative they can achieve "perpetual peace."

Kant started with a series of recommendations ("preliminary articles") for avoiding or limiting war (see "Concept in Context"), such as (a) make agreements that fully resolve issues rather than just temporary truces, (b) avoid standing armies and governmental borrowing for war, which intensify other nations' fears, (c) refrain from continued occupation after war, and (d) avoid using extremely cruel and alienating means of war (e.g., poisoning or assassination). Then Kant proposed "definitive articles" of peace: that national governments should be republican (with the executive power separate from representative legislatures, which must approve declarations of war), that nations should assure hospitality to temporary visitors, and most importantly, that nations should join in a federation of free states under international law to help resolve their disputes and regulate their commerce.

_____

* Philosophers refer to this branch of philosophy as epistemology.

The international institutionalist perspective on international relations is sometimes labeled the "liberal" one, and in some ways it is derived from classical liberal impulses. Recall from chapter 6 that classical liberal ideology emphasizes the autonomy of rational individuals. They could unite as equals under democratic governments to assure peace and security for free behavior in the economy and in sociocultural relations. But the label "liberal" can be confusing here, not only due to its multiple meanings related to ideology (see chapter 6), but also because some analysts of international relations use it narrowly to refer to an explanatory emphasis on the roles played by contending domestic interests and individuals in the making of nations' foreign policy.

Another sometimes-used word for the international institutionalist approach is "idealism," but this term carries the connotation of looking at the world through "rose-colored glasses." To its supporters, international institutionalism is ultimately quite real world and practical. They firmly believe that diplomacy is the tried-and-true, hard-headed road to countries' long-term national interest.

As noted above, the term institutions is meant very broadly. It can apply to established customs, agreements, and protocols as well as to bodies such as the U.N. General Assembly or the European Central Bank. Notably, a prominent early expression of internationalist institutionalism was Europe's Treaty of Westphalia in 1635. It ended a century of bloody wars fought among European monarchs in order to, among other things, impose their religious views on others. The treaty assured to each monarchy the right to govern its own affairs and deal with religion in its own way within the country's boundaries, without interference from other nations. (Today, of course, most nations support freedom of religion within their borders as well as internationally.)

The international institutionalism model does not deny each country's concerns for its own national interest and influence. It is understood that nations may have their own self-interested goals, such as national security, national wealth, and even the spread of certain social or religious values. However, the model assumes that national governments can recognize that other nations have their distinctive goals, too, and that one country's safe pursuit of values can accommodate the pursuits of others. International interactions can produce multiple winners (in contrast to the zero-sum aspects of realist attitudes described below). Established procedures and institutions can help coordinate nations' contention and cooperation by facilitating rational discussion and exchange of information.

It has been noted that well-established democracies, which generally accept a level of contention and cooperation among ideas and perspectives internally, tend not to go to war against each other.[2] Two major factors might help explain this pattern. Authoritarian leaders may be more confident in their ability to unite their country against an external threat, because they can forcefully quell any domestic opposition to war. Democracies, on the other hand, tend to accept the idea of disunity and can allow opposition to a war policy prior to actual conflict (not least because of the economic costs of war). And under representative democratic political frameworks, norms of negotiation, accommodation, and compromise have become commonly accepted. If the potential adversary nation is also a democracy, it too is likely to be accustomed to such patterns. International political frameworks and the norms and customs around them may be viewed as an extension of the practices of representative democracy.

Embassies, Consulates, and Bilateral Relations

Governments have specialized units and personnel to deal bilaterally (between two units) with other nations and their citizens in centers called **embassies**. Each embassy is located in the foreign capital and has an official head, the ambassador, with other staff under him or her. The ambassador takes direction, when necessary, from the foreign ministry back home, headed by the foreign minister.

The security of embassies in other countries is a crucial norm of cooperation in international relations. A nation's embassy staff in another country are accorded a guarantee of autonomy and security called **diplomatic immunity**—protection from detention and trial for actions taken in performance of their duties. Even if the host country thinks that some embassy staff are involved in spying, its main practical option is to expel the suspected diplomats rather than arrest and prosecute them. (If a diplomat is expelled, the guest nation may retaliate by expelling one or more of the host country's diplomats in the guest nation.) The strength of this norm explains the international shock which greeted the 1979 failure of the Iranian revolutionary government to protect the American embassy against the seizure of its diplomats by militants. This incident began several decades of hostility between the Iranian government and that of the United States.

Another component of a nation's foreign service is the **consuls** and their staff, who may be located in different cities in the host country. They do such things as processing visas and helping their countries' nationals in certain commercial matters. Embassy and consular staff also gather information about their host nations and sometimes serve as spokespersons for their native countries' governments. Thus embassy and consular officers function as go-betweens to foster ongoing international communication and to handle minor matters so that they don't blow up into major ones.

In addition, sometimes a state will designate a special **envoy** and a supporting delegation to go to another nation, or sit down with representatives of multiple nations, to help resolve a particular issue. Striking past examples of such negotiations include the nuclear weapons limitation agreements such as the 1963 treaty banning atmospheric nuclear tests, the 1968 treaty banning nuclear proliferation, the Strategic Arms Limitation treaties between the United States and the Soviet Union, and the Comprehensive Test Ban Treaty of 1996.

International Law

The idea of "natural law" governing the relations between nations is an ancient concept. Such rules originate in long-established and well-understood custom. For example, diplomatic envoys customarily enjoyed immunity long before the practice was spelled out formally at the Congress of Vienna in 1814–1815, which reorganized the boundaries of Europe after the Napoleonic Wars.

Official agreements (sometimes referred to as treaties), are a prominent form of international law. These agreements can be bilateral (between two nations) or multilateral (among a number of nations). But there is no overseeing power to guarantee that either type of agreement is observed. Under the aegis of the United Nations there is an International Court of Justice in The Hague, the Netherlands, which has handled over seventy cases since 1945. But its judgments have weight only with the affected nations' consent.

To be sure, breaking a provision of international law, particularly if a rule is rooted in long-followed custom among nations, can bring retaliation from other countries. This can be a significant deterrent. For example, a key part of the American debate about the treatment of enemy combatants in the War on Terror—including whether torture may be employed—concerns whether such treatment would invite other nations or groups to use such techniques on captured American soldiers. When the German military in World War I broke agreements and used poison gas, they soon discovered that it was a big mistake (bringing retaliation in kind), and Germany did not use poison gas in World War II. Alternatively, a community of like-minded nations may apply economic sanctions against a nation perceived to be violating some sort of international law, as in the case of the withdrawal of investment in South Africa over its racist system of apartheid in the 1980s, the trade restrictions against Iran in the 2000s over its uranium enrichment program, and in 2014 and 2015, the economic sanctions applied against Russia over its intervention in neighboring Ukraine.

If such sanctions are not widely observed, however, they won't be effective. Sometimes provisions in international law are not sufficiently clear or detailed, or don't seem to address important issues. In the end, formal agreements among the majority of nations often serve mainly as statements of shared aspirations. They reflect a consensus among nations concerning what rules enable people and societies to be secure and thrive, and thus ought to be respected. Backed only by the threat of retaliation, they fall short of the force of law within a nation.

The United Nations

In multilateral relations (among multiple nations), international law and inter-governmental interactions are handled in international organizations. As the global economy becomes more and more connected, nations have become increasingly interdependent. Not surprisingly, most nations have preferred to band together to deal with international challenges, rather than going it alone to protect their national interests. Increasingly, where interventions occur across national boundaries, only multilateral interventions are considered legitimate. These often include participation by nations whose strategic interests are not directly involved in the issue at hand.[3]

The United Nations, the most global international organization, was founded in 1945 in the aftermath of World War II by members of the victorious Allied forces. The founding goals of the U.N. were (a) to assure collective security against any attack by one nation against another, (b) to provide a political framework to resolve nations' differences short of war, (c) to cooperatively enhance well-being internationally, and (d) to enhance respect for human rights, especially after the Universal Declaration of Human Rights in 1948.

The United Nations has bodies whose members represent nearly all of the world's nations. The General Assembly represents the 193 member states with one vote each, usually cast by the nation's ambassador to the U.N. The General Assembly debates issues and gives developing nations the opportunity to express their views. However, it lacks the capacity to enforce its resolutions, such as those calling for withdrawal of Israeli occupation of the Palestinian West Bank and Gaza after 1967. The Economic and Social Council provides a venue for nations to discuss social, economic, and development problems, particularly those fac-ing the developing world. But it is powerless to actually redistribute significant resources to address problems of inequality.

The U.N.'s executive units operate independently of the particular member nations who supply the units' civil service personnel and funding to carry out U.N. resolutions and programs. The most prominent bodies for U.N. action are the Security Council and the Secretariat, located in New York City in the U.S. The Secretariat also has administrative centers in other places that oversee an array of offices and operations around the world, including programs for technical assis-tance to developing nations. The United Nations International Children's Fund (UNICEF), for example, has its main headquarters in New York, but the World Health Organization (which provides vaccines, for example) is headquartered in Geneva, Switzerland, and the Food and Agriculture Organization and the World Food Program are headquartered in Rome, Italy. And as we saw in chap-ter 13, there is the World Court in The Hague, the Netherlands, but it resolves cases only when the national parties choose to submit to its jurisdiction.

U.N. interventions in conflict situations must be approved by the Security Council, which is made up of fifteen member states at a time. Five nations, the United States, Britain, France, Russia, and China, have the special status of being permanent members, and each has a veto over U.N. action. Other nations rotate to fill the other ten seats. During the Cold War period of 1947–1991, the Security Council rarely took major actions because either the United States or Russia vetoed most proposed actions. The Security Council was able to approve U.N. intervention (led by the United States) in response to North Korea's invasion of South Korea in 1950 only because the Soviet Union was boycotting the Council at the time, and hence was not present to cast its veto. Nonetheless, the U.N. did take smaller actions during this period, such as stationing troops in zones between contending forces to monitor and bolster peace agreements, and setting up and supplying refugee camps for people displaced by conflicts. The Security Council continues to play this key role. In 1991, the U.N. authorized the American-led effort to roll back Iraq's invasion of Kuwait.

The United Nations, Secretariat Building, New York City.

To be sure, there have been failures and mixed outcomes. In the early and middle 1990s, the U.N. attempted unsuccessfully to intervene in fighting among Somali warlords that threatened the delivery of food aid to avert famine. In the case of the mid-1990s' genocide in Rwanda, the U.N. failed to respond (see Country Case Studies below). Efforts to set up safe havens for refugees in Bosnia in the middle 1990s met with mixed success; in 1995 in Srebrenica, the small number of poorly armed Dutch U.N. peacekeepers stood by as Serb forces abducted and later murdered over 8000 men and boys. Finally it was the North Atlantic Treaty Organization (NATO), under American leadership, that intervened with force to resolve the Balkan conflict.

Human Rights Institutions

A notable feature of U.N. activity is its attention to human rights. To be sure, human rights problems normally arise internally within countries where their national governments remain sovereign. But in the U.N.'s view, human rights problems in nations commonly spur international conflict, as well as offending widely held moral principles. As we saw in chapter 3, the Universal Declaration of 1948 was followed up in 1966 by the two international Covenants of human rights, one civil and political and the other economic, social, and cultural. These two Covenants went into effect for signatory nations in 1976. The United Nations Human Rights Commission (UNHCR), with fifty-three member nations, meets in a yearly conference of over 3,000 delegates and observers to discuss and pass resolutions on human rights challenges around the world.

Notwithstanding these formal international treaties and structures concerning human rights, real-world respect for human rights is driven primarily by national initiative, partly to support these formal international rules but also independently of them. In practice, the most important aspect of the international civil-political rights system is regular communication. As was noted in chapter 3 (the Human Rights Connection), the U.N. has a set of requirements for reporting on situations of possible human rights infringement and an administrative structure for assessing those reports and making recommendations. These requirements serve to highlight human rights values and enhance publicity of human rights infringements. But in terms of concrete action addressing human rights conditions, the effectiveness of this process depends heavily on voluntary national cooperation (see Country Case Study on Serbia below and the Rwanda case in chapter 18).

Given the basically voluntary nature of national human rights enforcement, the commitment of individual national governments and nongovernmental organizations often makes the biggest practical difference in human rights outcomes. Some governments go out of their way to support international human rights efforts. For example, the Norwegians, Dutch, and Belgians frequently supply troops for peacekeeping duty around the world. But many nations, especially the most powerful ones, such as the United States, tend to weigh carefully their own national interests before making commitments under U.N. or regional human rights systems. The American political executive did not sign the civil-political Covenant until 1977, more than a decade after it was drawn up in 1966. And the American Senate did not ratify the treaty until 1992, and it qualified its approval with stipulations ruling out the use of the U.S. court system to apply the Covenant. In the late 1970s, U.S. president Jimmy Carter, who put human rights on the American political agenda, nonetheless tended to criticize Soviet human rights practices more than those of America's Cold War allies.

To publicize human rights problems, some nations have increased their efforts to monitor human rights around the world. Faced with the early 1970s' upsurge in human rights violations in developing nations, the U.S. State Department began a comprehensive yearly publication reporting on civil-political human rights conditions in countries around the world. In the mid-1980s, the Scandinavian governments and their countries' human rights institutes began publishing a human rights yearbook reporting on both civil-political and economic-social human rights conditions in developing nations that received Nordic development aid.[4]

Nations can apply conditions to the foreign aid that they provide as a way of encouraging respect for human rights. Requiring aid recipients to improve their human rights conditions as a prerequisite for receiving foreign aid is called **conditionality**. In the early 1970s, for example, the U.S. Congress passed a law requiring conditionality. But subsequent administrations were selective in applying it. In the late 1970s, conditionality was applied to some of the most abusive military regimes in Latin America, for example, but not to the Marcos regime in the Philippines or the Shah's regime in Iran. Nonetheless, around the world in the 1980s and 1990s, increasingly donor nations and aid agencies pressed authoritarian regimes to democratize as a condition for continued development aid. In many cases, elections (though not necessarily free and fair ones) and greater civil-political freedom did ensue (see chapter 16).

Nongovernmental organizations (NGOs) have played a crucial role in fostering respect for civil-political rights. These NGOs tend to be specialized; for example, Amnesty International focuses on political prisoners, Human Rights Watch is concerned with freedom rights generally, attorneys in the International

League of Human Rights do legal work in human rights cases, journalists and other writers who are members of PEN International work for freedom of expression and the press, and there are many others.[5] Numerous NGOs are domestic, within the nations experiencing the human rights problems. Such groups play a crucial role in publicizing those problems, either through their formal access to the Human Rights Committee set up under the civil-political Covenant or through other channels.

Viewed as interest groups (see chapter 9), these associations are value related, typically without a tangible stake in human rights (at least until the violator regimes turn their repression on the NGO activists themselves). Information from them tends to be trustworthy, but regime intimidation and repression tends to keep their membership small. They tend to be very short on the resources needed to do their work.

Economic Organizations and Agreements, and Path Dependency

A major positive impetus behind international diplomacy has been the desire to increase international trade and mutual economic benefit. Despite governments' efforts to protect and enhance their own domestic economic potential (as in the economic-nationalist ISI strategies discussed in chapters 7 and 15), nations also tend to recognize their practical interdependence. They perceive incentives to build international economic relationships that might foster prosperity in the long run and further reduce incentives to go to war. The Great Depression of the 1930s showed that uncoordinated national economic policies could greatly worsen economic conditions for everyone.

In 1944, shortly before the end of World War II, representatives of the Allied nations met in Bretton Woods, New Hampshire, to discuss a new postwar international financial structure. They mapped out a system of stable exchange rates among currencies, established such entities as the IMF and the World Bank to help damaged and poorly developed economies to reconstruct and develop, and planned a series of recurring negotiations to reduce tariffs among nations.

Since the postwar recovery period, these arrangements have evolved. Exchange rates have since been freed to "float" (change in response to supply and demand) in currency markets. The IMF has evolved from overseeing exchange rates to acting as a creditors' bargaining agent in dealing with debtor nations. In that role, the IMF steers debtor countries' economic policies toward freer markets (see chapter 16). The World Bank has become a major conduit of aid for poorer nations' financial stabilization and development projects. The GATT (General Agreement on Tariffs and Trade) rounds of negotiated tariff reductions evolved into the World Trade Organization (WTO) in 1995, which can now impose sanctions on nations that violate trade agreements. The world's most economically powerful nations meet periodically in G-8 and G-20 conferences to discuss matters of mutual concern.

Other more specialized organizations and agreements have been created to regulate and resolve conflicts in specific areas. Some of these patrol particular multinational economic sectors, such as commercial fishing or whaling. Others address international environmental problems, such as the Kyoto Accords of 2001 to limit greenhouse gas emissions.

Implicit in the international institutionalist view of international relations is a key causal factor in the development of such institutions and arrangements: **path dependency**. Path dependency is the tendency of policymakers facing new situations to stick to the working methods and structures that they are accustomed to. The optimistic take on path dependency is that new institutions and practices can build habits of cooperation and trust in and around them, and achieve a train of partial successes. Over time, this can develop momentum down a path toward more elaborate and regularized practices and institutions to resolve intense contention and coordinate national policies. For example, the European Union (described below) developed out of the European Economic Community, which had developed out of the earlier European Coal and Steel Community in the immediate postwar era. As was noted above, the current WTO emerged from the success of the prior several rounds of GATT, in reducing tariffs on industrial goods to roughly a tenth of their prior levels.

Regional Organizations and the European Union

Some international organizations are regionally based. Their foreign ministers or other representatives meet periodically to discuss shared problems and disputes, and on occasion send a peacekeeping mission to a member country. Examples are the Organization of American States in the Western Hemisphere, the Organization for African Unity, and the Arab League in the Middle East. In addition, economic institutions have developed to foster free trade on a regional level, such as the North American Free Trade Agreement (NAFTA, including Mexico, the United States, and Canada), Mercosur (including Brazil and the southern cone of South America), the Asia-Pacific Economic Cooperation group, the Association of Southeast Asian Nations, the Southern African Development Community, and the East African Community.

Europe has by far the highest degree of regional coordination. Most of the region is now a free trade area with a common currency, the euro, and shared guidelines on such policy issues as national government budget deficits and social welfare policies. The European Community (EC) emerged in 1967 out of earlier economic agreements and initially included only France, Germany, Italy, Belgium, the Netherlands, and Luxemburg. Later Britain, Ireland, and Denmark joined the EC. Each nation was given a veto over measures that impacted it. By the mid-1980s, the EC was planning to become a free trade area with a single currency. The Maastricht Treaty signed in 1992 formalized this commitment, and in 1993 the European Union (EU) was born. A core group of countries within the EU began using a single currency, the euro, in 2002. Other nations in eastern Europe joined the EU after the fall of Communism, bringing the current number of member states to twenty-eight (see Table 17.1).

In its legislation, the EU has moved cautiously beyond trade regulation into other policy areas, which are traditionally the preserve of its nation-states. But it has gained importance now that its law is recognized by the courts as superseding national laws where the two conflict. The European Court of Justice (ECJ), though limited in scope, has played an important role in boosting and standardizing respect for human rights in Europe, alongside the larger Council of Europe (see chapter 14). In the 1970s, over half of ECJ cases concerned trade restrictions, whereas by the 1990s the percentage of such cases had dropped to around a quarter. The number of cases that address environmental protection,

TABLE 17.1	Date of Entry into the European Union or Its Predecessors		
Country	**Year of Joining**	**Country**	**Year of Joining**
Belgium	1958	Sweden	1995
France	1958	Cyprus	2004
Germany	1958	Czech Republic	2004
Italy	1958	Estonia	2004
Luxembourg	1958	Hungary	2004
The Netherlands	1958	Latvia	2004
Denmark	1973	Lithuania	2004
Ireland	1973	Malta	2004
United Kingdom	1973	Poland	2004
Greece	1981	Slovakia	2004
Portugal	1986	Slovenia	2004
Spain	1986	Bulgaria	2007
Austria	1995	Romania	2007
Finland	1995	Croatia	2013

consumer rights, taxes, worker freedom of movement, and gender equality has risen significantly.[6]

The European Union has a two-part legislature: a 785-member elected representative body, the European Parliament, and a more powerful Council, composed of ministers from member states. Votes in the Council are allocated primarily according to their countries' populations. The Parliament and Council are intended to consider proposals in policy areas that states cannot effectively address on their own. Generally the proposals are first formulated and presented by the Union's executive, the European Commission located in Brussels, Belgium. In the early stages of European integration, important proposals required the Council's unanimous approval. However, under the Maastricht Treaty, significant legislation can now pass with "qualified majority voting," which

"Yes" campaigners outside Dublin Castle celebrate the result of the favorable EU Lisbon Treaty vote (with nearly two-thirds supporting) in Ireland in 2009, backing closer integration with Europe. The vote was necessary because in Ireland, accepting the new reforms required amending the Irish constitution.

means the support of both a majority of member states (two-thirds for proposals not coming from the Commission) and 74 percent of the votes in the Council.

EU treaty revisions must be ratified by all member states. By the early 2000s, a proposal was afoot to create a European constitution to strengthen and clarify the Union's institutions and procedures (including strengthening the role of the European Parliament) and help address common issues such as climate change, terrorism, energy, and humanitarian efforts. In 2004, however, voters in France and the Netherlands rejected the idea. The Treaty of Lisbon of December 2007 tried a softened version of the reforms by only amending the previous treaties. It proposed, among other things, to change the qualified majority approval required of the Council to 55 percent of the votes representing 65 percent of the Union's population. The new provisions finally passed in all member states and went into effect in 2009.

Cooperation Outside Formal International Institutions

In addition to formal structures, established customs and patterns of cooperation can also be considered international institutions. As we have just seen, in key situations formal international institutions have relied on groups of individual nations to approve and take the lead in carrying out broad institutional commitments and resolutions. In terms of limit-setting power, this is reflected in the veto power possessed by each of the five permanent members of the U.N. Security Council (the United States, Great Britain, France, Russia, and China). In terms of positive action, path-dependent negotiations toward freer trade were spearheaded by the world's leading trading partners and the patterns of cooperative interaction in organizations that developed among them. And nongovernmental associations, ranging from international interest groups and multinational corporations to international and domestic human rights groups, can sometimes affect whether and how international commitments are implemented.

This aspect of international institutionalism has been stressed in the work of political scientist Robert Keohane. He began by recognizing the basic absence of a world government with the same domestic authority as that of national government, and how individual states' national interests can counteract widespread good intentions. In the light of such limitations, Keohane maintained that international cooperation and dispute resolution was not merely the product of existing formal institutions alongside incentives presented naturally by an interdependent world desiring peace and prosperity. He argued that clusters of countries that share common interests must make a conscious effort to cooperate to pursue and implement principles of international law.[7]

Indeed, recent experience has illustrated the need for coalitions of nations, cooperating in order to carry out widely supported international resolutions and commitments. Examples range from the coalition assembled in 1991 to reverse

CONCEPT IN CONTEXT | Peace Recommendations in the Real World

Early in Kant's essay on "perpetual peace" noted above, he listed a series of "preliminary articles" of peace. They amount to hypotheses regarding which factors encourage war, and which discourage it. It is interesting to trace how Kant's hypotheses have fared recently. The record is mixed.

One key Kantian recommendation for nations is to enter into peace agreements that really resolve the divisive issues, rather than only into truces that postpone them. Here, arguably, nations mostly do their best. However, they do sometimes resort to temporary, partial agreements like the 1990s' Oslo Accords on the Middle East, which have failed to secure lasting peace between Israel and the Palestinians in ways that illustrate Kant's point. On the other hand, the same process shows that insisting on, and waiting for, the resolution of all issues in a comprehensive agreement can make the best the enemy of the good, preventing any progress at all. Resolution of major contentions sometimes has to be one issue at a time, which can gradually build a momentum of trust and cooperation.

Second, Kant wanted nations to steer clear of two options that are perceived by other nations as threatening: standing armies (Kant found reserve armies and training permissible) and governmental borrowing for war, which provides easy access to funds for potential aggression. On their face, these proposals are unrealistic; obviously nations have long ago adopted standing armies and the option of borrowing money to fund wars. But a kernel of empirical truth remains in Kant's warnings about their negative consequences. With standing armies and borrowing capacity unequal between countries (see "offensive realism" below), advantaged nations might be perceived as especially threatening, encouraging suspicion and hostility in weaker nations. For example, the technological might of the American standing army and the seemingly unlimited American capacity for national borrowing to pay for its activities (without asking for tax increases to pay for war)—as in the case of the American war in Iraq in the 2000s—might make the United States appear especially menacing. This situation may invite fearful nations trying to deter the Americans to ramp up their tools for threatening the United States in return, perhaps including developing nuclear weapons that undercut nonproliferation agreements (e.g., in Iran today).

Kant's third article focused on refraining from colonial occupation of other nations or interference in their governments. Progress has been made on the first of these two points, with the mid-twentieth-century decolonization in the developing areas. But despite U.N. stipulations protecting national self-determination, at times invasion and continuing occupation occur and remain a barrier to lasting peace, as in the case of Israel and the occupied Palestinian territories. And the invasion itself may be judged afterward to have been a mistake, creating more instability, as most Americans now think about their country's 2003 invasion of Iraq. Notably, however, sometimes invasion by a neighboring country has proved to be the only realistic way to end genocidal behavior, as in the cases of Vietnam's invasion of Cambodia to remove the Pol Pot regime in 1978, and Tanzania's invasion of Uganda to oust the murderous dictator Idi Amin the same year.

Kant's fourth article provided that if you do end up in war, avoid using means that are so nasty, destructive, and alienating as to rule out any future mutual trust (e.g., assassinations or poisoning; in today's world, biological or chemical weapons). The "laws of war" have made progress, with (for example) the absence of poison gas in World War II after its use in World War I, and the dismantling of weapons of mass destruction programs by Saddam Hussein's Iraqi regime in the 1990s, by Muammar Gaddafi's Libyan regime in the 2000s, and by the Syrian Assad regime in 2014. But when a potential chemical agent cannot be entirely destroyed (e.g., chlorine, which has essential civilian uses), a group under siege may still be tempted to use it, as has been alleged of the Syrian government in its civil war in 2015.

Saddam Hussein's invasion of Kuwait and the NATO intervention in Bosnia in the mid-1990s (not U.N. sanctioned due to the Russian veto), to the 2014–2016 bombing of the Islamic State (IS) in Syria and Iraq and the emergency intervention to counter the Ebola virus epidemic in West Africa in 2015.

How could anyone fault international institutionalism's effort to build cooperation among nations around international political frameworks? Surely the benefits of broad cooperation outweigh those of unstructured contention and the outright conflict that can result from it. However, the appeal of international institutionalism's goals does not guarantee that national governments will always agree on the terms of cooperation, or follow them once agreed to. Regarding Kant's recommendations for avoiding war, for example, the track record is uneven (see "Concept in Context").

National governments are keenly aware that international agreements can be difficult to enforce, and that within and outside of international agreements, sometimes nations do push their own self-interests. In the end, the sovereignty of the nation-state still looms large. This brings us to another broad approach to explaining international relations, one that is focused on each nation pursuing its own national interest in an anarchic world.

REALISM AND INFLUENCE

As was noted at the beginning of this chapter, the realist model of international relations emphasizes contention between nations and the role of the influence of individual nations in international interactions, as each nation pursues its national interest. The **national interest** may be defined as a particular country's pursuit of a value (e.g., some form of public well-being such as national security) for the nation. Pursuit of the national interest sometimes undermines efforts at international organization and the application of international law. A prominent nation may refuse to sign an agreement at all, setting an example that weakens the agreement or the organization, as in the case of the United States refusing to join the League of Nations after World War I (see below), or to ratify the Kyoto Treaty in the 2000s. Some nations may refuse to enter into a multilateral agreement without certain exemptions in their favor, as in the case of key developing nations' (e.g., China and India) demand for exemptions from the greenhouse emissions requirements of the Kyoto Protocol.

Also, many agreements allow loopholes, explicitly or implicitly, that permit nations to act in ways contrary to the spirit of the agreements. For example, a nation that generally favors free trade agreements may insist on a tariff (a tax on a type of imported item) to protect a sector in its own economy from another nation's exports. It may cite such reasons as other nation's unfair subsidies of their exports, the exporting nation's own protective tariffs and regulations against imports, or the absence of labor or environmental protections in the exporting nation. A nation may simply want to protect a local sector that has been long associated with national survival (e.g., France's and Japan's tariffs, subsidies, and regulations to protect their farm sectors), or that it considers vital to its potential in world trade.

It is even possible to be suspicious about whether an international agreement has in the end served to further the national interests of powerful countries. The United Nations itself has persisted partly because each of the five most influential nations in the postwar era was given a veto in the Security Council, an important limit-setting power over the U.N. that those nations have used at times to protect their interests.

As was noted above, realism stresses the importance of differences in national power as countries contend with one another. The model's focus is more on international contention than on cooperation. According to the realist model, where cooperation exists it is mostly within each contending alliance and usually stems largely from the influence of the leading nation(s) within the alliance. In the writings of Thucydides on the history of ancient Greece, for example, concerns about relative power certainly governed much of the behavior of Athens and Sparta toward each other in the fifth century BCE.[8]

Offensive Realism

The mid-seventeenth-century British political philosopher Thomas Hobbes (see chapter 5) suggested a deep concern in human nature for "power after power." For him this stemmed from the insecurity that people feel when they find themselves in the "state of nature," outside the protective umbrella of government and its enforcement of laws and contracts. Without an overall government to compel peace and lawfulness through fear of punishment, Hobbes argued, competing individuals or groups will always worry about their safety and possessions, and will try to grasp for more power to protect themselves. For Hobbes, this view supported the establishment of national government to get individuals out of the state of nature and into assured security. Internationally, however, for Hobbes governments inevitably remained in this power-seeking state of nature in relation to each other. The focus on national security stemmed from human nature itself.

In the twentieth century, American political scientist Hans Morgenthau suggested that nations could be concerned with more than basic security; often they also want to pursue other values, whether religious, social, or territorial/material (e.g., Hitler's pursuit of territorial expansion to provide additional "living space" for Germans). But whatever values they are concerned about, nations need power to pursue them.[9] The realist viewpoint suggests that behind all of the appearances of international organization, cooperation, and mutuality, national governments also are—or should be—watching their backs, and may also be gazing over at greener pastures.

A recent model of realism, proposed by political scientist John Mearsheimer,[10] embodies the original Hobbesian idea of unlimited contention for power. Mearsheimer's argument for what he calls **offensive realism** follows a feature of Hobbesian contention in the state of nature: that everyone is uncertain and suspicious about the aims of other people, and thus never satisfied with the power that they possess. To assure its safety, any large power seeks to increase its power, ultimately to become dominant, in a condition called **hegemony**. In this view, international stability and cooperation can stem only from one dominant power calling the shots to assure its own security and control the outcome of major contentions in international relations. But each powerful nation cannot help struggling to become the hegemon, and the rise of a new challenger is always a potential upsetting factor. For Mearsheimer, full hegemony cannot be achieved and the struggle is endless.

Mearsheimer's picture seems to fit much of the first half of the twentieth century, when the balance of power strategy (see below) did not produce stability for long. Alliances frequently shifted as powerful nations rose and fell in international influence, and ultimately failed to prevent war. Defeat in World War I led to the collapse and dismemberment of the Austro-Hungarian Empire in Central Europe and the Ottoman Turkish one in the Middle East and southeastern Europe. The Japanese Empire rose rapidly in East Asia from the 1930s through the beginning of World War II, but collapsed with Japan's defeat. The German Empire quickly rose around 1940, but survived only during the war years of 1939–1945. The British and the French, after sharing strong international influence especially from the late nineteenth century up to World War II, saw the war weaken their empires, which subsequently yielded to decolonization between the 1950s and the 1970s.

Today, much projection of influence by individual nations is regional in scope, as donor nations provide aid to influence events and policy directions in nations around them. This capacity may have its roots in a nation's possession of valuable resources such as oil and gas. Especially if energy prices are high, exports of such resources bolster state budgets, enabling governments to exert more international political influence than they might otherwise have. Examples of this touch on some of the most important phenomena in recent international relations. Russia uses its role as a key supplier of gas to Europe to ward off attempts to curb its influence in Ukraine and Belarus. For decades, Saudi Arabia has used some of its oil wealth to enable the country's Wahabbist clerical establishment to fund Islamist religious schools and encourage the observance of strict Sharia law in Muslim communities in the Middle East and Asia. Shia Iran's oil profits have enabled its leaders to support the Shia majority in Iraq, the minority Alawite (a Shia offshoot) regime in Syria, Hezbollah in Lebanon, the Houthis in Yemen, and Hamas in Gaza. Venezuelan leader Hugo Chavez spread some of his country's oil wealth in the region to try to influence neighboring countries in the direction of his left social democratic ideological agenda.

However, when world oil and gas prices drop significantly, as they did in late 2014, such financially based influence may recede. For example, the fallback in oil prices has weakened Iran's capacity to extend aid to protect Shias from radicalized Sunnis in places like Iraq, Syria, and Yemen.

Offensive Economic Realism

Realism is normally viewed in terms of military strength and related political influence. But it is also possible to consider realism in economic terms, viewing nations as pursuing economic power.

The European colonial powers such as Great Britain, France, the Netherlands, Portugal, and Belgium displayed economic realism as they exploited their colonial possessions as sources of cheap raw materials (and as markets for their finished goods) without developing them much in other ways. As the colonies gained their national independence beginning in 1945, a new variant of economically based north-south realism emerged. Political sociologist Immanuel Wallerstein[11] characterized the early postwar globalization in terms of the unequal relationship of the world's economically powerful northern nations (what he called the "core" of the international economic system) to the underdeveloped south (the "periphery"). The south remained dependent on the northern nations not only as the prime markets for southern raw-material exports but also, increasingly, as suppliers of loans to finance development strategies. How so?

The 1970s saw a big spurt in northern lending to southern countries for development projects at very low interest rates, especially by banks who were deluged with "petrodollar" deposits from the windfall profits of the new oil cartel that had massively increased oil prices. Like any bank deposits, such money had to be lent out. By the 1980s when interest rates shot up to restrain inflation, many southern nations owed a lot of money to northern banks, governments, and other international financial organizations (e.g., the World Bank) that had financed their development efforts. The volume of such debt and the skyrocketing interest on it far exceeded what the debtors could realistically repay.

As the northern economic powers then offered new loans to help developing countries repay old debt (typically through the IMF), they made the aid conditional on the developing countries adopting free-market policies domestically, such as greatly reducing tariffs, regulations, and government spending. In effect, the northern economic powers were using their influence to impose free trade (sometimes called neoliberal) policies on the poor nations of the world's south. In the economic realism perspective, the aim was to allow the northern economic powers to continue their high rates of economic growth and prosperity while keeping most southern nations in their traditional role of poor, dependent suppliers of cheap raw materials. With the exception of a few export-oriented "**semi-periphery**" nations (e.g., South Korea, Taiwan, and Singapore; see chapter 7), the developing nations of the world's "periphery" could not become competitive contenders in world trade.

Today, for example, Germany pursues policies within the common-currency Eurozone that serve both to exercise and to consolidate its leading economic position and influence in continental Europe. In another example, China uses some of the proceeds of its large trade surpluses to affect its currency exchange rate (with the dollar), in ways that keep its products cheap in world trade and thus preserve and expand its penetration of world markets. Because the topic of economic realism is central to one of the major foreign policy challenges facing nations today, I postpone further exploration of it to chapter 18.

Defensive Realism and the Balance of Power

Traditionally, realism in international relations has been related primarily to military power. Following World War II, the United States and the Soviet Union emerged as the two strongest nations, with their vastly different systems of government and economics. International contention between these two great powers and their alliances initially seemed to stabilize international relations somewhat. How so?

Political scientist Kenneth Waltz has offered a new realist model to help explain this relative stabilization.[12] He suggested that in their international interactions, nations are alike in important ways. They recognize that while each government is sovereign over its own territory, the international political space is fundamentally one of anarchy, so that "self-help" is the starting point for foreign policy. Moreover, in contrast to Morgenthau's view that power may be pursued for a variety of purposes, Waltz argued that nations are focused primarily on security, and could rationally identify strategies that could usually, pretty reliably, assure that security. Where nations differ is in their relative power (principally military power). So achieving security means assessing the relative power of other nations in relation to their own power and acting accordingly.

The resulting pattern is a more moderate form of realism called **defensive realism**. Nations will form and join alliances to counter whatever power seems most threatening at the time. Sometimes referred to as "structural realism," this view stresses that strong nations in particular will try to cooperate and combine their forces to "balance" and check a rising aggressive power. Success in achieving a **balance of power** would be a rough balance in the military power and political influence between leading powers and their alliances. To be sure, such alliances are not so tight that one or more of their national members cannot shift alliances to better check a rising power. This behavior was common among the city-states of Renaissance Italy in the fifteenth century. Arguably, from the seventeenth-century Treaty of Westphalia on, and especially among the leading European powers after the defeat of Napoleon in the early nineteenth century, nations formed alliances to check whatever power seemed to be rising too rapidly and threatened to dominate the others.

In the last half of the twentieth century, peace among the big powers was more or less maintained for a forty-year period, from the late 1940s to the late 1980s, by a bipolar balance of power. The North American and Western European market-based nations faced off against the eastern bloc of Communist-run bureaucratic-socialist countries. Each alliance was spearheaded by a leading power: the United States and the Soviet Union, respectively.

After Stalin had driven back the Germans in World War II and imposed compliant Marxist-Leninist regimes on Eastern Europe, the United States adopted two primary strategies to balance the rising power of the Soviet Union: (a) the Marshall Plan, a massive aid package to get Western Europe back on its feet economically, and (b) the doctrine of **containment**—that every effort would be made to prevent any other countries, such as Greece, Turkey, South Korea, or Malaysia, from falling to Communism. Communism could be contained where it existed with the help of the North Atlantic Treaty Organization (NATO), which included the key Western allies. In response to NATO, the Soviet Union formed the Warsaw Pact with its East European client states. Cooperation within each alliance allowed it to contend effectively with the other.

As the two sides developed nuclear weapons (and later, powerful intercontinental missiles to deliver them), the capacity arose for "mutually assured destruction" (MAD) between the United States and the Soviet Union. Realists contended that MAD largely deterred both sides from aggressive moves, and kept the contest a "cold war" rather than a hot one. Although small regional conflicts might occur, as in the Korean conflict of the early 1950s and Vietnam in the 1960s, they were contained and kept from escalating into a larger war between the United States and the U.S.S.R.

Notably, however, the defensive realist model with its reliance on balancing power doesn't claim to be a strategy that will always guarantee stability and prevent wars. Its key aim is to explain the bases for whatever degree of stability and peace can be achieved, realistically speaking. But such values may not always be achievable; power balance may fail.

War: When Power Balance Fails

For realists in international relations, the key consequence of the failure of power balance is war. In chapter 15, we defined war as the application of physical force to defeat an enemy and gain control over a territory or some other strategic advantage. International war is between the armed forces of contending nations. The military theorist Karl von Clausewitz famously called war the "continuation of politics by other means." Again, however, in important ways, war represents the failure and abandonment of politics. War begins at the point where contention has become so extreme that the cooperation aspect of international politics disappears, and contention deteriorates into outright conflict. War may be bilateral, such as a war between two neighboring countries, or it may be between alliances of nations, referred to as world wars.

World War I was prompted in part by secret alliances among numerous nations, but was fought primarily by Great Britain, France, and Russia (the Allied powers) on the one side, against Germany, Austria-Hungary, and the Ottoman Empire on the other (until the United States entered the war in 1917 on the side of the Allies and shifted the balance of power). In only one morning during the 1916 Battle of the Somme, British forces suffered over 60,000 dead and wounded in an attack that failed and took no significant ground. The combination of World War I's horrific toll and its seeming senselessness spurred the first real attempt at an international organization in the form of a League of Nations. But requiring unanimous consent to act, and without the United States as a powerful member, the League proved weak and failed to restrain the rise and rearmament of Germany. World War II ensued, and its worldwide death toll was the greatest in human history. One country, the Soviet Union, suffered over 20 million civilian deaths (mostly from starvation) and 7 million combatant deaths.

American President George W. Bush speaking on an aircraft carrier just after the 2003 invasion of Iraq, declaring (under the banner "mission accomplished") an end to major combat operations in Iraq. Many years of combat operations against insurgencies were yet to come.

As indicated above, in principle, war is not politics; it begins where politics fails and ends. However, after World War II, some local wars resembled Clausewitz's conception of wars as events in international politics. For example, the United States intervened in the Korean War in the early 1950s, first against North Korean troops and later against the Chinese, and then again in the Vietnam War in the late 1960s and early 1970s against the south Vietnamese Communists and North Vietnam. In 1983, the United States invaded the small Caribbean nation of Grenada, and the 1980s saw a long war in Afghanistan between Soviet troops and rebel groups that included numerous Islamists. Many in the American and Russian foreign policy establishments saw these undeclared local wars as part of maintaining the power balance, alongside the nuclear standoff.

Today's Power Balances

After the fall of Communism in Eastern Europe and central Asia in 1989–1991, at first it appeared that America's supreme conventional military power might lead to an offensive realist American hegemony. Indeed, the Americans led the 1991 rollback of Saddam Hussein's Iraqi invasion of Kuwait, spearheaded the checking of Serb power in Bosnia in 1995 and Kosovo in 1999, ended Taliban control of Afghanistan (and its protection of al-Qaeda there) after the terrorist attacks of September 11, 2001, and invaded Iraq in 2003 to remove Saddam Hussein from power. The United States also provided key air support for the 2011 defeat of Gaddafi's regime in Libya.

These actions could be interpreted as the United States imposing hegemony in the aftermath of its triumph over the former Soviet Union in the Cold War. In most of these cases, the United States aimed to end oppression by authoritarian regimes that in the past had been, to some degree, allied with the Soviet Union. The implicit or explicit goals in each case included the installation of representative democracy and freer capitalism (and in Iraq and Libya, freer Western access to major oil reserves).

As early as the mid-2000s, however, Iraq and Afghanistan reminded the Americans of one of the lessons of the U.S. experience in Vietnam in the 1960s, and of the earlier French experiences in Vietnam and Algeria in the 1950s: that military technological superiority from the air does not always translate into power on the ground in the face of determined guerilla forces. By 2013, the United States had largely withdrawn from Iraq, was withdrawing from Afghanistan, and only gingerly supported some rebel factions in Syria. In Mali and the Central African Republic in 2013 and 2014, it was France that intervened to check the radical Islamists. The continuing American involvement in the Middle East has been to use air power selectively to weaken the new Islamic State threat and to aid local ground forces in trying to roll it back, not to directly invade.

Today the world is multipolar, with sometimes shifting alignments. Realist power thrusts tend to be regional as well, such as Vladimir Putin's resurgence of Russian influence in his region. Russia recovered in the 2000s (bolstered by the financial recovery brought by high oil and gas prices) from the economic weakness and disorganization of the immediate post-Communist era in the 1990s. While most of Central Europe has turned toward the European Union, Russia has reasserted influence over some of the former Soviet republics. While Putin was not able to prevent the Western recognition of Kosovo's independence from Russia's traditional ally Serbia in the late 1990s, nonetheless he achieved the world's tacit acceptance of the division of Bosnia and of security for its Serb-dominated sector. And Putin has halted the spread of NATO links and Western-style democracy to several of his closest neighbors. In response to a Georgian attempt to reassert control over areas with ethnic Russian majorities, in mid-2008 Russian troops marched into two breakaway regions of neighboring Georgia. And when the 2014 regime change in Ukraine removed a ruler friendly to Russia, Putin was able to back eastern Ukrainian resistance to the new regime and gain direct control of Ukraine's southernmost province, Crimea. Putin's late 2015 bombing in Syria, primarily to bolster the faltering regime of his traditional ally, Syrian president Bashar al-Assad, keeps Russia a key player in the Middle East.

The Middle East offers another example of regional power balance amid shifting alignments. In the 2000s, Shia Iran and its allies, the governments of Iraq and Syria and Hezbollah in eastern Lebanon, faced an informal alliance of the Sunni powers Saudi Arabia and Turkey with Israel (seeking to check Iran's nuclear capability, for example). Each alliance was backed by an outside patron: Russia supported the Syrian government and Iran, and thus, implicitly, the Shia alliance, while the United States backed the Sunnis and Israel. During the same period in Iraq, however, the United States and Iran remained in an informal alliance in support of the Shia-majority Iraqi government. And with the rise of the militant Islamist IS in Syria and Iraq in 2014, with its strategy of rule by terror, to some extent the regional alliances have been reshuffled. The Sunni oil states now find themselves in opposition to IS (at least officially), and Saudi Arabia has formally (though only nominally in practice) joined the air war against IS in Syria. But the

Saudis remain hostile to other groups that are aligned with each other in fighting IS: Shia Iran, the Syrian government (with the Shia-offshoot Allawites at its core) and the northern Yemeni (Zaidi Shia) Houthis.

In mid-2015 after a temporary election reverse for the dominant Islamist party (within a few months it had won back its parliamentary majority), even Sunni Turkey joined the air war against IS in a limited way, and allowed the United States to use some Turkish bases in the air war. Things are further complicated by the ethnic Kurds, who control territory in northern Syria and Iraq. They are among the most effective fighters on the ground against IS in Syria (where they are supported by the United States and Germany) and Iraq, but Turkey remains hostile to them due to their links with the Kurds of eastern Turkey struggling for autonomy there (including terrorist acts by the radical PKK).

By the autumn of 2015, a nuclear deal with Iran had eased tensions between the United States and Iran and Russia. And the Syrian government, suffering from troop shortages and battlefield reverses at the hands of IS, seemed to be tentatively reaching out to begin peace talks with the moderate Sunni opposition, brokered by officials of the emirate of Oman (though an important Saudi-backed salafist and jihadist Syrian group, Ahrar al Sham, had backed out of the talks, hostile to the prospect of a secular Syrian regime). In late 2015, IS extended its terrorism to include bringing down a Russian airliner, mass attacks in Lebanon (against Shias) and Paris, and a smaller attack (by IS supporters) in the United States. The result was stepped-up bombing and closer alignment—despite continued tensions over other issues—among the United States, Western Europe, Russia, and Iran, in fighting IS.

Nonetheless, these complex and sometimes fluid cross-cutting regional alignments, with cooperation characteristically mixing with contention, seem to limit the usefulness of any straightforward balance of power analysis. (As we shall see in chapter 18, additional light may be shed by another approach, stressing social identity ties such as religious and ethnic identity affinities, regarding international alliances in the Middle East today.)

Another factor complicating the decentralization of power balance is the increasingly important role played by nonsovereign actors. Multinational corporations often find themselves beyond the effective regulatory authority of any one national government. NGOs get involved in issues involving civil-political human rights and basic needs such as for minimal food and health care. International examples include Greenpeace in the environmental and wildlife policy areas, the French group Doctors without Borders (Médecins sans Frontières) in health, Amnesty International, which assists political prisoners, and the regional Human Rights Watch organizations concerned with political repression in general. Numerous NGOs are local, arising within one country. NGOs play increasingly important roles in highlighting, and sometimes influencing, how international problems are dealt with. In realist terms, the world certainly looks more ragged, complex, and multipolar than in the past.

Objections to Realism

As was noted above, realism in international relations most commonly refers to power-based politico-military relationships and patterns. A number of objections have been made to this approach by international institutionalists. First, realism cannot be the *whole* story. Powerful nations often take actions, join international

CONTENTION AND COOPERATION IN FOCUS | Shifting Issues and Alliances in Syria and Iraq

In Syria and Iraq, the idea of stable power-balancing (defensive realist) coalitions seems to have limited relevance. Alliances have shifted rapidly in response to new events and issues.

In recent decades, the traditional American stance in the Middle East and North Africa had been geared toward ousting authoritarian regimes that were former Soviet allies and introducing democracy and free-market capitalism. This meant supporting rebellious oppositions in Iraq, Libya, and Syria, for example. Russia has been on the other side diplomatically, opposing intervention to remove the regimes of Saddam Hussein in Iraq, Muammar Gaddafi in Libya, and Bashar al-Assad in Syria. But new developments in 2013 and 2014 led to shifts in alliances and position taking.

One example arose in Syria in 2013 around prominent incidents of use of chemical weapons in rebel-held territory. The chemical attacks were generally blamed on the regime (which denied responsibility for them), and initially led the United States to threaten to use its air power against Assad's chemical weapons capability. The Syrian rebels hoped that this might lead to direct American military involvement to support their rebellion. The Syrian government's allies, Iran and Russia, sharply opposed such intervention. However, this pattern of contention soon seemed to be overtaken by fears that Islamist rebels might capture these chemical weapons stocks and use them in Syria or elsewhere. Russia and the United States cooperated in a solution: have the regime's chemical capability removed and destroyed. Russia pressured the Assad regime into agreeing to get rid of the regime's chemical weapons, and by 2014 the United States and Syria had cooperated to eliminate them.

A parallel shift in the American position toward the Assad regime and its allies surrounded the rise of radical Islamists within the Syrian rebellion. As we shall see in chapter 18, the militant Islamist group Islamic State (IS) rapidly gained control of much of eastern Syria, and then in 2014 attacked eastward into northern and western Iraq. In the face of IS's violent and coercive imposition of strict Sharia law on controlled Sunni areas, the United States, Russia, and Shia Iran shifted from contention to partial cooperation to help shore up the various forces contending to stop the IS onslaught. Even pro-Sunni governments around the Persian Gulf (e.g., Saudi Arabia and the United Arab Emirates) declared themselves to be against IS's savagery and joined in the American air strikes (at least symbolically) against IS. However shaky, this new, broad coalition of previous opponents muted and/or replaced the previous coalition alignments.

organizations, cooperate with them, and deliver on commitments in ways that cannot be justified solely by go-it-alone national self-interest in wealth or security. For example, the Americans intervened (under the NATO umbrella) to protect Muslim populations from human rights abuses in Bosnia and Kosovo in the mid-1990s on moral grounds (see Country Case Studies below). And the Norwegians have applied significant resources, for a small country, to help impoverished nations. Even within balance of power strategies, nations often do not act solely on their own. They have to cooperate to maintain the alliances that balance the power.

Other objections to realism relate to the threat of war. According to the strategy of defensive realist power balancing, the threat of war can maintain an orderly peace. But in reality, efforts to balance power may contribute to war rather than preventing it. In some ways, World War I resulted from just the sort of commitments underlying the prewar alliances that were supposed to prevent war. In what has been called the **security dilemma**, mutual suspicion between powers and their alliances about the possibly aggressive intentions behind those alliances and military capacities drives arms races. The result can be destabilizing preemptive aggression. Are alliances and their spread of military capacities meant to be defensive, or offensive? Nations focusing on power can misinterpret each other's intentions, which can heighten tension and increase the risk of war. The same dilemma applies to the cyberwarfare capabilities of the 2010s; the same sorts of knowledge that are necessary to defend against electronic communications attack and terrorism can be used in offensive ways, as well.

Today it seems questionable whether the threat of war between major powers that underlies realism is still credible. The terrible consequences of the use of nuclear weapons continue to render them unthinkable for nation-states in practice. And globalization has created such a degree of international economic interdependence that even major conventional war may have been rendered unacceptable due to the catastrophic consequences of a large-scale war's disruption of financial, economic, and energy arrangements. Given the array of nuclear and conventional weapons that are currently available, and the economic and financial disruption that would result from large-scale conflict, world war simply cannot be allowed to happen. Arguably, power-balancing strategies need to be at least supplemented with international institutionalist efforts.

Further objections to conventional realism come from within the realist camp itself. One critique points out that nations are not all locked into the focus on relative power among nations that both Waltz and Mearsheimer stress. As the mid-twentieth-century realists had indicated, nations could vary in their goals in both offensive and defensive efforts.[13] Political scientist Stephen Walt has argued that conventional realism to some extent ignores the domestic politics of foreign policymaking, in which contending groups and their perceptions of threats and goals can play an important part.[14]

Opening up the inquiry to the role of domestic politics in foreign policymaking, and its contention among groups and goals, however, invites a more deeply critical approach. It suggests that international relations is seldom a matter purely of each national government being propelled by a single logic derived from external relationships, involving either international institutions or military power relationships among nations. In international contention and cooperation, there is often a role to be played by ideas and *shared social perspectives* behind nations' foreign policies—shared by members of groups both within the nation (e.g., nationalism) and across international boundaries. This outlook is referred to variously as the "social" or "constructivist" orientation. We shall explore its most substantial alternative motivational theory, focusing on the role of social identity groups such as ethnic, religious, or value-based affinities, in chapter 18.

SUMMARY: CONTENTION AND COOPERATION IN INTERNATIONAL INSTITUTIONALISM AND REALISM

In this chapter, we have examined two perspectives on international relations. One major approach structures international contention around cooperation with international institutions, from consulates and embassies to broader international law and the United Nations. Those institutions include customary practices and past agreements as well as formal international structures. World regional organizations are important too, the strongest of which is the European Union.

Realism, on the other hand, de-emphasizes participation in international institutions. This strategy stresses contention more than cooperation. It emphasizes each country's pursuit of its national interest, especially by maximizing national power. The result may be hegemony (dominance) by one nation that imposes cooperation on others with the implicit threat of superior military force. More often, alliances of nations contend with each other, as expressed by the defensive school of realist strategy. Usually each alliance has a leading anchor nation that exhibits a patron-client style of cooperation with its allies.

COUNTRY CASE STUDIES

Serbia and Mali are both countries in which international interactions are having major impacts. Most recently, international institutionalism-motivated human rights interventions have curbed realist-motivated efforts to exert power. Under Communism, the Yugoslav Federation had maintained a large degree of independence from Soviet preferences, so when the country broke apart in the early 1990s, Serbia, the federation's largest republic, continued a largely independent foreign policy that focused on supporting ethnic Serb populations in neighboring countries. Mali, on the other hand, was a former French colony that remained connected to its former colonial master. Both countries, however, have experienced intervention from the outside to check human rights challenges.

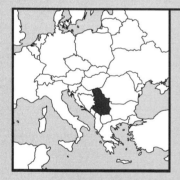

Serbia: Nationalist Realism and Human Rights Protection

The foreign relations of Serbia have focused most on realism, related to the country's regional neighbors. This realism has a long history. Five centuries after the still-remembered defeat of the Slavic and Christian Serbs by the Muslim Ottoman Turks (in 1389), Serbian nationalist struggles in the nineteenth century were finally rewarded with independence for the kingdom in 1882. As required by the Versailles Treaty that ended World War I, Serbia formed the center of a regional unit that also included Croatia, Slovenia, and Montenegro, and in 1929 was renamed the kingdom of Yugoslavia.

In World War II, it was the Serbian partisan guerillas, not the Soviets' Red Army, that spearheaded the liberation of Yugoslav territory from German control. By the middle 1950s, after a decade of Soviet aid and influence, Yugoslavia's League of Communists led by Josip Broz Tito had broken with Moscow, and joined an international "non-aligned" (with either Cold War protagonist) movement, along with India and other third world nations. By the 1960s, Yugoslavia was embarking on a competitive market system. Economic enterprises were publicly owned but autonomous, each controlled (at least in theory) by its elected workers' council. This approach presented a market-based socialist alternative to contend with the Soviets' centralized bureaucratic one. It sought to avoid the difficult questions of allocating resources among regions that would have arisen for Yugoslavia under a command economy. Tito sought to limit Serb control of the federation somewhat, but Serbs remained dominant in the army. In the early 1970s, the regime clamped down on tendencies toward Croatian autonomy among the League members there.

After Tito's death in 1980, tensions emerged among the republics as non-Serb regions renewed their desire for autonomy at the same time that Serb nationalism was on the rise. The popular Serbian leader Slobodan Milosevic adeptly crafted and intensified Serbian national Orthodox Christian identity. This identity-based strategy especially bolstered the Serb minority in the country's southernmost province, Kosovo, whose ethnically Albanian majority is primarily Muslim. Resurgent ethnic ultranationalism also reached beyond Serbia's borders to Serb populations in Croatia and Bosnia-Herzegovina.

With Croatia and Slovenia pressing for greater autonomy within the federation, tensions came to a head when negotiations failed in 1991. After limited military conflict, the independence of Croatia and Slovenia was established. The longest and most destructive ordeal, however, began when war broke out in the ethnically mixed state of Bosnia-Herzegovina in 1992. Hostilities commenced after Bosnian Serbs (over a third of Bosnia's population) opposed a referendum declaring Bosnia's independence from what remained of Yugoslavia. Milosevic informally backed the Bosnian Serb forces and sent volunteers and supplies from Serbia. In response, the U.N. imposed a trade and oil embargo on Serbia. The Bosnian Serb security forces used terror (particularly rape and murder) for "ethnic cleansing," to coerce Bosnian Muslim and Croat populations into leaving their villages. This human rights disaster proceeded for years, and led to an alliance between Bosnian Croats and Muslims in 1994.

International institutions tried to negotiate agreements to protect human rights, but achieved little success. The United States favored international intervention, but Russia, sharing its broad Slavic ethnic identity with the Serbs and traditionally supporting them, would likely veto any aggressive intervention under U.N. auspices. The U.N. was limited to stationing small contingents of troops in certain areas that were declared "safe," and, in a war crimes tribunal in The Hague (the Netherlands), to prosecuting individuals found guilty of gross human rights abuse.

However, mid-1995 saw the above-noted brutal massacre of civilians by Bosnian Serb forces in Srebrenica (which killed 8000 Bosnian Muslim men and boys despite attempts by the few Dutch peacekeepers in the area to protect them), along with more artillery attacks on civilians in Sarajevo. Soon came a development that illustrates the above-mentioned point by political scientist Robert Keohane[15]: that the implementation of international institutionalist goals must at times be spearheaded by direct action by clusters of allied nations. Air attacks were mounted by NATO, the main Western alliance (led by the United States).

These air strikes heavily weakened the Bosnian Serb forces, as leading Bosnian Serb figures were being indicted in the U.N. war crimes proceedings in The Hague. Finally the Yeltsin government in Russia was willing to join the United States in pressuring Serbia's leader Milosevic into meeting in Dayton, Ohio in 1995 to negotiate an agreement to end the Bosnian war, which became known as the Dayton Peace Accord.[16] The truce left Bosnia divided roughly in half, one part Serb controlled and the other Bosnian and Croat controlled.

None of this, however, had resolved the longstanding conflict in the Serbian province of Kosovo. Kosovo's population is primarily ethnically Albanian and Muslim (with a small Serb minority), but it had never been a distinct republic in the Yugoslav Federation, and the area contained a historical site revered by Serb nationalists. Kosovo had gained some autonomy from Belgrade in the 1980s, but lost it to Milosevic at the end of the decade. In the early 1990s, the Albanian majority undertook a peaceful movement to secede from Serbia, which was unsuccessful. In the wake of the negotiated end of the Bosnian conflict in late 1995, a Kosovo Liberation Army (KLA) arose to engage the Serbs in guerilla warfare. KLA attacks alternated with violent Serb reprisals. International institutionalist efforts such as new U.N. sanctions against Serbia and attempts at peace talks failed.

In early 1999, Serb security forces undertook what appeared to be a massive terror-driven ethnic cleansing against the ethnic Albanian majority. They used violence and the threat of it to force the Albanians out of their villages, producing huge numbers of refugees. In response, NATO began air attacks not just in Kosovo but also on targets in Serbia. This halted the forced exodus and led to a peace agreement. Serb security forces withdrew from Kosovo and the U.N. Security Council established a U.N. protectorate in the region. Some returning Albanian refugees attacked Serb civilians and drove many into Serbia, where some 200,000 Serb refugees still reside. Periodic attacks against Serbs in Kosovo in the mid-2000s have now subsided. Gradually, the rule of law came to prevail. In 2008, Kosovo's provisional assembly declared independence, though Kosovo remains formally a U.N. protectorate. The Serbian government contests Kosovo independence, and it does not affect an area in northern Kosovo containing three Serb-dominated towns, which remains under Serb control. Throughout Kosovo, many small Serb enclaves participated peacefully in recent local elections. Kosovo is essentially independent, though Russia continues to block its official U.N. recognition as a nation in the Security Council.

In Serbia itself, an international institutionalist factor increasingly came into play in the 2000s: the pursuit of membership in the European Union. First, this required that Serbia confront and resolve its past of human rights infringement. Milosevic was defeated by reform parties in the 2000 elections, and by mid-2001 had been handed over to the U.N. tribunal in The Hague for a Kosovo-related war crimes trial. (He subsequently died in prison during his trial.) In mid-2008 former Bosnian Serb president Radovan Karadzic, after many years in semi-hiding, was captured and brought to The Hague for trial. Notably, in early 2010 the Serbian parliament itself passed a resolution condemning the July 1995 Serb massacre of 8000 Bosnian civilian men and boys at Srebrenica, the most conspicuous single act of human rights abuse of the Bosnian war of the 1990s. In 2011, two other fugitive Serb leaders were captured and extradited to The Hague for war crimes trial: the Bosnian Serb military chief, Ratko Mladic, and the former leader of the Croatian Serbs, Goran Hadzic. And in early 2015, seven men were arrested in connection with the 1995 Srebrenica massacre in Bosnia.

Political contention within Serbia has continued to be affected by tensions between international institutionalist-oriented support for EU membership and more realist and identity-oriented support for closer links with Russia instead. In the early 2010s, the momentum toward international institutionalism seemed to be winning out, supported by the main parties. From 2012 to 2014, the majority coalition was made up of the (democratic socialist) Socialists along with the larger conservative and nationalist Serbian Progressive Party. But in the parliamentary elections of 2014, the Serbian Progressives scored a big victory, winning nearly half the votes and a parliamentary majority. The new prime minister, Alexander Vucic, has been unwilling to join in EU sanctions on Russia for its intervention in Ukraine, and hence Russia has exempted Serbia from its embargo on EU agricultural imports to Russia. In addition, Russia's gas giant Gazprom owns most of Serbia's main oil company, and Russia has pressed Serbia to participate in the planned southern pipeline project to convey Russian gas to Europe by going around Ukraine. All this makes the EU unhappy.

Regarding Russia's annexation of Ukraine in 2014, though, Vucic has favored Ukraine's claim, citing the parallel with Serbia's wanting to continue its hold on Kosovo. Nonetheless, many Serbs support Russia's intervention in Ukraine, and a few have even joined it (opposed by Vucic). Serbia continues to walk a fine line between pro-Russian realism and pro-Europe international institutionalism.

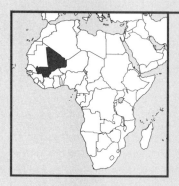

Mali: Regional-Religious Cleavage and French Intervention

Mali illustrates two of chapter 18's four foreign policy challenges facing nations today: poverty in the developing world and militant Islamist terrorism. Mali's colonial economy depended on rural production, with cotton as the main cash crop for export. Recent development of some gold mining has helped, but Mali continues to depend heavily on foreign economic aid, especially from France. In recent decades, donor aid has been increasingly conditioned on Mali transitioning to representative democracy. As we shall see below, after some reversals and a near fatal recent attack by militant Islamists, Mali seems to be making that transition.

Beginning in the fourteenth century, Mali was the site of powerful Muslim empires that encompassed the upper Niger River basin and connected trade routes across the southwestern Sahara. In this period, the city of Timbuktu was a center of Muslim learning and trade. But in the last half of the 1800s, France conquered Mali and folded it into its empire in West Africa, under the name of French Soudan. French colonial rule ended in 1959 with the creation of the Mali Federation, which included Senegal. By late 1960, the federation had broken up into independent Mali and Senegal.

For several decades, Mali followed the common pattern of that era for poor developing countries:

authoritarian rule by either a single party or the armed forces. The party that had spearheaded the anticolonial movement in Mali established a socialist one-party state under its leader, Modibo Keita, who cut Mali's ties with France and allied with the Soviet bloc. But with the economy failing by the mid-1960s, the regime turned back toward economic relations with France. In 1968, a coup led by a junior officer, Moussa Traore, brought Mali under military rule. President Traore ruled in his first decade as the head of a military regime, and then, after 1979, he led a military-backed single-party regime (the Democratic Union of the Malian People, or UDPM). Many banking and commercial enterprises remained state owned, including one controlling the marketing of cotton.

In the early 1990s, however, aid donors were pressing debtor nations to adopt multiparty democracy, as a pro-democracy social movement was challenging the regime from below. Between 1989 and 1991—a period of democratic transition in much of the developing and post-Communist worlds—many groups protested against one-party rule. After sharp clashes in early 1991, a military coup installed a transitional government led by Amadou Toumani Toure, which organized elections for the following year.

A French-style semi-presidential system with two-stage elections was drawn up and ratified by a "social pact"-style conference (see chapter 16) of a wide array of groups in mid-1991. Notably, in the style of several new African democracies in the period, the new constitution barred the registration of parties based on region or religion. In 1992, Malians elected a president and a parliament, whose PM would be nominated by the president but would be responsible to the parliament. The Malian government's budget continued to depend heavily on development aid from the international donor community, ranging from the IMF and World Bank to the French and American governments.

Mali's first elected president was Alpha Oumar Konare, a former education minister who had become a leader in the pro-democracy uprising. Konare's party, the Alliance for Democracy in Mali (ADEMA), won the parliamentary elections of 1992. ADEMA had evolved from a faction of the former single party (the UDPM) of the 1980s. Most of ADEMA's early allies soon went into opposition to the party, and in 1997 the opposition parties boycotted the vote following a dispute about election irregularities. Thus the 1990s had not solidly consolidated democracy; a single party was dominant, and voting turnout was low. For Mali to continue to maintain the donor support on which the government's budget depended, the keys were an evolution toward a genuinely multiparty democracy and a plan to address Malian poverty.

The 2000s did see an increase in multiparty contention and toleration of it. In the run-up to the 2002 elections, factional contention within ADEMA produced splits. Over the course of various election outcomes in the 2000s, other parties emerged: the Rally for Mali (*Rassemblement pour Mali*, or RPM) led by former PM Ibrahim Bubacar Keita, and the Union for Republic and Democracy (URD) led by a reform-oriented technocrat, Soumaila Cisse. In practice, ADEMA was led by the independent Amadou Toure, who had headed the 1991 transitional military government that had first established multiparty democracy, and retained substantial popularity among the people because of this past pro-democracy role. By the late 2000s, Toure was leading a coalition of ADEMA and URD, which generally won elections, while the main opposition was supplied by a coalition led by RPM. But Toure sought to include representatives of the other parties in his governments.

Mali's foreign relations continued to be dominated by its economic needs that had prompted the essential donor support. In the 1990s, the Malian economy had undergone much privatization and liberalization, reduction of government budget deficits, and improved tax collection, under pressure from the IMF and the World Bank. But little overall progress was made in fighting poverty. Over the 2000s, though, international institutions gained some confidence in Mali due to Toure's antipoverty plan and the country's continued representative democracy. A large portion of Mali's unpayable past debts were forgiven, reducing its yearly interest payments, and aid continued to flow to support its budget and development efforts in such areas as road building and education. Partly with help from increased gold mining, significant gains were made in some areas. For example, the proportion of Malian children attending primary school went from under a quarter to over half by mid-decade. But economic improvement was uneven by region, providing a key challenge faced by Mali and the donor community in recent years.

Periodically drought takes a heavy toll on Mali, and overall poverty statistics have been slow to improve. Extreme poverty continued in Mali's north, where the reach of government is weakest. The most politically active group in the north, the nomadic (Berber) Tuaregs, had rebelled in the 1990s, demanding autonomy or full independence for the north. That rebellion had been quieted only by a 1996 agreement that included establishing a new administrative region in the area of Kidal in the northeast. But Tuareg poverty continued, and a new Tuareg insurgency arose in the mid-2000s. Again, this was temporarily settled in 2006 by an agreement (mediated by the government of Algeria to the north) that promised development aid.

By 2011, however, the Tuareg leaders of MNLA, the National Movement for the Liberation of Azawad (their name for northern Mali), argued that the promises of development aid had not been fulfilled. In their quest for at least autonomy and at most national independence, they demanded the reduction or withdrawal of central government military troops in the north. At the beginning of 2012, reportedly with the benefit of weapons from the deposed Libyan Army and victorious Libyan rebels, the MNLA sought control of the whole region. An important ally in this effort was a radical Islamist group, Ansar Dine, which had been prominent in the MNLA. A March military coup in Mali's capital provided the occasion for MNLA units supported by Ansar Dine to take the important urban centers of Kidal, Gao, and Timbuktu, and to declare the national independence of the north.

The cooperation between MNLA and Ansar Dine reflected opportunism; each seemed to need the other for the regional rebellion to succeed, but their aims differed sharply; the Twareg MNLA was largely secular and wanted national independence for its region, while Ansar Dine, with growing resources and fighters from outside Islamist groups, wanted to establish a theocratic Islamist regime and rigid Sharia law throughout Mali. By the end of June 2012, the groups' cooperation broke down into contention, and Ansar Dine drove MNLA troops out of the big northern towns. Increasingly the lines blurred between Ansar Dine and other Islamic groups such as (a) the Movement for Oneness and Jihad in West Africa (MOJWA), centered around Gao, and (b) most importantly, al-Qaeda in the Islamic Magreb (AQIM), which seemed the biggest financier of the effort and the main orchestrator of the flow of jihadi fighters into Mali from neighboring countries. The imposition of Sharia law in the north by violence (or the threat of it) seemed very unpopular among ordinary northern Malians (especially the Songhi farmers), and produced over a million fleeing refugees and a humanitarian disaster.

These events of early 2012 led eventually to increasing cooperation in southern Mali to deal with the rebellion in the north, but not right away. A military coup in March 2012 by a faction of the under-resourced and poorly trained Malian military was no help against the rebels on the ground. More Islamist jihadis converged on Mali to consolidate administrative control and impose Sharia law on the north. The coup in the south served only to alienate donors and the most relevant international group at the time, Mali's neighbors in the regional Economic Community of West African States (ECOWAS), which immediately sanctioned Mali with a blockade.

In early April, however, ECOWAS mediation (led by the president of neighboring Burkina Faso) led to an agreement between the southern military and political leaders to formally restore constitutional government. President Toure (then in hiding) agreed to resign, and the presidency was passed to the speaker of the National Assembly, Dioncounda Traore, a longstanding ADEMA leader and prominent minister in the 1990s under then prime minister I. B. Keita. The military junta, though, continued to exert power behind the scenes under its leader, Amadou Sanogo. It obstructed outside military help, and allowed (if not encouraged or conducted) human rights abuse in the south against Tuaregs, Islamists, and other perceived opponents of the junta, including violence and disappearances. Meanwhile, the armed forces were making no significant military progress in the north.

By late 2012, an international institutionalist consensus was evolving among France, the United States, ECOWAS, the African Union, and eventually even the U.N., that some sort of outside intervention would be necessary to retake the north from the Islamist jihadis. It was in this cooperative context that at the beginning of 2013 the jihadis—by then evidently under AQIM control—suddenly mounted a drive into the south that threatened to approach the capital. This finally precipitated outside intervention. French forces, by then welcomed by President Traore, entered and drove the Islamists back and out of northern Mali. Having secured the populated areas, over the course of 2013 the French troops were mostly replaced by a U.N.-coordinated peacekeeping force made up of units from other African nations. But actions by small Islamist units still occur at times, and French special forces units continue to be active. International cooperation obviously continues to be necessary to contend with the international jihadist threat.

The climate for the aid has been bolstered by the continuing vitality of multiparty politics in Mali. By mid-2013, conditions were stable enough for presidential elections to be held. The leading candidates were those of the three long-standing parties: ADEMA, the RPM, and the URD (There was no significant independent candidate like Amadou Toure who had won in 2002 and 2007). Probably the best known was Ibrahim Bubakar Keita, the leader of the RPM since its creation in 2001 (when it split off from ADEMA). Keita had formerly served as PM in the ADEMA cabinet of the mid-to-late 1990s, as president of the National Assembly from 2002 to 2007 (with ADEMA's support), and as the main rival to Toure in the presidential election of 2007. Having left the PM position in 2000 under a cloud of alleged corruption, in 2013 Keita pledged to pick a cabinet of ability rather than politics. He won the presidency, chose a technocratic former bank official to be his PM, and subsequently dissolved the military junta committee that had ruled Mali briefly in 2012 and had continued to exist under the subsequent civilian government.

However, through 2015 the situation in the north remained unresolved. Armed groups, mainly Tuareg and their allies seem to run most of the area. Various militia groups at times fight among themselves for control of trade routes to profit from commerce and smuggling. Finally in mid-2015, U.N.-sponsored talks produced a peace agreement, including a government pledge to the Tuaregs of local elections, greater northern autonomy, and greater representation in the national government in Bamako.

With French special forces and air units still active in the north, the jihadists have not yet returned there in force. But it may only be a matter of time. Many ordinary northerners remain disgruntled, often still suffering from local corruption and extortion, and from lack of education, health, employment, and even food in some areas. In the late summer of 2015, discontent among the nomadic Fulani ethnic group of central Mali had contributed to the emergence of a new militant Islamist group there (apparently with links to al-Qaeda), the Massina Liberation Front.

Mali's government in the south has made gains toward democratization, and will likely continue to receive international aid, but more of it will have to be applied effectively to develop the north if stability is to be achieved.

◁ PRACTICE AND REVIEW ONLINE

CRITICAL THINKING QUESTIONS ——————

1. How does international institutionalism further the national interest of countries?

2. To what extent does the United Nations Framework achieve its goals?

3. How and to what extent do human rights institutions and agreements affect national governments' behavior?

4. To what extent do national power-based strategies achieve their goals?

5. What part does realism play in the global economy?

KEY TERMS ——————

realism, 506
international institutionalism, 507
collective security, 508

embassies, 510
diplomatic immunity, 510
consul, 511
envoy, 511
conditionality, 514
nongovernmental organizations (NGOs), 514
path dependency, 516
national interest, 520
offensive realism, 521
hegemony, 521
semi-periphery, 523
defensive realism, 524
balance of power, 524
containment, 524
security dilemma, 528

FURTHER READING ——————

Art, Robert J., and Robert Jervis, eds. *International Politics: Enduring Concepts and Contemporary Issues.* New York: Addison-Wesley Longman, 2000.

Baylis, John, James Wirtz, Eliot Cohen, and Colin Gray, eds. *Strategy in the Contemporary World.* New York: Oxford University Press, 2002.

Diehl, Paul F. *Politics of Global Governance: International Organizations in an Interdependent World.* Boulder, CO: Lynne Rienner Publishers, 2001.

Fasulo, Linda. *An Insider's Guide to the UN.* New Haven: Yale University Press, 2003.

Gilpin, Robert. *Global Political Economy: Understanding the International Economic Order.* Princeton: Princeton University Press, 2001.

Holsti, K. J. *Taming the Sovereigns: Institutional Change in International Politics.* New York: Cambridge University Press, 2004.

Keohane, Robert O., and Joseph S. Nye. *Power and Interdependence,* 3rd ed. Glenview, IL: Scott, Foresman, 2003.

Morgenthau, Hans J. *Politics Among Nations: The Struggle for Power and Peace.* Boston: McGraw-Hill Higher Education, 2006.

Nau, Henry. *Perspectives on International Relations,* 2nd ed. Washington, DC: Congressional Quarterly Press, 2010.

Nye, Joseph S. *The Paradox of American Power: Why the World's Only Superpower Can't Go It Alone.* New York: Oxford University Press, 2002.

Scholte, Jan Aart. *Globalization: A Critical Introduction.* New York: St. Martin's, 2000.

Waltz, Kenneth N. *Theory of International Politics.* Reading, MA: Addison-Wesley Pub. Co., 1979.

NOTES

[1] See the discussion of international relations in terms of "liberalism" and "idealism" below.

[2] See James Lee Ray, *Democracy and International Conflict* (Columbia, SC: University of South Carolina Press, 1995).

[3] See Martha Finnemore, "Constructing Norms of Humanitarian Intervention," in *The Culture of National Security: Norms and Identity in World Politics,* ed. Peter J. Katzenstein (Columbia University Press, 1996), 153–85.

[4] For example, see the 1994 edition: Peter Baehr, Hilde Hey, Jacqueline Smith, and Theresa Swinehart, eds., *Human Rights in Developing Countries: Yearbook 1994* (Deventer, Boston, and Oslo: Nordic Human Rights Publications and Kluwer Law and Taxation Publishers, 1994).

[5] See Margaret E. Keck and Kathryn Sikkink, *Activists Beyond Borders: Advocacy Networks in International Politics* (Ithaca, NY: Cornell University Press, 1998), and Claude E. Welch, Jr., ed., *NGOs and Human Rights: Promise and Performance* (Philadelphia: University of Pennsylvania Press, 2001).

[6] See chapter 14.

[7] See Robert Keohane, "Theory of World Politics: Structural Realism and Beyond," in *International Institutions and State Power: Essays in International Relations Theory,* ed. R. Keohane (Boulder, CO: Westview Press, 1989).

[8] See *Complete Writings of Thucydides: The Peloponnesian War/the Unabridged Crawley Translation,* with an Introduction by John H. Finley, Jr. (New York: Modern Library, 1951).

[9] See Morgenthau (2006).

[10] See John J. Mearsheimer, *The Tragedy of Great Power Politics* (New York: W. W. Norton, 2001).

[11] See Immanuel Wallerstein, *The Modern World-system* (New York: Academic Press, 1974).

[12] See Waltz (1979).

[13] See Randall Schweller, "Neo-realism's Status-quo Bias: What Security Dilemma?" *Security Studies* 5 (1996): 90–121.

[14] See Stephen Walt, "The Enduring Relevance of the Realist Tradition," in *Political Science: The State of the Discipline,* ed. Ira Katznelson and Helen V. Milner (New York, W. W. Norton, 2002), 197–230.

[15] See note 8 above.

[16] See Richard Holbrooke, *To End a War: From Sarajevo to Dayton—and Beyond* (New York: Random House, 1998).

Social Identity and Today's Foreign Policy Challenges

FOCUS QUESTIONS

- **HOW** do internationally shared social identities and related values affect contention and cooperation in international relations?

- **HOW** do differences in interpreting religions affect the impact of religion on international politics?

- **HOW** might social identities reinforce realist strategies?

- **WHAT** are the biggest foreign policy challenges that nations face today? What lines of contention are at work in each, and how might the interplay of contention and cooperation resolve them?

IN 2011, A TRAGIC PROCESS BEGAN UNFOLDING: the civil war in Syria. Authoritarian regimes had been swept from power by mass uprisings in Tunisia and Egypt, so why not in Syria, to remove a regime with episodes of violent repression of opponents in its past? For some time, political discontent had been rising. (Among other things, a multiyear drought had hit Syria's agricultural areas, sending distressed farmers fleeing to the cities.) Most prominent among the frustrations was the authoritarian government's long-standing exclusion of the Sunni Muslim majority from participation in Syria's leadership. The government was run at the top by the Assad family and its associates from the Alawite sect, a minority offshoot of Shia Islam.

What began as peaceful protests in early 2011 were at times met with regime violence, and eventually escalated into rebellion and full-scale civil war. Neither the government nor the rebels had accurate, sophisticated weapons, so as the war dragged on, civilian deaths mounted into the hundreds of thousands, and those fleeing to squalid refugee camps now number in the millions.

In 2003, the United States and Great Britain had intervened to remove a repressive dictator in Iraq. That did not end well, but nonetheless many called for Western intervention to at least arm the Syrian rebels in a major way. At first, the U.S. government was reluctant. Americans had little reliable knowledge of the rebels they would be arming, apart from two facts: (a) a rising portion of the effective fighting seemed to be done by militant Islamist groups that the West did not want to see replacing the Assad regime, and (b) incidents had occurred in which arms provided to secular rebels had ended up captured by, or sold to, Islamists.

In 2014, however, a new development arose that produced a very different sort of international intervention. The Iraqi arm of al-Qaeda, which had been largely driven into Syria from its original home in Iraq, began conquering new territory in Syria. Along the way, it was capturing weapons and vehicles from other rebel groups as well as from the regime, and other resources such as oil for fuel. Soon the group controlled a significant chunk of territory in Eastern Syria, in which it imposed strict, medieval-style Sharia law (see chapter 6), through public killings of suspected dissenters and other coercive acts of terror. Declaring its independence from its parent, al-Qaeda, the group renamed itself the Islamic State (IS, sometimes called "ISIL"—the Islamic State of Iraq and the Levant). And following the custom of the medieval Islamist empires, IS declared its leader, Abu Bakr al-Baghdadi to be its "Caliph" (the old title given the supreme imperial leader).

Meanwhile, IS's numbers of fighters were constantly growing, fed not only from young men from conquered areas who were coerced and/or religiously indoctrinated into military service for IS, but also by a growing inflow of militant Islamist fighters from other countries. Bulging with territory, resources, and ideologically committed fighters, the group suddenly carried out an audacious and successful attack back into the northern and western Sunni areas of Iraq. (The Sunnis there felt little allegiance to the Shia-dominated Iraqi government that had been excluding and sometimes repressing them.) In their invasion, IS captured large amounts of fairly up-to-date American military equipment from the disintegrating Iraqi government forces, including tanks, artillery, heavy machine guns, and armored personnel carriers. IS had become an international entity, spanning large areas of both Syria and Iraq. In some ways, it was following the playbook of the Saudi Wahhabi jihadists of the late eighteenth and early nineteenth centuries, and the post–World War I Isfahan movement (See chapter 6).

If a medieval Islamist empire could arise and expand this quickly with modern weapons in hand, where would it end? In response, not only the United States and other Western military powers, but also the Gulf Arab states (intervening in Syria), joined in air strikes in Syria as well as Iraq. The aim of the Western powers was to support Kurdish, Iraqi government, and other local forces in their efforts to stem, and ultimately reverse, the IS onslaught. To some extent, this new international context tended to supplant the prior debate about trying to remove the Assad regime in Syria. (The earlier overthrow of the authoritarian state in Libya had led to no state at all in that country, with radical Islamists increasingly filling the void.)

Thus a domestic tragedy in Syria had become a large-scale exercise in international cooperation against a common foe. In many ways, the battle represents a clash of identifications and solidarities—IS with its intense religious identification and solidarity with a radical Sunni version of Islam, versus a diverse array of supporters of individual freedom, sharing a sense of identification with freedom values but with less of a sense of solidarity among them. The factors that gave rise to this conflict, and that prompt international interactions around it today, are things we need to understand.

SOCIAL IDENTITY IN INTERNATIONAL RELATIONS

Each of the two perspectives on international relations discussed in the previous chapter, international institutionalism and realism, tends to rely on its own pattern of logical reasoning from particular facts—for international institutionalism the facts of international institutions and their potential, and for realism the facts of the relative power possessed by nations and alliances. A third approach to understanding international relations suggests that policymakers can vary in how they interpret the facts of the case, and that nations' foreign policies are influenced by shared social perspectives on the challenges that they confront.

Spearheaded by political scientist Alexander Wendt,[1] this social approach, also known as **constructivism** (see "Concept in Context: Constructivism") stresses that states' conceptions of their identity and interests are affected by perceptions, attitudes, and meanings that emerge in their social and political interactions with other states. Even realist ideas—for example, international anarchy, the consequent necessity of national "self-help," and strategic participation in power-balancing alliances—are notions that actually emerge from such patterns of interaction, and thus may be interpreted differently by different actors in particular situations. As nations participate in international institutions, for example, the social norms and expectations that govern the institutions (e.g., the rule of law and customs of reciprocity) and the shared knowledge and trust that emerges from experience in them, in turn, affect nations' international behavior. And the

CONCEPT IN CONTEXT | Constructivism

Some analysts refer to the social approach to understanding international relations with the term "constructivism." But the idea of "construction" in this context can be a little misleading. It connotes something that is consciously invented or designed. Indeed, some shared social perspectives that influence foreign policymaking were originally spearheaded by individuals, small groups, or elites, who intentionally crafted and propagated them.* Examples such as al-Qaeda, American "neoconservatism," and the current ethnic ultranationalist campaigns in Russia and China come to mind. And at times leaders use public relations techniques to try to steer public opinion in support of their foreign policy agenda. For example, Russian president Vladimir Putin's interventions in Ukraine in 2014 and 2015 should be viewed against the backdrop of his long-cultivated campaign to arouse ethnic Russian nationalism in his country.

But while social identities such as shared ethnicity or religion, for example, may not be purely "primordial" in the sense of being set in nature, nonetheless

typically they do not seem to have come solely from intentional construction or invention, either. Shared social perspectives often seem to emerge gradually over time among groups that identify themselves with them. (Constructivists themselves often stress that identity groups result from "discourse" among multiple participants, involving "symbols" and "stories.") Religious affinities such as the Sunni and Shia identities in the Middle East are, at least in part, bigger phenomena than the individual leaders who try to activate, enhance, or even manipulate them. In the big picture of the development of socially shared perspectives, terms such as "emergence" and "evolution" may sometimes be more appropriate than the notion of artificial creation that seems to be inherent in the term "construction."

_____

* For a perspective that stresses the role of leadership in activating identity groups for political purposes, see Paul R. Brass, *Ethnicity and Nationalism: Theory and Comparison* (Newbury Park, CA: Sage, 1991).

social approach considers the impact of non-state actors, such as multinational corporations, other interest groups, and NGOs such as human rights groups that try to affect governments' policies by publicizing their misdeeds.

However, as I have presented it so far, this social approach to understanding international politics has less explanatory coherence than either the international institutionalist or realist approaches offer. Many supporters of the social approach do not defend a third motivational theory to contend with the other two. The social approach often seems only to be directing our attention to "everything else" in social attitudes that can affect foreign policymaking, beyond the rational logics of international institutionalism and realism, enriching our understanding of how realist and international institutionalist strategies play out in the real world. For example, a nation's international institutionalist strategy may be supported by the country's own democratic values. And a nation's realist strategy can be bolstered by domestic nationalism (see below).

Within the social approach, however, there is one factor that can be viewed as motivating particular sorts of international strategy and interaction: shared **social identity**. At times, social identities seem to play outsized roles in motivating international contention and cooperation, especially when it comes to international alliances. Social identity can take the form of shared identification and solidarity with a particular group, such as an ethnic or religious category that spans national borders, or an international social movement with its own values and world view. And as noted above, nationalism itself can be an impactful social identity.[2]

We usually think of identity groups as contenders in domestic politics (see chapter 9). But they can cross national boundaries, too, and affect international interventions, alliances, and agreements. Identity linkages with foreign actors can motivate a nation's foreign policy actions in ways that may contend with, or alternatively reinforce, strategies that stem from international institutionalism or realism.

After exploring the social identity factor thematically, this chapter considers several foreign policy challenges that nations face today in which social identity has been a contributing factor: global warming, poverty in the developing world, radical Islamist terror, and international financial instability. As we shall see, each challenge presents its own distinctive patterns of contention and cooperation.

Ethnic-Cultural Contention

A key factor that can cross boundaries to affect foreign relations is shared ethnicity. Border-spanning ethnic attachments can be enhanced by value-related concerns, such as greater freedom, dignity, or material prosperity for a particular ethnic group. Members who consider their ethnicity to be primary to their personal identity may be drawn to views associated with that ethnicity, perhaps "framing" a rival group or country (and past and present contentions with it) in a distinctive negative way. For example, through much of the middle and late twentieth century, Arab nationalism was a key factor in Middle Eastern nations' relations with the West and Israel, sometimes picturing the nation of Israel as a Western imposition as well as a Jewish state. In eastern Europe, shared ethnic identity has influenced Russian support of fellow Slavs in the former Yugoslavia and fellow ethnic Russians in Ukraine, Belarus, Moldova, and Georgia.

In parts of the world, democratic transitions (some related to the end of the Cold War) have ended the prior authoritarian suppression of ethnic or religious contention. In some cases, the subsequent intensification of ethnic conflict has crossed national (some new) boundaries. For example, in post–World War II Yugoslavia, the Serb-dominated army and regime kept a lid on potential tensions between Serbs, Croats, Bosnian Muslims, and other non-Serb groups; after the fall of the Yugoslav regime and the advent of the national independence of the regions of the former federation, conflict arose that crossed borders (see Country Case Study on Serbia, chapter 17). In Africa, conflict in Rwanda and Burundi between Hutus and Tutsis cut across national boundaries. Once the former Belgian colonial rule that had enforced Tutsi dominance over Rwanda and Burundi was removed and the area divided into two nations, international ethnic identities and interactions contributed to both the Rwandan genocide and how it was brought to an end (see Country Case Studies below).

Religion and the "Clash of Civilizations"

Recently, the most widespread form of identity-related international relations has emerged in the tension between radical forms of Islamism and the views of secularists and other religions. More than two decades ago, American political scientist Samuel Huntington suggested that increasingly a "clash of civilizations" between Islam and other great religions was replacing the old cold war ideological division as the most important source of cultural identification and contention in international relations.[3]

Certainly, divisions cited by Huntington between such civilizations as Anglo-European Christian, Islamic, Chinese, and Hindu have always existed. The Anglo-European Christian versus Islam cleavage is at least as old as the Moorish invasion of Spain in 711 and the Christian crusades of the twelfth and thirteenth centuries. Most recently, however, new West-versus-Islam tensions emerged in some areas in the aftermath of 9/11[4] and other subsequent al-Qaeda acts of terrorism, and the conquests of Islamic State in Syria and Iraq. Radical Islamist military efforts have also arisen in parts of northern Africa and in other areas of the Middle East.

In the Middle East, the spread of Islamism has largely replaced traditional secular Arab nationalism, and seems to be deflating optimism about the near-term spread of democracy there. The spirit of democratic cooperation represented by the Arab Spring has largely been replaced by secular versus Islamist cultural contention. In U.S. policy toward Syria and Iraq from 2014 on, the prior American power-balance contention with Iran was largely replaced by limited American cooperation with Iran to contend with the violent and totalitarian religious extremism of the Islamic State.

To be sure, in developing areas with weak states and out-of-control street crime, Sharia law with its swift and harsh punishments (see chapter 6) can appeal to some people. In this situation, fundamentalist Islamists may frame the crime problem in terms of what they see as a Western cultural overemphasis on personal freedom. Such Islamists advocate curbing a range of other activities that they associate with the West, from banning alcohol, dancing, and gambling to generally restricting the autonomy of women (see chapter 5). As noted above, by 2014, armed Islamic State militants who held territory were imposing strict Sharia law by coercive force. Often those who do not convert to IS-style Islamism are either killed or, in the best case, ordered to leave (without their possessions, which are confiscated). In the city of Mosul, Iraq, after the Islamic State took control, reportedly there were murders of both Christian and Muslim clerics as well as other dissenters.

As some commentators have observed, however, Huntington seemed at times to oversimplify the cultural dimensions of international contentions. In his "clash of civilizations" assessment, he places great emphasis on differences between the major religions. But religious divisions within civilizations can be important too, such as within Chinese civilization between Confucianism, Taoism, and Buddhism, within Christianity between Catholicism, Lutheran Protestantism, and Calvinism, and within Islam between the moderate Sunni, radical Salafist Sunni, and Shia branches.

The latter religious contention among Muslims has obviously affected international relations in the Middle East. Shia Iran works to protect the Shia majority in Iraq and the national government that it dominates, the Shia majority opposition in Sunni-run Bahrain, and the Shia minorities in Lebanon (with its Hezbollah militia) and Yemen (with its Houthi militia). Iran and Hezbollah help the government of Syria, which is led by a Shia-offshoot minority called the Alawites, in that nation's civil war. Iran cites the Syrian government's role as protector of the Shia and other minorities (including Christians) from the Sunni majority.

The Syrian rebellion is primarily Sunni, and increasingly spearheaded by its most potent groups militarily, the militant Islamists of IS and the Nusra Front. In Iraq, IS explicitly seeks to expand its social identity base by appealing to Sunni Arabs as such, claiming to be the Sunni Arabs' true representative and leadership against what IS considers to be the enemies of Sunni Islam. A similar project was underway in central Mali in 2015, where a new militant Islamist group, the Massina Liberation Front, appealed to the nomadic Fulani minority (about a tenth of the Malian population) as the answer to Fulani discontent about the Malian government's marginalization of the ethnic Fulanis.

The fact that broad religious "civilizations" are not monolithic also has implications for the chances for the international spread of democracy and individual freedom in Muslim-majority nations. Outside the minority of Koranic (and hadith) literalists, we see a range of views among Muslims on such issues as religion-state separation, democracy, the need to adjust Sharia law to today's world, and personal freedom for women. And some commonalities exist between civilizations. For example, Islam fully accepts private property and the market economy (though with more regulation than is favored by free-market advocates). To some extent, different interpretations of values such as freedom, well-being, order, justice, and equality cut across Muslim populations, as they do Anglo-European ones.

Thus we need to beware of making too sharp a distinction between Muslim-majority cultures and Anglo-European-influenced ones with their general acceptance of secular government. Certainly, Islamist political parties, especially when they hold majorities, have leaned more toward imposing Islamist cultural values than in the past (e.g., in Turkey and Egypt in 2012 and 2013), sharpening conflict with secularists. And often governing Islamists who present themselves as moderate have not been very vigorous in restraining radical Islamist groups. We saw this in the Morsi government in Egypt in 2012–2013 and Tunisia's Ennahda party government in 2013 (though not in 2014). To be sure, however, it is not clear that these experiences under Islamist party government actually reflect the preferences of ordinary Muslims in those countries.

Social Movements and Value-Related Identity

Another type of identity factor is the phenomenon of social movements and the values that they represent. In the 1950s and 1960s, Africa and Asia began an anticolonial movement for national independence that fundamentally changed international relations in the developing world. In Europe in the 1970s and 1980s, a broad peace movement arose to pressure governments to remove nuclear weapons and generally reduce East-West tensions; in some countries it produced a new foreign policy approach called **détente**, aimed at generally reducing contention and increasing peaceful cooperation between the United States and the Soviet Union. In the late 1980s, a democratization/human rights movement spread in East-Central Europe. Russian leader Mikhail Gorbachev ultimately lifted the threat of Soviet military intervention in Eastern Europe, which helped pave the way for the fall of Communism. In the 1970s, a worldwide environmental movement was born, which recently has focused increasingly on climate change as a pressing international emergency.

Less distinct identity communities have arisen over values tied to economic ideology, sometimes primarily among elites. As was noted in chapters 7 and 16, during the 1980s and 1990s a pro-globalization movement called neoliberalism arose among some economists, bankers, investors, and multinational corporations, and spread to others in government, business, and journalism, as well. Its central premise was that the values of overall economic growth (a particular version of economic well-being) and entrepreneurial freedom (a particular form of freedom) could best be pursued by freer trade internationally and domestically. The idea was to reduce (a) trade protection and subsidies, (b) government stimulus spending, and (c) regulation of economies. In response to the international financial and economic crisis and slump of 2008–2015, an identity community of sorts arose among many of the same groups, in pursuit of the strategy of austerity and its budget cuts (see chapter 7).

Often social movement identification seems to spread on its own. A key factor in the peaceful fall of Communism in Eastern Europe in 1989 and 1990 was the attractions of neighboring Western Europe, with its freedom, vigorous and autonomous civil society, democracy, and vibrant economies. As was noted above, by the late 1980s a broad democracy movement had arisen and spread in Eastern Europe.

Some of the one million-plus people at a demonstration in Prague during the Czechoslovak "velvet revolution" in 1989.

However, governments and other institutions may intentionally encourage the spread of certain values. In his concept of **soft power**,[5] political scientist Joseph Nye suggested that one country can influence another through efforts to promote its values. For example, in the late 2000s, the U.S. government under President George W. Bush undertook a campaign of soft power against the fundamentalist Ahmadinejad government in Iran to spread the ideas and values of political freedom and democracy there. Such efforts may or may not be successful, or the results may be much delayed. In the Iranian case, there were negative

consequences as well as positive ones; Iranian civil-society groups pressing for democracy were accused of being agents of America and suppressed.

In Latin America, from the late 1970s on, democracy movements from below pressed for the transfer of power from military regimes to civilian democratic rule. This movement had help from the Catholic Church (which had always played a major cultural and educational role in the region), fostering democracy education and pressuring military rulers toward democratization. The Catholic Church played a similar role in the Philippines under the dictatorship of Ferdinand Marcos. In the same period, some international efforts to support economic development in the world's south made aid conditional on political change toward democracy.

Nationalism and Its Economic Form

As we have noted at several points in this book, different models put forward to explain phenomena can converge in a situation, explaining it better in conjunction than each can separately. At times, realism can combine with the social identity factor of **nationalism**—intense identification with one's country and its interests. Here the focus of social identification is the nation itself, one of those groups for which intense social identification can yield hostile actions toward opponents (see "The Philosophical Connection"). A top group pursuing a realist strategy to project national power may bolster support for it by fostering nationalism generally, or framing proposals in ways that awaken nationalism. This is especially likely when the political executive wants the legislative assemblies to back a foreign policy initiative. Russian president Putin's interventions in eastern Ukraine in 2014 (including the annexation of Crimea) were accompanied by an orchestrated campaign of Russian nationalism and fear of NATO probing of Russian defenses. On the eve of the American invasion of Iraq in 2003, President Bush painted Saddam Hussein's regime as actively developing "weapons of mass destruction" that could even threaten the United States. When the invasion found no evidence of such weapons programs, the Bush administration shifted its main public rationale for the occupation to another identity-based appeal: the idea of spreading the American values of freedom and democracy in the Middle East.

Intensified national identity can also find expression in **economic nationalism.** As was noted in chapter 17, realism can take economic forms in international economic and financial policymaking. For example, Germany, with its steady and substantial trade surpluses, is the most successful economic power in the Eurozone, and consequently wields heavy influence. At times Germany uses its influence over EU institutions to pursue policies that, among other things, benefit the economic interests of Germany's banks and businesses (see below, under the heading of the challenge of national economic power). But this economic realism is also bolstered by the mobilization of national identity sentiment backing it up. Conservative Christian Democratic chancellor Angela Merkel and her finance minister Wolfgang Schauble often picture Germany as industrious and frugal in contrast to the Greeks, in German efforts to press austerity policies on Greece.

In response, a more defensive form of economic nationalism has emerged in southern Europe. In 2015 Spain saw the sudden rise to prominence of an anti-austerity, left social democratic party, Podemos, and in Greece such a party, Syriza, emerged victorious in the parliamentary elections of 2014. It fought to end

THE PHILOSOPHICAL CONNECTION | Reinhold Niebuhr

Reinhold Niebuhr (1892–1971) was an American Protestant thinker who was deeply concerned about the possible imbalance in power between groups. In *Moral Man and Immoral Society* (1932), Niebuhr emphasized the difference between human behavior in individual interactions on the one hand, and behavior in contending groups on the other. In individual, face-to-face interactions, people are capable of impartiality and even altruism, as they more or less contain their selfish impulses. In groups, however, people can easily lose their moral compass. Groups and nations can do awful things to their opponents if given the chance. In intergroup contention in politics, power relations often prove more important than rational arguments.

For Niebuhr, this dangerous potential sprang from human nature. In his view, humans have a survival impulse that is harmless in its raw form of the desire to live. But it can develop in human experience in two different ways. One can pursue the "will to live truly," to fully realize one's potential, including shouldering social responsibility in one's community. Here Niebuhr seems to favor self-development thinking (see chapter 5). Alternatively, however, the survival impulse may take a second, dangerous form: the "will to power," in pursuit of prestige and domination individually and collectively. Niebuhr thought that especially amid contention among nations and racial groups, the will to power seems to win out, with the help of self-serving rationalizations that try to put a good face on their oppressive behavior.

In a later work, however, *The Children of Light and the Children of Darkness* (1942), Niebuhr developed a more complex picture. He drew a difference between the approaches that he viewed as merely naive mistakes, such as those of the socialists and the free-market-oriented "children of light," and the approaches of the Fascist "children of darkness,"

who most clearly reflected Niebuhr's earlier picture of "immoral society."

According to Niebuhr, both capitalism and socialism shared the illusion that an economic system could fully harmonize individual interests with the common interest. On the one hand, free-market supporters assumed that pursuit of economic self-interest in the market led to equilibrium in the market economy. But for Niebuhr, the market, if left to itself, produced large inequalities and waste, with the strong devouring the weak and property becoming a source of injustice. In Niebuhr's view, the Marxists had the advantage of seeing that these things can happen. But for him they succumbed to a related illusion of possible harmony—the idea that on the other side of the socialist revolution, interests would harmonize. For Niebuhr, the rise to power of the managerial class in the Soviet Union showed yet again that a powerful group could arise to take what it could get. Even under democratic socialism, he suggested, the bureaucracy might be able to gain control of politics.

In Niebuhr's view, our visions of cooperation must not blot out the realities of contention. He wanted every contending group to recognize that absolute justice, love, and brotherhood exist only at the highest level of perfection, the divine. In the lower realm of historical political contest in pursuit of justice, every conception of the good is limited and relative. No one should consider his or her own moral idealism as full protection against the threat of collective selfishness. The best answer, then, is democracy and the balance of group powers that it can achieve. But democracy's basis must be humility and mutual respect between contending groups. In economic policy, for example, Niebuhr favored approaching property and the market pragmatically. He favored preserving private property as a defense against domination, but regulating it where necessary to prevent injustice. In short, he ended up a moderate left-of-center advocate.

the punishing austerity of the prior years, to reduce Greece's large and unpayable government debt, and initiate stimulus spending to try to get Greece out of its depression. In the end, Greece lost its fight and had to suffer continuing, relentless austerity (see below). Nonetheless, this episode illustrates that to understand such international contention, we may need to combine economic realism (whether offensive or defensive) with social identity in the form of economic nationalism.

	International Institutionalism	**Realism**	**Social Identity**
TABLE 18.1	**Characteristics of Motivational Factors in International Relations**		
Primary motivation	International order through peaceful negotiations among nations	National power, to pursue or assure national military security and wealth	Seeking and promoting values shared among those with a common identity
Key actors	Diplomats and international institutions like the UN and the EU	The individual state as a single unit	"Civilizations," religions, ethnic groups, social movements
Types of international linkages	Long-term cooperation following stable customary practices and rules	Alliances that last as long as they serve a nations' power interests	Long-term relationships with nations that share common social, religious, or ethnic identity
The nature of the international community	International order maintained through international law, institutions, and nations' mutual interests in peace and prosperity	Relative anarchy, structured only by informal hierarchies of power, prestige, and wealth	Persistent division of the world into contending identity blocs

Each of the three key motivational factors discussed in this book's last two chapters—international institutionalism, realism, and social identity—can suggest its own account of the main groups and aims that contribute to national governments' behavior in interacting with other nations. And each has its own distinctive portrait of the key linkages at work in the international community overall (see Table 18.1). But in explaining international politics, particular cases may require combinations of two or more of these approaches.

POLICY CHALLENGES

What are the most threatening global policy challenges that governments face today, and what are the prospects for resolving them? This chapter cannot survey the whole terrain of foreign policy issues, but we examine four that seem to this author to be most pressing at the time of publication: global warming, poverty in the developing world, radical Islamist terror, and imbalances in national economic power that can threaten international financial stability. Each of these challenges spawns contention involving, at some point, social identity as well as national power pursuit and the use and support of international institutions. And each of these policy challenges seem to require, in one way or another, both vigorous contention and concerted international cooperation if they are to be addressed.

For each policy challenge, we attempt to answer a few key questions. First, who are the main contending groups, and what interests and/or values are they pursuing? Second, what are the groups' preferred policy directions for pursuing their interests and/or values? Third, what are the empirical claims that are made or assumed by the contending groups, and how valid are they?

Global Warming

The threat of **global warming** is an unprecedented policy challenge facing the world today. Despite a few small debates about the data at the margins, the scientific world now recognizes that our climate is warming, due mostly to atmospheric carbon dioxide buildup from the burning of fossil fuels such as oil, gas, and coal for energy. (Methane releases, from cattle, production of oil and gas, and thawing of seabed, lakebeds, and permafrost, comprise a secondary factor.) As political scientist David Victor suggests, this situation threatens serious consequences, involves contention among key groups, and will require international cooperation to address it.[6]

The Problem The earth's average temperature is clearly increasing. According to a recent report by the U.S. National Oceanic and Atmospheric Administration, July 2015 was the warmest month since record keeping began in the 1880s, and the first seven months of 2015 comprised the warmest such period on record (following 2014 which was the warmest year on record up to then). What are the impacts that can most directly affect public perceptions (or lack thereof) of a global warming crisis? By far, the heaviest near-term impact would seem to be in the area of water shortage. Extended and intense droughts will directly deplete rivers, lakes, and water tables, undermining human and agricultural consumption. The loss of mountain snowpack and glaciers that normally feed the rivers on which huge urban populations depend for water (especially in south and east Asia) will lead to massive economic disruptions and human migrations. Secondly, polar icecap melting creates a rise in sea levels that threatens shorelines. For example, in lowland Bangladesh, tens of thousands of villagers have already been driven into the capital Dhaka and other cities by flooded homes and salt water encroachment on their rice plots. And weather-related calamities will intensify, because higher sea and air temperatures generate more weather turbulence. Together with rising sea levels, coastal storms will cause widespread flooding well in advance of large-scale loss of land to the sea.

Also, **feedback effects**—consequences of a factor that act to intensify its effect—may be worsening the situation: some scientists fear that CO_2-driven warming of the polar areas in the future might trip large-scale releases of methane—more than twenty times as powerful a greenhouse gas as CO_2 (though less long-lasting in the atmosphere)—from currently frozen seabed, lakebed, and permafrost sources.

The main fuels that produce carbon dioxide are coal, oil, and natural gas. Especially when the prices of oil and gas shoot up, as they did between 2008 and 2013, the desire for access to cheap energy for economic development and comfort (e.g., air conditioning) contributes to increased mining and burning of coal. Coal is plentiful in some countries and cheap to mine, but is the worst known source of CO_2 and other dangerous air pollutants. China alone is said to have large numbers of new coal-burning power plants at various stages of development. With the huge drop in oil prices that began in mid-2014, there has been less pressure to pursue coal, but the cheap availability of oil tends to discourage the use of expensive alternative energy sources that do not emit greenhouse gases.

In the United States, coal use (and overall emissions growth) has been reduced in recent years due to the explosion of new American production of natural gas—whose burning yields half the carbon dioxide emitted by coal—via a process called hydraulic fracturing, or "fracking." The new supply has lowered the price of natural gas in the United States to the point where coal cannot compete very effectively, and new American coal-burning electricity plants are not being built.

However, fracking requires large amounts of water (mixed with toxic chemicals) for high-pressure injection to fracture the shale. This heavy water use may deplete rivers, lower water tables, and drain aquifers that are already stressed by agricultural use and by increasingly frequent and serious droughts due to global warming itself. The necessary reinjection of the wastewater for underground storage can cause small earthquakes. And on occasion, claims have been made (still controversial) that the chemicals may leak into ground water. Moreover, reliance on natural gas has its own dangers; in late 2015 and 2016 a natural gas storage well in a Los Angeles suburb blew and produced a huge, continuous, dangerously flammable release of methane (again, twenty times as powerful a greenhouse gas than carbon dioxide, though lasting only twenty years in the atmosphere before turning into CO2), that forced evacuations and took months to cap.

Unfortunately, the main collective good at stake worldwide—long-term human well-being on the planet—takes the form (a) not of something concrete that we can see now, but rather something ill-defined that is off in the future,[7] and (b) not of an attractive new gain, but rather the avoidance of a predicted catastrophic loss. Neither of these aspects of the collective good are very compelling in the short run, when the key decisions and changes must be adopted.

As we saw in chapter 9 (on interest groups), economist Mancur Olson proposed a rational choice theory of collective group action. Among other things, it stressed that cooperation by a category of people or organizations in contributing to achieve a collective goal is most likely where each potential contributor sees a clear and substantial material stake in the outcome (e.g., a lot of money), and each individual contribution is perceived as a significant portion of the resources necessary to achieve the goal (most likely when the category is small, such as a trade association of corporations). If either of these requirements are not met, there is a widespread temptation of individuals to be free riders, receiving whatever benefits result without contributing to them. Free riding involves either not taking the goal very seriously or thinking that one's contribution would be just a "drop in the bucket," and that among the large numbers in the category there will be plenty of other contributors to take up the slack.

Those with the biggest material stake and incentive to cooperate are the big energy companies, who tend to cooperate to *avoid* major changes to address global warming. They remain among the most powerful influences on the government policies of nations, especially those with large deposits of oil, gas, or coal. Citizenries of the developed nations, hooked on the convenience of cheap energy, tend to cooperate with big energy rather than contend with it. Citizenries of the developing nations, hungry for more reliable and affordable access to (especially) electric power, want economic growth first, postponing addressing other concerns to when they become affordable.[8]

In some ways, most of the human race today comprises a huge identity group that shares an attachment to familiar styles and standards of living, and cannot imagine making significant changes. These identity attachments may have to be punctured in one area of each nation at a time. In 2015, the state of California, for example, was in an unprecedented (in modern times) four-year drought due to reduced rain and snowpack in the mountains, with only one year of water supplies left. California may be forced to lead the way in the United States in addressing one part of the global warming puzzle: finding ways to significantly conserve water and energy. Much of Iran is running out of water due to a seven-year drought, having exhausted ground water supplies in many areas to supply agriculture (especially for pistachio nuts).

Early Responses Early responses to the global warming challenge fall into two categories, independent initiatives involving energy technology, and international cooperation involving government policy.

Research and development of clean energy technologies is ongoing among those with the resources to pursue them. There seems to be a division of labor among nations able and willing to invest, such as the United States, the United Kingdom, Norway, and China. Each country supports its own approaches, but it will take time before we know which of their approaches will be most effective. "Clean coal" technologies to separate the CO_2 and pump it back into the ground[9] seem to be developing too slowly now to be of much use in the near future.

Nuclear power, the only non-carbon-emitting technology that is well established, has its own well-known downsides, which include nuclear waste disposal and the risk of further proliferation of nuclear weapons. Research is ongoing to more safely and permanently encase and deposit nuclear wastes. But ramping up conventional nuclear power to replace carbon burning is an expensive proposition. Scattered efforts are underway to develop smaller, cheaper, prefabricated nuclear power units that can be mass produced and installed more quickly than the large standard ones, but at present only a handful of prototypes are being built. Meanwhile, nuclear energy still requires large amounts of river water for cooling,[10] just as global warming's droughts reduce river water flow in many areas. Nonetheless, given the pressing CO_2 crisis many environmentalist experts say that nuclear energy will have to be part of any solution.

Rapid development and expansion of alternative energy technologies such as solar, wind and geothermal seems necessary. But these efforts are likely to require heavy government subsidies in an era of post-2008 budgetary scarcity, post-2014 cheap oil, and antitax ideological pressure in some countries. The high cost of these efforts—at least until they are compared to the costs of failing to slow global warming—remains an obstacle to developing the political will to act on the necessary scale. Usually short term oriented, people and governments remain largely unwilling to take seriously the massive future costs of inaction.

A few glimmers of hope seem to sprout from the parched earth. To be sure, by 2013, China had become the world's biggest national contributor to rising greenhouse gas levels, relying heavily on the worst carbon emitter, coal, to power its huge national momentum toward further industrial development. However, the Chinese government has begun to apply some of the proceeds of its large trade surplus to support experiments with alternative energy and cleaner use of coal. The recently elected conservative government in India is pushing ahead with coal, but simultaneously investing in some large-scale solar efforts.

Public opinion worldwide seems to be gradually accepting the reality of a global warming problem. This process received a boost in mid-2015 with an encyclical (an official papal message to Catholic congregations worldwide) by the new Pope Francis, accepting the agreed-upon science regarding global warming and human responsibility for it, expressing alarm, and urging action. But broad opinion change may be uneven. What is rising is worldwide *average* temperatures of the sea and air, allowing for cooler periods in some areas while others are warming, so that local doubts may arise. And politically, a few pockets of ideological opposition to the science have emerged (principally in the United States). In the early 2000s, by some measures global warming seemed to have leveled off somewhat—though still at very high levels historically. But by the mid-2010s, record-level warming was again evident, and there were indications that the seeming pause earlier might have been a statistical artifact related to changing methods of data gathering.

Global warming is clearly an international phenomenon; the atmosphere and the oceans are shared by all. Accordingly, any effective policy attack on the problem must involve international cooperation. Early U.N.-sponsored agreements were prominent here: the 1992 Framework Convention on Climate Change and the 1997 Kyoto Protocol to it. (To some extent, early efforts were modeled on the successful earlier mitigation of atmospheric ozone depletion by developing harmless chemical substitutes, a much smaller and more manageable problem.) But effectively, these agreements are voluntary, with only a minority of nations signing up, and sanctions for not meeting targets are weak.

The part of the world that has displayed the greatest degree of overall international cooperation is Europe. But even European efforts to curb greenhouse gases run afoul of a common facet of policymaking that was noted in chapter 3: the traditional political tendency to first try an incremental step that is, as much as possible, in accord with existing practices and interests. For example, Europe agreed on a **cap-and-trade** program in the 2000s: setting emission limits on enterprises and allowing those under their limit to sell their "cap space" to those over their limits. This somewhat market-oriented approach is considered to be politically much easier to swallow than carbon taxes or bans on certain kinds of carbon-producing energy sources. But cap-and-trade has produced very limited real reductions in greenhouse gas emissions, at least in relation to the global problem.

On its own, Germany is subsidizing alternative fuel development and raising energy costs, but the resulting gains are limited by the government's current effort to eliminate nuclear power use (originally touched off by Fukushima-related fears). Meanwhile, the Kyoto-related Clean Development Mechanism helped developed nations exceed targeted limits by supporting sometimes questionable projects in developing countries. Overall, the result was a patchwork of weak agreements sometimes referred to as "regime complexes," which so far have failed to coordinate serious efforts to head off global warming. What political scientist Charles Lindblom called policymaking by "muddling through" with "disjointed incrementalism"[11] did not seem to be working.

To a large extent, we can say that economic nationalism stands in the way. The most important question is whether growing awareness of global warming and its consequences can translate into political willingness to pay the higher prices for energy and the taxes to fund the transition toward alternative sources, and to undertake whatever lifestyle changes are required to actually address it. (How big those changes will be continues to be debated.)

Today's Main Options As was noted above, the most global efforts to date have been at international conferences aimed at getting the developed and developing worlds to agree on limiting carbon emissions. In advance of the

November 2015 climate change summit meeting in Paris (see below), a late 2014 agreement had provided for monitoring and reporting national emission conditions and improvements. But through 2015, emission reduction targets of the sort adopted by developed countries still had not been accepted as mandatory by the developing nations.

The developing nations point out that the world's north has already achieved modernization and development, after having created most of the problem of atmospheric carbon increase in the process. They argue that under these circumstances, it is unfair to require developing nations to make costly energy cuts and transformations (a) that will restrain their economic development, and (b) that their governments do not have the resources to undertake, in any case. From the point of view of empirical accuracy and shared values of well-being and fairness, the developing nations are right. But until countries such as China and India also cut their emissions, reductions by developed nations alone cannot effectively rein in CO_2, and northern incentives to take vigorous action on their own are reduced. Meanwhile, the planet's current pattern of human habitation is at risk, right now.

Now there seem to be two contending paths, each involving political contention and cooperation. One is to continue with conventional political approaches, as Europe has done. Conservation groups attempt to lobby for incremental policy change in the face of (a) resource-rich interests aiming to preserve the status quo, and (b) the natural human tendency to avoid sharp change and high cost until unacceptable conditions and disasters are already staring people in the face. To a degree, those favoring this go-slow approach amount to an identity group as well as a range of status-quo interests. Again, large numbers identify with their current style of life and material position to the point that they can hardly conceive of anything much different.

In December 2015, however, diplomacy took a big step forward, at least in advancing worldwide recognition of the problem. At a world climate change summit meeting in Paris, 195 nations agreed to submit carbon emissions targets and ultimately limit climate change to under 2 degrees Celsius (ideally, 1.5 degrees) over pre-industrial levels. As usual, the agreement did not address national means to reach those emissions targets or enforcement of them, but it did provide for a $100 billion fund of developed-nation help to developing nations in meeting their targets. To be final, by 1917 the agreement will have to be ratified by 55 nations representing 55 percent of the world's carbon emissions. It remains to be seen, of course, how successfully this unprecedented global recognition of the climate change challenge will be implemented. Country by country, identity-related and material stake interests in the status quo will have to be overcome.

On the other side is a direct, global problem-solving approach: (a) focusing on shared public values—especially well-being ones—over the long term, (b) accepting the scientific understanding of the reality, and (c) approaching the problem pragmatically rather than in identity terms. If the world's nations were to cooperate pragmatically, they would adopt an all-out approach like that of the American government's "Manhattan project" during World War II (to build an atomic bomb before the Germans could), or the Marshall Plan of aid to Western Europe in the late 1940s and early 1950s (enabling the region to get back on its economic feet after the devastation of World War II). Emergencies impose cooperation, or at least they should do so.

Beyond cooperation in conservation efforts, this second approach would involve immediately building huge solar and wind farms for power generation (in the short run paired with natural gas plants for when the sunshine and wind are absent), in both developing nations and developed ones. Almost wherever there is open space not occupied by people or carbon-absorbing vegetation, either solar panels or reflective devices (sending the light energy either back into space or to power generation) may need to cover non-forested land. In addition, new energy transmission and storage technologies need to be deployed to distribute the energy effectively, along with prefabricated nuclear power stations wherever cooling water is plentiful. Fossil fuel burning would be rapidly wound down. (Cars would need to become either hydrogen fuel cell-based or electric, using alternative-energy-powered electric grids.)

The cost, construction, and ownership of the new power generation efforts may have to follow the adage of "whatever works." It may be necessary to go back to the tried-and-true approach of the early-middle twentieth century: public utilities—in this case international ones funded by nations with the ability to pay. An expanded version of the Organization for Economic Cooperation and Development, for example, might serve as the parent owner of the public utilities. Avoiding the looming climate catastrophe is a planetary responsibility, not only an individual national responsibility.

As in the above-cited examples of crisis-driven spending by advantaged countries, the bulk of the cost must be borne by nations with the ability to pay: generally the developed nations and others (e.g. China) who have been very successful in world trade. (If we have learned anything from the southern European debt crisis of the 2010s, it is that you can't get what you want just by demanding money from people who don't have it and are already suffering and sacrificing.)

Some have suggested that the developed nations are less likely to make big financial sacrifices to aggressively reduce planetary carbon emissions, because they have the resources to adapt to the resulting damage from global warming as it comes, in ways that seem to benefit the nation directly. Over time, however, I am not sure whether this pessimistic observation will hold water (!). Certainly the poorer developing nations will suffer most from global warming, but in the developed nations, massive and hugely costly disruptions will occur that can have a potent shock effect. In the United States, already the multiyear western drought has no end in sight, and fires fueled by the dry brush and heat promise to devastate ever-growing expanses of precious carbon-absorbing forest. When much of California literally runs out of stored water and costs begin to skyrocket, American public opinion may shift. Down the road, hugely costly yearly flooding of parts of Manhattan and Miami can focus the mind. To be sure, antitax ideological identity, the material stake interests of today's energy companies, and the influence of wealth in political campaigns and media ownership are potent obstacles. But even they may be surmountable in a context of public shock over impacts of global warming on large numbers of people at once.

Poverty in the Developing World

Another key foreign policy issue concerns the developing world. As we saw in chapter 3, in the 1960s and 1970s, the U.N. promoted an economic-social Covenant of human rights. It called for governments to "take steps"—both domestically and through international cooperation—toward making an "adequate standard of living" available to the poor. While the ultimate goal was quite idealistic, the Covenant was formulated in a way that made several concessions to the real world. It aimed only for "adequate" well-being levels, set no timetable, left the "steps" undefined, and recognized that steps could only be taken within the limitations of available resources and workable strategies. Moreover, the Covenant did not posit a universal definition of "adequate" access to such needs as food,

A solar panel farm in Andalusia province in Spain, producing electricity.

health, employment, etc. Those standards were left to diverse states to interpret and apply in their own economic and cultural environments. And the formulation preserved the freedom of the beneficiaries. The aim was to make the components of minimal well-being readily available to would-be aid recipients—perhaps not without some effort by them to access the benefit—not to compel recipients.

Early Approaches and Current Conditions In the first years after the U.N. economic-social Covenant went into effect in 1976, much development aid pursued a "basic needs" approach. The most sophisticated versions of it (e.g., in some Scandinavian aid) emphasized strategies of "integrated" development, in which all parts of the picture would be addressed. In rural development, for example, education, clean water management, health clinics, reforestation, microcredit, and community participation in decision making should accompany the conventional economic needs, such as for improved farming methods, cheap fertilizer, and insecticides to assure affordable food supplies for both urban and rural areas. This comprehensive approach still has its defenders today. Regarding economic-social human rights, we have seen a recent focus on human "capabilities" for self-provision of minimal well-being, and the needs that must be met to assure the development of those capabilities.[12]

However, to many observers this comprehensive approach looked expensive and difficult. In the 1980s, it yielded to pessimism about the cost of meeting the needs of the world's poor. A more minimalist and empirically based refinement of the first steps of the basic needs strategy was proposed, called the **minimum threshold approach**. It aimed at targeting certain core needs areas such as food, water, health, and employment, to assure minimal levels of them first. The idea was to bring recipients to the threshold of a more self-reliant, bottom-up momentum toward self-provision of other benefits and higher levels of provision of these core benefits.[13] So far, however, this approach has not been widely embraced, and today's financial stresses and government debt difficulties render it even less likely to be applied.

The goals of the economic-social Covenant, however, are no less relevant in the twenty-first century. Astronomical numbers of people continue to experience unending hunger, pain, and struggle. (These are the breeding grounds for terrorist groups to recruit those with "nothing left to lose" and searching for meaning and dignity in life; see below.) Some developing nations have shown reductions in the percentages in extreme poverty (especially in China), some growth of the middle class, improvements in infant mortality rates and education, the spread of cheap cell phones to enhance communication, and growth in GDP (Gross Domestic Product) per capita. But GDP per capita is only a statistical average. It often primarily reflects gains among the upper and upper-middle-income strata, which conceal widening inequality between the extremes and worsening conditions among the poor.

Conditions are especially bad among the poor in much of sub-Saharan Africa and south and southeast Asia. Food insufficiency contributes to specific health threats and general health deterioration, amid poor sanitation, lack of safe water supply, and drastic shortages of health workers. From 2008 through early 2014 world-market prices of food and fuel increased significantly (due especially to increased Chinese demand), causing a spike in starvation and malnutrition. And global warming will take its worst toll in these areas, with drought and snowpack depletion causing rivers to wither, and coastal flooding (with sea level rise and worsening storms) driving huge numbers from their homes and agricultural plots. In addition, HIV/AIDS remains a terrible scourge in some areas.

Meanwhile, the economic policies of better-off nations often seem to wholly disregard their plight. An example is **biofuels** policy, undertaken in the 2000s in some countries to become more energy independent from (then) expensive and nonrenewable imported oil. But subsidies for ethanol and palm oil encourage taking agricultural land and food grains out of the world's food supply, in order to add only marginally to the fuel supply for cars and trucks. This can contribute to spikes in world food prices (such as occurred in 2008–2009) that can in turn lead governments in food exporting nations to reduce or cut off their exports to try to protect their domestic food affordability. Such economic nationalism can further reduce the international food supply and drive up world food prices, creating a vicious circle. Meanwhile, the high energy requirements of producing biofuels often seem to rival the energy that is produced.

To be sure, international organizations and advantaged nations continue their aid programs to address world poverty. The World Bank, whose biggest contributor is the United States, makes loans to developing nations for such things as development projects, education, and health. In the 2000s, however, World Bank leaders appointed by the United States were more skeptical of such aid, focusing more attention on the portion of aid money lost to corruption (which some northern European donors say is small and largely unavoidable).

The United Nations Development Program gives grants and help in development planning, and some regional organizations are active as well, such as the Europe-centered Organization for Economic Cooperation and Development. Efforts range from large scale to small scale. An example of the latter is the microcredit approach, which involves starting small self-managed lending groups that pool their resources for short-term lending to members. Among the results are the start of many small trading, service, and craft enterprises, often by women.

Today's Options On the food front, the U.N.'s World Food Program continues its work, but is hampered by the recent increases in food costs. Private international NGOs such as Oxfam, Save the Children, and (Irish) Concern, and the numerous small NGOs working within their own nations to help the least advantaged are also active in this area.[14] The World Bank, the IMF, and the World Food Program all highlight the need for tens of billions of dollars in emergency food aid and support for seeds, insecticides, and fertilizers necessary to sustain food production in poor areas.

Another sector of international aid that has become more prominent in recent years is philanthropic giving by private individuals and foundations. An example is the very large fund spearheaded by Microsoft founder Bill Gates and his wife Melinda (and supported by U.S. financier Warren Buffet), which has been making a difference in certain strategically targeted problem areas in health and education, such as the need for inoculation against disease.

As we saw above, one focus of effort in the developing world has been industrial development for export to the world's developed north. Early gains in countries such as South Korea, Taiwan, and Singapore were followed by growth in other areas such as urban pockets of Malaysia, Indonesia, and even Bangladesh. Most recently, however, export opportunities for such nations have been shrinking as China's subsidies and currency management have enabled Chinese producers to keep the prices of their exports low. Moreover, China can buy oil and mineral resources elsewhere in the developing world for its domestic needs, in effect raising the costs of these industrial inputs for other developing world producers.

Problems with industrial development also include environmental challenges. Industrial development provides jobs and higher living standards for many in China, but in the context of very unhealthy environmental conditions (especially air quality) and harm to forest, water, and fishery resources.

As to developing nations' governments themselves, they remain cash-strapped as they face both deteriorating infrastructure (especially in electric power and water availability) and unrelenting population increase. Civil wars such as those recently in Congo, Sierra Leone, Sudan, Sri Lanka, and Syria make conditions worse. Such wars, and environmental disasters such as earthquakes, tsunamis, and floods (such as the large-scale Pakistani floods of 2010 and the earthquake in Nepal in 2015), produce humanitarian crises that can only be addressed by international aid that is ad hoc at best.

To be sure, individual national governments provide bilateral loans and grants for development and poverty alleviation. For some of the most advantaged governments, however, aid is steered for politically related purposes rather than humanitarian ones. The United States heavily aids political friends such as Egypt and Israel. (This is in contrast to Norway, for example, which directs some of its North Sea oil income to ground-level poverty fighting in parts of the developing world.) China builds roads in parts of Africa, but normally only where the Chinese have projects developing mineral and fuel resources for the Chinese market.

Addressing these needs and conditions in the developing world must be an international matter. But post-2008, economic and financial conditions have slowed economic growth in the world's advantaged North. Large government deficits and debt problems have emerged among many of the world's developed nations, which create formidable political obstacles to increasing northern redistribution to the poor of the developing nations. Meanwhile, the recent economic and trade triumphs of China's enterprises (both state-owned and private) underline the impression that globalization and free trade serves primarily to benefit the haves, while the have-nots languish.

Perhaps the most that can be hoped for in the near term is curbing policies by the world's more successful nations that directly worsen conditions among the developing world's poor. For example, the American government seems finally to be shifting away from the above-noted biofuel policy. Future environmental problems in food production—including droughts and rising sea levels resulting from global warming—underline the importance of attention to international food policy.

Terror and Its Militant Islamist Forms

Another formidable international policy challenge is terror, especially in its militant Islamist forms. Most notably, al-Qaeda in Iraq has morphed into the Islamic State, controlling significant territory in both Iraq and Syria. And groups in Libya and northern Nigeria, for example, are publicly joining it. To begin with, we must focus on terrorism itself.

Terrorism's Aims and Methods As was noted in chapter 15, terrorism is an extreme form of political contention in which violence and the threat of it are used in mobilizing fear, to influence or coerce members of another group. This purpose behind terror distinguishes it from other forms of political violence, such as an assassination of a particular political figure that is driven by rage, hate, or the desire to eliminate the victim from political contention (e.g., the killing of Indian prime ministers Indira Gandhi in 1984 and her son Rajiv in 1991). Terror is also different from genocide, the attempted extinction of a victim group within a controlled territory, as in the Holocaust. In the case of an act of terror, typically part of the aim is to establish a credible threat of more terror in the immediate future, enhancing the spread of fear among members of the targeted group.

Terrorism can vary as to the type of group that engages in it, its ultimate goal, its tactics, its immediate victims, and the scope of group targeted for coercion. For example, tactics can range from hijacking a plane to car bombing a building, or beating or murdering someone who seems uncompliant. Tactics vary in the amount of attention that they get. A single huge bomb that brings down a big building in a city (at the extreme, planes used as bombs in 9/11 in the United States) may get more attention than a series of assassinations of policemen or other low-level government officials in a country's rural areas. But the latter may be more effective in driving the state out of those areas to open them up to terrorist control.

The goal of the terrorism affects the scope of the target group. Terror with a limited objective (e.g., Tamil independence in northern Sri Lanka) may occur on a smaller, more targeted scale than terror driven by an attempt to coerce a substantial population, such as Hitler's bombing of London during World War II (to break the British will to fight), or Stalin's removal of the Ukrainian harvest in the fall of 1932, starving Ukrainians to extinguish any remaining resistance to forced agricultural collectivization.

If terror is conducted or fostered by elements of the state toward people within its borders, we call it state terror. If a government's security forces indiscriminately burn villages or bomb urban neighborhoods where insurgents operate, we have state terror. But state terror may also involve a government's explicit or covert support of informal groups to execute its terror. For example, we saw this in the cases of some Latin American military governments' tacit support of the death squads that killed leftists (known as the "disappeared") in what have been termed the "dirty wars" of the 1960s through the 1980s in Chile and Argentina. In another example, in the 2000s, the Sudanese government seemed to support the Janjaweed militias' use of rape and murder to drive black African Muslims from their villages in Darfur.

Most often, however, when we think of terror we have non-state actors in mind. We think of a terrorist group as aiming either to remove the government, as in the case of the leftist Tupamaro guerillas in Uruguay in the early 1970s, for example, or to achieve a region's independence (called separatism), as in the case of the Tamils of northern Sri Lanka.

Terror may be an accompaniment to civil war. By itself, war's violence between the groups fighting each other is not called terror. Two armed forces locked in battle represent the breakdown of political contention in favor of outright military conflict. However, one side or the other may use terror to try to coerce noncombatants into refraining from supporting the other side's war effort. In Algeria in the late 1950s, the indigenous National Liberation Front was fighting an urban guerilla war and used terror to weaken the resolve of the ethnic French and the Algerians who cooperated with them.

Related to this is mass killing of innocent civilians of an ethnic or religious group by insurgents aiming to intensify intergroup ethnic or (religious) **sectarian** tensions, to the point of outright civil war and perhaps division of the nation. This seemed to be among the objectives of ethnic Serb attempts at ethnic cleansing against Bosnian Muslims in the 1990s, for example, and Islamic State's Iraq strategy of suicide bombings at Shia funerals, street markets, etc.

Where terror is ancillary to civil war, it may be limited by its military goals. For example, an insurgent group that seeks to expand the territory that it has "liberated" from government control may engage in terror against police stations and government offices in a neighboring area. The point is to drive out the area's agents of government (reducing civilian hopes for government protection), in preparation for a military offensive to take over that area. In the 1960s in Vietnam, Viet Cong guerillas assassinated village headmen in areas that they were moving into, to frighten government officials away and press villagers to cooperate with the guerillas.

Occasionally, terror has no doubt contributed to the political change desired by those who engage in it. In the above-noted Algerian case, the French ultimately withdrew, allowing the country its independence. Most often, however, terror does not achieve its goals. It may succeed only temporarily, until resistance hardens or some outside intervention occurs. In Somalia, thanks to the intervention of neighboring Kenya's military forces in recent years, much of the territory previously lost to Al-Shabaab Islamic militants was reclaimed by the Somali government. In 2013, intervention by French military forces drove most militant Islamists out of northern Mali (see Country Case Studies, chapter 17), though sporadic local attacks continue.

Terrorist acts (especially those against noncombatants) are infringements of human rights that are, on their face, criminal and immoral. They display what appears to be an inhuman side of the group or movement engaged in them.

Moral revulsion at such acts no doubt played a part (alongside American money) in the late 2000s' rise of "awakening" groups in some Sunni areas of Iraq against al-Qaeda-style terrorism there. The spread of such moral outrage was a key consequence of the IS killings of 130 innocent young people in Paris, France, in November 2015.

Today's militant Islamist terrorism and responses to it tend to make the fight an international phenomenon. As we have seen, if groups in neighboring countries or former colonial occupiers are not involved at the outset of terror, they often become so over time, whether in support or opposition to the terrorist group. And increasingly today, militant Sunni Islamist jihadis seem to be a fluid international force. Individual jihadis operate in a particular area at any given time, but many seem ready to cross borders to the next venue. For example, jihadis who were active in the militant Islamist takeover of northern Mali in 2012 came there from neighboring Algeria, Niger, or Mauretania, or even from more distant areas such as Libya, Yemen, or even Chechnya in the Russian Federation. Small numbers of young British and French Muslims are among the Islamic State's fighters, alongside the more numerous Saudis and Tunisians, for example. And the huge flows of Arab refugees into Europe in 2015 (roughly half from Syria) no doubt included a few terrorists determined to act in Europe.

To a remarkable degree, the terrorism of Sunni Salafist jihadis (see chapter 6) displays similar tactics regardless of where they are operating, whether in Syria, Mali, Somalia, northern Nigeria, or Afghanistan. They may first enter a country to support someone else's domestic resistance there, such as that of the Tuaregs in northern Mali in 2012, the Sunni opposition to the Shia-dominated Iraqi regime, or Sunni rebels fighting Syria's Assad regime (whose core is Alawite, an offshoot of Shia Islam). If the prior insurgency has been successful enough to clear some areas of government forces, its units tend to move on to the next front, leaving the area relatively lawless. Salafist jihadis may then move in, take over the area, and use terror against the civilian population to impose strict Sharia law. Under it, displays of Western (or any non-Islamic) culture, and even ordinary recreational activities such as beer drinking, gambling, smoking, or playing music, meet with warnings or violence. Independent female behavior brings beatings or worse, and schools for girls are often destroyed. Again, these tactics do not receive the attention garnered by the 9/11 attack on the World Trade Center in New York, but they are numerous and constitute a fairly uniform pattern of terror.

In Islamic State's social media efforts to attract devout foreign Sunni Muslims to come to the Caliphate, one of the selling points is the opportunity to actually live as the literal wording of the Koran and the Sunni hadith prescribe. This appeal is not without resonance among some Sunnis who feel oppressed. As was noted in chapter 6, the authoritative clerical establishment of Saudi Arabia adheres to the Shaf'i doctrine of Islamic thought, which advocates following the literal wording of the Koran and the Sunni hadith, and thus supports the application of Sharia as the law of the state. To be sure, the Saudi clerics do not advocate violent jihad as the strategy for overthrowing governments to establish rule by strict Sharia law. But they have used resources from the Saudi government in "soft power" efforts to establish madrassas (religious schools) throughout the Muslim world to, in effect, spread Shaf'i views and Salafism. Not surprisingly IS, sharing the same ultimate goal and doctrine (but with a different strategy), tries to expand its social identity base by appealing to Sunnis worldwide as the true representative of Islam. Wherever there are widespread grievances among a group that is mainly Sunni (e.g., the western and northern Arabs of Iraq, or the Fulani of central Mali), IS and al-Qaeda present jihad—to establish a regime of strict Sharia law—as the answer. Shared Sunni identity is a key factor.

Regarding strategy, Sunni Salafist terror groups see what they do as justified by Koranic verses about jihad, with their very general language about the obligation of Muslims to do battle with those—whether infidels or apostates—who in some way "fight" against Islam. The precise meaning of such terms as "fight," "infidel," or "apostate" does not seem to be clearly spelled out in the sacred books. It seems easy to claim, for example, that all Shias are apostates or infidels, and thus deserving of the ultimate punishment if they do not convert, or that anyone who continues to oppose IS control and strict Sharia law is "fighting" against Islam or Allah.

Responses to Terror Policy responses to such terrorism must involve international cooperation, but may differ in their effectiveness. Targeted aerial attacks to kill terrorist leaders (e.g., American drone strikes) can be a hindrance to terrorist groups, but usually little more. One dead leader will be replaced by another live one. And al-Qaeda and its fellow jihadis seem to be decentralized, for example, with al-Qaeda in the Islamic Maghreb operating across North Africa, Al-Shabaab in Somalia, Boko Haram in northern Nigeria, the Nusra Front in Syria, the Taliban in Afghanistan and Pakistan, and even local IS units acting autonomously.

Personal religious attachment, among fighters who have rejected their oppressed and hopeless past in their country of origin and have embraced a vision that continues into heaven, enables IS to widely employ suicide car bombings and vest explosions (while often in government uniforms) in their tactical repertoire. Such tactics can be potent militarily, breaking through gateway checkpoints to permit a sudden incursion by follow-on jihadi attackers into a village or government compound, taking full advantage of the psychological shock value.

Another factor is the technological superiority in weapons and vehicles that jihadists often enjoy. In the case of IS in Iraq and Syria, the large number of modern American weapons and vehicles (including over 2000 advanced "Humvees") that they captured in their 2014 sweep in Iraq has allowed them to mount successful attacks with limited numbers of troops. Lacking any reluctance to kill civilians who have not converted to their cause (who again, they label as infidel enemies or apostates), jihadis can swell their ranks of foot-soldiers by coercion. For their part, government troops in Iraq, are poorly armed and often demoralized by the corruption and poor leadership that they often see around them.

With their deep identity connection to their cause, most militant Islamic insurgents today cannot be persuaded to drop terrorist methods in favor of other forms of political contention (as some Islamist groups did in the late 1990s in Algeria, for example). Seemingly only counterinsurgency force can beat them back. But government attempts to fight the terrorists face special difficulties. Government patrols to search for individual terrorists are vulnerable to sniper fire and small explosive devices, and are often ineffective. IS operatives systematically lay mines wherever they control territory, so retaking ground once lost to IS requires slow and difficult minesweeping by engineers.

Meanwhile, terrorists are not reluctant to go into civilian residential areas that they are infiltrating, set up mobile firing positions there, fire their weapons (e.g., mortars or rocket-propelled grenades) into neighboring government-held areas, then quickly pack up and leave before return fire has had time to organize. In practice, the main antiterrorist option in response for government forces is weapon strikes from the outside at such firing positions, with conventional artillery, mortars, or rocket-propelled grenades. But such weapons tend not to be high-tech and surgical, so they often do "collateral damage" to the surrounding residential area, from which the jihadis have already made their hasty retreat. The result may be high costs in deaths of civilians, especially in urban areas. Such deaths in turn provide public relations gains for the insurgents as they (and often, reporters) lament how the government forces are "attacking their own people."

Much more surgical American air strikes with the latest precision weapons are more effective with much less collateral damage. But they are only as useful as the targeting intelligence that they rely on. Such strikes can be very effective in some local areas of Syria and Iraq. (e.g., they supported Kurds who were trained and equipped for target identification in retaking the town of Kobani in northwestern Syria in late 2014.) But these efforts are still too few and scattered to turn the tide overall. Specialist American (or French, in West Africa) military personnel seem to be necessary on the ground to identify targets and call in strikes. But introducing such troops is politically controversial, especially given the American experiences in Vietnam in the 1960s and Iraq in the 2000s.

Ideally, local Sunni tribes might resist the terrorists, but often they are too terrorized by IS murder threats to fight back. Many struggle to survive economically, so they need to be paid to take on the risks of resistance. If they do, typically they are not adequately supplied with modern weapons (e.g., in Iraq, where the Shia government is reluctant to equip Sunnis). International coalition and native governmental forces have a poor record of cooperating to adequately arm the antiterrorist fighters. And again, when areas are retaken from IS, typically they are full of booby traps and land mines, and may be vulnerable to subsequent IS counterattacks.

As for the ordinary people on the ground in the conflict areas, the response of many has been to flee. Millions of Syrians, for example, remain displaced internally or in refugee camps in other countries. Increasing numbers, now in the hundreds of thousands, try to make their way to the safety of Europe. On their attempted journey, whether across Turkey and the Balkans, or across North Africa and the Mediterranean (from lawless Libya), they tend to fall prey to extortion by those in the human smuggling trade on whom they depend, or to the weather, lack of food and water, or leaky boats. Those making it to Europe become part of the mounting refugee burden there. Not surprisingly, European nations share the sense of alarm about the challenge of militant Islamism in the Middle East and in central and northern Africa.

A Kurdish fighter looks over the destruction of the town of Kobani in northwestern Syria, after it was retaken from IS.

An important component of strategy against the risk and reality of such terrorism brings us back to the challenge of poverty in the developing world. Marginalized groups and poor neighborhoods, providing no prospects for young people, remain the primary recruiting grounds for ethnic-nationalist, religious, or ideological groups that use radicalizing propaganda (especially via Internet websites) and/or offer money to increase the numbers of their fighters. As was noted above, sophisticated development aid experts have long known that poor urban areas and villages must be helped, where needed, with such basics as food, water, jobs, and security against crime, to make acceptable lives for themselves. (Spikes in the scarcity and expense of water and food seem to have played a significant role in the "Arab Spring" uprisings in North Africa and the Middle East.) But aid must be accompanied by fostering the cooperation of community groups and involving them in the implementation of aid programs. Local government and security people must be community based as much as possible to receive the ground-level cooperation that they need to deter or capture terrorists without collateral civilian deaths and heavy losses of their own.

National Economic Power

A fourth recent challenge is the emergence of patterns of economic dominance by certain nations, whose economic position and influence may be backed by nationalism and may not always be exercised wisely. As was noted in chapter 17, realism in international relations can take economic as well as military and political forms. There we saw that during the colonial era of the nineteenth and early twentieth centuries, imperial powers such as Great Britain and France (and on a lesser scale, countries such as the Netherlands, Portugal, and Belgium) displayed economic realism in pursuing their economic dominance and advantage in their colonial spheres of influence. In the decades after World War II, colonialism wound down. But it is sometimes argued that in the latter decades of the twentieth century, the more developed and economically powerful nations of the world's north spearheaded global free trade organizations not in an international institutionalist spirit, but rather out of national economic self-interest. According to an economic realist perspective, the northern nations aimed to enhance their already advantaged positions, technologically and financially, in international economic competition. On this view, what is new amid twenty-first century globalization is that new big winners have emerged: China worldwide, and in Europe, Germany.

Worldwide China's combination of advantages in technology, still comparatively low wages in most of the country, and good infrastructure have brought massive export success and huge trade surpluses (exports exceeding imports) in international commerce. As the country builds its share in foreign markets at ever higher technological levels, domestically China continues to maintain tariff and regulatory barriers against imports.

The result for the Chinese government has been bulging revenues, which it uses in various ways to further press its competitive advantage in world trade. More than in other countries, the Chinese government pursues traditional policies such as building infrastructure (roads, rails, electric power) and subsidizing exporting companies' research and development with cheap credit, to further boost China's technology advantage. In addition, China's state-owned enterprises buy land and privileged, cheap access to key raw materials in Africa and other developing areas. Meanwhile often other nations' exporters are only allowed to sell to the growing (and potentially huge) Chinese market on condition that they move production to China, where, among other things, industrial espionage to gain Chinese access to foreign technology is easier. And in another government tactic, other countries' access to what are called "rare earth elements"—crucial in a wide range of high-tech products including smart phones—over which China now has a virtual monopoly, has at times been made conditional upon moving the high-tech production to China.

Moreover, with its huge financial reserves from past trade surpluses, the Chinese government can afford to buy other nations' currencies to keep the value of its own currency (the yuan) low. This keeps the prices of Chinese exported goods low for competitive advantage, and prevents the usual moderation of trade imbalances that can come from appreciation (rise) in the value of the currency of a successful exporting nation.[15]

To be sure, after keeping the yuan from appreciating in value against the dollar in the decade from 1995 to 2005 (called "pegging" its currency to the dollar), when China was building its formidable position in world trade, the Chinese government was under growing international pressure to relent. In the period from 2005 to 2015, China accommodated somewhat to the prevailing international practice of allowing exchange rates to float upward or downward in response to market forces. Its monetary authorities permitted the yuan to go up by 18 percent in relation to the dollar between 2005 and 2008, and by another 10 percent between 2010 and 2014. But whenever there were signs of export weakness and a slowing of China's remarkable 7–10 percent yearly GDP growth rate, such as during the world financial crisis of 2008–2009 and the international uncertainty of the late summer of 2015, China either resumed pegging (2008–2010) or devalued the yuan (as in the late summer of 2015, by 3 percent). Ultimately, economic realism seems to prevail.

Europe In Europe, the last decade has seen Germany's rise to economic dominance and heavy political influence over other nations' economic policies in the Eurozone and the larger European Union. In the years after reunification, policymakers in Germany perceived the country to be held back economically by costly high wages, labor market regulations, and generous unemployment benefits, especially amid the challenge of absorbing the former East Germany. The Hartz reforms of 2004 and 2005 opened up the labor market with a category of "temporary" employment that skirted traditional protections against easy layoffs, and cut back access to long-term unemployment benefits in ways that encouraged laid off workers to go back to work at lower wages. German firms established or expanded production not only in eastern Germany but also into a range of other low-wage post-Communist east European countries. As was noted in chapter 7, today Germany takes advantage of its trade success with high-tech exports (e.g., industrial machinery and chemicals to China) and its access to cheap east European labor to lead Europe in influence, as its wealthiest power.

In the recent past, Germany had the resources to navigate the financial crisis of 2008–2009 fairly well. The country's unemployment rate stayed low with help from the government's "short work" program of subsidizing businesses to keep workers on the payroll, rather than laying them off. In contrast, the southern European slump (in Greece and parts of Spain, depression) has continued through 2015, with high government deficits and debt and continuing unemployment rates above 20 percent in some areas (over 40 percent for the young).

The situation is worsened by the common currency itself. The shared use of the euro prevents southern European governments from using their own national monetary policies to recover. And the common currency prevents any appreciation (growth) in the value of Germany's currency to lessen Germany's competitive advantage and moderate the trade imbalance in Europe. The south's unpayable debts to German banks and European institutions under German influence mounted, giving the Germans clout which they have used to impose further austerity, producing yet further economic decline in Europe's south (see chapter 7). Meanwhile, the consequent budget and debt crises (again, especially in Greece and Spain) have kept the value of the euro low internationally, which in turn keeps the prices of German exports low and competitive in world trade outside the Eurozone. Thus, like China in 1995–2005 and 2018–2010, Germany has been able to avoid a rise in the value of its currency that otherwise would attend the nation's huge trade success.

All this might appear to be primarily a matter of economic realism by German policymakers and their allies (perhaps influenced by creditor interests in relation to southern European debt). But social identity factors also seem to be at work. Among the dominant policymakers in EU institutions, free-market austerity theories seem to be pervasive. According to them, austerity's spending cuts will quickly bring economic recovery by driving down wages, and thus the costs of exporters, so they can reduce product prices and be more competitive in international trade.

In contrast, as we saw in chapter 7, the contending theoretical approach, the Keynesian one, is more pragmatic and data driven. It points out that factually, applying austerity in a slump simply suppresses growth and employment, as was shown by recent research by IMF economists (and many others around the world).[16] As economists put it, wages tend to be somewhat "sticky," not going down fast enough to turn things around before the enterprises go bankrupt due to the surrounding depression. When the facts do not seem to carry weight, often intense social identity may be playing a key part—in this case, identification with free-market doctrine in a way that amounts to an elite social movement—alongside material stake interests like those of creditors.

In addition, a second identity factor may be reinforcing the first: economic nationalism that extends even to many ordinary Germans. For all the idealistic enthusiasm that some feel for a single European identity, the Eurozone remains a collection of distinct nations, each with its own national identity. Their citizenries are not under a single European governmental unit with welfare policies that automatically help the poor or unemployed in distressed regions (e.g., American food and medical aid provided for the poor in lower-income states such as Alabama and Mississippi as well as advantaged ones). Thus inequality involves contending national economic interests as well as contending economic strata. Germans tend to see themselves as citizens of a successful and hardworking nation that should not have to transfer resources to a nation such as Greece, which many Germans view as lazy, coddled, spendthrift, unsuccessful, and undeserving of such aid.

Thus two contemporary identity groups converge and reinforce each other in Germany: nationalism and free-market neoliberalism. In contrast, a more pragmatic view would accept the facts that (a) Greece is in a depression to which years of severe austerity have contributed, and (b) Greece's huge debts—fostered by past governments of both the left and the right—make it implausible to imagine Greece's government or its banks repaying on time. A pragmatic approach suggests negotiating down the remaining Greek debt to governments and international institutions, which has been part of the solution for a number of developing nations in past decades (and as private creditors of Greece have already agreed to do). Some even suggested that Greece exit the Eurozone, get back to having its own national currency (the drachma) and its own autonomous monetary and fiscal policy, and through devaluation of its national currency, grow its competitiveness in international trade.

This was not the outcome. In mid-2015, Greece lost its fight to renegotiate the demands of Germany and the EU apparatus for more Greek austerity. This was despite a referendum showing 60 percent Greek opposition to such terms. The Greeks were faced with a threat by the German finance minister, Wolfgang Schauble, that if Greece did not accept the full list of austerity terms, she would be excluded from the Eurozone. Thus Greece would have to return to its pre-euro currency, the drachma, and many Greeks with substantial savings feared that the drachma would then fall in relation to the euro and their savings would take a big hit. Moreover, Greek banks were being kept from failing only by support from the ECB, which maintained that such support would continue only as long as Greece was proceeding toward acceptance of the bailout austerity terms. A climate of fear and uncertainty prevailed in Greece, and rational, factual, pragmatic debate about whether Greek exit from the euro might be best in the long run did not take place. Meanwhile, the governing Syriza party's leadership had promised to keep Greece in the Eurozone. Under all these pressures, prime minister Tsipras switched to accepting austerity to get the bailout aid so Greece could make its next debt payments and stay in the Eurozone. Greek austerity intensified and the country's depression seemed likely to deepen.

By 2015, anti-austerity sentiment was running high in Europe. Defensive economic nationalism and anti-austerity "Eurosceptic" political parties were strengthening. Doubts were rising not only in southern Europe but also among some in northern countries that are traditional pro-austerity stalwarts but had begun experiencing faltering economic growth, such as the Netherlands and Finland. However, the prospects for effective anti-austerity cooperation to seriously contend with pro-austerity elites seem poor. Anti-austerity and Eurosceptic sentiment is diverse (including groups from both the far left and the far right, for example), without much of a unifying social identity beyond each nation's defensive economic nationalism and shared support for forms of minimal economic well-being for its citizens.

SUMMARY: CONTENTION, COOPERATION, AND SOCIAL IDENTITY IN FOREIGN POLICY

As we have seen, a third major cluster of factors behind foreign policymaking is related to social identity groups that span borders. Shared ethnicity or religious affiliation, for example, can help explain cooperation in international alliances, and differences over such factors can say a lot about international contention. Sociopolitical movements and related values, too, can amount to broad identity groups with international impacts. A social identity factor that can support and intensify realist strategies, including economic ones, is nationalism.

The policy challenge that promises to have the biggest long-term impact on the world is global warming. The coming droughts will affect tens and even hundreds of millions of people per river system. International contention over water supplies may bring conflict and war. Cooperation in accepting the science regarding the problem and acting on it in a significant way has been slow in coming. People are invested, both economically and psychologically, in the status quo regarding the use of fossil fuels. Promising strategies exist at the drafting stage, but cooperation by those with the resources to implement them to seriously contend with the challenge is so far lacking. The same applies to global poverty, which feeds both the rebellions in developing nations that invite militant Islamist intervention, and the numbers of terrorist fighters that intervene.

Militant Islamist terrorism involves identity groups, but contending with it requires cooperation in alliances of nations. But identity-related and realist contentions continue within those coalitions, such as between Shia Muslim nations (and groups), moderate Sunnis, and Western nations. Meanwhile, the militant Islamists themselves are difficult adversaries. This is due not only to their religious commitment to imposing strict Sharia law that supersedes other concerns for them, but also to their readiness to spill blood—their own, in suicide bombing attacks, and that of their opponents in using terror to enforce cooperation in the areas that they control. Driving them back requires not only the advanced precision military technology available to the West, but also, in the hands of allies on the ground, arms and vehicles that are at least the equal of those of Islamic State. All this requires more cooperation, and less contention, than we currently see among those without the unifying identity ties that the Islamic State enjoys.

Another challenge today is offensive economic nationalism. In different ways and settings, China and Germany provide examples of its impact. Each nation is wielding international economic influence in ways that, in effect, further the fortunes of its enterprises in world trade. Meanwhile, leaving economies to entirely unregulated and globalized free markets, a single dominant currency, and the bankruptcy courts—without even emergency government intervention—has a poor track record: of either the disaster of depression or the strong (especially technologically) devouring the weak, nationally and internationally. The contending austerity-minded and Keynesian groups must look to the values that they share, and find a way to recognize the empirical facts together and cooperate on the most effective strategies revealed by economic science.

COUNTRY CASE STUDIES

Here we consider two cases: Iran, which plays an active role in affecting its neighbors in the Middle East, and Rwanda, an African country that has suffered grievously from identity-based conflict across national borders, and from neglect by international institutions.

Iran: Alliance Leader, Ally, and Antagonist

Iran's recent foreign policy combines identity with realist factors. Historically, Iranian nationalism has a long heritage, dating back to the Persian monarchy in ancient times, which distinguished Persia from its Arab neighbors to the west. The rise of Islam reinforced this distinctive Persian identity when the Shia branch of Islam established its heartland in Persia. Since then, Iran's Shia identity has infused the realist role that it plays in Middle East politics, especially in Iraq and Lebanon.

The Islamist regime in Iran was born with the overthrow of the Western-oriented and U.S.-allied monarch, the Shah, Mohammad Reza Pahlavi. Many Iranian nationalists had remained bitter over the original installation of the Shah's monarchy, in a 1953 CIA-engineered overthrow of the elected government led by Mohammad Mosaddegh (which had nationalized Iranian oil). The United States continued to support the Shah's oppressive regime until it was removed in 1979 by a revolution led by traditionalist cleric Ayatollah Khomeini, who fused (anti-American) Iranian nationalism with a revival of Shia Islam. As we saw in chapter 11, the Iranian system provides the formalities of representative democracy, but it gives religious authorities like the Guardian Council such strong veto power over laws and candidacies to the legislature that Iran's government is best classified as a theocratic authoritarian regime.

In 1997, however, something different seemed to be emerging. A reformer, Mohammed Khatami, was elected president with the support of many women and students who favored greater personal and cultural freedom, and he was reelected in 2001. A number of reform-supporting organizations sprouted up, encouraged by Khatami's support for dialogue with the West. However, Khatami's democratization and reform efforts were ultimately frustrated by the religious clerical establishment, which (as noted above) can veto legislation and candidates for parliament. By 2004, most reformers had been banned from running for parliament in that year's elections.

When President Khatami's second term ended in 2005, a conservative firebrand, Mahmoud Ahmadinejad, won the presidency with a promise to alleviate poverty. In office, however, Ahmadinejad was known mostly for realist initiatives in security and foreign policy. These include enriching uranium (perhaps to a level that might be usable in nuclear weapons), aiding and seeking to influence the Shia majority in southern and central Iraq, and supporting the Lebanese Shia militia Hezbollah and its efforts to thwart Israeli incursions into southern Lebanon. Along the way, all of these moves highlighted and heightened nationalist confrontation with the United States.

By the late spring of 2007, the Iranian government faced the threat of Western economic sanctions (related to its nuclear program) and increasing domestic discontent. The domestic issues included the absence of reforms, poor economic conditions such as high unemployment and inflation, and contention about the seriousness and adequacy of the regime's antipoverty efforts despite large government revenues from high oil prices. At that point, Ahmadinejad mounted a major wave of repression. Activists of students' and women's organizations were imprisoned, and large numbers were detained or beaten up for displaying Western dress and hairstyles.

The government portrayed these harsh measures as a response to what it saw as a realist and identity-based offensive by the United States against Iran. In 2006, the United States had shifted from quieter modes of influence to an explicit public commitment of twenty million dollars in "soft power" aid to Iranian groups to try to bring about regime change there. Referring to the aid as a U.S. attempt to recruit Iranian agents to pursue its nationalist designs, the Ahmadinejad regime banned or suppressed many reform-oriented nongovernmental organizations (detaining their activists), which it accused of receiving U.S. funding.

When Ahmadinejad won reelection in mid-2009 by a large margin in the officially announced vote count, reformist opponents charged widespread vote fraud. The subsequent "green revolution" protest demonstrations brought numerous detentions and charges of torture in jail. After its own investigation, the regime declared the result valid, with Supreme Leader Khamenei backing the outcome and condemning the protesters.

Recent events, however, have focused on the confrontation between Iran and the West over Iran's nuclear ambitions. The nation had been enriching uranium on an increasing scale in what the Iranian government said was the pursuit of peaceful nuclear power development and its own production of radioisotopes for medical purposes. In early 2009, U.S. president Obama pledged a new effort in internationalist diplomacy. But the Iranian regime refused to cooperate fully with provisions under the Nuclear Non-Proliferation Treaty (NNPT) for monitoring and inspection of its nuclear program by the International Atomic Energy Agency (IAEA). IAEA inspectors could not verify conclusively that Iran was not working secretly to produce weapons-grade uranium fuel.

In the autumn of 2009, the Western powers proposed a deal—for Iran to trade the bulk of its moderately enriched uranium for a more highly enriched form suitable for a medically oriented reactor. The Iranian government refused, saying it would only offer a limited portion of its enriched uranium, and could not trust the West to follow through on the deal. In June 2010, the U.N. Security Council abandoned this effort and imposed a new round of sanctions on Iran, with the acquiescence of Russia and China. However, these sanctions were limited to restricting Iranian trade in military-related products and freezing Western assets of companies linked to Iran's Revolutionary Guards. The sanctions did not include a wider economic embargo, which would have significantly impacted the Iranian economy (which the U.S. government wanted but China and Russia declined to support).

In its approach to the nuclear issue, the Ahmadinejad regime, with the explicit support of the Supreme Leader, adopted a realist approach of power contest with the United States by rejecting established paths of internationalist diplomacy (e.g., full compliance with IAEA inspections) to resolving the dispute. A nuclear weapons capacity would be an especially important nationalist symbol and perhaps a source of new influence in the Middle East, a region where Israel is the only country with nuclear weapons, and in the Muslim world, where thus far only (Sunni) Pakistan has had nuclear weapons. If Iran got close to actually producing a deliverable nuclear weapon (how soon that could occur is debated), the risks of military attack from Israel to destroy or blunt that capability, perhaps supported by the United States, would rise significantly.

However, there may be a role for identity-related factors. If Iran gained nuclear weapons capability, this Shia Persian nation would be the only Islamic nuclear power in the Middle East, raising the Shia flag in the face of the Sunni Arab majority in the region as well as Israel. (In 2015, Sunni-partisan Saudi Arabia threatened to get nuclear weapons if Iran did so.)

Another aspect of the interweaving of realist and identity motivations in Iranian foreign policy may be seen in Iran's projection of influence in Iraq and Lebanon. The war in neighboring Iraq had the consequence of giving Shia Iran major influence over the Iraqi government, with Shia Muslims comprising the majority of the Iraqi population and making up the majority of the parliament elected in early 2010.

Iran has also extended its influence in the mid-2000s as the main supporter of the Lebanese Shia militia Hezbollah. Iran has supported Hezbollah economically and militarily via southern Iraq and Syria. Syria is primarily a Sunni nation, but a Shia-offshoot minority (called the Alawites) is entrenched in control of the Syrian government. Syria has traditionally exercised heavy influence in much of Lebanon, especially as the informal guarantor of the peace among the militias that ended the Lebanese civil war at the end of the 1980s. But in the 2006 war between Israel and Hezbollah in Lebanon, Hezbollah was able to blunt the Israeli incursion, while the weaker official Lebanese army remained on the sidelines. The political result for Hezbollah was a veto capacity in the Lebanese cabinet, and enhanced prestige and security influence well beyond its Shia home area in the Bekaa valley. Since Hezbollah's main backer is Iran (also a key supporter of Hamas in Gaza), Iran was able to present itself to Arabs in a new role, as the chief bulwark against Israel in the Middle East. All of this new regional influence by Iran has an identity-related base—the Shia belt from Iran through southern Iraq, the Alawite minority in Syria, to Hezbollah in Lebanon, and around to the Shia Houthis of Yemen.

Iran's legislature, called the Majlis (dominated by an alliance of conservative groups called the United Principalist Front) has a very limited role in foreign policymaking. Majlis candidates are screened to assure that they are sufficiently Islamic, and the body is heavily controlled by the limit-setting power of the conservative twelve-member Guardian Council—composed of six clerical figures appointed by the supreme leader and six nominated by a leading jurist and approved by the Majlis. The council can veto Majlis decisions as well as screen Majlis candidates. Today there seems to be much impatience among ordinary Iranians with the country's isolation and the economic privations that stem from Western sanctions over Iran's nuclear program. But any expression of that impatience in the Majlis is likely to be very muted and ineffective.

Foreign and security policy is generally the preserve of President Rouhani, Supreme Leader Khameni, and the forces that back these two figures, including the Islamic Revolutionary Guard Corps (IRGC). The IRGC began during the 1979 revolution as the key militia backing Ayatollah Khomeini and the new regime. It has developed into a special branch of the armed forces, separate from the regular army and responsible for domestic and foreign security and ideology. Internationally, Iran's dealings with Hezbollah in Lebanon, for example (e.g., training in the use of sophisticated weapons), are managed by IRGC troops there.

Domestically, the IRGC is a powerful political, economic, and ideological force. It manages a political militia called the Basij, which intimidated and repressed protesters following the disputed 2009 presidential election. Economically, the IRGC amounts to a large holding company involved in strategic economic sectors such as energy and telecommunications. As the government goes about privatizing state-owned enterprises in these key sectors, often it is actually transferring ownership from the government to the IRGC or other politically connected corporations.

Put all this together and one can see why observers debate which authoritarian force in Iran is most powerful: the religious establishment represented by the Guardian Council, or the Revolutionary Guard Corps? In fact, many observers of Iranian politics now describe two factions within the regime: (a) the IRGC, and the portion of the Principalist Front that supports it (often apparently supported by Supreme Leader Khamenei), and (b) a more moderate bloc of clerical figures with some representation in the Majlis, the Guardian Council, and the Assembly of Experts, supported by Iranian businessmen referred to collectively as "the Bazaar." But the two factions have expressed their differences mainly in domestic policy, over such matters as how harshly to treat protesters and how fast and far to go in reducing subsidies and imposing new taxes on the Bazaar businessmen.

Regarding foreign policy, the two groups have often seemed to be in agreement. However, in the late 2000s, the most prominent moderate leader, Ayatollah Hashemi Rafsanjani, showed discomfort with President Ahmadinejad's confrontational approach to relations with the West. Ahmadinejad's hostile foreign policy stance seemed to be aimed partly to distract Iranians from economic difficulties and shortcomings at home. Economic sanctions against Iran due to its nuclear development provided a useful excuse—and target for blame—for a poor economy at home. For the Iranian government, realist and identity themes always seemed ready to trump international institutionalism.

Nonetheless, economic sanctions have been the only peaceful weapon that the West has against Iran's program for uranium enrichment. In mid-2010, the United States and the European Community adopted new rounds of economic sanctions. The sanctions restricted such Iranian trade sectors as shipping, banking, and even access to European technology in oil and gas production, which are important for Iran. By the time of the next presidential elections in 2013, growing numbers of Iranians were unhappy at the declining economy, the seemingly corrupt distribution of resources by Ahmadinejad to the IRGC, and high inflation. A moderate, Hassan Rouhani, won the presidency promising a renewal of negotiations to end the sanctions.

Iran's continuing toll of unemployment and inflation is related to the sanctions, the drain on the country's resources due to its support of the Iraqi government, the Assad regime in Syria, and Hezbollah in Lebanon and Syria, and the mid-2014 drop in oil prices that cut sharply into its revenues. President Rouhani retained much public support for his pursuit of negotiations. (Despite occasional opposition from religious conservatives and the Basij paramilitaries, on the whole Islamist cultural control seemed to be receding.) In mid-2015, Western and Iranian negotiators finally signed a deal providing that Iran limit its uranium enrichment well short of weapons development, with robust monitoring, in return for a phased reduction in economic sanctions. Whether this signals a turning point in Iran's relationship with Europe and the United states, with implications for better cooperation in the fight against the radical Sunni IS in Iraq, remains to be seen.

Rwanda: Genocide in an International Context

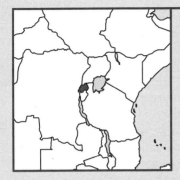

Rwanda in East Africa provides an example of a centuries-old pattern of superimposed ethnic and socioeconomic cleavages. For many generations in Rwanda and Burundi, ethnic Tutsis were a warrior herding minority dominating a feudal peasant class of ethnic Hutus, who had to do forced labor when the Tutsi lords asked. The German colonial authorities before World War I, and the Belgian ones after it, ruled indirectly, relying on the Tutsi dominance over the Hutu majority. Under the Tutsi monarchy that ran Rwanda and neighboring Burundi prior to independence in 1962, education, jobs, and other advantages from the Belgians tended to go to the Tutsi elite. All this was much resented by Hutus in their serf-like position. By the late 1950s, opposing movements for, respectively, Hutu "emancipation" and continued Tutsi dominance had formed in both Ruanda and Burundi.

As independence neared, an incident of violence in 1959 against a Hutu politician prompted a wave of thousands of killings of Tutsis by Hutus. By 1961, however, the situation had eased enough that pre-independence local elections could be held. The Hutus won and Belgium dissolved the united monarchy of Rwanda and Burundi. At this point, events in the two neighboring countries took different courses, but continued to influence one another. In Burundi, following a 1965 Hutu election victory, elements of the Tutsi military assassinated the Hutu leader. After coup and counter-coup, a Tutsi military takeover produced a brutal Tutsi military regime that ruled Burundi until 1993.

Rwanda, for its part, chose in a referendum to become independent as a Hutu-run republic. But after repulsing attacks by Tutsis from Burundi and other neighboring countries, the Rwandan government became a one-party regime under the Hutu emancipation party, Parmetu, which had led the anticolonial movement. After another Tutsi incursion in 1963, another pogrom against Tutsis occurred in Rwanda, with thousands of Tutsis slain. Large numbers of Tutsis fled into Uganda, Burundi, and other border areas. The reverberations in neighboring Burundi, with its Tutsi-dominated military regime, included a Tutsi-perpetrated genocide that killed 200,000 Hutus there. This in turn produced a wave of Hutu refugees fleeing into Rwanda, and exacerbated anti-Tutsi feelings in Rwanda.

Thus the Hutus and Tutsis had experienced genocidal violence thirty years before the much larger Rwandan genocide of 1994. A 1972 coup in Rwanda produced a one-party Hutu regime that was more repressive toward Tutsis than before. It was led by Juvenal Habyarimana and his party, the National Republican Movement for Democracy and Development (MRND), which ruled Rwanda for the next twenty years. Nationalist realism had fused with ethnic identity politics. International institutionalism was largely missing.

By the late 1980s, tensions between Tutsis and Hutus were further intensifying. In northern Burundi, Hutu violence against Tutsis was followed by a Tutsi military massacre of 20,000 Hutus there. And in neighboring Uganda, a new Tutsi armed group formed that included many émigré Rwandan Tutsis who had served in the Ugandan military: the Rwandan Patriotic Front (RPF) under the leadership of Paul Kagame. The RPF attacked Rwanda in 1990, beginning a civil war that lasted until 1993. Kagame presented the invasion (which brought RPF control of much of northern Ruanda) as an attempt to restore democracy to Rwanda and allow the return of some half million émigré Rwandan Tutsis currently living in neighboring countries. Habyarimana, on the other hand, portrayed it as an attempt to restore the old Tutsi domination and feudal enslavement of the Hutus. Each side set up its own radio station as a propaganda mouthpiece. Habyarimana formed a Hutu youth militia (called the Interahamwe), and began localized pogroms against Tutsis. Truces repeatedly broke down.

Under international pressure across Africa in the early 1990s for democratization, however, in the spring of 1992, Rwanda set up the forms of a multiparty regime. Meanwhile, as was noted above, when free elections in Burundi in 1993 led to a Hutu victory there, the Tutsi-dominated Burundian military assassinated the elected Hutu leader and a Burundian civil war ensued. Thus, for purposes of superimposed ethnic, economic, and political cleavages, the political field of Hutu-Tutsi tension included not just Rwanda, but also Burundi, the neighboring Kivu province of Congo (to which many Tutsi refugees had fled earlier), and portions of Uganda used as bases by the Tutsi RPF.

In August 1993 came a ray of international institionalism-style hope: the Rwandan civil war seemed to have ended with the Arusha Accords. This pact resulted from talks involving all sides that had been engineered by the United States, France (a traditional Hutu ally), and the Organization of African States. Under the Accords, which served both as a peace agreement and a democratic transition pact, a new transitional government was set up. It included the Hutu parties and the RPF in a multiparty cabinet, and formally weakened Habyarimana's presidential powers. Under the surface, however, the Tutsi-led RPF and the Hutu extremists led by the president remained deeply suspicious of one another. Hutus expanded their Interahamwe militia units and their radio broadcasts and published materials vilifying Tutsis. Government documents have since revealed that in 1993 the Rwandan government had imported from China an astonishing number of machetes, which were used in the subsequent wave of killings.[17] Apparently, government officials were meeting with the youth militias and military units to plan the systematic genocide.

The peace/transition plan went into effect after a striking incident in April. After a Hutu won the 1994 presidential election in Burundi, the two Hutu presidents met in April, apparently to pursue national reconciliation. However, in transit between the countries their plane was shot down, killing both leaders. Some leading Hutus blamed the attack on Tutsis, and the now notorious Rwandan genocide against Tutsis commenced.

Government-backed radio in Rwanda urged everyone to participate in the killing of all Tutsis. The Interahamwe militia, by then numbering over 30,000 and including portions of the military and some local politicians, went into action. At roadblocks, in homes, and in churches and other places of refuge, Tutsis, their children, and some moderate Hutus were murdered, most often with the government-provided machetes. Politicians associated with the Arusha Accords were systematically exterminated, along with any foreign personnel who tried to protect them (notably including ten Belgian troops trying to guard the prime minister). Other foreign security personnel were quickly withdrawn from the country. The genocide proceeded unhindered for over three months, ultimately killing 800,000 to a million Tutsis and many moderate Hutus.

The informal status of the Hutu militias allowed the Rwandan government to sow confusion about what was happening, claiming officially that any killings were spontaneous outbursts. Nonetheless, the genocide required a lot of government-led planning and coordination. Moderate Hutus were forced to cooperate, and even to sometimes join in wielding machetes, or risk being killed.

On the international institutionalist side, at least in theory the United Nations was another player in this fraught situation. By early 1994, the U.N. contingent in Rwanda had been informed that militias and Rwandan military units were concentrating arms and planning for a systematic massacre of Tutsis in the country. However, international actors did nothing despite the valiant efforts of some of their personnel on the ground to stop the genocide. Old realist alliances seem to have played a part. France (with old informal links to the Hutus) and Russia made clear they would block any U.N. Security Council action to intervene, and the American government was in no mood to risk repeating its recent failed intervention in Somalia. The genocide ended only with the victory of invading Tutsi RPF forces from Uganda in July. Over 2 million Hutu refugees fled to surrounding countries, especially Congo, where many died of disease in camps.

Over the next two years, Hutus were assured of safety in Rwanda if they had not been active perpetrators of the genocide. Partly stimulated by a Tutsi uprising in the Hutu refugee areas in Congo, by 1996 over a million Hutu refugees had returned to Rwanda. Apart from occasional skirmishes in these Congo areas between Tutsi raiders and former Interahamwe elements, the region remains peaceful. Notably, only invasion from a neighboring country was able to stop the murderous state terror.

The Tutsi-dominated regime of Paul Kagame is still in power. Hutu genocide perpetrators were mostly tried in official courts, though some remain across the border in Congo. Arguably Kagame has brought peace and prosperity to Rwanda, reducing poverty with limited corruption. But as president, Kagame brooks no rivals, and suppresses any real dissent or opposition. His RPF remains disciplined under his control, and only parties that support the president are allowed to operate unhindered. Multiparty democratic elections remain mainly a formal appearance that seems intended to keep up the flow of foreign aid, which makes up a significant chunk of the Rwandan budget. Kagame continues to try to invoke fear of guilty Hutus in the Congo, amid continuing concern about the Burundian Hutu government's threats to Tutsis in that country. The constitution says he must step down in 2017, but chances are strong that Kagame will get the restriction removed to allow him to continue in office.

✈ PRACTICE AND REVIEW ONLINE

CRITICAL THINKING QUESTIONS

1. Among identity groups that affect international relations, how are ethnic and religious affinities different from value-related social movements? Can the two overlap? If so, how?

2. Why and how might realist policymakers have to get involved in identity politics to pursue their aims?

3. How are poverty in the developing world and global warming connected? What is the connection between poverty and Islamist terrorism?

4. What are the differences between the economic nationalisms at work in China and Germany?

KEY TERMS

constructivism, 539
social identity, 540
détente, 543
soft power, 543
nationalism, 544
economic nationalism, 544
global warming, 547
feedback effect, 547
cap-and-trade, 550
minimum threshold approach, 553
biofuels, 554
sectarian, 557

FURTHER READING

Anderson, Benedict. *Imagined Communities: Reflections on the Origin and Spread of Nationalism*. London: Verso, 1991.

Barry, John, and Robyn Eckersley, eds. *The State and the Global Ecological Crisis*. Cambridge, MA: MIT Press, 2005.

Brass, Paul R. *Ethnicity and Nationalism: Theory and Comparison*. Newbury Park, CA: Sage, 1991.

Dessler, Andrew E., and Edward A Parson. *The Science and Politics of Global Climate Change: A Guide to the Debate*. Cambridge, UK: Cambridge University Press, 2006.

Dreze, Jean, and Amartya Sen, eds. *The Political Economy of Hunger*. Oxford, UK: Clarendon Press, 1995.

Gore, Albert. *An Inconvenient Truth: The Planetary Emergency of Global Warming and What We Can Do About It*. Emmaus, PA: Rodale press, 2006.

Huntington, Samuel P. *Clash of Civilizations and the Remaking of World Order*. New York: Simon & Schuster, 1996.

Kaplan, Stephen B. *Globalization and Austerity Politics in Latin America*. Cambridge, UK: Cambridge University Press, 2013.

Milanovic, Branko. *Worlds Apart: Global and International Inequality, 1950–2000*. Princeton, NJ: Princeton University Press, 2005.

Nau, Henry R. *Perspectives on International Relations: Power, Institutions, and Ideas*. Washington, DC: CQ Press, 2007.

Stiglitz, Joseph. *Making Globalization Work*. New York: Norton, 2006.

Taras, Raymond C., and Rajat Ganguly. *Understanding Ethnic Conflict: The International Dimension*. New York: Longman, 2006.

Thomas, Caroline. *Global Governance, Development and Human Security*. London: Pluto Press, 2000.

Victor, David G. *Global Warming Gridlock: Creating More Effective Strategies for Protecting the Planet*. New York: Cambridge University Press, 2011.

———. *Climate Change: Debating America's Policy Options*. Washington, DC: Council on Foreign Relations, 2004.

NOTES

[1] See Alexander Wendt, "Anarchy Is What States Make of It: The Social Construction of Power Politics," *International Organization* 46, no. 2 (1992): 391–425, and *Social Theory of International Politics* (Cambridge, UK: Cambridge University Press, 1999).

[2] For an exploration of international relations that considers the third main approach to international relations to be "the identity perspective," see Nau (2007).

[3] See Huntington (1996).

[4] For another early analysis of the West-militant Islam clash, see Benjamin Barber, *Jihad vs. McWorld* (New York: Random House, 1995).

[5] See *Soft Power: The Means to Success in World Politics* (New York: Public Affairs Press, 2005).

[6] See David G. Victor, *Global Warming Gridlock: Creating More Effective Strategies for Protecting the Planet* (Cambridge, UK: Cambridge University Press, 2011), and *The Collapse of the Kyoto Protocol and the Struggle to Slow Global Warming* (Princeton, NJ: Princeton University Press, 2001).

[7] See Alan M. Jacobs and J. Scott Matthews, "Why Do Citizens Discount the Future? Public Opinion and the Timing of Policy Consequences," *British Journal of Political Science* 42, no. 4 (2012): 903–35.

[8] See *Globalization, Political Institutions and the Environment in Developing Countries* (New York and London: Routledge, 2012).

[9] Examples are (a) gasifying the coal and separating the CO_2 before cleanly burning the remaining hydrogen for energy, and (b) burning coal with 100 percent oxygen so that the exhaust is almost pure CO_2 to be pumped into the ground.

[10] Research is ongoing into other potential cooling technologies, such as sodium-based cooling.

[11] See Charles E. Lindblom, "The Science of "Muddling Through," *Public Administration Review* 19, no. 2 (Spring, 1959): 79–88

[12] See Amartya Sen, *Development as Freedom* (Oxford: Oxford University Press, 1999), and Martha C. Nussbaum, *Women and Human Development* (Cambridge, UK: Cambridge University Press, 2000).

[13] See Asbjorn Eide, "Realisation of Social and Economic Rights and the Minimum Threshold Approach," *Human Rights Law Journal* 10 (1989): 35–51; and Bard Anders Andreassen, Alan G. Smith, and Hugo Stokke, "Compliance with Economic and Social Human Rights: Realistic Evaluations and Monitoring in the Light of Immediate Obligations," in *Writing Rights: Human Rights Research at the Chr. Michelsen Institute, 1984–2004*, ed. Ivar Kolstad and Hugo Stokke (Bergen, Norway: Fagbokforlaget, 2005), 131–47.

[14] For treatments of a broad range of international nongovernmental organizations, see John Boli and George M. Thomas, eds., *Constructing World Culture: International Nongovernmental Organizations Since 1875* (Stanford, CA: Stanford University Press, 1999).

[15] Under the usual international custom of free trade (and hence "floating exchange rates") in countries' currencies, a successful exporting country will see its market gains moderate as investors put money into it, producing a rise (appreciation) in the value of its currency, making its products more expensive.

[16] See chapter 7. An example is Olivier Blanchard and Daniel Leigh, "Growth Forecast Errors and Fiscal Multipliers," IMF Working Paper 13/1, IMF Research Department, January 2013. The results show that empirically, cuts in government spending have indeed suppressed GDP by roughly 1.5 (or more) times the amount of the cut—much more than the European authorities seem to have previously assumed.

[17] See Linda Melvern, *Conspiracy to Murder: The Rwandan Genocide* (London: Verso, 2004).

GLOSSARY

A

abstract review Judicial review of bills at the point of their passage.

ad hoc committee A special legislative committee, not permanently established, to examine a particular issue or problem.

administrative law Law specific to an administrative unit and its practice, applied by special courts separate from the regular justice system.

affective voting Voter choice due to personal feelings about one or more candidates or parties.

agency theory An explanatory approach that emphasizes the strategies, policy preferences, and decisions of leaders of elite groups and parties seeking to protect or further their interests during democratic transitions.

anarchy The absence of government.

anticipated reaction Influence due to a client thinking ahead to what the patron's reaction would be to a choice the client might make, and acting accordingly.

anti-system party A party that is critical of the democratic system itself.

appellate court A panel of judges who take a second look if the lower-level judgment is appealed by a party to the case.

aristocracy For the classical Greek and Roman political philosophers, the public-spirited rule of the few best citizens.

aristocratic traditionalism A strand in political thought that suggested that harmony could be best realized by sharing rule among an elite possessed of wisdom and justice of character.

associational group A group that exists for social and/or political purposes, with the association lobbying to gain benefits for the larger categoric interest that the association represents.

austerity An economic policy approach that focuses on balancing the government budget, primarily by cutting government spending.

authoritarian government A form of government in which the officials who set the main outlines of the government's key laws and programs are not chosen by the people in free and fair election.

authority Power that is widely accepted as a matter of formal or legal obligation.

autonomy Independence in decision making.

B

backbencher An ordinary member of parliament, not part of her or his party leadership in the body.

balance of power Internationally, a rough balance in the military power and political influence between leading powers and their alliances.

behavioral pluralism Scientific study of observable political phenomena that emphasizes the contention, bargaining, and often compromise among interest groups.

bicameral legislature A legislative branch with two assemblies, or "houses"; common among large nations with federal forms of government.

bimodal distribution A range of views which cluster at each extreme, with few in the middle.

biofuels Turning agricultural products (e.g., corn and palm oil) into fuel for cars and trucks.

broad party A party that tries to reach out to a range of interests with an eye to winning elections, while retaining a moderate ideological identity.

bubble An unrealistically large increase in the price of something (e.g., property or crude oil) due to speculative investment.

budget deficit The excess of government spending going out over tax money coming in.

bureaucracy The body of professional, career functionaries (also called the civil service) who carry out a government's laws and programs without regard to party partisanship.

bureaucratic authoritarian Authoritarian rule that relies heavily on an institutionalized bureaucracy to make many policy decisions.

bureaucratic politics model An approach to explaining executive branch politics that focuses on contention among actors representing different units within the executive, jockeying for influence.

C

candidate orientation voting Affective voting by individual candidate.

cap-and-trade A strategy of setting carbon emission limits on types of enterprises and allowing those under their limit to sell their unused "cap space" to those over their limits.

capitalism A market system in which productive property is predominantly privately owned.

capital Privately owned productive resources.

caretaker government A minority cabinet that lacks a support party in the parliament, and thus cannot pass new legislation and is limited to administering the executive departments under existing law until a new majority coalition or support party emerges.

case law The precedents of a legal system, referred to collectively.

categoric interest A category (classification) of people or organizations that is affected by government policy.

caucus A meeting of a party's members in a legislative assembly.

central bank A nation's independent governmental "bank for the banks."

centralized decision making A pattern in which key decisions originate among top members of its leadership and organizational hierarchy.

challenge of participation A rise in citizen contention with the government to allow more people to safely participate in politics.

charisma An individual's personal appeal on camera that can be a source of affective support.

civic culture A society in which a significant portion of the population is inclined to participate in politics, at least in voting.

civil liberties Individual freedoms such as those of expression, association, religion, and the press.

civil society Groups and their organizations that are thought to be close to the ground or the grass roots, such as labor unions, community organizations, professional associations, women's groups, student groups, ethnic-cultural minority groups, etc.

civil war War between contending forces within a single country.

classical liberalism Ideological thought that focuses on individual freedom in both economic and sociocultural policy, free market oriented economically but on sociocultural issues, moderately left of center and personal freedom oriented.

clientelist party A party that is based on patron-client relationships to particular groups.

code law Legal systems that apply an elaborate written code of laws and rules directly to cases, associated with traditional continental European judicial practice.

coercion Influence that involves compelling an individual to obey by threatening or using force or other extremely harsh penalties.

coinciding cleavages A situation in which society is divided into two or more groups with multiple sources of difference between them, such as over religion, ethnicity, language, region, or economic stratum.

collective responsibility The customary rule under parliamentary government that if you are a minister in the cabinet, you must publicly support all bills proposed by the cabinet to parliament.

collective security The pursuit of national security through cooperation with other nations in international institutions based on agreement to come to each other's defense in attacked.

common law Principles and practices that emerged from specific judicial decisions arrived at by higher-level courts in classic cases.

communal group A group based on a shared identity and a sense of solidarity around it.

communitarian Thought stressing that conceptions of justice and the common good originate with and depend on society, rather than on the rationality of individuals or on state intervention.

concrete review Judicial review after a case concerning the law has arisen in the courts.

concurrent Occurring at the same time, as in legislative and presidential elections happening on the same day.

conditionality Requiring certain human rights improvements as a prerequisite for giving foreign aid.

conference committee Where different versions of a bill have been passed by two houses, a Committee formed from leading members of both houses' relevant committees, to iron out the differences.

conservative An ideological stance that is right of center on economic issues (free market oriented), sociocultural intervention (favoring it), and military strength.

consolidation Representative democracy taking hold and persisting

constituent service Helping citizens who live in the representative's district with particular problems that they may have with government.

constitution A set of explicit, formal rules for governmental decision making, including the basic structures, procedures, powers, and limitations of government.

constitutional law Law pertaining to the constitution and the powers of units of government in relation to each other and to the rights of citizens under the constitution.

constructivism The idea that international interactions issue from "discourse" (communication) within and among communities that are themselves the products of such phenomena as "stories" (historical narratives) and symbols, rather than straightforward empirical facts.

consul The leading diplomatic representative of a foreign country in a local area within a nation.

consumer demand Consumer spending on goods and services.

containment The strategy by the U.S.-led capitalist countries of making every effort to prevent any other countries, such as Greece, Turkey, South Korea, or Malaysia, from falling to Communism.

co-optation Incorporating opposition leaders into the regime's structure by offering positions and other attractive inducements in return for cooperation.

cross-cutting cleavages A situation wherein each group is internally divided by other lines of social division that cut across multiple groups, so that members of the same group are opponents on some issues and members of different groups are allies on some issues, in effect softening the intensity of intergroup political contention.

D

decentralized decision making A pattern in which key decisions are dispersed to various groups or lower levels within an organization (e.g., a political party).

defensive realism Nations cooperating and combining their forces to "balance" and check a rising aggressive power.

deflation Declining prices for goods and services, due to insufficient consumer demand.

delegate model A model of representation suggesting that the representatives' main duty in the assembly should be to support policies that are favored by the majority of the voters back home in their districts (sometimes called the "mandate model").

democratic socialism Having a socialist economy governed by democracy, established by peaceful change through the democratic process.

dependent variable The result, or outcome, of the impact of one or more factors on something else.

détente The 1970s and 1980s policy of generally reducing contention and increasing peaceful cooperation between the United States and the Soviet Union.

diplomatic immunity The international custom of protection for diplomatic personnel from detention and trial for actions taken in performance of their duties.

direct democracy The citizens themselves making policy decisions.

directive power Power that is aimed at getting people to take specific actions.

E

economic nationalism Intensified national identity in support of national economic interests in international economic and financial policymaking.

economic policy Policies that affect the economy, including domestic spending (e.g., in such areas as welfare, transportation, and education), taxation, and regulation.

Electoral College In the United States, a special assembly of slates of representatives, chosen by the voters, which on the ballot were pledged to vote for one presidential candidate or another, and which formally choose the president by majority vote.

electoral system A country's system of voting.

elite model The view that the preferences of some dominant minority within a group are the main influence over the group's policymaking.

embassy A special office in a country that officially represents the government of another country to facilitate relations between the nations and their citizens.

empirical theory Explanatory hypotheses regarding patterns of cause and effect in politics.

empirical An approach to understanding something that focuses on observed facts and looks for patterns that shed light on why phenomena occur.

envoy A special representative of a state designated to deal with one or more other nations' diplomats regarding a particular issue.

ethnic ultranationalism An ideology that centers policy on the dignity, flourishing, and power of an ethnic group, usually one that comprises the majority in its society.

exchange relationship A relationship of mutual influence between two people who are inclined to help each other, governed only by the customary norm that if possible, favors should be returned.

executive office In the American political executive, a cluster of agencies (established by law) that help coordinate governmental functions that cut across departmental boundaries, whose chiefs must be confirmed by the Senate.

exit poll A sample survey of those leaving representative polling places after voting, asking the voters about themselves, how they voted, and why they voted the way they did.

F

failed states States with hardly any state capacity, with anarchy prevailing over much of the territory.

Fascism An ideology that stresses intense ethnic identification, control of the state by the leaders of the dominant ethnic group in the country, and extreme nationalism.

federalism The inclusion in governmental structure of a regional level of government, to which some responsibilities are delegated (such as education, roads, and criminal justice).

feedback effect Any consequence of a change that serves in some way to further intensify the original change.

fiscal policy Policy on government spending and taxes, referred to collectively.

flat tax A tax at the same rate for everyone, regardless of income.

focus party A party with a narrow appeal.

formal political equality Having each person's vote count equally, and allowing virtually every citizen to aspire to office.

fractionalization The presence of a very large number of parties in parliament, requiring several of them to cooperate in a majority coalition to pass bills into law.

free market (strand) A strand in political thought that pursues entrepreneurial freedom above all else.

free rider An individual or organization in a category who doesn't join its association, but nonetheless does receive the benefits that the organization gains from influencing public policy.

free self-development A strand in political thought that pursues the free development of the potential of each citizen.

G

global warming The gradual rise in air and sea temperatures that results from emissions of greenhouse gases, principally carbon dioxide from burning coal, oil, and natural gas, and methane, that trap the sun's energy in the atmosphere.

government party A party that controls the government and is held together mainly by its desire to stay in power.

governmental institutional group An institutional group comprised by a sector of the executive branch of government.

government The leading organizational units with the authority to make policy and carry it out for a territorial community.

grand coalition An alliance between the largest parties on the left and the right, in a majority coalition and cabinet.

Green ideology An ideology that seeks to rally people concerned about the environment, focusing especially on selective government intervention to protect environmental health.

H

habeas corpus Protection against being detained without being charged with a crime, and the right to face one's accusers.

hardliners Groups within an authoritarian regime in transition who are very reluctant to yield power.

head of state A nation's chief ceremonial figure, symbolically representing the nation for some formal purposes (may or may not coincide with the position of chief executive).

hegemony The dominance of one nation globally or in a region of the world.

humanitarian law A strand in political thought that pursues the reconciliation of contending interests around wise law and mutual good will, aimed at addressing the needs, and gaining the consent, of all citizens.

hypothesis A prediction about how one or more variables are likely to affect something else.

I

ideological focus party A party that is focused more on persuading people to its ideological outlook than on winning numerous votes in elections.

ideology A general outlook and prescriptive strategy for dealing with society and its problems, linked to particular values and empirical perspectives that support the strategy.

import substitution industrialization (ISI) A government policy strategy in a developing nation to support domestic industries in producing goods that were at first imported, through subsidies for domestic producers, state-owned startups, and high taxes on imports (tariffs) to give domestic producers a price advantage.

independent leaner A voter who fairly regularly votes for a party's candidates but does not identify with the party as a member.

independent variable A factor that has a causal impact on something else.

independent voter A voter who not only fails to identify as a member of a party, but also does not regularly lean toward support for one party or another as a voter.

indirect election Having a government official elected by other elected officials, not by the voters directly.

inflation Prices rising faster than production.

influence Informal power that is typically less intense than coercion, and may work through positive as well as negative inducements.

insistence powers A president's formal powers to force assemblies to vote on legislation within a certain time period or without amendment.

institutional interest group An organization originally formed for purposes other than social and political ones, with benefits from lobbying flowing to or through the organization itself.

interest aggregation Moderating and merging the aims of like-minded interests into a common policy platform (e.g., of a political party).

interest group Any group of people or organizations with shared concerns relevant to politics, or any association representing such a group, that tries to influence policymaking without running candidates for office under its own banner.

interest-based focus party A party that is focused on representing a group interest or a cluster of closely related interest groups.

international institutionalism Foreign policy that emphasizes diplomacy, negotiation, and rule following in international interactions, structured by international institutions and customary cooperative practices, in pursuit of peace, mutually guaranteed security, and economic progress.

intervening variable A factor that affects how an independent variable affects a dependent variable.

J

jihad In Islam, struggle against injustice, evil, or any perceived enemy of Allah or the prophet Mohammed, most often in violent holy war but also in other forms of struggle with sin or injustice.

judicial activism A high court stepping in to resolve key issues where the regular democratic process has been unwilling to do so.

judicial review Court judgments on the consistency of legislation, rules, and decisions with the constitution, which can nullify the law or rule if it is considered unconstitutional.

junta In a military regime, a small group of officers leading the supreme military council.

K

keynesian policy An approach that focuses on addressing economic downturns and slumps by focusing especially on increasing government spending to reduce unemployment and stimulate more consumer spending.

L

left of center Policies that generally favor government intervention in the economy to solve problems (e.g., spending, regulation,

or taxation), while opposing significant government intervention to restrict personal freedoms or to enlarge national defense.

legislative assembly A governmental body that is made up of many members who are equal in voting power, and approves laws by majority vote.

liberal democracy The combination of free market-leaning capitalism, representative democracy, and protection of civil liberties and group autonomy.

limit-setting power Power that sets boundaries and leaves people free to act within those limits.

line authority The central operational hierarchy of managerial authority in an organization.

line item veto A president's power to veto only one part of a bill.

lobbyist An interest group representative who interacts with government officials on its behalf.

M

majority preference model The view that policymaking by a group carries out the preferences of the majority of its members.

majority rule Requiring the support of more than half of the members (50 percent plus 1) to make a decision.

Marxism A strand in political thought that sees the capitalist market as leading to class conflict and a socialist revolution that would bring equality and well-being.

Marxism-Leninism The ideology of "Communism," which borrowed from Marxian class conflict theory but emphasized seizing state power and using it to control the economy and sociocultural life.

material stake group A group for whom tangible consequences are the main focus, whether in economic or other physical forms.

meaningful voter choice Voting in which success for the voter-preferred candidate, party, or coalition will make a significant difference in government policymaking.

membership People who are formally enrolled in an organization.

militant Islamism A worldview portraying sharp contention between Islam and Western values, with the goal of a non-democratic government dominated by the Muslim clergy (theocracy), that enforces strict Sharia law on the people as the country's criminal justice system.

military coup A takeover of the government by military officers.

minimum threshold approach A development aid strategy that targets certain core needs areas such as food, health, and employment first to assure minimal levels of them that can bring recipients to the threshold of a more self-reliant, bottom-up momentum toward self-provision of other benefits and higher levels of provision of these core benefits.

minimum winning coalition The predictive model that suggests that multiparty parliamentary cabinets will represent no more parties and seats than are necessary to assure a bare majority of votes for the cabinet's bills in parliament (fits office-seeking motivation).

minority government A cabinet composed of leaders of a party or coalition that does not hold a majority of the parliamentary seats.

model A simplified impression or picture that aims to represent what is really happening on a larger and more complicated stage.

moderate left-of-center ideology An ideological stance that is left of center in favoring government intervention in the economy (in taxes, spending for well-being, and regulation)—but moderately and selectively—and strong protection of civil liberties.

monarchy Established, institutionalized rule by one person.

monetarism An austerity-minded strategy focused on monetary policy, contending that downturns and slumps can be addressed by the central bank adding to the supply of money for bank lending (reducing interest rates), and that overheated economies can be reined in by contracting the supply of money for bank lending.

monetary policy Central bank adjustments to the overall supply of money potentially available to a country's banks for lending (usually by buying or selling government bonds or adjusting short-term interest rates paid by banks when they borrow from the central bank itself).

monopoly Having only one producer of something, who can dictate prices and quality to consumers.

multi-issue group An interest group based on a defined population that deals with any issues that affect it.

multiparty A party system with a number of significant parties, usually five or more.

multiplier Regarding the consequences of a change in government spending or taxation, the ratio of (a) the resulting change in GDP for the local or national economy to (b) the amount of money involved in the preceding government policy change.

N

national identity Widespread self-classification by people as citizens of their nation-state.

national interest A value (e.g., some form of well-being) pursued on behalf of a particular country.

nationalism Social identification focused on the nation itself.

natural law A body of principles of conduct that the Stoics had observed to be common to the practices of harmonious and flourishing societies (e.g., "no harming").

necessary condition A factor that must always be present for a certain outcome to occur, but does not always produce it.

negative freedom The protection of individual thought and action from inappropriate barriers presented by society or government.

neoconservative Conservative thinking that stresses nationalism and tends to advocate military intervention in foreign countries in the service of the national interest.

neo-corporatism The incorporation of representatives of important interest groups in formal government bodies or executive functions.

new public management A recent approach in public administration favoring greater autonomy, flexibility, and entrepreneurship for lower-level administrative units to achieve greater efficiency and cost control.

nomenklatura In the old Soviet systems, the ruling Communist party's list of all of the significant managerial positions in government, the economy, and society, for which the party could review and veto appointments.

nongovernmental organizations (NGOs) Organizations that are not part of any government and that aim to represent interests, usually international value-related concerns.

normal distribution A range of views that are concentrated at moderate levels of intensity or support for a view, with fewer at the extremes.

normative theory Theory that suggests, examines, and justifies one or more values as the key consequences of politics, and explores what are the most effective means to pursue them, as paths that ought to be followed (alternatively, "political philosophy").

normative Inquiry, explanation, or discussion that concerns what someone believes ought to be the case, or that evaluates phenomena, positively or negatively.

O

offensive realism The idea that to assure its safety, any major power must seek to keep growing in power.

office seeking An approach to explaining coalition formation and maintenance in multiparty cabinets that assumes that the main motivation of parties is to share in the influence and status that accompanies holding positions in the political executive.

officials People who work in formal positions in an interest group organization.

oligarchy Self-interested rule by a property-tied and wealth-oriented elite.

open-list proportional representation An unusual form of PR voting in which the voters pick the candidates that they favor from the party's list on the ballot, giving the seats to those with the most votes.

operationalize To put a term into practical operation in referring to clearly identifiable behavior.

oppositional voting Voting driven mainly by opposition to a party or candidate.

organizational density The extent of organization at the national, regional, and local levels.

P

pacts In democratic transitions, formal or informal agreements between traditional elite groups and democracy supporters, which often serve to protect the prior elites somewhat as democratization proceeds.

parliamentary A form of representative democracy in which the leading executive officials also serve in the legislative branch, and the chief executive is chosen by a majority vote in the main legislative assembly, and normally serves only as long as her or his policies receive majority legislative support.

party branch In Europe, the members of a given political party in a local area (town, urban borough, county).

party discipline A party's legislators actually following its leadership and remaining unified in legislative voting.

party fraction The members of a given party who are serving in a legislative assembly.

party identification Considering oneself a member of a party.

path dependency The tendency of policymakers facing new situations to stick to the working methods and structures that they have become accustomed to in the past.

patron-client relationship An exchange relationship in which one of the two parties (the "patron") has much more to offer than the other (the "client").

peak association An umbrella association representing other related associations.

peers People sharing a characteristic, such as a neighborhood, social group, or age cohort.

penetration by state authority The extension of state authority throughout the country.

permanent secretary In the British civil service, the chief among the senior civil servants of a department.

personal autocracy A form of rule in which the chief executive is also the chief lawmaker, and there is no explicit role for other institutions or organizations in key decision making.

personal dictatorship A form of personal autocracy that lacks both institutions and traditional legitimacy, relying only on force and personal loyalty.

personal leadership model The view that policymaking tends to follow from decisions and interactions of individual leaders.

personalistic party A party that is held together to a substantial degree by the charismatic appeal of the party's leader.

plaintiff The party in a civil law case that believes it has been wronged and is suing for damages.

plural elites A model of multiple elites dominating politics and policymaking in areas affecting them.

policy direction voting Voter choice due to preferences regarding the directions that the candidates and parties seem to want government to take on policy issues (e.g., toward a value, an ideology, help for an interest group, or a particular policy on an issue).

policy seeking An approach to explaining coalition formation and maintenance in multiparty cabinets that suggests that parties primarily pursue policy directions whether related to their values, ideological identity, interest group ties, or particular favored policies.

policy An organization's practical approach to solving a problem or achieving a goal.

policy-significant party A political party whose legislators' support, either now or in a plausible future, might prove necessary to maintain an ongoing legislative majority.

politburo In a Marxist-Leninist single-party regime, the ruling party's central board of directors, in which the top party secretaries (e.g., one each for the economy, ideology, and party organization) meet with the most important cabinet ministers.

political accountability The capacity of the citizens to hold leading public officials responsible for their performance in office, usually via elections.

political attitudes Values, beliefs, and preferences related to politics.

political cleavage Any enduring division within a population that can contribute to political disputes.

political culture Widespread and long-held values, beliefs, and related customs concerning what citizens expect from their government and how they relate to it.

political executive The top stratum of offices in the executive branch of government, chosen through a political process of some sort, that gives overall direction to the professional civil service.

political legitimacy The widespread sense among the public that their system of government is rightful and just for them.

political party An organization that runs candidates for office under its own banner.

political science The systematic investigation and explanation of what happens, why things happen, and the consequences of what happens, in politics and government.

political socialization People conveying to others their values, norms, and beliefs concerning politics and policies.

politics The interplay of contention and cooperation among individuals and groups to affect decision making in authoritative organizational frameworks.

positive freedom Society providing, through government action, positive benefits that expand individual choice, such as minimal health care, public education, work-day limits, and laws against child labor and unhealthy work conditions.

post-materialism Concern about sociocultural issues such as minority rights, the environment, peace, and gender equality, rather than traditional economic issues.

power checking A strand in political thought that assumed self-interest as the main motivation of political participants, feared governmental power, and focused on how to check and divide that power.

power concentration A strand in political thought (epitomized by Thomas Hobbes of the mid-seventeenth century) that sought order and physical security through political unity under an all-powerful single leader or assembly.

power The causal impact of the preferences of an individual or group on the actions of others.

precedent A key judicial decision made by a higher-level court in an important case that serves as an example for lower courts to follow.

preference intensity The strength of someone's attachment to their views.

presidential A form of representative democracy in which the chief executive is elected directly by the people and serves a fixed term of office, with no one serving in both the legislative and executive branches at the same time.

primary election Having all party members or supporters vote to choose the party's nominees for elective office.

primary group A group with ongoing face-to-face interaction, such as a fraternal organization, office, or economic enterprise.

privatization Governments selling off their state-owned enterprise to the private sector.

progressive taxation Taxing higher incomes at higher rates.

propaganda Intentional bias or distortion in representing reality, for political purposes.

proportional representation A voting system in which large election districts each send a number of representatives to the key legislative assembly, and these seats are allocated to the parties in proportion to their shares of the vote in the district.

public goods Goods that serve the whole population and tend to be impractical for the private market to provide profitably.

public interest group A value-related group pursuing a public good.

public opinion The public's views and preferences concerning the issues, leaders, and parties of the day.

public value A particular form of a broad value category such as order, justice, freedom, well-being, or equality, pursued for the whole community rather than only for oneself or one's group.

R

random selection Identifying respondents for polling purposes without any source of steering or bias.

realignment An election that yields long-term change in patterns of party support among groups in society.

realism Nations' independent pursuit of their self-interest and national influence in security, political, and economic matters.

reapportionment Periodic adjustment of the boundaries of legislative districts, usually to adjust to changes in the distribution of the population.

recall Remove from office by a vote outside the regular election procedures.

redistribution Transferring resources from the economically better-off to the less advantaged of a society.

referendum A vote by citizens directly on whether a policy proposal will become law.

regulate Impose rules on.

regulatory policy Applying rules to the economy.

regulatory strings Minimum requirements and standards set for the use of subsidy money.

representative democracy A form of government in which the people, in free and fair elections, choose the officials who set the main outlines of the government's key laws and programs.

representative sample A portion of the population that fairly accurately represents the array of opinions in the whole.

retrospective voting Voting for or against a candidate or party due to positive or negative consequences of government policymaking while the candidate or party was in office, without much reference to the policies themselves.

revolution A decisive, forcible, and thorough replacement of the prior regime, over a limited timeframe, that is spurred partly by unconventional political participation by some sort of mass movement, and has a major and enduring impact on politics and society.

right of center Policies that generally oppose government intervention in the economy to solve problems (e.g., spending, regulation, or taxation), while favoring government intervention to restrain personal freedoms and to strengthen national defense.

rule of law A government's consistent application of rules that apply equally to everyone.

runoff election A second election, usually a few weeks after the first round of voting, in which the top vote-getters (usually two) from the first stage contend for the final selection by the voters.

rupture A model of democratic transition in which the authoritarian regime is confronted by mass demonstrations and is quickly forced to yield, retaining little influence over what comes next.

S

Salafism Support for state imposition of strict Sharia law, based on a literal reading of the Koran and the early Sunni hadith as instructions for living.

sales tax A tax paid by consumers when they purchase a good or service.

scope of authority The particular field that the authority covers, and who is subject to it.

sectarian Pertaining to religious differences.

security dilemma Mutual suspicion between powers and their alliances concerning the possibly aggressive intentions behind those alliances and military capacities, inviting arms races and preemptive aggression.

semi-periphery Developing nations who have carved out niches of success in the international economy.

semi-presidential government A type of representative democracy that has a popularly elected president with significant powers that include appointing a prime minister, alongside a parliament that must approve the president's choice for PM.

separation of personnel In presidential democracy with separation of powers, the rule that no one may serve in both the legislative and executive branches of government at once.

separatist war A war fought over whether a part of a country will be allowed to separate and form its own nation.

Sharia law An Islamic system of law derived from the Koran and the hadith (reports of Mohammed's life and actions

and commentaries on them) that some areas use in their courts.

signing statement A declaration by a president upon signing a bill that some part of it will not be carried out, due to the president's concerns that it may not be consistent with the constitution.

single-issue group A group that arises around only one issue or a cluster of closely related issues.

single-party-dominant, electoral authoritarian rule Authoritarian rule in which the dominant party permits multiparty elections, but aggressively disadvantages other contending parties to the point that they are not really competitive in those elections.

social capital A community's fund of good will, mutual confidence, and mutual trust, that stems from local civic participation and tends to support the political legitimacy of democracy.

social identity Shared identification and solidarity with a group or community of some sort, such as an ethnic or religious category, a social movement with shared values and a world view, or nationalism itself.

social movement A value-related categoric interest that is especially large and important in a nation.

social pact A broad agreement, drawn up by a large conference representing all key groups in society, to structure a new democracy.

social welfare Services that aim to assure minimal well-being to the disadvantaged, such as the elderly, the unemployed, the ill, or the poor.

socialism Public or state ownership of the bulk of a country's productive property.

societal institutional group A nongovernmental institutional group, such as a religious hierarchy or an economic enterprise.

sociocultural policy Policy concerning the bounds of acceptable personal freedom, in self-expression, individual and group autonomy, and politics.

soft power One country exercising international influence through efforts to promote its values in other countries.

softliners In a democratic transition, individuals or groups from the prior authoritarian elite who are flexible and willing to make pacts with pro-democracy reformers.

spoils system An American bureaucratic practice dating from the 1830s (during Andrew Jackson's presidency) whereby each

new chief executive would sweep out most of the administrative employees and fill their positions with his followers.

staff Positions and/or structures that are attached to key decision makers in an organization, to provide them with advice, planning, services, or specialized information.

standard operating procedures (SOPs) Specific, detailed rules employed by bureaucratic units for handling particular situations.

standing committee A regular, specialized legislative committee for handling bills or examining the work of an executive branch ministry or department.

state capacity Sufficient government strength to enforce laws and implement programs.

state terror The systematic threat and use of violence by government officials, or by others with the backing of government officials, to compel obedience.

strand (current) A group of normative political thinkers who broadly agree on what are the main problems that should be addressed regarding contention and cooperation, which primary values government should pursue, and at least some aspects of their practical solutions.

subsidy A government grant, low-cost loan, or special tax break for an organization or activity that serves the national interest in some way.

sufficient condition A factor that always produces a certain outcome.

supermajority A vote of significantly more than 50 percent plus one, required to pass legislation.

support party A party outside a minority cabinet that is willing to approve its proposals in one or more policy areas.

surplus majority cabinet A multiparty cabinet that includes the leaders of more parties than are necessary to comprise a parliamentary majority.

T

tariff A tax on an imported good.

the pluralist model The view that influence over policymaking is dispersed among a wide range of interest groups that contend and bargain with one another.

the state All units of a country's government considered as a single entity with comprehensive and sovereign authority over a territorial community.

theocracy Government by a religion's clerics.

totalitarian A nondemocratic government that imposes an official ideology on social life, the media, and education, requires organizational leaders to be members of the ruling party, monitors society, and infringes the human rights of anyone about whom it has suspicions.

tracking poll A survey over an extended period that samples a new batch of respondents each day, and on a daily basis releases the results only for the most recent three or four days.

traditional monarchy A personal autocracy that exists as a long-standing, formalized system with a degree of legitimacy available due to traditional familiarity.

trustee model A model of representation suggesting that a territorial representative should act on her or his own judgment on behalf of the nation, rather than trying to follow opinions in the district.

two-party A party system in which political contention is dominated by two main parties, normally with one or the other holding the majority in any given legislative assembly.

U

unicameral legislature A legislative branch with only one house.

unitary state A governmental system which does not grant a regional level of government independent responsibility for any policy areas.

V

value-added tax A tax applied to commercial transactions between businesses.

value-related group A group that exists to pursue a public value.

veto player Any group whose support is necessary for policies to be adopted by government.

voter turnout The percentage of eligible voters who actually vote on election day.

W

war The application of physical force to defeat an enemy and gain control over a territory or some other strategic advantage.

weak states States those with poor state capacity.

INDEX

Arctic Ocean

Beaufort Sea

Greenland

Baffin Bay

United States

Canada

Hudson Bay

Iceland

Gulf of Alaska

Labrador Sea

North Pacific Ocean

North Atlantic Ocean

United States

Hawaii (United States)

Mexico

Gulf of Mexico

The Bahamas

Cuba

Dom. Rep.

Belize

Jamaica

Haiti

Honduras

Guatemala

Nicaragua

Caribbean Sea

El Salvador

Costa Rica

Panama

Trinidad & Tobago

Venezuela

Guyana

Suriname

Colombia

French Guiana

Galapagos (Ecuador)

Ecuador

Peru

Brazil

Bolivia

Paraguay

South Pacific Ocean

Chile

Argentina

Uruguay

Falkland Islands

South Georgia

South Sandwich Islands

Weddell Sea

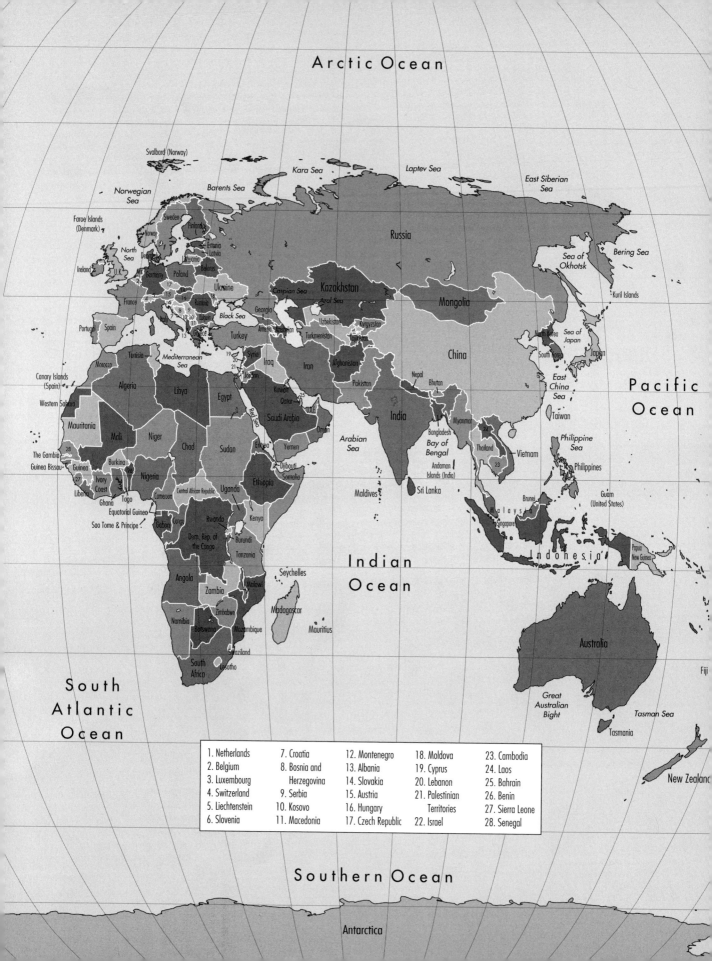